1979

# CLINICAL AND EXPERIMENTAL STUDIES IN PERSONALITY

Morton Prince
1856-1929

# CLINICAL

## AND

# EXPERIMENTAL STUDIES

## IN

# PERSONALITY

BY

## MORTON PRINCE

Revised and Enlarged
*(with an Introduction and Notes)*

BY

## A. A. ROBACK

GREENWOOD PRESS, PUBLISHERS
WESTPORT, CONNECTICUT

Originally published in 1929 and 1939
by Sci-Art Publishers, Cambridge, Massachusetts


First Greenwood Reprinting 1970

Library of Congress Catalogue Card Number 72-100197

SBN 8371-3995-3

Printed in the United States of America

# PREFACE AND HISTORICAL RETROSPECT

For several years I have been urged by a number of my colleagues to collect in published form selected papers from my writings and lectures on abnormal psychology and allied subjects that have been printed in medical and psychological journals during the last forty years. I have not felt inclined to yield to these sympathetic requests until this moment. What finally decided me to do so has been the recent publication of Prof. W. S. Taylor's little volume (*Morton Prince and Abnormal Psychology*) in which he has done me the honor of giving an exposition of my theories and a critical digest of my studies. As Professor Taylor's book is based upon my published papers, and makes constant reference to them, I have thought it would be advisable, in accordance with the requests I have received, to collect in an easily accessible and permanent form at least the more basic of them, the original papers, as well as a few unpublished lectures. I have particularly in mind the possible needs of those students, the newer generation, who may wish to re-examine the theories of the different modern "schools" of abnormal and dynamic psychology and study, as Professor Taylor has done, the findings obtained by methods which, I fancy, have been more or less peculiar to my own investigations. This thought has been reinforced by the fact that many of these papers were published in the *Journal of Abnormal Psychology* when it was pioneer in its field, and before it had attracted, in any marked degree, the attention of psychological or medical circles. Some were also published in medical journals where, for the most part, they have lain buried, hardly accessible to students of psychology. Quite a number of papers have been omitted from the present collection in order to keep the volume within reasonable proportions from a book-making point of view. Several more recent papers I should like to have included, but three of these "Three Fundamental Errors of the Behaviorists and the Reconciliation of the Purposive and Mechanistic Concepts"; "Awareness, Consciousness, Coconsciousness and Animal Intelligence from the Point of View of the Data of Abnormal psychology — A Biological Theory of Consciousness"; and "The Problem of Personality — How Many Selves Have We?") have been already published in book form in *Psychologies of 1925* (Clark University, 1926) to which the interested student can easily refer, and one ("Can Emotion be Regarded as Energy?") has just appeared in the collection of papers on *Feelings and Emotions* (Wittenberg Symposium, 1927). I have also been unable, owing to the limitations of space, to include a number of selections from numerous lectures on abnormal and dynamic psychology which it has been my privilege to deliver in courses given in a number of universities in this country and abroad — the University of California, London, Cambridge and Oxford Universities, the University of Edinburgh and Harvard University. A sufficient number of papers, however, are here presented to give, I think, the views I have felt justified in advancing as to the interpretations of well-known phenomena, the theories reached regarding various problems of human personality, and the principal data, derived from research, on which they are based.

With this end in view, I have included "My Life as a Dissociated Personality" because, although not written by me, it was written under my direction by one of my subjects (B. C. A.), a case of multiple personality. It is not only a very remarkable introspective account of subconscious life, but the phenomena described occurred during my long and intensive experimental study of the case, and were checked up by my own observations. So it properly belongs in this collection, as did the "autobiography" of "Sally," a coconscious personality in the study of Miss Beauchamp (*The Dissociation of a Personality*). The two autobiographies should be compared. Moreover, this contribution to dissociated personality was largely made use of in an article entitled "The Psychogenesis of Multiple Personality" (*Journal of Abnormal Psychology*, vol. XIV, no. 4, 1919), incorporated in the 2nd edition of *The Unconscious*, 1921 (Lectures XVIII-XX). This article and "My Life" supplement the paper in this volume entitled, "Miss Beauchamp: The Theory of the Psychogenesis of Multiple Personality."

Looking backwards, in historical retrospect, the author has had the advantage of having lived through the whole period of growth of abnormal psychology, from its first beginnings some forty years ago. He has thus been able to follow its growth, to keep in contact with the successive discoveries and the accumulating data in its field, the progressive development of thought and attention which it has awakened, and the changing theories and interpretations of phenomena that have been advanced during this period. To have been in touch with all these various phases of this field, and perhaps have taken a small part in them, he feels, has provided a background of accumulated data (many of which are liable to be forgotten) and a perspective which are helpful in weighing and judging the value to be attributed to any particular findings and to the probable truth of any theory based upon them.

It seems incredible that forty years have elapsed since the gateway to the unknown field of abnormal psychology was first opened by Pierre Janet in 1887 in his classical studies of hysteria. It was a long time, after this beginning, before this field was recognized as a legitimate one for research, and the discoveries made in it accepted as established. Few were the prospectors in this virgin soil and few the diggings which, for the most part, had their aim in searching the subsoil of the subconscious. Few were interested and few read the limited literature; and fewer still, of those that read, understood. I remember well that even so late as 1906, when I made the venture of founding the *Journal of Abnormal Psychology*, there was so little understanding that it was said by some of my outstanding colleagues in the medical profession that it was to be a "spook" journal! The number of those engaged in research was small. Progress, consequently, was slow. The main reason for this was that psychopathology met with distinct antipathy, on the part of neurologists and psychiatrists, and indifference in academic psychological circles. The conception of the neuroses and psychoneuroses as having an organic physical basis, and a scientific antipathy to a pathology that was not objectively physical and could not be seen under the microscope, were so deeply ingrained in us, of the medical profession, that the newer findings and theories based upon them were actually resented and resisted as heresy, with all the force of conservative medicine — as some of us had reason to know. Papers along these lines before learned neurological societies were almost taboo.

In this country the influence of the distinguished and able Weir Mitchell, of whom I was originally a disciple, and whose conception of the psychoneuroses was that of the now discarded neurasthenia, was also all-powerful; and his so-called "rest-cure," based upon the therapeutic physical principle of making "fat and blood," had spread throughout Europe as well as America.

This resistance was difficult to break down and took a long time. The suspicion is not ill-natured — and as an explanation is justifiable — that unconsciously it was thought, if the new school of psychopathology was right, then that which had been traditionally accepted had to be thrown away, and a new knowledge acquired, which the medical profession was not fitted by training to pursue and which found no place in the curricula of medical schools.

As to academic psychologists, their indifference was natural in that the material for research in the early years was confined to patients to be found in hospital clinics or the private practice of physicians. From such sources they were necessarily shut out, or, if inquisitive, attending such clinics took them away from their academic laboratories and was laborious and time-consuming. So they left the field alone as a mystical one, in which physicians could play to their hearts' desire. But, nevertheless, as a defense reaction, they not seldom, from their arm-chairs, threw out rather contemptuous criticisms.

Perhaps, here, I may make a personal reference as it illustrates these points. I remember that in 1906, when *The Dissociation of a Personality* was published, the work done outside of the psychoanalytic school was so little read that I determined I would, if possible, at least make "them" read. So in writing the *Dissociation*, I purposely, with "malice aforethought," constructed it in the form of a dramatic story of great length, 563 pages. As a scientific account it might well have been condensed within the compass of fifty pages. I think my little ruse was successful.

One wonders how long this resistance, on the one hand, and indifference, on the other, would have persisted if it had not been for Freud. It was Freud who broke down the resistance and turned the indifference to interest. In this he was aided, in this country, by public opinion, which had been awakened by various religious and lay movements in psychotherapy. The public began to insist that the medical profession should give an answer to the questions which were asked about the influence of the mind on the body in producing ill-health; and the profession had to take some notice. But Freud's sexual theories, which were promulgated by a gradually growing host of enthusiastic exponents, were too alluring and appealing to each one's own personality not to awaken interest sooner or later. There is something about sex that has always been attractive. Freud did what no one else had succeeded in doing; he made the psychological world and the medical world take notice. He gained the attention of both. But not all at once. For his theories to gain a hearing and eventually a firm footing, it required a number of years and the efforts of a band of early converts who, as devoted disciples, went forth to spread the new gospel. Some of these, though at first absolutely cocksure and hopelessly dogmatic, later recanted and abandoned the master. The conservatives of the medical profession offered even stronger resistance than they had done before to less radical offerings. But a goodly number of younger progressives were captivated by the new theories and, undeterred by criticism or ridicule, organized their special psychoanalytic societies and pursued their studies, seeking to apply their doctrines in wider and wider fields. Psychoanalytic methods, observations, and doctrines soon displaced or obscured those of all other workers in the field, and, in fact, captured abnormal psychology.

I know of one pathetic figure, a colleague of mine, whose heart was well-nigh broken. In the popular mind and, indeed, in that of conventional psychologists, the two were erroneously identified. Indeed, Freudian psychology had flooded the field like a full rising tide, and the rest of us were left submerged like clams buried in the sands at low water. Clams, I take it, must be philosophers, or belong to William James's "tough-minded" group. My poor colleague was neither, though psychoanalysts considered us all clams. Still, "we few, we happy few" continued on the even tenor of our way, pursuing our observations and practising successfully psychotherapy according to our own views. We were pleased to speak of ourselves as the "Boston School" of abnormal psychology. One of the outstanding figures in this group was (and is) Dr. George A. Waterman, whose extraordinarily large experience and enviable reputation for success in the treatment of the psychoneuroses and maladjustments of personality bear testimony to the soundness of the principles upon which this "school" was founded.

However, the Freudian tide is slowly receding and a safe and sane dynamic psychology is coming into its own again.

In time the psychoanalytic school became firmly seated in the saddle. All students, even though unbelievers, must be grateful to Freud; for no one else, at the period to which I am referring, had succeeded in making the world "stop, look, and listen." Not long thereafter abnormal and dynamic psychology became legitimatized as a department of psychology and medicine and accepted by universities and medical schools.[1] And yet it may be questioned whether the general acceptance of psychoanalytic technique did not retard the development of research by more scientific methods. However, a full and general acceptance of the soundness of a psychological pathology, whatever theories be held, as the basis of the psychoneuroses, dates from the World War, when it was forced upon a doubting profession. Owing to the same influence as those I have sketched, the academic psychologists dropped their indifference and became attracted

---

1 Tufts College Medical School was the first, I believe, in this country to establish a systematic course in this field of medicine (1902).

to a dynamic psychology which held out to them the fascinating problems of motivation, behavior, and purpose. Coming late into the game, as they did, and being, therefore, without the background of familiarity with all the earlier work, they failed, as a rule, to realize that abnormal psychology had offered as interpretations of phenomena other theories which were equally dynamic, and there were other motivations than that of a libidinous wish. But notwithstanding the popularity of Freud's theories, and though I felt their fascination, I never was able to accept his basic principles nor many of his mechanisms. This was not because of failure to try out his methods of analysis and faithfully test his observations. The former I used and still use as a valuable addition to my own technique, but I did not reach the same results. There were too many facts of observation and experiment which the Freudian theories (proclaimed as facts) neglected. The methods of investigation were too inexact and unreliable to justify the conclusions, and the findings were open to other interpretations than those laid down by his theories. And, in particular, I was never able to accept his concepts of the unconscious and the libido. Both are irreconcilable with *all* the facts furnished by other methods of investigation as well as by those of psychoanalysis. Of course, there is much, very much, in Freudian psychology that every experienced investigator accepts, but this "much" is not specially Freudian, but is common dynamic psychology. Then, again, to be further specific, I never have been able to accept the metaphysical principle of a single entity, whether libido or *élan vital,* as the sole motivation of all our desires, mental perturbations, maladaptations, and behavior, however complicated the mechanisms through which it carries out its purpose.

This retrospect will, I hope, tend to justify my acceptance of the idea — very likely a subconscious unavowed desire; who knows? — of publishing these papers.

I wish here to acknowledge my indebtedness to Dr. A. A. Roback, who has undertaken the whole of the laborious task of editing and preparing the volume, including the index, for the press. In fact, he has zealously undertaken and carried through this work as if the volume were his own, allowing me to wash my hands of the job. Without this aid I never would have considered publication. I extend to him my grateful thanks.

I wish also to thank Dr. Meyer Solomon for his generous and valuable help in reading the proofs. It was, perhaps, Dr. Solomon's repeated insistence and proffers of help that overcame my inertia and reluctance to gather together these papers. May I hope that they will not prove lacking in interest, if only historical, to students of human personality and that they may stimulate some to carry further than I have done, by improved methods and more fruitfully, researches in this absorbingly interesting field.

M. P.

Boston,
December 20, 1928.

## EDITOR'S PREFACE

THE volume which is now republished in a revised and enlarged edition first appeared in 1929. It was fortunate that I could consult Dr. Prince at every step in my editing his essays. Neither of us then supposed that a new edition would be necessary in less than a decade.

It soon became evident, however, that the repeated demand for the book from various institutions, both here and abroad, would have to be taken into consideration. Surely an important work like Dr. Prince's *Clinical and Experimental Studies in Personality* could not be allowed to remain out of print indefinitely.

In a sense, this may be called a memorial edition to commemorate the tenth anniversary of Dr. Prince's death. It happens also to be ten years since the volume first appeared. When we further note that 1939 marks the sixtieth anniversary of the author's graduation from the Harvard Medical School, when he received his M. D. degree, and also the thirtieth year since Prince introduced psychopathological instruction in our medical schools (Tufts College Medical School), the occasion becomes more eventful in retrospect.

It was not an easy matter to select from the hundreds of papers, those which would be most representative, as well as most worthy of survival. Ideas shift, interests change, and what seems significant in one age may sound trivial to another. It is to the credit of America's pioneer in abnormal psychology that he possessed the perspicacity to realize what was bound to be antiquated in his writings and what would likely weather the onslaught of time.

In a period when the term "personality" had, at the most, a philosophical connotation, Prince was helping to create a *psychology of personality*. It is a mistake to associate him with the study of multiple personality alone. He was in reality concerned with personality as a whole, using, however, the synthetic, instead of the customary analytic, method. Confronted with conditions, phases, states or aspects of personality, he investigated these parts first and then integrated them. Hence the title of the book which I suggested and which Dr. Prince accepted after considerable deliberation and consultation with some of his younger associates. The studies in this volume are, of course, primarily in the realm of the abnormal; but their value lies in *pointing to the constituents of the normal personality*, thus transcending the immanent interpretation of the data.

For a whole generation Dr. Morton Prince had been in the forefront as an investigator of those remarkable phenomena of the human mind we hear so much of and know so little about, as hypnotism, the subconscious, double personality, automatic writing, etc., as well as the psychoneuroses and allied problems.

Before him, abnormal psychology was a speculative field. He has turned it into an experimental soil. By virtue of his long practice as a physician and nerve specialist, he has been able to study the hidden nooks of the mind not from books but at close range; and the results of his labors over thirty-five years apear in convenient form in the shape of a voluminous book replete with interest and humanism.

Many have *written* on personality. Morton Prince alone has *probed* it from angles that are not accessible except to very few. Gifted with an ingenuity and skill for handling patients, he has actually experimented on the personality of his patients, both in order to effect a cure and to demonstrate the underlying cause of the trouble. It is no exaggeration to say that he was the leading experimentalist of his generation in abnormal psychology.

Far from interest waning in Dr. Prince after his death in 1929, there has been a feeling of late, as expressed in a number of studies and in biographical sketches of the man, that some of his investigations are almost classics.

There are numerous textbooks in abnormal psychology. Morton Prince's *Clinical and Experimental Studies in Personality* may be regarded as the *fundamental text,* comprising crystal-clear presentations of cases he had personally investigated.

The present edition differs from the first in but few particulars, aside from the added preface, introduction, and editorial notes, as well as portrait. The volume has been thoroughly revised, a number of words modernized, and the misprints corrected. In addition, several extended passages from Dr. Prince's essays, not originally included, have been appended in order to present a broader view of the man's mind.

In changing the orthography of names like "Tarchanoff" (to Tarkhanov), and words like "biologic" or "psychologic" to *biological* and *psychological,* the standard usage was followed but the word "coconscious" which is hyphenated in reference works, appears in Dr. Prince's essays, as the coiner of the term had always written it, without a hyphen. In my own introduction, however, I have adopted the hyphenated form.

While some of the papers, from which fragments have been reprinted, may be out of date at present, it is interesting from a historical angle to trace Dr. Prince's mental and professional growth. At the same time we gain through them a picture of the various *étapes* of psychopathology in this Country. It is noteworthy that even in these early essays, Prince shows that he has sensed the trend of his science and of world affairs.

His résumé of the work on thought-transference and estimate of the results, notwithstanding the half a century which has elapsed since its publication, are more than of historical interest today; and we are again reminded, on reading his acute observations on the subject, of the verse in Ecclesiastes which questions the possibility of novelty.

The inclusion of the passage from his "A World Consciousness and Future Peace" is especially germane at this time; and his allusion to the rights of China in an address which was delivered at a garden party given by a high Japanese official in Tokyo, in 1916, rings, in view of the circumstances today, like a prophetic irony.

A biographical sketch of Dr. Prince had been prepared for this volume, but in view of the size of the book, it was decided to defer publication of that part of the memoir. The introduction has been condensed for a similar reason. Morton Prince deserves a full-size biography; and it is not at all unlikely that such a *Life* will be undertaken in the near future by one of his many admirers.

It is a pleasant duty to acknowledge the assistance rendered by Mrs. Prince and also to thank Miss Minny H. Moran, Dr. Prince's secretary over a long period of years, for her valuable assistance in re-reading the proof-sheets, and for her helpfulness in procuring some of the necessary material, in the preparation of both the original and the revised editions.

A. A. R.

May 20, 1938

# CONTENTS *(analytic)*

# CONTENTS

# TABLE OF DIAGRAMS AND ILLUSTRATIONS

# INTRODUCTION

## MORTON PRINCE'S PLACE IN PSYCHOLOGY

THE value of Dr. Prince's contributions has often been discussed in private psychological circles, where differences of opinion had been heard. Many think of him only in connection with his study of the Beauchamp case and multiple personality in general, ignoring his more solid investigations. There are those who regarded him as a junior partner of the dissociation firm of Janet and Prince (although Prince was the older of the two men). Some wondered how lasting Prince's views would prove in the annals of psychology and there are always the few who will question the matter because of the manner. Prince had not striven to achieve systematic unity, therefore, they concluded, he was unsystematic. A number of the younger psychologists, trained in the behavioristic schools, looked upon him as a charming dilettante. He had neither set himself up as a god nor did he wish to be known as an iconoclast. To most psychologists he was a medical man and to probably just as many neurologists and psychiatrists he was a psychologist. That is often the price one has to pay for keeping abreast of two sciences or arts.

Professor W. S. Taylor, who has given us an able exposition of Dr. Prince's chief doctrines in a little book entitled "*Morton Prince and Abnormal Psychology*," tells us that "the great majority of students and workers in psychopathology as well as in general psychology are not familiar with Morton Prince's important modern contributions," while in his article on Prince in the *Dictionary of American Biography,* he even intimates that our author was too enthusiastic in his statements, almost justifying the neglect which Prince to some extent had met on the part of academic psychologists.

The truth of the matter is that every pioneer in psychology, with the exception of James and Freud, has been and will be neglected in course of time. Men of the towering stature of Wundt, Ebbinghaus, Külpe, Stumpf, Hall, Münsterberg and Titchener have been more or less shelved, although twenty-five years ago, theirs were names to conjure with. There is much to be said on this score, but this must be reserved for another occasion. Let this remark suffice for the present. The average psychologist can see only a narrow portion of the psychological panorama; and if he is concerned with the present the past is occluded from view.

Only those who have formed schools, who have brought up a generation of disciples rigidly adhering to the traditions of the master, can be said to live on in the psychological world, but with the exception of Freud, we do not see that even the founders and builders of the science have had much success. The chief reason for this decline is the progress which psychological thought and experimentation is making almost every year, so that problems which loomed large ir the last generation hardly seem to exist at present, giving place to others which were scarcely dreamed of then. There is, however, a subjective reason. Too many psychologists are interested in the last word, the last study, regardless of whether it deserves a reck or not, just as swing fans wish to forget that there is a vast amount of dance music superior to the caterwauling, crooning, and machine rasping, which they think is new every week. Before we can reach an evaluation of Prince's contribution to psychology, we must become oriented as to his general trend.

Although he set out as a practising physician expecting, as he wrote Dr. Taylor "that it would be patients with organic diseases, diseases of the heart, lungs and kidneys, typhoids and other infectious fevers, etc., that would ring my doorbell or send their calls in urgency," he soon began to see that "these were but a small part of the ills for which a physician's services are needed." It was then, that is to say just fifty years ago, that Prince inaugurated a new movement, which we now take for granted, just as the youngsters accept radio as something that had always existed, a movement to include systematic instruction in functional diseases in the medical schools.

Prince did not experience a sudden illumination in his change of heart from the organic to the mental and functional. He had already been impregnated with the germinal ideas, possibly, while at Harvard, but certainly during his short stay in Paris and Nancy, where Charcot and Bernheim had given direction to his thought.

Long before "dynamic psychology" as a phrase occurred to anyone, Prince had entertained views which established his pioneer claim in this field. While differing widely with Freud in essentials, he nevertheless may be regarded in certain respects as a collaborator of the founder of psychoanalysis. Prince's concept of the *coconscious* is not altogether remote from Freud's *unconscious*. His doctrine of meaning, as set forth in Chapter 1 of the present book, is the counterpart of Freud's system of complexes, and is one of the most valuable contributions toward the understanding not alone of abnormal phenomena but of normal occurrences too.

His conception of purpose, too, while avowedly akin to McDougall's hormic notion, is more in line with Freud's exposition of the interplay between the individual's *superego* and the experiences which go to make up the *id* and affect it so powerfully. Prince's reasoning does not sound so novel because he was always endeavoring to employ existing terms and to bring his data in accord with accepted principles.

It is to his credit that in his search for explanations, he would not, even in those early days, move, so to speak, in a psychical vacuum. In spite of his metaphysical commitment that the ultimate essence of matter was psychic (psychical monism) he insisted on a psychophysical foundation in everything pertaining to the mind. His concept of the neurogram, as a system of neural processes (synaptic connections) where dispositions of memories are stored up which lend themselves to various degrees of activation is not only interesting but seems to be a sound principle in accounting for most types of human behavior.

We note then, that Prince was far-sighted enough to sense the direction psychology would take a generation hence when he rejected the generally accepted tenet that only what is in consciousness, what we are aware of, is psychological subject matter, while at the same time, he was realistic enough in grounding his inference in physiological, or rather neurological, concepts, often using analogies from physical theory (electron, proton) to clarify his procedure.

In all his professional vicissitudes, Prince managed to steer clear of the mechanistic whirlpool. Not that he believed in the absoluteness of introspection. The observation of objective behavior to him was a *sine qua non* of science, but the patient's testimony surely had to be taken into account. In one sense, he has gone beyond Janet, who, doubtless, influenced his line of inquiry; for he was not satisfied with half-way explanations like "incompleteness" or "exhaustion." Prince was anxious to apply the experimental method to abnormal cases. The result was that in some of his findings, he affords us significant material toward the understanding of personality. In a number of investigations he had come upon results which show him to be an ally of Pavlov and the conditioned reflex school. The chapter on "Association Neuroses" which originally was a paper published in 1891, gives us the analogue of the conditioned reflex principle applied to psychoneurotic patients. Yet the subjective factor, which is excluded by animal objectivists and behaviorists, is not eliminated in Prince's study. On the contrary, it is utilized in integrating hysterical patients whose afflictions appear to be organic.

The artificiality of the division between the normal and the abnormal has been recognized by Prince several decades ago. He has dealt with conflict in a truly dynamic manner, making it almost a property of every mental process, similar to inhibition. To be sure, he has not treated it in the magisterial manner of Freud, who was not hampered by psychological knowledge, and was not influenced by his physiological training, but Prince's task was to supply a physical basis for the mental phenomenon.

Prince's catholicity is not the same as eclecticism. He does not *agree* with Freud and with Pavlov, with Janet or McDougall. His position happens to be a sort of intersection of roads. He has not, it is true, explored the roads that others have taken. Nevertheless the byways he has taken, leading him into some of the hidden recesses of the human mind — his masterly exposition of multiple personality, his experimental studies of hallucination, visions, and other processes which have been associated with the occult deserve a place among the prescribed readings for students in psychology along with his more systematic work on the *Unconscious*. His method is ingenious, his descriptions are vivid, his procedure scientific enough to satisfy the most exacting objectivist and his reasoning sound. He does not start with questionable premises, nor does he overstep the boundaries of his results in reaching his conclusions.

The writings of Dr. Prine, with but one or two exceptions, are marked by a moderation and levelheadedness which sometimes cause the reader to wonder whether anything new had been said. His aim is not to startle or shock but to expound. Nowhere is this quality so manifest as in his long study of the mechanism and interpretation of dreams (chapter XVIII. Here the author very painstakingly and yet without betraying any labored effect, unravels the dream tangle in such a manner as to disclose the underlying symbolism without taking recourse to all-embracing theories which may be fascinating though not convincing.

Prince's account of the mechanism of dreams is, to my mind, superior to Freud's treatment because it is so eminently sane. In the six dreams which he analyzes, the procedure is so straightforward and the steps so measured that we can follow and accept every move. Here dreams are not reduced to one principle alone and we are not told beforehand what to expect or what key to use to unlock the mystery. It is more the experimental method of the laboratory that is recommended. The results in many ways tally with those of the psychoanalytic school, but there is less deviousness apparent in the inferential process.

### PRINCE AND FREUD

The question of how Freud has influenced Prince, or what constitutes their chief difference has occurred to many students of abnormal psychology. Sometimes it has been thought that Prince deliberately rejected *ab origine* the psychoanalytic method, viewing with suspicion and alarm the incursion of the Vienna master, and his growing prestige.

To the credit of Morton Prince it must be said that he

was a "good sport" not only in games but also in serious matters. While many of his colleagues deprecated the new doctrine striking at its vulnerable spot — sex — Prince would often at least tentatively make use of it, although not apparently with any measure of success. Psychoanalysis was not beneath him. If he could not see eye to eye with its founder it was because he was trained in a different milieu, and was by nature, too, perhaps an empiricist — in the line of Locke, Hume, John Stuart Mill and Huxley.

Far from decrying Freud's contribution, he has on more than one occasion acknowledged it, "rendering unto Caesar what was Caesar's." He has been equally liberal with Janet as with McDougall; for it was one of Prince's fine traits not to "steal the show" of someone else, or, indeed, to wish the limelight all to himself.

In some cases, Prince pays homage to the genius of Freud. In others, he shows his indebtedness by employing some of his ideas and terms, e. g., secondary elaboration. Here and there a result points to a Freudian mechanism like condensation (page 409). We see there was no repression in that regard; yet there is a marked difference between the scientific attitudes of the two men, although both could be placed in the category of dynamic psychologists.

Freud is primarily an *affective* dynamist; Prince is in large part, an *ideational* dynamist. The latter recognizes the potency of the instincts and the emotions, but is not willing to relinquish the cognitive claim on our *psyche*. To paraphrase a Kantian dictum, one might say, "Meanings without affects are barren, while affects without meaning are blind." The meanings in this connection need not be envisaged in the light of absolute truth. It would seem that in the field of therapy, at least, Prince is a pragmatist or an instrumentalist. Perhaps, had he lived today, he would align himself with the operationalist school in psychology.

There is, of course, some hope of seeing possibilities for a Vienna-Boston axis in that complexes, on the one hand, and sentiments, on the other, offer some ground for a *rapprochement*, but, in the last analysis while Freud's therapy ends with the abreaction, Prince's method consists essentially in re-education, that is to say in supplying new meanings to the patients, thus arguing more for a kinship between Prince and Jung.

It would take us too far afield in an introduction of this sort to enter into Prince's view of repression, sublimation, libido, conflict and other characteristically Freudian concepts. That they were held to be one-sided and speculative may readily be imagined. On the other hand, the psychoanalytic criticism of Prince has been that he is not far-reaching, that his explanation is too localized and that his motivation psychology does not reveal any depth.

### MULTIPLE PERSONALITY

Morton Prince will be remembered for his thoroughgoing researches in multiple personality, for his concepts of "coconscious" and "neurogram" and for his method of re-education in psychotherapy, which although nothing novel, had emphasized the subject from a new angle.

Since a large part of this volume is devoted to cases in multiple personality, little need be said on this head. It would, however, be somewhat shortsighted or, shall I rather say, majestic to ignore some of the objections, usually repeated *sotto voce*, against his studies, the chief of which was that he had unwittingly suggested the crucial data he had been able to elicit from the various subjects.

Prince must have been aware that such a stricture would be possible; for he had called in two of his colleagues to witness the sessions, in one instance, and obtained their statement as to what had occurred then. Furthermore, he had gone to the trouble of checking up carefully on every detail. This meticulousness may strike some readers as a fault, reminiscent of the boring testimony presented in court trials. The investigator makes sure to record the fact that revelations about the various personalities, references to "she," etc., came from the subject, never from him, through so much as the slightest intimation.

As to the possibility that during the treatment and experimentation, Dr. Prince may have made a rift in the original personality, so that different states or moods might have drifted apart to such an extent as to form apparently different personalities, the answer to that cavil is that, if that were so, it still is a remarkable performance, one that throws a great deal of light on the subject of personality, and comparable to the artificial induction of cancer in order to study its etiology.

That the experiments were not harmful to the patients could be inferred from the integration which followed. It may interest the readers to learn that all three cases described in the present work have been cured — all three, Miss Beauchamp, B. C. A. and the "Susie-Juliana" are still alive, and so far as I know, there is nothing abnormal about them. All of them had been married. A very recent letter, dated April 28, 1938, from the "Spanish Juliana" ("Susie") contains the following sentence, "Some people who know nothing of psychology have told me I would have been better off if I had not met Dr. Prince, but I do not think so. I did not [however] have the same vocal power after the treatment."

There have been others who have either discovered or treated cases of dual personality both before and after Dr. Prince. There is no reason to suppose that all of them have been deluded or succeeded in creating a *persona ex machina*.

The cases, it is true, are rare, but so are certain organic maladies.

In reply to a question addressed to one of Dr. Prince's close associates as to why cases of multiple personality were scarcely met with these days, the following statement was made:

"I would be very glad to express myself more fully on this subject. As a matter of fact only last week when I talked with Dr. C. about his cases on the Neurological Ward, I asked him why they no longer had such classical cases of major hysteria as we used to have on the wards 30 years ago. He had no satisfactory answer and my feeling is that in the method of study employed in these neuroses now-a-days such conditions are not so easily recognized."

### THE CO-CONSCIOUS

A concept which has not had much favor with either psychologists or psychiatrists is that of the "co-conscious," a term coined by Prince to designate, as the *Dictionary of Psychology* puts it (I believe I formulated the definition there, so I can readily accept it) "mental states which co-exist in the individual's personal consciousness, but are dissociated from it, *i. e.*, states of which the individual is not aware, yet which are dynamically active and may account for various mental phenomena, both normal (*e. g.*, lapses of the pen) and abnormal (*e. g.*, crystal gazing, visions, hallucinations, dual or multiple personality)."

The "co-conscious" was thought of in connection with the subconscious which was much heard of about 50 years ago. Freud's *unconscious* had not yet come into being as a term. When the term "unconscious" was employed, as it was by Carpenter, Maudsley, and Münsterberg, it was intended to connote the physiological process of cerebration.

The controversy then revolved around the question whether acts which we perform during abstraction or absent-mindedness, or problems solved during sleep are attended by consciousness in the slightest degree. There seemed to be several different views of the "subconscious" theory. Prince, on the strength of his inquiries into dissociation, held that there may be parallel lines of awareness or consciousness; and furthermore that below the tempestuous surface of the delirium consciousness, the unruffled normal personality may still possess its own consciousness, accessible under hypnosis. Once the facts of multiple personality and visions, as brought out by Prince, are accepted on their face value, the conclusion that there is a co-conscious level, or better, phase of personality is inescapable.

Prince does not of course, give up the term "subconscious." It has its place as a generic designation for all the gradations of consciousness which are below the threshold of actual awareness, from the marginal stage to the brain processes known as cerebration (unconsciousness).

Mental states, as well as brain processes and physiological dispositions or "residua," come under the head of the "unconscious" in Prince's usage.

### THE NEUROGRAM

The mental states depend upon the latter and derive their *meaning* from the neural pattern which has been formed through the experience of the individual, and which has been designated by Prince as the "neurogram." The neurogram is the record which conserves the conditions of re-arousable mental states. This pattern is not merely a series of tracings, but contains a potential meaning for the individual. The neurogram is not something static, but gathers momentum in time, or else more or less fades out, in accordance with the circumstances surrounding the original experiences and their association with or dissociation from other elements.

Perhaps it would be possible to say that for Prince, the neurogram is the *unit of personality organization*. Latent or "quiescent" neurograms may be constellated into a larger pattern which, when it acquires sufficient elements out of the *disjecta membra* dissociated from the general system and floating about, so to speak, assumes the form of, or emerges into a secondary personality. We all have the germs of such personalities, but our neurograms are sufficiently integrated to prevent the formation of new alliances. Yet under certain conditions: fatigue, delirium, hypnosis, abstraction, the latent neurograms may show signs of activity. A depersonalization and at the same time, naturally, a repersonalization takes place. We often hear and use the expression ourselves, "I felt like a new person."

Prince was ever anxious to link the psychological with the physiological. The psychogenesis of neuroses was for him a psycho-physiogenesis in the last analysis. In this respect then he was true to the principles of traditional psychology.

### MEANING

The cardinal factor in the origin of neuroses is the nature of the root-ideas, the setting which gives any experience its meaning and which again is conserved or stored in the particular neurogram. Dr. Prince was never tired of relating the anecdote of the great naturalist, Louis Agassiz, who when his terrified wife cried "Louis, Louis, there is a snake in the house," exclaimed "What! only one? What could have become of the other?" In our own era of political strife we can think of hundreds of names and labels which would re-activate a setting with entirely different meanings for different people. And is not the complex which forms on the basis of this or that setting akin to the psychoneurosis, if not actually to be identified with it?

Prince's conception of meaning is not only a contribution to abnormal psychology. It constitutes a chapter in theoretical psychology; and again it is brought home that merely to associate Prince's name with psychopathology, as is commonly done, is somewhat of an injustice to the man, as well as possibly an oversight of a large part of the bridge which connects two important branches of science.

RE-EDUCATION

It was as early as 1898 that Prince emphasized the rôle of education in the treatment of psychoneurotics. To say that he was the first to have advocated this method would, of course, be an overstatement; for all forms of psychotherapy include it as an integral part of the treatment.

Prince, however, has supplied the theoretical basis of such re-education, through his conception of meaning and root-ideas. Re-education does not become merely a phase of suggestion — ideas implanted on the mind of the sufferer; rather it affords the patient a new *point of view*. We perceive here again the rational note in Prince's system. "It is surprising", wrote Prince, exactly forty years ago, "to find after a searching inquiry . . . how often what seems to be a mere chaos of unrelated mental and physical phenomena will resolve itself into a series of logical events, and law and order be found to underlie the symptomatic angle."

That may be said to be the groundwork of the psychoneurosis, which must have its counterpart in the behavior of the patient. Prince does not mention the Freudian term *displacement,* but he might well have done so. The displacement, as I understand it, would then lead to a distortion of perspective, a warping of viewpoint, a metamorphosis of value. The displacement is on the unconscious level; the distortion, on the conscious level, and the queerness or instability on the behavior plane. Any type of element may be displaced; but only a rational unit may be distorted.

Prince's re-education then consisted in restoring the healthy, normal or reasonable point of view, often through a sort of dialectic method which causes the patients to see light, of their own accord. The procedure involves autosuggestion perhaps as much as suggestion. Above all, it requires the establishment of a balanced approach to the particular problem. Re-education loosens the pendulum of common sense, which, in some instances, is fastened on one side, so as to oscillate regularly in order to traverse the necessary ground of a situation. In some cases re-education merely regulates the too impetuous tempo.

Re-education must be understood in two senses. First of all it is a theory. Secondly it is a method, or perhaps rather an art; and Prince excelled particularly in the art. It must be borne in mind that this brief exposition of Prince's notion of re-education does not refer to its earlier phase, when often electricity would be applied to the patient, partly for effect.

The late stage, as practiced by Prince, necessitated a search for the underlying causes or motives. Indeed, it may be said that there was a re-activation of the original trauma, or at least a re-enactment of the primary (although not "primal") scene, so that the patient could pick up the thread from that point and experience an illumination. This method may be in some degree related to the induction of artificial fever in order to produce a shock that serves to clear up the befogged mind.

The concept of re-education, then, while by no means an innovation on the part of Morton Prince, has undoubtedly been formulated or crystallized in such a way as to be connected with his system of psychology, as a whole. Of its practical aspect, particularly the skill, the adroitness, employed in achieving his objective, only those who have worked closely with him as associates could present an adequate idea. Naturally part of the art was to be found in the charm of his personality, in his ability to set up a *close rapport* between himself and his patient on a cordial plane.

## SHREWD OBSERVATIONS

In addition to the fundamental concepts in Prince's system which have been briefly discussed in the foregoing sections, there is yet to add that Prince had made a number of shrewd observations in various articles, which have scarcely been noticed in the literature.

Let us take but one, which he originally brought to light in the *Boston Medical and Surgical Journal* (April 28, 1898) and in a chapter on "Traumatic Neuroses" in *American System of Practical Medicine* (1898). Some one, in the widely accepted belief that neurosis might result from any physical shock or accident, had remarked in the Journal mentioned that the marines, because of the limited space available for their operations on boats, would always be in danger of developing neuroses in the rough and tumble of their activities aboard.

Prince replied to this by pointing out that the physical shock was not necessarily a condition of neurosis, that the injury inflicted in many railroad accidents which leads to severe mental trouble may be much less than the physical blows received in being suddenly tackled on the gridiron, yet he had never heard of a "traumatic neurosis" developing from such rough treatment. A questionnaire addressed to managers and physicians in charge of the principal college teams did not disclose the existence of such neuroses; and he further cites the fact that blows of the fists in pugilistic contests have not been known to bring about neurosis.

Dr. Dana, a colleague of Prince, had, as a matter of fact, reported on three cases of football neurosis, but these seem to constitute such an insignificant proportion as to be negligible.

The theory behind this is that with the players, boxers, and sailors there is a different "set" than in the case of the passenger who sustains an injury in an accident on his travels. There is a prepared attitude, a reservoir of meanings entirely disparate in those who are hurt while indulging in sport.

May we not apply this explanation to account for the remarkable absence of war neuroses or shell shock cases, at least in the Loyalist ranks, during the present Civil War in Spain, whereas the World War had presented many thousands of such cases? Certainly one must admit that the defender of his ideals has a different mental set than the drafted soldier who is not sure what he is fighting for, and for whom the enemy is merely an abstract creature, "built up" through propaganda. In other words — although Prince has not drawn this necessary conclusion — the *sense of values* is a determining factor in the development or non-development of neuroses. We should expect, on this hypothesis, a far greater number of war neuroses among the aggressors than among the defenders on any battlefield. Naturally there is some allowance to be made for the cultural or personality level of the individuals involved. The ignorant coolies in China making their stand against the Japanese cannot be compared with the high-minded men who have left comfortable homes and fine careers in other countries to fight in the International Brigade on behalf of the Loyalists in Spain.

## SOCIAL AND POLITICAL PSYCHOLOGY

When Morton Prince entered the political arena, in 1915, to bolster the cause of the Allies and began to discourse on such topics as "The Psychology of the Kaiser" and "The Creed of Deutschtum", many of us, including myself, then only a student, viewed these activities with some misgivings.

It was still the age when science was supposed to remain aloft, transcending all the conflicts and foibles below. A psychologist who dabbled in politics was of course in danger of being discredited by his colleagues; for his motives would soon be questioned.

Prince, however, was not merely getting "mixed up with politics". He had no need of it; for he was reared in a political atmosphere and had even been urged to accept the nomination for the office of mayor of Boston. It was not politics which had concerned him but rather society. His idea of a "world-consciousness" which, could it have been truly realized, would have saved the League of Nations from becoming but a helpless puppet in the hands of hypocritical ventriloquists, was just then taking shape. Prince, it would appear, had inherited a spark of the Prophets. He could envision a world where the lion could dwell side by side with the lamb, but they would first both have to be united through some ideal.

Fully two decades have elapsed before many of us have begun to appreciate that even if psychologists will not attempt to tackle politics, politics is apt to tackle psychology, and that far from decrying Prince's efforts on behalf of an eventual world peace, we must admit that he was in advance of his time. It is heartening to think that many of the American psychologists, at present, are interested in international issues, and that the Society for the Psychological Study of Social Issues, which is devoted to the examination of the very questions that at one time would have been considered taboo in academic circles, is the lustiest offspring of the American Psychological Association.

Since an extract from Prince's essay on a world consciousness is included in the present volume, it is not necessary to expatiate further on the subject, except to add that with the nations arrayed against one another along the lines of certain ideologies, we could envisage the world as a case of multiple personality with the erstwhile more or less integrated personality, which represented the world in normal periods, being dominated by a secondary personality that had been forming out of the disintegration incidental to the World War. Abnomal psychology would, in the past, draw on political philosophy or government for its metaphors. For the nonce, let us reverse the process.

### CONCLUSION

Morton Prince, like so many other progressive spirits, has not restricted himself to the field which he had started out to cultivate. A versatile investigator, he could not confine himself to medicine. His earliest papers dealt with such prosaic topics as vaccination, tonsillitis, electrolysis, and disinfection. He soon branched out into neurological problems, and thence into the highroads of psychology and psychiatry.

It was natural for medical men to look upon him as somewhat of a renegade, while psychologists, particularly of the younger generation, regarded him as an interloper. Undoubtedly he gave the impression sometimes of being a "Saul among the prophets." How much of the ambivalent attitude toward him in some quarters had been due to the fact that he had been brought up in a wealthy atmosphere (and perhaps his surname, as well as his bearing, was a subliminal factor) will, of course, never be known, but his position in the scientific world, when compared with that of a number of his colleagues, was somewhat puzzling.

With the rise of Freud, Prince became more and more eclipsed, as was his more famous associate, Janet. It should be borne in mind that Prince had never been a pretender to the throne. He was not even set on being a *primus inter pares*. He could always take his place as a peer in the world of psychological medicine.

The paradox about his influence is that while he was always looked up to as a distinguished representative of his profession, his theories did not take root academically, although they were widely discussed. They seemed to have fitted into the grooves too readily. Perhaps, had he elaborated mechanisms that were a bit more speculative, he might have met with greater success.

To my mind, it was not the matter so much as his manner that proved a stumbling-block. He was clear-headed and systematic, yet he would often go into such details that the reader's attention would become diverted from the main issue. His handling of the multiple personality cases over the course of various studies (hallucinations, co-conscious imagery, visions) is especially to be criticized in this connection. There is a repetitious process which runs through several of his chapters and papers. While it is true that he wishes to put before us all the data upon which to base our opinion, there is produced the feeling that a good deal of what we are reading is too trivial.

A writer with a decidedly publicistic style would have been able to impress not with the wealth of the protocol but with the selection of the particulars and distributed emphasis. Prince was at his best in his more compact statements, when he did not employ stereotyped expressions like "when and as" or "as she maintains, and I am inclined to believe." In nearly every one of his essays, there was a message but it usually would be packed in a barrel of excelsior.

Some, no doubt, grow impatient, and become lukewarm toward the nugget after finding it. Others skim over it without realizing its value. In this way, we are prone to forget sometimes that he was a pioneer in American psychopathology; and that at a time when Weir Mitchell's "rest cure", designed to build fat and blood in the patient was the widely acclaimed treatment for psychoneurotic individuals, Morton Prince had already laid the foundation here for the psychogenic view of mental disorders.

This designation, "A pioneer in American psychopathology", which is inscribed over the portal of the Prince Room in the Boston Medical Library, and which was taken from the title-page of the commemorative volume in his honor, is as appropriate an estimate of his life-work as can be conceived.

It was not only, however, as a creative force that Prince figures in the annals of psychology. He has other merits to his credit. Perhaps in this connection, it will be fitting to quote from my editorial preface to the volume just cited, *Problems of Personality,* which included contributions from a galaxy of distinguished psychologists and psychiatrists in the United States and abroad.

"In the case of the present volume, there is a further complication in that Dr. Prince, as will be seen from a glance at the bibliography of his writings, has not maintained any one single intellectual interest throughout life. His earlier years he had devoted partly to philosophy but mainly to purely medical studies. Thence he advanced to neurology and later to psychopathology and abnormal psychology, in which field he had acquired his fame, largely in connection with his multiple personality researches.

. . . . . . . . .

"To point out his merit as a pioneer in psychology would be quite unnecessary here, but since his unique position as a mediator between two or more branches of science is often lost sight of, let it be remembered that it was Dr. Prince who, at any rate in the United States, supplied the bridge between abnormal psychology and what is ordinarily called general psychology. Through the establishment of the *Journal of Abnormal Psychology* and the publication of symposia he was able to bring about an exchange of views which otherwise would have remained inarticulate; and, furthermore, through his travels and extra-academic accomplishments he has succeeded in promoting the cause of psychology in distant countries and of American psychology in particular by effecting a *rapprochement,* more or less international in its scope, among the various workers in psychology, psychopathology and allied fields.

. . . . . . . . .

"In this connection, Dr. Prince's merit lies not only in his original contributions, but in bringing his findings into accord with the body of accepted facts, and thus ensuring a clarity of presentation which few specialists even care to acquire. It is through such a careful orientation that Dr. Prince has done much to break down the barriers which divide the several schools in his field of science; and by his generous appreciation of the work of others, he has been instrumental in bringing to a focus, under the purview of psychology, a number of divergent views which but for him might have remained detached and scattered."

A. A. ROBACK

# BIBLIOGRAPHY

## BOOKS AND ARTICLES ON PRINCE *(and in his honor)*

A. A. ROBACK (ed): *Problems of Personality*. Studies Presented to Dr. Morton Prince, Pioneer in American Psychopathology, 1925, IX, 434.

W. S. TAYLOR: *Morton Prince and Abnormal Psychology* (1928) XI, 137.

### ARTICLES AND OBITUARIES

(Titles preceded by † refer to obituaries)

[G. W. ALLPORT] Editorial. *Jour. Abnormal and Social Psychology*. 1938, vol. 33, pp. 3-13.

*Cyclopedia of American Biography*, (suppl. ed.) 1931, vol. 12, pp. 38-40.

*Harvard College, Class of 1875*. Fiftieth Anniversary Report, 1875-1925, pp. 94-98.

† *Herald-Tribune* (New York) Sept. 1, 1929.

L. H. HORTON: "Prince's 'Neurogram' Concept — Its Historical Position", in *Problems of Personality* (1925) pp. 387-419.

J. JASTROW: "Morton Prince". Encyclopaedia of the Social Sciences, vol. XII, page 405.

† *Jour. Amer. Medical Assoc.*, Sept. 14, 1929, vol. 93, page 864.

M. MOORE: "Morton Prince, '79". *Harvard Medical Alumni Bulletin*, 1938, vol. 12, pp. 23-25.

M. MOORE: "Morton Prince, M. D., 1854-1929". *Jour. Nervous and Mental Disease*, 1938, vol. 88 (in press) about 10 pages.

† [H. T. MOORE]: Editorial, *Jour. Abnormal and Social Psychology*, 1929-30, vol. 24, pp. 249-250.

† G. H. MONKS: "Morton Prince." *Harvard Graduates Magazine*, 1929, vol. 38, pp. 185-193.

† H. A. MURRAY: "Dr. Morton Prince." *Jour. Nervous and Mental Disease*, 1929, vol. 70, pp. 663-666.

T. K. OESTERREICH: "Zur Einführung" in *Die Spaltung der Persönlichkeit*, 1932, ninth volume of the Beiträge zur Philosophie und Psychologie, pp. VI-IX.

A. A. ROBACK: Preface to *Problems of Personality* (1925), pp. xi-xiii.

A. A. ROBACK: "Morton Prince; a Memoir" (in press) about twenty pages.

† E. W. TAYLOR: "Morton Prince, M.D., LL.D.; 1854-1929," *Archives of Neurology and Psychiatry*, 1929, vol. 22, pp. 1031-1036.

W. S. TAYLOR: (ed.) *Readings in Abnormal Psychology and Mental Hygiene*, 1926.
There are twenty extracts in this anthology taken out of Prince's writings. Prince's name occurs 63 times in the index, almost twice as often as any other name, Freud and Janet included.

W. S. TAYLOR: "Morton Prince." *Dictionary of American Biography*, vol. 15, pp. 230-232.

† *Times* (New York), Sept. 1, 1929, section 2, page 5.

† *Transcript* (Boston), August 31, 1929.

Shorter sketches of Morton Prince appear in the *International Encyclopaedia* (1923 edition), and supplement volume 2, 1930, *Who's Who in American Medicine, American Men of Science*, first — fourth editions (1906, 1910, 1921, 1927), *Who's Who in the East* (1930), *Who's Who in America*, 1908-1909 *to* 1928-1929, *The Psychological Register* (1932), vol. 3, *Enciclopedia Universal Ilustrada*, (Barcelona) vol. 47, and (†) *New England Jour. Medicine*, Sept., 1929, vol. 201, p. 501.

### BIBLIOGRAPHIES OF PRINCE'S WRITINGS

There are four bibliographies of Morton Prince's papers and books, none of which is exhaustive:

(a) The first, compiled by Miss M. H. Moran, appeared in *Problems of Personality*, 1925 (ed. by A. A. Roback), pp. 420-427, and is classified under the heads of general medicine, forensic medicine, neurology, psychology, psychopathology, psychiatry and philosophy — a total of 96 papers. The books and collaborations are listed separately.

(b) The second, which appeared in W. S. Taylor's *Morton Prince and Abnormal Psychology* (1928), pp. 128-132, enumerates only those writings (46) which the author made use of in the preparation of his exposition.

(c) *The Psychological Register* (1932), pp. 394-397, presents the fullest list of Dr. Prince's contributions and collaborations (136 titles in all).

(d) A bibliography by Merrill Moore (privately printed, 1938), includes several references to writings about Prince.

Nearly all of Prince's papers are to be found in the Prince Room at the Boston Medical Library, which also houses his manuscripts, among them a neatly written out lecture, with diagrams and with sketches executed in his own hand, on "The Architecture of the Brain." Apparently completed in 1881, it was to serve as material for a course he expected to offer in some medical school.

## TRANSLATIONS

"Experimentelle Untersuchungen über psycho-galvanische Reaktionen," etc.; *Jour. der Psychol. und Neurol.*, 1908, vol. 13, pp. 249-262.

"Die Psychopathologie eines Falles von Phobie," *Intern. Ztschr. f. Psychoanal.*, 1913, vol. 1, pp. 533-546.

*La Psychologie du Kaiser;* Etude de ses sentiments et de son obsession. (Transl. by J. Pineau), Paris, 1915. The same booklet has been translated into Japanese, and was published in Tokyo.

Ueber die Notwendigkeit das systematische Studium der funktionellen Krankheiten in die medizinische Studienordnung Aufzunehmen." *Intern. Ztschr. f. Individual Psychologie*, 1928, vol. 6, pp. 2-5.

"Der Fall Miss Beauchamp" in *Die Spaltung der Persönlichkeit*, 1932, pp. 1-30 (translated by W. Hermes) Stuttgart, 1932 (Beiträge zur Philosophie und Psychologie, No. 9).

PART I

# CHAPTER I

## The Rôle of Meaning in the Psychoneuroses[1]

THERE is no more fascinating study in psychology than that of meaning. The more intimately one probes into this component of the mind, the more interesting it becomes and the clearer our conception of the nature of perception and "ideas" of which it is the most important ingredient for human behavior. The same is true of meaning as a factor in many other problems of personality. An understanding of meaning gives an insight into the genesis of our likes and dislikes, our attachments and aversions and prejudices, our sentiments and ideals, — in short of numerous traits of personality and the behavior which they incite. Meaning is the core of perception and ideation in that it underlies both. It is a component which is intimately bound up with our whole intellectual and affective life in its various ramifications — a component so fundamental that it is the key to many problems in both normal behavior and the psychoneuroses.

As to the latter conditions, in meaning we can find the basis of an interpretation and solution of their pathology and therapeutics, which may well be adopted as a working principle for a school of abnormal psychology. Through meaning alone we can satisfactorily explain — and I believe correctly explain — that for which other schools have introduced hypothetical concepts requiring unconscious entities (e. g., libido) incapable of scientific demonstration.

It is not necessary, indeed it would be tedious in this connection, to repeat in any detail the conventional account

---

1 This paper, here revised and abridged, was presented under the title, "The Meaning of Ideas as Determined by Unconscious Settings," before the American Psychopathological Association, May 29, 1912. *Journal of Abnormal Psychology,* Oct.-Nov. 1912.

of the psychology of perception; for it is extensively treated by writers of text-books. So much attention is commonly given to it that it would seem that little remained to be said about it. Yet the conventional exposition oversimplifies the situation and thus prevents us from viewing perception as a true and complex *integrate* in which many ingredients function in different combinations. Consequently, from the point of view here taken, the generally accepted conception of perception is inadequate and incomplete.[1] This is particularly true of meaning which, as one of its elements, is so intimately bound up with perception (and "ideas"). Consequently it will conduce to clarity and help lay a foundation for my main theme, if I point out in a general rough way certain facts regarding perception and meaning. This is also essential in order to show the application of meaning to the treatment and genesis of the psychoneuroses as well as the light which therapeutic methods throw on the psychology of perception.

Perception may be regarded both as a process and a group of conscious elements, some of which are within the focus of attention or awareness and some of which are outside this focus. As a *process* it undoubtedly may include much that is entirely unconscious and, therefore, without conscious equivalents, and much that appears in consciousness. As a group of conscious elements, it is an integrate, or compounding of many elements.

It is commonly agreed that your perception of Dr. X, for example, whom you recognize as your physician, is much more than a visual image, a cluster of visual sensations, — I mean the sensations of color and form that come from your retina when you see him, and which combined constitute an image of his person. Besides the latter it includes a number of memory images, some of which are only in the fringe of consciousness, and can only be recognized by introspection, or under special conditions. These images may be (as they most often are) visual, orienting him in space and in

---

1 The traditional view takes into account only a limited number of the data at our disposal and neglects methods of investigation which provide data essential for the understanding of this psychological process.

past time, or in various associate relations, according to your previous experiences; they may also include auditory — the imaginal sound of his voice, — or verbal images of his name; or they may be the so-called kinesthetic images, etc., and all these images supplement the actual visual sensations of color and form I have mentioned.

It is the integration of these secondary images with the primary visual image of X that converts the latter into a perception. Otherwise it would be only an image of a face, any face. But a perception includes more than images, it includes cognition and meaning; in this case a simple meaning, namely, that what you see is not only a face but it is X. (Undoubtedly other factors, particularly *affects,* take part in meaning, and we shall see later what they are.)

Even to be aware of (recognize) the image as a human face and not a monkey or chair, of course, implies cognition, as indicated by the term "recognize," and, to this extent, it carries with it a certain amount of meaning. Now, this meaning must be derived from past experiences with human beings acting as a context or setting, all of which goes to show what a complex affair a perception is. It is much more than a single sensation or a simple image, though it may embrace form and color.

That secondary images take part in perception is, of course, well recognized in every text-book on psychology, where they will be found described. Everyone knows that. But what is not generally known is whence they come. What thrusts them up into the content of awareness to make a perception? Academic psychology is satisfied to say that they are there as associated elements, and rests content with that. But dynamic psychology is not content with that, and from its data seeks to explain them in terms of the unconscious; that is to say, to refer them to unconscious processes and dispositions of which they are integral elements. In normal everyday life it is easy to become aware of them under certain conditions. For instance, to take an auditory perception; you are listening through the telephone and hear a strange voice speaking. Aside from the meaning of the words, so far as concerns the voice, you are conscious of little more than auditory sensations, although you do perceive them as those of a human voice, and not of a phonograph.

Then, of a sudden, visual images of the speaker's face, and perhaps of the room in which he is speaking, and his situation therein, of the furnishings of the room, etc., become associated with the voice. Instantly you recognize, perceive the voice as that of your acquaintance, Y. Your perception of the voice now takes on a fuller and different meaning in accordance with these imaginal elements. (Your perception, also, may acquire feeling-tones, affects of pleasantness or unpleasantness corresponding to your previous experience with Y.) In such an experience, probably common to everybody, the secondary images which take part in perception are unusually clear and easily detected. But the point to be noted is: these images play an important part in giving a meaning to the auditory images — the voice — and make the latter a perception. And this meaning is a more or less common meaning, common, that is, to all those who know Y and have had substantially the same experiences with him that you have had. Obviously, then, perception includes meaning besides sensory elements.

But, as I shall presently argue, a perception of one and the same object may have several meanings corresponding to the different contexts in which it is set; that is, to the different experiences a given individual, you or I, may have had with the object. And of these several meanings, one or more may be peculiar to and possessed only by you or me. It may be called an egocentric meaning. This watch, for example, may have for you only the meaning of a mechanism to keep time, but for me it may, also, in addition have another meaning, that of a souvenir, with strong feeling-tones, of a dead friend, and in each of these perceptions of the watch, different secondary images are incorporated in accordance with this difference in the meanings. Consider what different meanings the above perception of Y would have had for you and me if he had been your father.

Another common everyday experience,[1] which I have frequently had, may be taken as one more example. I meet an apparent stranger in the street. He bows to me. Who is he? I am wondering until suddenly an image of his face flashes into my awareness, not isolated as it was a moment ago, but integrated with a lot of secondary images of the interior of a jeweler's shop; images of a showcase filled with jewelry, etc., and one of this man standing behind the showcase; perhaps even of people moving about. I may even have auditory images of the sound of his voice; and to all this may be added certain feeling-tones — pleasant or unpleasant. We see then that with the emergence into the content of awareness of these images, my perception is no longer that of a stranger without egocentric meaning, but of a salesman in a particular jeweler's shop, and as such it has a particular meaning for me which it does not have for another person. My perception is derived from personal experience of the jeweler's shop, in which experience, as a setting, conserved as memories, the image of the salesman is incorporated. These memories necessarily have been conserved as dispositions in my "unconscious," as residua. Now, at the moment of recognition, this whole setting has been switched into functional activity, secondary images emerge, and my perception of a stranger becomes that of a known salesman.

This phenomenon is precisely the same as that of the conventional illustration of text-books, in which one and the same design is perceived at one moment with the meaning of a flight of steps and at another as an overhanging wall, according as one unconscious setting is switched into activity or another. Let us keep constantly in mind that the experiences from which the associative images of a perception are derived and which provide the context and meaning must, by the theory of memory, be conserved as organized unconscious residua or dispositions and, as a working hypothesis, that these organized unconscious dispositions become functionally activated and take part in every per-

---

[1] Introspection following everyday experiences, I think, is fully as, if not more accurate than, laboratory experiments, as in the latter, images as artefacts are liable to be created unwittingly by the subject.

ception. *Images, setting, context, meaning function as a psychic whole.*

But we are not obliged to rely upon the method of introspection to demonstrate the integration of secondary images as elements essential for perception (and meaning). This can be done experimentally by objective methods, by which the perceptual integrate can be broken up, the perception shorn of certain of its images and thereby made to lose its meaning and cease to be that particular perception. Then, with the reintegration of the images, the original perception is reformed. By way of illustration, let me cite the following observation, which is possibly unique. As a preliminary, it is well to point out that if memory images are habitually synthesized with sensations to form a given perception, and if perception is a matter of synthesis, then theoretically, it ought to be possible to dissociate these images. Further, in that case, the perception as such ought to disappear. That this theoretical assumption correctly represents the facts I have been able to demonstrate by the following experiment which I have repeated many times.

I should first explain that, as Janet was the first to demonstrate by certain technical procedures, some hysterics can be "abstracted" (dissociated) in such a way that the experimenter's voice is not consciously heard by them, but is heard and understood subconsciously. The ordinary procedure is to whisper to the subject while his attention is focused on something else. The whisper undoubtedly acts as a suggestion that the subject will not consciously hear what is whispered. The whisper has a meaning and the whispered word-images are accordingly dissociated but are perceived coconsciously, and whatever coconsciousness exists can thus be surreptitiously communicated with, and responses obtained without the knowledge of the personal consciousness. In this way, I have been able to make numerous observations showing the presence of dissociated coconscious complexes, which otherwise would not have been suspected. Now, the experiment which I am about to cite was intended for the purpose of determining whether certain experiences for which the subject had amnesia were coconsciously remembered, but the results obtained, besides giving affirmative evidence on this point, furnished certain instructive facts indicative of the dissociation of secondary images, and with this dissociation the disappearance of a previous perception as such.

The subject, Miss B, was in the state known as B IV a, an hypnotic state, *her eyes closed*. While she was conversing with me on a subject which held her attention, I whispered in her ear with the view of communicating with coconscious ideas as explained above. While I was whispering she remarked, "Where are you? Where have you gone?" and later asked why I went away and what I kept coming and going for.

On examination, it appeared that during the moments when I whispered in her ear, she not only ceased to hear my voice, but actually believed I had gone away. That is to say, she could no longer visualize my body in particular juxtaposition to her own, the secondary *visual* images being dissociated with my whispered words. The dissociation of the auditory images of my voice had carried away also the associated visual images necessary for a perceptual idea of me in a particular space. At these times, however, she continued the conversation and was alert and not at all in a dreamy state.

But this was not all. Testing her tactile sense later, I found that there was no dissociation of this sense during these moments. She felt tactile impressions while she was not hearing my voice, but she explained afterwards (while whispering, of course, I could not ask aloud questions regarding sensations) that when I touched her and when she held my hand, palpating it in a curious way as if trying to make out what it was, she felt the tactile impressions, or tactile sensations, but not naturally. It appeared as the result of further observations that this feeling of unnaturalness and strangeness was due to a dissociation of the secondary visual images which normally occur with the tactile images. When this occurred she could not perceive the hand as *my* hand. (She described the tactile impressions of my hand as similar to those she felt when she lifted her own hand after it had "gone to sleep." It felt dead and heavy as if it belonged to no one in particular. She perceived the hand but not as *my* hand. My hand felt as though it might be anybody's hand.)

Further testing revealed that when, *before* abstraction, she held my hand, she could and did definitely visualize my hand, my arm, and even my face, and then perceived the hand as *my* hand. While she was thus visualizing, I again abstracted her auditory perceptions by the whispering process. Presto! At once, the secondary visual images of my hand, etc., disappeared: and with this disappearance of visual images, the perception of the hand as *my* hand again disappeared.

Desiring now to learn whether these dissociated visual images were perceived coconsciously, I whispered, at the same time holding her hand, "Do you see my hand, arm, and face?" She nodded (automatically), "Yes." "Does *she* (meaning the personal consciousness) see them?" (Answer by nod), "No." (The personal consciousness (B IV a) was unaware of the questions and the nodding; the latter was performed subconsciously.)

This experiment was repeated several times. As often as she ceased to hear my voice, she ceased to visualize and perceive my hand, though she could feel it without recognizing it.

Interpreting these findings, I think we are compelled to conclude that for a perception of the tactual impressions as *my* hand, the associated visual images of my body were necessary to give them a particular meaning; and that when these images were dissociated (by technical methods) from the tactual impressions, this particular perception including meaning was lost to consciousness.

Here is another observation bearing on this mechanism of perception. We have seen that a tactual perception of the body includes visual and other sensory images besides the tactile sensation.

Now, B. C. A., in one hypnotic state, spontaneously develops general anesthesia so complete that she has no consciousness of her body whatsoever. She does not know whether she is standing or sitting, nor the position of her limbs, nor her location in space; she describes herself as simply *thought without a body — as thought, in space.* More than this lack of objective perception, she cannot *visualize* any part of her body. In contrast with this she can visualize the experimenter, the room, and the objects in the room, but not her body. Further, strangely enough, the dissociation of the tactual field from consciousness is so complete that she cannot evoke tactual images of any sort. As a consequence the dissociation of these images carries with it the inhibition of the visual images that were synthesized with them through experience. In other words, both tactual and visual images of her body have disappeared, and with them perception of her body. Visual images of the environment, however, not being synthesized with the tactual body-images, can still be evoked.

So we see from observations based on introspection and experimentation that perception includes, besides primary simple images (sensations) of an object, secondary central images of various kinds and in various numbers; and, what is more important for our theme, that these latter images play a part in determining the character of the perception, *i. e.*, its meaning.

Furthermore, these images are readily traceable to past mental experiences with which they correspond and which, as a setting, have been conserved in the form of residual dispositions, organized as an unconscious complex or integrate with the object. And so far as these images provide meaning of whatever kind and however limited and specialized, this meaning must originate in this setting. These facts are elementary, as every first-year student of psychology knows. But the principle underlying them is, as we shall see, of fundamental significance for the understanding of many psychoneuroses, though this may not be generally recognized.

## II

*The Setting and Meaning of Ideas.* What I have said thus far refers to the content of an idea or perception only so far as it is a compound of images and so far as these images contribute to meaning. But meaning ordinarily includes more than images. It includes concepts, as well, with affects or feeling-tones. The idea of a lion, for example, includes the concept of a fearful, dangerous animal, or of exciting "big game," or of a carnivorous mammal, a species of the family *Felidae*, according as our experiences have been respectively those of an ordinary mortal, or of an enthusiastic hunter, or of a scientist. And these concepts are particular meanings of the idea "lion" corresponding to and determined by those past experiences. And evidently these meanings are of a personal character insofar as they are characteristic of any individual. Such personal meanings may be called *egocentric*. But, of course, a lion may have all these and more meanings for the same individual according to the situation, and these meanings may be shared in common with other individuals; and in so far as this is the case they are common or group meanings. But the point, now, is that the idea or perception of a lion includes as meaning more than images; namely, concepts and feeling-tones; otherwise our responses and behavior towards a lion would be little or nothing more than tropisms and the same for all individuals. If this be admitted, as, I think, everyone will agree it must be, we may describe the content of ideas or perception (P) as images (I) plus meaning (M)[1]:

$$P = I + M.$$

The concepts and affects of meaning, then, are, like images, *acquired* and, if so, meaning must be derived from and determined by associated past experiences.

These antecedent experiences that are the origin of meaning, though not always remembered and brought into the light of awareness, are easily discovered by any one of

---

1 For an able discussion of ideas and meaning see R. F. Hoernlé "Image, Idea and Meaning"; *Mind* (N. S.), 1907, no. 61.

the technical methods of so-called psychological analysis. And such methods, as well as everyday observations, show that our associative experiences become, by the fact of being so experienced, organized into integrates, *i. e.*, complexes and systems; and thus the meaning of our ideas, our ideals, beliefs, prejudices, judgments, etc., are formed and acquired.

All this, it will be said, is only a platitude. And so it is, or ought to be; for everyone knows it, or ought to know it. But how can antecedent experiences that are past and gone persist as an organized system and determine persisting meanings? The only conceivable way is as conserved residua or dispositions in the unconscious. That is to say, associated antecedent experiences (from which meaning is derived) are represented in the unconscious as conserved integrates or complexes of dispositions. If this be not true, memory and the relation of the past to the present are unintelligible. If it be true, then these unconscious integrates of dispositions must play an active part in maintaining and determining the meaning an idea has for us. They must have an active functioning part, even if the source of that meaning — the antecedent experiences — cannot be voluntarily recalled to consciousness but has fallen into the shadow of oblivion.

Thus it is that, in this sense, ideas are said to have their *roots* in antecedent experiences; but when we say this what we really mean is that their *roots are conserved unconscious dispositions*, otherwise what we say has no meaning at all. And when ideas have acquired a common meaning for a group, whether that group be a caste, or a society, or a nation, they have roots in a setting of common experiences conserved in the unconscious in the manner here stated. These conserved integrates of dispositions may be called the *"setting."* Obviously this setting (antecedent experiences) determines the images, the point of view, the relation of the object to the individual, the concept of the object, and through the incorporated affect the emotional attitude, interest, etc., towards the latter. All this spells meaning. Just as the context in a printed sentence determines the meaning of any given word, so in the process of all perceptions the setting of antecedent experiences gives the meaning to the perception. Perception or idea thus takes one meaning according as it is constellated with one integrate of dispositions and another meaning according as it is constellated with another integrate. We may, then, enlarge our formula for a perception or idea so that it will include *setting* (S) and *root-dispositions* (R-D) as well as images and meaning.

P=I+M+S+R-D.

This may be illustrated by the following: let us suppose that three persons, in imagination, perceive a certain building used as a department store on a certain street I have in mind now, in a growing section of the city. One of these persons is an architect, another is an owner of property on this street, and the third is a woman who is in the habit of making purchases in the department store. When the architect thinks of the building he perceives it in his mind's eye in an architectural setting, that is, its architectural style, proportions, features and relations. His perception includes a number of secondary images of the neighboring buildings, of their styles of architecture, and of their relations form an esthetic point of view. In the perception of the owner of property there are also a number of secondary images, but these are of the passing people and traffic, of neighboring buildings as shops and places of business. In the woman's perception, the secondary images are of the interior of the store, the articles for sale, clothes she would like to purchase, and possibly bargains dear to her heart. Plainly each perceives the building from different points of view. Each might perceive the building from the same point of view, but in fact the point of view differs because of differences in the past experiences of each.

In the case of the architect, the root-experiences were those of previous observations on the architecture of the growing neighborhood. In the case of the property owner, they were of thoughtful reflections on the future development of the neighboring property, on the industrial relations of the building to business, and on the speculative future value of the property. In the case of the woman they were of purchases she had made, of articles she had seen and desired, of scenes inside the shop, etc. Out of these different

root-experiences a complex or integrate was built and conserved in the mind of each — conserved, that is, as unconscious dispositions. The idea of the building is set in these
respective dispositions which, therefore, may be called its
setting. The perception of the building obviously has a dif-
erent meaning for each of our three observers, and plainly
out of this setting of unconscious dispositions emerges the
conscious meaning, *i. e.*, an architectural, industrial, or shopping meaning, as the case happens to be; and we may further say the setting determines the point of view or attitude
of mind or interest. *Either the perception proper —
images — of the building or the meaning may be in the
focus of attention, and the other then recedes into the background or the fringe of awareness.*

Further, different *affects* may enter into each setting
and therefore into the perception and meaning. With the
architectural meaning there may be linked an esthetic joyful emotion; with the industrial meaning a depressing
emotion of anxiety; with the shopping meaning perhaps one
of anger, if the shopper had lost her temper with a salesgirl
and still has a feeling of resentment. These affects determine
the mental attitude towards the department store and were
plainly organized with the concepts pertaining to meaning.
They, largely, through their impulsive tendencies, determine the overt behavior of the individual towards the situation. (This incorporation of an emotion of course is of
considerable importance for psychopathic states.)

The humorous story of the bus conductor who tried to
reassure the old lady, exposing her legs as she climbed the
steps to the roof of the bus, with the comforting remark,
"Lor' ma'am; legs don't mean nothing to me," takes on much
psychological significance. Perhaps he little knew that legs
still had a meaning for him in the fringe of his awareness.

### III

*Settings May Be Partly Unconscious.* Now the thesis I
wish to present is one which is not so readily accepted by
psychologists, namely, the setting of an "idea" is a complex

*functioning* mechanism of which certain elements only may emerge into the focus of awareness or into the fringe of consciousness to be the meaning, while the rest of the elements (dispositions) remain as roots buried, so to speak, and hidden in the soil of antecedent experiences beyond all conscious recognition until they are dug up by psychological analysis. Thus, although in this case the meaning is conscious, *it is a part of a functioning complex which is largely unconscious.* Functioning, not inert, I say, for the evidence at hand compels the interpretation that the *complex, as a whole, or largely as a whole,* that which is unconscious as well as that which is conscious, takes on functional activity during ideation. And, indeed, though functioning, the greater part may remain unconscious while that which emerges into awareness as meaning may be only the affect and a verbal abbreviation or other symbol of the antecedent experiences (meaning). The roots may then have to be dug up to obtain the significance of the symbol and affect. *But the fundamental principle is that images, meaning, setting and root-dispositions are a psychological (or psycho-physiological) whole (P=I+M+S+R-D), and may function as a whole if adequately stimulated.*

The data supporting this theory are numerous, although its actual demonstration is difficult. The theory would explain the behavior of ideas in prejudices, affections, aversions, jealousies, etc., and in obsessions, such as the phobias, and even impulsions. The data are derived from the analysis of associative neuroses, synthetic experiments and pathological phenomena.

The theory, indeed, offers, I believe, the only intelligent explanation of these insistent affective states and particularly the abnormal anxiety and other states of obsession. It renders entirely unnecessary the conception of infantile sexual complexes (Oedipus complex, etc.) and the fantastic Freudian concept of the unconscious and its libido and many suppositious symbolisms and mechanisms invented to explain behavior.

The theory makes use, of course, of another theory — that of unconscious processes, just as a theory of gravitation or magnetism might make use of the theory of ether. It is beyond the scope of this paper to adduce the evidence for unconscious processes in general. I will merely say that this evidence is drawn from a large and varied number of normal, pathological and experimental phenomena.

It is obvious that all past experiences which originated the meaning to an idea cannot be in consciousness at a given moment. If I carefully introspect my imaginal perception or idea of an object, say of a politician, I do not find in my consciousness all the elements which have given me my viewpoint and attitude of mind and feeling towards him — the meaning of my idea of him as a great statesman or a demagogue, whichever it be — and yet it may not be difficult, by referring to my memory, to find the past root-experiences which have furnished the setting for this viewpoint. Very little of all these past experiences can be in the content of consciousness and much less in the focus of attention at any given moment; nevertheless I cannot doubt that these experiences really determine and are the roots of the meaning of my idea, for if challenged, I proceed to recite this conserved knowledge; and so it is with every one who defends the validity of the meaning of his ideas.

This theory is supported by the fact of common experience and knowledge, which it also renders intelligible, that we cannot change a person's idea (opinion) about anything without changing his viewpoint; that is to say, without so changing the root-ideas upon which the idea or opinion is based that he perceives the object from a different viewpoint. If and when this is done, the object of his idea acquires a new and different meaning derived from a new setting. Thus opinions notoriously undergo a change. Unless it is done, opinions persist, unmodified; and so it is with certain psychopathic states.

In the psychotherapy of pathological conditions, such as phobias, this principle is basic, as we shall presently see. In such conditions, the aim of therapeutics is to change the setting that determines the meaning of and therefore causes the disturbing idea. When this is done the obsession is cured.

The correctness of the theory is also borne out by the

fact that we can experimentally, almost at will, create settings from which not only images but a concept as meaning will emerge into awareness without the subject having any knowledge of how or why he acquired such a concept. This is done in hypnosis. In this state the subject is instructed, *i.e.,* educated, about any object chosen for the experiment. Thus a complex in which feeling is incorporated is organized as a setting to the object. After waking, if the subject has amnesia it will be found that the object (whatever it may be, the weather, a person, a place, or a disease) has acquired a meaning for the subject corresponding to the information suggested in hypnosis. If asked why he has such a concept, why the object has such a meaning for him, he will be unable to explain. He will have to say, "I don't know." And yet it is obvious, as can be shown by re-hypnotizing him, that it has emerged from a setting of root-ideas acquired in the hypnotic state.

The application of this procedure and principle to therapeutics is obvious.

The question at once comes to mind in the case of any given perception, how much of past experiences (associated ideas) is in consciousness as the setting which provides the meaning?

Although all past experiences which are responsible for the meaning of any idea cannot be in the content of consciousness, yet the meaning, however much verbally abbreviated as a concept or symbolized, must be in consciousness, else the term "meaning" would have no meaning — it would be sheer nonsense to talk of ideas having meaning. As I have said, the meaning may be in the focus of attention, or it may be in the fringe or background, according to the point of interest. If in the focus of attention, meaning plainly may include a succession of memories of quite a large number of past experiences, and if in the background, it will have various elements, which we are coming to. In either case, it may be held, and probably in most instances quite rightly, that meaning is a short verbal equivalent of past experiences, or summing up in the form of a symbol, and that this equivalent, or surrogate, or symbol is in the focus of attention or in the fringe of awareness, *i. e.*, is clearly or dimly conscious. Thus, in one of the examples given above, the industrial meaning of the owner's idea of the building might be a concept, the final summing-up of his past cogitations on the business value of the property; in the case of my idea of the politician, the symbol *statesman* or *demagogue*, might be in consciousness as the meaning. The rest of the past associative root-experiences, in either case, would furnish the origin of the meaning and setting, and as a part of a functioning whole would determine that which is in consciousness.

## IV

*Contents of the Fringe.* That meaning may be hidden or half hidden in the fringe is a matter of considerable practical importance for the understanding of certain psychoneuroses and even certain unavowed attractions, aversions and prejudices of everyday life.

When speaking colloquially of the content of consciousness, we have in mind those ideas or components of ideas — elements of thought — which are in the focus of attention, and therefore that of which we are more or less vividly aware. If you were asked to state what was in your mind at a given moment, it is the vivid elements, upon which your attention was focused, that you would describe. But, as every one knows, these do not constitute the whole field of consciousness at any given moment. Besides these, there is outside the focus a conscious margin or fringe of varying extent (consisting of sensations, perceptions, and even thoughts) of which you are only dimly aware. It is a sort of twilight zone in which the contents are so slightly illuminated by awareness as to be scarcely recognizable. The contents of this zone are readily forgotten owing to their having been outside the focus of attention; but much can be recalled if an effort to do so (retrospection) is made immediately after any given moment's experience. Much can be recalled only by the use of special technical methods of investigation. I dwell on these elementary facts because I believe that the more thoroughly this wonderful region is explored, the richer it will be found to be in conscious elements. And these play a more important part in everyday and pathological life than is generally supposed.

It must not be thought that because we are only dimly aware of the contents of this twilight zone, the individual elements necessarily lack definiteness and positive reality. To do so would be to confuse the awareness of something with that something itself. To so think would be like thinking that because we do not distinctly recognize objects in the dark, they are therefore but shadowy forms without substance. When, in states of abstraction or hypnosis, the ideas of this fringe of attention are recalled, as often is easily done, they are remembered as very definite real conscious elements; and the memory of them is as vivid as that of most thoughts. That these marginal ideas are not "vivid" at the time of their occurrence means simply that they are not in such dynamic relations with the whole content of consciousness as to be the focus of awareness or attention. What sort of relations are requisite for "awareness" is an unsolved problem. It seems to be a matter not only of synthesis but of dynamic intensity within the synthesis.

However that may be, outside that dynamic synthesis which we distinguish as the focus of attention, we can at certain moments recognize or recall to memory (whether through technical devices or not) a number of different conscious states. These may be roughly classified as follows:

1. Visual, auditory, and other sensory impressions to which we are not giving attention (e. g., the striking of a clock; the sound of horses passing in the street; voices from the next room; coenesthetic and other sensations of the body).

2. The secondary sensory images of which I spoke at the beginning of this chapter as taking part in perception.

3. Associative memories and thoughts pertaining to the ideas in the focus of attention.

4. Secondary independent trains of thought not related to those in the focus of attention (as when we are doing one thing or listening to conversation and thinking of something

else. Very likely, however, what appear to be secondary trains are often only alternating trains. I have, however, a considerable collection of data showing such concomitant secondary trains in certain subjects.) Such trains can be demonstrated as a precisely differentiated "stream" of consciousness in absent-minded conditions, where they may constitute a veritable doubling of consciousness.

Some of these marginal elements may be so distinctly within the field of awareness that we are conscious of them, but dimly so. Others, in particular cases at least, may be so far outside and hidden in the twilight obscurity that the subject is not even dimly aware of them. In more technical parlance, we may say, they are so far dissociated that they belong to an ultra-marginal zone and are really subconscious. Evidence of their having been present can only be obtained through memories recovered in hypnosis, abstraction, and by other methods. These may be properly termed *coconscious*. Undoubtedly, the degree of awareness for marginal elements, *i. e.*, the degree of dissociation between the elements of the content of consciousness, varies at different moments in the same individual according to the degree of concentration of attention and the character of the fixation, *e. g.*, whether upon the environment or upon inner thoughts. It also varies much in different individuals. Therefore some persons lend themselves as more favorable subjects for the detection of marginal and ultra-marginal states than others. Furthermore, according to certain evidence at hand, there is in some persons, at least, a constant shifting or interchange of elements going on between the fields of attention — the marginal, and the ultra-marginal zone. What is within the first at one moment is in the second, or is entirely coconscious, the next, and *vice versa*.

Amnesia develops very rapidly for the contents of the twilight region as I have already stated, and this renders their recognition difficult.[1]

---

1 The development of amnesia seems to be directly proportionate to the degree of awareness, provided there are no other dissociating factors such as an emotional complex.

## V

*Meaning in the Fringe.* Let us now return from this general survey of the fringe of consciousness to our theme — the setting which gives meaning to ideas.

It is obvious that theoretically, when I attend to the perceptual images of an idea, the meaning of the idea not being in the focus of awareness, may be found among the conscious states that make up the fringe of the dynamic field. For instance, if my idea of a certain "oil magnate," my knowledge of whom, we will say, has been gained entirely from the newspapers, is that of a "crook," this verbal meaning may be dimly in the fringe of my awareness. It may be, perhaps, only a summary or symbol of all the knowledge I have acquired regarding him. The *origin* and setting of this meaning — a crook — I can easily find in my associative memories of what I have read. But there would seem to be no need, indeed it would be impossible for all these roots to come to the surface and emerge into awareness — a short summary in the form of a secondary image, a word or symbol of a crook may be sufficient, and this conscious meaning may be relegated to the fringe. The same principle is applicable to a large number of the simple perceptions of objects in my environment — a book, an electric lamp, a horse, etc., where the meaning is likewise in the fringe.

Passing over such normal ideas of everyday life as incidental to our main purpose, when we examine certain pathological ideas (phobias) we find that the principle of "fringe and meaning" is supported by the actual facts of technical observation. We find in the fringe of consciousness, judging from my own observations, conscious elements which in particular cases may even give a hitherto unsuspected meaning to the pathological idea. For this and other reasons I am in the habit when investigating a pathological case, like an obsession, of inquiring into the whole content of consciousness and particularly the fringe of attention, and reviving the ideas contained therein, particularly those for which there is amnesia. It must be borne in mind that a person may be only dimly aware or totally unaware of the thoughts, images, sensations, etc., which make up the fringe of consciousness at any given moment. Moreover, as amnesia for this fringe, even when there is more or less awareness for its contents, ensues very rapidly, the memory of the same cannot be recovered by the ordinary methods of retrospection. And yet these thoughts, images, etc., contribute to the whole content of consciousness of the moment.

Obviously when the meaning is in the fringe, the emotional response that is excited by the perception of some object may be entirely incomprehensible to the subject. Though the object, and often the very thought of it, arouses a strong feeling-tone, even an intense emotion, it has no meaning, of which he is consciously aware, that justifies or explains the emotion. Yet this meaning, in such a case, can be found by analysis in the fringe.

The principle is easily demonstrable in individuals who are victims of "anxiety attacks," or attacks of fear, a very common form of psychosis, or obsession. In obsessions, an intense emotional innate disposition or "instinct" — most commonly fear, or anger (hatred) or affection — is integrated in the setting and, dominating the content of consciousness, characterizes the psychosis. There are several types. In one the subject suffers from recurrent attacks of fear without knowing what he is afraid of or what excites the attacks, because the object is in the fringe.

In another type the fear is excited by some well-recognized object, but the object has no conscious meaning that renders the fear intelligible. The subject can give no explanation of his viewpoint. The fear may be of fainting, of church steeples, or of thunder storms, or of a particular disease, say cancer, or of open spaces or closed places, or what not. The fear recurs in attacks which are excited by the object or stimuli of one kind or another that are associated with the object.[1] The patient can give no explanation of the

1 These associated stimuli that excite an attack can always be traced to some associated element — subjective or objective — that was a part of an antecedent situation from which the obsession developed. In consequence of this associa-

meaning of this perception that renders intelligible his fear. There is nothing in his consciousness, so far as he knows, which gives a meaning to it and explains the fear.

Such cases lend themselves admirably to the demonstration of meaning as a concrete integral component of a perception and the part it plays in the pathology and genesis of an obsession and other fixed ideas (prejudices, affections, aversions, etc.) The following case is an example of both types.

C. D. was the victim of attacks of fear; the attacks were so intense that at times she had been almost a prisoner in her house in dread of such onsèts when away from the refuge of her home. And yet she was unable, even after two prolonged searching questionings, to define the exact nature of the fear which was the salient feature of the attacks, or from her ordinary memories to give any explanation of its origin. During the last twenty years the fear had come upon her with great intensity, but she could not recall the date of its inception and, therefore, the conditions under which it originated; consequently nothing satisfactory could be elicited. She could consciously recall, however, that originally she had had attacks of idefinable fear of great intensity attached to no specific idea that she knew. These had occurred years before the patient came to me (in 1903), and therefore no examination into the content of consciousness at these moments had been made. During recent years, however, the fear, as she herself expressed it, had become particularized, but had varied at different times. At one time, as she thought, it was a fear of illness, then of losing consciousness (or fainting), then of her mind flying off into space,

tion, the stimulus, that would be otherwise inadequate, excites the attack. Thus the sound of running water excites an attack of anxiety or depression or aversion, as the case may be, because in an episode from which the obsession originated, a running brook happened to be associated in the situation. In principle, this conversion of an ordinarily inadequate stimulus into an adequate stimulus is a conditioned response (reflex). Since this paper was published, H. L. Hollingworth has argued that this principle, for which he uses the curious term "redintegration," provides a psychological explanation of the pathology of obsessions, etc. But while it offers an explanation of an attack in terms of stimulus and response, it does not answer the deeper question — the "why" of the response. That must be sought in root-dispositions which provide the setting and meaning of the original episode and determine their persistence.

then of being alone. She was not clear as to the specific nature of her fear at the time when she came under observation, although it was somewhat vaguely of losing consciousness.

As a result of searching investigation by technical methods, it was brought out that the specific object of the fear was *fainting*. When an attack developed, besides the usual physiological disturbances and confusion of thought, there was in the content of consciousness a feeling that her mind was flying off into space and a *definite thought of losing consciousness*, and that she was going to faint. There was amnesia for these thoughts following the attacks. She never had fainted in the attacks and, as it later transpired, had fainted only once in her life. Here then, in the content of consciousness, was the object of the fear in an attack. But the object was afterwards forgotten: hence she could not explain what she was afraid of. Why fainting should be such a terrible accident to be feared, she also could not explain.

The question now was: what possible meaning could fainting have for her that she so feared it? This she did not know.

Probing the matter further, I found that there was always in the *fringe of consciousness* during an attack, and also during the anticipatory fear of an attack, *an idea and fear of death*. This, to use her expression, "was in the background of her mind"; it referred to impending fainting. It appeared then that in the fringe or ultra-marginal zone was the idea of death as the meaning of fainting. Of this she was never aware. It was practically subconscious. It was the meaning of her idea of herself fainting. In consequence of this meaning, fainting was equivalent to her own death. She would not have been afraid of fainting if she had not believed, or could have been made not to believe, that in her case it meant death. We might properly say that the *real object and meaning of her fear was death*.

When this content of the fringe of attention was recovered, the patient voluntarily remarked that she had not been aware of the presence during the attacks of that idea, but now she realized it plainly, and also why she was afraid of fainting — what she had not understood before. (It must be borne in mind that this meaning of fainting as a state equivalent to death did not pertain to fainting in general, but solely to herself. She knew perfectly well that fainting in other people was not dangerous; it was only an unrecognized belief regarding a possible accident to herself.) Besides this content of the fringe of attention, it was also easy to show that the fringe included the thought (or perception) which had been the immediate excitant of each attack. Sometimes this stimulus-idea entered the focus of attention; sometimes it was only in the fringe. In either case there was apt to be amnesia for it, but I found that it could always be recalled to memory in abstraction or hypnosis.

The content of consciousness taken as a whole, i. e., to include both the focus and the fringe of attention, then, would adequately determine the meaning of this subject's idea of fainting as applied to herself.

But why this meaning of fainting? In what dispositions of experiences was it "set"? It must have been derived from antecedent experiences and, therefore, must have had its roots in dispositions left by them. An idea can no more have a meaning without antecedent experiences with which it is or once was integrated, than can the word "parallelopipedon" have a geometrical meaning without a previous geometrical experience, or "Timbuctoo" a personal meaning without being set in a personal experience whether of missionaries or hymn books.

It would take too much space to give the detailed results of the investigation by hypnotic procedures that followed. I will merely summarize by stating that the fear of death from fainting had its roots in an experience that occurred more than twenty years before, when she was a young girl about eighteen years of age. At the time, as the result of a nervous shock, she had fainted, and just before losing consciousness she thought her symptoms meant death. Ever since, she has been afraid of fainting.

But this again was not all. Why should death be such a fearful thing as to become an obsessing phobia? A searching investigation of the unconscious in deep hypnosis revealed the fact that death from fainting was constellated with still wider experiences involving a fear of death. At the moment of the nervous shock just before fainting (fancied as dying) she thought of her mother, who was dangerously ill in an adjoining room, and a great fear came over her at the thought of what might happen to her mother if she should hear of the cause of her nervous shock and of her (the patient's) death. It further appeared that the idea of death and fear of it was set in a still larger series of experiences. It dated from a childhood experience when she was eight years of age. At that time she was frightened when a pet animal died, and a fear of death had been more or less continuously present in her mind ever since, but not always consciously so; *i. e.*, sometimes it was in awareness and sometimes in the ultra-marginal zone of consciousness. She had been able to conceal the fear until the fainting episode occurred, and, as she in hypnosis asserted, the fear afterwards had continued to be present more or less persistently, although she was not conscious of the fact when awake, and it had attached itself to various ideas. Until put into hypnosis she had no knowledge of all this.

The idea of death became constellated, too, with a fear of acquiring *cancer,* in consequence of certain incidents of her mother's illness and death; this apprehension had been constantly in her mind, but never previously confessed, and had been the real meaning of her fear of illness — a fear (lest any given illness might prove to be cancer) that had been conspicuous and puzzling to her physicians. Illness and death from cancer she had persistently believed awaited her.

Without pursuing further these and similar details, it must be evident that the meaning of fainting and death is set in a large constellated group of experiences.

How are we to explain the persistence during more than twenty years of an unsophisticated fear of fainting, a reproduction (as memory) of the content of consciousness of a youthful episode? Or more specifically, the thrusting of the thought of death, as an element (meaning) in the fainting complex, into the content of consciousness, not, to be sure, within the focus of attention but still in the content, even if so far outside the focus that there was no awareness of it? The theory of unconscious processes, established, as I think we are justified in saying, in the mechanism of numerous and varied psychological phenomena, offers an adequate explanation. As brought out in the associative memories in hypnosis, *the youthful episode, fainting, had become constellated with a larger complex in which death was the obtrusive element. This complex was conserved in the unconscious and, as the real setting, was an active functioning process.* It furnished the conscious "meaning" to fainting and its affect, fear. It was derived from antecedent root-experiences which were still very real to her and *believed in.* This belief, based on these experiences, determined the viewpoint of herself, particularly as one destined to die of cancer. During the phobia attacks, a portion of the unconscious complex — fainting, death, fear — emerged as conscious elements. *The remainder persisted as an unconscious functioning process.* The content of consciousness, including therein the focus and marginal zones of awareness, would, according to the analogy of a clock, correspond to the chimes and hands, while the unconscious process would corresond to the concealed works.[1]

I forbear to cite the analysis of other cases which give the same results.

It must be borne in mind, however, that analysis, meaning thereby the determination of associated past experiences, cannot beyond question demonstrate the continuing unconscious functioning of the dispositions of such experiences and the causal factor of a present conscious process. It can demonstrate the sequence of events and, therefore, each successive link in a chain of evidence, as in a criminal trial,

---

1 After the root-idea had been changed by therapeutic re-education, the viewpoint of the patient was changed and the anxiety attack ceased. A certain school of psychologists, I know, will want to go one step further and postulate a repressed subconscious wish to which the fear complex is a reaction; but I see no justification for this. The biological instinct of fear has tremendous conative force, and any idea to which it is linked (as a sentiment), so long as the setting determining its meaning persists, tends to express itself by this force, just as much so as a wish. Through the sophistication of the idea the sentiment becomes dissolved.

or it can demonstrate the material out of which we can select, with a greater or less degree of probability, the factor which in accordance with a theory — in this case, that of unconscious processes — seems most likely to be the causal factor. Just as in the analysis of a bacterial culture we can select the germ which seems on various considerations to be the most likely cause of an etiologically undetermined disease, but for actual demonstration we must employ synthetic methods, that is, actually reproduce the disease by inoculation with a bacterium, so with psychological processes synthetic methods are required for positive demonstration.

For synthetic proof, hypnotic methods are available and give more positive results.

If a subject is hypnotized and in this state a complex is formed as a setting, it will be found that this setting, after the subject is awakened, will determine his point of view and meaning of the central idea when this comes into consciousness, and this although the subject has complete amnesia for the hypnotic experience. Accordingly, if the idea is one which previously had a very definite and undesirable meaning which we wish to eradicate, we can build a new setting to that idea and so give it a very different meaning, provided it is one which is acceptable to the subject.

To take simple examples, and to begin with a more or less hypothetical case, but one which in practice I have frequently duplicated: I hypnotize a subject, and although, in fact, the day is a beautifully fair one, I point out that it is, on the contrary, disagreeable because the sunshine is glowing and hot; that such weather means dusty roads, drought, the drying up of the water supply, the withering of the foliage, that the country needs rain, etc. In this way I form an integrate of ideas as a *setting* to the weather and give it, fair as it is, an entirely different and unpleasant *meaning,* and one which is accepted. The subject is now awakened and has complete amnesia for the hypnotic experience. When attention is directed to the weather, it is found that his point of view, for the time being at least, has changed from what it was before being hypnotized. The perception of the clear sky and the sunlight playing upon the ground includes secondary images of heat, of dust and of withered foliage, (such as have been previously experienced on hot dusty days), and has acquired a new meaning corresponding to the new setting, and this setting has its roots in the dispositions of the associated thoughts suggested in hypnosis. For some of these thoughts — perhaps only a few — arise in consciousness, but, if he continues to think about the weather, or his opinion is challenged, perhaps nearly all the secondary images mentioned are brought up. Manifestly the new setting formed in hypnosis has induced the secondary images and associated thoughts. Much of this setting is manifestly unconscious. Nevertheless it must with its associated root-dispositions take an active functioning part in the perception. Images, meanings, setting and root-dispositions form a functioning whole $(P=I+M+S+R-D)$.

In similar fashion I made a subject view as an unpleasant cesspool for sewage a river which was being converted into a beautiful water park by a dam.[1] In this instance the main ideas of the setting suggested in hypnosis became the conscious meaning of the perception; but this meaning had its roots formed in the whole hypnotic experience. In hundreds of instances, for therapeutic purposes, I have changed the setting, the viewpoint, and the emotional meaning of the ideas of the patient by suggestive procedures, often during hypnosis and therefore without his conscious knowledge. This is the goal of psychotherapy, and, in my judgment, the one fundamental principle common to all technical methods of such treatment, different as they appear to be when superficially considered.

It is obvious that in everyday life when, by arguments, persuasion, exhortation, suggestion, punishment, or prayer, we change the viewpoint of a person, we do so by building up sentiments (complexes) which shall act as settings and give new meanings to his ideas. But these meanings always have roots in dispositions which take part in a functioning whole. I may add, if we wish to sway him to carry this

1 The Unconscious, *Journal of Abnormal Psychology*, April-May, 1919.

new viewpoint to fulfillment through action, we introduce into the complex an adequate emotion which, by the driving force of its impulses, shall carry the ideas to practical fruition.

It is well at this point to emphasize a fact which I have already mentioned, namely, that the secondary images, which occur in the fringe of every perception, are the images pertaining to the unconscious complex from which they have emerged into the fringe. They are, therefore, determined by a functioning unconscious complex; and as nearly all ideas may have a number of different contexts or settings, and, therefore, various meanings, so the secondary images will vary according to the character of the unconscious complex which has been switched on at any given moment. For instance, the river which I see out of my window may, at one moment, have a setting which will present it in my consciousness as an object in a beautiful landscape; at another moment, as in the above mentioned experiment, as an unpleasant sewage basin. And introspective analysis will show that the secondary images will vary correspondingly in each perception. These images, as elements in the unconscious complex of past experiences, emerge into the fringe of consciousness.

## VI

*The Setting in Obsessions.* We are now in a position, on this theory, to look a little more deeply into the structure and mechanism of an obsession, and thereby realize why it is that the unfortunate victims are so helpless to modify or control them. Indeed this behavior of the obsession could be cited as another piece of circumstantial evidence for the theory that the functioning setting is largely unconscious and that only a few elements of it enter the field of consciousness. If you simply explain to a person who has a true obsession (*i. e.,* an insistent dominating idea with a strong feeling-tone such as a fear of cats, closed spaces, etc.), the falsity of his point of view and the foolishness of his emotion, he will agree with you, but the explanation has no effect in changing his viewpoint and feeling. The patient cannot modify his idea even if he will. But if the original complex, which with its root-dispositions is hidden in the unconscious and which determines the meaning of the idea, is discovered and so altered that it takes on a new meaning and a different feeling-tone, the patient's conscious idea becomes correspondingly modified, and ceases to be insistent. This would imply that the insistent idea is only an element in a larger functioning unconscious complex which is the setting, and unconsciously determines the viewpoint. The reason why the patient cannot voluntarily alter his viewpoint becomes intelligible by this theory because that which determines it is unconscious and unknown. He may not even know what his point of view is, owing to the meaning being in the fringe of consciousness. The obsessing idea may be only an unrecognized symbol and one element in the unconscious setting, as, for example, the fear of ringing-of-bells in a tower, which in one of my cases was a symbol and associated element in a complex that involved a sense of guilt of being the cause of her mother's death.[1]

If this theory of the mechanism is soundly established, the difficulty of correcting obsessions becomes obvious and intelligible.

In the study and formulation of psychological phenomena there is one common tendency and danger, and that is of making the phenomena too schematic and sharply defined, as if we were dealing with material objects. Mental processes are not only plastic but shifting, varying, unstable, and sometimes undergo modifications of structure almost from moment to moment. We describe a complex schematically as if it had a fixed, immutable, and well-defined structure. This is far from being the case. As I have already insisted, like a vine it has many and far-reaching roots. Although there may be a fairly fixed nucleus, the integrate, as a whole, is ill-defined and undergoes considerable modification from time to time. New elements enter the integrate

1 See next chapter.

and replace or are added to those which previously took part in the composition.

The same indefiniteness pertains to the demarcation between the conscious and the subconscious. What was conscious at one moment may be subconscious the next and *vice versa*. Under *normal* conditions there is a continual shifting between the conscious and subconscious. I have made numerous investigations to determine this point, and the evidence is fairly precise, and to me convincing, that this shifting continually occurs,[1] as might well be inferred on theoretical grounds. Nor, excepting in special pathological and artificial dissociated conditions, is the distinction between the conscious and subconscious at any moment always sharp and precise; it is often rather a matter of vividness and shading, and whether a conscious state is in the focus of attention or in the fringe. Experimental observation confirms introspection in this respect.

In view of the foregoing, we can now appreciate a fallacy which has been too commonly accepted in the interpretation of therapeutic facts. It is quite generally held that it is a necessity that the underlying unconscious processes cannot be modified without bringing them to the "full light of day" by analysis. The facts of everyday observation do not justify this conclusion. The recovery of the memories of the unconscious complex is mainly of importance for the purpose of giving us exact information of *what* we need to modify, not necessarily for the purpose of effecting the modification. Owing to the fluidity of complexes, whether unconscious or conscious, our conscious ideas can become incorporated as dispositions in unconscious processes. This means that any new setting which we may incorporate in the disposition of our conscious ideas to give them a new meaning can be made to enter into dispositions contained in unconscious complexes. The latter is able to assimilate from the conscious new material offered to it. Practical therapeutics and everyday experience abundantly have shown

---

[1] I am excluding conditions like split personalities, automatic writing, etc., and refer rather to normal mental processes.

this. I have accomplished this, and I believe every therapeutist has done the same time and again. We should be cautious not to overlook common experience in the enthusiasm for new theories and dramatic observations. After all is said and done, we have only one mind. The difficulty is in knowing what we want to modify, and for this purpose analytical investigations of one sort or another are of the highest assistance, because they furnish us with the required information. If we recover the memories of the unconscious complex our task is easier, as we can apply our art with the greater skill.

# CHAPTER II

## THE PSYCHOPATHOLOGY OF A CASE OF PHOBIA — A CLINICAL STUDY[1]

THE case of phobia, of which this is a clinical study, was one of church steeples and towers of any kind. The patient, a woman about forty years of age, dreaded and tried in consequence to avoid the sight of one. When she passed by such a tower she was very strongly affected emotionally, experiencing always a feeling of terror or anguish accompanied by the usual marked physical symptoms. Sometimes even speaking of a tower would at once awaken this emotional complex, which expressed itself outwardly in her face, as I myself observed on several occasions. Considering the frequency with which church and schoolhouse towers are met with in everday life, one can easily imagine the discomfort arising from such a phobia. Before the mystery was unraveled she was unable to give any explanation of the origin or meaning of this phobia, and could not connect it with any episode in her life, or even state how far back in her life it had existed. Vaguely she thought it existed when she was about fifteen years of age, and that it might have existed before that. Now it should be noted that an idea of a tower with bells had in her mind no meaning whatsoever that explained the fear. It had no more meaning than it would have in anybody else's mind. In the content of consciousness there was only the perception plus emotion, and no corresponding meaning. Accordingly, I sought to discover the origin and meaning of the phobia by the so-called psychoanalytic method.

When I attempted to recover the associated memories

1 Read at the Fourth Annual Meeting of the Psychopathological Association at Washington, D. C., May 8, 1913.

by this method, the mere mention of bells in a tower threw her into a panic in which anxiety, "thrills," and perspiration were prominent. Before making the analysis I had constructed a theory in my mind to the effect that a phobia for bells in a tower was a sexual symbolism, being led to this partly by the suggestiveness of the object and partly by the fact that I had found sexual symbolisms in her dreams.[1]

Analysis was conducted at great length, and memories covering a wide field of experiences were elicited. When asked to think of bells in a tower, or each of these objects separately, there was a complete blocking of thought in that her mind became a blank. Later, memories which to a large extent, but not wholly, played in various relations around her mother (who is dead) as the central object, came into the field of consciousnss. Nothing, however, was awakened that gave the slightest meaning to the phobia even on the wildest interpretation. The patient, who had been frequently hypnotized by another physician, tended during the analysis to go into a condition of unusually deep abstraction, to such a degree that on breaking off the analysis she failed to remember, save very imperfectly, the memories elicited. Such an abstraction, as we shall see in a later chapter, is hypnosis.

Finally, after all endeavors to discover the genesis of the phobia by analysis were in vain, I tried another method. While she was in hypnosis I put a pencil in her hand with the object of obtaining the desired information through automatic writing. *While she was narrating some irrelevant memories of her mother,* the hand rapidly wrote as follows: "G—— M—— church and my father took my mother to Bi——, where she died, and we went to Br——, and they cut my mother. I prayed and cried all the time that she would live and the church bells were always ringing and I hated them."

When she began to write the latter part of this script, she became depressed, sad, indeed anguished; tears flowed

---

[1] In making the analysis, therefore, I was in no way antagonistic in my mind to the Freudian hypothesis.

down her cheeks, and she seemed to be almost heartbroken. In other words, it appeared as if she were subconsciously living over again the period described in the script. I say "subconsciously," for she did not know what her hand had written or why she was anguished. During the writing of the first part of the script she was verbally describing other memories; during the latter part she ceased speaking.

After awakening from hypnosis and when she had become composed in her mind, she narrated, at my request, the events referred to in the script. She remembered them clearly as they happened when she was about fifteen years of age. It appeared that she was staying at that time in G—— M——, a town in England. Her mother, who was seriously ill, was taken to a great surgeon to be operated upon. She herself suffered great anxiety and anguish lest her mother should not recover. She went twice a day to the church to pray for her mother's recovery, and in her anguish declared that if her mother did not recover she would no longer believe in God.

The chimes in the tower of the church, which was close to her hotel, sounded every quarter-hour; they got on her nerves; she hated them; she could not bear to hear them, and while she was praying they added to her anguish. Ever since this time, the ringing of the bells has continued to cause a feeling of anguish. This narrative was not accompanied by emotion as was the automatic script.

It now became evident that it was the *ringing* of the church bells, or the *anticipated ringing* of bells, that caused the fear, and not the perception of a tower itself. When she saw a tower she feared lest bells should ring. This was the object of the phobia.[1] She could not explain why she had

---

1 I want to emphasize this point because certain students assuming the well-known alleged sexual symbolism as the meaning of steeples and towers will read, and have read, such an interpretation into this phobia. As a matter of fact, although these objects had been originally alleged by the subject herself to be the object of the fear, it was done thoughtlessly as the result of careless introspection. Later she clearly distinguished the true object. Steeples and towers were no more the object than the churches and schoolhouses themselves. They bore an incidental association only, and only indicated where the ringing of bells might be expected to be heard, having been an element in the original episode. Nor were bells *qua* bells the object of the phobia, but the ringing-of-

never before connected her phobia with the episode she described. This failure of association, as we know, is not uncommon, and in this case was apparently related to a determination to put out of mind an unbearable episode associated with so much anguish. There had been for years a more or less constant mental conflict with her phobia. The subject had striven not to think of or look at belfries, churches, schoolhouses or any towers, or to hear the ringing of their bells, or to talk about them. She had endeavored to protect herself by keeping such ideas out of her mind. Before further analyzing the case, there are two points which are well worth calling attention to.

1. When the subject subconsciously described the original childhood experience by automatic script there was intense emotion — fear — which emerged into consciousness without her knowing the reason thereof. When, on the other hand, she later from her conscious memories described the same experience, there was no such emotion. In other words, it was only when the conserved residua of the experience functioned coconsciously and autonomously as a dissociated independent process that emotion was manifested. So long as the memories were described from the viewpoint of the matured adult personal consciousness there was no emotion. As a subconscious process they were unmodified by this later viewpoint. This suggests at least that when the phobia was excited by the sight or idea of a tower, it was due likewise to a subconscious process, and that this was one and the same as that which induced the experimental phobia.

2. The phraseology of the script is noticeable. The account is just such as a child might have written. It reads as if the conserved thoughts of a child had awakened and functioned subconsciously.

From this history, so far as given, it is plain that the

bells, of the kind that recalled the mother's death. In other words, the fear was of bells with a particular meaning. Nor was the fear absolutely limited to tower-bells, for it transpired that the subject had refrained from having, as she desired, an alarm bell arranged in her house in the country (in case of fire, etc.) because of her phobia. (This note is, perhaps, made necessary by the violent shaking of the heads of my Freudian friends that I noticed at this point during the presentation of the paper.)

psychosis in one sense is a recurring antecedent experience or memory, but it is only a partial memory. The whole of the experience does not recur but only the emotion in association with the ringing of bells. The rest of that experience: *viz.*, the idea of the possible death of her mother, with its attendant grief and anguish associated with the visits to the church, the praying for recovery and finally, the realization of the fatal ending — all that which originally excited the fear and *gave the ringing-of-bells-in-a-tower meaning* was conserved as a setting in the unconscious. That this rest of the experience was conserved was shown by the fact that not only could it be recalled by automatic writing, but brought to conscious memory, although not through association with the phobia. From this angle, the fear of bells ringing may be regarded as a recurrence of the original fear — that of her mother's death — now derived from a subconsciously functioning setting. The child was afraid to face her grief and so now the matured adult was also afraid.

From another point of view, the ringing of bells may be regarded as standing for, or a symbol of, her mother's death with which it was so intimately associated, and this symbol awakened the same fear as did originally the idea itself of the death. An object may still be a symbol of another, although the association between the two cannot be recalled. (The transference of the emotional factor of an experience to some element in it is a common occurrence, *e. g.*, a fear of knives in a person who has had the fear of committing suicide.)

The discovered antecedent experiences of childhood then give a hitherto unsuspected meaning to the ringing of bells. It is *a* meaning — the *mise en scène* of a tragedy of grief and a symbol of that tragedy. But was that tragedy with its grief the *real* meaning of the child's fear, or, perhaps more correctly, the *whole* of the meaning? And is it still the meaning in the mind of the adult woman? Does the mere conservation of a painful memory of grief explain its persistent recurrent subconscious functioning during twenty-five years, well into adult life, so that the child's emotion shall be re-awakened whenever one element (bell-tower) of the original experience is presented to consciousness? And, still more, can the persistence of a mere association of the affect with the object, independently of a subconscious process, explain the disorder? Either of these two last propositions is absurd on its face as being opposed to the experience of the great mass of mankind. The vast majority of people have undergone disturbing, sorrowful or fear-inspiring experiences at some time during the course of their lives, and they do not find that they cannot for years afterwards face some object or idea belonging to that experience without being overwhelmed with the same emotion. Such emotion in the course of time subsides and dies out. A few, relatively speaking, do so suffer and then, because contrary to general experience, it is called a psychoneurosis.

We must, then, seek some other and more adequate factor in the case under examination. When describing the episode in the church, the subject stated that on one occasion she omitted to go to church to pray, and the thought came to her that if her mother died it would be due to this omission, and *it would be her fault*. The "eye of God"[1] she thought was literally upon her in her every daily act; and when her mother did die, she thought that it was God's punishment of herself because of that one failure. Consequently she thought *that she was to blame for her mother's death*; that *her mother's death was her fault*. She feared to face her mother's death, not because of grief — that was a mere subterfuge, a self-deception — but because she thought she was to blame; and she feared to face towers with bells, or, rather, the ringing of bells, because they symbolized or stood for that death (just as a tombstone would stand for it), and in

1 This idea had its origin in a child's fairy tale, and had been fostered by the governess as a useful expedient in enforcing good behavior. The child, accepting the fairy legend, believed the eye of God was always on her and every one in the world and observed all that each did or omitted to do. The legend excited her imagination, and she used to think about it and wonder how God could keep His eye on so many people as there were in the world. At a still earlier age, when she was about eight, she had thought her little brother's death was also her fault, because she had neglected one night, at the time of his illness, God's eye being upon her, to say her prayers. For a long time afterwards she suffered similarly from self-reproach. It is interesting to compare the outgrowing with maturity of this self-reproach with the persistence of the later one, evidently owing to the reasons given in the text.

facing that fact she had to face her own fancied guilt and self-reproach, and this she dared not do. This was the real fear, the fear of facing her own guilt. The emotion then was not only a recurrence of the affect associated with the church episode but a *reaction to self-reproach*. The ringing of bells, somewhat metaphorically speaking, reproached her as Banquo's ghost reproached Macbeth.

All this was the child's point of view.

But I found that the patient, an adult woman, *still believed and obstinately maintained* that her mother's death was her fault. She had never ceased to believe it. Why was this? Why had not the unsophisticated belief of a child become modified by the maturity of years? It did not seem to be probable that the given child's reason was the real adult reason for self-reproach. I did not believe it. A woman forty years of age could not reproach herself on such grounds. And even if this belief had been originally the real reason, as a matter of fact she had outgrown the child's religious belief. She was a thoroughgoing agnostic. Further probing brought out the following:

Two years before her mother's death, the patient, then thirteen years old, owing to her own carelessness and disobedience to her mother's instructions, had contracted a "cold," which had been diagnosed as incipient phthisis. By the physician's advice her mother took her to Europe for a "cure," and was detained there (as she believed) for two years, all on account of the child's health. At the end of this period, a serious chronic disease, from which the mother had long suffered, was found to have so developed as to require an emergency operation. The patient *still believed* and argued that if her mother had not been compelled to take her abroad, she (the mother) would have been under medical supervision at home, would have been operated upon long before, and, in all probablity, would not have died. Furthermore, as the patient had heedlessly and disobediently exposed herself to severe cold, and thereby contracted the disease, compelling the sojourn in Europe, she was to blame for the train of circumstances ending fatally.

All this was perfectly logical and true, assuming the

facts as presented.  Here, then, was the real reason for the patient's persistent belief that her mother's death was her fault, and the resulting persistent self-reproach.  *It also transpired that all this had weighed upon the child's mind, and that the child had likewise believed it.*  So the child had two reasons for self-reproach:  One was neglecting to pray and the other was being the indirect cause of the fatal operation.  Both were intensely believed in.  The first, based on the "eye of God" theory, she had outgrown, but the other had persisted.

Summing up our study to this point: all these memories involving grief, suffering, self-reproach, bells and mother formed an unconscious setting which gave meaning to bells in towers, and took part in the functioning to form a psychic whole.  The conscious psychosis[1] was, first, the emergence into consciousness of two elements only, the perception and the affect; and the fear was a reaction to self-reproach, a fear to face self-blame.

Now, even if the mother's death were logically, by a train of fortuitous circumstances, the patient's fault, why did an otherwise intelligent woman lay so much stress upon an irresponsible child's behavior?  The child, after all, behaved no differently from other children.  People do not consciously blame themselves in after-life for the ultimate consequences of childhood's heedlessness.  According to common experience such self-reproaches do not last into adult life without some continuously acting factor.

A search, in this case, into the unconscious brought to light a persisting idea that when events in her life happened unfortunately, it was due to her fault.  It had cropped out again and again in connection with inconsequential as well as consequential matters.  She had, for instance, been really unable on many occasions to leave home on pleasure trips for fear lest some accident might happen within the home and, consequently, it would be due to her fault; and if away she was in constant dread of something happening for which she would be to blame.  It was not a fear of what might hap-

---

1 Dr. Prince uses the term "psychosis" here and elsewhere in the sense of any functional disorder (or even mental state. See p. 99).          — A. A. R.

pen, an accident to the children, for example, but that it would be her fault. I have heard her, when some matter of apparently little concern had gone wrong, suddenly exclaim, "Was it my fault?" At the same time her voice and features would manifest a degree of emotion almost amounting to terror. When her brother died (still earlier, before her mother's death) she had blamed herself for that death, as later with her mother, on the same religious grounds. This self-reproach for happenings, fancied as due to her fault, has frequently appeared in her dreams.

It would take us too far afield to trace or discuss the psychogenesis of this idea. Suffice it to say, it can be followed back to early childhood when she was five or six years of age. She was a lonely, unhappy child. She thought herself ugly and unattractive and disliked, and that so it always would be through life, and it was all her fault because she was ugly, as she thought.[1] The instinct of self-abasement (McDougall)[2] or negative self-feeling (Ribot) dominated

1 Another example of this idea, and of the way it induced a psychosis, is the following: She had an intense dislike to hearing the sound of running water. This sound induced an intense feeling of *unhappiness and loneliness.* This feeling was so intense that whenever she heard the sound of running water she endeavored to get away from it. The sound of a fountain or rain water running from a roof, for example, would cause such unpleasant feelings that she would change her sleeping room to avoid them. Likewise, drawing water to fill the bathtub was so unpleasant that she would insist upon the door being closed to exclude the sound. She could give no explanation of this phobia. It was discovered in the following way. She had been desirous of finding out the cause, and we had discussed the subject. I had promised that I would unravel the matter in due time, after the other phobia had been cured. I then hypnotized her, and while she was in hypnosis, and just after we had completed the other problem, she remarked that a memory of the running water association was on the verge of emerging into her mind. She could not get it for some time and then, after some effort, it suddenly emerged. She described it as follows: "It was at Bar Harbor. I was about eight years of age. There was a brook there called Duck Brook. The older girls used to go up there on Sundays for a walk with the boys. I went with them one Sunday, accompanied by the governess, and was standing by the brook with a boy. It was a very noisy brook, the water running down from the hillside. While I was standing by the brook watching the running water the boy left me to join the other girls, who had gone off. I thought that was the way it would always be in life; that I was ugly and that they would never stay with me. I felt lonely and unhappy. During that summer I would not join parties of the same kind, fearing or feeling that the same thing would happen. I stayed at home by myself, and when I refused to go it was attributed to sullenness. They did not know my real reasons. Ever since, I have been unable to bear the sound of running water, which produces the feeling of unhappiness and loneliness, the same feeling that I had at that time. I thought then that it was all my fault because I was ugly." It was then tentatively pointed out at some length to the subject that as she

the personality as the most insistent instinct, and from its intensity within the self-regarding sentiment (McDougall) formed a sentiment of self-depreciation. She wanted to be liked, and believed it to be her own fault that, as she fancied, she was not, and reproached herself accordingly. This sentiment of self-depreciation, with its impulse to self-reproach, has persisted, as with many people, all her life, and has been fostered by unwise and thoughtless domestic criticism. The persistence to the present day of this impulse to self-reproach is shown in the following observation: Quite recently this subject began to suffer from general fatigue, insomnia, distressing dreams, hysterical crying, indefinable anxiety, and sort of twilight states of mind, or extreme states of abstraction. In these states she became oblivious of her environment, did not hear the conversation going on about her, nor answer when directly spoken to. This became so noticeable that she became the jest of her companions. In these states, her mind was always occupied with reveries, though mostly pleasant, regarding a very near relative who had died about six monthss previously. Her distressing dreams also concerned this relative. It appeared, therefore, probable on the face of the symptoms that they were in some way related to this relative's death.

Now it happened, as I already knew, that the relative had died under somewhat tragic circumstances, and that our subject's experience during the last illness was unusually distressing and sorrowful. *This experience, she asserted, she could not bear to speak or even think about, and over and over again she had refused to do so and put it out of her mind. She further asserted that her reason for this attitude*

now knew all the facts, which had been brought to the "full light of day," etc., she of course would no longer have her former unpleasant emotions from the sound of running water. Hereupon, to put the question to the test, I reached out my hand and poured some water from a carafe, by chance standing by, into a tumbler, letting the water fall from a height to make a sound. At once she manifested discomfort and sought to restrain me with her hand. The setting had to be changed. This was easily done by leading her to see that her childhood's ideas had been proved by life's experiences to be false. When this became apparent she laughed at herself, and the disturbance ceased at once.

2 *Social Psychology*

*was the distressing nature of the scenes in which she took part.*

Now, I did not believe that this was the true reason, although given in good faith. It was improbable on its face. To say that a grown woman, forty years of age, could not do what every woman can do, *viz.*, tolerate sorrowful memories simply because they were sorrowful, and, perforce, put them out of mind, is sheer nonsense. There must be some other reason.

On examining a dream I found it to be peculiar in one respect: It was not an imaginative or fantastic composition, but a detailed and precise living over again of the scenes at the death-bed; that is to say it was a sort of somnambulic state. In recalling this dream[1] she could not for some time recover the ending. Finally it "broke through," as she expressed it. The dream was as follows: First came many details of the vigil of the last night of the illness; then she returned to her room and to bed to snatch a few moments' sleep; she was awakened by the husband of the dying relative appearing in her room. He sat on the edge of her bed and said to her, "All is over." Up to this point the facts of the dream were actual representations in great detail of the actual facts as they had occurred, but at this moment the dream presented a fact which had not occurred in the real scene; she suddenly, in the dream, sat up in bed and exclaimed, "My God! then I ought to have sent for the doctor!"

Here was the key to the intolerance for memories of the illness of the relative and the death-bed scene. What had happened was this: the question had arisen early in the illness whether or not a doctor should be sent for from London in consultation. The expense, owing to the distance, would have been considerable. The whole responsibility and decision rested upon the subject. Against the opinion of other relatives she had decided that it was inadvisable. After the fatal ending the question had arisen again whether or not she ought to have sent for the consultant, and she had been

---

1 This was done in hypnosis; the dream being forgotten when awake.

tormented by the doubt as to whether she did right. *Was the fatal result her fault?* Although she had reasoned with herself that her decision was good judgment and right, still there had always lurked a doubt in her mind. She was also somewhat disturbed by the thought of what the husband's opinion might be.

The real reason why she could not tolerate the memories of the last illness of this relative, and the psychogenesis of the symptoms now were plain; they were not grief but self-reproach with its instinct of self-debasement. The memories brought to her mind the thought that the fault was hers, and with the thought came self-reproach. *This self-reproach she was afraid of and unwilling to face.*

Now follows the therapeutic sequel: The relative's illness at the beginning was in no way of a dangerous nature, and the proposed consultation had nothing to do with the question of danger to life. The death was due to a purely accidental factor and could not have been foreseen. When I assured her in hypnosis, *with full explanation,* that her decision had been medically sound, as it really was, the change in her mental attitude was delightful to look upon. "Wasn't it my fault? Wasn't it my fault?" she exclaimed in excitement. Anxiety, dread, and depression gave way to exhilaration and joyousness. She woke up completely relieved in mind, and retained the same feeling of joy, but without knowing the reason thereof. The explanation was repeated to her in the waking state, and she then fully realized (as she did also in hypnosis) that her previous view was a pure subterfuge, and fully appreciated the truth of the discovered reason for her inability to face her painful memories. The twilight states, the insomnia, and the distressing dreams, the anxiety, and other symptoms ceased at once.

Returning to the phobia for bells, in the light of all these facts, the patient's belief that her mother's death was her fault and the consequent self-reproach were obviously only a particular concrete example of a lifelong emotional tendency originating in the experiences of childhood to blame herself; and this tendency was the striving to express itself of the instinct of self-abasement (with the emotion of self-subjection) which, incorporated within "the self-regarding sentiment" (McDougall), was so intensely cultivated and had played so large a part in her life. Indeed, this instinct had almost dominated her self-regarding sentiment, and had given rise time and again to self-reproach for accidental happenings. It now specifically determined her attitude of mind towards the series of events which led up to the fatal climax and determined her judgment of self-condemnation and self-reproach. These last most probably received increased emotional force from the large number of roots in painful associations of antecedent experiences (particularly of childhood) in which the self-regarding sentiment, self-debasement, and self-reproaches were incorporated.[1] *Nevertheless the fear was of a particular self-reproach.* The general tendency was of practical consequence, only so far as it explained the particular point of view and might induce other self-reproaches.

As a general summary of this study it would appear that we can postulate a larger setting to the phobia than the grief-inspiring experiences attending her mother's death. The unconscious complex[2] included the belief that she was to blame plus the sentiment of self-reproach; and the whole gave a fuller meaning to the ringing-of-bells in a tower. The fear, besides being a recurring association, was also a reaction to the subconsciously excited setting of a fancied truth or self-accusation. Although excited by towers and steeples, the fear was really of self-reproach. Towers, steeples and bells not only in a sense symbolized her mother's death, but

1 For instance, when I came to the therapeutics I found in abstraction that the patient did not want to give up her point of view "because," as she said, "it forms an excuse so that when I feel lonely, if there is nothing else to be lonely about, I have that memory and point of view to fall back upon as something to justify my crying and feeling lonely and blue."

When she now feels blue and cries, as happens occasionally, and she asks herself, "Why?" she drifts back in her mind to childhood and remembers she was lonely, and then cries the harder. Then she vaguely thinks of her mother's death being her fault. She likes, therefore, to hold on to this as a peg on which to hang any present feeling of blueness and loneliness.

2 I distinguish between unconscious and subconscious in that the former (according to my terminology) is a subdivision of the latter and relates only to the conserved residua of past experiences and processes which have no psychological equivalent, while subconscious besides these also includes co-conscious processes.

her own fancied fault. It was in this sense and for this reason that she dared not face such objects. The conscious and the unconscious formed a psychic whole.[1]

Now, in reaching these conclusions, see how far we have traveled: Starting with an ostensible phobia for towers, we find it is really one of ringing-of-bells, but without conscious association: then we reach a childhood tragedy, then a self-reproach, on religious grounds, then a belief in a fault of childhood behavior culminating in a lifelong self-reproach — the causal factor and, psychologically, the true object of the phobia. And between this last self-reproach and the phobia no conscious association.

The *therapeutic* procedure and results are instructive. As the fear was induced by a belief in a fancied fault exciting a self-reproach, then obviously if this belief should be destroyed the self-reproach must cease and the fear must disappear. Now, when all the facts were brought to light, the patient, as is usual, recognized the truth of them. She also recognized fully and completely the real nature of the fear, of the self-blame and of the self-reproach. There remained no lingering doubt in her mind; nevertheless the bringing to "the full light of day" of all this did not cure the phobia. As the first procedure in the therapeusis it was pointed out that it was contrary to common sense to blame herself for the heedlessness of a child; that all children were disobedient; that she would have been a little prig if she had been the sort of a child that never disobeyed, and that she would not have blamed any other child who had behaved in a similar way under similar circumstances, and so on. She simply said that she recognized all this intellectually as true

1 Some, I have no doubt, will insist upon seeing in towers with bells a sexual symbol, and in the self-reproach a reaction to a repressed infantile or other sexual wish. But I cannot accede to this view, first, because a tower was not only not the real object of the phobia, but not even the alleged object, which was the ringing of bells; second, because it is an unnecessary postulate unsupported by evidence; and third, because in fact the associative memories of early life were conspicuously free from sex knowledge, wishes, curiosity, episodes and imaginings, nor was there any evidence of the so-called "mother-complex" or "father-complex" or any other sexual complex that I could find after a most exhaustive probing. The impulses of instincts other than sexual are sufficient to induce psychical trauma, insistent ideas and emotion. To hold otherwise is to substitute dogma for the evidence of experience.

and yet, although it was the point of view which she would take with another person in the same situation, it did not in any way alter her attitude towards herself. In other words, the bringing to the full light of day of the facts did not cure the phobia. It was necessary to change the setting of her belief. *To do this, either the alleged facts had to be shown to be not true, or else new facts had to be introduced which would give them a new meaning.* This, briefly told, was done in the following way.

She was put into light hypnosis in order that exact and detailed memories of her childhood might be brought out. Then, through her own memories, it was demonstrated, that is to say the *patient herself demonstrated*, that there was considerable doubt about her having had phthisis at all; that she was not taken to the usual places of "cures" for phthisis, but sojourned in the gay and pleasant cities and watering-places of Europe; that her mother really stayed in Europe because she enjoyed it and made an excuse of her daughter's health not to come home; that she might have returned at any time but did not want to do so; and that the fault lay, if anywhere, with her physician at home. When this was brought out, the patient remarked, "Why, of course, I see it now! My mother did not stay in Europe on account of my health but because she enjoyed it, and might have returned if she had wanted to. I never thought of that before! It was not my fault at all!" After coming out of hypnosis, the facts, as elicited, were laid before the patient. She again said that she saw it all clearly, as she had done in hypnosis, and her whole point of view was changed.

The therapeutics, then, consisted in showing that the alleged facts upon which the patient's logical conclusions had been based were false; the setting was altered, and thereby a new and true meaning given to the real facts. The result was that towers and steeples no longer excited fears, the phobia ceased at once — an immediate cure.[1]

---

1 It is worth noting that between the bringing to the "full light of day," the facts furnished by the analysis and the cure, a full year and a-half elapsed during which the phobia continued. The "cure" was effected at one sitting. The original study was undertaken on purely psychological grounds; the cure for the purpose of completing the study.

# CHAPTER III

## THE SUBCONSCIOUS SETTINGS OF IDEAS IN RELATION TO THE PATHOLOGY OF THE PSYCHONEUROSES[1]

THAT our points of view, attitudes of mind, sentiments, and the meaning which ideas have for us are determined by the experiences of life and are, therefore, *acquired* can scarcely be traversed. This is only to say, as observation shows, our thoughts, ideas, perceptions, and feelings, become, by the fact of being experienced, organized into complexes or systems and correspondingly conserved in the subconscious. This, when interpreted, means that the residual subconscious dispositions (psychical or neural) acquired through conscious experiences are thus organized. Consequently we may say that nearly every idea, the elements of every thought (*e. g.*, wars make patriotism) are organized with a large number of antecedent experiences through the medium of subconscious residual dispositions. So much we may agree upon as our starting-point. Now, it is necessarily these antecedent personal experiences that form the context or setting which gives to the idea that particular meaning for the individual which may be called its *experiential egocentric meaning*. This is my first thesis.

The psychological content of every idea is a complex affair. An idea of any given object, of a violet, for instance, a snake, a particular building, contains of course sensory elements conveniently called images — visual, tactile, olfactory, etc. — or what Hoernlé calls "signs." You all remember Charcot's classical diagram to represent the concept "bell" — a diagram copied freely in our text-book explanations of aphasia. This diagram consists of a lot of little

---

1 Read by title at the Sixth Annual Meeting of the American Psychopathological Association, 1915.

circles, each representing both a brain centre and a sensory memory picture — a visual picture of a bell, an auditory memory of the sound of a bell, a tactile and temperature memory, a word-hearing, and a word-seeing, and a word-uttering memory, and so on.  And all these little circles are joined to one another by conducting tracks; and thus the picture of the bell excites the centres and the memories.  The combination of all these sensory memories or pictures is supposed to make the concept bell.  And on this principle, in our textbooks, aphasia has been very simply and satisfactorily explained — satisfactorily to the anatomists.  But an idea or concept is much more complicated than this.  I will say parenthetically, for it has nothing to do with my present subject, it is because of this inadequate notion of the content of an idea, whether of a bell or anything else, that the classical theory of aphasia has proved to be so inadequate and unsophisticated.

Besides the sensory "images" accepted by every psychologist, the content of an idea, psychologically speaking, contains what is called "meaning."  If we call, following Hoernlé, the sensory elements, in Charcot's diagram, "signs," we may say every idea has, besides signs, meaning of some sort.  Even nonsense syllables have the meaning "nonsense."  A given man may have the meaning "father," or "son," or "physician," or "murderer, or "emperor" — one meaning for one person and one for another.  Now sign and meaning make a complex or "psychical whole," a "psychosis," using the word in a psychological not pathological sense.  This "psychical whole," whatever it may be, is the content of consciousness so far as concerns the idea.

But the whole content is not vivid, clear, in the focus of attention.  The meaning may be in the focus, while the signs are dim, in the background or fringe, or *vice versa.*

The important point is that "meaning" is a very definite concrete part of the idea.

Again, while the sensory signs may be constant for a given idea, the meaning is a varying component, varying for different individuals, and varying at different moments in the same individual.  It may be only the dictionary meaning representing the use or purpose of the object, substantially such as is contained in the definition given in the dictionary. In the content of many ideas, meaning is limited probably to a dictionary meaning. But with a great many ideas, in addition to this, the content of meaning is much fuller and takes on a specific personal or egocentric character. In other words, the objects of ideas have acquired by the personal experiences of life a very personal relation and, therefore, meaning to the individual. This meaning has been formed by the individual's experiences with the object and these experiences have become closely organized with his own "personality." This meaning of a given idea may, accordingly, be spoken of as the *experiential egocentric meaning.* Let me explain by an example:

The idea of blood contains sensory signs (color, fluid, smell, etc.) plus the dictionary meaning ("The fluid which circulates in the principal vascular system of animals," etc.) and these signs and this meaning may make up the "psychical whole" of the idea with a given individual. But with others, who have had very specific personal experiences with blood, the idea may have an extra meaning corresponding to those experiences. Thus to a physiologist, like Harvey, the meaning may contain memories in detail of the whole vascular system and of the various organs of the body; and, to a more modern physiologist, memories of the blood corpuscles and various constituents of the blood. All these memories, with biological theories of his own regarding the physiology of the blood, may be contained more or less specifically in the content of meaning and be a part of the psychical whole. To a layman, who knows nothing of physiology and has had no biological experiences, blood may have a meaning in which are contained ideas and feelings of danger to life. To a soldier who has had experiences in the trenches and has seen blood poured out as a result of ghastly wounds made by shrapnel, there may be contained in the meaning ideas of slaughter, horror, shell-fire in the trenches, according to his experiences; and if he has himself been wounded or has seen a comrade mutilated by the shells of the enemy, there may be contained in the meaning of the idea memories related to his own personality and associated with strong emotions of horror or pity, or aversion. To the butcher in the slaughter-house the meaning may be only that of a great pool of red slimy liquid in which he is obliged to wade, with memories of his daily occupation. To a Jack-the-Ripper it has a sexual meaning. To each and all, blood has a distinct and personal meaning. All these different meanings have plainly been acquired from the life experiences of the individual; consequently the same idea has a different meaning for different persons according to the differences in the antecedent experiences of each. Consider the differences in the meaning of the word "son" according as the context shows it to mean your son or my son; and so consider the differences in the meanings which a snake may have for an ordinary person, a naturalist, and a Freudian psychologist. These differences plainly depend upon the differences in the antecedent ideas with which a snake is associated and organized in the mind of each. Similarly consider the differences in the meaning which X, your friend and college classmate, has for you, and the meaning which he has, respectively, for a grateful, adoring patient, and an ungrateful, dissatisfied one. Thus there may be as many experiential egocentric meanings as there are individuals, but, of course, there may be such a meaning that is common to a group, or community of individuals, though differing slightly in each member of the group or community. These different meanings, peculiar to each individual, are plainly extra, or over and above the dictionary meaning, and are experiential and egocentric, in that they are, on the one hand, derived from his own experiences and, on the other, organized about his own personality. We may say that the idea is *set* in his antecedent mental experiences, which may be called the *setting* that gives the idea meaning.

Going one step farther, we know that the setting is necessarily represented, according to the principle of conservation, by subconscious (neural) dispositions. Consequently, every idea, or nearly every idea, that has egocentric meaning must have roots in such dispositions. From them (or determined by them) a greater or less number of memories of antecedent mental experiences, organized with the sensory signs of a given present idea, emerge into the content of consciousness, either into the focus or fringe, as meaning. *Idea and meaning, or perhaps more correctly expressed, signs and meaning, thus become a psychical whole.*

It is obvious that not all but only a small part of the memories of antecedent experiences can emerge into consciousness as the meaning of an idea. Consequently there must still remain, below the conscious threshold, a number of these subconscious (neural or psychological) dispositions, likewise organized by previous experience with the idea. These form subconscious *roots* or ramifications. What subconscious elements emerge into meaning must, of course, be determined in each case — and this is a matter of considerable importance — in interpreting a psychosis. And a still more important question is the determination of what part, if any, the subconscious elements of the setting — the roots — play in psychological processes.

As to the first question: although only a relatively small part of the numerous egocentric experiences of the setting can enter the content of consciousness at any given moment, and much less the focus of attention, nevertheless the whole content of consciousness may be much richer in conscious elements of the setting than is commonly supposed. I say this, because when we speak of the content of consciousness we have usually in mind only the focus of attention, meaning thereby those elements which are vivid — of which we have vivid awareness, Whereas, we know that besides these there are other conscious elements of which we are only dimly aware. These constitute the fringe of awareness, a sort of twilight zone. Into this the vivid region of awareness shades.

Now it often happens that technical investigation reveals in this twilight zone conscious elements, derived from the setting of past experiences, which not only contribute to but may be the chief elements in the egocentric meaning of the idea. Indeed the content of this twilight zone may furnish the explanation of the viewpoint, previously inexplicable, towards an object.

Going still further, we find an ultra-marginal zone for which there is no awareness at all — a true coconscious zone; and in this too, according to my observations, we find elements of meaning.

And so it happens, particularly with ideas of emotional value, where for instance there is intense antipathy, or fear, or hatred of an object, that the subject cannot explain his viewpoint, does not understand the meaning of his sentiment of antipathy or hatred, because in certain cases, at least, the meaning is in the twilight zone or ultramarginal zone of the content of consciousness.

Numerous psychological investigations have convinced me of this fact. In phobias, therefore, a complete examination must include these zones. Because the contents of these zones are dim, it must not be inferred that therefore their elements have no functional intensity. On the contrary, judging by the reactions which they excite and which can be easily traced, they may have very great impulsive intensity.

But even such findings will not reveal the *why* of the meaning — *why* an object has such an egocentric meaning for the subject. For this we must search still further into antecedent experiences — into the setting from which these elements, whether of emotion or memories, emerge into various zones of the content of consciousness.

This search necessarily leads us into the *subconscious part of the setting* from which meaning is derived. As we have seen, only a relatively small number of elements of antecedent experiences can enter at one moment into the content of consciousness to become meaning. There must always still remain below the threshold of consciousness many subconscious dispositions deposited by life's experiences and organized with the idea — all forming a dynamic psychic whole. And from whatever viewpoint we approach the subject, we are compelled to believe that in many cases at least, these furnish many active integral elements in a *functioning system*. The conscious meaning is but part and parcel of a larger system of which, as with an iceberg, the larger part is submerged — that is, subconscious. The conscious and the subconscious thus form a functioning whole — a psychosis. Thus it comes about that many of the elements of the fringe of consciousness, the content of the background of the mind, will be found to be only the dimly, but consciously emerging part of a subconscious mechanism. The subconscious, conceived as functional residual dispositions, thus plays an important dynamic part in conscious thought, and it is easy to understand how it can play a dominant part in certain abnormal psychoses.

We may use the analogy of the hidden works of a clock to represent this subconscious mechanism, while the chimes, the hands and the face would represent that which is in consciousness. Though the visible hands and the audible chimes appear to record the time, the real process at work is that of the hidden mechanism.

If we would know the *why* of the meaning of any object of consciousness, it is obvious theoretically — and practically investigations confirm this theoretical view — that we must discover all the dispositions derived from antecedent thoughts (experiences) systematized within the setting, or from which the setting in a restricted sense is in turn derived. These give us the root-ideas, to use the language of common parlance, of the setting and therefore of the egocentric meaning. This is what we mean when we say that the root-ideas of two persons, or the people of two communities, or nations, are the same in regard to some questions of common experience.

It is also obvious that the systematized dispositions of the antecedent experiences, root-ideas, settings and "meanings" pertaining to any object of thought determine and furnish the "point of view" or "attitude of mind" in regard to that object. This would be, for example, the psychological interpretation of a truth expressed in a letter to me by the late distinguished statesman, Joseph Chamberlain — "We English and Americans are one people, not merely because of blood and religion and literature and history, but above all because our root-ideas are the same, because we approach every question from the same standpoint, because we are alike in all essentials and only differ in minor characteristics."

Similarly, to use a more concrete illustration, **A** has a strong antipathy for **B**. He cannot adequately explain this antipathy, excepting that B means for him an arrogant, overbearing man. Let us suppose investigation discloses previous experiences of wounded self-pride, which he does not or cannot voluntarily, for one reason or another, bring into consciousness. These would furnish the reason for the antipathy — for the egocentric antipathetic meaning which B has for him. These experiences have formed a subconscious system of dispositions of which the antipathetic meaning of B is an emerging part — perhaps an unconscious and unrealized defense reaction. Its roots, in any case, are in the subconscious system. It is also obvious that at any given moment a very small part of such a system can become conscious thought. Though it is theoretically possible — so long as such a system is conserved — that the whole may be brought piecemeal into awareness, either voluntarily as an act of memory, or through various technical devices, nevertheless the greater part must ordinarily remain as a subconscious system of dispositions (neural or psychical?). And indeed it frequently is the case that a person cannot voluntarily reproduce but a small part of the setting of antecedents which furnishes the point of view and egocentric meaning of an idea. Hence it is that in such cases he is ignorant of its origin, of the *why;* and then it is said he is unconsciously motivated. It may or may not be that repression, because of the unpleasant character of the antecedent experiences, is the reason for the failure of reproduction. Sometimes it is and sometimes not. I am not here concerned with mechanisms of amnesia but only with subconscious systems of dispositions that determine points of view and meaning.

It follows, again, theoretically that a change of "attitude of mind," of the point of view regarding any object of consciousness involves a change in the "meaning" of the object. And such a change in meaning involves a change in the root-ideas pertaining thereto, the fundamental ideas of what we here call the "setting." Obviously the setting may be so changed by introducing into the conscious and subconscious systems of experiences composing the setting —

new experiences, new thoughts, new knowledge — new ideas or knowledge that was not previously organized, or systematized with the experiences out of which the setting was built up. Thus, suppose that in the above example there were artificially introduced into the wounded self-pride setting of A ideas of B's admiration of A, of new knowledge that explained A's antecedent experiences with B in an entirely new light and wholly favorable to B. As a result the setting and meaning of A's ideas of B would be changed and the antipathy would cease. This is common everyday experience and requires no psychologist to formulate the principle. The only thing required of the psychologist is to discover in obscure cases the root-ideas from which given points of view, attitudes of mind and meanings have originated. These are often almost impenetrably hidden in the subconscious and require considerable and cunning research for their discovery.

If all this is true, then it is going far afield to introduce the Freudian conceptions of symbols, unconscious infantile sexual wishes, a metaphysical "libido" and what-not into the formulas.

Let us now see how far, through these fundamental psychological principles, we can interpret the phenomena of the psychoneuroses. For this purpose we must consider in more detail the content of the subconscious mechanism.

Before doing so, however, we must consider the psychology of the emotions.

### EMOTION AND SUBCONSCIOUS PROCESSES

We have thus far considered only *acquired* dispositions. There are a number of dispositions or tendencies to specific reactions which are admittedly *innate*. These reactions are determined by a discharge of force in various directions along neural pathways. To say they are innate means that these reactions are conditioned by congenital preformed pathways and central dynamic arrangements and dispositions. Among these dispositions are those instincts which have emotion as a correlated conscious element or accompaniment. Whatever psychological theory of the emotions we may adopt we must admit that they are psychophysical instincts which serve a biological aim. Fear and anger, for example, protect the individual, by flight or pugnacity, from threat of danger or actual harmful attack.

It is generally agreed that in the make-up of personality, in man and animals, there are a number of such primary emotional instincts, although there is some question as to which shall be regarded as primary and which are merely compounds of the primary. We may safely say, however, that in every man and higher animal there are, besides anger and fear, the instincts of curiosity, self-assertion, self-abasement, repulsion, and the parental and sexual instincts. Eact of these has its peculiar emotion — wonder, elation, subjection, disgust, tender feeling and libido. All these instincts, the most advanced psychologists believe, have through the force of their emotions tremendous impulsive or driving force which tends to carry out the aims of the instincts. The emotional impulse in one plays in principle exactly the same part as the impulses of the others, and there is no difference in this respect between the impulses of the sexual instinct and those of the others. What is true of the former is true of the latter. Biologically, the libido stands in exactly the same dynamic position as fear, anger, wonder, etc. One of the most astounding things in the Freudian philosophy is that it either totally disregards everything that has been written by capable students of psychology upon the emotions, or, when it recognizes these important innate dispositions, it does so in a most superficial and inadequate way and subordinates them all to the use of one instinct, the sexual, which it makes paramount and promotes to a hegemony in a confederation of instincts. One hardly knows whether to ascribe this attitude on the part of psychoanalysts to an amazing ignorance of psychology or to that Freudian mechanism which represses from consciousness disagreeable and intolerable facts.

The Freudian conception may be right or it may be wrong, but in either case, to dismiss without discussion well-known facts and plausible interpretations, sustained by capable psychologists of world-wide reputation, is not cal-culated to render Freudian interpretations more acceptable to those who have a wider or different culture.

Considerable complaint is made (and with justice) by psychoanalysts that their critics have not made themselves acquainted with Freudian data and conceptions. Is not the boot on the other leg, or at least on both legs?

In the study of emotion by psychologists in general, attention has been as a rule, I believe, too strongly focused upon it as a psychological state, thereby over-emphasizing this one factor to the neglect of the instinctive process as a whole and particularly of the factor of discharge of energy, known as the impulsive force of the emotions. This dis-charge takes place in at least three directions: (1) to the skeletal muscles determining coordinated movements that manifest instinctive expression of a given emotion, on the one hand, and, on the other, tend to carry out the aim of the instinct (flight in the case of fear, pugnacious movements in the case of anger: (2) to the viscera, through the sympathetic nervous system. These discharges have been admirably studied by Pavlov, Cannon, and others. Cannon has also pointed out how the discharge to the adrenal glands, liver, blood-vessels and other viscera co-operate in the fulfill-ment of the aim of the instinct: (3) finally, it is necessary for the discharge to move in directions which inhibit incom-patible mental dispositions and active mental processes on the one hand and, on the other, those antagonistic instincts, bodily movements, and functions which would conflict with the aim of the given instinct. Thus thoughts and actions motivated by the instinct of anger are at once inhibited by fear, if that instinctive process be excited to activity. Thus stated, the inhibition means antagonism and conflict between two opposed processes. This is a general principle of func-tioning of the nervous system and conditions all coordinated activity as shown by Sherrington.

Emotion then cannot be regarded as a "free, floating" conscious state, or even force, or libido, or energy, that "attaches" itself to this or that, but as only one element in an innate instinctive process conditioned by congenital nervous dispositions and pathways.

My next thesis is that by experience the dispositions thus acquired become organized with innate dispositions into a complex which functions as a whole. In this way not only ideas of objects — father, friend, snake, or fatherland — take on an emotional tone, but the ideas acquire the impulsive force of the emotional instinct which strives to carry them to fruition.

An idea organized with one or more emotional instincts has been aptly termed by Mr. Shand a *sentiment*. We thus have sentiments of love and hatred and jealousy of a person, of self-interest, of self-abasement, of reverence for an object, etc. From such sentiments are necessarily evolved wishes, aspirations, longings, aversions, etc. — a wish or striving to possess a loved person, to injure a hated person, to supplant an object of jealousy, to escape from a feared object, or a self-reproach, etc. So far, however, as a wish or striving includes a foresight of the future, of the goal to be attained, it includes acquired dispositions, acquired by experience. These acquired dispositions of the wish become of necessity integrated with the innate instinctive dispositions of the sentiment from which it derives its impulse or craving. A sentiment, then, is more complex than the simple organization of an idea with an instinct. It may include a wish.

Furthermore, we have seen that an idea has "'meaning" as well as perceptual images. The emotional dispositions belonging to a sentiment, therefore, are necessarily organized also *with the dispositions of meaning, i. e., of antecedent experiences.* Hence it is more than a figure of speech to say that the emotion of a given sentiment has its *roots* in subconscious antecedent experiences. Indeed, observation shows, I think, that the origin of the emotion of a sentiment is almost always, if not always, to be found in the setting of antecedent experiences from which the meaning is derived. Consequently, as all these experiences do not recur to consciousness, it often happens, as psychological studies of obsessions and hysteria have shown, that a subconscious complex of acquired dispositions provides the emotion which emerges into consciousness along with an idea. We may then conservatively speak of subconscious emotional complexes, in the sense of complexes of acquired dispositions (psychological or neural) organized by experience with innate emotional dispositions or instincts.

A sentiment then is, or may be, a much more complex affair than the simple organization of an idea with innate instinctive dispositions. It may be a large complex that includes dispositions, acquired by experience, which provide a meaning to the sentiment and foresight of a goal to be attained, so essential to the wish.

In speaking, then, of a "sentiment" I would have it understood that I include this whole complex as a "psychic whole," the various factors of which cannot be separated or changed without destroying the sentiment. In fact this is what we do when we wish to change or destroy a sentiment.

Now to go back for a moment to the impulsive force of an emotion manifested as discharge:

As Shand *(The Foundations of Character)* and McDougall *(Social Psychology)* have so forcibly argued, the impulsive force of the emotional instincts (organized about an idea to form a sentiment) largely provides the driving force which tends to carry the idea (and wish) to fruition; and the idea guides an awakened instinct in its striving to fulfill its aim. Without such a driving force, on the one hand, the idea would be, *comparatively* speaking, inert, lifeless; on the other hand, without such organization with ideas, instinctive activity would be unregulated, uncoordinated and chaotic. Thus ideas are energized by being organized with emotional instincts. The impulsive force of the instinct becomes a motivating force, a striving of the idea to express itself in mental and bodily behavior. The so-called striving or craving of a wish, for example, on this theory, is due to the tendency of the instinct to discharge its motivating force. From this viewpoint we find the key to the explanation of the observed fact that the conserved *dispositions* of sentiments organized by experience strive to find expression, consciously or subconsciously.

When by reason of some conflicting force or dissociation, their conscious equivalents cannot enter awareness, they tend, activated by their emotional instincts, to become active autonomous subconscious processes.

## CONFLICTS

This brings us to a consideration of *conflicts*. The realization of the fact that human personality is disrupted by emotional conflicts is as old as the literature of the world. In modern times psychology has attempted to formulate their laws — that is all.

Now when an emotion is aroused, a conflict necessarily occurs between its impulse and that of any other existing affective state, the impulse of which is antagonistic to the aim of the former. Consequently an awakened instinct or sentiment which is in opposition to that of some other instinct or sentiment, also in activity, meets with resistance. Whichever instinct or sentiment, meaning whichever impulse is the stronger necessarily downs the other; inhibits the central and efferent parts of the process — ideas, emotions and impulses — though the afferent part conveys the stimulus to the central factor. Thus processes of thought which the inhibited sentiment or instinct would normally excite, or with which it is systematized, are likewise inhibited and behavior correspondingly modified. These statements are only descriptive of what is common experience. If one recalls to mind the principal primary emotions (instincts) such as sex impulse, anger, fear, tender feeling, hunger, self-abasement, self-assertion, curiosity, etc., this is seen to be an obvious biological truth. Fear is suppressed by anger, tender feeling, or curiosity (wonder) and *vice versa;* hunger and the sexual instinct by disgust.

There is one difference, however, between the repression of an instinct (anger, fear, etc.) and that of a sentiment. The former may be simply inhibited. A sentiment, however, being an idea about which a system of emotional dispositions has been organized, when repressed by conflict, or when simply out of mind, whether capable of reproduction as memory or not, is still conserved, as we have seen, as an unconscious neurogram or system of dispositions. As we have also seen, so long as it is conserved it is still a part of the personality. Even though repressed it is not necessarily absolutely inhibited but may be simply dissociated and then be *able to take on dissociated subconscious activity.* As a subconscious process, the idea with its setting, meaning, wish, etc., continues still organized with its emotional dispositions, and the conative forces of these, under given conditions, may continue striving to give expression to the idea.

All sorts of phenomena may result from the emotional discharge of such a subconscious "sentiment." Into these I will not enter. I may mention here only one phenomenon of this striving, namely, the emerging into consciousness of the emotional element of the sentiment while the idea remains subconscious, thus producing an apparently unaccountable fear or joy, feelings of pleasure or pain, etc.

I forbear to mention illustrative examples of the phenomena of conflict, which I might easily cite from both clinical cases and experimental studies.[1]

### THE SETTINGS IN THE PSYCHONEUROSES

Now let us return to our examination of the subconscious part of the settings which give meaning to the conscious or dimly conscious or subconscious ideas of a psychoneurosis. Such an examination will always disclose, I believe from my own investigations, conserved subconscious sentiments, or dispositions of sentiments, of a varying nature; and, organized in all of them, intensely developed emotional instincts. The sentiments, as I have said, may include that of guilt ("guilty conscience"), self-reproaches, or anxieties, jealousies, self-abasement, fear, hatred, resentment, wishes, doubts, or scruples, or what-not; and the instincts are one or a number — centred about each idea.

These are integral and dominating elements in the settings. One or the other has acquired a hegemony in the

1 For examples and a fuller description of conflicts see *The Unconscious,* chapters XV and XVI.

confederacy of the setting. Such elements, particularly wishes, sense of guilt, jealousy or tend to be activated by the motivating impulses of their emotions, that is, by the tendency of their instincts to fulfill their aim. When so activated they express themselves in psychological and bodily behavior. They thus give rise to conflicts with other sentiments with resulting phenomena, and they excite reactions from other instincts which may be defense reactions, such as fear or anger; and from one or other of these reactions certain elements arise in consciousness. These may be simply an affect, such as anxiety, or a phobia or an insistent fixed idea, or it may even be an hallucination. Indeed, hallucinations may be shown by experimental methods to be emergences from subconscious processes of this kind; and consequently the hallucinations of the insane can be logically explained as phenomena determined by more or less autonomously functioning dispositions, motivated into processes below the threshold of consciousness.

Of course, a stimulus of some kind, either from the environment, such as a perception, or from within — an associated idea — is the spark which touches off this psychological explosive. According to this interpretation *any sentiment, that is to say, any conserved idea (wish, e. g.) activated by any of the innate emotional dispositions, if sufficiently strong, may thus become the motive that determines mental and bodily behavior, whether conscious or subconscious.*

When, owing to some specific mechanism, an activated sentiment is prevented from emerging into awareness as a conscious process, observation has shown that it may manifest itself as an autonomous and entirely subconscious process. This process, which is then said to be dissociated, may, by methods of analysis, ofen, as in hysteria, be identified with the dissociated sentiment (subconscious idea).

This brings us to the question: why do not such ideas (or processes) wholly emerge into the content of consciousness; that is to say, why are they subconscious?

To this difficult question various answers have been given, each being a different interpretation of the facts.

According to Janet, the dissociation is due to the inability of the personal consciousness to synthesize the ideas because of physical weakness *(épuisement)*. According to Freud, it is due to repression which occurs because of the peculiar character of the repressed idea. This idea for him is always (or nearly always) a sexual wish, generally of infantile origin, motivated by the striving of the sexual force or libido. The wish is one which, because of its character, is unpleasant to the personal consciousness and is therefore consciously or unconsciously repressed.

According to my own view, if I may venture to formulate it in general terms, the dissociation may be effected by any mental conflict. The impulsive discharge of an emotion, whether that of a purely instinctive reaction such as fear and anger, or that of a sentiment, tends, as observation shows, to inhibit or dissociate antagonistic instincts and sentiments, and whole systems of ideas in which such instincts and sentiments are systematized. Hence in the conflict of antagonistic sentiments, wishes, doubts and scruples, of antagonistic interests evoked by unsolved problems, in the conflict of anxieties with the desire for mental peace, in a conflict with self-reproaches or the fear of self-blame, in a conflict with an overwhelming emotion discharging its impulsive force in almost every direction, in short, through any one of the multitude of conflicts, by which the human mind may be literally torn and distracted, one or other of the contending factors may be inhibited by an antagonistic impulse and so dissociated as to be incapable of taking part in the processes of thought and thus prevented from emerging into consciousness.

But it may not be absolutely inhibited. If its own motivating impulses are sufficiently strong, it may take on autonomous dissociated subconscious activity, and manifest itself by various phenomena. The consideration of these belongs to special psychology and is beyond the scope of our subject. I only wish to point out that, according to my observations and interpretation of such phenomena, any conserved disposition motivated by almost any emotional impulse, that is to say, almost any of the motives of life —

any of the longing or fears, or resentments, or antipathies, or jealousies, or hatreds, or affections, or curiosities — which torment poor human nature, may become a subconscious process. Any of these may activate a process which may continue entirely outside of the personal awareness and exhibit all the characteristics of intelligence — of volition, imagination, emotions, etc.

Under other conditions any subconscious motive, although not emerging itself into the personal consciousness, may indirectly determine the content of that consciousness — that is, mental behavior — in that it is a dynamic factor in that "psychic whole" of ideas which we have discussed, and also in that the *secondary or sequential processes* to which it gives rise, not being in conflict with the dissociating force, may emerge as conscious processes. Thus, for example, a wholly or dimly subconscious sentiment of jealousy may determine secondary rationalization, such as moral reprobation of the object of the jealousy. These ideas may emerge as a conscious interpretation of certain concrete acts of a given individual who is the object. These ideas, thus emerging, become conscious processes of thought without the individual realizing the motivating factor. He is then said to be "unconsciously" motivated by jealousy. Or, similarly, certain ideational processes may emerge, producing falsification of reasoning, self-deception, delusive viewpoints, delusions, etc. Or certain elements of a subconscious process may emerge into the focus or fringe of the personal consciousness as indefinable emotion, insistent ideas, obsessions, impulsions, and hallucinations. When the emotion of anxiety pertaining to a subconscious process alone emerges into awareness we have a pure anxiety state. When an idea with its emotion emerges we have a phobia. In this case it often will be found that the meaning of the obsessing idea is to be found in the fringe or background of the mind. When sensory "images" pertaining to the subconscious "ideas" emerge we have hallucinations. On the other hand, the whole process may be subconscious, producing automatisms of various kinds. Different combinations and interactions of subconscious and conscious processes may produce multiform phenomena, normal and abnormal. Among these, occurrences of conflict are conspicuously important. These facts are easily demonstrated experimentally in subconscious personalities, and other pathological conditions. The details of mechanisms by which such phenomena are produced constitute problems which by themselves still need to be worked out.

In the light of these fundamental principles, we can realize, through such phenomena, the importance of a knowledge of the functions of the subconscious for psychiatry. Without such a knowledge no psychiatrist is properly equipped to understand the problems set before him.

### THERAPEUTICS

The therapeutic end of it is simple in principle. It consists only first in discovering the dominating sentiments in the subconscious setting, and secondly, in altering, through educational processes, these sentiments to others which change the egocentric meaning of ideas, viewpoint and attitude of mind, and thus adapt the patient to his environment. In the functional psychoses I find in practice that it works.

# CHAPTER IV

## Association Neuroses[1]

### A STUDY OF THE PATHOLOGY OF HYSTERICAL JOINT AFFECTIONS, NEURASTHENIA AND ALLIED FORMS OF NEURO-MIMESIS

*Prefatory note:* This study is included in the present volume because it seems to derive some interest from and is supported by the fact that since its publication in 1891 the underlying physiological principle of association neurosis is identical with that of the "conditioned reflex" which has been so beautifully demonstrated experimentally by the physiological researches of Pavlov. By approaching the problem as one of physiology, and by experimental methods on animals, Pavlov has formulated the principle in physiological terms and established it in a way that is impossible in a clinical study. It is obvious that the "inadequate" stimulus of the conditioned reflex is the "associated" stimulus of the association neurosis.

Incidentally I would further point out that in the mechanism of the conditioned reflex, even in Pavlov's dogs, there is undoubtedly, as in association neurosis, a psychical factor as a constituent derived from previous experience. Being subjective, this factor, of course, must be left out of account in investigations on animals. Nevertheless it cannot be disregarded in a complete account of the mechanism.

Every practitioner is familiar with a class of nervous affections, commonly known as neuro-mimesis, typified, when occurring as a local disease, by so-called hysterical joints, and, when occurring as a more general neurosis, by certain forms of neurasthenia and hysteria. Both types frequently follow traumatism or some acute disease. The different forms which the affection may take are numerous, and, though generally characterized as hysterical, should be distinguished from the classical types of that protean disease. They, as a rule, resemble in the grouping of their symptoms other diseases which are essentially organic. For example: hysterical joints imitate very closely true joint lesions; neuroses of the stomach simulate true dyspepsia or gastritis; localized pain and tenderness resemble the same symptoms due to sprained ligaments and muscles; hypochondriasis, true neurasthenia; neuralgic pain, true neuritis or neuralgia; painful crises, true spinal disease, and so on. One of the most sharply defined of these symptom-groups — and one which is best known — is that of hysterical joints. I have chosen this in illustration of the points I wish to bring out. It is a very common affection. Brodie, who should have the credit of first describing it, says:

"I do not hesitate to declare that among the higher classes of society, at least four-fifths of the female patients who are commonly supposed to labor under disease of the joints labor under hysteria, and nothing else." While Brodie tended to exaggeration in placing the proportion as high as four-fifths, and was in error in limiting the disease to the higher classes, the general truth of this statement will be substantiated by all surgeons, as it has been by Esmarch, Paget, Skey and Shaffer. The affection is just as common among the poor as among the rich.

There is no symptom present in true joint disease that may not be present in this spurious affection: pain, limitation of motion, shortening, swelling, atrophy of muscles, contractures, and, if in the leg, limping. The combination of all these symptoms, however, is seen only in the severer types. The more usual form is represented simply by local pain and tenderness, with the consequent inability to use freely the affected arm or leg; very little, if any local deformity is then present. Such an affection is commonly called an hysterical joint; but if I may call attention to what is apt to be overlooked — dubbing such affections hysterical is not an explanation, and in no way adds to our knowledge of their pathology. At most it is merely saying what they are not, *i. e.*, that they are not due to organic causes.

There is no objection to the use of the term hysterical if one insists on retaining it as a generic term to include various but distinct functional neuroses; but it has its objections, since the word connotes so much, and is associated with such varied pathological processes that it tends to obcure our understanding of them and to prevent our obtaining an insight into their true nature. Hysteria, as at present used, embraces a large number of types of functional affections, which vary greatly among themselves and essentially differ in their nature, pathogenesis, clinical picture and course. It is important that these differences should be recognized and the different types classified according to their pathology. After this has been done it will be found that hysteria can be retained only as a generic term, like the word functional, or else must abitrarily be limited to a single type of such diseases.

Now, that theory of the pathology of affections of the kind which are about to be discussed is based upon the psychological law of the association of mental processes. This law may be stated in general terms as follows: ideas, sensations, emotions and volitions occurring together tend by constant repetition to become so strongly associated that the presence of one of them reproduces the others. This law is so well-known that it is hardly necessary for me to dwell upon it here. But it has not been made use of to the extent that it might have been in the elucidation of the symptomatology of disease. If this law is true of normal sensations and ideas, it must be true as well of sensations of pain, of nausea, of vertigo and similar morbid phenomena. But more than this, one at first sight would naturally infer that if it is true of mental states and their underlying brain processes, it is presumably true of pure physiological activities such as are represented in the spinal cord and the lower nervous centres. Inasmuch as all nervous processes are fundamentally alike in their nature, it is to be presumed that if brain processes, with their correlated mental states, can be welded together into an automatic mechanism, it is similarly true that the pure physical activities of the spinal cord, although not correlated with subjective states, may also be welded together by association in the same manner; and that this is true whether these neural activities are simply physiological and normal or pathological in their nature. This is the thesis which I hope to establish, and I believe that with this law so extended, we shall find that many so-called hysterical af-

fections, many neuroses and psychoses, which otherwise are
unintelligible, may be readily explained. They may be termed
*association neuroses and psychoses.*

## ASSOCIATION OF MENTAL STATES WITH NORMAL PHYSIO-LOGICAL PROCESSES

It is a well-known fact that not only may two mental
states be associated, but a mental state and a purely physio
logical function may also be linked together; for example
increased action of the heart may be associated with various
emotions; flow of saliva or gastric juice with the visual picture or memory of certain foods; diminution of saliva with
the emotion of fear; spasm of the bladder with the occurrence of various periodic habits of life, and so on.

A neurasthenic patient of mine, who has had several
children, but now past the age of child-bearing, tells me that
she never hears a child cry without having a feeling of swelling or fullness in her breasts as if the milk were running
into them. This feeling is the same she always had when she
was nursing her children. On a late occasion, when she was
taking care of a friend after confinement, this feeling was so
strongly excited by the crying of the child that at the end
of a week her breasts ached as of old. The pain persisted for
a whole week during which she was in attendance.

## ASSOCIATION OF MENTAL STATE WITH PATHOLOGICAL PHYSIOLOGICAL PROCESSES

The act of blushing may be so strongly associated with
a single idea, that whenever the idea is present the individual
cannot help blushing, no matter how much he try. Indeed
this may be carried so far that blushing may become almost
a pathological phenomenon, to the annoyance of the unfortunate victim of the habit; and when this act is strongly
connected with a particular idea or set of ideas, we may
fairly say that we have the first rudimentary association of a
normal mental state with a pathological physiological condition. A more marked example of this association may be

seen in sea-sickness. I have known a person to be so affected by the motion of the sea that merely looking at the water while standing on dry land has caused the severe pain in the eyes and forehead, and vertigo. Actual sailing always produced the same sensations, which were described as being much worse than the classical nausea which always followed them. Again, vomiting is certainly a pathological condition; and yet I know of a young woman who was so unfortunate that the act of kissing was always followed by uncontrollable vomiting. On one occasion the result was particularly embarrassing, it being the moment when she consented to give up her state of single blessedness, and was obliged to leave her accepted *fiancé* standing in the middle of the room while she hurried off to avoid what would have been a mortifying accident. In each of these instances we have a normal mental state associated with a pathological one, and in the act of kissing, a not at all unpleasant task, associated with a very disagreeable function. The mechanism, by which these associations and resulting pathological conditions were brought about, is easy to understand. In the case of the person in whom severe frontal pain and vertigo were provoked by the sight of the sea, the association of the two mental states — the *visual* picture and the sensation of *pain,* etc., — is plainly to be found in the past experience of the subject, who had many times had the same sensations produced by the actual *motion* of the sea. By this means, the *visual image* of the water, although not the primary cause but an associated idea, had become so firmly bound with the sensation of vertigo and pain, that when the former was present the latter was necessarily reproduced.[1]

One cannot here doubt the efficacy of the law of association of ideas to account for the whole pathological process. But in this case the excitant of what is now only the consequence of the association of two mental states was originally an *external* agency, *viz.,* the actual motion of the ship. The impression made by this upon the nervous system was so deep that afterwards the presence alone of an asso-

[1] In the recent literature, this is referred to as the "inadequate stimulus."

ciated idea — the visual picture of the water — was suffi
cient to arouse the other elements of the pathologica
process. This is a fundamental which I wish to emphasiz
and make use of later on when we come to study more com
plex conditions, *viz.*, *that a pathological process in the nerv
ous system, once engendered by an external agency, ma
afterwards be awakened, on the cessation of that agency, b
means merely of a physiological action or a psychologica
state previously associated with it.*

The original cause of such pathological processes is no
always easy to determine, but that it may sometimes hav
its origin in the revival of past experiences (*i. e.*, pure menta
states) may be seen by the following incident: A youn{
physician, in whose family had occurred an appallin{
epidemic of diphtheria, resulting fatally to one of its mem
bers, found himself shortly afterwards near the diphtheriti
wards in one of our large hospitals. Owing to the publicit{
which had been given to the epidemic in his family, he wa
urged very strongly by the physicians and attendants not t
enter the wards. But desiring to see one of the patients, an{
feeling that as a member of the profession, *noblesse oblige*
he persisted in going in. It is probable that, as so much wa
made of the matter, a profound impression was made upor
his mind. Shortly after leaving the ward he was was taker
with a severe pain in his throat, which was strongly increaser
by swallowing. The pain and local sensations in every way
simulated that of tonsillitis. Now, the subject of this wa
absolutely convinced that his pain was entirely subjective
or hysterical, and could not possibly be due to local causes
and he endeavored to control it by an act of will. But no
mental effort made the slightest impression upon the loca
symptoms, which were as accentuated as if due to inflam
mation. It was only by persistent effort directed toward ab
sorption of his mind in professional duties that he was able
to free himself from them. In this case we must assume that
the experiences of a past sore throat were revived by
the visual image, etc., of the diphtheritic throat, and having
been once revived, no mental effort could control it; or, put
ting this into physiological language, we may say the sensory

centres of the pharynx were reflexly excited from the visual centres, and, owing to the profound mental impression created, continued thus to be excited as a pure association neurosis.

This association of a mental state with a pathological process is frequently seen following a traumatism, where the revived idea of the accident awakens one or more symptoms which originally formed part of a psychosis long since subsided. For example: a patient of mine, who suffered from nausea, vomiting, headache and dizziness, following a shock in a railway accident, suffered from these same symptoms for several months afterwards whenever he rode in the cars, although between times he was practically free from them. He has since recovered.

The following is an example of the association of two pure *psychical* states following traumatism: A friend of mine, at present in absolutely good health, was knocked down, some years ago, in the streets of New York by a coach drawn by four horses. The accident was unusually startling, the coach coming upon him unawares, so that he was knocked down without warning. Almost the first thing he was conscious of, beyond the nervous shock, was the fact that he was lying on the ground, while over and above him, as he looked up, was the white belly of a horse. To-day, if this person is suddenly startled by any noise, he tells me that he sees before him as a vivid mental picture the white belly of a horse. Here is an association of the mental state of fear and a visual image.

I know of no more beautiful illustration of the association of a single *mental state with a pure physical* process than that furnished by a case of Dr. Mackenzie, of Baltimore. It was that of a lady who had been for years a terrible sufferer from rose cold or hay fever. The disease became aggravated by the addition of asthmatic attacks which complicated the coryza. She had become so sensitive that the number of exciting causes of an attack was very large. She was so sensitive to roses that the mere presence of a rose in the same room was sufficient to induce an attack. Suspecting the nature of her trouble, Mackenzie obtained an artificial rose of such exquisite workmanship that it presented a perfect counterfeit of the original. One day, when the lady came to his office, after assuring himself by careful examination that she was perfectly free from coryza, Mackenzie produced the artificial rose from behind a screen where it had been concealed, and held it in front of her. Almost immediately a violent attack of coryza developed. Her eyes became suffused with tears, the conjunctivae injected, the puncta lachrymalia began to itch violently; her face became flushed, the nasal passages obstructed, her voice hoarse and nasal; she complained of a desire to sneeze and tickling and intense itching in the back of the throat and in the auditory meatus; there was also photophobia and secretion of fluid from the nasal passages; to this was added a feeling of oppression in the chest and a slight embarrassment of respiration. Examination showed the nostrils almost completely obstructed by swollen, reddened and irritable turbinated structures and filled with fluid. The mucous membrane of the throat was injected. At this point Mackenzie stopped the experiment, thinking it had gone far enough, and the patient left the office with a severe attack of coryza.

The sequel is equally interesting. The true nature of the rose was shown to the patient, with the result that on her next visit she plunged her face into a bunch of real roses without ill effect.[1]

I know nothing more instructive than this case. We have all the phenomena of inflammation, a series of apparently organic processes set into activity by the force of an associated idea. It would seem as if the physiological processes of secretion of tears, secretion of mucus, vasomotor action (causing injection of tissue), pain, etc., were united into an automatic mechanism, and the whole connected (associated), as with a spring, with a higher visual centre, which when touched set off the whole mechanism. The principle here involved is an important one, and it will be well to bear

---

1 *Amer. Jour. Med. Sciences,* 1886, vol. XCI, p. 45. The reader is referred to this interesting paper for accounts of numerous cases of neuroses of various kinds associated with a fixed idea.

t in mind when we come to consider other complex associations. It shows conclusively the possibility of an automatic nervous process of considerable complexity becoming
established, and afterwards excited anew as an independent
neurosis by a purely physiological stimulus.

I have myself seen a young woman who has suffered
from frequent attacks of nervous coryza and sore throat;
but although the nervous origin has been apparent, the automatic mechanism is not so sharply associated with a single
idea as in Mackenzie's case.

The whole process in this case may be set down diagrammatically as follows:

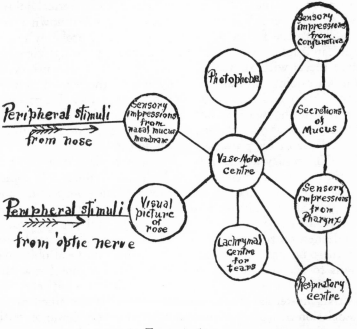

FIGURE 1

Originally, the peripheral stimuli which created the
neurosis came from the nasal mucous membrane. Afterwards, when the different centres had become welded to-

gether into an automatic whole, the entire process wa
exploded by the visual impressions from the optic nerve
stimulating one of the associated centres.

### HYSTERICAL JOINTS

I think I have given enough to show that a pathologica
process may be the expression of an association of menta
states or of physiological activities, or the combination o
both, although the examples cited have been drawn from
very simple, perhaps rudimentary, forms of neuroses; bu
I wish to illustrate the principles of the law by the simple
examples before applying it to those in which the condition
are more complex. Let us now return to hysterical joints
which we selected as an illustration of a well-known type
I will cite the following simple case, which probably every
one can duplicate in his own experience. A strong, vigorou
man meets with an accident causing more or less injury to
the knee-joint. Motion and any use of the leg, of course
causes pain and makes locomotion impossible. He is confined to his house or his bed, takes care of his knee, nurses it
bandages it, applies the usual remedies, and treats it, under
the advice of his physician *secundum artem.*

The injury at the outset was only a slight one, and ye
at the end of six or eight weeks he is still disabled. He come
to you for examination, and after carefully inspecting the
leg you are unable to detect any local deformity, but he
complains of pain on walking, he limps, and you find some
tenderness on pressure about the joint, and pain located here
or there on passive motion: but you find no local objective
signs to account for his condition. Such a case I saw the
other day. I was satisfied that the disability was entirely subjective, hysterical if you please, and to be explained as an
association neurosis. I found also, what is very common with
such patients, a mental timidity about using the leg for fear
of aggravating the mischief. I told him to throw away his
cane, to walk without limping and disregard his leg, assuring
him at the same time that his knee was well, and only required use for the pain to disapppear. This advice was fol-

lowed by a prompt recovery. The mechanism of the neurosis in this case I conceive to be as follows: a *bona fide* lesion about the knee is produced. At every attempt to use the limb, every time the knee is bent, pain is felt in the joint; in consequence of this, the sensory centres, stimulated by the kinesthetic sensations due to bending the knee, are firmly associated with the sensory centres of pain excited by the same act. Later the local lesion entirely disappears, but the two central sensory processes remain so firmly associated that the mere act of bending the knee awakens both processes — the pathological one of pain as well as the physiological one of sense of movement.

This may be diagrammatically represented as follows:

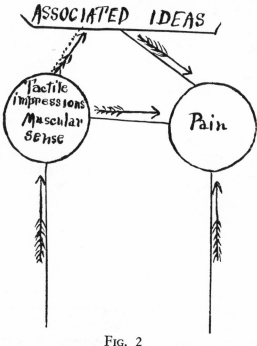

FIG. 2

At first the centres of pain are excited directly by the peripheral stimuli from the joint; later, indirectly from the associated centre of muscular sense, etc., as indicated by the arrows.

I have no doubt that in most of these cases the sensory centres in the central nervous organ are maintained in this condition of association by an *auto-stimulation dependent on the condition of mind of the subject,* which is generally that of anxiety regarding the future of the injury.

But leaving this point for the present and passing on to the study of more complex conditions, I will cite in illustration the case of a little girl who was brought to me for trouble in her leg. On examination I found that not only was there pain on motion in the knee-joint, but there was also marked contracture of the hamstring muscles, so that when the patient attempted to walk, the heel was drawn up, and the weight of the body was for the most part supported on the ball of the foot. There was also decided atrophy of the muscles of the calf and thigh. The electrical reactions, however, were normal. Repeated examinations by Drs. Burrell and Cushing, as well as by myself, failed to detect evidence of organic disease of either the knee or the hip joint. In Dr. Burrell's report I find it stated, "the length of limbs are the same, although the right leg is apparently $\frac{1}{4}$ inch longer than the left; limitation of motion in the right hip; right leg in position of extreme rotation; slight abduction and slight flexion of the knee" (at this time flexion had diminished decidedly owing to treatment). "No heat or tenderness about either knee or hip joint; left side of pelvis rotated forward toward the left, right scapula held higher than left, apparent lordosis. Diagnosis — neuro-mimesis, atrophy from disuse." There was in this case a history of traumatism. Some six or seven months previously, a schoolmate pulled the girl off her seat at school, and she fell to the ground with her leg crossed under her. She sprained her knee, and, according to her mother's statement, she complained of pain in the joint for some days after. Her mother thinks there was a little puffiness about the knee at the time, and asserts that the girl soon began to limp, that the leg was in a constant state of slight flexion, and that it was difficult to straighten it. This limping and bending of the leg had increased up to the time she came under my observation.

Under treatment, which consisted principally of electricity and moral encouragement to use the leg regardless of pain, and especially to extend it, the girl improved in the course of a month or so. She was soon able to walk with the heel on the ground, and had no pain except when attempts were made to extend the leg passively. She was then lost sight of for nearly a year. At the end of this time she presented herself again for examination. She was then found to be in practically the same condition as she was when last seen, no further improvement having taken place. The difference in size, however, of the two legs was more marked, and it was found to be impossible to straighten the leg. One day, it was noticed, on examination, that when she was told to make a strong effort to kick with the disabled leg, although she appeared to do so with considerable force, yet the patella and its tendons did not rise up in relief as did those of the other knee, and that when extension reached a certain point, namely, that corresponding to the position in which the leg was habitually held, the extensor muscles on the front of the thigh ceased to contract, and instead of becoming hard to the touch, like that of the sound limb, remained soft. At the same instant, the hamstring tendons stood out in strong relief from contracture of these muscles. In other words, at first sight, there seemed to be simultaneous with the contracture a paralysis of the extensor muscles. But a simple test showed that there was no real paralysis, for when she was told to raise and lower herself on one leg, or to step on a chair she was able to do so with ease. The only explanation, then, of this phenomenon was a sudden *inhibition* of control of the extensor muscles at the same instant that the *contracture* of the flexor muscles took place. Another element was thus added to the symptomatology. In measuring the leg, it was further found that although the difference in the size of the two legs was somewhat increased, it was not due to increase of atrophy, but to increase of growth of the sound leg. The atrophy was apparent rather than real. The electrical reactions were perfectly normal. The pathology of the case seemed now, for the first time, to be clear, and the clue to rational treatment was obtained, as will presently appear from the sequel.

The conditions in this case, then, were as follows: probably at the beginning local inflammation, pain and muscular spasm; later, pain, contracture, muscular inhibition, atrophy.

How are these, and in particular the contracture, to be explained? A little consideration, I think, will enable us to do so without difficulty. Contracture of this kind is only persistent spasm. If we examine a normal joint, we shall find that any attempt on our part to move it is accompanied by more or less spasm of the muscles controlling it, and only by a strong effort of will, if at all, can a person inhibit such involuntary contraction. In the case of an inflamed joint any motion sufficient to cause pain is followed by marked spasm of the muscles, which may be so intense as to hold the joint perfectly rigid. Now this spasm is, in my opinion, nothing more or less than an exaggeration of a normal condition; but, whether this be admitted or not, spasm of a muscle moving a joint is a classical symptom of joint disease. Further, by extension of the reflex process, limitation of motion in the neighboring joints may be induced; for example, when movements of the hip are limited by disease of the knee.[1]

Now in the case of A. F., during the first days following the accident, when there was more or less local injury to the joint, the slightest effort to extend the leg was followed by pain and spasm of the hamstring muscle. At the same

[1] Much light is thrown upon the mechanism of contracture from peripheral irritation by a study of the simpler forms, such as are observed in "paradoxical contraction," and the similar phenomena, observed in hysterical subjects, to which Charcot and Richet have called attention. In such subjects the pain of movement of a joint induces a contracture of the muscles of definite duration. Massage of a muscle or friction of the skin in certain hysterical subjects also causes more or less persistent contraction. I have already reported ("Boston Med. and Surg. Jour.," 1887) a case of persistent spasm of the *tibialis anticus* and extensor muscles of the toes maintained by peripheral irritation from the great toe joint. This spasm was in all probability begun as a volitional contraction to relieve pressure, but was afterwards continued for at least twenty-five years by peripheral stimulation, as a mere automatic process, similar to that we are considering; and this, although no signs of local disease could be made out.

time there was voluntary disuse or inhibitoin of the extensor muscles owing to the pain. The slightest motion, that is to say, the slightest centripetal impression from the joint, due to change of position, excited not only the sensory centres of muscular sense and pain, but the motor centres as well. By constant repetition these centres became physiologically associated together. Sense of movement, pain, muscular inhibition, spasm — became firmly united into one automatic process. In course of time the local injury subsided, and with it the local causes of pain; but now, the centres having become thoroughly welded together, the peripheral impressions of movement are alone sufficient to excite the whole process; and pain, muscular inhibition and spasm are excited as before. The automatic process having become once established, it continues as an independent neurosis after the original exciting cause has ceased to exist.[1]

The moment the knee is extended beyond a certain point, the kinesthetic sensations are sufficient to work the automatic process and stimulate not only their own sensory centres, but those of pain and motion. This process is represented by the following diagram.

[1] It is interesting to compare this study of contracture made nearly 50 years ago with the Freudian approach, with the conditioned reflex view, which it certainly resembles and with the most recent investigations in neural function.

In Louttit's *Clinical Psychology* (1936) pages 499-504 we find a case of partial paralysis of the left leg ascribed to witnessing of parental scenes over extra-marital affairs.

Prince's detailed neural picture does not exclude the psychoanalytic etiology; for the "primal scene" or any other repressed experience may be in Prince's language an "integrate" of the association neurosis. No one, however, to my knowledge, has afforded us a sounder physiological theory of what happens in the case of such neuroses and hysterical phenomena than the author, who has at the same time always stressed the psychic factor in inducing such conditions.

— A. A. R.

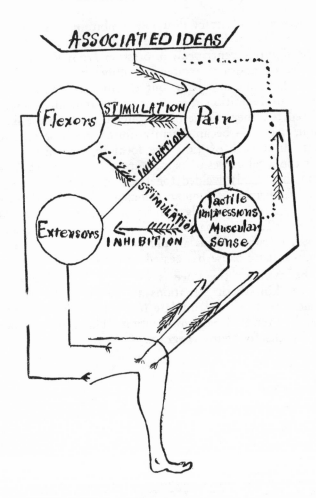

FIGURE 3.

So much for the theory; now for the proof. It will be remembered that this girl has been in this condition for over one year and a-half. During the first few months that I saw her, about six months after the accident, she improved to this extent that she could get the heel down to the ground, and the contracture was much diminished, but the leg never could be absolutely straightened. It will be remembered that at the expiration of nearly another year, on her return to me, she was in the same condition as she was when I saw her ten months previous. No improvement had in that time taken place. It was then that on re-examining her I made out the condition of things already described and obtained the first clue to intelligent treatment. It was based on this theory of an association neurosis, and on the fact that she had lost control, by long habit, over the extensor muscles of the leg. When directed to draw up the patella of the affected leg she was unable to do so. She could draw up the patella of the left leg with ease. Therefore the first step in treatment was directed toward teaching her to regain control over the right inhibited patella. She was first practiced in moving the left patella, and then both in unison. After a few minutes I succeeded in teaching her to draw up the right patella, and when she did so the spasm of the hamstring muscles began to relax; and soon, for the first time during my whole observation of her, the leg straightened out and the deformity dissolved. Still forcible passive extension of the leg at that time resulted in spasm and she was unable to straighten the leg while the weight of her body was upon it. After she had learned to draw up the patella while lying down, she was taught to extend the leg completely by kicking — that is, to continue contraction of the extensor muscles after the knee had arrived in the position so long maintained, and until the full extension of the leg was accomplished. This was finally successful. She was then made to stand on the leg and throw the knee back; later still, to walk throwing the knee back with every step.

Although this training had been carried on under most unfavorable circumstances, that is, during an occasional visit to the hospital, about once a week or ten days, and under the supervision of her mother at home, the result has been that she can now extend one leg as well as the other, and the contracture has disappeared, though the limb occasionally relapses into its former position when she is not observed. The pain has disappeared.

It should be said that to induce these exercises, a great

deal of moral and physical influence was necessary, as the child was very rebellious and complained of pain about the joint at every effort to straighten the leg, and pretended to be unable to do what was wanted and to suffer in the doing of it. It was not difficult to make out that this was mostly simulated. Otherwise the child showed no hysterical condition. With this result, I think I may fairly say that our theory has been proved.

It will be noticed that the consideration of the atrophy has been omitted in this discussion. This was necessary, because there is still much difference of opinion regarding the pathology of atrophy in true joint disease. While orthopedists tend to regard it as due solely to disuse, neurologists generally regard it as due to some neuropathic process. Until this question is decided, one must speak with caution in these hysterical cases; but there are several explanations, any one of which would be sufficient. In the first place, the atrophy, as has been said, was not as great as appeared at first sight. The great difference in the measurements of the leg was shown to be due to increased growth of the sound leg, rather than to retrograde process in the injured limb, so that the whole may be regarded rather as a hindrance of growth than an atrophy. Or it may be that at the beginning there was a slight atrophy due to the true joint trouble,[1] and since then there has been simply a retardation of growth. If atrophy of true joint disease is really due to disuse, it would explain everything that is present in this case. If, on the other hand, as I believe, the pathology is more complex, it may be readily supposed that the same inhibitory influence which paralyzed the extensor muscles inhibited the cells in the anterior cornua of the spinal cord and inhibited the growth of the limb. In this case the atrophy would be introduced into the automatic process.

---

[1] I have known this to occur in a case of paralysis and atrophy from neuritis. The paralysis passed into hysterical paralysis, which was suddenly recovered from in a moment of mental excitement. The atrophy, which was marked, persisted during the hysterical stage.

## PSYCHICAL ELEMENTS AS A FACTOR IN THE PROCESS

The study of the pathology of these affections would be far from complete if no account were taken of the psychical elements as a factor in the generation of the neurological process. The mental element undoubtedly plays a very important part, and particularly in maintaining the neurosis after it has been once established. That pain and various other nervous phenomena may be kept alive by the mind dwelling on them is a well-known fact. It is not, however, so well recognized that symptoms may be maintained in this way in sufficient prominence to constitute by themselves alone a distinct neurosis; although it is well known that when limited to the intellectual side of consciousness they may become so persistent as to form a well-recognized psychosis, known as "fixed ideas." In this way, an association neurosis may be kept from subsiding and may be maintained for an indefinite period of time. A very good illustration of the effect of this element may be seen in the following case: I was consulted by a neurotic patient of mine for a very sharp pain in the foot below the inner malleolus. On examination of the foot I found the tissues decidedly puffy at this place and exquisitely tender to the touch. She walked with considerable pain and limped badly. I could obtain no traumatic history. From the puffiness of the tissues and the tenderness, I was inclined to the belief that there was a local injury of some kind — probably a neuritis — but was in much doubt. However, I assured her in a confident tone that the case was plain and that the trouble was "pododynia." The word evidently struck her imagination and she seemed to be contented. Presently she said to me, "What is pododynia?" I laughed and said, "Pododynia is pain in the foot." Upon this she laughed heartily and said, "Never mind. I feel much better already. It is a great comfort to know what it is," and then she added, "If you doctors would always tell us what is the matter, we should not suffer half so much and would get well much quicker." In the course of a few hours or so she was walking about without limping and free from pain.

Whatever the origin of the pain in this case, it had evidently been maintained by a fixed idea of disease. The number of symptoms that may be maintained in this way as fixed ideas is numerous, and may be severe enough to lead to the absolute disability of the patient. Pain, nausea, vomiting, tired feeling and paralysis are very common; the last especially after railway accidents; and, in my opinion, they constitute a considerable proportion of traumatic neuroses.

### MIMICRY PROPER

This leads me to another class of hysterical affections closely allied to those following traumatism; one in which the neuro-mimesis is due to mimicry, in the popular sense of the word, without traumatic history. Weir Mitchell has devoted a very entertaining chapter to this class of diseases in general. It is most instructive to see to what extremities mere mimicry may reduce the human body. There is hardly any function which may not be disturbed. Paget records the case of two brothers, one of whom had true joint disease, the other the hysterical form contracted by pure mimicry; and Shaffer tells of two sisters, similarly affected.

The exciting cause, however, seems to have been, in Shaffer's case, a slight traumatism. The one with neuro-mimesis had nursed the other during her illness.

Weir Mitchell, after detailing from his great clinical experience a number of cases of mimicry, many of them extraordinary in their details, says that he has often pondered over them trying to satisfy himself whether the pain so often complained of was really true pain like that suffered by other people. He says he has found it difficult to answer this question; but, after hearing the autobiographies of a number of his patients, he believes the pain is real, though due to the mind constantly dwelling on itself. I should say that in such cases there can be little question about the correctness of this opinion, and that pain of this sort is the true psychical equivalent of stimulated centres; but these centres are excited by an auto-stimulation, the result of discharges along association tracks from higher (psychical) centres.

In other words, we must look for the solution of the primary excitation of these psychoses not in external causes such as traumatism, but in internal stimulation from previous ideas or mental pictures which secondarily lead to the development of an automatic process similar in every respect to that produced by traumatism. Such a mental process would be identical with that known as the psychosis of fixed ideas — a well-recognized type. Taking a specific case — that of facial spasm recorded by Weir Mitchell — in illustration, we have the following data to explain just how the automatic process would be developed.

While showing a case of facial spasm to one of his *confrères,* Dr. Weir Mitchell noticed that that gentleman's face was suddenly affected with spasm in a way similar to that of the patient which he was exhibiting. His medical friend was entirely oblivious of the fact and the spasm was absolutely involuntary. In this case the excitation of the visual centres corresponding to the visual image of the muscular spasm was reflected along the association tracks to the centres of the facial nerve, the stimulation of which resulted in facial spasm. The whole process was absolutely automatic.

Cases of pure mimicry of this sort are not very uncommon. Nearly all are familiar with the dancing mania of the Middle Ages, which spread like a great plague through a large part of Central Europe. The contagion passed from city to city and from province to province until thousands were affected with this strange disease. In Strassburg it obtained the name of St. Vitus' dance, from which the name of our modern disease is derived. Individuals were attacked with convulsive seizures from merely watching others dancing in their presence. In Italy the disease was known as tarantism, and was supposed to be due to the bite of the spider, the tarantula. The spasmodic movements, once generated, were beyond the control of the will and continued as automatic processes. A number of years ago Weir Mitchell observed a very interesting epidemic of convulsions in a children's ward in a home in Philadelphia. The convulsions were epileptiform, sometimes choreiform, in their character, and often very severe. One child after another became affected until finally more than a dozen were attacked. Some of the cases were very violent and very rebellious to treatment. It became necessary to isolate them from one another and to distribute them among the different hospitals of the city, where they finally recovered, after varying periods of from one to three months. In these cases, although the convulsions were primarily due to a mental impression, the neural process became so firmly engrafted in the nervous centres that it persisted as a neurosis beyond the control of the will. It is well known that many neuroses, although they may have originated in volitional attempts to deceive, nevertheless pass in time beyond the control of the will and persist as true pathological processes. Let us cite, *e. g.*, the fact that, though vomiting primarily may have been begun by a malingerer or hysterical patient, with the direct desire to deceive, it may afterwards persist in spite of the subject's desire to stop it. *When the various neural processes have been well amalgamated, no matter what the original excitant, they seem to be carried on in the lower centres as an automatic mechanism in the form of a neurosis.*

Physiologically, this is well-recognized and is the basis of education and most of our daily actions. Sewing, reading, writing, piano playing, telegraphing, skating, walking, etc., though primarily begun as a series of individual volitional acts, later become welded together in lower nervous centres as automatic processes, and are carried on for the most part without the intervention of volition. In a similar way, processes that are pathological may be originated.

Taking the case of hip disease recorded by Paget, and due to mimicry, the explanation is obviously as follows: the condition of the one brother who was genuinely suffering from this ailment had excited, through suggestion, the sensory centres in the other brother's highly sensitive nervous organization. The result is real pain located in the hip. The limb is held rigidly in one position, partly by volition and partly as a reflex process from the sensory centres, in consequence of the physiological law of spasm in muscles moving a joint in which there is pain. After the pain and spasm have been long continued in association, the spasm becomes contracture. Limp necessarily follows, vaso-motor and trophic centres may eventually be included in the association, owing to diffusion of the stimuli along the physiologically connected reflex tracks. In this way all the symptoms of true joint disease may result, and an independent automatic neurosis may be established.

## NEURASTHENIA, TRAUMATIC PSYCHOSES, ETC.

There is another class of diseases in which the association process plays a conspicuous part, and often stands out in relief as the dominant feature in the symptom picture. I mean that large group of diseases known as neurasthenia, including some forms of hypochondriasis and hysteria. I may say in parenthesis that neurasthenia, as a term, means very little. As ordinarily used in practice, it embraces a variety of very different and distinct pathological conditions. At best I think it represents a bodily condition upon which are grafted various neurotic processes of different pathology. It may be compared to a pool in which, when the water is low, various forms of animal and vegetable life previously hidden out of sight emerge from its depths and approach the surface, while numerous foreign fungi and algae find in the stagnant water a suitable culture for their development; but when the water is high and its circulation is quickened by the inflowing springs, the organic life at the bottom sinks out of sight, and the parasitic growths on its surface perish from contact with the freshened and oxygenated water. It is thus in so-called neurasthenia, when the general vitality is lowered, the individual seems to become conscious of every response of the body to the outside world, and to feel the vital friction, as it were, of the various functions carried on by the internal organs; at the same time neural processes become engrafted upon the nervous system as the expression of the reaction of the depressed organism to the surroundings. On the restoration of the general vitality to its normal level, these processes are, as a rule, broken up, but they may persist as independent automatic neuroses. These neuroses may constitute a considerable portion of the symptom-picture of neurasthenia and allied affections.

And I may say here that I believe that the symptom-picture of many cases of *traumatic psychosis* is to be explained in this way. The persistence of the symptoms in such cases is to be accounted for by the law of association, which also enables us to understand the early recovery of many cases after the award of damages has been made, without imputing fraudulent motives.

The origin and development of this symptom-picture offers a field for study which deserves the attention of the clinician, and, if approached from the point of view already laid down, will amply repay the labor given to it. One will be surprised to find how intelligible many symptoms become, which before could not be explained, or which were simply set down as "neurasthenic."

A few cases in illustration will make clear the application of the principle:

A woman, forty-one years of age, came to me complaining of paroxysms of pain, from which she had suffered for ten years past. The pain was located in the epigastrium and sometimes was accompanied by pain under the right eye, and in the soles of the feet.

It was described as hot and burning in character, "just as if you put your finger on the stove." These paroxysms came on nearly every day, and lasted from one minute to half an hour; when occurring at night, she was unable to obtain any sleep. As a rule, during the day "she could not go over two hours without pain" of greater or less severity. Physical examination showed nothing abnormal beyond a tender spot at the junction of the sixth or seventh rib with the sternum on the left side. She was of a nervous, anxious temperament, easily worried and disturbed by trifles. Cross-examination revealed the fact that ten years before, she received a great nervous shock in the form of some "terrible news." She thinks the first pain came simultaneously with the nervous shock, and she ascribes her condition to that accident. At that time she became "numb all over," "for four or five months could not sleep at all," "felt dazed and confused in mind; if spoken to, the voices sounded 'away, away off.' " This is the best description I could obtain of her condition at that time. At present any mental worry or excitement causes a paroxysm; for example, after waiting two hours in my office without seeing me, she went away, under the disappointment, "all doubled up with pain." Physically she is in good condition. She is strong and can walk long distances, her spirits are easily depressed or elevated; over-fatigue, worry, disappointment, in fact anything that upsets her mental equilibrium, brings on a paroxysm.

The treatment in this case was static electricity. After a few sittings, the paroxysms of pain ceased; she was in every way better mentally and physically. She said "she felt like a different woman." She was free from any attack while under observation, for a period or four or five weeks, when she was discharged.[1]

The order of events in this case I conceive to be as follows: Ten years ago this patient was attacked with an acute nervous illness, of which two prominent symptoms were mental distress and epigastric pain. These two processes were so frequently associated together, that a reflex physiological connection became established between their nervous centres; the presence of the one then necessitated the reproduction of the other; and when later recovery from the acute illness occurred, the association being persistent, the presence of any physiological excitement or anxiety was necessarily accompanied by a paroxysm of pain. The pathological condition lay in the association of two centres, and not in the centres themselves. The treatment resulted in the breaking up of this association, probably by means of suggestion.

A young woman consulted me in October, 1890, in consequence of peculiar attacks of distressed breathing from which she suffered. The description of these attacks was that of wheezy respiration and a sensation of suffocation. They were sufficiently frequent and severe to oblige her to give up her occupation. Besides this she was anemic, drank tea to

1 She reported herself several months later still free from attacks.

excess, and had very little appetite and suffered from loss of strength; in other words, the usual condition of general debility. Careful inquiry elicited the fact that these paroxysms of suffocation were preceded by a train of minor symptoms, which developed in the following sequence; ball in throat, fright, feeling of blood rushing into eyes, trembling, palpitation, chill, distressed breathing, crying spell, aching of heart. It further appeared that menstruation did not come on till she was 20 years old, but previous to this she had had numerous attacks of epistaxis. Ten years ago she suffered from slight attack of hemoptysis, which has been recurring about once a year ever since. These attacks always precede by a day or two the catamenia. Lungs are normal. When the hemoptysis comes on, she has the following sensations: feeling of blood in throat, fright, trembling, palpitation, pricking feeling in chest, chill, crying spell.

I was struck with the similarity between these two groups of symptoms, and further inquiry brought out the fact that when in her later attacks she felt the lump in her throat, she always imagined it was blood, and was frightened in consequence. The rest of the symptoms then followed by association. The attacks were brought on by almost any mental excitement, such as being obliged to hurry, being in a crowd, cross words, and so forth.

The paroxysms of distressed breathing had another origin. This first came on during an attack of grippe, during the preceding December, and was apparently one of the neuroses so frequently seen following that disease, probably caused by the poison. It was then tacked on to the other group of symptoms, and the whole formed an association group.

The treatment consisted in forced feeding and static electricity. She rapidly gained in weight, and at the close of December she was discharged perfectly well. She had been ill nine months.

I may also cite here the case of a neurasthenic patient who exhibits a very irritable nervous system. This patient suffers considerably, when pregnant, with a variety of symptoms largely referable to the abdomen. When in this condition — she suffers from great exhaustion, considerable nausea, abdominal pains of all kinds, tympanitic distention of the abdomen, paraesthesia of the left side, and various other symptoms. The exhaustion, faintness and abdominal distention are extreme. At present almost any strong irritation of the abdomen, such as massage, electricity, jolting in a carriage, etc., muscular and nervous fatigue, will result in the production of the same set of symptoms; and all the phenomena of pregnancy, or at least of disturbance of the pelvic organs, are exhibited. It is proper to say that this patient, at one time in the past, suffered from some sort of pelvic inflammation, accompanied, so far as I can learn, by a very similar train of symptoms.

The explanation of such groups of symptoms is properly to be found not in peripheral nerves, nor in spinal or cerebral centres, but rather in associations established by previous acute processes between such centres, or to diffusion of stimuli along physiological channels. It may be regarded as a hyper-excitability of the association systems of fibres, or a species of pathological physiology.

The practical corollary from this theory is that in a large class of neuroses we are to look for the causes not in diseased nerves and centres, but rather in a pathological association of normal anatomical elements, and the treatment is to be directed to the breaking up of this association, and the re-grouping of the nervous centres.

# CHAPTER V

## Suggestive Depersonalization and Repersonalization

### THE PSYCHOPHYSIOLOGY OF HYPNOTISM[1]

#### I.  WHAT IS HYPNOTISM?

In presenting this topic of hypnotism for discussion, I have thought it opportune to reconsider the subject, notwithstanding all that has been written about it, for in my judgment, more superficial, unscientific observations have been made, more specifically selected data to bolster up particular hypotheses have been collected, more ill-considered conclusions have been drawn, and more nonsense has been written here than in any other important field. The terms hypnotism and hypnosis have acquired unfortunate implications and connotations and are not free from stigma and prejudice even in the minds of physicians. In the minds of lay people, they border on the occult. Furthermore, they do not correctly define the phenomena. Some new and more correct term is therefore desirable — one that will represent the psychophysiological principles involved and will be descriptive of the phenomena.

For there is a general misunderstanding of the nature of hypnosis, leading to many foolish questions, such as: "How many persons can be hypnotized?" This and many other questions indicate a misunderstanding of the nature of hypnosis. It is equally correct to answer: "Very few can be hypnotized," or "Every one can be hypnotized," according to the understanding of hypnosis.

1 Presented at the 52d Annual Meeting of the American Neurological Association, Atlantic City, N. J., June 1, 1926.

However, this is of small importance. My main thesis is that hypnotism has always been treated as if it were something bizarre, a mental condition that stood apart as something distinctly different from all other conditions; whereas it is only one of a large category of conditions characterized by alteration of the personality. In this category are to be found various clinical types of alteration, some normal and some abnormal, all due to the same processes and mechanisms, and therefore fundamentally resembling one another, in that they are all types of depersonalization and repersonalization from the standpoint of the modern conception of the structure of personality. Specifically, these types are known as attention, abstraction, revery, sleep, hypnosis, moods, ecstasy, trance, fugues, somnambulisms, multiple personality, etc. The only reason for differentiating hypnosis is that it is an artifact most commonly induced by a specific external stimulus (suggestion); on the other hand, it is not always so induced, but may be induced by endopsychic stimuli (autosuggestion), while, correspondingly, the other types may also be induced as artifacts by external suggestion, though they are more commonly induced by endopsychic stimuli.

A popular conception, shared by many medical men, is that there is some definite specific state into which a personality becomes transformed when hypnotized. Of course there is no specific definite state constituting hypnosis, any more than there is any specific waking state, in which alertness or torpidity, absent-mindedness, abstraction, fantasy or day-dreaming, intoxication, moods with alterations of character traits, acute emotional states, etc., are present. These states all vary in their psychological and physiological traits. Consequently, the states of hypnosis are as varied and multiform as there are possible combinations of the psychological and physiological components of personality. Even in the same person several different states may develop, each exhibiting different memories, traits, and other personality characteristics, and physiological aberrations, such as anesthesia and paralysis.

The recognition of this fact is important practically,

because when hypnosis is employed for experimental research, psychological analysis, or therapeutics, an examination of the reports often reveals that it has been assumed by the author as a matter of course that the succeeding hypnotic states, induced in the course of successive observations in the same subject or patient, are always the same as that first obtained; whereas it is the case, as a careful reading of such a report makes clear, that a different state, or integrate, was unwittingly obtained exhibiting different memories, traits and other phenomena. This error may vitiate the conclusions.

However varied and multiform the states of hypnosis, there are certain general principles to which every state conforms. These are inhibition, dissociation, and synthesis or reintegration. It is generally agreed that every hypnotic state involves inhibition and dissociation, but it is not so generally realized; and it is certainly not emphasized that hypnosis also involves reintegration, often as the preponderant alteration, with a total result of depersonalization and repersonalization.

This is true because the induction of this state is and must be governed by the normal mechanisms of the mind, for every act of attention, thinking, reasoning and perception, however motivated, involves inhibition, dissociation and integration, just as on the physiological side, as Sherrington has shown, the same holds true for the sensori-motor activities of the nervous system and must be true of the brain as well as of the spinal cord. All conflicting mental systems of activity mutually tend to inhibit one another, so that when one system, say, of thought or perception, is in activity, it tends to inhibit other systems that would conflict or would be incompatible with it during such activity. This inhibition is particularly intense when the inhibiting system is motivated by an emotion. Unless this were true, the functioning of the mind and nervous system would be chaotic. The simple normal states, for example, of active and passive abstraction, attention, contemplation, revery, "brown-study" and absent-mindedness, are the product of these three processes — inhibition, dissociation and reintegration; abstraction is, as I will later point out, identical in principle with light hypnosis.

In other words, light hypnosis, the stage to which the great majority of subjects are hypnotized, is nothing more or less than a particular type of abstraction.

## PHENOMENA

Let us take the two extreme types of hypnosis, the so-called lighter and deeper states (mere figures of speech, by the way) and tabulate the phenomena as determined by observation. Between the two extreme types, every degree and variety of dissociation, inhibition and integration occur. Dissociation and inhibition with resulting depersonalization may predominate, or it may be integration; or both may exist in equal proportions. The final repersonalization may have for an end-product such an extreme alteration of personality as to result in a complete change of character and be identical with what is known as a secondary personality.

It will be well to examine first the extreme type, so-called somnambulism, for in this type the phenomena resulting from the three processes are so obtrusive that they cannot escape recognition.

## DISSOCIATION AND INHIBITION

It is advisable to consider dissociation and inhibition together, for though they are not co-extensive or identical as phenomena, nevertheless in practice it is often difficult to distinguish between them, for they are undoubtedly only different results of the same process. Though the terms are commonly used synonymously, this use is not strictly correct. Dissociation is the more generic term, for, while that which is inhibited is also dissociated, that which is dissociated is not necessarily inhibited. A sensation, for example, may be only split off from the content of the consciousness of the moment, as perceptions in the fringe of the conscious field are split off from the attentive consciousness (*i. e.*, the focus of attention). In this split-off state the sensation may function involuntarily or automatically, as it is called, or it may be capable of so functioning, and then is not inhibited but only dissociated from the field of awareness.

*Mental Dissociations.* — On the mental side, dissociation (and inhibition) may involve the memories of whole epochs in the subject's life, so that he reverts to a period long antedating the day of hypnosis. There is, therefore, complete amnesia for the succeeding periods, and he lives again in a preceding epoch. Thus, Mrs. J., when hypnosis is induced, reverts suddenly and unexpectedly back nine years to the day just before she received an emotional shock, and imagines it is that day. There is complete amnesia for the whole intervening time of nine years. Similarly, Mrs. B., a widow, reverts two or three years to a period when her husband was alive and under that illusion mistakes me, to my embarrassment, for her husband and proceeds to enter into confidences of family life of a specific day in the past.

Again, the dissociation may involve intellectual acquisitions such as languages, and it is well to bear in mind that different states mean different dissociations; thus, Miss B., at one time in hypnosis, has complete amnesia for Latin, and at another for French, although she knows both well.

Some of the most striking alterations of personality (depersonalization) result from the dissociation of traits characterized by sentiments, deeply cherished beliefs and ideals. Thus, intensely held religious sentiments and beliefs may be completely dissociated and lost in one or another phase. Likewise, sentiments of aversion or affection toward persons may disappear and may be replaced by their opposites. This substitution may be traced to a reversion to the sentiments that obtained toward the same object at an earlier epoch of life. B. C. A. acquired in an *A* phase a most intense aversion amounting to scorn and hatred toward a certain person X with whom, at an earlier epoch, she had held pleasant and friendly relations; in the *B* phase, the earlier sentiment of friendship recurred and became reintegrated with the personality of this phase.

The parental sentiment may likewise be completely dissociated and lost, only to be immediately recovered on emergence from the hypnotic phase. In consequence of this dissociation, a repersonalized subject took not the slightest interest in her young son, who she felt, as she said, was not her son, although she was conscious of the fact that he was born of her body. Do not imagine that this was a phenomenon of suggestion. On the contrary, it occurred spontaneously as the result of psychic conflict.

Equally instructive is the disappearance through dissociation of the self-regarding sentiment, and its replacement through reintegration of its opposite. I could cite several examples of this. One will suffice. Mrs. O. has a conception of self characterized by a feeling of inferiority, incapacity and weakness of will. In the hypnotic phase, this is replaced through reintegration by a sentiment of self-pride, superiority, dominating capacity and will, self-assertion, superior intelligence, etc.

A curious and psychologically interesting phenomenon that I observed in one case was the dissociation in one phase of hypnosis, known as "alpha and omega," of the conception or idea of self. This state described her consciousness as only "thought" without any conception or feeling or idea of being an ego or I — nothing to which the word "I" could be applied — just thought without an I.

Equally curious was the loss of the time sense that "Sally" exhibited. One minute, or an hour, or a day was the same to her.

A phenomenon of dissociation effecting a marked alteration of personality is difficult to formulate. It involves a psychological principle for which I have contended for a long time. This dissociation is of a large system of mental dispositions which, with their roots, acquired by experience, gives as the setting that particular "meaning" to objects and ideas that they have for the individual, and determines the attitude of mind and point of view of the individual toward such objects and ideas. A good example would be the difference in the meaning of "mother" to you and to me, according to whether it is your mother or my mother. The difference, of course, depends on the difference in our individual experiences. In consequence of the dissociation of such a system, particular meanings of persons, places, objects, situations, etc., and emotional attitudes toward them are completely lost and perhaps replaced by others belonging to an earlier epoch of life. For example, an outdoor life, the wood and canoeing are objects of intense distaste to Mrs. B. and are avoided so far as possible; in the *B* phase an absolutely opposite meaning and point of view with corresponding tastes and behavior emerges, and determines her choice of activities. In my view, this principle is of the utmost practical importance and is the basis of psychological therapeutics. I could cite example after example of this principle if space permitted.

In the affective field, dissociation and depersonalization may be equally distinctive. Here one may have to do with primitive unintegrated emotional instincts and appetites. This form of depersonalization has for the most part been overlooked, although, I may say, I have frequently described it as of great importance in my studies of dissociated personality. I will content myself with a mere enumeration of some of the dissociated or inhibited instincts. Fear was totally absent in more than one case; the loss of hunger was noted in another. The sex appetite or instinct may likewise be totally inhibited in some one hypnotic phase of personality and may be present in another phase. Thus in one phase of hypnosis, Mrs. O. was totally asexual, and in another, intensely sexual. The same loss of the instinct occurred in one phase with Mrs. B., in which phase the term had lost all but a dictionary meaning.

Similarly, anger and the other emotional instincts may be dissociated with corresponding depersonalization. I will further cite in this category only the complete loss of the instinct of self-assertion with the consequent dominance of self-abasement in one hypnotic phase of Mrs. O., while in another phase the reverse was the case, and the subject exhibited the most exalted self-assertion and domination of her environment.

All these mental dissociations occurred spontaneously

ndependently of suggestions, and characterized the hypno-
ic phase.

*Physiological Dissociation.* — On the physiological side
he personality may lose spontaneously a variety of func-
ions, the most conspicuous being those of sensation and
notility. Thus B. C. A. could be put into a number of dif-
erent hypnotic states. In one, there was not only general
oss of tactile sensibility over the whole body, but also com-
lete loss of coenesthesia. She had no consciousness of having
 body at all, no awareness of muscular movements, including
he mimetic movement of the facial muscles. She did not
now whether she was standing or sitting. She described
erself as "thought in space." In another state, there was
oss of the special senses of taste and smell. In the state I
all "alpha and omega," tactile sensibility was lost.

The sensory functions, dissociated in one hypnotic
tate, were reintegrated in another. Likewise, spontaneous
paralyses have been noted in the literature, although I have
not observed them. As with the mental dissociation, these
physiological forms occurred spontaneously.

## INTEGRATION

I now come to integration and repersonalization. The
most familiar phenomenon is the integration in hypnosis of
dispositions pertaining to memories of past experiences, forgotten and beyond recall in the waking state. These may include experiences of another state for which there is
complete amnesia in the waking state. Among the latter are
those of sleep (dreams), trances, fugues, intoxication, delirium, nocturnal somnambulism, amnesic state, and the experiences of a second, third, or fourth dissociated personality.
These are all phenomena of integration and constitute a new
integrate.

Less familiar is the integration as well as the recall of
memories of the environment that never entered consciousness at all but were only subconsciously experienced, or at
most were in the fringe of consciousness. I have made various experiments demonstrating this phenomenon. It should

also be recognized that such perceptions may be integrated in one hypnotic state (*a*) but not in others (*b* and *c*).

Sometimes such subconscious perceptions become integrated in dreams; or they may become manifested in strikingly dramatic form, as visions simulating "thought transference" or spiritualistic phenomena, as I have on several occasions observed. Thus, for instance, a telephone message received by my secretary from a distance and transmitted as a cablegram to the cable company was read in a crystal by a subject of mine. She had subconsciously heard the message as it was transmitted, without being consciously aware of the fact.

Repersonalization through the process of integration is particularly striking when large systems of memories, thoughts, reflections and fabrications, in the form of fantasies, become so integrated with the personality as to stamp the make-up with a character of dramatic individuality. Mrs. O., for instance, in a dissociated state known as Maria, manifested a dominating fantasy of being the reincarnated soul of a Spanish peasant girl and (later) a courtesan of the thirteenth century. She spoke broken English and a supposed Spanish dialect (a neologism, of course) and sang, danced and acted the part in a most characteristic and entertaining way. In other respects, she appeared to have a normal personality.

The fantasy was the reintegration of youthful day dreams which had undergone subconscious incubation and had grown until finally they burst into flower. This fantasy was thoroughly believed in, became the dominating trait of the personality, and combined with a number of other reintegrated sentiments, instincts and traits. These day-dreams and fantasies, as well as sentiments, were components of a large, highly organized integrate, the psychogenesis of which I was able successfully to unravel. The case was one of complete thoroughgoing repersonalization.

Of the common traits that make up personality, the reintegration of sentiments is the most instructive from the point of view; but I have already, when discussing the phenomenon of dissociation, cited examples enough of the eversion to sentiments entertained at an earlier period of life, and the substitution of an earlier and opposite sentiment for a later one, regarding one and the same object. The alterations of personality occasioned by such integration may be readily recognized. I have likewise spoken of the substitution of earlier meanings of objects, ideas and situations, and of corresponding attitudes of mind and points of view. The repersonalization effected by such reintegrations must be obvious.

I have already said enough, too, about the emotional instincts as such. I will merely add that I have more than once observed the reintegration of the sex instinct and some others (anger and self-assertion) that were repressed and inhibited in the normal waking state.

*Moods.* — The depression and exaltation of a waking state may be spontaneously replaced by their opposites. Depression gives place to exaltation, and *vice versa*. Of course, a mood involves, besides the affects peculiar to it, large systems of mental dispositions determining the point of view and attitudes of mind toward and meaning of the situations of life. I cannot enter into this here. However, it is easy to understand how the integration of one system with its effects, in place of another, may effectively contribute to the repersonalization of the individual.

In illustration I might cite many experiments and observations of my own, but to eliminate personal bias, I shall mention an interesting experiment by another observer.

While engaged in some hypnotic experiments on a man, aged 22, who was "essentially normal and responsible, of robust character and of decided intellectual ability," "Greenwood"[1] found to his surprise that suddenly, without the slightest influence of suggestion and as if by accident, the young man fell into at least four distinct phases or moods, each of which may be well characterized as a self.

The first phase, the ordinary or quiet mood, was

1 Edward Greenwood: *Society for Psychical Research, Proceedings* in 1903, vol. XVII, p. 279.

similar to his normal self when awake. He was of a quiet
nature, speculative and restrained, well-bred and courteous
ous in demeanor and of a religious and idealistic temperament.
perament. If a suggestion was made not consonant with
this character, it was rejected at once, and any amount
of insistence would be in vain.

In the second phase, called the "gay mood," into
which, on its first appearance, he suddenly, *without
warning* and to the surprise of the experimenter, changed
out of the first phase, the subject became extremely hilarious
arious and absurd, jested in an easy way, displayed a
tendency to practical jokes on the experimenter, kicked
his clothes about the room and was generally obstreperous
ous and fantastic, both in speech and in behavior. Then
of a sudden, without warning or suggestion of any kind
he reverted to his former quiet, gentle, restrained self
On other occasions, in this gay mood, which frequently
occurred, he showed himself to be a "gay Lothario,"
for he displayed an astounding lack of the ordinary conventions
ventions or proprieties, professed a complete contempt
for either religion or morality and a disregard for any
responsibility in his actions, becoming, in his own language,
guage, a child of nature, non-moral, though not vicious
Any suggestion not consonant with this mood was, as
in the first phase, instantly rejected.

The third phase was a "malicious" mood. In this he
became a sort of "Jack-the-Ripper." He exhibited a
strong wish to inflict pain and frequently asked permission
mission to stab the experimenter in order to have the
gratification of seeing blood flow. Indeed, he was detected
tected surreptitiously extracting a pen-knife from his
pocket with a view to satisfying this inclination. He
confessed to a wish to vivisect, or, failing that, to
strangle.

The fourth phase into which the young man fell
in the same way, was a "depressed" mood, the very opposite
posite of the gay phase. Now he exhibited himself as a
melancholic — a melancholy Jacques — utterly and be-

yond bounds, miserable and ready, for no reason that was apparent, to burst into tears.

Each of these moods, or so-called selves, carried its own different set of emotions, tastes and mental attitudes. As I have said, suggestions not consonant with the particular mood he was in were rejected. The whole manner of the man in each exhibited an absolute contrast of expression, conduct and mode of speech, just as is the case with all of us in our different moods, but not like those of this young man, I hope.

As to the reintegration of physiological functions, sensibility and motility that have been inhibited in the waking state, manifested by functional anesthesia and paralyses, may be reintegrated in the hypnotic state. As evidence of the integrating effect, as contrasted with the dissociating effect of the hypnotizing procedure, nothing is more instructive and convincing than the results of a certain technic I have successfully used in restoring the complete normal personality out of two different phases of multiple personality. The technic has been to hypnotize one or both of the different dissociated personalities, A and B, into deeper and deeper states until one, C, is obtained that is a completely integrated composite of the two. Each is thus reintegrated in this one C, which is found to be the whole normal personality. The technic is precisely the same as that of conventional hypnotizing. The suggestions have been precisely the same; namely, "sleep," or "sleep deeper" and yet the process was almost entirely that of integration. The combined memories of A and B were integrated in C; the instincts and other traits dissociated respectively in A and B were restored, and so with the other components of personality. Likewise, I may cite a classical case, one of Jules Janet's, that was supposed to be the normal personality but was a dissociated hysteric state with various stigmata. When the patient was hypnotized, the stigmata disappeared, and he became perfectly normal and lived a normal life in this state. It was thought to be an hypnotic state, but far from that it was the normal personality that had been "waked up" unwittingly by the hypnotizing procedure. The previous hysteric state was the dissociated personality, which now by the hypnotic procedure had become reintegrated into a normal one.

Passing in review all the phenomena I have cited as observed in so-called "deep hypnosis," I think there can be no question that they were the product of the three processes I have dwelt on and that the results obtained may be properly characterized as suggestive "depersonalization" and "repersonalization."

It will be objected that some of these examples are cases of so-called multiple personality. Of course some are, but what of it? Every one who has made intensive studies of dissociated personalities will agree that they are identically the same as the somnambulic or the deepest stages of hypnosis as produced by hypnotic suggestion. This is well exemplified by Greenwood's case that I have quoted. In the second place, in some cases the secondary personalities were first obtained by hypnotizing as hypnotic states, as happened in three cases I have cited; it was only later that they broke loose and emerged as full-fledged secondary personalities. In the third place, one finds that as the result of autosuggestion similar repersonalization frequently occurs, as exemplified by the trance states of mediums, which are generally accepted as identical with hypnotic states, on the one hand, and with secondary personalities on the other.

Moreover, in light hypnosis the same phenomena of dissociation, inhibition and integration are found, differing only in degree and in their combinations. Between the lightest states and the more extreme repersonalizations of somnambulism, one finds among the dissociations nearly every variety of mental and physiological component of the mind-body (personality). And the same is true of integrations.

### LIGHT HYPNOSIS

I shall now consider the phenomena of light hypnosis.

*Mental Phenomena.* — By the force of suggestion (whatever that may be), the attention is focused on a limited number of objects — the experimenter and his suggestions, bodily sensations and feelings of sleep. These are ntegrated into the content of attentive interest. The composition of this "integrate" varies largely in accordance with the suggestions of the experimenter and the expectations of the subject. It is thus an artifact. As in abstraction, it may or may not include perceptions of the environment and associated memories, which are either impossible of voluntary recall or not ordinarily recalled by the subject. It may be such a limited system of conscious processes as to constitute what has been called *monoideism*. Indeed, there may be a complete "blocking" or inhibition of "thought." The subject cannot "think."

When the integrate does not include perceptions of the environment (auditory and tactile), these may still function and may be only dissociated without being inhibited, for they may be recorded. This is shown by recovering memories of such perceptions in another state of hypnosis. Here, it should be noted, is found a similarity between light hypnosis and abstraction, revery, absent-mindedness and analogous states; for perceptions of which the subject is not aware in these states have been shown in numerous observations to occur subconsciously. This is done by recovering memories of them in hypnosis and by other technical methods.

In light hypnosis, by the law of inhibition and dissociation, mental and physiological dispositions are prevented from functioning. Incompatible ideas, the emotional instincts (fear, anger, sex, etc.) and the sentiments are in abeyance. Thus, on the one hand, critical thoughts, reflections on the suggestions given, reasoning, perceptions and images are inhibited and do not enter the content of consciousness of the moment; on the other hand, various traits peculiar to the individual, such as the instinctive emotional reactions and sentiments, for the same reason are not in functional activity and do not give a response. Thus shorn of many of its traits and reactions, the personality is more or less depersonalized.

In this way the composition of the integrate, or content of attention, is limited and may be held more or less stable by the continuing motivating force of the suggestion. But the composition, being an artifact, depends in part on the integration effected by the suggestion, wittingly or unwittingly given, and the expectancy of the subject, and in part on the field of dissociation and inhibition similarly induced. In the integrate of this light state, then, there is a slight or limited but still recognizable repersonalization of the subject.

*Physiological Phenomena.* — There is an inhibition of the musculature of the body in accordance with which the muscles fall into a state of relaxation as in sleep, or in the first stages of sleep — when one is "going to sleep." This is particularly true of the elevators of the eyelids, 'which tend to close. Whether this relaxation is brought about by specific external suggestion or autosuggestion, by the direct volition of the subject, or by other inhibiting agencies, it is not necessary to inquire. At any rate, it is not an essential phenomenon of hypnosis.

I have said that the field of the content of awareness in light hypnosis is limited to a few specific objects, such as I have mentioned, and is apt to be stable, but this is not necessarily so. If express directions are given to the subject, a succession of associated memories will stream through the mind and will constitute a changing content of consciousness, just as is the case in abstraction, the state commonly used to obtain so-called free associations.

*Amnesia.* — Absence of memory for the hypnotic experience may or may not follow on light hypnosis. The same is true of abstraction, *mutatis mutandis.*

After obtaining free associations in the ordinary state of abstraction, I have occasionally noted extensive amnesia for certain memories on "waking," and I have no doubt that others have also. Whether or not there is amnesia following such light dissociated states depends, in my judgment, on various factors and particularly on the degree and extent of the dissociation of the personality and possibly on the intensity of the previous repression of the memories from conflicts.

*Suggestibility.* — Much has been made of the increased suggestibility in hypnosis, but whether there is a greater degree in the light stage under consideration than in some types of abstraction remains to be proved. Crystal visions and automatic writing are common suggested phenomena in normal abstraction. If suggested contractures are taken as a criterion, as is commonly done, they can often be produced in the normal alert state. Coué, in his public demonstrations, has notoriously induced them in apparently alert subjects. Various observers have reported striking examples of contractures produced in alert subjects. I induced strong contractures in an alert subject by using a tuning fork, which, to impress her, was represented to be a powerful magnet. On the other hand, it must not be overlooked that probably only in a minority of cases of light hypnosis can contractures be induced. They belong more characteristically to somewhat deeper stages of depersonalization. Likewise, suggested analgesia is a common phenomenon in alert subjects, when expertly handled.

*Comment.* — When the phenomena of hypnosis are considered from this point of view as phenomena of integration, dissociation and inhibition, it would seem plain that the state is one of depersonalization and repersonalization. Personality, according to the theory that offers the more intelligible and adequate explanation, as I have frequently argued on the basis of studies of abnormal as well as of normal conditions, is an organized integration, on the one hand, of the sensory and motor functions and, on the other, of the innate instinctive dispositions — the so-called emotional "instincts" — plus the dispositions and systems of dispositions acquired through the experiences of life. All these, roughly speaking, include the "traits" of the individual. These traits consist of the emotional urges and tendencies, the habit reactions, the sentiments, ideals, beliefs, etc. Obviously, so far as and so long as any of these components of personality are dissociated from the whole integration, there is a depersonalization. And so far as and so long as there is a new and different integration of the remaining components there is a repersonalization.

A tabulation of the negative phenomena observed in hypnosis, then, shows that there is a dissociation or inhibition of many of the component traits and reactions of the normal alert personality, resulting in what one is entitled to call depersonalization.

Between the light phases of hypnosis and the deep phases (somnambulism) there is an infinite variety of phases differing from one another only in degree and complexity of dissociation and integration.

The next point I want to make is that light hypnosis is substantially nothing more nor less than abstraction, or at least a type of abstraction. There are several types of abstraction, all conforming to the same principles of integration, dissociation and inhibition and differing only in the structure of the final integrate, according to the source and specificity of the stimulus (suggestion, intrinsic interest of the subject, endopsychic stimuli, instinctive impulses, etc.). No two types and no two states are precisely the same in respect to the elements of personality that are integrated and dissociated.

If this is true and light hypnosis is a type effected artificially by suggestion, one must not forget that it is an artifact, and that therefore the type and its phenomena are artificially determined and tend to conform to the suggestions given.

It would follow from this interpretation that any physician who uses passive abstraction for the purpose of obtaining free associations in psychoanalysis (as every one does) or suggestive therapeutics, uses hypnosis.

Again, it follows that, as every one can be induced to go into a state of passive abstraction, every one can be repersonalized (hypnotized) to this extent.

Hypnosis, then, does not stand apart as a bizarre condition of mind and body; it is one type of a large category of conditions, the essence of all of them being a normal, artificial, or abnormal alteration of the structure of personality. All types are the resultants of the same processes and are characterized clinically by depersonalization and repersonalization of the whole structure of personality. The differences of type are brought about by differences in the motivating impulses that effect dissociation and integration. The only and insufficient reason for differentiating hypnosis from the general category is that it is a suggested artifact, though this is not always the case.

In view of these principles and the facts of observation, I have suggested the term "repersonalization," or "suggestive repersonalization," in place of hypnotism. The former correctly characterizes the facts; the latter does not, but it expresses an outgrown theory that identifies hypnosis solely with sleep and neglects other allied forms of altered personality.

This point of view — depersonalization and repersonalization — is important and fruitful in that it allows us, on the one hand, to relate hypnosis to fundamental principles governing the functioning of the mind and, on the other, to class it in a large category of normal states such as sleep, abstraction, revery, mystic ecstasy, moods, absent-mindedness and emotional crises, and abnormal states, such as trances, hysterical crises, fugues, somnambulisms and double personalities.

## II.  THE MOTIVATING FORCES

Although it is not strictly within the scope of this paper, I feel that some consideration of the forces that induce suggestive repersonalization is called for, as the question is sure to be raised. Several theories have been offered, but, in my judgment, none can be said to have been substantiated.

All students agree, I believe, that the phenomena are induced by suggestion in some way. It is therefore around the nature of suggestion, the nature of the force or forces which it evokes, and the mechanisms which are brought into play by those forces that the discussion revolves as the real problems.

According to the original Freudian hypothesis, the essential characteristic of hypnosis and suggestion is a dissociation of consciousness (an assumption that I have tried to show is inadequate), but this dissociation is not primarily, as commonly believed, "an artificial state brought about by the hypnotic procedure. The dissociation is already present for the operator to make use of."[1] It exists in the form of "infantile incestuous thoughts" in the unconscious (the mother or father complex) which have been repressed from infancy; that is, ready to be fixed on the operator. The essence of hypnosis resides in the unconscious fixation of sex hunger (the libido) on the person of "the hypnotizer." And the "capacity to be hypnotized and influenced by suggestion depends on the possibility of transference"; i. e., on the "unconscious sexual attitude" of the hypnotized to the hypnotizer — the deepest root being in the repressed parental complex (Freud, Jones, Ferenczi and Sadger). When this is translated into ordinary everyday language, it means that the subject unconsciously becomes sexually in love with the hypnotizer. By what mechanism the phenomena of hypnosis are induced because of this fixation is not clear. After as critical a study as I have ever given to anything, the reasoning by which hypnotic phenomena are induced on this theory of "transference" seems to me a mere hodge-podge of logic. It is useless to discuss it here; yet I think that this sexual theory may be modified and restated in a form to give it a certain plausibility, although it would no longer be Freudian.

In the language of the psychologist, there is a response to the stimulus (suggestion) of the hypnotizer on the part of the subject, in the form of an unconscious reaction of the "libido" contained in the repressed infantile thoughts. The urge of this libido, then, becomes unconsciously integrated with the suggestion given and supplies the impulsive force or drive that carries the suggestion to fruition; that is to say, produces the phenomena of dissociation, inhibition and integration and finds satisfaction.

Even when so formulated, the theory is, to my mind, unsound for many reasons. Certainly, if the thesis for which I have argued here is true, this modified Freudian hypothesis is incredible, for surely, if, as I have insisted, hypnosis is only a type of repersonalization not differing in principle

1 Ernest Jones: *Papers on Psycho-Analysis*, William Wood & Co., New York 1919, p. 321.

from abstraction in its several forms, sleep, trance, spontaneous somnambulism, etc., it is almost unthinkable that sexual love induces all of these common and (some of them) everyday phases of personality.

The most commonly advanced theory (called by McDougall the "ideo-motor" theory) holds that the suggestion of the operator awakens as a reaction an "idea" in the subject. This "idea" (which is a representation of the state expected by the subject), reinforced by any emotion organized within it as a sentiment, has in itself an adequate driving force to bring about dissociation (and integration?) and, therefore, the phenomena corresponding to the representation in the consciousness of the subject.

McDougall rejects this theory on the ground that so-called "ideas" have no motive force of their own, but derive their impulses solely from becoming linked up with one or more emotional instincts. He proposes, accordingly, what is really a necessary corollary to and application of his theory of the nature of instincts and the purposive part they play in mental behavior. His explanation of suggestion and *rapport* therefore demands careful examination.

To appreciate the full meaning of his theory, it must be borne in mind that, according to him, "ideas," so-called, are of themselves lifeless, inert things, incapable of carrying themselves to fruition. To become effective, they must become linked up with one or more of the emotional instincts (fear, anger, curiosity, etc.). The drive, urge, impulse, or craving of these instincts provides the driving force that renders the idea capable of being carried to fulfillment in accordance with the aim of the instinct. Among his instincts is that of submission or self-abasement. It is this instinct, in his view, that is always awakened by the hypnotizer and, thereby becoming linked with the suggested idea, gives the suggestion the force which induces the dissociation of the personality, on the one hand, and creates the submissive *rapport* of the subject with the hypnotizer, on the other.

The reason for the awakening of this particular instinct is to be found in the attitude of mind of the subject toward the hypnotizer. He looks up to the latter as a being of superior power whom he endows with prestige, authority and knowledge and therefore to whom he feels inferior. In fact, this instinct is the basis of the feeling of inferiority — the so-called "inferiority complex." I am ready to accept the facts that there is such an instinct with a "drive," even if not of the purposive nature attributed to it by McDougall, that it is awakened in many cases of hypnotic suggestion, and that it then provides the main driving force to the suggestion, or at least co-operates in doing this.

However, my objection to the theory is that it is overworked. A priori, there surely is no reason why other instincts may not be equally effective. I am unable to accept the statement that the submissive instinct is universally applicable to all instances of hypnotic suggestion, or to all, or many suggestions in everyday life (which must also be explained); or that in many cases of hypnotic suggestion, the awakened and efficient impulse is not that of another instinct or interest, such as self-assertion, curiosity (scientific curiosity), or some such interest as apparently is the effective force in normal abstraction, or that it may not be faith or expectancy. It also leaves out of account hypnosis induced by autosuggestion, contagion, and even by a secondary coconscious process or personality.

Many persons can hypnotize themselves or learn to do so. Mediums hypnotize themselves, producing the so-called trance state, which is identical with hypnosis, as shown by the fact that it is often produced by "hypnotic" suggestion.

Furthermore, the fact is significant that hypnosis can be induced in the primary personality by a coconscious secondary personality. It may be recalled that Sally, a coconscious personality, repeatedly hypnotized the principal personality, Miss Beauchamp, by coconscious "willing."[1] Also in the case of B. C. A., a coconscious intelligence repeatedly induced a trance state in the principal personality.[2] Is one to infer, in such observation, that the hypnosis was induced by

[1] Morton Prince: *Dissociation of a Personality*, 1906, p. 319.
[2] My Life as a Dissociated Personality, by B. C. A. *Journal Abnormal Psychology*, October, 1908, and December, 1909.

the force of the instinct of submission, notwithstanding the fact that she was unaware of the coconscious personality and could not know that she was being hypnotized by herself in this bizarre fashion?

Human motives are too complex to be reduced in all cases to one simple instinct, whether it is sex, submission, fear, or any other.

Nor will any instinct, though it may be the driving force of the suggestion, explain all the phenomena that characterize the hypnotic state, such as many of those I have marshalled in the foregoing as phenomena of dissociation and integration (anesthesia, paralysis, contractures, somnambulism, hallucination, etc.).

It seems to me, also, that ideas have an intrinsic driving force in themselves, however much this force is reinforced and strengthened by the more powerful forces of the emotions; consequently, I cannot wholly reject the ideo-motor theory.

That the force of the suggestion inducing hypnosis may be derived not from the instinctive emotion of submission but from that of self-assertion is shown by the case, as I interpret it, of Mrs. J., which I cited as an example of epochal amnesia.

When I first attempted to hypnotize her, it was without the slightest success. Whereupon she turned to me and said, with some strong feeling of self-assertion and pride, "No one can hypnotize me. My will is stronger than any one's will. You can't do it." Thereupon I said, "You are right. I can't. But the reason is you are afraid. You have not the courage to be hypnotized; you are a coward; you haven't the 'sand.' " At once, as if to show me not only that she was not a coward but also that she could do anything she willed to do, she promptly went into the deep somnambulic state I have described. In this state, it will be remembered, she reverted to a previous period in her life, with epochal amnesia for the nine succeeding years. She also exhibited a delusional phenomenon which is not uncommon in such conditions of reversion. I have observed it often. At the period to which she reverted, she was relatively slim and slight, with a corresponding waist measurement. When I showed her the tape measure recording the increased size of her waist, she insisted that the figures were several inches less, reading them in accordance with her illusion of living at the time when that was her girth.

Even if her attitude at the outset was bravado and a reaction to the submissive instinct, the motivating force must have been the instinct of self-assertion.

But whatever the driving force is that gives effect to suggestion — whether it is derived from the sexual impulse or that of the instinct of submission or self-assertion, or any other — no theory so far advanced will give an adequate explanation of all the phenomena of hypnosis, and especially of the integration, though it may explain the simpler phenomena of dissociation, particularly of the lighter stages. Nor will it throw light on the more important problems of the mechanisms by which many phenomena are affected, even such simple ones as automatic contractures. Why, for instance, was the hypnotic state, in the case just cited, characterized by retrograde amnesia and the delusional phenomena? Whether or not the instinct of submission or self-assertion was the motivating force, it will not explain these and other specific phenomena.

Likewise, many of the more complex phenomena of integration are left totally unexplained and require some other principle. McDougall himself admits that a number of phenomena remain obscure.

Let us take, for example, somnambulism with the integration of large systems resulting, without apparent rhyme or reason, in a secondary personality with the loss or dissociation of particular instincts, and other functions. To explain such phenomena one must, it appears to me, introduce the principle of conflict, as I have done when interpreting the psychogenesis of multiple personality. The suggestion that the subject be hypnotized (*i. e.,* "sleep") for some reason, obscure at the time, strikes some sentiment or other psychological component in a large integrated system (in

B. C. A., as elsewhere, I have endeavored to show[1] a rebellion against the conditions of life) and thereupon the whole system, in conflict with the rest of the personality, springs into life and becomes the secondary personality. Through conflict, the rest is repressed. But why should certain fundamental and native instincts like fear, anger or sex become dissociated? This is a riddle.

And why, in the same subject, in one hypnotic phase should there be a dissociation of one set of traits and certain functions with integration of certain other specific traits and functions, while in a second and third phase the dissociations and integrations are entirely different? Why, for instance, in one phase of hypnosis is there general anesthesia; in another, anesthesia of a special sense, and in a third no anesthesia at all? This applies to other functions and mental traits (sentiments, etc.). The suggestion in each case was identical, being simply "sleep," without any specific implication and expectation of the resulting phenomenon, which was a surprise. Here one is dealing with mechanisms and forces that are totally obscure. One must look for endopsychic forces as explanations, and among them internal conflicts between mental systems.

These and more phenomena are unexplainable on any theory that neglects to take into consideration all the phenomena of hypnotism, particularly the integrations and their motivations, as well as the same phenomena occurring in allied states like abstraction, sleep, trance, double personality.

---

[1] The Unconscious; 1919. Lectures XVIII to XX; also Jour. Abnormal Psychology, 1919.

PART II

# CHAPTER VI

## WHY WE HAVE TRAITS — NORMAL AND ABNORMAL

### (An introduction to the Study of Personality)

I KNOW of no problem of more practical importance than that of personality. Upon its correct solution depends our understanding of character and human behavior. And this is true not only of individuals but of groups of individuals — of communities, nations and races. It is not too much to say that without a comprehensive insight into the psychology of personality, we cannot understand the reactions of the individual to his environment, or of social and political groups and even of nations to each other and to their respective situations. Such an understanding must include, besides the individual traits of which personality is composed, the motivations which are the springs of action and which determine behavior.

But before entering upon our theme, let us have a somewhat more precise conception of what we mean by personality. It is commonly agreed, as I think must be admitted, that, from a descriptive point of view, personality is the sum-total of traits, and that differences of personality depend upon differences in traits, on the one hand, and on the varying combinations of them, on the other.

But what are traits? All writers do not mean the same thing by traits and consequently do not accept the same definition. What one would include as a trait, another would not. In the present discussion, from a purely descriptive point of view, by traits is meant the sentiments and ideals with their meanings for the individual; the more complex habits; the fixed acquired beliefs and prejudices and likes and dislikes; the accepted ethical and social codes of conduct; the aspirations and enduring desires; the innate cravings, or urges, or impulsions and appetites and inherited tendencies in general; and many other analogous characteristics of human nature, all of which, according to their varying combinations, distinguish one individual from another and determine behavior.

All of those I have mentioned, however, are not basic and primary. Some are secondary in that they are compounds of primary traits or resultants and modes in which the primary basic traits find expression. In any case, the terms are descriptive and not explanatory.

Let us be a little more specific, and for this purpose turn to a few historical personages for illustrative traits.

Bismarck's will-to-power, his pugnacity, his contempt for his political foes and his colleagues as well as the masses; his egotism and sense of superiority; his distrust of the people; his ruthless ambition to dominate every situation for the aggrandizement of Prussia; his fearlessness and courage to grasp power and responsibility; his assertion of personal dictatorship; his rancorousness, impatience and irritability when thwarted, and his resentment of opposition; his sentiment of love for his wife and children and dogs and the forest; his aversion to his mother; his pride of self and caste and Prussia; his reverence for monarchy and hatred of democracy; his lust for revenge even to cruelty; his egotistic domestic habits; his habits of deceit, trickery and actual lying to achieve diplomatic ends, and his belief in "blood and iron" to accomplish political aims, were all traits of his personality; and they manifested themselves in characteristic behavior.

It requires no psychologist to recognize these peculiarities of the man as traits. But for the most part they were not basic. Rather many of them were the mode of expression, the resultants, so to speak, of, and secondary to, other more fundamental units of personality, such as his self-regarding sentiment and idea of self, his pugnacity instinct and that of self-assertion, his belief in the divine right of his king to rule, his political ideals of government, his aspirations for the hegemony of his native state over all Germany, etc. Some of these fundamental units were instinctive and inherited. Others were acquired in the course of life's experiences. These instinctive urges, sentiments and systems of ideas were the true basic traits out of which sprang the many qualities for which he was noted and which determined the behavior that bullied his world of politics and social life. So his traits may be defined in terms of behavior or of the basic mental and instinctive springs of action.

Likewise, we all recognize, to take another historical illustration, that Lincoln's personal uncouth habits, his sense of humor and tendency to melancholic moods, his moral ideals and faith in God, his charitableness, intellectual honesty, sympathy with the unfortunate and the slave, his abnegation of self and absence of pride, his moderation and marvelous patience and tolerance of opposition, his hatred of slavery but reverence for law, the constitution and the Union, his faith in the common people and belief in democracy and government by the people, his "hatred of violence in any form or by anybody," his "passion for fairness" and his abhorrence of "iron and blood" were traits of his personality.

Could there be any greater contrast than that between the personalities of Bismarck and Lincoln? An appraisal of these two great statesmen by the standard of ethical values would beyond question award to Lincoln the greater character. But for psychology, which takes no account of such values, Bismarck had the more interesting and intriguing personality. And can it be denied that the personality of each was the sum-total of its traits?

If I may take one more interesting historical personage for illustration, Disraeli's youthful habits of foppery, theatrical playing of the mountebank and love of personal display, as well as the political ambition, the will-to-power, the self-assertion, the love of imperial tinsel and of his Queen, characteristic of his maturer political life, were traits. The traits of Napoleon and of the ex-Kaiser, William II, might be cited in similar fashion. Biographers have recognized the traits of historical personages by their behavior, but, not being psychologists, they have not traced them to the basic units of personality. Indeed, it would take a psychological examination of the individual to do so, particularly as objective behavior is, as everyone now-a-days knows, frequently the expression of subconsciously working traits; and too often it happens that, even after an intensive psychological analysis of the personality, the conclusions are matters of interpretation and doctrines on which many may differ.

And here it is as well to remember that *phobias, impulsions, and other obsessions are traits of personality,* and belong in the same category as deep-rooted prejudices and aversions and normal fears. They are pathological simply because they prevent proper adaptation to the situations of everyday life. Likewise, criminal and delinquent habitual tendencies and behavior are traits. In my judgment, we shall never understand the criminal mind and the problem of crime until we recognize that the behavior of the criminal is the manifestation of traits that, in principle, are created and organized precisely in the same fashion as are those of the socially behaving individual.

The traits of personality are the springs of action, the principal motivating forces that determine the logical and other intellectual processes of thought. Some of them consciously — others, such as desires, aversions, fears, and sentiments of self, of hatred and affection and pride, subconsciously, and therefore, unwittingly marshal associated memories, originate, guide and control processes of creative imagination and other processes of thought, which carry the urge of the traits of fulfillment and determine behavior.

A study, then, of human nature resolves itself into a study of traits. Poets, dramatists and fiction writers in general, by combining a number of selected psychological traits into one character, seek to create theoretical personalities. Sometimes their creative imagination eventuates in a psychological success; at other times, in a psychological impossibility. But in any case, it is rare (if ever attained) that the constructed personality is the whole personality. Only a few selected traits are drawn in full light, while the rest are left in shadow or entirely out of the picture. For the purpose of art, this method is a necessary canon. It would be impossible to draw a picture of an individual that would include all his traits, for traits are manifested as reactions to situations, and the situations would have to be multiplied beyond all bounds to exhibit them all.

Hamlet lets us see only one side of his personality, which comes to light as a reaction to a simple situation, the death of his father and re-marriage of his mother to his uncle, who turns out to be the murderer of his father. Iago discloses also only a single trait. It is safe to say that, if these two characters were real human beings, they had many other traits which would have been manifested in situations of a kind that would have called them forth. Very likely, one who had known Iago intimately would have recognized that his devilishness was only a compensatory reaction to a feeling of inferiority and was a mode by which he was trying to get square with the world. It would make an amusing, as well as a psychologically sound skit, to have Hamlet portrayed in an entirely different situation — to have him carried off by his fellow students of Wittenberg to a festive Kneip. Then we would see no longer a melancholy Hamlet but an uproarious, convivial one, drinking bumpers with the rest and wishing his father's ghost back in the shades of Hades. Or we might have a domestic scene from the life of Iago in which he would be surrounded by a happy family, an adoring wife and admiring children. Then we should see a kindly loving husband and father, romping with the youngsters, the feeling of inferiority gone and with it the malicious trait, sunk out of sight into the unconscious. Create whatever situations you like, only make them such as evoke different traits from those which we have been allowed by Shakespeare to see, and we would not recognize our Hamlet or Iago, though they would be the same personalities, but exhibiting themselves in different situations. Wordsworth's celebrated "Happy Warrior" might well appear to us in a less admirable light if he had a shrew for a wife; and even Sir Galahad, the noblest and purest knight of the Round Table, might not have appeared so noble if he had fallen under the wiles of Helen of Troy. *Cherchez la femme!*

Personality, in other words, is many-sided, one side being manifested in one situation, another in another, and so on. Thus, apparently, a person in actual life exhibits contradictory traits, but it is the situations that are responsible for the seeming paradox. It is only when the individual responds in a contradictory way to the same situation, that we can be said to have a paradoxical character which, it is safe to say, never exists in real life, but only in fiction.

Popular writers, publicists, politicians and criminologists take a deal of satisfaction in talking about human nature without the least conception of the psychological problems involved. Consequently they generally end in erroneous deductions regarding the probable or improbable behavior of individuals, communities and nations.

Probably not many would agree on a psychological definition of traits, and, therefore, on what should be included in a classification of them. Most commonly, perhaps, traits are defined in terms of behavior. From this point of view, a trait may be defined as specific habitual behavior characteristic of the individual in given situations. But if "behavior" is taken in the narrow sense of objective behavior, as is customary, this definition of a trait becomes too narrow.

On the other hand, if behavior is used in a more comprehensive sense, as I think it should be, to cover mental reactions as well as bodily reactions, so that we may speak of mental behavior as well as objective behavior, then such a behavioristic definition becomes adequate. For although it is true that, for the most part, it is through objective behavior that traits are manifested and we become cognizant of them in another person, nevertheless, in ourselves we recognize a number of mental traits which do not expose themselves to another through our behavior. Many people have sentiments, ideals, desires, aspirations, beliefs, cravings, mental habits (e. g., feelings of inferiority) and other traits in the make-up of their personalities which are only recognizable by an introspective analysis of their inner life, or of their behavioristic habits that are not objectively discernible. One reason for this is that such traits are often repressed or held in check from overt expression by other traits; as when ambitious desires are restrained by shyness.

To be sure, the impulses of such restrained traits undoubtedly affect and, it may be, determine the attitude toward situations, and the mode of life, habits of thought and feeling, and compensatory activity. And they, also, when activated, find expression in visceral manifestations. All such reactions undoubtedly may be logically interpreted as objective behavior, but the behavior is too subtle for detection by ordinary observation and is open to doubtful interpretations. Any definition of traits, then, should include characteristic activities of mental life that are not obtrusively manifested in objective behavior. And it should be in terms of mental processes that *determine* behavior rather than of the resultant behavior. From this point of view, *a trait may be defined as an habitual mental reaction characteristic of the individual to an actual or ideal situation.* This definition would exclude simple habits, which are little if anything more than conditioned reflexes (such, for example, as the common habit of smoking a cigar or cigarette immediately after meals; acquired tastes for food, odors, etc.; customs, habits of manners, etiquette and dress, and a hundred and one other simple habits of everyday life). On the other hand, it would *include and give full weight to repressed subconscious desires, aversions, apprehensions,* etc., that, through conflict or otherwise, and by various mechanisms, may be regarded as the determinants of what, on the surface, so far as consciousness is concerned, is apparently unrelated behavior. Repressed subconscious desires, etc., by whatever behavior they may be manifested, and by whatever mechanisms, are just as much traits as conscious desires and their behavior. This conception of a trait is a more fruitful point of view, as we shall see; for a study of mere behavior can tell us nothing of the *why* —of the structure of personality and of the motivation that determines one mode of behavior rather than another. As a method, it is true, it is the only approach to the objective study of behavior. But that does not negative or belittle the fact of there being conscious traits not open to this method.

Now, what is characteristic of traits is that they are obstinately persistent, enduring; otherwise they would not be habitual and characteristic of the personality. This does not mean that traits are necessarily everlasting throughout life, or that they cannot be modified or eliminated in accordance with new experiences and replaced by others of even an opposite character, with corresponding changes in the personality. The traits of childhood give way to new ones during adolescence, and these, in turn, are replaced by those of the adult, though it is not uncommon for some to persist throughout life.

As an editorial writer, discoursing on the heroism of John D. Rockefeller, Sr., in revisiting the scenes of his youth, remarks: "The libraries are full of books relating the sad experiences of these seekers of youthful memories. There is the amusing *Conrad in Quest of His Youth,* for example, in which the hero falls asleep at the critical tryst hour [with a former love of his early years, after having disappointedly sought out the companions of his youth only to find them all changed in their personalities]. There is an old poem, *Twenty Years Ago,* in which the pilgrim is disillusioned. The boy and girl friends of school days develop so strangely, and in looks, talk, and action are so different from what they were! Even the sweethearts of youth seem to have changed for the worse! The gods of youth are simply not the gods of later years. In extremely old age, there is more likely to be a re-awakening of the old fondness for childhood haunts, but it does not usually induce a visit. Mr. Rockefeller distributed dimes to those he met. Most persons would not consider the experience worth two cents."

Indeed, by technical psychological methods, traits can be artificially modified or eliminated and others newly created, with a corresponding modification of the personality. This is the goal of psychotherapy. Nevertheless, until such modifications occur, effected under the influence of new experiences of everyday life, or education, or psychotherapy, traits are enduring and the personality persists unchanged.

Why do traits thus endure? And why do we have them

at all? And why should we not be the sport of our environment from moment to moment? What makes our personalities stable, consistent things within certain limits? If traits are mental processes, why can we not change them at will, and so change our personalities — change our sentiments, our prejudices, ideals, attitudes and feelings, as we can change our thoughts from one topic to another, or change our clothes? This is what fiction writers make their characters do, and what old-fashioned penologists and sociologists thought they could do to reform the wayward, the delinquent and the criminal. Think and wish as we please, our personalities remain as before. No account, limited to behavior, can give an answer to this question. It is an important question, for it is the key to the problem of personality.

The most satisfying theory is that of *"integration of dispositions."* According to this theory, traits depend upon the organization of inherited and acquired psycho-physiological dispositions. That is to say, they are the functioning of organized integrates of such dispositions.

Dispositions? What are they? They are "tendencies" of something, of course. But of what? You never heard of a "tendency" off somewhere in space without its being a tendency of something. Alice said that she had seen a cat without a grin, but never before she came to Wonderland, had she seen a grin without a cat. We must go to Wonderland if we would see a disposition without its being a disposition of something. Inherited dispositions, admittedly, are tendencies of preformed physiological arrangements of the nervous system. Acquired dispositions are tendencies of conserved experience. For my part, I cannot conceive of experience being conserved in any way excepting as physiological records. This is the theory of memory — physiological, because it is impossible to imagine such records to be mental. For how can a mental experience be conserved as such, and where? Let us call a spade a spade and speak of acquired dispositions as physiological, created and organized and integrated by experience. I have called such dispositions "neurograms." How the activation of them is accompanied by, or manifested by, correlated mental processes is the old mind-body problem, which we need not go into.

If this be so, then personality is a structure as much as is the brain and spinal cord. But the important difference is that the structure of the latter is innate and inherited, while that of personality is in part inherited, as primitive instinctive dispositions, and for the most part acquired through experience. Personality, if I may quote from my previous writings,[1] may be considered *"as a composite structure built upon a foundation of preformed inherited psychophysiological mechanisms (instincts, etc.) by experience."*

The inherited mechanisms, of course, are the instinctive dispositions. (Whether they be called instincts or by some other name does not matter, it is only a question of terminology, which depends upon what is held to be connoted by the concept of instinct.) The point of importance is that the behavior of the infant (aside from that of simple physiological reflexes) consists wholly of responses to the environment of these inherited dispositions. It is little more than an instinctive and reflex robot. But — and in this our infantile robot differs from a mechanical robot — as it comes in contact with the world it acquires experience, and this experience modifies the specific responses of the inherited instinctive mechanisms to specific situations. Every biologist agrees to this. From the first peck of the chick, whether it hits the grain of corn or misses it, its pecking mechanism is conditioned, modified and controlled by the experience of pecking. And likewise with the human organism, "the instinctive behavior of the individual becomes conditioned, modified and adapted by experience to the specific situations of the environment. Necessarily, these modifications of the workings of the innate mechanisms by the imposition of experience upon and within them become very complicated, and the problems of instinct and experience thereby evoked have been the object of much study and debate."

1 The Structure and Dynamic Elements of Human Personality: *Jour. of Abnormal Psychology*, December, 1920; *The Unconscious*, 2nd edition, chapter XVII.

But how can the organism, whether a chick or a human being, "acquire" experience? How can a past experience that has come and gone determine the character of a future experience? Here, too, every biologist accepts the theory that what is acquired forms "dispositions," that an experience tends to leave in the nervous organization "dispositions," which become integrated with the instinctive dispositions and thus form a functioning whole in respect to the specific situation. The instinctive impulses are accordingly modified by the acquired dispositions.

All this is elementary enough. Yet it is worth while to recall it here because it is the fundamental principle underlying acquired traits of personality. For "there is a body of evidence which leads to the conclusion that upon the innate mechanisms as a basis, the composite structure of personality is built up by experience.

"By experience, new 'dispositions' are deposited (i. e., acquired), organized and systematized, not only among themselves but integrated with the inherited mechanisms. Thus, on the one hand, are formed new structural mechanisms, which in their functioning manifest themselves as those mental processes we call traits, and the outward behavior which they determine; and, on the other, the instinctive mechanisms are conditioned and brought under control by experience and mental processes, and acquire an extra driving force from the impulsive forces of the integrated instinctive mechanisms. This conception, which we owe to McDougall, I consider of great importance for an understanding of traits in the growth of the mind."

Accordingly we may say as a final analysis of traits: *Personality* is the sum-total of all the biological innate dispositions of the individual and of all the *acquired* dispositions and tendencies — acquired by experience. And it is limited to these.

The former would embrace the emotions, feelings, appetites and other tendencies manifested in instinctive reactions to the environment; the latter — the memories, ideas, sentiments, habits and other complexes of intellectual and affective dispositions, acquired and organized within the personality by the experiences of life. But all are integrated into one functioning organism, or whole.

As to the mode of this integration, "it is well recognized that the acquired dispositions are, by the very experiences through which they are acquired, organized into complexes and systems of complexes which are conserved as such in the storehouse of the unconscious, to be drawn upon by memory or to be awakened again to activity as occasion may demand to serve the purposes of mental life. By such complexes *are meant habits, sentiments, ideals, beliefs prejudices,* with their roots, settings or meanings, systematized thoughts, etc., in short, systematized experience in almost any domain."[1]

Many of these become traits that characterize the individual and determine his reasoning processes, his feelings, his attitudes, and his behavior in specific situations. For they have not only an organized structure but possess a dynamic potentiality, a drive, largely due to the fact that within the complex are incorporated one or more emotional or other instinctive mechanisms from which its chief, but not whole energy is derived.

*The important corollary of this theory of dispositions is that we should not look for the springs of human behavior to a single vital principle, such as the urge of a libido, or an élan vital, or other metaphysical entity, but rather to the motivating energy, derived from and inherent in the different inherited instinctive dispositions, and the many multiform integrated and organized systems of acquired dispositions created by the experiences of life.*

It is a common popular aphorism that human nature cannot be changed. And on the basis of this pessimistic proposition the cynically-minded criticize all attempts to outlaw war and to modify the asocial or illegal behavior of groups of the community. The proposition is true if human nature is limited to the primitive instinctive urges with which every child is born. But it is not true if human nature is taken to include personality, through which those

1 *The Unconscious;* chapters IX and XV.

rges manifest themselves. Personality can be changed by modifying or reconstructing its traits and organizing new ones by the creative force of new experience. This I have done time and again, and I believe my colleagues have done so also. I venture to say that Dr. Macpherson, Dr. Waterman and others will testify that on the basis of these principles and by these methods they have equally successfully reconstructed personalities, sometimes with dramatic results.

It is obvious from this theory of personality why we have traits, why traits are so obstinately persistent and why they cannot change arbitrarily at will. Having a structure of integrated dispositions, brain "patterns," to use the terminology of the day (but a concept formulated by Descartes three centuries ago), created and organized by experience into complexes and systems of complexes, they necessarily persist, unless erased by the corroding effect of time, until modified or transformed by new experience. But, as they must have widely ramified roots and settings in dispositions left by experiences of the distant past, often reaching back to childhood and conserved, perhaps, as cravings, in the unconscious beyond the reach of awareness, the new modifying experiences, whether educational, therapeutic or those of everyday life, must, in order to be effective, create new roots and settings that will construct new meanings, new points of view, new habits, new attitudes, and provide new cravings and drives.[1] Such modifications result in new brain patterns, new structures — which mean new traits or the elimination of old ones.

For these reasons and on these principles, the physician, who would adjust his psychopathic patient to the situation of his everyday environment; the sociologist, who would reform the asocial behavior of the maladjusted delinquent or criminal and substitute traits that conform to the demands of the social organization, knows that he must re-organize, modify, reconstruct the dispositions that underlie the traits of each. And until this is done, he knows that all efforts at reform will be useless. And, likewise, the experienced states-

1 Cf. chapter I, "The Role of Meaning in the Psychoneuroses."

man knows that until he has created new sentiments, change
the habits of thought, and the traditional attitudes of mind
of the people, and thereby public opinion, any proposal o
reform will fall on deaf ears, even though it be the abolitio
of war and preservation of world peace.

"You're nothing but a pack of cards!" exclaimed Alic
as she awoke from Wonderland. Perhaps she had better sai
"a pack of robots!"


### EDITORIAL NOTE

"A pack of robbers" would perhaps fit in better wit
this particular context, and Dr. Prince, had he lived today
might have thought of the assonance. The exposition o
traits, which was his last piece of scientific writing, is in lin
with the most recent views of psychologists (G. W. Allport
*e. g.*). His distinction between overt and potential trait
is at present taken care of by the terms "phenotypical" an
"genotypical" (not in Kurt Lewin's sense, however, but i
that of Hoffmann and the Kretschmer School.

— A. A. R.

# CHAPTER VII

## Miss Beauchamp

## The Psychogenesis of Multiple Personality[1]

### I "sally"

### An Alternating and Coconscious Personality

### I. Foreword: The Data

A NUMBER of years ago (1905) I published a study of the Beauchamp case (The Dissociation of a Personality).[2] It was one of multiple personality and exhibited three different personalities alternating with one another. One of them, however, "Sally," besides alternating with the others, had a coconscious existence, in that she persisted as a self, *i. e.*, as a separate mental system possessing a differentiated self-consciousness, while each of the others was present. Thus there were two selves existing at one and the same moment, one coconscious to the other.

The account, as published, was limited largely to a study, from a descriptive point of view, of the numerous psychological phenomena of all sorts manifested by the case and to the reconstruction of the normal self out of the disintegrated fragments.

The discussion of the theoretical problems involved was deferred for a later volume. This had been nearly completed some years ago, when it seemed best to postpone the

---

1 *Jour. of Abnormal Psychology*, 1920, vol. XVI, no. 1.
2 Second (enlarged) edition, 1908, Longman's Green & Co., New York.

discussion until certain fundamental problems were studied. Accordingly, these studies were incorporated in a volume *The Unconscious,* published in 1914. Then came the outbreak of the war and since then the manuscript has been laid aside owing to other interests.

While the literature is fairly rich with descriptive accounts of multiple personality, the psychogenesis of this phenomenon has not received much attention, probably owing to the difficulties involved and, I venture to say, to a lack of understanding of the phenomenon as well as of the problem itself.

For those who have not read the first book *(The Dissociation of a Personality)* and to refresh the memories of those who have read it, a brief *résumé* of the chief characteristics of the different personalities, (B I, B IV, and "Sally") will be necessary for an understanding of this study.

Miss Beauchamp manifested three secondary personalities, B I, B IV, and "Sally." B I, known as the *"Saint,"* was characterized by extreme piety, religious scruples, and moral traits that are commonly regarded as the attributes of saintliness — meek and dependent, never feeling anger or resentment or jealousy, bearing her hard lot with almost inconceivable patience, never rude or uncharitable, never self-assertive, she might well be taken as typifying the ideal of Christian morality.

B IV was the *"woman:"* strong, resolute, self-reliant, "sudden and quick in quarrel," easily provoked to anger and pugnacity, resenting interference and obstruction to her own will, determined to have her own way in all things at all costs, intolerant of the attributes of saintliness, the antithesis of B I, she belonged to womankind and to the world. She may be called the *"Realist."*

Sally, the *child* in character, thought, and deed — a mischievous delightful child, loving the outdoor breezy life, free from all ideas of responsibility and care, and deprived of the education and acquisitions of the others — belonged to childhood to which she was in large measure a reversion.

Here are three personalities sharply differentiated in traits, health, educational acquisitions, tastes, feelings, etc., yet all derived from one and the same person and alternating with one another.  The problem is:

(1)  To find the elements of the normal personality (a) lost by, *i. e.*, dissociated from, the secondary personalities, and (b) those retained by the same;

(2)  To find in each secondary personality complexes of ideas, traits, sentiments, instincts and innate tendencies, if any, which at any period of the normal development had been repressed or dissociated from the normal whole self, but which now re-animated had, by a synthetic re-arrangement with other elements of that self and by secondary incubation, become constellated into a new secondary personality;

(3)  The formulation of the psychogenetic mechanisms and forces by which the dissociations and re-arrangements were brought about.

Sally, psychologically, is the most interesting of Miss Beauchamp's personalities because of the fact that she was not only an alternating but, like B in the B. C. A. case, a coconscious personality.  Of course, when B I and B IV alternated with each other, the memories of the experiences of each respectively, and the constellation of the various complexes, instincts, sentiments, dispositions and other elements of personality belonging to one or the other, as the case might be (according as to which was extinguished), remained dormant, conserved in the unconscious.  In this sense each might be said to be subconscious to the other, but in a dormant state.  The same was true, naturally, of both when they disappeared and Sally was in evidence as the principal phase of consciousness.  This is more accurately expressed by saying that with each alternation there was, as is always the case, a re-arrangement and new synthesis of the elements of personality: some were utilized in the new combination and some discarded.  But with the emergence of the combination characterizing the one phase, the combination characterizing the other became dormant.

When Sally, however, disappeared, the case was entirely different.  This personality then still persisted.  This was possible because she became not dormant but coconscious;

that is to say, the combination of elements of this phase still continued to function (and often to express themselves as automatic phenomena) though the principal consciousness (B I or B IV) was unaware of this coconsciousness. This is a very important distinction. It meant the co-existence of two different combinations at one and the same time, each with a self-consciousness. There were two I's then in existence. As with Bimi, the ape in Rudyard Kipling's tale, "there was too much ego in her cosmos." I have elsewhere described the main characteristics of Sally[1] and must refer any one desiring a more detailed statement to what was there said but will reiterate the essentials.

## (A) DISSOCIATIONS

### (1) Sensory Defects

That Sally included a dissociated psycho-physiological condition is made manifest by certain mental and physiological stigmata which she exhibited. Amongst the latter may be placed the peculiar anesthesia which was present. With her eyes closed she could feel nothing; the tactile, pain, and temperature senses were lost; you could stroke, prick, or burn any part of her skin and she did not feel it; you could place a limb in any position without her being able to recognize the position which had been assumed. All this was true not only when her eyes were closed but when she was not allowed (as by the interposition of a screen) to look at the tested parts. "But," to quote what I have elsewhere said, "let her open her eyes and look at what you are doing, let her join the visual sense with the tactile or other senses, and the lost sensations at once return. The association of visual perception with these sensations brings the latter into the field of her personal consciousness. The same thing is true of auditory perceptions. If Sally hears a sound associated with an object she can feel the object. For instance,

---

1 *The Dissociation of a Personality*, chap. IX. (The chapters and pages referred to in this study always have reference to this work unless otherwise designated.)

place a bunch of keys in her hand and she does not know what she holds. Now jingle the keys and she can at once feel them, as is shown by her being able to recognize the different parts of their forms [with her eyes closed]." Sensation could, however, be restored *temporarily* by suggestion. That an anesthesia with this peculiarity is due to dissociation is obvious and is a well accepted fact.

To quote again, "Sally's anesthesia extends to the somatic feelings. She is never hungry or thirsty. If she eats she does so as a matter of form or social requirement. There is also an entire absence of bodily discomforts. This anesthesia probably explains in large part Sally's *freedom from ill health*. She does not know the meaning of fatigue, of pain, of ill health. She is always well. It is probably, in part at least, in consequence of this anesthesia that Sally does not share the pain or other physical ailments of Miss Beauchamp or any of the other personalities. Let Miss Beauchamp be suffering from abdominal pain, or headache, or physical exhaustion, and let her change to Sally, and at once all these symptoms disappear. Sally knows of the symptoms of the other personalities only through their thoughts or their actions. She does not feel the symptoms themselves. The same is true of the sense of muscular fatigue. Sally can walk miles without being conscious of the physiological effect. Curiously enough, however, Miss Beauchamp may afterwards suffer from the fatigue effects of Sally's exertions.

"What is true of Sally in these respects as an alternating personality is also true of her as a coconsciousness. *Coconsciously, Sally is always anesthetic.* If Miss Beauchamp's eyes are closed and any portion of the skin is touched or pricked, or if a limb is placed in any posture, coconscious Sally is unaware of the tactile pain or muscular sensations, although the other personalities are not anesthetic but perceive each sensation perfectly."

## (2) Dissociations of Emotions and Instincts

When she emerged as an *alternating* personality, some of the emotions (and consequently the innate instinctive mechanisms to which they belong) though components of the other personalities, even obtrusively so, were dissociated from Sally and hence were not incorporated in her make-up. This, as I have found it, is one of the most important and determining phenomena in alternations of personality and to a large degree, is responsible for the contrasting traits. It requires a special study by itself. I shall here content myself with pointing out merely the lacunae in her personality.

*Fear.* This instinct seems to have been entirely eliminated from Sally's composition. The objects, circumstances etc., capable of arousing this instinct are so numerous that, of course, it is impossible to assert dogmatically that any person is absolutely devoid of it until put to every concrete test, and yet Sally showed herself without the fear reaction in so many situations, physical and moral, which would ordinarily arouse fear in the average person, that I am almost compelled to believe that the instinct was lost in her. So far as I could see, none of the causes, such as a thunderstorm, or darkness, or social consequences of conduct, or illness, or fear of inanimate or animate objects, like fire, snakes, spiders, etc., or the numerous other things that awakened fear in the other two personalities — none of these things affected Sally. I have known her also to be in the most dangerous situations, such as climbing out on the eaves of the roof and preparing to jump from the fifth story window, without apparently experiencing the slightest fear. It is significant that Sally was also free from the pathological phobias which were so conspicuous in the other personalities. The most reasonable interpretation, therefore, is that the instinct of fear was dissociated from this personality.

*Sexual Emotion (Instinct or Appetite).* This instinct also was completely dissociated from Sally who, like B in the B. C. A. case, was a stranger to the emotion and psychologically sexless. As this cannot be said of her normal personality, it could not have been a matter of organic development, but only a phenomenon of dissociation. Though she knew the meaning of sexual language as defined in the dictionary, the terms conveyed no notion of that which they expressed. Dissociation of an instinct, as an explanation of the lack of normal reaction in the individual, is proved, in principle, by study of the *sexual instinct* (appetite). This instinct is manifested by such a definite reaction that it is easily recognized and studied. It is not uncommon for this instinct to be absent under conditions that can only be interpreted as those of dissociation. For example, Mrs. F. S., as a result of an emotional trauma, completely lost this instinct — a matter of considerable consequence, as the conjugal conditions were on the verge of leading to divorce. A suggestion in hypnosis readily restored the instinct and conjugal happiness. If one chooses to distinguish by definition between inhibition and dissociation, insisting that what is inhibited is not dissociated, it can be shown that in many instances the instinct is not inhibited because it functions in dreams and in another phase of personality. It is dissociated from the psycho-physiological composition of a given personality.

*Parental Instinct.* The data do not permit us to form a definite opinion regarding the presence or absence of this instinct, but Sally's attitude towards children, when contrasted with that of the alternating phase (B I) makes one very doubtful of her having retained it. The love of children in B I was very marked. Sally simply dislikes them, and certainly no tender emotion was evoked by them as it was in B I. Whether this emotion was evoked by other objects is a matter of doubt.

*The emotion of disgust* belonging to the instinct of repulsion or aversion, frequently observable in B I, seemed to be absent in Sally. At least objects which excited this emotion in the former phase not only did not do so in the latter, but were often attractive. This, however, might be attributed to the formation of different sentiments with these objects, as will be presently explained. Still, if the instinct was retained, a sentiment of aversion to some object, punctuated by disgust, ought to have been formed, but this was not observed.

*The Feeling of Subjection (Self-Abasement).* I do not think any one would have exhibited Sally as a shining example of this emotion and instinct. If this child of nature possessed it I failed to observe it. She was certainly free from any shyness, or self-consciousness, or sense of inferiority, which so often torments and spoils the lives of normal people. Nor did she exhibit any sentiments in which self-abasement is incorporated.

It was probably due, in part at least, to this loss that she never inherited from Miss Beauchamp or acquired any religious sentiments, though they were predominant in her other self — B I. The "saintly complex," a religious ideal, intensely motivated by the instinct of self-abasement, which had characterized and colored the whole life of the original self, was left out in our young scapegrace. No, Sally did not know the meaning of self-subjection even before an ideal of Divinity.

Whether *hunger* (like sexual feeling) be regarded as an instinct or appetite, or simply a craving-reaction, Sally was devoid of it. This, perhaps, may be explained by the somatic anesthesia by which all bodily sensations were dissociated. However that may be, the contrast between the absence of appetite of this alternating self and the enjoyment of food by the one known as B IV, who was the butt of Sally's jokes because of her appetite, could not be overlooked.

These were the principal emotions and instincts which were not incorporated in the composition of Sally, and which I interpret as dissociated inasmuch as they were manifested in one or other of Miss Beauchamp's selves.

On the other hand, there was one instinct or innate craving (whatever it be considered) which was dominating and insistent in the childlike Sally. It stamped the character of her personality. It completely governed her behavior. It was all the more striking in that it was left out of B I's composition. This was the *play disposition*. The significance of this we shall see when we study the psychogenesis of this alternating and coconscious self to which the dissociation of Miss Beauchamp gave birth.

### (3) Sentiments

Corresponding in a general way to the loss of particular

emotions and retention of others was the absence, on the one hand, in Sally, of sentiments which characterized the normal self and, on the other, the possession of sentiments peculiar to herself. Thus the differences in the characters of the original Miss Beauchamp — the real self — and of the secondary youthful child, Sally, became strikingly manifested. When we come to the study of the psychogenesis of the other two alternating selves we shall find the same variation in the sentiments, and corresponding variations of character. It is well to understand clearly the meaning of "sentiment," the precise sense in which it is here used, otherwise the significance of these variations or alterations of personality will be missed.

The modern conception of "sentiment" we owe to Shand. By "sentiment" I mean an object, or idea of some object, which has been organized by experience with one or more emotional *dispositions*. As an emotional disposition is an instinct or part of an instinct, a sentiment is an idea structurally organized with one or more instincts from which it derives its motivating force. Thus, the idea of mother may be organized with the instincts possessing the emotional dispositions of tender feeling, reverence, etc., that of God with tender feeling, awe, subjection, etc. Sentiments, then, become complex units in the structure of the mind. In the psychological terminology of the day, a sentiment may be defined as an emotional complex. This concept, a modification of Mr. Shand's, we owe in *principle* to him. Mr. Shand's conception, or some modification of it, like the one I have formulated, is, I believe, pretty commonly to-day adopted by psychologists. Such differences as exist relate to the exact structure of the organization of the complex. With the latter we need not concern ourselves here. This concept accords fairly well with the usage of popular speech, but it has certain important implications, supported by observation, which popular usage does not realize and take into account. It is popularly recognized that emotions become linked by experience to objects or ideas of objects. But that is not the point. There is nothing new in that. That has been understood ever since Adam kissed Eve. The point is that in the linking of an idea to an emotion, what happens is this: the idea becomes structurally organized with an instinctive psycho-physiological disposition, of which an emotion, such as fear, or anger, or curiosity, is a component, and which has an aim or end. Now, when the instinct is excited not only is there felt emotion, but the impulse of the disposition is an urge or drive which carries the instinct to fulfillment and satisfies its aim.[1] If the instinct is that of flight (fear) the urge is to escape; if of pugnacity (anger) — to break down opposition, and so on. Further, in consequence of the organization of the idea of an object with the instinct, the presentation of the object in consciousness necessarily awakens the instinct which then determines behavior in relation to the object, in that it impels escape from the object if the emotion is that of fear; to possess it, if the emotion is of love; to injure it, if of hate. Idea and instinct, then, in this sense form a sentiment. A sentiment, thus, though a complex, behaves as a unit, as a psychic whole, possessing an aim which it strives to satisfy. And it is important to bear in mind, for the purposes of a study such as this, that with the awakening of a sentiment in consciousness there are let loose impulsive forces discharged by their instincts (emotions?), which not only determine behavior, but control, inhibit, dissociate, repress, excite, or otherwise affect other mental processes.

But this is not the whole story of a sentiment; it is too schematic. A sentiment is a product of the growth of the mind and organized by experience. This means that it has its *roots* in a greater or less number of antecedent experiences related to its object. It is a growth from these roots. It is a product of these experiences and because of and by them it has been organized. You cannot functionally and dynamically isolate a sentiment from these root-experiences,

---

1 To say that such a psycho-physiological disposition has an end or aim which it strives to satisfy is not equivalent to saying that it has a purpose with a foresight of that end. Purpose presupposes foresight as indispensable; without foresight purpose seems to me meaningless. I conceive that *foresight* is derived solely from experiences and is not innate. "Instincts" are serviceable rather than purposive. Purposive behavior, though served by instincts, is guided by and depends upon experience.

that is, from the dispositions acquired by these experiences. It is, therefore, more or less strongly organized with them. They *as a setting or context* give it meaning, just as every idea is dependent upon its setting for its meaning. This is very neatly shown by a study of pathological sentiments, such as the phobias. Practical examination of these sentiments shows that they are so strongly and intimately rooted in a complex of antecedent experiences that the origin and true meaning of the phobia can often only be understood by bringing to light these root-experiences. They furnish the viewpoint and attitude of mind towards the object of the sentiment. Nor can you kill a sentiment except by killing these roots; that is without changing the setting, which means the viewpoint. Alter the setting and you alter the point of view, the attitude towards the object, and then destroy the sentiment.

From all this it follows, if this theory of the sentiments is true, that sentiments are integrated with larger systems of dispositions, deposited by the experiences of life, from which experiences "foresight" and "purpose" are derived. In these larger systems there are also organized other instincts of which the drive or urge co-operates with the drive of the sentiment in determining the mental attitude and behavior in given situations: *e. g.*, fear, when the loved object is in danger; anger, when it is injured. Sentiments and their roots, the settings, thus are organized in still larger complexes or "psychic wholes." At least this is my interpretation of the facts. (In my view both Shand's and McDougall's conceptions of the structure of a sentiment fall short in that they are both too schematic and theoretical and fail to take into consideration all the facts of observation, particularly as revealed by pathological studies.) At any rate, sentiments and their "settings" are integrated in mental systems in the course of the growth of the mind — and characterize personality.

It is hardly possible to overestimate the part played by sentiments (including their root dispositions or settings) in the determination of personality and character and, hence, in alterations of personality. Upon the sentiments, among other things, largely depend the habits of thought, the behavior, and reactions of the individual to the environment, and, therefore, those traits which we select as particularly marking the character of the personality. This principle was readily recognized in Miss Beauchamp, whose sentiments stood out in high relief and strongly contrasted with those of Sally. That Miss Beauchamp had built up, as a result of her self-education and day-dreaming habits, a large number of sentiments possessing more than usually intensive emotional dispositions, not only in connection with the "saintly complex" but with many other ideas and objects, is apparent from the biographical history of her case. These sentiments were the basic structure of her idealism. The church and religious services and music, the Madonna, Christ, all that pertained to religious worship had become invested with emotions of love, and reverence, and self-subjection, and feelings of exaltation and pleasure, and thereby had become objects of sentiments.[1] Likewise, the divinity-worship of her mother, in which afterwards several other persons were successively incorporated, indicated a similar sentiment. An opposite sentiment which included fear and dislike involved her father. Seeing people and the world about her not as they were, clearly and truly, but as they were colored by her imagination, she built up strong sentiments of an idealistic sort which gave a peculiar stamp to her character, and she was known as "an original." People, natural objects, and animal life (snakes, spiders, etc.) became endowed with intense emotional dispositions of one sort or another and thereby formed sentiments.

Sally, as contrasted with Miss Beauchamp and the other two alternating personalities, presented three peculiarities in respect to her sentiments. The first was that some of the most characteristic and dominating sentiments of her whole original self were entirely lacking in this secondary mutilated self. Sally, like a shorn lamb, emerged absolutely denuded of these. Likewise, many of the sentiments of the other two alternating personalities B I and B IV did not exist in Sally. Expressed in a different way, the same ob-

1 Chap. XXI and Appendix R. *(Dissociation of a Personality.)*

jects or ideas, which in Miss Beauchamp were organized with certain particular emotions, were entirely devoid of these emotions in Sally's mind, or, as I will presently explain, were organized with a quite different emotion. And likewise with respect to the ideas of B I and B IV. Furthermore, such sentiments were necessarily organized with different settings and consequently acquired different "meanings." Thus it was, for example, that religious ideas which stirred with intense emotional reaction the other personalities, particularly Miss Beauchamp and B I, awakened no such emotions in this young scapegrace. Their ideas had for her not only no religious emotional tone but also no religious meaning. In her mental composition they were not organized with emotions into sentiments. Hence they did not stir her. She considered them all fol-de-rol and was simply bored. The "saintly complex" with its sentiments of sainthood, which largely dominated Miss Beauchamp and B I, is a good example. Sally had no such complex. It was the same way with persons, and places, and scenery. Sally was devoid of the sentiments, which, often intense in their emotions, many of these objects formed in the minds of the other personalities. In other words, the emotions which were centred about certain persons, places, scenery, etc., found no such association in Sally's consciousness and hence were not animated by these objects. The failure to acquire such sentiments corresponded as a rule, I think, with the loss of the appropriate instinct. When dealing with the psychogenesis of the case of Sally, this point will be more fully considered.

The second peculiarity which Sally manifested, as regards the sentiments, was the organization, about an object, of emotional dispositions entirely different from those organized with the very same object or idea in the consciousness of the real self, or of one of the other secondary personalities. The consequence was that an object for which Miss Beauchamp had a sentiment of reverence, or gratitude, or awe, or affection, or fear, or self-abasement, etc., awakened in Sally, in her turn, a sentiment of jealousy, or humor, or playful sport, as the case might be. Likewise the former personality might have a sentiment of repugnance, or aversion for objects which excited joy and wonder in the latter.

The third peculiarity was the fact that Sally had sentiments of her own for objects which were entirely indifferent to Miss Beauchamp. These were chiefly of a childlike order such as pertain to childhood.

The second peculiarity often gave a dramatic setting to the situation when the change from one personality to the other took place; as for instance when Miss Beauchamp, coming to herself, found herself talking familiarly and joyously with a person for whom she had an aversion and of whom she disapproved; or handling a collection of spiders and snakes, of which she had an intense horror.

In accordance with the third peculiarity, Sally manifested sentiments some of which were, coconsciously, of long standing since childhood. For instance, the disposition to play, long since dissociated from Miss Beauchamp, remained conserved subconsciously and, as I have said, was conspicuous in Sally's make-up. In accordance with this disposition, a large number of sentiments pertaining to sports, outdoor life, etc., had been organized in her personality. Similarly, in the course of time, she built up sentiments of her own in connection with the persons and objects that came into her life; she had her own little "keepsakes" and treasures not shared by the others. Some of these persons and objects were common to the lives of all the personalities, but, as I have said, the sentiments of each phase differed; with one and the same object — B I would have the sentiment of veneration, Sally of play, B IV of hostility.

This change in the composition of the sentiments, involving the same idea as its object, may seem somewhat strange at first thought, but if we stop to think a moment we will recognize that the same thing is often observed in everyday life in moods. In each mood one and the same object is organized with different emotional dispositions and in different settings, so that the object is accompanied by different affects and has a different meaning for the individual.[1]

This difference was interestingly and instructively ex-

1 Probably nearly everyone, for example, has experienced in one mood a strong aversion for a person for whom in another mood he has a real affection.

hibited in the facial expressions of the different personalities of Miss Beauchamp. As objective signs of the fundamentally governing sentiments of each I have described these in the full account of the case.[1] Referring to B I and Sally it was remarked: " . . . with both Miss Beauchamp and Sally, every mood, feeling, and emotion is accompanied automatically by its own facial expression, so that, as each individuality has a dominant, and for the most part continuous, emotional state of mind, each wears a corresponding expression, different muscles coming into play in each. By this expression alone, it is generally possible at a glance to recognize the personality. As this expression is purely automatic and the accompanying resultant of the emotion, it is impossible for one personality completely to simulate any other. When Sally tries to impersonate Miss Beauchamp, the best she can do is to try to look serious; but as she does not *feel* serious, and actually lacks the emotion or mood of Miss Beauchamp, her face does not really assume the expression of that personality. Occasionally Sally will have for a moment, under the influence of some event, such as a scolding or threat of punishment, a depressing or anxious emotion identical with that of Miss Beauchamp; then her face will wear an expression indistinguishable from the latter's, but as a rule these variations are only momentary."

In view of the large part emotional dispositions, as elements of instinct and sentiments, and the other innate dispositions play in the determination of personality, it may be instructive to tabulate the emotions as present or absent in the three personalities for purposes of comparison. With this purpose in mind it will be convenient to follow chiefly McDougall's classification of the primary and compounded emotions and of the innate dispositions.[2] In doing so, it is not necessary to commit ourselves to an entire acceptance of

1 Page 123. *(The Dissociation of a Personality.)*

2 There is considerable difference of opinion as to what emotions should be regarded as primary and what affective states as compounds of these or others. The analysis of an affective state is no easy matter. It is largely one of interpretation, of the correctness of which we have no absolute test — no test by which it can be determined that all the elements have been differentiated, or even that the true elements have been discovered.

its correctness or of the soundness of the analysis upon which it is based. For the purpose I have in mind it makes no difference whether an affective state is primary or composite. It is not easy or always possible, of course, to determine the retention, and still more difficult the total absence, of affective dispositions in an individual. The disposition may exist but its emotional reaction may be excited only by some special situation in which the person may be placed. If a person flies into a rage in a given situation, as B IV did on numberless occasions, we know he possesses the anger reactions (and instinct), but if he does not exhibit this emotion it may be that the situation is not one that will excite the disposition in him, but it might be that another situation would do so. Still such simple everyday emotions as anger, fear, tender feeling, subjection, etc., are easily determined under prolonged observation. The difficulty is with the more complex and rarer affective states (sentiment) like awe and gratitude. Special situations peculiar to each individual are necessary to elicit these states, and particularly to build them up as sentiments. When, however, a person has been under continued and close observation in all sorts of situations during six years, with every opportunity to examine the content of consciousness, it is possible to determine with certainty the presence and absence of many affective states, though we may not be able to satisfy ourselves regarding others. In the following table, when the evidence has been insufficient to form any opinion, the fact has been recorded alone by a query. It should be further said that the personalities were not absolutely fixed in respect to their emotions; they had their moods as well as normal people. And, although these moods were mainly characterized by feelings of pleasantness or unpleasantness and of exaltation and depression, nevertheless in one mood an emotional reaction might be excited by a given situation which would not yield any such reaction in another mood. This is also true of normal people. There was however always, I believe, some situation, as with all people, which would induce the reaction peculiar to the personality. Whatever the amiability at a given moment of B IV, for instance, she could not be trusted too far, for there was always some irritant that would arouse anger; on the other hand, in no mood could B I be excited to anger, which must be rare in normal people. Sally was the least changeable and rarely showed differences of moods.

### Instincts[1]

|  |  | Sally | B I | B IV |
|---|---|---|---|---|
| Primary Emotions | Anger | Present | Absent | Present |
| | Wonder | " | Absent ? | " |
| | Elation (Self-assertion) | Present | " | Present |
| | Fear | Absent | Present | " |
| | Disgust | " | " | ? |
| | Subjection | " | " | Absent |
| | Tender Emotion | Present | " | ? |

[1] It will be noted that throughout this chapter, the author is following McDougall's analysis of the emotions, instincts, and sentiments. Even if the doctrine of instincts should be impugned, we can still talk of traits, attitudes and interests, in addition to emotions, moods, and sentiments. The tables on this page and the next are, therefore, still illuminating instruments in the dissection and synthesis of the various states constituting the multiple personality of the Beauchamp case.

— A. A. R.

## *Sentiments*

| | Sally | B I | B IV |
|---|---|---|---|
| Love | Present ? | Present | Present ? |
| Hate | Present | Absent | Present |
| Admiration | ? | Present | ? |
| Awe | ? | ? | ? |
| Reverence | ? | Present | Absent ? |
| Gratitude | Absent | " | Absent |
| Scorn | ? | Absent | ? |
| Contempt | ? | " | ? |
| Loathing | ? | " | ? |
| Fascination | ? | ? | ? |
| Envy | Present | Absent | ? |
| Reproach (self) | ? | Present | ? |
| Anxiety | Absent | Present | Present |
| Jealousy | Present | Absent | ? |
| Vengefulness | " | " | ? |
| Resentment | " | " | Present |
| Shame | Absent | Present | Absent |
| Bashfulness | " | ? | " |
| Joy | Present | Absent[1] | Present |
| Sorrow | " | Present | Absent ? |
| Pity | Absent ? | ? | ? |
| Happiness | Present | Absent ? | Present |
| Surprise | " | ? | ? |

Compound emotions and other affects

## *Other Instincts and Innate Tendencies*

| | Sally | B I | B IV |
|---|---|---|---|
| Play | Present | Absent | ? |
| Sexual desire | Absent | " | Absent |
| Acquisition | Present | " | ? |
| Sympathy | " | Present | Absent |
| Suggestibility | " | " | Present |

[1] Excepting when in a special condition of ecstasy (chap. XXI). Joy and sorrow are not accepted by McDougall as true emotions.

## (4)  Intellectual Defects and Characteristics

Of the *intellectual stigmata,* the dissociation of many of the educational acquisitions of Miss Beauchamp is noteworthy. In a general way it may be said that Sally had lost Miss Beauchamp's culture — the knowledge of foreign languages, shorthand, mathematics and general higher culture. This means that she did not have access to the unconscious storehouse of these conserved dispositions. Their complexes could not be switched on to those constellations which constituted her personality. It is interesting to note that when attempts were made by her — in experiments to test her intellectual faculties — to make use of this culture, for example, to make different calculations, with the synthesis of the lost knowledge she changed to Miss Beauchamp (B I). That is to say, the B I constellation replaced in mass the Sally constellation. For this reason the latter objected to the experiments. The same phenomenon often happened when she was forced to recall certain intense emotional experiences.[1] The impulsive force of these emotions, which were dissociated from Sally, when thus awakened, determined the awakening of the whole B I (or B IV) constellation.

### (B)  SYNTHETIC DATA

The ideas which took a dominating part in Sally's personality and stamped individuality upon her character were, as we shall see later, derived from conserved complexes which had been formed by the experiences of childhood and youth. Invested with emotions of joy and happiness and feelings of pleasure and excitement, they were the centres of sentiments. They were also to a large extent organized with the innate disposition or instinct of play. The mental systems into which they entered, and which may be summed up as play complexes, formed the settings or context which determined her point of view and perceptions. Other ideas, of course, belonged to her memories; for, with the exception of book

---

1 Page 221. (*The Dissociation of a Personality.*)

learning and general culture, of which I have already spoken, she possessed all the memories of Miss Beauchamp and B I[1] and was aware of all their experiences. But, as has been stated, these ideas were devoid of the emotions with which they were invested as sentiments in the other personalities. In the Sally phase, ideas of outdoor pastimes, sports, games, riding, hunting, skating, boating, and sailing, ideas of these and similar pleasures appealed to her imagination, and, invested with complex emotions — joy, happiness, play, curiosity, interest, etc. — aroused feelings of pleasure and excitement; and tales of adventure and hair-breadth escapes; of hunting and fishing and outdoor sports, and all that excites the spirit of youth — the spirit that bubbled over within her — awakened an intense interest and emotional excitement.

It was this sort of ideas which, invested with emotions, formed the main sentiments and, therefore, determined the character of the personality; it is also to be noted that the sentiments were those which are generally characteristic of childhood and youth, and there is evidence that they were the persistence and *recrudescence* of sentiments formed during those early years, but long since dissociated, or repressed, from the consciousness of the self-cultivated personality — Miss Beauchamp — and dormant.

It should be further noted that these ideas are such as are normally associated with the play "instinct," particularly in immature years, and in Sally this was the dominant instinct. One might almost say that everything naturally connected with this instinct awakened a response and expressed itself in impulsive tendencies. Even her fondness for and habit of teasing and mischief, much to the discomfiture of her other selves, was merely the expression of this instinct; for teasing was only a game which she, like a child, loved to play.

We may further say, from what we have been able to learn of Miss Beauchamp's early history and our knowledge of child life, that the Sally complexes were once, far back in

---

1 Excepting, also, of course, certain sensory memories.

childhood, a side to her character, just as they re-appeared as a side to the character of the restored resurrected real self. With the restoration of the normal self, in situations which would naturally awaken the play instincts in a healthy normal person, Sally's sentiments and feelings and instincts bloomed again in Miss Beauchamp. In other words, to a large extent Sally was a *reversion* to a stage of childhood — to the complexes and reactions of that period.

But the Sally complexes, we shall have occasion to see when studying the psychogenesis of this phase, were the result of something more than a simple reversion to and re-awakening of conserved dispositions deposited by the experiences of youth. There undoubtedly had been going on for years a subconscious *incubation* of these dispositions which had been continuously gathering into themselves new experiences, conscious and subconscious. The youthful dispositions had thus been receiving fresh accretions of formative material until they had flowered into a personality. To this we shall presently return.

It remains to mention one other class of processes which entered into the constellation that formed this phase. As already intimated, Sally was a coconsciousness as well as an alternating personality. As a coconsciousness she had perceptions of her environment which never entered the awareness of the principal consciousness. In this state she saw, heard, and was generally cognizant of much that neither B I nor B IV consciously recognized. She often perceived correctly external relations which were incorrectly perceived by those two. When Sally became an alternating personality, this unusual and accessory knowledge was retained by her. Consequently her experiences and her knowledge of the environment differed to a certain degree from those of the others and contributed to this extent in differentiating the personalities. Likewise a large mass of evidence goes to show that as a coconsciousness there were trains of thought and feelings that did not enter the conscious stream of the principal consciousness. This large coconscious mental life tended further, by coconscious elaboration, to build up complexes which later appeared in consciousness as memory when she was an alternating personality, and thus to further characterize and differentiate this phase.

In this analysis of the Sally phase I have done little more than to give a descriptive account of the facts and observations. Sally was in everything, save psychological experience, a child. Her instincts, her mental reactions, her perceptions, were those of a child. Her perceptions of W. J., for example, were of a person who would give her candies, take her on excursions, give her youthful outings, etc., while by contrast the perceptions of B I for the same person were of an exalted being to whom reverence and admiration were due as to a preceptor and religious guide. In each phase the meaning of the perception was determined by the complexes forming the context which contained the corresponding sentiments. Sally's complexes were, therefore, those which were characteristic of youth. This youthful personality, however, was modified, more or less, by the fact that she was aware of the social and worldly experiences and knowledge gained by the other personalities, and therefore knew, as a matter of expediency, that her activities must be correspondingly curbed and her behavior modified to fit the exigencies of conventional life. This she was in a degree accustomed to do voluntarily, but her sentiments and impulses were those of the youthful ideas I have described.

By way of summary, then, we may say that primarily Sally was made up of split-off fragments of personality repressed from the main consciousness during childhood. Secondly: she was a reversion to a stage of childhood. Thirdly: in her mental composition there was a recrudescence of sentiments of early life, long ago repressed. Fourthly: there were incorporated complexes which were the result of the subconscious incubation of dispositions deposited by the experiences of youth. Fifthly: her mental composition included independent coconscious perceptions and thoughts elaborated into complexes and systems of memory distinct from those of the other personalities.

If this be a correct summary of the facts it remains to determine, on the basis of the given data, by what genetic influences this personality was created.

## II.  The Genesis of Sally

The genesis of Sally is another and psychologically more interesting problem. Thus far, our study has been confined to its composition as an alternating phase, but the genesis of the phase cannot be understood without relating it to its roots in the subject's subconscious mental life in which it had its origin and development long before it appeared as an independent alternating personality. For the details of the phenomena, through which this subconscious life was manifested, I must refer you to the full account of this case. It is enough to say here that a large mass of evidence went to show that when the Sally phase changed to one of the other phases it did not become dormant, as was the case with the B I and B IV phases after they changed to one another or to Sally, but continued in activity as a segregated coconscious self of which the principal consciousness was unaware. In other words, while B I or B IV was in existence as an alternating self, Sally still persisted as a self, incarcerated, so to speak, in her subterranean abode where she lived her coconscious life. There she had thoughts, perceptions and feelings of her own. Whether her coconscious life was uninterrupted and continuous, or whether it came into being from moment to moment in response to stimulation, it is difficult from objective evidence to affirm with positiveness. She herself insisted, as other coconscious selves have insisted, that it was continuous, that is, that there was a continuous stream of coconscious thought just as when she was an alternating self. It is possible that this was an illusion on her part. However that may be, it is not a matter of consequence for our present purposes. Certain it is that as a coconsciousness she could manifest herself by so-called automatic phenomena (speech, writing, movements) and by influencing the principal consciousness by hallucinations, aboulia, inhibitions, etc., almost whenever she saw fit; and it was possible to elicit evidence of her coconscious existence whenever one desired.

When she became an alternating personality, she retained memory of her coconscious life, and many of these memories could be demonstrated experimentally to be true reproductions of actual subconscious experiences. This phase needs to be considered, then, both as a coconscious and as an alternating consciousness.

Now how comes it that such a large coconscious life came into existence? It cannot be explained on the simple principle of alternation of phases, that is to say, as a necessary consequence of one constellation of mental complexes, B I or B IV, replacing another constellation (Sally), for observation of numerous cases of alternating personality shows that ordinarily one phase of personality does not become coconscious to its successor. When alternation occurs one phase simply replaces the other which in turn becomes dormant, ceases to have conscious activity. Neither B I nor B IV became coconscious to the other nor to Sally after replacement took place; nor did No. 1 and No. 2 in the case of C. N., nor C and A in the case of B. C. A., become coconscious after replacement, but simply dormant, and so with numerous cases in the literature. Mere alternation, then, is not sufficient to account for the persistence of a phase as a coconsciousness.

On the other hand, Sally does not stand alone as a unique phenomenon. We have seen that B, in the B. C. A. case, also became coconscious when replaced by A or C.[1] These two cases exhibited a phase which manifested itself both as a coconscious self and as an alternating self. In "A Divided Self" — the case reported by Charles E. Cory,[2] which I have been permitted to verify — the same phenomenon was observed. As a phenomenon it is of frequent occurrence, though not often as a phase of multiple personality. A phase of this kind needs to be studied, therefore, in both relations. To fully understand the Sally phase, and the same is true of the B phase (B. C. A.), it is necessary to take up this question of autonomous dissociated coconsciousness. To do so *in extenso* would carry us into a wider field of inquiry and anticipate studies to which I shall devote

1 See next chapter, and *The Unconscious* (2nd edition), chapters XVIII-XX, 1921.
2 *Jour. Abnormal Psychol.*, Oct. 1919.

another contribution.  We may, however, touch upon it sufficiently to allow us to understand the psychological conditions involved in the genesis of Sally.  All experienced students of abnormal psychology have had frequent opportunities to observe and study autonomous coconscious activity and therefore are familiar with its various types.  They range all the way from sporadic discrete ideas, restricted to very narrow limits and manifested as segregated psychological activity independent of the personal consciousness, to complex systems of thoughts and feelings constellated into a self.

Coconscious activity of this kind is most frequently observed under conditions where alternations of personality are not observed.  As a phenomenon it is quite common by itself.  It is in cases like those of "Lucie" and Mme. B, made classical by M. Janet, and that of Mlle. Hélène Smith, an unprofessional medium, so admirably studied by M. Flournoy, that coconscious activity can be observed in its most highly developed form.  Indeed, the phenomena manifested by mediums, who claim through automatic writing and speech to give expression to the thoughts of spirits and send messages from the spirit world, often present the best examples of autonomous coconscious life.  These have been too much neglected by psychologists.

In the simplest cases as, for example, in hysteria, or when automatic writing has been experimentally cultivated, the coconscious idea is some memory which has been dissociated from consciousness, perhaps with a strong affect like fear linked to it, or it may be some memory of a past experience which has been forgotten.  Such a memory may be one of childhood or something read or heard; the content of the idea may be of the most diverse nature.  In the more complex forms, the subconscious ideas may involve an extensive series of thoughts and feelings synthesized into a large system capable of constructive imagination, and, drawing upon the storehouse of conserved knowledge possessed by the normal self, it may fabulize ideas of considerable originality.  It may thus rival, in extensiveness of mental processes, the primary self.  Such a subconscious system then becomes a veritable secondary self (though coconscious) having experiences of its own.

In pathological cases the beginning of such a system is apt to be some strongly emotional experience (memory) which had been dissociated by some psychological trauma (shock), or mental conflict, or voluntary repression. The memory of this experience is conserved in the unconscious, and from time to time, excited by some stimulus, takes on coconscious activity. In other cases, as with the development of mediums, the beginning may be some idea which has been awakened, from its dormant condition in the storehouse of unconscious experiences, by experimental or environmental stimuli. Whatever the origin may be, beginning in a small way as a few dissociated ideas, they may undergo a sort of subconscious incubation, rob the personal consciousness of some of its functions and possessions, and by the synthesizing effect of repeated experiences (hysterical attacks, experimentation, so-called *séances*, etc.) develop into a large egocentric system capable of thought, feeling, and volition.

Such a subconscious system commonly gives expression to its ideas through automatic writing (or mechanical contrivances like the ouija board) and speech, or, particularly in hystericals, through other forms of automatic motor phenomena of one kind or another. The system is then entirely coconscious. But it may be made experimentally to replace the primary consciousness which then temporarily becomes extinguished and dormant. When this happens, the previously coconscious system becomes an alternating consciousness or self. The method by which this is accomplished is that of external suggestion (hypnotism) or, what in principle is the same thing, that of the subject going voluntarily into the trance state (autosuggestion) as with mediums. In either case the personal consciousness becomes dormant and the coconscious system comes into being and replaces it. The subject will now be found to be in either one of two states; either in the trance state, which is a lethargic condition in which the previously coconscious system continues to express itself by writing or speech, having only control of the hand or tongue, the remainder of the body being in a paralytic condition, corresponding to the dormant personal consciousness; or in a somnambulic state.

In the former state, the consciousness present seems to casual observation to be still coconscious because it continues to make use of the same methods of expressing itself as it did before the personal consciousness became dormant. As a matter of fact, however, it will be found that the personal consciousness has become dissociated and that there is only one consciousness in existence, namely, that which was previously coconscious. This has, therefore, become an alternating consciousness.

In the somnambulic state, the previously coconscious system becomes enlarged, taking on some of the functions, which it had not previously possessed, of the personal consciousness (e. g. general and complete muscular control of the body). The somnambulist is then capable of an independent mental and physical life comparable in every way to that of the personal self. This state is commonly spoken of as a secondary self or personality. In other words, through the induction of dissociation a previously existing coconscious system[1] replaces the personal consciousness and becomes an alternating system. After the alternating phase has become once established and has built up independent experiences of its own, the change from the normal to the secondary phase is readily evoked. There are, of course, other ways by which alternating systems are developed (e. g., B I and B IV[2]) ; I am only describing the way in which a coconscious system may become alternating. It was in this way, as I interpret the evidence, that Sally became an alternating somnambulic personality.

---

1 Of course other dissociated states may be induced in the same individual.

2 An alternating system, originating by dissociation of the personal consciousness, may later become coconscious, as was the fact with B (B. C. A.).

THE ORIGIN OF THE COCONSCIOUS SYSTEM

But how did the coconscious system originate, and how did it come to develop? This is the problem with which we are concerned.

We have already seen that as an alternating personality this phase was a secondary system of mental processes, the centre of the system being certain complexes, instincts, and innate tendencies which once had belonged to the principal system but which at some early time had become dissociated and conserved as dispositions. The recrudescence of these dispositions formed the nucleus of a secondary system which at first, as we shall see, was solely coconscious. It remains to discover the forces which determined the primitive dissociation and to trace the growth of the subconscious system. We shall find, I believe, according to the evidence at hand, that, as the result of conflicts within the consciousness of the child, ideas at an early date in childhood were repressed, split off, and segregated as coconscious ideas. Later they received constant increments from the same source from which they derived their own origin. Thus subconscious complexes began to be formed which later became organized into a system. This subconscious secondary system then began to have experiences of its own, in the form of thoughts and perceptions, distinct from those of the primary system, and thus became in time enlarged into a self. The final and accidental emergence in hypnosis of the complete secondary personality was only the awakening by the force of conflict of an already preformed submerged conscious system under favoring conditions. These conditions were a personal consciousness already dissociated, first by trauma (conflict) and then further artificially by hypnosis. Substantially, the same sort of series of psychological events and the same sort of history I have obtained in another case, that of Maria.[1]

1 This case has been interestingly studied and reported by Mr. C. E. Cory, ("A Divided Self," *Jour. Abnormal Psychol.*, vol. XIV, no. 5) through whose kindness I have been able also to study it from the point of view of this problem.

The source from which we are obliged to draw for information bearing on the origin and development of a subconscious personality is necessarily the fund of subconscious memories. Fortunately we have a fairly full account of these in "the autobiography of a subconscious self" by Sally.[1]

According to the memory of the coconscious personality, the beginning of doubling of consciousness dates back to the time when the child was learning to walk. "Learning to walk," she writes, "was the first experience of separate thoughts. I remember before this there wasn't anything but myself, only one person. . . . It was at this time, too, that I was conscious, not exactly of being a different person, but of being stronger in purpose, more direct and unswerving than I appeared, and of being in a certain sense *opposed* to myself. This feeling was much stronger at some times than at others. Why, I do not know. Then first began my *impatience* with C., who instead of attending to whatever she might be doing would suffer herself to be distracted by a thousand and one things. For instance, in walking, just as I would get interested and eager to go on, down she would flop in a heap to study her shoes, to gaze at the people in the room, or to play with some treasure she had discovered on the floor [curiosity instinct]. *Then* I was conscious both of the child on the surface, so easily affected and diverted, and of the other child who was years and years older (I insist I was older) and stronger."

Sally, when cross-examined about these statements regarding the date of the beginning of double consciousness, and asked for specific instances, made the following additional statement:

1 *Dissociation of a Personality*, chap. XXIII. At first disposed to accept with considerable reserve these subconscious memories, the wider my experience with such phenomena, and the more intensive my studies in other cases, the more credence I am disposed to give to them. Today I am satisfied that this subconscious account is substantially correct, so far as it goes. The hypermnesia exhibited by subconscious processes is truly remarkable, and, if evoked under stringent conditions which will exclude artifacts, is reliable, as has often been demonstrated. This hypermnesia must of course be distinguished from fantasies and fabrications. It is noteworthy that some of Sally's statements of the forces at work in producing dissociation accord with present-day conceptions, although she could not possibly have foreseen and therefore have had even an inkling of these psychological theories.

"She was just a very little girl just learning to walk, and kept taking hold of chairs and wanting to go ahead. She didn't go ahead, but was all shaking in her feet [fear instinct]. I remember her thoughts distinctly as separate from mine. Now they are long thoughts that go round and round, but then they were little dashes. Our thoughts then went along the same lines because we had the same experiences. Now they are different; our interests are different. Then she was interested in walking, and I was too, only I was very much more interested, more excited, wildly enthusiastic. [Instincts of play and self-assertion with emotions of joy and elation.] I remember thinking distinctly differently from her; that is, when she tried to walk she would be distracted by a chair or a person or a picture or anything, but I wanted only to walk. This happened lots of times."

Sally's use of the pronouns "I," "myself," "me," implies a self-consciousness pertaining to this separate train of *opposing* thoughts and feelings as if they were systematized into a self at this period. But we need not be misled by this phraseology or interpret it as meaning that such an organized system existed at this time. There is no reason to suppose that these memories indicate the functioning of anything more than emotional impulses linked with particular ideas so far outside the focus of attention as to be coconscious. I have already pointed out[1] that whenever isolated subconscious perceptions and feelings, like the lost tactile sensations of hysteria, anesthesia, and perceptions and images in the fringe of conscious attention, etc., of which the individual is unaware, are recalled afterwards in hypnosis, the hypnotic personality speaks of them as its own, as if the hypnotic self had a self-existence at the time of the perceptions. The same is true of the personal consciousness when, as is sometime the case, we are able to bring back in abstraction the dissociated ideas of absent-mindedness. We say "*I* thought," "*I* perceived such and such things," "such ideas occurred to *me* and that is why *I* did so and so absent-mindedly." And ye

1 *Loc. cit.*, p. 395.

he recollection represents dissociated coconscious ideas out-
ide the focus of the personal self.  We shall see in the next
hapter that the secondary personality B, in the case of B.
C. A., makes a point of this when describing the early re-
•ellious B complex of "floating thoughts, impulses, desires,
nclinations," which, at first repressed and thereby disso-
iated, developed later into the coconscious personality B.
he insists over and over again that this complex of disso-
iated thoughts and impulses in no sense was constellated
nto a self, an "I," although she finds herself obliged to use
he personal pronoun in describing it, as at the later period it
eemed to be a part of her life-history.  At first it seems to
ave been little more than conflicting *impulses*.  In the case
)f Miss Beauchamp, the hypnotic personality, B II, made
he same distinction in describing the discrete unsystematized
houghts which occurred outside the focus of attention.
he likewise insisted that the necessities of language obliged
ier to use the personal and possessive pronouns "I" and "me"
n describing them, although at the time of their occurrence
hey in no sense constituted a coconscious self.

In interpreting Sally's phraseology, then, we may right-
:ully assume that she "retrojects" her later self or ego into
:he past when speaking of the beginning of the doubling of
:onsciousness, or, more correctly speaking, assimilates and
dentifies the dissociated thoughts with her own life-history.[1]
The first cleavage was undoubtedly in the form of impulses
·*onflicting* with the impulses of the thoughts that occupied
he focus of attention, and the personal pronoun "I" covers
10 more than this.  The former were those of the joy of
walking, of self-elation and play, which tended to carry the
ict to fruition; the latter of interest in "her shoes," "the
people in the room," or some "treasure . . . discovered on
the floor," which suddenly entered the focus of attention
while in the act of walking.  Sally in her ignorance of the
psychological principle of conflicts, merely indicates these
conflicts by such phrases as: "I was conscious . . . of being

---

[1] Like B (B. C. A.), however, she never identifies the ideas of the principal
:onsciousness with herself.

in a certain sense *opposed* to myself"; "my *impatience* with C"; "she would be distracted by a chair, or a person, or a picture, or anything, but I wanted only to walk"; "I wanted to go farther than she did."

Of course at the beginning, these conflicting impulses were only occasional, but it is easy to understand that with the constant repetition of such experiences, the conflicting thoughts and impulses would become more and more disaggregated from the dominating personal consciousness, and as they acquired a wider range, would gather to themselves other ideas, and form organized complexes. As the child grew older and her habits of thought and traits of character began to be formed, the predominating conflicting complex appears to have been a *rebellion,* as in the case of B. C. A., against her own personal attitude of mind and interests. When she was old enough to go to school, for example, the rebellion seems to have been made up of desires and impulses for childhood's pleasures, those of outdoor life, and those which her companions were enjoying while C. (Miss Beauchamp) imaginative and conscientious and serious-minded, was interested in literature (fairy stories), her lessons, and her teachers. It was at this time that she (Miss B.) "used to spend most of her time curled up in the garret away from everyone, and then she was quite happy with her books and day-dreams and visions."

But the other children, her schoolmates, were having a good time enjoying fun and frolics, and C. felt imperative impulses to do these things too; for, as a part of her innate nature, she also enjoyed play. "She was awfully fond of outdoor things — climbing, running," etc., but with the cultivation of the intellectual interests she necessarily had put, to a large extent, these childhood pleasures out of mind, had repressed them. Nevertheless the instincts were all there — conserved. By repressing an instinct we do not get rid of it. We may control it, keep it in subjection, but it remains, conserved as an innate disposition and may function unconsciously. This conservation of a repressed instinct is well exemplified by the behavior of the sexual instinct. Though repressed from childhood, and ever through years of married life, it may later be aroused into activity with the full force of its emotions and impulses. It is only a question of dissociation and synthesis.[1] And so with thoughts. We say we put thoughts that interest us, and, though tolerable, trouble us, or that we cannot bring to completion, questions we cannot solve — *out* of our mind. What we really do, or may do, is to put them *into* our mind.[2] They go into the unconscious or coconscious, and there, under certain conditions, function with happy or unhappy results. In saying this, I am not indulging in theory but merely stating the results arrived at by experimental research. By the use of certain technical methods, the memory of these dissociated thoughts which have been put out of the mind, and which have become thereby coconscious, can be recovered. So when the child gave up the instinct to play and put out of mind certain thoughts, she simply pushed both into the subconscious (unconscious and co-conscious).

One of the things the other children, the boys, enjoyed was playing "hookey" or truant. On the contrary, C. "liked going to school immensely and used to get awfully enthusiastic over her lessons and over her teachers, but I [the coconscious complex] never cared for either. They were so tiresome and uninteresting." Here were conditions that invited a conflict of impulses. The desire for school was antagonized by the desire for play which had been pushed into the subconscious; so, in spite of this liking and enthusiasm for school she, C., played "hookey" but, strangely enough, against her will. "She didn't want to do it but she did"; and what is more, got punished for doing what she didn't want to do. The reason was, as with the B complex

---

1 I fully believe, as the result of observation and experiment, that the sexual instinct is never absent in healthy people of either sex excepting from senility; it is only dissociated when apparently absent.

2 "Some of the Present Problems of Abnormal Psychology." *Congress of Arts and Sciences*, St. Louis, (Transactions) 1904; also, *Psychol. Rev.*, vol. XII, nos. 2 and 3, 1905.

I am not referring to repression in the Freudian sense of intolerable wishes, but in the sense of everyday thoughts that are acceptable, and occupy our interest, though they may involve anxieties and responsibilities we must and properly desire to fulfill.

in B. C. A., the innate impulses to play broke through the subconscious; there was a conflict and the impulses won. As thus stated, you will say there was nothing unusual in this, nothing more than we all have experienced when subjected to temptations, *i. e.*, impulses coming from different sides of one's character. What was unusual was that the impulses came from emotions linked to ideas of which she was not aware, *i. e.*, coconscious ideas. "I," the autobiography recites, "I" [the coconscious complex] suggested things to her sometimes by thinking hard. *I* didn't really do them; *she* did them, but I enjoyed it. I don't know that I made her; I thought about them very hard. I didn't deliberately try to make her, but I wanted to do the things and occasionally she carried out my thought.[1] Most times she didn't, when my thoughts were entirely different from her own. Sometimes she was punished for doing what I wanted; for example, I didn't like going to school; I wanted to play 'hookey.' I thought it would be awfully exciting because the boys did it and were always telling about it. She liked going to school. One day she stayed away all day, after I had been thinking about it for a long time. She didn't want to do it, but she did. She was punished and put to bed in a dark room, and scolded in school and made to sit on one end of the platform; she was shy and felt conspicuous.

"I always knew her thoughts; I knew what she was thinking about on the platform. She was thinking partly of being penitent and partly of fairy tales, so as not to be conscious of the scholars and teacher, and she was hungry. I was chuckling and thought it amusing.[2] I did not think of anything else except that her fairy tales were silly. She believed in fairies, that they were real. I didn't and don't. At this time she was a little girl. I was there during all the life with J.

[1] The same phenomenon was observed in B. C. A. It is analogous to the phenomenon of post-hypnotic suggestion.

[2] This reminiscence reminds us of the trait, later exhibited by Sally when a full blown coconscious self, of which so many examples have been already given. I refer to the coconscious enjoyment of Miss Beauchamp's discomfitures and of teasing her. The latter seems to have had its source in the play instinct as I have already pointed out. The appearance of this trait at this early period is of interest.

nd at ——— College. I never forced her to do things till
ntely. Lots of times when she was a little bit of a thing I
was angry when she wasn't."[1]

The statement in the last paragraph of coconscious joy
nd anger while the personal consciousness was under the
nfluence of an opposite emotion tallies with what I have
many times observed in Miss Beauchamp. Again and again
have seen her features momentarily ruffled with anger, or
t least with unmistakable manifestations of anger, while
he herself was calm and placid, and, *vice versa,* her face
ssumed a merry pleased expression while she herself was in
 state of anxious depression. This momentary expression
ould always be traced to coconscious emotions and thoughts
which often expressed themselves in automatic speech.[2] I
lave experimentally obtained the same phenomena both in
3. C. A. and Miss Beauchamp.

By this time, at the school age, it will be seen the cleav-
nge of consciousness had become more sharply marked, and
he coconscious ideas had increased in complexity and range;
hey had begun to take on functional activity independent
of that of the principal consciousness, and to form a parallel
tream of thought; they had their own sentiments, chiefly
o play, differentiated from those of the main stream of conciousness. The result was that the impulses from the play
nstinct erupted from the subconscious and determined the
oehavior of the personality. In consequence, C. found herself doing things against her will, doing what "she did not
want to do," and not knowing why she did them.

The psychological conditions, when Miss Beauchamp
as a child found herself doing things against her will, were
substantially similar to those described by B. C. A., when
that personality found herself doing things she strongly objected to and was horrified because she did them.[3] The B

1 It is worth noting that this is in entire accord with what used to happen
later when Miss Beauchamp was under observation and Sally was a full-fledged
coconscious self. The former would find herself doing things she did not want
to do and not knowing why she did them. These actions could always be traced
to the thoughts and impulses of Sally.

2 *The Dissociation of a Personality,* p. 275.

3 See next chapter.

complex ruled B. C. A. at times just as the Sally complex ruled Miss Beauchamp. Whether the coconscious complexes in the latter were at this early period, of which I am speaking, constellated into an egoistic system, one that can be properly characterized as a self, it is at this date impossible to say. Nor does it matter. The principle of coconscious activity is alone of importance. The repressed play instinct and sentiments tended to express themselves and, functioning, to develop the coconscious system.

As the child grew older and became occupied with the moral problems of her unhappy life — serious problems for a neurotic, sensitive, visionary child brought up in an unsympathetic atmosphere — she withdrew more and more within herself and gave herself up to introspection, self-criticism, and day-dreaming. Now two consequences followed. The one was the formation of a fixed idea — complex-building — which ruled her life and appeared later as the dominating idea in B I; the other was the widening and deepening of the rift between conscious systems of thought to which different and antagonistic instincts were linked. By this rifting, the coconscious system became still further developed and separated from the personal consciousness.

The fixed idea was the "saintly complex"; visionary that she was, "she believed that God wanted her to save her mother from some dreadful fate, and that in order to do this she must, before the day should come, have attained a certain ideal state mentally, morally, and spiritually. Everything that came up was tested in its relation to this; she was always fretting about it, always dissatisfied with herself, and fancying that she fell short (as she did)." This impossible ideal haunted her day and night — there was no escaping it. She fancied her mother's illness (the autobiography goes on to state) "had all come because of her; that she had fallen short of God's requirements. She tormented herself, and me[1] too, night and day with going over and over and over everything that had happened since she was born, thinking this, that, and the other — that she had not been earnest

1 Note the conflict.

nough, that she had not loved mamma as deeply as she hould, that she had been dreaming away her life instead of cting. It was all rubbish. She had never done anything hen." In other words, she sought spiritual perfection, not s an end but as a means of obtaining something else. This neans was the *repression* of all other sides to her character, he human sides with their instincts of anger and self-asser-ion as well as the play instincts with the joy of youthful pleasures. One effect of this repression was to produce the B I and B IV systems. This is another problem which will be considered in the study of those systems.

Another effect of repression was to push into the cocon-cious certain ideas which were unacceptable and incom-patible with the saintly complex, but which were compati-ble with the already existing coconscious complex. Some of hese ideas consequently became synthesized with this com-plex, which thus became still further enlarged. "Ruled by one idea," the personal consciousness continued, "steadfast and unswerving," striving for one end and seeing and in-terpreting the world about her through this idea, all other points of view and interpretations were disregarded. Per-sons, scenes, incidents were perceived and interpreted through his idea; "seeing things," as the autobiography says, "always rather through her own thought than clearly and truly." Things *were* seen, however, clearly and truly, but cocon-ciously, just as things not perceived in hysterical anesthesia nay be perceived coconsciously. This expansion and autono-mous activity of the coconscious probably would not have happened if another and more effective factor had not been at work to cause a splitting of consciousness; this was her habit of putting herself into abstraction, extreme absent-mindedness, or dreamy states. "She used to go mooning about, not knowing half the time what she was doing." In these absent-minded states she would be day-dreaming of fairy stories (at an earlier period) or of her fancied sins. One incident indicates the depth of this condition of abstrac-tion; it was the occasion of the death of the baby. "C. had been very restless and nervous during the day, had been scolded and sent to bed several times that evening, but had finally managed to steal unnoticed into the room where the baby was kept to prevent its disturbing mamma, for it cried incessantly. She took it in her arms. . . . to soothe it, and after a time it grew quieter; then still more quiet, until finally it gave a curious little gasp and stopped breathing altogether. But C. had not noticed it, for she had entirely forgotten the child in going over and over for the ten thousandth time her sins. She sat there gazing into space until morning, until the nurse came, and for a wonder the nurse wasn't cross. . . . C. did not know until late that afternoon, when she heard the nurse telling some one, that the baby had died in her arms, although I knew immediately that it must be dead."

Abstraction means not only repression but it may be a dissociation, or splitting of the elements of the content of consciousness. Indeed, Janet went so far as to explain the peculiar dissociation of hysterical anesthesia with the formation of coconscious perpetual ideas as chronic absent-mindedness. Here was a powerful factor making for the splitting of personality and the developing of a coconscious system. In the frequently repeated "dreaminess," the stream of perceptions of the environment, neglected by the absent-minded personality, absorbed in one idea, to say nothing of the constant normal stream from the fringe of the conscious field, helped to swell the subconscious reservoir, to form a large coconscious system, independently apperceiving the environment and retaining memories thereof until it became organized into a self with memories and feelings and impulses of its own, and possessing a self-consciousness. At what period this system acquired a self-consciousness it is impossible to say, but it must have been at an early period in youth, about the time the saintly complex began to be formed, and its growth was probably gradual. With dissociation, those apperceptions of the environment which were taken in by the personal consciousness and those which were taken in by the coconscious system differed materially. "As a rule," the autobiography states, "in any given scene or incident, C. would take in only what might be expressed as the thing itself. C II would be conscious of more details, while I would be conscious not only of the thing itself with all its details *but also of much besides.*[1] I say 'C II,' because I do not know how else to express what was in C.'s mind as apart from mine, which she was not conscious of at the time, but which she remembered when hypnotized." It is noteworthy that the memory of these early perceptions accord with the experimental findings at a later period. I was able to demonstrate that a large number of details of the environment were not perceived by the personal consciousness. Many of these were outside the focus of attention (some, indeed, outside the fringe of consciousness). These could be recalled in hypnosis (in the state of B II). They seemed to be simply discrete visual and auditory images, etc., not organized into a system; for instance, those images that occupy the periphery of the field of vision and are not ordinarily perceived unless the individual gives attention to this field. They also, however, included details of the objects in the focus of attention. For, although attention was focused on the object, it was not on the details. For instance, although the personal consciousness would perceive a book in certain relations, it would not perceive certain discolored spots on the cover of this book. In this case the images of these spots would afterwards be remembered in hypnosis (B II) *as having been previously present outside the field of the personal consciousness.* Again, when a scene was reproduced experimentally in a crystal vision, all the subconsciously perceived details would be pictured in the vision — details, of which Miss Beauchamp had not been consciously aware and could not remember. The perception of the coconscious personality (Sally) would include not only all this but also very "much besides" as the autobiography points out. If the object, let us say, was a person, he would be perceived coconsciously in a different mental setting or context from that in which he was perceived by the principal personality, and thus the perception would have a different meaning to the coconscious Sally. Miss Beauchamp perhaps would perceive a certain person as an important personage, interested in

1 Italics mine.

what she was saying, but Sally would perceive the same per
sonage with comical idiosyncrasies, with peculiarities of dress
and disinterested, his mind being on other matters and only
pretending to pay attention. Sally's perceptions would
probably be at the moment more nearly correct, although
there would be truth in both. The difference would depend
upon the difference in the perceptions — Sally's being more
complete in detail — and in the settings into which the perceptions would be assimilated. It is in this sense that the
statement of the autobiography that the coconscious self
was conscious not only of all that the personal consciousness
perceived and of details not so perceived, "but also of much
besides" is to be understood, as I was able experimentally to
verify. Exactly the same coconscious phenomena I have observed in numerous experiments with B. C. A. So the two
systems in Miss Beauchamp "always saw people differently
and hence cared for them in different degrees."

The effect of repeated experiences in distraction in
bringing about a cleavage of the personal system of consciousness I have observed in another case, C. N. This patient for many years has been in the habit of voluntarily
putting herself, many times a day, into a deep state of abstraction, or light hypnosis, for the purpose of fixing facts
in her memory or of recalling past experiences. She has also
indulged the habit with the purpose of deliberately influencing her behavior and attitude of mind. In this state she
puts ideas into her subconsciousness, i. e., builds complexes
in the subconscious, which it is her intention shall not be
overcome by external influences but shall determine her conduct, etc. In this way she has built up a large subconscious
system which emerges from time to time as an alternating
personality and behaves also coconsciously.

In the case of Miss Beauchamp, the coconscious self thus
began to have dissociated experiences of its own — perceptions, thoughts, interests, points of view, feelings, and memories, which necessarily became organized into an independent system. In the beginning of the dissociation in early
childhood, so long as the experiences of the two systems were
the same, the thoughts of the two ran along the same lines

as respects the objects of thought, although the thoughts were different. Later, when the experiences of the coconscious system differed from those of the personal system, and their interests differed, the two systems thought about different things at the same time. This became more marked after the coconscious system had become an alternating phase; then, as each phase had a different life temporally and environmentally, each having its own friends, occupations, pleasures, and experiences in general, the experiences of each radically differed. Each had its own instincts, mental attitudes, desires, and impulses. Each phase had its own storehouse of conserved experiences (memories) upon which it could draw for thought. When the alternating phase became coconscious it still had access to its own storehouse, and thought along the same lines as when an alternating self.

One more factor undoubtedly was at work in the evolution of the subconscious self. I refer to what has been called by James *incubation*. William James, with his remarkable insight into the meaning of things and capacity to open promising vistas for future psychological research, applied this principle to explain the phenomena of sudden religious conversion. He explained these "phenomena as partly due to explicitly conscious processes of thought and will, but as due largely also to the subconscious incubation and maturing of motives deposited by the experiences of life. When ripe, the results hatch out, or burst into flower.[1] Or, in other words, the elements of the ethical complexes of ideas which dominate the mind have been deposited from time to time as the result of the day-to-day experiences of life and conserved in the unconscious storehouse of the mind. The elementary ideas of experiences, of course, have had their source in early education, the "social consciousness," and the everyday occasional, cursory, fleeting or sustained thought of the individual. They have given rise to doubts and scruples of greater or less intensity leading to conscious conflicts disturbing the mind, and desires unfulfilled. They in-

---

1 *Varieties of Religious Experience*, p. 238. *Cf.* also *The Dissociation of a Personality*, chap. XXI, The Psychology of Sudden Religious Conversion; also *Jour. Abnormal Psychol.*, vol. I, No. 1.

clude motives for the solution of the ethical problems of life. All are repressed, "put out of mind," as with an unsolved problem. Conserved in the unconscious, they furnish the formative material out of which the religious belief is to be formed. Such experiences were conscious processes at the time of their occurrence but they were not systematized into a religious belief and linked with the driving emotions required to give a belief its force. In the subconscious, however, they undergo incubation, i. e., undergo re-arrangement and become systematized with one another and all other experiences which are compatible with them. A subconscious torch, so to speak, to change the metaphor, has thus been manufactured out of the formative material deposited by the experiences of life, ready to be set ablaze by a spark when the favoring occasion arises. The spark is some new internal or external experience occurring often in a moment of distraction (dissociation). More literally, a conflict arises between the submerged complex and the personal consciousness; the former becomes the victor and the individual is overcome by the sudden emergence of the unconscious complex. The conversion seems to him miraculous in his ignorance of the unconscious processes that have been at work.

That this principle of incubation is general in its application and soundly based on numerous facts of observation and experiment there should be no doubt. I need cite here only those of the unconscious solution of problems — mathematical, logical, literary, social and scientific — and compositions showing a constructive imagination.[1] After a problem has failed to be solved by conscious consideration, its elements pass into the unconscious where they apparently lie dormant. But active incubation goes on and the solution emerges into consciousness in an apparently mysterious way. The correctness of the principle can be demonstrated experimentally, as when, for examle, a mathematical problem is given in hypnosis to a subject who is awakened before the task is undertaken. Later the answer emerges into con-

---

1 I have quite a collection of such stories, verses, etc., composed by subconscious processes.

sciousness according to the conditions of the experiment.[1]

Applying this principle to the evolution of the coconscious self in the case of Miss Beauchamp, we are entitled to assume that this self was partly due to the "subconscious incubation and maturing of motives deposited by the experiences of life," including in this life both the conscious and coconscious experiences (perceptions, thoughts, etc.). In other words, the early primitive dissociated ideas (wishes for pleasure) assimilated much of this material, so much as was compatible with the subconscious instincts and impulses, and the whole became, by a process of incubation, systematized into a self-conscious system. In view of the fact that from a very early date the personal consciousness was in the habit of repressing many of its instincts, natural innate dispositions, and all wishes and thoughts unacceptable to and incompatible with the saintly complex, a rift being thereby made in the unity of the personal consciousness, a large amount of material must have been dissociated and set free ready for incubation and assimilation by the already existing coconscious complex. The active motive in the incubation was the repressed disposition to play — wishes for pleasure incompatible with the serious interests of the morbid child and the saintly complex. These furnish the motive force for the coconscious system.

By way of summary then we may say that the psychogenesis of Sally was due to several co-operative and successively active factors:

1. Primitive early conflicts between opposing impulses — those of the play disposition and joy *versus* those of curiosity and possibly fear, leading to the dissociation of the former.

2. Formation later of studious interest and of a fixed idea — the saintly complex — in antagonism with the joyous play instinct and frivolous sentiments, etc. By the force of the former the desire for youthful pleasure, such as "outdoor things, climbing, running, etc.," of which "she was

awfully fond," was further and repeatedly repressed into the coconscious system.

3. Dissociation of consciousness through the force of self-cultivated habits of abstraction (absent-mindedness, day-dreaming).

4. General habit of repressing all expression of inner conflicts and innate tendencies of youth.

5. Autonomous subconscious functioning.

6. Subconscious incubation.

7. General synthesization of the coconscious systems thus formed with the experiences of the alternating phases.

There remains the question: What caused the eruption of the coconscious system as an alternating personality?

It will be remembered that the coconscious system first emerged as an alternating system accidentally in hypnosis. On one occasion, after Miss Beauchamp had been hypnotized a few times, it was found that the usual hypnotic consciousness was suddenly replaced by another and unexpected personality, afterwards known as Sally. This personality, at the time, appeared to have spontaneously and suddenly sprung into life as a new creation, fully developed, without antecedent germination — as something totally unlike the normal Miss Beauchamp. But we have already seen that this was far from being the case and that as a coconscious system it had long been in existence; that it had its germ in dissociated ideas split off far back in childhood; that there had been a gradual coconscious growth, passing through the embryonic period, and a prolonged gestation to reach the full maturity of a coconscious self. Its final appearance as an alternating personality was only the parturition of an already developed subsystem.

How came this system to erupt as a personality after so long being held in quiescence? The explanation is to be found in the principle of conflict acting during an unstable condition. This condition was that of an enormously increased state of dissociation of consciousness. It will be remembered that Miss Beauchamp, although supposed at the time to be an ordinary neurasthenic, was in reality a secondary dissociated personality, B I. The discovery was only

made at a later period, but such was the fact. This dissociated personality was again still further dissociated by being
hypnotized. The state of hypnosis is, as is well known, characterized by increased suggestibility and diminished resistance to subconscious influences. This is not only a generalization but was particularly true in this case as was evidenced
time and again by objective manifestations. In the hypnotic
state, as well as in dissociated hysterical states, to which Miss
Beauchamp was subject, the coconscious system easily influenced the personal consciousness and produced automatic
phenomena.[1] The state of a secondary personality in hypnosis was then a particularly favorable condition for the impulses of the coconscious system to repress the personal consciousness and emerge as an autonomous system. That the
impulses of the pleasure-loving, childish, coconscious self
were antagonistic to and in conflict with those of the morbid
saintly personal self almost goes without saying. They had
always been in conflict and they continued in conflict during
the six years while the case was under observation. Any
stimulus which awakened the desires and impulses of this
coconscious self was liable thereby to repress the personal
consciousness, push its constellated system into the oblivion
of the unconscious, there to remain for the time being quiescent, while itself emerged as the dominant consciousness.
When, therefore, in hypnosis, coconscious Sally came to life,
the conditions of the experiment gave not only the opportunity but the stimulus which awoke the desires and impulses that won the victory. Previously the influences of
the principal personality had successfully repressed those of
the coconscious personality; now those of the coconscious
personality were the stronger and repressed the principal
personality.

The final fate of Sally is instructive and, I think, confirmatory of the theory of her psychogenesis here expounded.
She always insisted that if Miss Beauchamp were made well,
if the dissociated systems, B I and B IV, of that divided self
were reintegrated into the original single normal self, she,

1 For example compare *Dissociation*, etc., Index (automatic phenomena,
automatisms, etc.).

Sally, would, as she frequently complained, "go back to where I came from." What she meant was an enigma until the genesis of this coconscious and alternating self was, as a result of this study, understood. The remark was passed over as being inconsequential. But it is now plain it had deep significance. Sally, from the standpoint of her own knowledge, had an understanding of the case, and an insight into some of the psychological principles of personality, as she frequently demonstrated, which psychologists might well regard. "I thought you psychologists knew this," or, "if you psychologists don't know this you don't know much," she would often comment. Now we see what Sally meant when she looked forward to the fate that awaited her.

With the reintegration of the divided self, the previously repressed desires and sentiments of childhood were repressed once more into the realm of the unconscious storehouse of personality, and not only repressed but *suppressed* by the stronger autocratic systems of the real self. Sally "went back to where she came from."[1]

## II. "The Saint" (B I) and "The Realist" (B IV)

### Two Alternating Personalities

#### (a) "the saint"

In the foregoing study of "Sally," we have seen the distinguishing characteristics of the three secondary personalities evolved out of the disintegration and reintegration of the elements of the normal personality. It remains now to make a similar study of the remaining two alternating personalities, B I, the Saint, and B IV, the Realist and practical woman.

The problem of B I is comparatively simple, for her characteristics were essentially, on the one hand, an exagger-

---

1 This, of course, requires fuller explanation; but it is out of the question, even if possible, to go into the details here of the disintegration of Sally and the reintegration of the elements of her personality into one psychic whole.

ation of those habits of mind, of the sentiments and settings and systems of ideas and innate dispositions which from the time she was a child she had intensely cultivated and brought to a high degree of sensitiveness and excitability; and, on the other, a suppression of those sentiments and systems, instinctive dispositions, etc., which were directly antagonistic in their conative tendencies to the former systems. The latter had receded from the field of consciousness and ceased to take part in her personality. To understand the traits of B I emerging out of the break-up we must envisage those of the original Miss Beauchamp.

## (1)   The Psychological Traits of Miss Beauchamp

It should be recalled to mind that Miss Beauchamp was a dreamy and visionary child,[1] and these traits persisted during girlhood, up to the time of the shock that caused the split of personality and the development of B I, which occurred when she was 18 years of age. Her life was a lonely one, particularly in the long school vacations when she "used to spend most of her time curled up in the garret away from everyone, and then she was quite happy with her books and day-dreams and visions." Morbidly impressionable, shut within herself and given to day-dreams, she was unduly under the influence of her emotions. She took everything intensely, lived in a land of idealism, and saw the people and the world about her not as they were "clearly and truly,"[2] but as they were colored by her imagination. That is to say, she saw people as they were colored by her own ideas which dominated her judgment and tended to be insistent. Even as a child she appeared to have hallucinations, or, at any rate, she so mixed up her day-dreams and imaginings with reality that she did not have a true conception of her environment.

---

1  For details see *The Dissociation of a Personality*, chaps. II and XXIII.

2  The autobiography runs: "She was dreamy and visionary . . . in seeing things always rather through her own thought than clearly and truly; . . . She holds to certain beliefs and ideas with unwearying patience. It makes no difference that the facts are all against her. It makes no difference that people never or very rarely live up to her expectations. She still ignores the facts, still idealizes the people."

"As a child and as a girl she had been so much alone, so dependent upon herself for the solution of all problems that troubled her, that she had gradually come to be governed by laws of her own making, ignorant of those already existing for mankind." She was the "shut-in" kind. In spite of her dreaminess, she threw herself with great intensity into whatever she might be doing or had in mind. These traits might have been corrected if there had been any one interested in doing so; as it was, they became habits.

Now, there were three concrete expressions of her idealism which affected her life in years to come. One was the logical reaction to the other two. They were three "*sentiments*," each of which had become incorporated in a large emotional setting of idealism which gave an ethical meaning to the sentiment. These were the dominating dynamic factors in her mental composition.

The first was an out-of-the-ordinary very intense religious sentiment which may be termed *divinity worship*. It involved the *Madonna and Christ* as its object. Miss Beauchamp had developed within herself a religious idealism of a high degree which took on a romantic aspect and sometimes expressed itself in mild mysticism and states of ecstasy. When troubled and perplexed she resorted to prayer for aid and consolation, and then not infrequently a vision of the Madonna or Christ brought peace and comfort to her troubled mind and solved her perplexities.[1] The habit was, undoubtedly, largely due to the condition of her unhappy child-life, in consequence of which there was no one to whom she could turn when in need, and she was thrown back into herself. She lived within herself and dreamed. She thus created a very intense personal sentiment for the Madonna and Christ to whom she turned when in distress. This sentiment was one of *love, reverence, admiration and self-abasement*. William James divides human beings into the "tender-minded" and the "tough-minded." I think we can also divide them, according to the types of their mental processes, into the "mystics" and the "realists." There are more

1 Chap. XI and Appendix L (*Dissociation*, etc.).

mystics of a mild type than is generally realized. Miss Beauchamp might well be classed as a mild mystic. The vividness of the images accompanying her thoughts, the extreme emotionability and tendency to deep revery, the ease with which she experienced actual visions, particularly of Christ and the Madonna, the ecstatic emotions felt at such times and the feelings of direct communion with these divine beings amounting, I think, to what appears to have been at times the direct knowledge of them — all these experiences indicated the mystic type.

The second sentiment was what I have called the *"Mother-worship,"* a similar and related sentiment involving the mother as its object. As far back as the period when she went to school the "shy, nervous, and imaginative" child was "terrified by the appearance of her father," but "worshipped, literally worshipped, her mother," "who," according to the autobiography, "did not, however, care for her and paid her slight attention." "Her whole life, all her thoughts and actions and feelings centred about her mother." Her mother become her Divinity. Perhaps we may say her Divinity was personified in her mother, in that her sentiment for her mother was intimately associated with that for the Madonna; for there is reason to believe that there was much in common in their settings, and that there were organized in both sentiments the same religious emotions, reverence, self-abasement, etc., characteristic of divinity-worship. These emotions with their impulses, striving to give expression to the ideas of divinity and motherhood, would necessarily determine, in many directions, her reasoning, judgments and conduct.

The psychogenesis of these two sentiments offers an interesting subject for speculation, but there is no need for the purpose of this particular study — centering on the forces and mechanisms which brought about disintegration of personality — of our entering into it and I shall not do so.[1] We

---

1 Of course it will be held by many of the psychoanalytic school that the genesis of the divinity-mother worship sentiments was due to an unconscious infantile homosexual wish — the attachment of the sexual libido to the mother and Madonna. I do not accept this interpretation, as a number of facts, not

need only deal with the fact that, at this epoch, two closely related sentiments had been organized, had attained to a large degree the hegemony of the personality and, therefore, were capable of determining behavior and reacting as organized psychic wholes in an autonomous fashion to conflicting impulses. In other words, these organized complexes were capable independently, regardless of any hypothetical subconscious motives, of entering into mental conflicts and disrupting the personality.

The third concrete expression of her idealism was an idea of self as the object of a sentiment which may be defined as *saintliness*. The most obtrusive instinct organized with this idea was that of self-abasement, of which the emotion is negative self-feeling (Ribot) or self-subjection. This instinct was contributed to the idea of self by the "self-regarding sentiment." For the idea of self, regarded as a complex or integrated whole, has, according to this theory, structurally organized within it this sentiment in which two opposing instincts, self-abasement and self-assertion, are incorporated by experiences, but either may be the dominating one. McDougall has argued, and I think soundly, "that the idea of self and the self-regarding sentiment are essentially social products; that their development is effected by constant interplay between personalities, between the self and society; that, for this reason, the complex conception of self thus attained implies constant reference to others and to society in general, and is, in fact, not merely a conception of self, but always one's self in relation to other selves." But, as I shall argue later when considering the realist's conception of self (p. 251), this formulation must be considerably broadened. Every sentiment (and therefore the self-regarding sentiment) has roots in and is consequently related to many dispositions deposited by the experiences of life; it is

necessary to cite, warrant another explanation. They may have it so if they wish. The point is that whatever the origin of these sentiments and the large religious setting in which they were integrated, the sentiments once organized and however formed, contained in themselves their own driving forces or urges (derived from their emotions) which enabled them to act as autonomous psychic wholes and determine behavior. As such psychic wholes they could and did, according to my view, dominate the character, enter into conflicts, and produce various phenomena as will appear later.

related to what has gone before. And the experiences on the part of the self of what has gone before, *i. e.*, what the individual has previously experienced (ideally or realistically) in reference to the object of the sentiment, determines the attitude of mind and point of view towards that object, and is responsible for the organization of the object and emotion into a sentiment. The sentiment is the resultant and the expression of those antecedent experiences. They form its setting and give it meaning beyond the mere emotional tone. *You cannot separate sentiment, conceived as a linked object, and emotional instincts, from such setting. They form a psychic whole.* This is not only theoretically true, but actual dealings with pathological sentiments (in which the principle can be most clearly studied) called phobias, and other emotional obsessions, bring out this intimate relation between the sentiment and the conserved setting of antecedent experiences. Such practical dealings also show not only that the sentiment is the outgrowth and the expression of this setting, but that by changing the setting, the sentiment can be correspondingly altered. I am now little more than repeating what I have said above in the study of Sally. *But I want to emphasize that in the dynamic functioning of a sentiment, the setting co-operates in maintaining and carrying it to the fruition and satisfaction of its aim.*

The content of Miss Beauchamp's idea of self was derived from an ideal of perfection inspired by religious teachings and exemplified by the Madonna, and, therefore, closely associated with the other two sentiments just mentioned. This idea of self was thus referred not only to an object of the environment (society), her mother, but to God, Christ and the Madonna and religious ideals, so that her conception of self included her conception of her relation to Divinity.

Such a conception would be motivated by several emotions — love, self-subjection, awe, reverence, etc. And this ideal she strove to reach in her own person by artificially moulding her character to conform, and by incorporating in her idea of self the concepts of moral and spiritual perfection and obedience to God's wishes. The sentiment thus became set in a context of religious ideas (experiences) forming an organized psychic whole which gave meaning to it as the fulfillment of the Divine Will, etc. It naturally followed that this volitionally cultivated idea of self largely governed her conduct at this time.

The motive for this self-cultivation of perfection was not at first religious but related to her mother.

For some unexplained reason she conceived the idea that some calamity was hanging over her divinity; "She believed," according to the autobiography, "that God wanted her to save Mama from some dreadful fate, and that in order to do this she herself must, before the day should come, have attained a certain ideal state, mentally, morally, and, I think, spiritually. Everything that came up was tested in its relation to this; she was always fretting about it, always dissatisfied with herself, and fancying that she fell short (as she did)." "This impossible ideal haunted her day and night — there was no escaping it, although . . . it was not perfection as an end that she strove for, but perfection as a means of attaining something else." This something else was the saving of her mother. And so she set about perfecting herself in saintliness for this purpose, repressing all the thoughts, ideas, feelings, and instincts that were incompatible with her ideal, and cultivating those that led to ethical and religious perfection. These notions so ruled her that when her mother fell ill — the illness from which she died — the child fancied, the autobiography goes on to state, that it "had all come because of her; that she had fallen short of God's requirements. She tormented herself, and me, too, night and day with going over and over and over everything that had happened since she was born, thinking this, that, and the other — that she had not been earnest enough, that she had not loved Mama as deeply as she should, that she had been dreaming away her life instead of acting. It was all rubbish. She had never done anything then." In other words, it was all her fault that her mother was ill; her mother was suffering because she, the child, had failed to attain perfection.[1] Here was self-reproach with resulting conflicts but it does not appear that at this epoch the latter gave rise to pathological consequences beyond the repression of normal instinctive tendencies and ideas of child life.

This complex sentiment of saintliness, which had been cultivated for years, later, when the disruption of personality occurred as the result of conflict, emerged, as we shall see, and became the dominating characteristic in one of the secondary dissociated personalities (B I). Then, becoming freed from the controlling influences of counteracting and balancing ideas motivated by other instincts, it ruled her conduct and, as a character trait, became developed to a degree that seems almost unbelievable. For to the mind of this later emerging dissociated personality B I, "the Saint," disobedience, selfishness, impatience, distrust, rudeness, uncharitableness, unforgivingness, anger, a failure to tell the truth or a suppressing of half the truth were literally sins and their manifestation wickedness to be cast out by fasting, vigil, and prayer. But this is anticipating a later emergence and development of character traits to be considered in their proper place. For the present, I want to confine myself to a different and earlier formative period.

Her mother died when she was thirteen years of age. Then followed a period of five years between that event and the shock that caused the disruption. The first three of these, when she lived with her father, were characterized by nervous stress and strain, a succession of nervous shocks,

1 This attribution to one's self of the fault of a calamity occurring to a loved person is not uncommon, as we know, in everyday life. In a morbid unreasonable childlike form I have observed it with pathological consequence in another case. The subject, when a child, attributed the death of her mother and of her brother to the fact that she had neglected to pray for them at the times of their respective fatal illness. There resulted a persisting fixed idea that the deaths of these relatives were her fault, and consequent self-reproaches. The original complex, for the most part, remained unconscious, but during the course of her life, even to a late period, it absorbed into its setting (which gave a meaning to her idea-of-self) the common events of everyday life to a remarkable degree and affected her happiness and conduct. Everything unfortunate that happened, or might happen, was apt to be judged as due to her fault, in almost a superstitious way. It required the methods of hypnosis and automatic writing to trace the obsession to its original childhood source. By changing the setting and therefore the viewpoint, the cure was effected. (Cf. above, chap. II; also The Unconscious, chap. XIII.)

frights and unhappiness. At sixteen she ran away from home and never saw her father again. Thus ended the first hystero-genetic period.

It must not be thought that during the succeeding five-year epoch mentioned, particularly the last two years, Miss Beauchamp was yet a saint, or, if you will, even a religious prig. After her mother's death, and more especially after running away from home, she had come under other influences that allowed free play to the expression of her whole personality — to her idealism, to her love of intellectual culture, to her practical adjustment to reality, to her play instinct. In other words there were other sides to her character and these other sides found, to a certain extent at least, expression. Thus, for instance, she took part in more than one youthful, but harmless, escapade, even to donning boys' clothes on several occasions in search of adventure, and giving vent to her play instinct. She was "an original" fast enough, and a new life had come to her. On the other hand, in adjusting herself to reality, her practical side came into activity and found expression as a nurse in a hospital where we find her when the catastrophic disruption of personality occurred. Emancipated from the old environment and conditions of life, and their hystero-genetic forces, she had become relatively normal though probably still somewhat psychasthenic. Nevertheless the artificially cultivated sentiments either still persisted or left their conserved dispositions, organized as unconscious residua, ready to be awakened by an appropriate stimulus.

The divinity-worship persisted, as did also the mother-worship, but in an altered form. While the sentiment of self (saintliness) determined the character of the resulting personality, emerging out of the psychological wreck induced by the shock of conflict, the sentiments of divinity-worship and mother-worship played the principal part in causing the conflict and break-up. For, after her mother's death, another person, known as J—— became incorporated in the mother-complex, substituted — if you like — for the mother, and thereby invested with the same emotions.[1]

1 Later other persons successively became the objects of this divinity sentiment — became her "divinity."

J—— in turn became her human divinity, and in a way personified the closely associated and integrated sentiments of divinity-worship, for he became in her mind invested with many of the heavenly attributes of perfection and of a superior being. Indeed, coming into her life in the time of her distress, she conceived him to be a "heavenly messenger" sent to her in her affliction. Here was an earthly person, a living human being, one of pre-eminently fine character, culture, and ability to whom the shut-in child could turn at last. Save to the Madonna and Christ, never before could she turn to any one. Her mother had disliked her, although the child was not consciously aware of the fact. Coconsciously she knew it and the reason why,[1] and to the mother, the child, yearning for a mother's love, never turned. And so the one person who brought aid, and comfort, and happiness into her troubled mental life and who alone gave opportunity to her longing for self-expression — that imperious demand which if unsatisfied results in individual and social unrest — became invested with the emotions of reverence and self-abasement and was actually felt to be a heavenly messenger, a personification of the divinity sentiment. It was when this ideal came later into conflict with the realities of life that there followed a shattering of the mental structure. Thus in one direction or another her whole life, until recovery occurred and she became adjusted to reality, was largely governed by this sentiment.

1 In this knowledge we have a clue to the genesis of the seeking for saintly perfection. Quite possibly, if not probably, the child *consciously* demanding the mother's love and *subconsciously* being aware of her dislike, there was a subconscious wish or motive to overcome this dislike. The natural thought of a child would be to attain this wish by being 'good,' i. e., attain moral perfection. But how could the subconscious motive induce the personal consciousness to seek this end in this manner without a conscious motive, seeing that the child was not consciously aware of the maternal dislike? If we assume that the unhappy marital relations suggested some unhappy fate for the mother and that there was a natural conscious wish for divine assistance or intervention (in such conditions religious people almost "instinctively" turn to God, as did this child), the subconscious wish could, through communion with God, easily convert itself into the idea of a *divine* wish that the child should be good (attain saintly perfection) to save her mother. Thus the subconscious wish to win her mother's *love* appears in consciousness through rationalization in a disguised form as God's wish that she *save* her mother from a "dreadful fate." But this, of course, is largely speculation although based on facts.

Before attempting the study of the mechanism of this disruption, itself, of the personality and the conflicting forces which occasioned it, it will be well to consider the effect of the formation of the three sentiments I have described upon the personality as it existed at the age of thirteen, during the mother's lifetime.

The building of such sentiments involved two processes — one of synthesis, the other of dissociation or repression. The former consisted in the organization, about the objects of the sentiments, of the innate instinctive emotional dispositions appropriate for the sentiment. These emotional dispositions have been already described — love, reverence, self-subjection (submission), etc.

The impulses of these dispositions not only tend to carry the ideas of the sentiment to frution, but to repress and suppress the impulses of the antagonistic instinctive dispositions and the sentiments in which they are organized. This is the second process. If this were not so, a sentiment or ideal would not be effective in determining behavior. There would be constant conflicts of impulsive wishes; and which impulse would get the upper hand and determine the character of the personality would always be a matter of doubt. We might have a vacillating and an oscillating character, such as so often is met with, never fixed, but first governed by one ideal and then by another. When moral issues are involved, such characters oscillate between good and evil impulses — weak characters, we call them. For a sentiment to dominate the character, for Kant's "categorical imperative" to take control, antagonistic impulses must be repressed and suppressed. Hence it was that in the successful building up of the three dominating sentiments in Miss Beauchamp's character — saintliness, divinity-worship, and mother-worship — the opposing innate dispositions and tendencies and the sentiments in which they were incorporated were repressed. Thus *self-assertion and pride* were repressed and suppressed by the impulses of self-abasement (submission). And likewise, by the conative forces of the other cultivated emotional dispositions, it resulted that *anger*, the disposition to *play, jealousy, hatred, ingratitude* and other compounded emotions, and the sentiments formed with them, were suppressed and cast out of her character. This continued so long as the three dominating sentiments were successfully cultivated.

We shall see what happened when the disruption of personality occurred, and what were the forces which brought it about.

## (2)  The Emergence of the Saint, B I

Miss Beauchamp, notwithstanding a certain degree, perhaps, of hysterical instability that may have existed, was, at any rate, a practical unity, an integrated single consciousness from at least the time of eloping from home to the summer of 1893 when the catastrophe occurred. Whatever coconscious mentation (later synthesized and emerging as "Sally") may have gone on, it did not practically affect the unity of the personality. At the time she was following the vocation of a nurse in a hospital, a vocation for which she had for long had an idealistic longing.

The shock occurred during a dramatic interview at the hospital door in the setting of the darkness of night and a terrific thunder-storm, with peals of thunder and flashes of lightning which at intervals lit the face of her companion and revealed expressions of human feeling. Her companion was her "divinity" — the "heavenly messenger," who had been the object of her sentiment of reverence, self-subjection and gratitude. We must keep this in mind if we would understand the psychical trauma. In her mental complexes he was one to be worshipped as a being of a superior order. Much older than she, he was the embodiment of the spiritual and the ideal and not to be thought of in ordinary human relations.

What happened was this, according to the testimony of the different personalities. Its emotional significance may be best understood through the vision by which it was reproduced in the mind of B IV. (This personality, be it remembered, had amnesia for the episode, her memory for her life ceasing just before its occurrence and beginning again only at the moment of her emergence as a personality six years later.) [1]

To obtain the vision I said:

"Fix your mind [for a vision], and *see* whether you saw him again that night." She looks straight forward and falls into a dreamy state. "I have got it, Dr. Prince. It is curious. I see there are two. No, I don't get it." [Then, much agitated, and withdrawing from what she sees]: "No, it is impossible! No, it is not true! No, no, no! I see nothing true! I hear nothing!" [She shrinks as if in great mental distress.] I urge her on, saying, "Look, you see yourself outside the hospital." She repeats again, "It is not true! That did not take place! I see nothing true! I hear nothing true!" She continues denying and resisting. I insist, though she seems in mental anguish, as if re-enacting what is before her. She again "fixes" her mind, and apparently follows a scene. "I can see two — [a pause]. No! I would tell you if what I see were true! We separate — [a pause]. No, I can't tell you!"

"Do you see yourself?"

"Yes, I see myself."

"With whom?"

"Jones; but not like himself. All is dark except for the flashes of lightning." She seems abstracted and answers dreamily: "It is not Jones at all — his face is all drawn, and he is very much excited." Then, coming more to herself, "He was very nervous and excited — not like himself — and as I saw myself I seemed so, too. It was dark, and lightning flashes lighted up my face and his. I was frightened."

"Where were you?"

"It must be outside the hospital door. I am absolutely sure it is not true. The vision is gone. It was all very horrid. I don't like visions like that. It never happened. [Looking again.] I can't tell you more. No, I can't hear anything. Now, I see only the trees. He seemed perfectly mad. [She shrinks and shudders.] Don't ask me to tell you more; I can't!" [She moves her lips inarticulately, as if physically

---

1 *The Dissociation of a Personality*, p. 223.

ınable to speak (aboulia?) and I allow her to come to
ıerself.] . . .

Sally now bounced into existence, highly excited, and
)egan vehemently to contradict B IV's statement that the
vision "was not true." "It is true. It is true," she ex-
:laimed. Then Sally, *while thinking about the vision,* became
ad, dreamy, and depressed; then suddenly changed back to
} IV, who said the vision had come again but that it was
ıot true.[1]

The veridicality of the facts revealed in this vision was
:onfirmed by the memories of the other personalities B I
ınd B II (the normal reintegrated self) as well as by Sally.

This traumatic episode had for a consequence two rev-
:lations: one actually known, the other more or less infer-
:ntial. The first was the intellectual revelation that her
'divinity" was, after all, no "heavenly messenger" but only
mortal, and the realization of this fact — nothing very extraordinary in itself — was the disillusionment of her ideal.
The second, somewhat inferential but one which I have
strong reason for believing, was a revelation of herself to herself. It was the awakening of the previously dissociated sexual
emotion. Rightly or wrongly, in the, to her, excited features
of her companion she thought, at least, that she recognized
this emotion, and she herself probably momentarily experienced manifestations of the same instinct without realizing
their meaning. This accounts for her intense *horror, aversion,* shrinking and agitation, and the force of the two dis-
illusionments — the discovery of the human side of her
divinity, on the one hand, and of her own sexual nature, on
the other.

The effect of these two revelations was twofold: first
the awakening of the two instincts, repulsion and flight, with
their strong impulses and emotions of aversion and fear. We
are not obliged to imagine, or depend upon the statements
of the subject for the complex emotional state that ensued,
for in the crystal vision of the scene it was reproduced and
lived over again and exhibited in a dramatic form before

1 *Loc. cit.,* pp. 220-222

my eyes.[1] In both the original scene and the reproduction
she was horrified by the revelation and this feeling was
heightened by the dramatic situation in which the scene
occurred and which was reproduced.

In another and older person, the reaction to the revelation of the facts probably would have been different. The
first disillusionment might have brought on anger and self-
assertion coupled with aversion. But the pugnacious anger-
reaction and that of self-assertion had long been repressed
and dissociated. To the second disillusionment, the revelation of herself to herself, she might have reacted by submit-
ting to the force of the awakened sexual instinct. In this
young divinity-worshipping soul, in whom the instinct of
self-assertion had long been suppressed, there was special
danger of such submission owing to the domination of the
contrary instinct of self-abasement sedulously cultivated. In
face of this danger, the first defensive reaction, therefore,
was a composite of the two instincts, fear and aversion —
and she fled, horrified.

The secondary effect of the two revelations, after a
period of incubation, may also be called a defense reaction
if that aspect of such reactions appeals to one. This effect
was the later-awakening of and bringing into dominance
once again the conflicting saintly complex, the evolution of
which, by cultivation, and its hegemony during the life-time
of the mother has been described.

This did not occur immediately but only gradually,
after a period of so-called incubation, in the course of a
week. Such a period, as we know by experience, is common
in the traumatic hysterical psychoses, such, for example, as
"shell shock" and "railway-spine." During this week the
saintly complex, awakened by the experiences she had just
gone through, came to the rescue of her anguished mind.

---

1 This vision occurred spontaneously several times. I want to say again that
I do not believe that what occurred justified socially the intense reaction on the
part of Miss Beauchamp, or that to-day, in her normal condition, the episode
would appear to her as anything very extraordinary. It must be remembered
that the subject was then dominated by an extravagant ideal and the saintly
complex, and saw things, "not truly as they were," but only the ideal which
exaggerated or distorted the perceptions.

And necessarily the processes of repression and dissociation of antagonistic sentiments and tendencies, by the force of the impulses of the emotions organized in the revived complex, began to get in their work. Impelled by the instinct of flight (and fear) she fled, and broke off (probably unjustly and unreasonably) all relations with the person who was the cause of her distress. She refused to answer or read explanatory letters, she avoided the society of others, and, so far as her duties permitted, all alone she walked the fields by day and the wards of the hospital by night, brooding over her twofold disillusionment.[1]

The flight from the cause of the trauma was identical in principle with the psychological flight and shrinking of the "shell-shocked" soldier from the dangers of the trenches. And in the one case as in the other, the revival, even in memory, of the experiences which caused the mental trauma re-induced the same emotional effects — hysterical stigmata.

Thus stimulated into activity, the saintly complex, or idea of self in relation to God, came to life and occupied the content of consciousness to the exclusion of all else in her broodings. Under the domination of this idea with its powerful emotions (love, reverence, awe, subjection, etc.), not only the sexual instinct but all the instincts and sentiments opposed to it and incorporated in the realistic side of her character became unacceptable and intolerable. They were therefore repressed and dissociated. So likewise was it with the instincts of pugnacity and self-assertion and play and others which were also repressed.

Described in everyday language, without psychological technicalities, all this might be told in very simple words. Her reactions were not very different from what occurs to any one who has received an intense emotional shock from the revelation of a truth which has come in conflict with and shattered his previous expectations, hopes, or ambitions. Under the influence of a great grief, from the loss or disgrace of a loved one, or overwhelming anxiety over

---

1 The shock from a somewhat similar disillusionment caused a disruption of personality in the case of B. C. A.

an inevitable calamity, or even violent anger from an affront
the average person withdraws from his social environment; his mind is dominated by his emotion; a single group
of ideas, representing the painful memories of his disillusionment and his present situation, occupies his mind
to the exclusion of all else; to these ideas and affects
he gives himself up, perhaps nursing and worshipping
them; all his previous ideals and other counterbalancing
thoughts and points of view and feelings are excluded
from his consciousness and thereby dissociated. Those instinctive processes with their emotions which are incompatible with those which overwhelm and direct his personality are necessarily inhibited. Such a person, for the time
being, is in an acute dissociated state. We recognize this
fact when we say he is shaken by his grief or whatever the
shock may be, and say, "give him time and he will 'get hold
of himself'; or, 'regain himself.' " It is also popularly recognized that the condition is an hysterical one. But it is only
an acute dissociation with an obsessing idea.

As time goes on, he follows one of two courses: either,
as most commonly happens, he awaits the effect of time —
the painful emotions begin to lose their intensity; the memories begin to fade and become less insistent; the repressed
systems emerge again and the person "becomes himself
again," in full possession of his former interests, tendencies,
and instincts; or, he turns for defense against the painful
memories to some interest that has counter impulses and
emotions. In a change of occupation or scene he finds new
pursuits and interests, and gradually readjustment of his disturbed equilibrium takes place. If the person is a woman
and, like Miss Beauchamp, has deep religious traits, she is
likely to turn to religion for solace and compensation, and
to find relief in prayer and communion with God. Her mind
is then dominated by religious ideas to the exclusion of the
realistic side of her character. In mediaeval times, such persons often entered the cloister as a refuge where, isolated
from the world and associations that would keep alive the
painful memories and their conflicts, they pursued their
new religious interests; and the disrupted personality was

again established. In psychopathic individuals, like Miss Beauchamp, the reaction to an emotional "shock" is often extreme; the synthetic restitution of the dissociated elements fails to occur and the condition then becomes prolonged and chronic as a state of hysteria.

But to return to the analysis, what became of the sentiment of divinity-worship of the "heavenly messenger" — the messenger to whom her sentiment of mother-worship (grafted upon and derived from the Madonna-worship) had been transferred? (p. 239). Was it repressed? Not at all. By the new experiences of the 1893 shock, the setting of this sentiment was altered, the old roots were thereby killed, new roots were established, *a new point of view created*, and *the sentiment was disintegrated and killed.* The "messenger" became just an ordinary mortal as seen from the new point of view. This is precisely what happens in the cure of a pathological sentiment (obsession) by whatever therapeutic method it is accomplished.

But the original sentiment, divinity-worship of the Madonna and Christ, as might be expected under the circumstances of disillusionment, and its intimate relation to her idea of self, with its love of God, persisted in intensified degree. To it she fled from the harrowing reality of life and in it she found consolation.

Thus, by such mechanisms, there was a re-awakening of the dominating complexes of her former self, the basic structure of her idealism — divinity-worship and saintliness-idea of self — and a reversion to those components of that self. But there was more than this. There was by the force of conflict a suppression of all antagonistic complexes and tendencies, and, therefore, of the realistic side of her character. By these two processes, there ensued a change of personality, which included an exaggeration and intensification of the idealistic side of her former self. Thus she became B I, the Saint — the Saint in whose thoughts pride, disobedience, selfishness, impatience, distrust, rudeness, uncharitableness, unforgivingness, anger, a failure to tell the truth, or suppressing half the truth were literally sins, and their manifestation wickedness to be cast out by fasting vigil and prayer.

## (B) "THE REALIST," B IV

The genesis of B IV, the Realist, is a much more difficult problem than that of B I. To understand the psychological mechanism that came into play, one ought to be familiar with the principle and the phenomena of *displacement* and *substitution*. By this principle a particular complex, or system of complexes, is crowded out of, *i. e.*, switched out from the personal consciousness and another previously dormant complex, or system, is substituted for it. This is effected by an appropriately attuned stimulus, a conflict and repression. Of course it is a normal phenomenon of everyday life; and the principle governs many of the changes that daily occur in the hegemony and consequent behavior of the normal personality. It is exemplified, for example, in changing *moods*. But in pathological conditions it is often seen in sharply outlined concrete form; and its resulting manifestations are manifold. The solution of the problem of B IV which I offer involves this principle. But before touching it let me rehearse briefly the historical facts.

It so happened that the first appearance of B IV occurred in my presence. Miss Beauchamp, in the personality of B I, had lived a continuous existence for six years.[1] One day, shortly after leaving my consulting room in good condition, she suffered an emotional "shock" of the following character. She had received a letter, the tone and language of which recalled the scene on the memorable night of August, 1893, when she received the shock which had changed Miss Beauchamp to B I. It brought the whole experience vividly back to her. She became highly nervous and excited, and then and there *had a vision of the scene when she met the writer of the letter outside the hospital door. She could hear his voice speaking as he did then;* and

---

[1] Excepting, of course, for the interruptions due to the emergence of the subconscious Sally during the last year after coming under my observation, as already described.

he emotional whole — the letter, the visual and auditory
allucinations and the memory — gave her an overwhelming
iock, agitating her as she had *been agitated six years before.*
*he was profoundly moved and upset.*[1] This was accentu-
ted by a second shock received a few moments later from
isreading the headlines of a newspaper, probably through
allucination. After returning home, her mental condition
as such that even coconscious Sally became alarmed, wrote
er a letter correcting her delusion to calm her, and sent for
ie. Visiting her a few hours afterwards, I found her in a
ondition of intense nervous agitation, fatigue, depression
nd reticence, such as indicated great mental strain. She
:arcely spoke, answering questions only in monosyllables.
he was, as it afterwards became clear, in a semi-delusional,
: not "twilight," state. Suddenly, and without apparent
ause, an extarordinary change came over her. She became
ranquil, natural and apparently normal and sociable.

It was a new personality, B IV.

## (1) Character Traits of B IV

Let us study the character of this personality from the
oint of view of innate and acquired dispositions. B IV in
iost respects was the antithesis of the Saint, and properly
iay be called the Realist. She had individual peculiarities
f character, of disposition, of temperament, of tastes, of
abits, of memory, and of physical health, which sharply
istinguished her from B I. Even many of her physiological
eactions to the environment were different.[2] But the points
f chief interest for us now are that a number of the emo-
ional instincts and other innate dispositions which were dis-
ociated from the personality in the synthetic composition
f B I, left over, so to speak, were gathered up and retained

1 The emotional effect of this letter may be gathered from the effect produced
n the normal whole personality in hypnosis (B II) when I put the question to
licit a memory of the occurrence. At once she was thrown into a state of
error, shrinking from me as one might from a horrible dream. Her mental
istress was manifested in her features.

2 A large number of these contrasted traits peculiar to each personality have
een tabulated and are worth studying. (*Loc. cit.*, p. 288.)

in that of B IV, while *vice versa*, certain ones which, we have seen, were retained and appeared extraordinarily active in B I, were dropped out in the construction of B IV. And, correspondingly, certain sentiments for which the lost emotional dispositions were essential constituents were respectively absent in one or the other; and even the same object was sometimes organized with a different set of emotions in each, giving rise to different kinds of sentiments in regard to it.

Thus the *instinct of self-abasement,* which was so dominating a characteristic of the Saint, was entirely left out of B IV; while on the other hand the opposing *instinct of self-assertion,* dissociated from the Saint, was retained in B IV and was an equally dominating characteristic. Correspondingly, *the idea of self,* incorporated with the "*self-regarding sentiment,*" was organized with self-abasement in the Saint and with self-assertion in the Realist, B IV. In consequence, the former was submissive to the degree of humility and dependent on authority, while the latter was self-assertive, independent, self-reliant, masterful, and resentful of control. McDougall, with keen insight and analysis, has argued that the self-regarding sentiment is organized with these two innate dispositions, but in different degrees in different individuals, and with the growth of the mind one may replace the other in the adaptation of the individual to the changing environment. Taking two extreme types, he draws a picture of the proud, arrogant, self-assertive, domineering person, with the feeling of masterful superiority and angry resentment of criticism and control, one who knows no shame and is indifferent to moral approval and disapproval. In this personality the instincts of self-assertion and anger are the dominating innate dispositions of the self-regarding sentiment. On the other hand we have the type of the submissive, dependent character, with a feeling of inferiority, when the contrary disposition is the dominating one. McDougall's analysis was beautifully illustrated by these two personalities, fragments of the original self, which were actual specimens from real life of his theoretic types. Again, McDougall's theoretic analysis of the conception of self, showing the idea to be one "always of one's self in relation to other selves," is concretely illustrated and substantiated by the dissection of this mind, effected by trauma. But, as an important addition to this theory both from a structural and dynamic point of view, I would insist, again, that the complex conception of self includes a setting of mental experiences of much wider range, in which the idea of self is incorporated and which gives the idea meaning. The range of this setting extends beyond other "selves" and may include almost any of life's experiences. Concretely, and more correctly, the psychological interpretation of the "reference to others and society in general," of the relation of one's self to other selves, would in this particular instance be as follows: The Saint's conception of self (with the self-regarding sentiment) was related to an ideal world and ideal selves contained in religious conceptions; and hence it became organized in a larger setting which gave it a meaning of divine perfection such as is obtained, or aspired to, by saints, and in which were incorporated the emotional dispositions of awe, reverence, love, self-abasement, etc. This conception was not a product of, or related to, the social environment. Rather it was the product of an ideal world. She, as has been said, lived in a world of idealism, oblivious of the realities round about her, which she saw not "clearly and truly" but as they were colored by her imagination. Her idea of self thus became the "saintly sentiment" of self-perfection.

On the other hand, the conception of self of B IV, the Realist, was related to and set in the realities of this social world as they clearly are, the world of her objective environment. And in this conception of self, the instinctive dispositions of self-assertion and anger contributed the promptings and motive force to dominate these realities and bend them to her will. Corresponding to this conception, it was the persons and conditions and affairs of actual life that touched her interest rather than religion and the church to which she was antipathetic. This relation of this self to the actual world of realities was *displayed in certain corresponding traits* which were manifested by B IV and which were absent in B I, who exhibited diametrically opposite traits *corresponding to her own conception of self.*

Thus the former never voluntarily entered a church nor read devotional books; the latter was very fond of church and read many devotional books by preference.

The former, with an eager interest in general affairs of the world, devoured newspapers; the latter never read them and cared little about what was going on in the world.

The former delighted in meeting new people;[1] the latter was morbidly averse to them and confined herself to old friends who belonged to her world of idealism.

The former, who read very little, as a realist preferred books dealing with facts, the latter, who read a great deal, as an idealist loved books of devotion, poetry and novels in which she could live in a world of imagination.[2]

Similarly, corresponding to the instinct of self-assertion, incorporated in the self-regarding sentiment of B IV, and to the instinct of self-abasement in that of B I, could be traced, respectively in each, certain logically resulting traits. For instance, the former self was extremely self-reliant and self-assertive; the latter very dependent and submissive.

The former exhibited the vanity of a consciousness of superiority and felt she was quite capable of running the world; the latter was free from such vanity and conceit.

The former was unwilling to take advice or submit to control; the latter was ready to take the one and submit to the moral help of the other.

The former had an indomitable will and obstinacy, if only to have her own way; the latter was easily influenced and yielding.

The former was selfish in that she considered only herself and her personal convenience; the latter was the exact opposite, always considerate of others.

It will be remembered that the Saint was absolutely devoid of the instinct of anger. But the innate disposition was

1 Possibly the herd instinct (if there is such an instinct) took part in this trait.

2 For a tabulation and discussion of the distinguishing traits of character see *The Dissociation of a Personality,* chapter XVII.

not absolutely *suppressed;* it was dissociated only and switched off from the personal systems of B I and on to those of the Realist. It followed the principle of *switching.* In B IV, anger was a paramount instinct and gave rise to traits that obtrusively distinguished her; so much so that I frequently used it as a test to recognize which personality I had to deal with. I would make a remark which would, as I knew, be accepted submissively by the Saint, but if the Realist was before me, the tapping of the foot on the floor, or the compression of the lips would betray the boiling anger within.

Thus it was that B IV was quick-tempered and subject to violent rages which nothing could restrain; while B I was amiable, even-tempered and never angry;

That B IV was rude if opposed and apt to be intolerant at all times; but B I never;

That B IV was quick to take offense and to retaliate; she wore a chip on her shoulder, while B I never took offense;

That B IV fought Sally day and night, while B I never quarrelled with Sally, no matter how deeply she suffered from her tormentor.

This "switching" of an organized disposition is most aptly illustrated by the transference of *acquired* dispositions from the personal system of one phase to the other. For instance, there were times when the knowledge acquired by B I through study, such as French, Latin and shorthand, was lost by B I but switched on to B IV, who conversely did not possess it if possessed by B I. Likewise what was learned by B IV was often not possessed by B I unless lost by the former; it was thus switched off from B IV and on to B I. What forces brought about this switching was not inquired into. It may well have been some kind of conflict, for conflicts were in continual operation between the two systems.

The presence or loss of the chief *innate dispositions with their emotions* has been tabulated in the preceding study of Sally. To this the reader is referred, but a few words may be added about one or two of them.

*Sympathetic innate tendencies:* Without stopping to

inquire into the somewhat difficult problem of *sympathy*
but assuming that this is equivalent — to use McDougall'
phrase — to the "sympathetic induction of emotions" an
that it requires (?) a specialized innate mechanism, ther
was a marked difference in the characters of the two per
sonalities in this respect. The Saint, as might be expecte
from such a character, was intensely sympathetic. The joy
and sorrows, the pain and suffering of others induced th
same lively emotions in herself, while the Realist remaine
apparently unmoved. I say "apparently," for, as will b
presently told, she so objected to the idea of being the sor
of person the Saint was, that she repressed and suppresse
such emotions with might and main. At any rate, the differ
ence manifested itself practically in different and opposin
traits. For instance:

B IV hated illness and had a morbid horror of every
thing connected with it; while B I loved to be with peopl
who were ill and suffering.

B IV hated charitable and altruistic work, visiting an
reading to invalids and old people, visiting the poor, etc.
B I loved such things.

B IV detested old people; B I was devoted to them.

*Tender feeling; the parental instinct; love.* It is difficult to decide to what extent these were present or eradi-
cated, if such was the case, from the Realist. She had suc
a strong aversion to feeling these and, indeed, any emotions
that she concealed them if she had them. At any rate, sh
manifested no traits that can be ascribed to them but di
show some that suggested their absence. Thus B IV regarde
children as a great nuisance while B I was very fond of them
Likewise, while the latter did not hesitate to exhibit her fondness for certain friends, I did not note that B IV ever did
and further she was decidedly averse to forming friend-
ships. She kept every one at a distance.

*Suggestibility.* B IV was equally suggestible with B I, a
would be expected with dissociated personalities. This fact
when contrasted with the difference in the respective sympathetic reactions of the two, is some evidence in favor of dis-

inguishing between sympathy and suggestibility as psycho-
ogical mechanisms.

*Emotionalism.* Notwithstanding the failure of B IV to
react sympathetically to emotions, she was far from free from
hem. They were intensely induced by other objects and
hrough other channels. "Music, religion, scenery, a poem,
a story, or the personality of an individual aroused intense
feelings, pleasant or unpleasant, which swayed B I irresistibly
and threatened to dominate IV. Even in recalling to memory
a scene of the past, each lived over again all the feelings experienced at the time. Of the two, probably the feelings of
IV were the more intense. But there was a great difference
in the behavior of I and IV to these emotions. B I's life was
given up to their influence. In the play of her mobile features every feeling could easily be read. But IV fought
against them, trampled upon them, resisted them with all
her might and main. She was determined that she would
not be under the influence of her emotions, whether of religion or music, or of those coming from the personal influence of another. She, indeed, concealed this side of her
character successfully for a long time, pretending that she
was indifferent to all that really affected her intensely."[1]
The explanation of this behavior is that remembering, as
B IV did, her early emotional character and life as an idealist, she, being a realist, was determined she would no longer
be that kind of a character and fought against her emotions
or avoided everything that gave rise to them. And here an
apparent paradox is presented, but it is only an apparent
one. B IV had an aversion, as already stated, to religious
services, including the music, and yet she was emotionally
stirred by them. This is easily accounted for on a well-
known psychological principle. The emotions emerged from
the religious complexes of B I, which, though dissociated and
dormant, were technically, of course, subconscious. Vibrant
with emotion, they sent their thrills of feeling through her
whole being. (Numerous and varied examples of this principle were observed in this case. It is the same as that governing some types of phobias in which the emotion derives

1 *Loc. cit.,* p. 295.

from the conserved dispositions of long forgotten experiences.) The principle of habit also played a part.

*Acquired dispositions.* Here we have to do with *intelligence.* Of the major sentiments, that of the conception of self was the dominating one in determining behavior, and practically the most important. Of this sufficient has been said. But the negative aspect is equally important; that is to say, the elimination from the character complex of the great dominating sentiments of the Saint — the divinity one, and the saintly conception of self — with which the Realist's conceptions of the realities of life and her sentiment of self were in conflict. These conceptions and sentiments of the *one* and the *other* were irreconcilable and necessarily led to an irrepressible conflict. On the minor sentiments, relating to the unessentials of everyday life, there is no need to dwell, as we are only concerned with the forces that took part in the disruption of personality.

The general intelligence of the Realist needs only a word. It was on the same level with that of the Saint, but being freed from the emotions and unpractical sentiments of the latter, particularly the saintly conception of self, on the one hand, and being in contact with the world of realities, on the other, her judgments were better balanced. The self-regarding sentiment with its masterful instinct of self-assertion, reinforced by anger, enabled her to cope with the realities of life. And yet, being a dissociated personality, her judgments were unbalanced when a problem involved the whole self. Thus she could not appreciate the necessity of reconstructing the complete normal personality and the impossibility of her own dissociated self continuing as a persisting personality.

The general intelligence and culture, however, were of a high order, although as has already been pointed out, certain acquired dispositions — knowledge of French, Latin, shorthand, etc. — were at times switched off.

Such were the main character-traits of the Realist. The difference in the reactions of the two personalities to one and the same stimulus should be pointed out before leaving this aspect of the problem. This difference was due, of course, to the differing innate and acquired dispositions retained and lost by each. Thus, for example, when feeling anxious and worried about some circumstances, the Saint would react with depression, a feeling of helplessness, submission to fate, patience and recourse for relief to prayer and church; the Realist, with violent anger, defiance and rebellion against the world, self-assertion with rejection of all previous good resolutions to accept rules of conduct, and, as an outward act of behavior, perhaps, the destruction of the product of intellectual work that had involved hours of laborious effort.[1]

In this description of the character-traits of B IV, and in contrasting them with those of B I, I have simply assembled facts of observation. It is an obvious interpretation, if not wholly such a fact, that in the one phase were mobilized into a functioning whole certain of the innate and acquired dispositions which were repressed from the other phase; and that of these acquired dispositions, certain important ones (sentiments) were the product of the social environment. And conversely in the other phase (B I) were mobilized certain other of the innate and acquired dispositions; and that of the latter, certain sentiments were the product of an intensive, artificial self-cultivation — artificial in the sense of not being the natural outgrowth of the environment, but of a volitional premeditated self-education. Of course some dispositions (innate and acquired) were common to both. In other words, the elements of personality were mobilized into two differentiated integrated systems forming two different resulting and contrasting characters.

That these two mobilizations should come into *conflict* was inevitable in view of the irreconcilable instinctive impulses of their instincts, sentiments and ideals. As this antagonism has an intimate bearing on the theory of the dissociation of the normal self into these two phases, it needs to be more concretely introduced into the evidence.

The respective mental attitude of the Realist and the

---

1 *Loc. cit.*, p. 298.

Saint toward each other, and of the former toward her character as a young girl are noteworthy. Thus, the B IV phase, in the course of the reconstruction of the complete normal self, raised intense objections to being infected with the points of view, the ideals and the emotions which dominated the personality of B I; she equally objected to being the kind of person she used to be as a girl, before her emancipation after her mother's death, for these same traits were then dominant, as we have seen, although not in so exaggerated a form. It was this intense resistance, manifested by angry rebellion and shrinking, that was at the bottom of the obstacle which I so long encountered in amalgamating the several personalities into one whole. It was a force which was well nigh insuperable. "Don't make me B I, Dr. Prince, it is giving me all that I most dread," she wrote (p. 412). She was afraid of being "infected," as I have already explained in my first publication, "with B I's saintliness," and all that it carried with itself. It maddened her to think she was that kind of a person. So strong was the antagonism that she systematically gave suggestions to herself that were intended to counteract, when hypnotized, any suggestions that I might give to bring into consciousness the complexes of B I and fuse the personalities (pp. 446-450, 492). In hypnosis, as B IVa, all the concentrated essence of this antagonism broke out and for hours resisted every suggestion with constantly repeated counter autosuggestions. It prevented fusion in that it induced the replacement of the hypnotic state by the waking phase of B IV, or inhibited my suggestions. When, at times, I was in a measure successful in overcoming this antagonism and fusing the personalities, the B IV phase, then recovering memories of the sentiments and ideals of her other side, became maddened at the thought of becoming transformed into such a character. "Not like B I, not like B I! Never!" she exclaimed (p. 490).

On the other hand, the other phase, B I, was equally antagonistic to the B IV side. When this phase learned what sort of ideas ruled her in the B IV phase, she was inexpressibly ashamed, humiliated, frightened, and begged forgiveness. She repented in sack-cloth and ashes. These ideas shocked her saintly conceptions and were intolerable (pp. 407-409, 415). Submissive though she was, the one thing she could not accept was to be like B IV or Sally.

These observations would seem to permit of only one interpretation, namely, that the traits that characterized the B IV phase represented those elements of the original personality which were incompatible with the cultivated saintly and divinity sentiments and their settings, and had been repressed and dissociated. These elements included certain innate dispositions, such as anger and self-assertion; and certain acquired dispositions, such as the conception of self in relation to the realities of society and a clear and realistic understanding of the outer world. In a sense, the phase as a whole was a side to the original character. This latter point of view would not imply that on the one side Miss Beauchamp was bad-tempered and self-assertive and dominating, but only that anger and self-assertion are two instincts inborn and inherent in every personality and *potentially* capable of being aroused and also of being repressed. In this case, they were temporarily excluded by repression from the original personality as active instincts. The acquired dispositions likewise were a side of the original character in that they were acquired by experiences involving contact with the social world of realities during that happy period following her mother's death, after her elopement, when she was following the congenial occupation of a nurse. But when following the catastrophe of 1893, the personality reverted, in a greater or less degree, to that "dreamy and visionary" period of girlhood, when she saw things "rather through her own thought than clearly and truly," and it made "no difference that the facts were all against her," this acquired realistic conception of the world became incompatible with the idealistic sentiments of B I and was necessarily repressed. Otherwise there could have been no reversion to and resurrection of those ideals.

That the Saint and the Realist were thus varying composites of the elements of personality derives considerable support from another set of phenomena.

B I and B IV could be, technically speaking, hypnotized, really synthesized into a single personality known as B II. It developed that B II was the whole original personality called the "Real Self," but in a state of hypnosis. This self had complete memory or knowledge of herself as the Saint and the Realist — of herself, I say, for so she considered the relationship and so it was. Asked who she was, she replied,

"I am myself."

"Where is B I?"

"I am B I."

"Where is B IV?"

"I am B IV. We are all the same person, only *now I am myself.*"[1]

Now the points I want to bring out are: first, that this self was a well-balanced and synthesized normal self, with the memories of both B I and B IV. The instinctive disposition of self-assertion was balanced by the opposing disposition of self-abasement, and so the self-regarding sentiment was not overdominated by either; and, likewise, the anger reaction was balanced by a complete and healthy appreciation of the circumstances of her situation; the sentiments that dominated B I were balanced by an understanding of realities; the memories of B I were balanced by the memories of B IV; the points of view of the one were balanced by the points of view of the other; and the emotionality of both was restrained by a rational understanding of ideals and the environment.

That this self was a synthesis of many of the elements of each (memories, instincts, etc.), was an obvious fact; and that it was a complete synthesis was a logical interpretation.

The second point is that this self was clearly conscious and fully realized that sometimes she awoke as B IV, meaning that then she became "rattled" and said and did all sorts of "mad things," prevaricated and fibbed, etc.; and that sometimes she awoke as B I, when she was morbid, nervous and not herself. But nevertheless they were all herself,

---

1 Loc. cit., pp. 273 and 520.

though she exhibited different traits at different times corresponding to those phases, and consequently she used the personal pronoun, "I," in speaking of herself in each phase. In accord with this conception of the phases, she explained that, as it seemed to her, after the hospital episode she had simply changed in character and that the result of the change was that character known as B I. As to B IV, it seemed to her that in this phase she became, for some obscure reason, "rattled" and was dominated by the traits observed in herself in this character.

It is difficult to find any other satisfactory interpretation of this observation than that we had first integrated into a normal psychic whole (B II) two previously dissociated psychic systems (B I and B IV) of innate and acquired elements of personality, and then, on the subject's "waking up," this whole had become disintegrated again and its elements reintegrated into two differing psychic systems or wholes (capable of alternating with one another) producing two different characters out of the sum-total of one original personality.

## (2) The Genesis of the Realist

There remains the question: what forces induced on June 7, 1899, the first integration of the dissociated elements, founded in the B IV system, and the emergence of this system into consciousness, *i. e.*, its substitution for the B I system.

It should be remembered that this occurred six years after the original normal personality, Miss Beauchamp, had been transformed by the shock of 1893 to B I the Saint. The Realist, B IV, therefore emerged and displaced not the normal self but B I, a dissociated self from which many innate and acquired dispositions had been repressed. Furthermore, B I had just passed through and was still under the influence of a tremendous emotional experience. In consequence, she was still further dissociated at the moment and in a quasi-delirious or so-called "twilight" state, like a "shell-shocked" soldier.

In such disintegrated states, we know from experience that subconscious ideas and systems of ideas (*i. e.*, organized innate and acquired dispositions) more readily are excited and take on autonomous independent activity and, in so doing, their emotional impulses in turn repress, or otherwise disturb, any conflicting conscious processes functioning at the moment. And amongst these phenomena of conflict is the displacement or switching out of the latter from the personal consciousness followed by the substitution of the previously dormant and conflicting dispositions which then emerged into consciousness. This phenomenon is observed when such dispositions are "struck" by any stimulus which excites their emotional constituent.

This psychological principle, demonstrated by experimental observation on dissociated states, is a very important one. If space permitted I could cite numerous examples from clinical and experimental observations[1] and covering a variety of conditions — hypnotic suggestion, psychopathic states, dream complexes, multiple personality, etc. This phenomenon is something more than the mere "blocking" of thought, the inhibition of the processes of associative memory, for a recognition of which we are indebted to Freud. And it is quite different from the "compromise," "conversion," and other alleged phenomena of conflict of the Freudian psychology. It is rather the displacement in mass of a system of innate and acquired dispositions by another system through the force of its antagonistic emotional impulses, and the substitution in consciousness of the latter. An hypnotic consciousness may by such forces be replaced by the waking personal consciousness or by another hypnotic one, and *vice versa;* one psychopathic state may be replaced by another; the personal consciousness may be replaced by a psychopathic or disintegrated one. In such displacements and substitutions, there may be and often is *amnesia* in one state for all the experiences belonging to the displaced state, as when, to take a simple illustration, one hypnotic state is replaced by another or the waking state. In more complex

---

1 My original manuscript cited a number of such observations illustrating the various types of this phenomenon.

conditions there may be a disintegration of the normal personality of such a kind that one or more emotional instincts and sentiments and other acquired dispositions, even that of the conception of self, may be displaced and suppressed, with the substitution of their antagonists. There thus results a splitting and reintegration of the elements of personality — an alteration of character. In all such instances some antagonistic but dormant sentiment is "struck" by the stimulus and awakened, and the awakening brings into being the whole system with which it is integrated. From one point of view such reactions are often, not always, defense reactions,[1] but this is not an explanation of the *how*, but only of the *why*.

By the technique of so-called "tapping" the subconscious (automatic writing, speech, etc.), in favorable subjects, the precise antagonistic and resisting sentiment that has been struck can be reached and identified. The whole process can then be brought to light and the *why* disclosed. Thus, in such cases we are not limited to *inferring* that the phenomenon is due to the resistance of subconscious conflicting ideas, but, by this tapping of the subconscious, we can actually obtain direct evidence of and identify the specific subconscious ideas and impulses which did the resisting and caused the phenomena.[2]

1 Many writers seem to be satisfied that they have reached a complete solution of a phenomenon by calling it a "defense" reaction. This may explain the motive but in no way the mechanism. Pretty nearly everything that involves resistance may, from one point of view, be called a defense against something, but the mechanisms of the behavior in defense may be widely different. From another point of view they are not defenses but the awakening of stronger impulses (desires?) for the gratification of something else. The awakening of subconscious Sally's impulses to play may be called a defense against the boredom of Miss Beauchamp's religious sentiments, but it was also the awakening of the urge of joyous emotions for their own gratification.

2 The phenomena of conflicts of the kind I am now dealing with are not always displacement and substitution. I have literally, without exaggeration, in the course of an intensive study of the subconscious, covering many years, made countless observations on the influence of the subconscious upon the waking consciousness and upon other subconscious processes. In the pages of the study of Miss Beauchamp, already published, will be found numerous examples of subconscious conflicts of this kind. The resulting phenomena by which they have been revealed have been aboulia, hallucinations, inhibitions, and abolition of consciousness, emotion, mistakes and falsification of speech, writing, visual perception and hearing, amnesia, motor acts, etc. *(over)*

Finally, I may say the demonstration of this principle of the displacement of one constellated system by another which puts up the resistance was time and again obtained in this case of Miss Beauchamp by the behavior of the very systems we are investigating. Thus, when the antagonism between the personalities was most intense and ideas pertaining to the personality of B I, but objected to by the other two personalities, were suggested to the normal state in hyp-

When the subconscious elements become constellated into a personal self, possessing a self-conciousness, and the faculties of willing, wishing and expressing itself in muscular acts, as is sometimes the case in dissociated personalities (e. g., Miss Beauchamp, C. N., M. R., and B. C. A.) : the subconscious factors become more complex and the phenomena of resistance and conflict become multiform and take on a more volitional, purposive, and intellectual character. The principle, however, is the same. There is a conflict between the personal consciousness and a subconscious complex. The fact that the subconscious complex belongs to a highly constellated subconscious system, capable of independent thinking, willing, and action, and of intending the consequences of a conflict with the principal consciousness, gives a more purposive and often more elaborate character to the resulting phenomena. For this reason they often have a dramatic aspect which withdraws attention from the psychological mechanism underlying them. In principle, these phenomena produced by a constellated subconscious self do not differ from those produced by simpler subconscious complexes in less complicated pathological conditions and everyday life. Cases of multiple personality are, therefore, often peculiarly fitted for experimental investigation of the influence of subconscious complexes upon the personal consciousness, as we are able in these cases by technical procedures to discover and identify the precise subconscious processes (motives, volitions, etc.) which have determined the disturbances of the personal self. I will recall here, as a few instances, the following observations in the case of Miss Beauchamp:

First, the occasion when in consequence of a suggestion to the hypnotized personality, meeting resistance from the subconscious self, there resulted an inhibition or blocking of thought (pp. 275, 306, 457).

Second, the occasions when a similar resistance resulted in false hearing, e. g., the words "badly" and "B I" being heard as "beautifully" and "B IV" respectively (pp. 321, 416, 497); or in word deafness (p. 457).

Third, the occasions when the hypnotized personality became dumb under similar conditions (pp. 275, 537).

Fourth, the occasions when the subconscious personality spoke automatically (pp. 157, 275, 459, 501) in opposition to a suggested idea are examples of the same kind of resistance and reaction to a suggested idea, although the expression of the reaction in the form of volitional speech involves more complicated processes.

Fifth, falsifications of writing were frequently observed in Miss Beauchamp's letters, produced by purposive interference by the subconscious self. One of the more elaborate of these was a letter in which the letters of every word were misplaced (p. 205). The fact that this letter is a product of intelligent subconscious thought does not in any way controvert the principle.

Sixth, negative and positive hallucinations, both visual and auditory, were very common (pp. 190, 210, 440, 483, 484, 486, 507, 538, 539, 561). One of the most elaborate of these was an hallucinatory letter which the subject read on a blank sheet of paper (index and pp. 283-285).

nosis, B II, the latter was immediately displaced and replaced by B IVa (pp. 450 and 503). Likewise, similar intolerable suggestions to B IVa resulted in a displacement of this hypnotic state by the waking personality, B IV (p. 494). Expressed in other words, the constellated systems which offered the resistance to the suggested ideas replaced, by conflict, the systems to which the suggestions were given. This is a common experience in giving unacceptable suggestions to hypnotized persons.

In other and numerous instances, when there was object n (resistance) on the part of the one intelligence inbein₁ to suggestions designed to awaken constellated complexes belonging to one of the dormant personalities, it was then very difficult to awaken that dormant personality; that is, to change one personality to another. This is in principle the same as the common resistance to hypnotism.

After this digression let us return to the birth of B IV, The Realist. We left B I in a "rattled" dissociated, semidelusional state while I was interviewing her (p. 248 above). She was still, as I have said, under the influence of a tremendous emotional experience. Now, as I interpret the succeeding phenomena (the sudden change of personality to B IV),

Seventh, aboulia (pp. 120-469), falsification of vision (pp. 432-433) and purposive motor acts (p. 157).

Eighth, displacement and substitution were common phenomena.

Many of these, and other phenomena, could be shown to be due to the volitional action of an integrated subconscious self upon the personal consciousness. The former was constantly in conflict with the latter and expressed this conflict in such purposive phenomena. On the other hand, some of the most marked examples of these conflicts were seen in the resistances to suggestions, which were met with, not from a subconscious self (Sally) but from ideas which had belonged to the consciousness of the personality B IV, and were conserved as dispositions in the unconscious. These resistances offered some of the greatest obstacles to the reconstruction of the dissociated personality and the cure of the case. Thus, even when B IV desired to be hypnotized for therapeutic purposes, the previous autosuggestion which she had given herself, to the effect that no suggestions should affect her, came at once into conflict with my therapeutic suggestions and counteracted them. Owing to this antagonism at these times it was almost impossible to hypnotize her, i. e., to change the mental synthesis, and every suggestion was counteracted and inhibited (pp. 447, 450).

Although I have cited examples from only one case, they are not unique, for I have observed a large number of identical phenomena in other cases, notably B. C. A., C. N., and M. R. It is not necessary at this time to pursue such observations further. It is obvious, I think, that the principle has been sufficiently well established.

the vivid revival, in the form of memories, hallucinations and emotions, of the emotional experience of that tragic night, acted as a stimulus and "struck" the associated complex of "realistic" dispositions (acquired by contact with the social world of realities)[1] and instincts which had been integrated in the normal personality at that period, in 1893, but being incompatible with the resurrected religious sentiments and innate dispositions of the altered personality (B I), had been suppressed and had lain dormant. They, nevertheless, were linked in associative experience and were struck as associative unconscious memories. These dispositions now excited came to life, and by the force of their emotions repressed in turn the complexes of the B I personality with which they were incompatible and in conflict. It was a veritable defense reaction against the emotions awakened by the memories and vision of the original "shock" (1893), and which now, once more, swayed B I with overwhelming and painful force. Thus, the complexes of B I, the Saint, were displaced, and those characterizing the phase B IV, the Realist, were substituted.

This displacement and substitution was made easy because of the dissociated condition in which B I was at the time, and for this reason I have emphasized the latter in some detail.

Is it mere assumption to postulate a conflict between the dissociated "realistic" dispositions (conceptions) and the sentiments of B I? This doubt is disposed of by the continual, actual and observed conflicts between these sentiments, conceptions, etc. These have already been described. (See p. 257 above.)

Furthermore, corroboration is found in the following observation which was, in principle, a repetition of the episode which first resurrected the B IV complexes. As a reaction to a proposition of mine which recalled the hospital episode, B I fell into a state of revery, so deep that she did not seem to hear my voice. Her mind had become occu-

---

1 See p. 259, above.

pied with memories of that experience and of the sentiments, etc., held by herself as B IV. Suddenly the B I phase
was displaced and B IV took its place.[1] This was not an
isolated occurrence. In the innumerable alterations of phases
that took place, it was possible to detect in many of them
that the change was effected by the stimulation of a conflicting complex. The same was true of many of the alterations with "Sally." Of course it was not possible to follow
the psychological factors in all the constant shiftings of
personalities.

This interpretation or theory of dissociated personalities — for after all every interpretation is a theory[2] — is opposed to present-day attempts of a monistic psychology to
refer the phenomena of the psychoses to a single subconscious motive, a wish, whether sexual or one to "escape from
reality" (so-called defense reaction) or some other, a motive which would only use organized complexes of innate and
acquired dispositions to effect a philosophic purpose. Such
unconscious wishes, if existent, may have been determinants
in the structural development of such complexes, but these
complexes, once formed, act as dynamic psychic wholes, *en
masse*, according to their aims and the ends they seek. In
this respect they are mass reactions. Of course, in them there
may be, and usually are, paramount forces of instinctive and
acquired dispositions corresponding to wishes, fears, ideals,
etc. Every sentiment is organized in a larger setting of dispositions (experiences) possessing a variety of dynamic tendencies which will take part in determining the direction
which the impulsive drive of the sentiment will take; or the
direction may be a resultant of all the forces. Perhaps a
good analogy is one of the late alliances between nations.
The most powerful may be the dominating power, but the
wills of the others will modify and perhaps even overrule the
former; or the final action of the alliance may be a com-

---

1 *The Dissociation of a Personality*, p. 249.

2 Anyone who attempts to postulate an interpretation as a demonstrated
fact shows that he has a mind incapable of distinguishing between theory and
fact and one that disqualifies him both as an observer and interpreter. Unfortunately we have too many examples of this kind of investigator of problems
in abnormal psychology.

promise, *i. e.*, resultant of all the wills. In the alliance of the psychological dispositions, the conception of a primitive unconscious sexual or other desire, sitting apart and underneath, as an "anima" or an "animus" (as Tristram Shandy's father would have said) "taking up her residence, and sitting dabbling, like a tadpole, all day long, both summer and winter," in an unconscious puddle, or like Descartes' soul in the pineal gland, pulling the wires and directing the dynamic forces of organized systems constituting personality, both "shocks the imagination" and is, to my mind, untenable. The present-day tendency to find a quasi-philosophic single principle to explain the complex psychological phenomena of personality, a sort of psychological monism, is not only fallacious but is bound to remove psychology from the field of science. Psychology deals with concrete phenomena which are the resultants of a complexity of forces driving in different directions. The law of the final drive is more comparable to the physical law of the "resultant of forces."

### EPILOGUE

I have frequently been asked what was the final outcome of this case. Did Miss Beauchamp remain well, a complete, united normal personality? I am happy to be able to answer that question in the affirmative. In my account of the case I cautiously left the question in doubt, not knowing whether her reintegration would prove stable and withstand the stress and strain of life. But it proved durable, and Miss Beauchamp not only has remained well, but, like the traditional princess in the fairy story, soon married and "lived happily ever afterward."

# CHAPTER VIII

## My Life as a Dissociated Personality

### BY B. C. A

[An account of the various phases of dissociated personality, written by the patient, after recovery and restoration of memory for all the different phases, cannot fail to be of interest. If the writer is endowed with the capacity for accurate introspection and statement, such an account ought to give an insight into the condition of the mind during these dissociated states that is difficult to obtain from objective observation, or, if elicited from a clinical narration of the patient, to accurately transcribe. In that remarkable book, *A Mind that Found Itself,* the author, writing after recovery from insanity, has given us a unique insight into the insane mind. Similarly, the writer of the following account allows us to see the beginnings of the differentiation of her mind into complexes, the final development of a dissociated or multiple personality, and to understand the moods, points of view, motives, and dominating ideas which characterized each phase. Such an account could only be given by a person who has had the experiences, and who has the introspective and literary capacity to describe them.

The writer in publishing, though with some reluctance and at my request, her experiences as a multiple personality, is actuated only, as I can vouch, by a desire to contribute to our knowledge of such conditions. The experiences of her illness — now happily recovered from — have led her to take an active interest in abnormal psychology and to inform herself, so far as is possible by the study of the literature, on many of the problems involved. The training thus acquired has plainly added to the accuracy and value of her introspective observations.

A brief preliminary statement will be necessary in order that the account, as told by the patient, may be fully intelligible.

The subject has been under my continual observation for about two years. When first seen, the case presented the ordinary picture of so-called neurasthenia, characterized by persistent fatigue and the usual somatic symptoms, and by moral doubts and scruples. This phase was later termed and is described in the following account as state or complex A. Later another state, spoken of as complex B, suddenly developed. Complex A had no memory for complex B, but the latter not only had full knowledge of A, but persisted coconsciously when A was present. B was therefore both an alternating and a coconscious state. Besides differences in memory, A and B manifested distinct and markedly different characteristics, which included moods, tastes, points of view, habits of thought, and controlling ideas. In place, for instance, of the depression, fatigue, and moral doubts and scruples of A, B manifested rather a condition of exaltation, and complete freedom from neurasthenia and its accompanying obsessional ideas. With the appearance of B, it was recognized that both states were phases of a dissociated personality, and neither represented the normal complete personality. After prolonged study, this latter normal state was obtained in hypnosis, and, on being awakened, a personality was found which possessed the combined memories of A and B and was free from the pathological stigmata which respectively characterized each. This normal person is spoken of as C. The normal C had, therefore, split into two systems of complexes or personalities, A and B. This relationship may be diagrammatically expressed as follows:

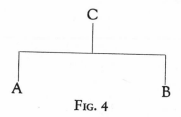

FIG. 4

This account is followed by one written by the dissociated personality B, describing the point of view of the patient in this state and also her subconscious (coconscious) life (which she claims to remember) in its various relations and functionings. The analysis, however it be interpreted, cannot fail to be a remarkable contribution to the subconscious. — Morton Prince.]

MY DEAR DR. PRINCE,

You have asked me to give you an account of my illness as it seems to me now that I am myself and well; describing myself in those changes of personality which we have called "A" and "B."

It is always difficult for one to analyze one's self accurately and the conditions have been very complex. I think, however, that I have a clear conception and appreciation of my case. I remember myself perfectly as "A" and as "B." I remember my thoughts, my feelings, and my points of view in each personality and can see where they are the same, and where they depart from my normal self. These points of view will appear as we go on and I feel sure that my memory can be trusted. I recall clearly how in each state I regarded the other state and how in each I regarded myself.

As I have said, I have now, as "C," all the memories of both states (though none of the coconscious life which, as B, I claimed and believed I had). These memories are clearly differentiated in my mind. It would be impossible to confuse the two, as the moods which governed each were so absolutely different, but it is quite another thing to make them distinct on paper. I have, however, been so constantly under your observation that you can, no doubt, correct any statement I may make which is not borne out by your own knowledge.

I am, perhaps, of a somewhat emotional nature and have never been very strong physically, though nothing of an invalid, and have always been self-controlled and not at all hysterical, as I would use the word. On the contrary, I was, I am sure, considered a very sensible woman by those who know me well, though I am not so sure what they may think of me now. I am very sensitive and responsive to impressions, in the sense that I am easily affected by my environment. For instance, at the theatre I lose myself in the play and feel keenly all the emotions portrayed by the actors. These emotions are reflected vividly in my face and manner, sometimes to the amusement of those with me and, if the scene is a painful one, it often takes me a long time to recover from the effect of it. The same is true of scenes from actual life.

Before this disintegration took place, I had borne great responsibility and great sorrow with what I think I am justified in calling fortitude and I do not think the facts of my previous life would warrant the assumption that I was, naturally, nervously unstable. It does not carry great weight, I know, for one to say of one's self — I am sensible, I am stable, I am not hysterical — but I believe the statement can be corroborated by the testimony of those who have known me through my years of trial. What I should like to point out is that my case shows that such an illness as I have had is possible with a constitutionally stable person and is not confined to those of an hysterical tendency.

A year previous to this division of personality, a long nervous strain, covering a period of four years, had culminated in the death of one very dear to me. I was at that time in good physical health, though nervously worn, but this death occurred in such a way as to cause me a great shock, and within the six days following I lost twenty pounds in weight. For nearly three months I went almost entirely without food, seemingly not eating enough to sustain life, and I did not average more than three or four hours' sleep out of twenty-four, but I felt neither hungry nor faint, and was extremely busy and active, being absorbed both by home responsibilities and business affairs. The end of the year, however, found me in very poor health physically and I was nervously and mentally exhausted. I was depressed, sad, felt that I had lost all that made life worth living and, indeed, I wished to die. I was very nervous, unable to eat or sleep, easily fatigued, suffered constantly from headache, to which I had always been subject, and was not able to take much exercise. The physician, under whose care I was at this time, told me, when I asked him to give my condition a name, that I was suffering from "nervous and cerebral exhaustion."

It was at this time that the shock which caused the division of personality occurred. Before describing it, I should mention a few of my most pronounced minor traits which, though of no importance in themselves, will enable, through the change that took place in them, the marked alteration of character following the shock to be recognized. Among these characteristics were a great dislike of riding on electric cars, an almost abnormal nervousness about bugs and mosquitoes — I always disliked going into the woods for this reason — an aversion for exercise in summer, and a fear of canoeing. I had never enjoyed sitting out from under cover or on the ground as the glare of the sun was apt to cause headache and I abhorred all crawling things.[1] I was reserved with strangers and not given to making friends quickly; devoted to my family and relatives, fond of my friends and not in the habit of neglecting them in any way. I felt much responsibility concerning business matters and had given a good deal of time and thought to them. Many more peculiarities might be mentioned. The change which took place in me in these respects will be presently related. But shortly before the complete change took place, to my surprise, there were times when I did some of the things above referred to, such as sitting in the woods, etc. I felt a sense of wonder that

---

1 I have put this in the past tense because I have changed in some of these characteristics. I enjoy an out-of-door life more than I used to; am fond of the woods and the water in spite of the insects and the fact that I am afraid of a canoe.

I should be doing them and a still greater wonder that I found them pleasant. There was also a sense at times of impatience and irritation at being troubled with business matters or responsibility of any kind and an inclination to throw aside all care. I wondered at myself for feeling as I did and rather protested to myself at many of my acts but still kept right on doing them. It seems to me that these ideas and feelings formed a complex by which I was more or less governed, and that this complex gradually grew in strength and could be identified with that of the personality (B) which first developed.

The shock I received was of an intensely emotional nature. It brought to me, suddenly, the realization that my position in life was entirely changed, that I was quite alone, and with this there came a feeling of helplessness and desolation beyond my powers of description. I felt, too, angry, frightened, insulted. For a few minutes these ideas flashed through my mind and then — all was changed. All the distressing ideas of the preceding moments left me, and I no longer minded what, a moment before, had caused me so much distress. I became the personality which we have since called "B." I do not feel now that the episode was of a character that would have affected a person of a different nature, or even myself had I been in good health. Psychologically speaking, I suppose I was already in a somewhat disintegrated condition and, therefore, more susceptible. At any rate it did affect me. From the moment of that shock I was, literally, a different person. The episode itself became of little or no importance to me and I looked upon it rather as a lark and really enjoyed it, as I did — in this character — succeeding events. With the change to "B" there was no loss of memory, as sometimes occurs under such conditions. It seems very curious to me that the effect of this shock was to change me not to the despondent, despairing mood of "A" which came later, but to the happy mood of "B."

In describing the two personalities I shall sometimes have to refer to them by the letters A and B to avoid the constant repetition of "myself as A — myself as B."

As B, I was, apparently, a perfectly normal person, as will

be seen from the description which follows, except that I was
ruled by a fixed idea that upon me, and me alone, depended
the salvation, moral and physical, of a person who was almost
a perfect stranger to me. I had known this person but a few
weeks. This idea became an obsession; all else sank into in-
significance beside it; *nothing* else was of any consequence,
and I went to all lengths to help this person, doing things
which, though quite right and proper, indeed imperative,
from my point of view as B, were unwise and unnecessary.
I believed that I was the only one in the world who would
stand by him; that every one else had given him up as hopeless and that his one chance lay in his belief in me.

With the change of personality, which will be clearer as
you read, there was also a complete change of physical conditions. Previously neurasthenic, I, as B, was perfectly well
and strong and felt equal to anything in the way of physical
exercise. The minor traits I have above mentioned were replaced by their opposites. A walk of three or four miles did
not tire me at all; I tramped through the woods during the
hottest days of summer, with nothing on my head, feeling
no discomfort from the heat and no fatigue; I sat on the
ground in the woods, hours at a time, not minding in the
least the bugs and the mosquitoes; canoeing I was very fond
of and felt no fear of the water. I also took long rides on
the electric cars and found them perfectly delightful. These
are small things but, as you see, it was a radical change and
seems as strange to remember as the more important ones.
As B, I was light-hearted and happy, and life seemed good
to me; I wanted to live; my pulse beat fuller, my blood ran
warmer through my veins than it ever had done before. I
seemed more alive. Nothing is stranger to remember than
the vigorous health of B. Never in my life was I so well,
before and since. I felt much younger and looked so, for the
lines of care, anxiety, sorrow, and fatigue had faded from
my face and the change in expression was remarked upon.
I neglected my family and friends shamefully, writing short
and unsatisfactory letters and leaving them in ignorance of
my health and plans; business affairs I washed my hands of
entirely. I lost the formality and reserve which was one of

my traits. My tastes, ideals, and points of view were completely changed.

I remained in this state for some weeks, enjoying life to the utmost in a way entirely foreign to my natural tastes and inclinations as described above, walking, boating, etc., living wholly out of doors; and also doing many irresponsible things which were of a nature to cause me much distress later.

Some of this might, perhaps, be ascribed to improved health; and yet it was different from anything I had ever been before.

After a period of a few weeks I received a second shock, which was caused by the discovery of deception in matters which my "obsession" had taken in charge. The revelation came in a flash, a strong emotion swept over me, and the state B, with all its traits, physical characteristics, and points of view disappeared, and I changed to another state which we have since called A. In this state, my physical condition was much as it was before the first shock, that is, I was neurasthenic. From a state of vigorous health, I constantly changed to one of illness and languor; could hardly sit up, had constant headache, insomnia, loss of appetite, etc. My mental characteristics were different. As before, however, there was no amnesia either for the state when I was B or for my life before the first shock.

Now, though as A, I was filled with most disproportionate horror at what had occurred during the weeks of my life as B, I was ruled by the same obsession, but with this difference: what I, as B, had done with a sense of pleasure, I, as A, did with a sense of almost horror at my own actions, feeling that I was compelled to do so by what seemed at the time a sense of duty. I felt that I must carry out certain obligations, and I doubt now, as I afterwards expressed myself to you, if I could have resisted had I tried. I would not refuse the demand for help which was made upon me because I, as B, had promised my aid, but in complying I was obliged to do things which seemed to me, as A, shocking and unheard of. I felt that my conduct was open to severe criticism but I had promised and must fulfill though the skies fell. It seems to me now, in the light of our present knowledge of B, that I was in a sort of somnambulic state governed by what I have learned were coconscious ideas belonging to B; that the impulses of the B complex were too strong to be resisted; but in my memory my ideas as B were at this time so curiously intermingled with my ideas as A that it is useless to try to analyze my mind more accurately. In mood, point of view and ideals, I was A, but I *did* the things B would have done, though from a different incentive. For a few days I remained A and then, owing, I think, to a lessening of nervous tension, I changed again to B and remained in that state for two or three weeks during which time I was physically well and happy again. At the end of this time, as a result of another realization of the actual situation, A reappeared and was the only personality for some weeks. These changes were due to successive emotional shocks.

When you first saw me, I was A at my worst. I had no amnesia for the events of the preceding months when, as B, I had been filled with the joy of living. There was no thought on my part of any "change of personality" — I had never heard of such a thing — but I was like one slowly awakening from a dream. I was equally aghast at what I (B) had done for pleasure, and at what I (A) had done from a sense of duty; one seemed as unbelievable as the other. One of the most shocking things to me, as A, was the fact that I had enjoyed myself. Had I committed the most dreadful crimes, I could not have felt greater anguish, regret, and remorse. I was dominated by the fixed ideas and obsessions of B; I felt that I *must* respond to any call for help made by this person even though it was against my inclination and judgment to do so; there seemed no choice for me in the matter — I *had* to; I could see no point of view but my own. To do what seemed my plain duty, I was willing to sacrifice myself in every way, but could not see that I (A) was now causing as much anxiety to my family as I had previously done as B; that I was sacrificing them also, or

that my idea of duty was entirely mistaken. A, it would
seem, was the emotional and idealistic part of my nature
magnified a thousand times. My emotions and ideals as A
were not different in *kind* from those of my normal self
but were so exaggerated as to be morbid.

As A, I was full of metaphysical doubts and fears, full
of scruples. I did not attend church because I felt that I
could no longer honestly say the Creed and the prayers.
The service had lost all meaning to me and so it seemed hypocritical to take part in it. I felt that I had utterly failed in
the performance of every duty, and tortured myself with
the remembrance of every act of omission and commission.
I accused myself of selfishness, neglect, in fact, of nearly all
the crimes in the calendar including, in an indirect way, that
of murder. My conversation was always of the most serious
character — religion (I believed in nothing), life after
death (of which I found no hope), and I dwelt much upon
the fact that none should be judged by their deeds alone,
that no one could tell what hidden motive had prompted
any given act. This was because I had (as B) done so many
things which (as A) I wholly disapproved of and felt might
be misunderstood. I did not understand them myself but
knew that my motive had been good. I was frightened, bewildered, shocked, agonized — concentrated anguish and
remorse. During these weeks I suffered more than any one
ought ever to suffer for anything, and always, over and over
in my mind went the same old thoughts — "*Why* did I do
as I did? *How* could I have done it? Why did it seem right?
What would my friends think if they knew? I was mad! I
*was not myself.*" Finally I decided to end it all — I could
not live under such a weight of humiliation and self-reproach.
I am sure, Dr. Prince, that you must remember how impossible it was to reason with me as A, for it was at this time
and in this state that I was sent to you.

Shortly after I came to you I began to alternate frequently and it is well to emphasize that one marked change
in the state of A developed. In this state I now had *complete amnesia* for my whole life as B; for everything I

hought and did.[1]  In other respects, however, these states
vere identical with what they had been.  The presence of
mnesia made no difference in the fact of change of per-
onality.  As I see it, I was just as much an altered personality
efore the amnesia developed as afterwards.  As B, I had no
mnesia.  I claimed not only as an alternating personality
o remember A, *but to be always coconscious with A and to
emember my coconscious thoughts.*  As a coconsciousness,
f course, I (B) would know A.  As stated above, I have
ow no remembrance of that coconscious life and cannot
peak of it from my own knowledge.  Why my memory of
B should not include that of her (my) coconscious life, I
nust leave to you to explain.

The amnesia made life very difficult; indeed, except for
he help you gave me I think it would have been impossible,
nd that I should have gone truly mad.  How can I describe
r give any clear idea of what it is to wake suddenly, as it
vere, and not to know the day of the week, the time of the
lay, or why one is in any given position?  I would come to
nyself as A, perhaps on the street, with no idea of where I
ad been or where I was going; fortunate if I found myself
lone, for if I was carrying on a conversation, I knew noth-
ng of what it had been; fortunate indeed, in that case, if I
lid not contradict something I had said; for, as B, my atti-
ude toward all things was quite the opposite of that taken
y A.  Often it happened that I came to myself at some so-
ial gathering — a dinner, perhaps — to find I had been

1 This came about in the following way: One day, while A was in hypnosis,
he suddenly and spontaneously changed to a different hypnotic state, charac-
erized by change of facial expression, manner, speech, etc.  It was afterwards
ecognized that this was the B complex in hypnosis.  I had not before seen or
eard of the B complex as such.  I had only known that the subject, from her
wn account, had been in a neurasthenic condition and had been through periods
f improvement and relapses.  I did not suspect that these phases of improve-
nent and relapses represented phases of personality, such as was soon discovered
o be the case.  A few days after the B complex had appeared in hypnosis, this
hase spontaneously awoke, and alternated, as it had previously done, with the
A complex.  But now, as the writer says, there was amnesia on the part of A
or B.  The explanation for this is undoubtedly to be found in the fact that a
ew synthesis and more complete dissociation of the B complex had taken place
hrough the experience of hypnosis.  Analogous phenomena I have observed in
naking experimental observations but it would take us too far away to enter
nto this question here.  (M. P.)

taking wine (a thing I, as A, felt bound not to do)[1] an
what was to me most shocking and horrifying, smoking ;
cigarette; never in my life had I done such a thing and my
humiliation was deep and keen.

I would often wake in the morning, as A, to find a not
on my pillow or on the table — usually of a jeering tone —
telling me to "cheer up," to "weep no more," etc.; some
times these notes would be in rhyme and nearly all advised
me not to trouble Dr. Prince so much.[2] These notes wer
written by B and when I "changed" in the night, but, as A
I supposed, when I first found them, that I had written then
in my sleep. If my condition had been one of remorse, i
was now one of despair. After a time, as A, I destroyed al
the notes I found, without reading them, hoping in this way
to discourage B's fondness for writing. As a result I foun
one morning a sheet of paper pasted directly in the middl
of my mirror. It was fastened at each corner with larg
red seals and bore the inscription "READ THIS" and con
tained information which it was quite necessary A shoul
have. As B, my attitude toward myself, as A, was somethin
like that of a gay, irresponsible, pleasure-loving girl towar
an older, more serious-minded sister. I, as B, had no pa
tience with A's scruples and morbid ideas and actually en
joyed doing things which I knew would shock or anno
myself as A, though occasionally as B, I felt a little sorry fo
A. It must be remembered that while I, as A, recognized n
division of personality and considered B's acts (of which i
must be kept in mind I had no memory) as my own, I, a
B, did not look upon A as any part of myself. As B, I fel
myself to be a distinct personality and insisted upon it t
you over and over again. I realize that I was not normal bu
thought that A was not normal either. I believed that my

1 During the first weeks of my existence as B, I had pledged myself to drin
no wine. The promise was made under such conditions that no reasonable per
son could have felt bound by it. As B, I realized this and felt no obligation t
keep it, but as A, I could not feel so, though you had assured me over and ove
again that I was not in honor bound.

2 Some notes were of a different kind, and you have told me that they wer
written in nocturnal somnambulism.

own views were more correct than A's and were entitled to
as much consideration, and could never understand why you
should prefer to keep A in existence rather than B. I felt
that with the restoration of the normal self, I could not
"come" as an alternating personality but I believe that I
should always be coconscious. As B, I felt very grateful to
you for treating me as if I were a "real" person and allowing
me to express my own personality. With everyone else I had
to pretend to be A, and my feeling of gratitude and the fact
that you asked for my co-operation — put me on my honor
as it were — were the underlying motives in telling you so
much of A's inner life. I, as B, thought A was very silly not
to tell you all the things which were troubling her — as was
indeed true — and it seemed to me (B) a great joke on A to
get up in the night and write you a long letter telling A's
most secret thoughts and perhaps enclosing something I, as
A, had written but had not really intended to send you. It
is true that, as B, I was perfectly willing to tell you things
which, as A, I would rather have died than disclose. Would
this not seem to show that even when a personality becomes
disintegrated, the real self, the ego, remains unchanged and,
in a way, governs the whole, even if imperfectly? Even as
B, feeling sure that the integration of the whole self meant
my own extinction, I still, for the most part, gave my help
toward that end.

As B, I was very extravagant and spent money in a most
lavish way, buying things which, as A, I felt I could not
afford, for though A was not, like the famous Mrs. Gilpin,
"upon pleasure bent," she did, like her, have "a frugal mind."
Being, as B, very fond of all sorts of gayety, I constantly
made engagements which, as A, who had no heart for social
pleasures, I did not care to keep; I constantly encouraged vis-
itors whom, as A, I did not care to receive; a volume could
be filled with the troubles of this ill-assorted pair of *me's,*
some of which were tragic and some very funny.

As A, I was all emotion as regards people, but I never
felt anger nor resentment. In this and other respects, the
change from what I was before the first shock was marked.
I had become absurdly grateful for every attention shown

me, though I felt myself separated from all my relatives and friends by the, as I thought, strange experience I had had. It seemed to me as if my heart were frozen and that an invisible barrier was between me and everyone else, and that I did not love my family as I had formerly done; it seemed to me that I *felt* nothing; but at the same time I was racked by the agony of the thought. Any tale of sorrow, suffering, or sin stirred me to the depths, but I experienced no sensation of pleasure or happiness. The outdoor world was unreal to me. I realized that it was beautiful; that the trees were green and stately, that the sky was blue, the wind soft, the water smiling; but I saw it only with my eyes; and to feel beauty, one must see it with the soul also. I felt myself no part of it — I was in the world but not of it.

As B, I felt no emotion except that of pleasure, using the word pleasure as meaning a "good time," — social gayety, driving, motoring, walking, boating, etc., but my enjoyment of these things was very keen. As B, I was always the gayest of the company, but for people I cared nothing. The little acts of affection which we all perform in daily home-life I never thought of. The habit of shaking hands with one's friends, kissing or embracing those nearer and dearer had no meaning to me. Ordinarily, I think, when one shakes hands with a friend one feels the individuality of the person, more or less, and the clasp of hands means something, but, as B, it meant no more to me than clasping a piece of wood, and the acts of shaking hands, embracing, or kissing were all alike — it made no difference to me which I did — one meant just as much as the other. This lack of feeling applied only to people, for I loved the outside world; the trees, the water, the sky, and the wind seemed to be a very part of myself. The emotions by which, as A, I was torn to shreds, as B, I did not feel at all.

My taste in reading differed greatly in the two states. As B my reading consisted largely of the magazines and short stories, though after becoming interested in the study of psychology I enjoyed reading on the subject as much as A did. Aside from that one subject, however, I preferred the lighter reading and, curiously enough I liked to read stories which portrayed the very emotions which I never felt. Kipling fascinated me. As A, I read Victor Hugo, Ibsen, Tolstoi, Maeterlinck, a great deal of poetry, the "Rubaiyat" of Omar Khayyam until I knew it by heart, and anything that touched upon the deeper problems of life.

In matters of dress and social pleasures, A and B were diametrically opposed. At the time of the dissociation of character, I was wearing mourning, but black was distasteful to me as B, and so far as was possible, I wore white — not even a black belt or buckle would I put on. This fact was far more strange than it seems, and caused much friction, for B's manner of carrying out her ideas was, under the circumstances, eccentric, to say the least, and, as A, it offended my sense of propriety and my pride. As A, I cared almost nothing for social pleasures, dress, etc., though my tastes in such matters did not materially change, but life was much too serious and painful to think of such frivolities; I went to the theatre and places of amusement because you said I must, not because I cared to.

B usually kept A's engagements, unless they conflicted too much with her own wishes, and kept A informed as to what had happened or was to happen, by notes, unless the changes of personality were too rapid. The diary, which has, at your suggestion, been kept, was also of great service in keeping A informed as to the course of events. I will copy a few extracts from this diary, as it gives a very good idea of the different moods and points of view.

Under the date of July 23, 190–, B writes: "I am here again tonight, B, I am. I may as well tell all I have done, I suppose. For one thing I had a facial massage — there is no need of being a mass of wrinkles. I know A doesn't care how she looks, but I do. The Q's spent the evening here and — if I don't tell, S will, I suppose — I smoked a cigarette. S was *terribly* shocked and angry with me. Now, A, don't go and tell Dr. Prince, you don't have to tell him everything — you do it, though. I *must* have a little fun."

The following day A writes: "I have struggled through another day. B has told what she did. How *can* I bear it? How explain? I am so humiliated, so ashamed. Why should

I do things which so mortify my pride? Quite ill all day —
I am, as usual, paying for B's 'fun.' It is not to be borne."

August 20, "Terrible day — one of the worst for a
long time. I *cannot* live this way, it is not to be expected. I
am so confused — I have lost so much time now that I
can't seem to catch up. What is the end to be? What will
become of me?"

August 21, B writes: "Good gracious! how we fly
around. A has been ill all day — could not sleep last night.
I hope he (Dr. Prince) won't send for us; for he will put a
quietus on me, and as things are now I am gaining on A.
Had a gay evening — no discussions of religion or psychology, no dissecting of hearts and souls while I am in the flesh."

August 25, "I wonder if A is really dead — for good
and all? It seems like it. The thought rather frightens me
someway, as if I had lost my balance-wheel. She wants to
die, she really does, for she thinks it to herself all the time.
I wish I were myself alone, and neither A nor B; I cannot
bear to hear A groan, she cannot bear my glee."

August 26, "Such a day! A got away from me for a
little while and tried to write a letter to Dr. Prince. It was
a funny looking letter for I kept saying to her 'you cannot
write, you cannot move your hand,' but she had enough
will-power to write some and directed it. The effort used
her up, however, and I came and the letter was not mailed."

August 27, A writes: "I am too much bewildered to
write. I have succeeded in writing Dr. Prince, if I can only
mail it. Oh, but I am tired! Such an awful struggle!"

To show how strangely the physical condition changed
as I alternated between A and B, I offer the following entry
from the same diary: September —, "A was used up and had
to stay in bed all the morning but I came about one o'clock
and Mrs. X asked me to motor down to Z. Had a gorgeous
ride and got home at seven nearly famished, for A had eaten
nothing all day — she lives on coffee and somnos — nice
combination — steak and French fried, for mine, please. Y
was delighted with the cigarette case; you must grin and
bear it, A."

As B, I had given a cigarette case as a birthday gift to a young relative to whose smoking A seriously objected.

November —, "What a day! Now you see it and now you don't — A ill, B well — first one and then the other. I got ready to go to the dentist — then A came; and her head ached and she was too ill to go. Then I came again and practised — etc." I remember this day distinctly. As A, I could not sit up, my head ached so badly. Then I would lose myself, that is, change to B, and feel perfectly well and go on with the work in hand. Changing to A again, with amnesia for the time I had been B, I would feel very ill and have to lie down. I think I changed from one state to the other at least half a dozen times — and A's day was one of suffering and B's day one of health and activity.

Again B writes: "I am really thinking seriously of going away. I am sure I could get along all right by myself. Dr. Prince says I am a 'psychological impossibility' (absurd), I am a psychological *fact* — more real than A. I could easily go away — Dr. P. could not help it." As A, I was stricken with terror by an entry like the above, for I knew that, as B, I could carry out my threat if I chose.

November —, "Well, once more I am permitted to write in this old diary. — After we got home C went to pieces, I never saw such a lot! — and then poor old A came, again anguish, wringing of hands, finally tears, then, thank goodness! I came myself. I *cannot* see why Dr. Prince would rather have that *emotional, hysterical* set than have *me!* It passes comprehension. I know *everything, always,* and they only know a few things for a few minutes."

This gives an idea of A's point of view: August, 190–, "Ill again — headache all day — these memories rack me. O, why, why, *why* did I ever feel and do as I did feel and do! — and it all seemed so right to me, so impossible to do anything else. I *cannot* understand where my common sense was — it is so incredible. I can't believe sometimes that it is not all a frightful dream — if I could wake and find it so! — the irony, the cruelty of it. Time is an 'arch satirist' indeed! He is having a little joke with me. There is *one* way to end it — how long before I avail myself of it? How much must I suffer?"

B feels quite differently: "I could have the loveliest time in the world if A would stay away long enough. There are lots of things to do and I am going to do them if I have half a chance. 'A short life and a merry one' shall be my motto."

This diary was kept for about a year and is a most curious document. Both as A and B, I often wrote at length my own theories and explanations of my case. Sometimes, when I was writing as A, *coconscious* B would take control of my hand and I would write, automatically, most decided objections to the idea I had just expressed.

I hesitate to write of the times when I was influenced by coconscious B, for I have no memory of the coconscious process. I remember, in the *alternating* state of B, telling you that I could, when *coconscious*, control A by *willing*, but of that "willing" as a process I have no knowledge. But, as a fact, on numerous occasions I was prevented from doing something I wished to do, or made, in some mysterious way, to do something I objected to. Afterwards as B, I claimed, as I remember well, to have coconsciously influenced my other self by willing. I will give one instance of the effect on A of this coconscious willing. As A, I felt it my duty to go often to the cemetery to which, as B, I objected. In fact, B said she would not go there nor allow A to do so. A writes in the diary as follows: "Another queer thing happened today. I have not been to the cemetery for a long time, so started to go there. I had gone only a little way, when I began to feel that I could not go on. I do not mean that I did not wish to, but that I could not easily move my feet in that direction. It was as if some physical force was restraining me, or like walking against a heavy wind. I kept on, however, and finally reached the entrance, but further I found it impossible to go — I was *held* — could not move my feet one inch in that direction. I set my will and said to myself, I *will* go, I *can* go and I will, but I could not do it. I began to feel tired — exhausted — and turned back. As soon as I turned away, I had no trouble in walking but was very tired."

I do not think I can make the living of such a life at all lear to those who know nothing of such conditions. It vould seem impossible for one to get on at all, and it was at nce more, and less, difficult than could be imagined. The ocial situation was often most complicated; the nervous train was intense; the anguish of mind frightful; but, as B, had amnesia. As A, I stayed very closely at home, was very ntuitive; and one grows extraordinarily quick in guessing; t works wonders to look intelligent and say nothing, paricularly when no one suspects such a condition, for if one eems forgetful or absent-minded, the last explanation o suggest itself to one's friends would be "change of ersonality."

It all seems very strange to me now that I have become nyself with all these memories. I feel quite differently about everything. The memory of those months of B's existence eems like the memory of a delirium. I feel, in a way, no responsibility for what, as B, I did. I remember those acts as my own; I deplore many of them; I cannot understand why they gave me pleasure for they would give me none now; I am sorry about them just as I would regret having, n the delirium of fever, done something which I would not n my right mind do, but I do not feel so humiliated, so ashamed of them as I did as A. They are so foreign to anything I would naturally do that they seem to be their own excuse. If, as A, I could ever have realized that B was only an illness, I should have been spared untold mental agony. But, as A, remembering as I did in the first part of my illness all my neglect of my friends and family, my indifference to their anxiety about me, the pain I caused them, and the many unconventional things I had done, I could not excuse or forgive myself; and never, as long as the state A remained, did I cease to be terrified and ashamed by the state B. I thought there must be something fundamentally wrong in my nature; that if any one knew the things I, as B, had done, I should be forever disgraced. Everything I did as B, I, as A, disapproved of. The things that gave me pleasure as B, caused me, as A, the bitterest mortification. As A, I condemned myself as B, utterly without mercy; and I suffered intensely.

I have said that I remember both A and B as myself and that is true, but there is a certain difference in my memory of B which I cannot quite describe. I do *understand* myself as B. It seems like delirium. A seems somewhat like a delirious state also, perhaps *dazed* would be a better word, but I understand why I felt as A did. A seems exactly like myself in an absurdly morbid, emotional, and unreasonable condition, but B seems foreign, though I was naturally of a gay and light-hearted disposition.

I could have lived my life, after a fashion, in either one of these states, had either one been stable enough to maintain itself without changing. Apparently my mental powers underwent no great change, but now that I am myself, I can see that in neither state was I capable of forming a well-balanced judgment. As A, I could see only one side of a subject. I could not compare, adjust, and shift my point of view nor look at anything in an impersonal way. Perhaps such a state would account for the fanatics and faddists who hold so tenaciously to their illogical ideas and who go to such extremes in carrying them out.

As B, I should have been in trouble all the time over money matters, and the pleasure of the moment would have determined my course of action, regardless of consequences. I should probably have lost all my friends, also, as I felt no affection for any one and was bound by no conventions. As A, I should have been in trouble all the time over everything on account of scruples, doubts, and fears, etc.

A and B are a good illustration of the psychological law, which you yourself have cited, that "States of pleasure are concomitant with an increase, and states of pain with a decrease of the vital functions." If I may so express it, A was a state of pain and B was a state of pleasure, and their physical and psychical conditions corresponded. As A, my psychical state was one of depression, hopelessness and despair, and my physical condition was one of neurasthenia. As B, my psychical state was of exaltation and happiness and the physical condition was one of vigor and ambition. When these conditions and relations are better understood by all physicians there will perhaps be hope even for the poor "neurasthenic."

Should this report be read by any but those who have some knowledge of such conditions, I am afraid they will say, "she was crazy," but I was not and never have been for one moment insane, though, as A, I used to fear I might be. During all this time, I lived my life, to all appearances, like any ordinary person. I directed the daily routine of my household, took entire charge of extensive repairs to my house, and managed my business affairs to a large extent. These things were done perhaps in a somewhat erratic manner, because as B, I neglected them very frequently, and this made it doubly hard for me as A, but not one of my family or friends suspected the true state of the case. I believe they all realized that I was in a serious nervous condition, very changeable as to mood, and felt much anxiety about my health, but that was all.

I have not spoken of my recovery in the restoration of my normal self as "C." As to how this was accomplished, I know nothing except what I have been told, which is very little. Everything was done through hypnosis, and I have no memory of what occurred. I only know that I went to you one day in a more than usually disintegrated state; that I was hypnotized and that I woke up *myself* with a feeling of strength and self-poise to which I had long been a stranger. There were no blanks in my memory — I remembered everything. This had been partially accomplished before, but the resulting state had not been stable, and it would involve too wide a digression to explain it. Every improvement in my condition has been made by the use of hypnotism. I have complete amnesia for my hypnotic states, but the results obtained I can speak of with conviction. Over and over again I have gone to you, as A, feeling utterly discouraged and hopeless; worn with insomnia and aching from head to foot from nothing but mental strain; so fatigued that the slightest exertion was an effort. I have, in this condition, been hypnotized, and when I woke a change so complete had taken place as to be little short of miraculous. The depressing emotions had disappeared and were replaced by a feeling of courage and ability to endure the trials of my life; the sense of physical and mental fatigue had given place to a sensation of lightness and well-being; the aches and pains were gone. I have then returned to my home comparatively happy, had a good night's rest and bore the strain of my peculiarly trying life for a longer or shorter period, as the case might be, with some degree of fortitude.

This was the change which could be wrought by suggestion in hypnosis in the state called A, for I am speaking of the earlier part of my illness, before a synthesis of memories had been effected, and A was the personality most in evidence. The same statement, however, holds good for the unstable state above referred to, when my memory was approximately complete but when I was easily disintegrated by any emotional strain or physical fatigue. Even now, being my normal self, I wake from hypnosis with a marked increase in my feeling of strength, stability, and ambition. As I have stated, I have never been in vigorous health (excepting during the time of my existence as B) and have suffered all my life from so-called nervous headache. For this trouble I have been treated by a number of physicians and I have no doubt that I have taken every known drug for headache, but nothing has ever given me such prolonged relief as therapeutic suggestion in hypnosis, and my health is better now than it has been for a number of years.

I realize the inadequacy of this description, Dr. Prince; it needs a mind trained to such study to do the subject justice and I cannot find the words to make the distinction between the two personalities as sharp as it really was. Moreover, I have touched only upon the lighter side of the case. The many deep experiences, some of them so bitter to remember and some of which have caused me lasting sorrow, I cannot bring myself to relate, and "the half has not been told." Few, I hope, have ever had or ever will have such an experience as mine. It seems to me, however, that similar conditions must often prevail when they are not recognized, or, if recognized, are but vaguely understood; there is little knowledge of the necessary treatment and the case is considered hopeless. As I have recovered, so may others similarly afflicted, and it is for this reason, and with the hope that a more general knowledge of the phenomena exhibited may be of some value in the treatment of such disorders, that I am willing to have the facts published. If it does serve that end I shall feel in it some compensation for the suffering and turmoil of the past few years.

# CHAPTER IX

## An Introspective Analysis of Coconscious Life

### MY LIFE AS A DISSOCIATED PERSONALITY — *(continued)*

#### BY A PERSONALITY (B) CLAIMING TO BE COCONSCIOUS

*Prefatory Note:* The preceding chapter gave an account of the different phases of multiple personality as they appeared to the subject after restoration to health. The account which is here presented was written by the same subject in one of her states of dissociated personality known as B, and gives the point of view of the subject in this condition. This personality, it will be remembered, although an alternating personality, claims also to be *coconscious* with the other phases of personality, including both the dissociated state A and the integrated normal state C, and to have a stream of mental life contemporaneous with the stream of the main personal consciousness of either state.

This second account derives its chief interest from the fact that it is an introspective analysis of coconscious life made by a person who remembers, as she claims, this life. It is not, therefore, an interpretation of objective facts, as must be any conclusions drawn from coconscious phenomena, like automatic writing and hysterical automatism, but the *remembered conscious experience of the person herself.* In this respect, it is a record of conscious processes similar to that which any one might give by introspective analysis of his own thoughts.

Not the least interesting part of the analysis is the genesis of the coconscious stream, which the writer traces to a complex (B) which had previously existed for a long period as a phase for her character, but without *un*awareness for the same, and which continued without interruption *after* un-awareness had developed, and thereby became independent and coconscious by definition although it had really existed before. This complex, however, as will be seen, is not the whole of the coconscious life, which also embraces a synthesis of perceptions of which the subject is not aware. The relations of this coconscious stream to the personal consciousness, its influences upon the latter, etc., are also described as they appear to the writer. The only aid given the writer in the preparation of this account was to indicate some of the various points upon which it seemed desirable to have such introspective testimony, such as "The Content of Coconsciousness," "Separateness of Coconsciousness," etc. These are given as headlines and have largely determined the form of the account. (The first headline, "Genesis of Dissociation," was inserted by myself after the account was written.) Every care has been taken not to influence the writer in her introspective observations. The rough draft, however, was criticized, some statements were challenged as interpretations, and the writer made to defend her statements as far as possible and make explicit what seemed too general or vague, or not clear, and to distinguish between fact and interpretation. I feel positive, however, so far as anyone can feel positive in such matters, that the introspective observations have not been influenced in any way, as the main object was to obtain an uninfluenced account free from artifact.

While it is difficult to accept as fact such an extensive and continuous coconscious life, the only alternative explanation is more difficult of credence. The truthfulness of the writer is beyond question. There remains, then, only the hypothesis that all the memories of this life are dream-like fabrications and hallucinations. It is difficult, if not impossible, to reconcile this interpretation with numerous facts; among them, that in numerous instances it could be proved that the claimed memories of B (not possessed by C) have corresponded accurately with the facts of the environment,[1] even when the subject, in one instance, was dreaming

---

1 Some of these data will be found in the following chapter.

and "walking in her sleep" (somnambulism); that they included the contents of automatic writings, of which the subject was unaware, and various other peculiarities; that the personality is otherwise a clear-headed, intelligent person capable of close reasoning, and is not subject to fabrications of memory of any other sort; that the memories were definite, precise, logical, and could not be broken down under cross-examination, etc. These memories certainly do not resemble fabrications as manifested in certain well-known cases (*e. g.,* those of Flournoy, Hyslop, Angel, and others).

The facts pertaining to the memories of coconscious life were narrated to me, in the course of my study of the case, by B *before* the subject had begun the study of the literature, and when, therefore, she was ignorant of the theories of the subconscious, multiple personality, etc.

It is interesting to note that the introspective observations of B agree, in principle, with those in the account given by the coconscious personality in the case of Miss Beauchamp. It is also in harmony with the objective facts observed in numerous pathological cases, like that of Miss Winsor, and in artificial dissociations of which the phenomena of automatic writing are examples. Whatever interpretation be put upon such an account, the importance of having an introspective analysis of this kind cannot be questioned.

One other point needs to be explained. Personality C, spoken of in this account, is not wholly the same personality as that which wrote the preceding account "My Life as a Dissociated Personality." To avoid confusion in the reader's mind I have not hitherto explained that, in the attempt to reintegrate the various dissociated states, a personality was first obtained and labelled C, which was not absolutely normal nor a complete integration. It was nearly so, however, but was unstable and varied in certain details, which would be confusing to go into here, from the final integrated normal personality C, who wrote the first account. Later this completely integrated and stable personality was obtained. The writer, B, claims to have the same coconscious life with this apparently normal stable personality, only she has not the power to influence her, and therefore cannot "come" voluntarily. She can, however, perform automatic writing (as many normal persons can), and thus give evidence of a coconscious existence. Through hypnosis, too, the alternating state B can be obtained. Afterwards the normal C becomes integrated again and retains memories of this state, as explained in her account.

Some of the phrases were italicized by myself to make the points of the writer clearer.

The writer desires it to be known that an opportunity was not allowed her to polish the style and give it a literary finish. An attempt was made by her only to weigh and note the facts as accurately as possible.

A complete experimental account of this case has been reserved for future publication.

M. P.]

[*Prefatory note by Dr. J. J. Putnam and Dr. George A. Waterman:* The undersigned, having had the privilege of seeing, on several occasions, the writer of the following report, and of witnessing the remarkable transformations of personality which Dr. Prince has learned to bring about in her at will, desire to add to the very interesting story which she tells a few words of endorsement and appreciation.

In the first place, we are convinced that the patient is a truthful witness, a conscientious observer, an intelligent and right-minded person. In the next place, we believe that what she describes as memories were memories and not vaporings or fabrications. The facts which she gave to us, as "state B," are faithfully transcribed in this account. As she told them, she made on us the impression of a person narrating her experiences and ready to be cross-questioned on them. Furthermore, a number of her statements were susceptible of verification and were verified by us.

JAMES J. PUTNAM, M. D.

GEORGE A. WATERMAN, M. D.]

## B'S ACCOUNT

I have been asked to write an account of my alternating and my coconscious life, and I have endeavored in the following pages to present the facts as they seem to me, but the task has been an extremely difficult one. The whole paper is, of course, retrospective and introspective, and it has been quite impossible at times to draw sharp lines of demarcation between the personalities. No doubt I may have read into the facts somewhat, and no doubt my account may be colored more or less by my present knowledge of abnormal psychology, for I have read a good deal of the literature and informed myself on the subject as much as possible. Had I not done so, I could not have written this account at all in any intelligible language — I should have no vocabulary in which to express myself. I find great difficulty now in making my meaning at all clear, for I have no words subtle enough. For example: I am in great need of a word that will express something in C's mind that is between a picture and a thought, and should be much obliged to any one who will supply it. I find myself in much the same position as a stranger in a foreign land — my words do not convey my meaning. Moreover, this paper has been written largely at odd times and at long intervals, and, consequently, is more or less disconnected. The main facts, however, of memory, though possibly the description of them may be tinged by what I have read, are, I am sure, absolutely correct. I suppose everybody's description of a fact is more or less colored by his general knowledge. The condition of the mind has been constantly changing, and what was true of A's mind was not true of the C first obtained, and the mind of the wholly integrated C is different from either of the other two; so my task, as I said, has been beset with many difficulties.

I have referred to the different personalities as A, B, and C, and in describing the system of ideas out of which, it seems to me, I developed, I have used the term "the B complex." The reader must not confuse the *B complex* with the *B personality*. The B complex was made up of floating thoughts, impulses, desires, inclinations, of which A was quite aware, but which had been for years suppressed; or, at least, she had been endeavoring to suppress them. It seems to me that the B personality (myself) grew out of this group of ideas, for in my character as a personality are all the ideas of the B complex. The two are distinct in the same sense that the seed is distinct from the flower, if I may be allowed to use metaphor. The B complex seems to me to be the seed from which I, the B personality, developed. I say that the B complex and the B personality are distinct, yet in referring to the B complex I find myself continually saying "I"; it is difficult not to do so. This, I think, must show the intimate relation between the two. I think of the B complex and I find I think of it as myself, although I do not think of A and C as myself, and they do not seem to be my own personality. You may say that I am C transformed, if you choose, but a thing transformed is not the same. I am, at any rate, a distinct personality.

### GENESIS OF DISSOCIATION

A very long time ago, C received an emotional shock which it seems to me, as I look at it now, resulted in the first little cleavage of personality. This emotion was one of fright and led to *rebellion* against the conditions of her life, and formed a small vague complex which persisted in the sense that it recurred from time to time, though it was always immediately suppressed. This complex, it seems to me, was the same, though only slightly developed, as that which appeared later and is described as complex B (corresponding to her second period). In trying to explain this condition, which, it seems to me, was the first starting of what ultimately resulted in a division of personality, I will divide the time into periods and I will call this *period I*.

Twelve years later she received a great shock in the sudden illness of her husband. The events of this period I call *period II*. This illness was of such a nature that C knew no complete recovery was possible, and that death might result at any time. This second shock aroused the same emotions of fright and *rebellion,* and seemed to revive and intensify the old complex. Then came the nervous strain of sorrow, anxiety, care, and the inability to reconcile herself to the inevitable. This nervous strain continued for four years. C's life during this time was given up entirely to the care of her husband; she tried to live up to her ideal — which was a high one — of duty and responsibility, and always having the sense of failure, discouragement, and apprehension. That old complex of rebellious thoughts, revived for the second time by the shock I have spoken of, became intensified and more persistent during the four years following. It was a *rebellion,* a longing for happiness, a disinclination to give up the pleasures of life which the conditions required; and there was a certain determination to have those pleasures in spite of everything, and this resulted in a constant struggle between C and this complex. For the sake of clearness I shall call this the B complex, for, as I have stated, it seems to me that it later developed into the coconscious and alternating personality, B, myself. C was conscious of these thoughts, but they represented to her the selfish and weak part of her nature and she tried to suppress them; tried to put them out of her mind but they still persisted, and she was always to a greater or less extent aware of them. There was no lack of awareness and no amnesia. As the months and years went on, the sorrow and anxiety of the C group increased, and the conflicts and *rebellion* of the B group increased. C was ashamed of the latter and always tried to suppress such thoughts as they rose. If during those years anything happy had come to C, the formation of this rebellious complex would, I believe, have been retarded, perhaps stopped altogether, but nothing pleasant happened; it was all grief, and everything went wrong. This B complex, it seems to me, as I have above stated, was the evolution of that which, in the form of rebellious thoughts, developed in period I.

Finally her husband died away from home, and that was, to C, the one thing she had felt she could not bear. She did not recover from the shock and became more and more nervous, was very much depressed, easily fatigued, suffered constantly from headache, and was possessed by all sorts of doubts and fears, reproaching herself for things done and undone. She also overtaxed her strength in attending to business matters. *As she grew more and more neurasthenic,* it seems to me as I look back upon it, *the B complex grew stronger and more dominant,* and with this increase of strength of this complex, C began to live a life *corresponding to the impulses belonging to it* — staying out of doors entirely — and then there followed much improvement in health. She took long rides on the electric cars, which she had always previously disliked intensely; she had always been very much afraid of a canoe, but now she went canoeing often and enjoyed it. She was surprised and astonished that she should enjoy these things, as it was foreign to her natural and previous ideas and inclinations. There was no change of character, properly speaking, but she did things she disapproved of and knew at the time that she disapproved of them. There was a recognition that she was doing things she would not previously have done, and she protested to herself, but even this half-protest was suppressed. She would say to herself, "Why am I doing these things? I never cared for them before. Why should I care for them now?" The old doubts and fears were at this time out of mind. The personality was C, but influenced and dominated by the B complex of which, of course, she was perfectly aware. It seems to me that the ideas of the C complex and the ideas of the B complex occurred concurrently and simultaneously, so that it could be said that one was coconscious with the other. This is the way it seems to me, but I find it impossible to state positively from retrospection that the two complexes were not rapid oscillations or alternations from instant to instant.

At this time there came to C a third shock of a strongly emotional nature, giving rise to events which I call *period III.* It brought to her the realization of a fact of which she had been unconscious; she had never thought of the possibility of such a thing, and she was startled, frightened, angry, all in a flash — and I was there. James, in explaining "Sudden Religious Conversion," speaks of a "flowering of the subconscious," — well, I "flowered," and C disappeared somewhere; *the B complex had become a personality* and I lived a life of my own choosing.[1] How slowly this complex gathered form in this case may be seen from the fact that it was five years from the time of the beginning of her husband's illness before I came as a personality.

Now, when I came as a personality, I felt much younger than C; my ideas of what constituted pleasure were more like those of a girl of twenty, as C was when she received the first shock *(period I)*. But in character, points of view, tastes, emotions, in everything that goes to make up personality, I was quite different from anything C had ever been; also in health. I was strong and vigorous, taking long walks and feeling no fatigue. I was also very happy. Life seemed so good to me; everything was so beautiful; the outdoor world looked to me as it does to one who has been for months shut in through illness. I loved the trees, the sky, and the wind; but I did not love people. I felt no care or responsibility — this is why I was so happy. I remained the only personality for about one month, when there came the fourth emotional shock, producing *period IV*. It was I, B, who received this shock and it *brought back C as the dominant personality* but in a somewhat changed condition. Her mental perturbation was greater, she was more intensely nervous, full of doubts and fears and misgivings. This state is one which we have called A, for the sake of clearness, and will be presently described. As to myself, I still continue, in a sense, as the B complex in the same way as during the time when C lived the life which was in accordance with my nature and opposed to hers, *i. e.*, the out-of-doors life during the latter part of the second period; only, as a result of the time *(period III)* when I was the sole personality (though I did not think of myself as such) and had lived my own life, I had, it seems to me as I look back upon it, become more crystallized. There had before seemed to be a conjoining of two natures, and there was now; only the sec-

---

1 That is, the remainder of the C complex subsided into the "unconscious," where, of course, its experiences were conserved. They could be recalled as a memory by B. As a system of ideas the B complex had been "flowering" for five years. (M. P.)

ond one, myself, was more strongly integrated. C, or rather A, as I shall call this new phase, had no amnesia for the preceding period *(III)*, and, as before, was still perfectly aware of the B complex. She was ruled by this complex, as C had before been ruled, and kept right on doing things in accordance with the impulses of the B complex. She was something like a somnambulist, I think, partly realizing the difference in her conduct, which seemed strange to her, and unable to help herself. This condition lasted about a week. Then I came again as a personality — the whole personality — and stayed a month. Then A came as the result of another shock, fully awake, and still without amnesia and filled with amazement, horror, and despair at what she (I, B,) had been doing, but still dominated by the B complex, of which she was still aware. These changes were all caused by emotional shocks connected with the same subject. As I, B, seem to represent all the lighter, gayer, and more irresponsible part of C's nature, so A seemed to represent all the sad, gloomy, and morbid part. She could hardly believe that she had done, a short time before, the things which she remembered perfectly as her own acts; she saw everything from an entirely different point of view. All the old doubts and fears returned stronger than before. The state of vigorous health was gone in a twinkling; she was ill, hardly able to sit up; intensely nervous, unable to eat, sleep, or to put her mind on anything. In this condition she was strongly dominated by the B complex. She felt bound to keep promises which I (B) had made *(period III)*, though she disapproved of the course of action it involved. There was no self-consciousness in the B complex of personality. I did not think of myself as a different personality until after the development of amnesia and unawareness in A, but in looking back I realize the fact that I was a personality long before I knew myself as such *(period III)*. I came, in the first place, as a personality by accident, so to speak, and I became the B complex again in the same way, but in the meantime I had lived an independent life, and the B complex was stronger and more isolated. It was at this time that A was sent to Dr. Prince.

[The following paragraphs in brackets were dictated by B in hypnosis. Consequently, as will be seen, the writer, in this state, remembers her previous hypnosis, which is not the case when she is awake. — M. P.]

[Shortly after A went to Dr. Prince, one important change took place; she began to have amnesia for the time when I was in existence as the whole personality. The first time A had amnesia for me occurred at home after I had come spontaneously. I do not remember the exact circumstances of my coming or what brought me. It was in the morning, and it was raining when the change took place, and I realized my own personality. I wrote a letter to Dr. Prince and took it to the office to post it. Just as I dropped it in the box, the change of personality again took place and A came to the fore to find herself in the post office, with no knowledge of why or how she came there. *From that moment A had complete amnesia for me as an alternating personality and also was unaware of me as a coconscious complex.* I do not know what caused the amnesia and unawareness, but Dr. Prince tells me there was a reason for it which he can assign.[1] I however, had no amnesia for A as an alternating personality, which may be due to the fact that I was also coconscious with A, as well as an alternating personality.

A and I (B) alternated frequently for months, A having amnesia for me, but I remembering A. The change in personality was caused by any sudden shock, emotion, fatigue, anxiety.

After C (whose memory was approximately complete but who was unstable)[2] was obtained, the three personalities alternated, A and C having amnesia for me (B) and for each other, but I had no amnesia, being, as I will presently explain, coconscious with both states. As an *alternating per-*

---

1 B had appeared accidentally in hypnosis, *i. e.*, as an hypnotic state. Of this, awake, she has no memory. The next time the spontaneous change from B to A took place, the latter had amnesia for B and unawareness for the B complex. (M. P.)

2 This was not the final C but a preliminary one who was not quite complete. (M. P.)

*sonality,* I (B) remember both states and *my own coconscious life, but not the hypnotic states.* When I am *coconscious* (with A and C), however, I remember my own hypnotic state and A's[1] but not C's hypnotic state.

There was no change in my (B's) character after I became an alternating personality except in so far as I was broadened by my own independent experiences.

In hypnosis, I remember that I came as B once, but hypnotized, having changed spontaneously from A, who was then in hypnosis. After becoming A, awake, she had no memory of this, *i. e.,* of me or herself in hypnosis, any more than I (B) have, awake. On the first occasion after this, when A changed to me (B), as above narrated, A was no longer aware of her rebellious complex, and she had amnesia for me as an alternating personality.]

## COCONSCIOUS LIFE

In reading this description of my coconscious life, the reader must remember that I am not trying to prove anything, as that is obviously impossible. I myself know the facts to be as stated, but that is not proof for anyone else. I can only state these facts as they seem to me and describe my coconscious thoughts as anyone would describe his thoughts by introspection. I can only claim that they are distinct memories; this I know. If anyone can interpret them in any other way, I shall be much interested in knowing how it can be done. My memory of my coconscious life is just as sharp and distinct, even more so, than my memory of my alternating life. I also know that C does not have these memories. Should this story chance to be read by some other coconsciousness, we may get additional evidence.

I have been asked if it does not seem strange to me that I should be able to think my own thoughts while C is thinking hers. It does not, of course, seem strange to me at all, but I realize now how strange it seems to others. But how

---

1 Being in hypnosis now I remember this, but when I wake up as an alternating personality I lose this part of my *coconscious* memory.

can anyone say that there is not in his own mind a second stream of thought of which he is not conscious?

Besides an alternating life, then, as I have said, I have another life which I must describe; namely, that of my subconscious or coconscious existence. When I am not here as an alternating personality, my thoughts still continue during the lives of A and C, although they are not aware of them. I am coconscious with both A and C. That is to say, my mental life continues independently of theirs. This coconscious life of mine is a continuation of my alternating life after the change takes place to A or C. I still go on thinking my own thoughts and retain all the memories of my life as B, and of my previous coconscious life. I think my own thoughts, which are different from theirs, and at the same time I know their thoughts and what they do. My *coconscious* life is very similar to what my mental life was before the unawareness developed in A, except for certain peculiar developments and differences which, it seems to me, have resulted from this unawareness. Before the unawareness, the different complexes existed but as a part of one personality. Then A was aware of my (B) complex and resisted it; now she is not aware and cannot. Before the amnesia there were the same conflicting emotions and desires, but the division of personality was not complete. The A complex was aware of the B complex and *vice versa*, but until A was weakened by ill-health, she largely controlled or inhibited the B complex. After becoming weakened, as I have said, when A was present, she was influenced by the B complex according to circumstances. On the other hand, when the B complex was present, it was at this time aware of the protest of the A complex, but was not at the time influenced by it. A was completely dominated by B, but B was never influenced by A.

As far as ideas, emotions, and points of view go, I was as much a personality before the amnesia and unawareness on A's part as after, but still I do not speak of myself as an "I" at that time, chiefly because I thought nothing about it. Before the amnesia, I do not think there were any thoughts in the B complex of which A was unaware, but there were many which she did not understand.

After the amnesia and unawareness, I became a distinct personality in my own thought because I had a life completely my own, of which A was unaware. My thoughts, my experiences, she knew nothing of. The unawareness removed all inhibition[1] of my thoughts, and from that time I can speak of my thoughts as coconscious, because while they ran along with A's as they had done before, she was no longer conscious of them. They were the same kind of thoughts as had occurred in the B complex; the unawareness only made them more isolated, separate, compact, better crystallized, and the fact that A did not know them gave them greater freedom. Inhibition was removed. Before this she inhibited these thoughts. Otherwise, the fact of awareness or unawareness did not make any difference. I naturally, then, spoke of this group of thoughts and perceptions as a personality.

With the absence of awareness there was a growth of the coconscious experiences, and the fact of alternation gave me independent experiences, and all this added to and developed both the coconscious and alternating lives. As an alternating personality I retained my coconscious memories.[2]

When C[3] was obtained, the condition was the same, only I was less strongly organized coconsciously. I do not mean in separateness of thought or perceptions, but with C, when first obtained, I had less power to influence her, could not alternate with her by willing, and came less often spontaneously, but later this changed somewhat. The fact is that this C was so unstable that the content of her mind changed

1 This is more specifically expressed in the preliminary notes from which the final manuscript was written, as follows: "Before this (the unawareness) I had the same thoughts and inclinations, but A knew them and rebelled against them. Now when A ceased to be aware of my thoughts and life they were there all the same, but we speak of them as coconscious by the definition. They continue as they had before. The unawareness only made them more isolated," etc.

2 That is, of course, so far as she knows. As a fact she does not remember the hypnotic states, which coconsciously she does. See above. (M. P.)

3 This was not the final complete C whom she could not influence at all. See footnote, p. 302. (M. P.)

constantly. What was true one day would not be true another. Later I could at times influence her, as explained on page 310.

When I am coconscious, I see and hear many things of which neither A nor C is aware. Whether this is also true of me as an alternating personality, in comparison with A and C, I cannot say, for obvious reasons, but I think I do observe more closely and notice all little things more as a coconsciousness than when I am a personality.

### CONTENT OF THE COCONSCIOUSNESS

In attempting to describe by introspection the difference between my mind and C's, I shall have to use some sort of metaphor, and so will say that there are two streams of thought, one below the other. The upper one is C and the lower one is B. These two streams are not of the same quality. The upper one, C, is more opaque — thicker, less sensitive to perceptions; an *inward* flowing stream; brooding, questioning, very active in itself, but not so quick to take in outside impressions as the lower one, B. The lower stream, B, is clearer — crystal clear — and is an *outward* flowing stream, open to every perception, lighter, not introspective.

Now, nearly everything that happens is perceived by some part of C's mind — the rustle of a paper, the cracking of a stick in the fire, the sound of a bird chirping, the smile or frown on the face of a person whom we meet, the gleam of their teeth, etc., everything that can be seen or heard is recorded in her mind whether she is conscious of it or not. These illustrations are taken from actual occurrences which I distinctly remember. Now into my stream of consciousness most of these perceptions are absorbed, but C is conscious of only the more important ones. For example: Dr. Prince comes into the room and C rises and greets him, shakes hands and says, "Good morning"; she is conscious of nothing but a sense of relief at seeing him, and is thinking only of the woes she has to tell him; but I perceive things like this: Dr. Prince's hand is cold; he looks tired or rested; he is nervous today; he has on such and such clothes or cravat, etc. These perceptions become my thoughts. C does not take them into her consciousness at all. Later, if she were asked if she shook hands with Dr. Prince, she might or might not remember it; as to his hand being cold and all the rest of it, she would not have noticed; if she did, it would be an *automatic* memory; she had not *thought* about it. When C's mind is concentrated on any one thing, like reading or studying, it is closed to every other perception. She does not notice the sounds in the house or out-of-doors, but I, being coconscious, do. I hear the blinds rattle, I hear the maid moving about the house, I hear the telephone ring, etc. She hears none of these things. She does not know that she is tired, and that she ought to stop reading, but all these things I know and think of. When she stops reading she becomes conscious that she is tired, but of the sounds in the house she knows nothing. I have read the book also, but these other things are added to my stream of conscious thought. So, you see, I know all C's thoughts, and think my own besides. When she is talking with anyone, I often disagree with what she says. She does not think at all the same about many things. I think of replies I would make quite different from the ones she makes. Then sometimes I do not pay very much attention to her conversation, though I know all she says, but go on with my own thoughts. I do not say that every perception is taken into my consciousness. It may not be. Something else may, and evidently does, perceive things which escape me.

I do not remember *everything all* the time. I say this because some seem to think the "subconscious" is *always* conscious of *everything,* but that is not so with me. I forget sometimes, just as C does, but my memory is better than hers, especially when I am coconscious. I think this last is so because when C is dominant, *i. e.,* present, I can think my own thoughts undisturbed. I am in a clear, light place all my own. I do not have to think "I must do this or that, I must go here or there," as I must do when I am the alternating personality; I can just lie dormant, as it were, as far as physical activity is concerned, and think and remember.

Often when C is talking to someone, I know that she is

misunderstood; she does not know that the person has received a wrong impression, but I do.

Now, when we change, and I, B, am present as an alternating personality, it seems to me that the lower stream rises and the upper one is submerged, there is only one train of thought. The two streams are united in the sense only that I have no amnesia for C's previous stream of thought, but, of course, when I am the personality there *is* no C. I could no more think C's thoughts than I could think any other person's thoughts. When the change takes place I, B, have control of the motor powers. What causes the change I cannot tell you — a sudden shock does it, likewise a strong emotion does it, fatigue, anxiety, depression, etc. Sometimes C feels the change coming, that is, she knows from experience that her mood of depression will end in changing.

### SEPARATENESS AND CONTINUITY OF COCONSCIOUSNESS

As I retrospect, it seems to me that the two streams of thought are entirely separate even when we are interested in the same thing. My train of thought may be, and usually is, quite different from C's. When C is ill, for instance, she is thinking about her headache, and how hard life seems and how glad she will be when it is over, and I am thinking how tiresome it is to lie in bed when I am just aching to go for a long tramp or do something gay. We rarely have the same opinion about any book we are reading, though we may both like it. C, however, enjoys some writers whom I find very tiresome, Maeterlinck, for example. She considers him very inspiring and uplifting, and I think he writes a lot of nonsense and is extremely depressing. She enjoys poetry and I do not care for it. It happens often that when C is desperately unhappy, and her train of thought is black and despairing, mine is gay and happy. My tastes and points of view are just the same when I am an alternating personality. I have already given illustrations of separateness, when speaking of the content of my coconscious life. The two trains of thought are always going on, except when I am the personality. Then there is but one — my own.

## EMOTION

The only emotion that I remember to have experienced is one of pleasure and happiness. I know nothing of remorse, reproach, and despair. I know that C has these emotions; I know how she feels about everything, that is to say, I know what she *thinks* she feels, but I do not myself experience them. I am sometimes disappointed and sometimes provoked, but never really unhappy.

Emotion seems to me something like mercury. C is easily affected by the slightest change in her social atmosphere. Something happens and her spirits rise, she feels lighter, stronger, ambitious, and her heart seems to beat quicker; something else happens and her spirits sink, she feels heavy and dull and ill and has a return of neurasthenic symptoms. I never change in that way. I am the same, that is, I always feel happy, and that is a very fortunate thing, for I can't do what I want to half the time. Trivial things affect C as if they were great things, and she spends nearly the same amount of emotion over the former as she would over the latter.

### RELATIONS TO A AND C

My relations with the two personalities are not quite the same. With A, I do not feel or taste. If she closes her eyes, I cannot tell whether she is eating meat or candy unless I know beforehand. With C it is different. I know when she is touched and I know what she is eating. Should she be hurt, I would feel it but don't think it would cause me pain. It is the same with her emotions; I know what they are from her thoughts, but she *experiences* them. When she walks, my sensation is of being carried, though I see and hear and know everything and feel the ground under her feet. As an alternating personality, I have no pain. I can distinguish between touch and pain, but I do not suffer from the latter. The only difference is that pain is unpleasant. With A, I do not feel any pain at all, not even when she has a headache.[1] Even as the personality (B), I feel no pain, that is, what A and C think of as pain. I have nothing but an unpleasant sensation. When I am tested by pin pricks or pinching, I know it is a prick or a pinch and not a touch, but it does not hurt. I do not know whether this would be true for severe tests or not, but I do not feel pain at the dentist's, though A and C suffer intensely.

### ABILITY TO VOLUNTARILY INFLUENCE THE PERSONAL CONSCIOUSNESS

Voluntarily I can often, not always, make both C and A do the things I wish to do or go to the place I wish to go to. I do this by a process of willing. I fix my mind on C's mind and I say to myself, or rather to C, "you must go out to walk, it makes no difference whether you want to or not, you must; your legs feel all twitchy, you can't keep still," etc., and then she begins to feel nervous; she gets what she calls the "merry pranks" in her legs and goes to walk to get them straightened out. In the same way I make her go to see the people I like best when she is out paying visits. I think of the persons I wish to see, and how much I wish to see them, and C "changes her mind" and goes there. She sometimes suspects, now that she knows more about me, that I am influencing her and resists the impulses she feels. Then we have a struggle in which she sometimes wins. With A, I always came out best, but C is stronger. The greatest conflict of our wills comes when she tries to go to the cemetery. She feels it her duty to visit that place, and over and over again has tried to do so, but I *will not* go there. She has not been there for more than a year. I set my will and she sets hers, but I always win. I hold her, by my will, so that she can't walk in that direction. [A's account of this incident is given in the previous chapter, page 286.] This strong willing on my part produces a feeling of exhaustion in C; she

1 These differences in the perceptions have been the subject of experimentation, which confirmed the statement of the subject. (M. P.)

feels very tired, and that it is really no matter anyway, and finally gives up her intention and turns back; she feels as if she were being pulled in two different ways. Sometimes it is easy to do this and sometimes not. It depends a good deal on the state of her health and the state of her mind.

Many times I influence her when she does not suspect it, in making her read the book I wish to read or in making her go to walk. She considers herself changeable and nervous and wishes she knew her own mind five minutes at a time. For instance: one day it was raining and she did not want to go out, but I felt that I could not stay in the house another minute. So I willed that she should go to walk, and she changed her clothes and went out. She thought "what nonsense this is to go out in this rain. I wish I knew what I wanted to do five minutes at the time." She would think, "I guess I will go to walk," and then she would think, "No, I don't want to go out in all this rain," then in a few minutes, "I believe I *will* go to walk," etc., and finally she went, more for peace of mind than anything else.

Over the *normal* C, who now exists, I have no power to influence her voluntarily or involuntarily, directly or indirectly, so far as I know. There are coconscious influences that are received from other parts of her mind, but I am not writing of these in this account.[1]

I have made it impossible for A to telephone Dr. Prince. A was always telephoning him, and I thought it was very foolish to do so, particularly as it usually resulted in suppressing me as a personality. So when A started toward the telephone, I held her, by my will; she could not go to the telephone for the purpose of speaking to Dr. Prince. She did not know that I did it. It seemed to her that while she wished to speak to him she had better not bother him after all, and then she would be so blue and depressed that I would "come."

Sometimes, after hypnosis, the first unstable C to whom

---

1 Investigation has shown other coconscious phenomena and influences distinct from those of the B complex. (M. P.)

I am referring could remember, in a way, some of my acts.[1] The memories were in the form of visual pictures, and it always seemed to me that she remembered only the things that Dr. Prince knew about himself. I, in the alternating state, was thinking of this one night after I had gone to bed and wondered whether, if I should hide A's watch and rings, Dr. Prince could make C remember it — not knowing it himself. I felt too lazy, however, to get up and hide them, but in the morning they were gone. I knew where they were, for I remembered she got up in her sleep and hid them in a cuff box where they were found by her sister. Then another night, when I was *coconscious,* I wondered if I could by *willing* make A get up in her sleep and do the same thing. So I willed that she should get up in her sleep and hide her watch and rings that night. I did not designate any place. She did it, or, at least, in the morning they were gone and could not be found for some time, until Dr. Prince discovered that they had been hidden, in her sleep, under some cushions on the landing of the stairs.[2]

When A is present, I can "come" voluntarily by willing, *i. e.,* blot A out and then I "come." When C is present it is more difficult, but I can sometimes do it, *i. e.,* when she is excited or depressed or upset in any way, physically or mentally. I can always do it with A except when she has a bad headache. This seems paradoxical, because, with this exception, when she is in poor health I can come more easily. Usually, for a few days after A had had suggestion from Dr. Prince, I did not "come." I don't know whether I could not or did not feel like trying. By willing I mean I would say to A — "Get away," "Go away," "Get out of the way," "Let me come," "I *will* come," and then A disappeared. She was gone and I was there. It was almost instantaneous. With C, I had to make a different effort. I had to think more about it, when I wanted to come; that I must be the personality because of the things I wanted to do; that I must

1 These memories were brought back by suggestion. (M. P.)

2 This was done through hypnosis. The articles were found as remembered in hypnosis. B, of course did not remember that the hypnotic state b had told me. (M. P.)

ome; that I would come. It sometimes took a minute or two to get rid of C. Her thoughts stopped. I don't know what became of them. The times, however, when I came by willing were comparatively few compared with the times when I came spontaneously, but there were many times. Sometimes the wish to change would blot out A without actual willing. Example: There was a dinner party to which I was very anxious to go, and while A was dressing she decided she would not go, and started to cross the room to take up the telephone to say she would not be there, and I wanted to go so much that she lost herself before she reached the telephone. My thoughts were, "I want to go," "You must go," but not, "I must come," etc.

### INVOLUNTARILY INFLUENCING THE PERSONAL CONSCIOUSNESS

Ordinarily the two streams of thought run on side by side without interfering with each other. C may be reading or studying something that interests us both, and our minds are occupied in the same way. I am contented and all goes well. At other times C may be reading and I may not be interested. I may not like the book or may want to do something else. I feel restless and dissatisfied, and soon C begins to feel the same. She can't fix her mind on what she is reading, puts down the book, goes to the piano but can't play, starts a letter but does not finish it, etc. This is what I call an involuntary influence. In this case, I do not have the power to "come" or to make C do the thing I want to do, in fact, perhaps I do not know what I want to do myself, but my state of mind makes her nervous and upset. As an example of involuntary influence I will take the following incident, as it is fresh in my memory. A few days ago, Dr. Putnam kindly allowed C to see a patient of his who is suffering from a form of hysteria. She could not put her feet down flat on the floor, but turned her toes up and tried to walk on her heels and the side of her feet, and as she walked she trembled all over and breathed irregularly.[1] I was much

---

1  This was a case of hysterical astasia-abasia of a peculiar type. (M. P.)

interested in the matter, and after we got home kept won
dering how the girl managed to walk that way — it seemed
so difficult. There was in my mind a picture of the girl with
her toes turned up, trembling and breathing hard; I was im
agining how it would seem to walk that way and to tremble
all over. I was not paying any attention to C's train of
thought, being absorbed in my own, and did not consider at
all how my thoughts might affect her until I became aware
that she was trembling from head to foot, that her toes were
all curled up, and that she could hardly keep her feet flat on
the floor. She was in great distress of mind, as she thought
her condition was caused by her extreme suggestibility, and
that she must be very ill to be so easily affected. She was so
much disturbed that she telephoned Dr. Prince, asking him
to help her to steady herself. I did not intend to produce
such an effect. It would seem plain that my train of thought
influenced her.

At another time, C was asked to go for a long auto-
mobile ride and dine in the country, coming home in the
evening. I was very anxious to go, but I had promised Dr
Prince not to interefere with C. I did not try to "come,"
but I could not help *wanting* to go, and I thought to myself
"O! I wish she would go." C declined at first, as I knew she
would, but as my longing increased she began to waver, hesi-
tated, and finally said she would go. She felt that she ought
not to go, that it was better not to accept such invitations
and hardly knew why she should have changed her mind
She felt provoked with herself about it, but as she changed
to me as an alternating personality soon after we started, it
was all right.

C once had a visual hallucination of Dr. Prince, because I was thinking of him. She was thinking of entirely
different matters, but I was thinking that if it were not for
Dr. Prince I might, perhaps, stay all the time, and was wondering why it was that I did not go away somewhere; why
it was that I felt bound to keep C's appointments with him,
etc. As I was thinking all this, C suddenly saw Dr. Prince
standing before her. He was so real that she spoke his name,
saying, "Why, Dr. Prince!" She was not asleep, but was

ying in bed looking at the fire when she had this hallucination. She knew it was a vision, but it was very distinct.

I one day wrote something in the diary, which has been kept by all of us, which A did not understand, and she took the book to Dr. Prince. I did not care to have him read what I wrote in my diary, and so that night I wrote a note to A, saying that I was going to put the diary where she could not find it and that she should never see it again. I did not, however, do so, but left it in the drawer where it was always kept. A found this note from me in the morning and went at once to see if the diary was gone. It was right there, but she could not see it; she took it in her hand several times in searching through the drawer, but could not see it, and did not do so for a week or more.[1] When she did see it, she could not understand how it came to be there and thought I must have "come" in the night and put it back. She wrote it so in the diary at the time. A writes, Sept. 19, 1907: "It is the strangest thing about this diary  I have not been able to find it for a week or more and I know it was not in that drawer last night, but I have been myself all day and how could B have put it back again?  I cannot understand it at all — perhaps she came in the night. A had seen Dr. Prince that day[2] and I suppose that is why she could see the diary when she came home.

## DREAMS

Though C does not remember her dreams when she is awake she feels their influence, especially if it is a depressing one. She dreamed a few nights ago of a very distressing event which really occurred several years ago, and which gave her an intense emotional shock. In the dreams she lived over again all the emotion she experienced at the time, all the feeling of horror, sorrow, fear, and self-reproach; also the physical sensation of nausea and headache which followed

1 This was probably due to combined conscious and subconscious influences — a conscious suggestion from the note and an unconscious wish that she should not see it. (M. P.)

2 That is, had received therapeutic suggestions. (M. P.)

the shock. When she woke, she had no remembrance of he dream, but she felt the depression, the headache, and th nausea.

Last night she had a dream which affected her in th same way. She dreamed she was standing on the top of very high mountain where she could see all the country fo miles around. She was alone, and the wind was blowing he hair and dress. It was at sunset, and the sky was filled witl clouds which took various shapes and were colored by th setting sun. The upper part of the sky was filled with pic tures which were framed in small white clouds, touched witl gold on the edge where they curled over. Some were land scapes, some were portraits. One portrait was of her mother very, very beautiful—and all were in colors. Below these pic tures were flowers of every kind and description — rose gar dens, old-fashioned gardens, wreaths, single flowers — ; perfect mass of color. Above all this was one cloud whicl had no color and no particular shape, but which attractec her attention more than the rest; she was fascinated by i and watched it. The sun went down and all the picture vanished, but this one cloud remained and took the shape ol a man — Mr. —— (her husband). She reached her hand to him and said, "Oh, speak to me," but he looked at her very sorrowfully and turned away. Then she had that same feeling of nausea, headache, and weariness, and covered her eyes. When she looked again it was not her husband but Dr. Prince, and she called to him and said, "Dr. Prince, if *you* do not speak to me I shall throw myself down the mountain," and Dr. Prince stretched out his hand and looked very funny, and he said: "If all the world were apple pie and all the sea were ink, what *would* we do for cocktails?" And C said, "Dr. Prince, you are perfectly horrid." Then she woke up, but she felt ill, just as she did in the dream, and when she saw Dr. Prince that morning, she told him she felt very ill. Now all that $C^1$ remembers of that dream is of standing on the mountain, with the wind blowing her hair and dress, and of seeing her husband and Dr. Prince. She

1 This is correct. (C.)

oes not remember anything else. I was awake when she dreamed this dream, for I know what was going on in the house and C does not. She did not hear the maid go downstairs or any of the sounds in the house. Her dreams are usually depressing though occasionally they are amusing. C sometimes remembers the main features of her dreams but none of the details.[1]

1 C has been examined on numerous occasions for memory of dreams and it has been found that she rarely remembers them, though they are recovered in hypnosis. The persistence of headache, nausea, and depression following a dream has been frequently noted and removed by a simple suggestion. (M. P.)

PART III

# CHAPTER X

## EXPERIMENTS TO DETERMINE COCONSCIOUS (SUBCONSCIOUS) IDEATION

ALTHOUGH a large and still accumulating mass of evidence has shown, under certain pathological and other conditions, the presence of coconscious (subconscious) processes of which the subject is unaware, and yet which manifest themselves through intelligent actions, still all writers are not in accord as to the interpretation which shall be put upon these manifestations. While I believe all students of abnormal psychology — those who have done the experimental work — are in agreement in interpreting subconscious manifestations as the expression of subconscious ideas, more or less dissociated from the personal consciousness — that is to say, they are agreed on the psychological interpretation — there are certain theoretical psychologists who still insist that all such subconscious manifestations are compatible with the interpretation that they are a result of physiological processes, without any association with ideas whatsoever.[1] This is the physiological interpretation. It is, therefore, desirable to obtain evidence which will determine which of these two interpretations is correct.

The following experiments were undertaken to obtain, if possible, such evidence.

B. A. is a case of multiple personality of which one personality may be designated as A and the other as B. Observation extending over many months has shown that A has no knowledge of B, but B is completely aware of A; that is, A has amnesia for the state of B, while B has no amnesia. B can be hypnotized and in hypnosis is known as "*b*." On

1 See further, chapter XVII.

awakening from hypnosis, B has no recollection of *b*. Now
the important point for our present purpose is that B, both
when awake and when in the hypnotic state as *b*, claims to b
subconscious (coconscious) with A when that state is to th
fore; she claims to have perceptions, feelings, and strains o
thought distinct from and synchronous with the mental lif
of A; she describes them with precision and specifically.

Of all this claimed subconscious life, A has no knowl
edge. The question is, can B's (and *b*'s) claim be verifie
even in part? She herself says: "I *know* it is so, but that i
not proof for another person."

To obtain evidence that would justify the inference,
devised the following tests:

## TESTS IN COCONSCIOUS PERCEPTION

*Experiment* 1. The following experiment was mad
without the knowledge of any of the personalities.

While talking with A, I had her close her eyes for
moment and while they were closed, as silently as possibl
without moving from my seat, I hung a handkerchief ove
the back of a chair on my left within the range of her peri
pheral vision. I then directed her to open her eyes, to kee
them fixed on mine and to listen to what I had to say.
talked to her earnestly for a few moments, holding her at
tention. She kept her eyes fixed on mine, and did not onc
look toward the handkerchief or allow her eyes to deviate
(As every physician knows, it is easy to detect the slightes
deviation of the eyes under such conditions.) After th
lapse of about half a minute, she closed her eyes at my re
quest, and I surreptitiously removed the handkerchie
Then, after allowing her to open her eyes again, she wa
directed to describe any change she had noticed in the en
vironment while I was speaking to her; anything she ha
seen which had not been present before closing the eyes th
first time, or anything which she missed now. She was un
able to describe any change; she had seen nothing. She wa
now hypnotized; the hypnotic state *b* immediately said o
coming: "I know; there was a handkerchief hanging on th

arm of the chair; I saw it. A did not see it, or at any rate, did not think about it, for I only know what she sees by what she thinks." As to the content of *b's* coconscious perception, she testified, "There was no thought in my mind connected with the handkerchief, excepting that I thought Dr. Prince's handkerchief was hanging on that chair. I didn't know it was any part of an experiment — I thought you were going to hypnotize her without her knowing it. It seems to me that I was there as a personality, that I am there all the time, just as I am here now, only now I can move and do as I please. When A is here I can't." Here it is interesting to note that two other hypnotic states, which can be obtained in this case, did not see the handkerchief, but neither of these claims to be or has shown any evidence of being coconscious with A. Their testimony, however, corroborates A's statement of not having seen the handkerchief. Both these hypnotic states, known as *a* and *c,* have a complete knowledge of A's consciousness, or rather, *are* A hypnotized. Neither saw the handkerchief.

*Experiment* 2. A similar experiment was made under the same conditions with (the real) Miss Beauchamp. Awake as Miss B., she did not see the test object, but the hypnotic state B II described it. Afterwards, Miss B. could not be made to recall having seen it, though it was described to her.

Accidental failure on the part of Miss Beauchamp to notice objects, such as passing me in the street, with complete perception by some one of her subconscious states, was frequently observed; but, of course, it is not possible to exclude amnesia as a possible explanation. Amnesia is even a possible interpretation in the above two experiments. It was, therefore, necessary to test the subconscious by methods in which amnesia could not be a factor.

#### COCONSCIOUS PERCEPTION AND REASONING

The following experiments were made without A's knowledge of what was being done. C, and afterwards B, were informed of the nature of the tests and entered into them with interest. The point of the experiments was to communicate to subconscious *b*, without A's knowledge, a mathematical or other problem, of which even *b* did not previously know the factors. This had to be done while A was thoroughly alert, and without in any way disturbing (dissociating) her consciousness or allowing her consciousness to become aware of, and thereby possibly take part, in the problem. *b* must, therefore, subconsciously become informed of the given problem without A being informed at the same time. The problem also had to be one which presumably could only be performed by psychological processes so far as we know.

Accordingly, it was agreed with *b* that, when coconscious, she should do a particular sum in arithmetic while A's consciousness was engaged in another task. The sum would be to add mentally certain numbers and, as a more difficult problem, to calculate the number of minutes or seconds intervening between two given hours. The figures to be added and those indicating the time were not to be given until A was present, so that *b* thus far knew only the nature of the task, not the task itself. It was necessary, of course, to convey to subconscious *b* the information, without at the same time informing A, and without producing any of those artificial dissociations which frequently follow when communicating with the subconscious.

It was, accordingly, agreed that A's attention should be engaged by having her write some verse with which she was familiar on a sheet of paper, on the upper and lower margins of which the required figures for the sum would be unobtrusively written. Coconscious *b* was to perceive these figures and make the computation. It was expected that A would not notice the figures if her attention by a little art was centred upon the verse as the important thing but at the same time it is obvious that it did not matter if she did, as the figures could have conveyed no idea to her either as to their meaning, or as to the nature of the task or as to whether she was expected to do anything with them for A was kept entirely in the dark regarding the nature of the experiment, and was not even informed that an experiment as such was being made. If she had seen the figures, they could have meant nothing to her.

On the other hand, if *b* was truly subconscious, as she asserted, she should be able to recognize the figures, interpret them, and possibly make the computation. It was further arranged with *b* that as soon as A had completed the verse, she was to be changed to *b*, who was to give the answer immediately on "coming," without delay, before she could have time to make the computation from memory after the change to *b*, in case it had not been done coconsciously.

*Experiment* 3. A was brought and the number 53 was written, without her knowledge, in the left-hand upper corner of a sheet of paer measuring 8½ × 11 inches, and 61 in the lower right-hand corner. The task for the coconscious was to recognize these numbers and to add them together mentally.

A was then directed to write in the middle of the sheet the verse: "Tell me not in mournful numbers," etc. I distracted her attention, as a conjurer might, so that she would not and, apparently, as a fact did not examine the paper, though as already said, it would have been immaterial if he had.

As she wrote, she repeated aloud in all the experiments, whatever verse was chosen, sometimes commenting on the poet's thoughts, sometimes on the faults in her own memory as to the words, sometimes laughing at both. This is of importance as indicating that she was *alert* and did not go into a dreamy state as some automatic writers do.

Once only (in the first experiment) she stumbled a bit while writing, as if there was a momentary inhibition of her thoughts by the subconscious process. A different verse was elected for each experiment.

After the verse was finished, when questioned, she stated that she had not noticed, in any of the experiments, any other writing (the numbers) on the paper, which had appeared quite blank.[1] This was the case in every instance. Whether this was due to my distracting her attention or to the effect of what might have been equivalent to a post-hypnotic suggestion, due to the conditions of the experiment, is not material. She was then changed to *b*. Immediately on appearing, *b* exclaimed, almost shouted: "114," which was correct.

In addition to this sum in mental arithmetic, it was arranged that *b* was, subconsciously, to count the buttons on my vest (previously concealed) and multiply the number by six. *b* gave the number of buttons correctly in the same breath with the above sum — but, as she explained, she forgot to multiply by six. As to the way she subconsciously did the sum, she explained that she visualized the numbers, though they did not arrange themselves in a definite form before her mind, and the sum then did not do itself, as was the case with another subject; but she said to herself: "Three and one are four, six and five are eleven," etc. "I looked up and I looked down at the numbers, and I looked at the buttons on your vest." (I had noticed a movement downwards of the eyes toward the lower number, but did not detect the other movements; but, of course, the eyes were in constant motion as she wrote.)

*Experiment* 4. The numbers 1.20 and 2.47 were written at the top of the sheet of foolscap (8 × 12 in.), thus:

1.20

2.47

These indicated twenty minutes past one, and forty-seven minutes past two, and the problem for the subconscious was to calculate the difference in time in minutes. On appearing, *b* promptly gave the answer: "one hour and twenty-seven minutes."

1 This was probably due to the fact that I had picked up intentionally, but with apparent carelessness, a wad of loose sheets of paper lying on my desk some of which were blank and some written upon (notes of experiments, etc.) so that there was nothing peculiar in a couple of numbers written on a sheet to strike the attention or arouse suspicion.

*Experiment 5.* In the same way, the numbers 3.15 and 4.33 were written. The problem was, as before, to calculate subconsciously the number of seconds intervening between these hours. *b* correctly gave the answer: 4680. She further described her subconscious mental processes in doing these calculations. She said, for instance, to herself: three-fifteen to four-fifteen is one hour or 60 minutes; four-fifteen to four-thirty-three is 18 minutes. 60 and 18 make 78. 60 times 78 is 4680. (This multiplication was done in the usual way, *i. e.*, 6 × 8 = 48; 6 × 7 = 42; 42 + 4 = 46, etc.)

Personality B was now brought, and her memory for the subconscious processes tested. (It will be recalled that B claimed to remember the subconscious states of A as a part of her own personality.) B thus far knew nothing of the experiments. All the details had been arranged with her hypnotic state *b* of whom, of course, she had no memory.

B now remembered the numbers which had been written on the otherwise blank sheets on which A had written the verse, and that she had seen them, *but she remembered nothing of the subconscious calculations*, did not even know that there had been any calculations or that the numbers meant anything. In fact, she thought the figures stood for dollars and cents, as suggested by the decimal point.

The evident reason for this was that the calculation formed part of the system of ideas forming the synthetic group *b*. With the awakening of synthesis B, this calculating group naturally became dissociated, as is always the case on awakening B out of hypnosis *(b)*.

To prove this principle, the following experiment was made, this time the directions being given to B instead of *b*.

*Experiment 6.* The following figures were written as before:

12.11
1.20

The problem was to calculate the number of seconds intervening between these hours. After A had written her verse, she was changed directly to B, who immediately gave the answer 4860.

B now remembered not only the perception of the numbers, but the calculation, which she said had been difficult. She had made the number of minutes 81 instead of 79. This was due to the fact that she had taken the hour 1.20 as 1.30, then calculating 12.11 to 1.11 as 60 minutes. If it had been 1.10 there would have been 20 minutes more (to make 1.30), but it was 1.11; so she should have subtracted 1 minute — instead of which she added 1 minute, making 21 minutes in all (instead of 19) — 60 + 21 = 81; 81 × 60 = 4860. This answer was not correct, but the error was even more instructive than if it had been right. The answer should have been 4940.

*Experiment 7.* In order to meet the possibility (however improbable) of *b* and B having made the calculation after "coming," notwithstanding the shortness of time at their disposal — a few seconds — or during the transition period when A's consciousness was partially (or wholly) extinguished[1] it was arranged that the computation should be written automatically while A was conversing. The figures were 1.43 and 3.39. As a result the hand wrote out the calculation while A was alert as before but, of course, without awareness of her hand.

There was a slight error in the answer, the hand making the elapsed minutes 114 instead of 116. This obviously is of no importance. Of importance is the fact that the *hand* explained, in part, the steps of the problem, thus: "1.43 to 3.39 would be two hours less than [by four minutes]." (This sentence was unfinished.) Then the number 114 was written and multiplied by 60, which was placed under it in the conventional manner, and the answer 6840 obtained thus:

---

[1] During such a transition period, however short, it is obvious that the secondary personality ceases to be coconscious and becomes an alternating personality.

$$114$$
$$60$$
$$\overline{\phantom{000}}$$
$$6840^1$$

It must be remembered that the subject did not look at the paper while the hand wrote, so that the "coconsciousness" was obliged to keep the figures in her head, though she calculated on paper. B and *b* later explained that when doing a calculation coconsciously on paper, she could not visualize the figures as she did when the calculation was made mentally. She, therefore, could not keep the figures in her head. It was "like throwing them away," *i. e.*, they would drop out of her mind.

A number of similar experiments in which the calculations were written automatically were made. The results were substantially the same, the multiplication being always correct, though the elapsed minutes were wrong.

Again; I taught B some dozen characters of a shorthand which I make use of in note-taking. Most of these symbols, I believe, are purely arbitrary, of my own invention, and B A had never seen them before. As soon as B had memorized them I changed her to A and wrote the following: " I J ∟ a √ of |." This was shown to A, to whom it meant nothing; but the hand promptly translated it, writing automatically: "I *have had a time of it.*" (Correct.)

Now, here something outside of A's consciousness recognized the characters, read them and translated them; something that in our experience can only be defined as intelligence.

Considering the conditions under which these experiments were made; that A knew nothing of their nature, that *b* and B did not know beforehand what the particular problem was to be; that the figures were not visible until A began to write the verse, and that A did not know the shorthand

---

1 On the first trial, the hand made the mistake of multiplying twice by 60. (The second time incorrectly.) When told "wrong," it wrote: "I can't do it as well when it is on paper. Are the hours right? 1.43 to 3.39." Then, as above, multiplied 144 by 60 correctly.

characters — the conclusion seems inevitable that they, figures and symbols, must have been interpreted subconsciously, even if A saw the former (which apparently she did not do) ; for A could not have known what any of them meant, and that the calculations and translation must have been made coconsciously; accordingly the memory of *b* and B, when afterwards describing the calculations, must have represented the facts. That such perceptions, interpretations, calculations and translations could have been made by pure *physiological processes without thought* is inconceivable and not substantiated by anything that we know of physiological processes.

In conclusion, I may cite one of a series of experiments made, in conjunction with Dr. Frederick Peterson, by means of the psycho-galvanic reaction method to determine the

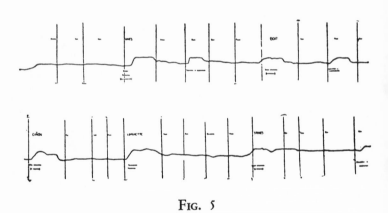

FIG. 5

presence of subconscious emotions of which the subject was unaware. This method, it will be remembered, depends upon the fact that an electric current, which is made to pass through the body, is increased whenever an emotion is aroused. The emotions are excited, as in ordinary association experiments, by test words, which are given to the subject, interspersed among indifferent words. The increase of current is recorded on a kymograph and appears as waves in the tracing. Advantage was taken of the fact that the hypnotic states, *a* and *b*, remembered dreams of which the subject was unaware on awaking. In one or the other of two nightmares, a boat, waves, a canyon and stones played a strongly emotional part, and these words, with the word "lorgnette," were interspersed in a list of twenty-five words. The word "lorgnette" referred to a subconscious experience of *b*, made up of perceptions and thoughts of which the waking personality had no knowledge.

The tracing obtained shows very marked rises in the curve corresponding to the words "waves," "boat," "canyon," "lorgnette," "stones." (See next chapter.)

The subject herself had connected with these words no associations which could explain the waves in the tracing and was not consciously aware of an emotion.

# CHAPTER XI

## EXPERIMENTS IN PSYCHO-GALVANIC REACTIONS FROM COCONSCIOUS (SUBCONSCIOUS) IDEAS IN A CASE OF MULTIPLE PERSONALITY

THE following experiments were undertaken with the view of determining: — first, whether in the psycho-galvanic reaction of Tarkhanov, we should be able to obtain physical corroboration of the evidence for coconscious or split-off ideas; and, second, assuming such ideas to have been demonstrated by other methods, to what extent, if at all, they could affect the galvanic reactions to word-stimuli. The term "coconscious" is used as equivalent to subconscious ideas actually present and functioning — i. e., co-active ideas. As to the first object, it should be explained that, although a large and still accumulating mass of evidence has shown, under certain pathological and other conditions, the presence of coconscious processes of which the subject is unaware and yet which manifest themselves through intelligent actions, still all writers are not in accord as to the interpretation which shall be put upon these manifestations. While, we believe,[1] all students of abnormal psychology — those who have done the experimental work — are in agreement in interpreting subconscious manifestations as the expression of coconscious ideas, more or less dissociated from the personal consciousness — that is to say, they are agreed on the psychological interpretation — there are certain theoretical psychologists who still insist that all such subconscious manifestations are compatible with the interpretation

1 These experiments were carried out in conjunction with Dr. Frederick Peterson, of Columbia University, whose co-operation I gratefully acknowledge.

that they are a result of physiological processes, without any association with ideas whatsoever. This is the physiological interpretation. It is therefore desirable to obtain evidence which will determine which of these two interpretations is correct. It seemed to us that Tarkhanov's "galvanic reaction" might throw some light upon the interpretation of subconscious phenomena. It will be remembered that Tarkhanov, Veraguth, Jung and others have shown that when a weak electric current is passed through the body and, at a given moment, an emotional tone is evoked by arousing some idea that has an emotion associated with it, at that moment the electrical current becomes increased. This increase is due, probably, to a diminished resistance of the skin brought about by the emotion. Now, if a galvanometer is placed in the circuit and so arranged that a ray of light, falling upon the mirror of the galvanometer, is reflected upon a scale, then with every increase of the current the light will travel along the scale. Accordingly, whenever, through a given stimulation, an emotional tone is aroused in the subject, there is an increase of electrical current and a movement of the light along a greater or less number of degrees upon the scale. By measuring these degrees of movement and plotting the oscillations upon a chart, a curve can be constructed, or, by the special contrivance of Jung, the oscillations of light can be recorded on a revolving drum (kymograph); this latter apparatus we used in our experiments. By using the well-known method of word stimulation, thus arousing various associated ideas with their emotions, a series of reactions can be obtained which record themselves through the oscillations of light on the kymograph.

In the experimental work thus far done, whether by the galvanic method or the more common word-association tests, the reactions obtained have been, in certain cases, interpreted as due to subconscious ideas, but the term "subconscious" has been rather vaguely used. It has so many different meanings that it is difficult to make sure in what sense it is used by those who would explain certain psychological phenomena by it. In this account, the term "subconscious" is used in the sense of "coconscious," which is also employed as a synonym, meaning split-off, dissociated ideas of which the subject is usually not aware, *but which, nevertheless, are in activity at a given moment.* "Coconscious," *therefore, implies doubling of consciousness.*[1]

In previous experiments, too, it has been necessary to infer the presence of coconscious (subconscious) ideas (if that has been the interpretation), from the occurrence of the galvanic reaction or word-association, and then to correlate the reaction with the inferred factor. It is desirable, therefore, that we should be able to have other evidence of the occurrence of both factors between which we seek a correlation — in this case, between "subconscious" processes (whether physiological or psychological) on the one hand, and the galvanic reaction on the other.

For this purpose, it is essential that the subject should be one in whom subconscious processes can be shown to exist by the methods commonly employed in investigation in abnormal psychology.

The subject, B. C. A., whom we made use of, is one who is particularly favorable for such experiments. She is a case of multiple personality in which one of the personalities claims to be coconscious with the other.

In order that the experiments may be intelligible, it will be necessary to briefly explain the relations of the personalities to one another.

The normal personality is known as C. This personality divides up into two others, one of whom is known as A, and the other as B. C is aware of herself in both the other states, A and B. On the other hand, A has no knowledge of either the normal self C, or of her disintegrated sister personality B. B, on the contrary, has a complete memory for the times when she is her disintegrated sister A, and the normal C.

This relationship may be diagrammatically expressed as follows. The arrows show the direction of knowledge.

[1] "Coconscious" is not the equivalent of "unconscious" (*das Unbewusste*) as used by Freud, Jung, and others.

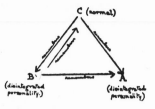

FIG. 6

The reason why B remembers the other two personalities is because, as she claims, *she exists as a coconsciousness during the lives of A and C respectively,* and as such a coconsciousness she claims to have a stream of ideas of her own, distinct from the stream of consciousness of the primary personality.

Accordingly, it is clear that B is both an alternating and a subconscious personality. That is to say, when A and C disappear, coconscious B remains as the sole personality in existence and is then no longer a coconscious, but an alternating personality. When A or C is present, B's memories persist coconscious with the respective primary personality. It will therefore follow that any experiences which B has had as an *alternating* personality she would remember as a coconsciousness when A is present, although A would have no recollection of them. And it is clear that, if these coconscious memories by certain technical methods could be awakened, we might get galvanic reactions therefrom, the source of which A would not be aware of. The same would not be true of C, however, because she has a memory of B as an alternating personality; but inasmuch as B, when *coconscious* with C has separate perceptions and ideas of which C is unaware, if these coconscious ideas and perceptions could be tapped, while C is present, we might get galvanic reactions from this source of which C would be necessarily unaware. Furthermore, there are other coconscious memories, to be presently described, of which neither A nor C has knowledge.

A, B and C can be hypnotized, and then there result three respective and distinctly different hypnotic states corresponding to each of the personalities, namely a, b, c. To show this more clearly, our diagram may be further enlarged as follows:

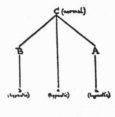

FIG. 7

None of the personalities, A, B, or C, has any memory for the hypnotic states.

As to the memories of these hypnotic states, it will be sufficient for our purpose here to state that only b (like B, as shown by other experimental evidence) is *coconscious* with the other two as well as with the primary personalities, A and C; b is not coconscious with B, but rather is that personality in the usual dissociated form; both are substantially one. Now it happens that the subject has dreams of which two of the three primary personalities, *viz.*, A and C, have no memory on waking. B and b, however, remember the dreams. Consequently if b is coconscious with *all* the other states, it would follow that, if we could tap these coconscious memories of dreams while the primary personalities were present, we might get galvanic reactions of the source of which A and C were unaware.

These principles were made use of in the following experiments. If they are not clear now, they will become so as the experiments are detailed.

I. *Experiments to test the presence of coconscious memories of dreams and other experiences of which the subject had no recollection when awake.*

As already stated, the subject frequently had dreams of which neither A nor C had any recollection after waking. The occurrence of such dreams was obtained from one or other of the hypnotic states, each of which remembered distinctly the dream and narrated it in all its details. The hypnotic state, b, gave the following accounts (corroborated by a and c) of two nightmares. I condense them, giving only the relevant details.

In the first dream, she thought she was in a *boat* with a companion, under particular circumstances which I omit. A great storm came up. The wind blew and the *waves* grew high and threatened to swamp the boat, which she was obliged to manage herself. "The boat went up, up, up and then down, down, down," and "the waves filled the boat and smothered us in foam." Then her companion was gone. Then the waves turned to *cats* which came down "all over her," filling the boat. (At this point, in describing the cats, the subject, who has a dread of cats, shuddered and seemed horror-stricken. In describing the scene, particularly in speaking of the waves and the cats, the subject was filled with lively emotions.)

In the second dream, she thought she was in a dark *canyon* through which she was making her way. It was very dark and the sides of the canyon were covered with *stones*. After reciting in an emotional manner how she tried to make her way through the canyon in darkness, she said that the stones turned to cats and overwhelmed her. As in the other dream, she was filled with lively emotions during the description.

*b*, it will be remembered, claims to be coconscious during all the waking states. In addition to reciting the dreams, she now gave an account of an episode which had occurred in the dining car on the journey, in company with the present writer, to New York when C was "awake." *b* claimed that, during dinner, she coconsciously had seen a lady dressed in black (Mrs. X, whom M. P. knew and who was sitting some seats behind) look her over with her *lorgnette* in, what appeared to her, a somewhat offensive manner. This action had made *b* coconsciously angry or at least resentful. She said that she (coconsciously) felt at the time that she would like to put the lady out of the car. *b* had seen her at a moment when C had turned her head and she felt certain that the latter had not noticed the lady, for if she had she would have *thought* of the affair, and *b* would have known her thoughts. *b* herself suggested this episode as a test, as the fact of the occurrence could be verified by questioning the lady in black, Mrs. X.

After the galvanic experiment was finished, C was questioned as to her memory. She had no recollection of having noticed the episode. Furthermore, as it was C who was in the dining-car, and as A, on whom the first experiment was made, has complete amnesia for the life of C, *she could not have had and, as a fact, did not have any conscious knowledge of the lorgnette episode*. The testimony of the "lady in black," later obtained, substantiated the account of the episode. It is important to bear in mind that *b*, when subconscious, as she claimed to be, remembered the dream of the episode.

*Experiment* 1. Accordingly, to test the presence of a subconscious emotion connected with the dreams and the dining-car experience, the words "waves," "boat," "canyon," "lorgnette," "stones" were interspersed among a number of other (indifferent) words, to wit:—[1]minister, [2]poor, [3]neck, [4]*waves*, [5]grass, [6]false, [7]belt, [8]flower, [9]*boat*, [10]kind, [11]pride, [12]seek, [13]*canyon*, [14]rich, [15]leaf, [16]travel, [17]*lorgnette*, [18]trust, [19]busy, [20]downstairs, [21]nobody, [22]*stones*, [23]big, [24]trees, [25]give, [26]sofa.

The galvanic experiment was made first, as I have said, with A. The curves obtained are shown in Figure 8. It will be seen that marked rises, in the curve occur at 4 (waves), 9 (boat), 13 (canyon), 17 (lorgnette), 22 (stones). All these rises must have been connected with subconscious associations, as the subject had no conscious knowledge whatsoever of her dreams or the lorgnette experience, while they corresponded with the actual dream and subconscious experiences as narrated by the hypnotic states a and b. It will be further seen that there are other rises at 6 (false), 11 (pride) and at 26 (sofa). These are referable to corresponding *conscious* experiences of A, the first two of which are known to the present writer, the subject herself explaining them.

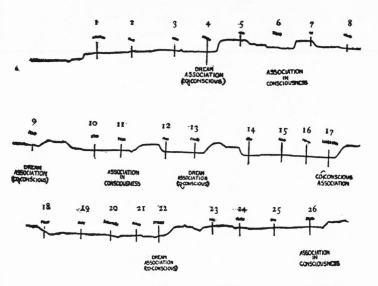

Fig. 8. Personality A. Dreams and coconscious experience (lorgnette). (The tracing is cut into three parts.)

*Experiment* 2. On the next day the same experiment was repeated with C. The alterations in the curve (of which only the portions corresponding to "canyon" and "lorgnette" are here reproduced, Figure 9) are not as marked as with A; and with two words ("boat" and "stones") connected with

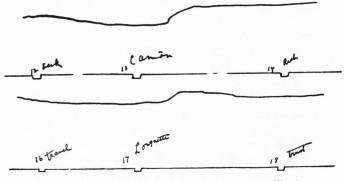

Fig. 9. Personality C. Test experiences same as Fig. 8.

subconscious experiences, and one word ("false") connected with conscious experiences, no rise occurred at all.

This may have been due to the fact that the experiment was a repetition, and therefore the words may have both consciously and coconsciously lost something of their emotional tone on the one hand, and on the other (as respects the word "false"), C, having a full knowledge of the previous experiment with A, not only knew what to expect, but, being more stable and normal, is less emotionally affected by any experience.

Nevertheless, it will be seen that there is a readily recognizable rise at 13 (canyon) and 17 (lorgnette).

These two tracings, and subsequent ones, should be compared with Figure 10, taken at rest. This tracing is, comparatively, a straight line.

Fig. 10.  Rest Curve.

II. *Relative coconscious and conscious reactions in different hypnotic states (a, b, and c) to same emotions.*

To test the relative reactions of the different hypnotic states, *a, b, c*, to the same subconscious and conscious memories, the test-words "Smith" and "ring" were used, and finally tactile stimulation was resorted to. Of the test-words, "Smith" referred to an experience in B's life, of which the corresponding hypnotic state *b* only (of the hypnotic states) had a memory. Of this experience, B *now felt ashamed*. It appeared that B, pretending to be A, had disclosed to a Mr. Smith the secret of her psychological disintegration into personalities. A and C[1] knew nothing of this and therefore *a* and *c* had also complete amnesia for it.

The word "ring" referred to a past experience in the life of B when there was disintegration of character without amnesia, so that both A and C knew it. It, therefore, was part of a *conscious* memory in all three personalities, A, B and C. B had enjoyed the experience: A, owing to the pecu-

1  This was one of the few hiatuses in C's memory, and has since been filled.

liarity of her character, had suffered intense remorse and anguish to a morbid degree. She had, emotionally, almost torn herself to pieces over it, wearing sackcloth and ashes, and the memory of the experience awakened similar feelings.

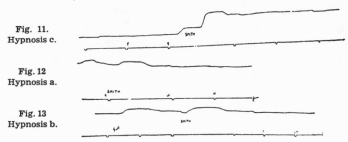

Figs. 11, 12 and 13. Reactions from coconscious memories in A and C and conscious memory in B for the same experience. A and C had amnesia for this experience (*Smith*).

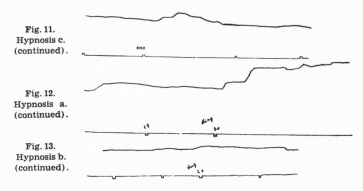

Figs. 11, 12 and 13, continued. Test-word, *ring*. Conscious memory in all three hypnotic states for the same experience.

C, however, now remembering the experience, is sorry but philosophical. While regretting, she in no way suffers.

Examining the tracings, of which we reproduce here only the portions corresponding to three stimuli (Figures 11, 12, and 13), we find rises corresponding to both these words. (The remainder of the tracing, corresponding to the indifferent words, showed nothing remarkable.) With "Smith," the greatest disturbance occurred with the hypnotic state *c*, who had no knowledge whatsover of the experience connected with the name. The reaction must have been, therefore, due to a *subconscious* memory (belonging to B).

With *a*, with whom the memory was also subconscious, there was a rise, but much less marked, and approximately the same as that obtained with *b*, with whom the memory was *conscious*. *c*, it should be said, was tested first, and, therefore, the surprise element may have been a factor in the height of the curve obtained with this state; and yet this explanation will not hold good with the word "ring," which gave curves with each of the hypnotic states, *corresponding to the intensity of the feeling which each experienced* in re-

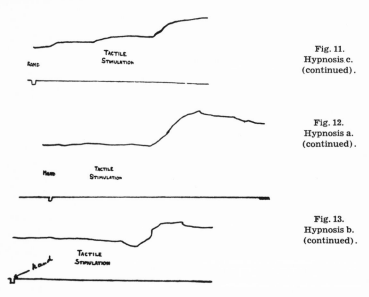

Fig. 11.
Hypnosis c.
(continued).

Fig. 12.
Hypnosis a.
(continued).

Fig. 13.
Hypnosis b.
(continued).

Figs. 11, 12 and 13, continued. Reaction to tactile stimulation, a and c were anesthetic and therefore the stimulation was not consciously felt. With b it was consciously perceived.

membering the episode. *c*, tested first, did not show the highest curve, but *a*, whose feelings were most intense, gave the highest, *c* the next, and *b* almost none at all. It also should be noted that when the word "ring" was pronounced, *c* gave a deep and apparently emotional inspiration, almost a gasp; *a* gave a sudden start and similar inspiration, while *b* laughed. Similarly with the word "Smith," *c* gave two deep inspirations of the same kind. Finally, after the last of the test-words, each of the states, *a*, *b* and *c*, was subjected to a strong tactile stimulation that presumably included an emotional tone. The significance of this lay in the fact that *a* and *c* are absolutely anesthetic, while *b* possesses complete preservation of sensation. Corresponding to this tactile stimulation there are marked risings in the curve in each of the anesthetic states as well as in *b*, showing that, *notwithstanding the anesthesia*, the tactile stimulation was coconsciously felt by *a* and *c*.

III. *To test coconscious reaction in A during automatic writing.*

For this purpose, A was engaged in conversation in order to hold her conscious attention. While she was conversing, in a perfectly alert state, her hand was directed to write automatically an account of the dreams made use of in the previous experiments and of the lorgnette experience with the "lady in black" in the car, of all of which A had no knowledge. The hand wrote a short account, as directed, bringing in the words "boat," "waves," "cat," "dark," "lady" (in black), "lorgnette," etc. Corresponding to these significant words, there were oscillations in the curve (Figure 14). It was not, however, easy, for technical reasons, to record accurately the time of the occurrence of a cocon-

Fig. 14. Personality A. Automatic writing of dreams and "lorgnette" experience, for all of which A had amnesia. Writing performed by coconscious memories (B).

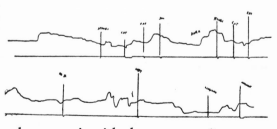

scious thought and connect it with the corresponding curve, as, of course, the thought arose before it was expressed in writing. The tracing was also much disturbed by the conscious emotional condition of A's mind, who awoke to find herself with a stranger, introduced to aid in the experiment, in a situation of which she had no previous warning. All sorts of collateral thoughts were running through her mind, as C afterwards explained, owing to her embarrassing situation and fear of betrayal of her secret, etc. The tracing is probably also modified by artifacts. Nevertheless the curve is interesting and shows certain approximate relations with the coconscious thoughts.

IV. *Experiments to test memories of personality B, coconscious with personality A, who was the subject.*

*Experiment 1.* The test-word was "Smith" and referred to an experience in B's life, already described, the memory of which was *now coconscious in A.* The indifferent words were: — ashes, blue, song, read, Mr. Skillings, bright, Mr. Gill, forceful, *Smith*, good, tip-cart, copper, foot, lazy, shovel, run, towel, cold, kitchen, ring, carriage, modest, floor, laugh, tongs, hot, hand. Examination of the curve (Figure 15)[1] shows a practically straight line until

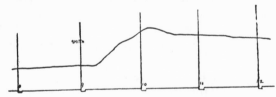

Fig. 15. Personality A. Reaction from coconscious memory for episode (Smith) for which A had amnesia.

the word "Smith" is reached, when there is a marked rise. The subject, when afterwards questioned, said that the word simply aroused associations with her sister, whose name it also was, but that these associations were emotionally indifferent and the word had no particular conscious significance

---

1 Excepting when the reproduction of the whole seems necessary, we give in this tracing and in the others only those portions which have a direct bearing on the experiment. The remainder of the tracings may be assumed to be negative.

for her. Of course, her sister was not the person referred to in the episode in which B played a part. This rise, therefore, can be interpreted only as due to coconscious associations.

*Experiment* 2. The test-word was "darling." The subject, as before, was A. The indifferent words were: coal, red, ong, reach, myopia, rake, Mr. Gill, signify, *darling,* Norfolk, hoe, tin, street.

The word "darling" referred to a very comical experience in the life of B of which A had no knowledge. The memory of the episode was, therefore, coconscious in A. It referred to a scene in which the word played a ridiculous

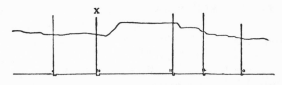

Fig. 16. Personality A. Reaction as in Fig. 15 from coconscious memory (darling = x).

part. The curve (Figure 16) shows a fairly straight line with a marked rise at "darling."

## V. *To test conscious memories in A.*

The test-words were "cats," "wall-papers," "hat," "black," interspersed as follows: [3]bad, [4]*cats,* [5]drink, [6]*wall-papers,* [7]good, [8]danger, [9]*hat,* [10]business, [11]walk, [12]hammer, [13]cry, [14]*black,* [15]round, [16]mouth.

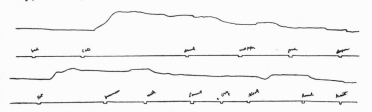

Fig. 17. Personality A. Reaction from conscious memories. "Cat" (4) upper tracing, and "hat" (9) lower tracing.

The word "cat" referred to an intense phobia for this animal, which the subject has had ever since childhood. Its probable origin is in a childhood experience revealed through automatic writing. The subject, in none of her personalities or hypnotic states, has any recollection of the episode. The dislike of cats is so intense that the mere mention of the word produces a strong emotional effect, and the presence of a cat has frequently produced an emotional shock. (See above account of dreams.)

The word "hat" is associated in her mind with several quarrels which she has had with her other self, B, over the kind of hat she should wear, B purchasing a light colored hat which A has as often exchanged for a black one. In fact, A is given to dressing in black, which B dislikes, preferring light colors. Hence the word "black" was inserted.

The word "wall-papers" referred to similar quarrels over the selection of wall-papers for her house.

Figure 17 shows a marked rise in the curve at 4 (cats) and a distinct, though not so high a rise at 9 (hat) and at 14 (black). The effect of "wall-papers" (6) was not especially marked.

VI. *To test perception in the peripheral field of vision. Subject: personality C.*

By a series of preliminary tests, the point in the periphery of the field of vision was determined, within which objects could be perceived but not recognized. This having

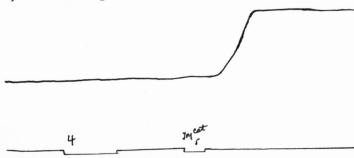

Fig. 18. Personality C. Peripheral vision of objects.

been determined, the following objects, with due precautions, were successively advanced from behind into this outer field. Although the subject perceived each, none was recognized excepting the last. The minute the last, which was a toy cat, was brought into this field, although, I think, it was not advanced beyond the position occupied by the others, the subject gave a start and shriek and exclaimed "Cat!" The tracing (Figure 18) shows a straight line until "cat" is reached, when a sharp, abrupt curve is recorded. The light of the galvanometer traveled 18 centimeters.

The objects were: 1, match-box; 2, pencil; 3, roll of paper; 4, watch; 5, toy cat. None of the first four objects were recognized visually by the patient, although she guessed the watch by hearing the tick, a complication which had inadvertently been forgotten. She could not describe in any respect any one of the other three objects.

When, however, the patient was hypnotized and put into state *b*, the state which claims to be coconscious, she was able to describe with minute accuracy each object, claiming that *she had seen them by peripheral vision, although the waking consciousness had not.*

VII. *Conscious reactions during "crystal visions."*
Subject: *personality A.*
The subject was asked to look into a crystal and reproduce a so-called "crystal vision" which, by suggestion, was made to take the form of the dream of the canyon, recounted above. As she looked into the crystal, she recited what she saw, the dream unfolding itself like a panorama before her eyes. She saw herself walking through this canyon exactly as she had dreamt it. The details exactly reproduced the dream. Whilst the vision unfolded itself, a tracing was taken.

While describing the vision, the subject, as is usually the case with crystal visions, experienced over again all the thoughts and emotions of her vision itself. At one place she saw the stones turn to cats (x, Figure 19). Then she saw

Fig. 19.
Personality A.
Crystal vision.

herself walking alone through this solitary place, sad and depressed by her helpless situation.

The tracing before "cats," not being remarkable, is omitted. The rise at "cats" was maintained by a succession of emotional states producing oscillations in the tracing. In the absence of a stenographer, it was impossible to take down the recital *verbatim*, nor was it possible, for technical reasons, as in automatic writing, to connect the curves accurately with the ideas as they were unfolded.

Fig. 20. Personality A. Crystal vision.

Another tracing, taken during a crystal vision, is represented in Figure 20. In this vision, she saw the representation of a previous actual episode in her life occurring during the interment of her mother in the cemetery, and also *during a trance state (supposed to be a faint) into which she fell at the time.* She had very little or no conscious recollection of this episode, owing to her having been in this abnormal condition, and yet she saw in detail everything that occurred in the trance. The correctness of the vision has been verified. The tracing shows the rise in the curve where she saw the scene in the cemetery. At this point, she turned her head away from the crystal and kept exclaiming: "I can't look! I can't look!" etc.

VIII. *Word-associations in the coconscious.*

An attempt was made to test the reactions to word-associations in the *coconscious,* as distinct from conscious associations. For this purpose A's attention was engaged in conversation and the hand was made to write automatically. By the well-known process of abstraction, words were given to the coconscious by whispering, and the hand was directed to write the words associated in the coconscious. By this method, the subject does not *consciously* hear the words, but they are heard coconsciously. The test-words used were those used before, *viz.*, "Smith," "ring," "lorgnette," "darling."

There was some difficulty in carrying out the experiment as the coconscious (B) rebelled after the first three words and refused to disclose its thoughts. It finally consented, however, to write a word in response, though that word might not be the first thought of.

| *Test-word* | *Coconscious associated word* |
|---|---|
| 1. sleep | dreams |
| 2. fruit | apples |
| 3. bad | +[1] |
| 4. mouth | ("I shan't speak"); teeth |
| 5. jolly | gay |
| 6. fun | pleasure |
| 7. Smith | lie[2] |
| 8. bed | rest |
| 9. pretty | lovely |
| 10. danger | ("I can't think") |
| 11. ring | Lowell[2] |
| 12. business | work |
| 13. dead | buried |
| 14. lorgnette | woman in black[2] |
| 15. cry | weep |
| 16. upstairs | attic |
| 17. darling | pencil[2] |
| 18. blood | cut |
| 19. offer | horrid man: |

1 This mark was made by B, because unwilling to disclose the name of a certain person.

2 These words disclose episodic associations with the test-words, and represented associated thoughts or judgments of the original experiences, *viz.*, "bad," "Smith," etc.

The tracing, made under the same conditions as Figure 14 (page 343), showed general irregular oscillations, due to conscious perturbation, as well as to the coconscious word reactions and possible artifacts. As these cannot be distinguished from one another, the tracing is omitted here.

The word-responses in this experiment are particularly interesting as bearing on the psychological interpretation of subconscious processes. It is difficult to explain such word-reactions through pure physiological processes.

*Conclusions.*

1. In certain pathological conditions, active subconscious processes, *i. e.*, memories of some kind, which do not enter into the conscious life of the individual, may exist.

2. Memories of conscious experiences which the subject can not consciously recall, *i. e.*, for which he has amnesia, may be conserved and give rise to the same galvanic reactions which are obtained from conscious emotional states.

3. The reactions are compatible with and, so far, confirmatory of the theory that these subconscious processes are psychical (coconscious).

4. To explain these reactions by the theory of physiological reactions is possible but far-fetched.

5. In dissociated (hysterical) anesthesia, tactile stimulation, though not consciously felt, may give rise to the same reaction as when consciously perceived.

6. Objects not consciously perceived by peripheral vision may be coconsciously perceived.

# CHAPTER XII

## SOME PROBLEMS OF ABNORMAL PSYCHOLOGY

*Prefatory note:* The following paper derives its chief interest from an historical point of view, although the one or two limited problems with which it deals cannot be said to have yet been solved by methods yielding scientific proof. Perhaps the problem is not accessible to such methods, but must remain in the domain of theory, and its solution accepted or rejected on grounds of probability.

The paper itself is an excerpt from an address entitled, "Some of the Present Problems in Abnormal Psychology," delivered about twenty-five years ago[1] and deals with only one of a number discussed at that time; namely, the evidence for the existence of dissociated subconscious processes in normal everyday life.

To ask for scientific evidence of such processes, and, much more, to question the validity of the theory of a normal subconsciousness, may sound strange to the ears of a modern student of psychology. But it must be remembered that at the beginning of this century, the concept of the subconscious, at least for abnormal psychology, was limited to split-off, dissociated processes, or a doubling of the mind. Such processes were discovered in abnormal conditions and, as artifacts, produced by methods of experimentation. They were indeed the starting-point for the modern conception of the subconscious (coconscious and unconscious) and gave impetus to subsequent researches. It is consequently historically interesting to see how far we have travelled in reaching our modern conceptions (which are far from uni-

---

1 St. Louis Congress of Arts and Sciences; Sept. 24, 1904.

fied even today) of the subconscious as a part of the mind, reaching far back into the past and embracing vast numbers of life's experiences, not split-off and dissociated, but organized as roots to, and complexes of, conscious and unconscious processes.

Nevertheless, there still remains the problem as originally formulated: Do dissociated, independent processes, such as occur as artifacts (automatic writing, solution of problems, incubation of thought, etc.), or as occur in abnormal conditions (hysteria, double personalities, etc.) function in normal everyday life and take part in the normal work of the mind? If so, they would explain much of our everyday thinking and much that is now mysterious. Certainly much happens *as if* they did, as Stout, for one argued. We may even say there is the highest probability that much of our mental work is carried on in great part by subconscious processes, or in co-operation with them. But scientific proof of the fact is difficult for reasons set forth in this essay. (I hope it is needless to warn the reader not to confuse this problem, which is that of the *mechanism* of thinking, with the entirely different one of *motivation* — the *why* of a subconscious or coconscious process.)

## DO SUBCONSCIOUS STATES HABITUALLY EXIST NORMALLY, OR ARE THEY ALWAYS EITHER ARTIFACTS OR ABNORMAL PHENOMENA?

I have already referred to the doubling of the mind and the formation of subconscious states that may result from this dissociation, even to the formation of a second personality. Now, if abnormal dissociation is only an exaggeration or perversion of normal dissociation, the question arises: to what extent is there a division of the healthy mind of such a character as to give it multiplicity? Are the well-known abnormal dissociations and automatisms, the manifestation of abnormal subconscious processes, merely perverted types of similar processes which go on in every healthy mind? This is one of the most pressing problems for abnormal psychology to settle, for the idea that there is a subconscious mental life of elaborate activity and which habitually plays a large part in all our mental processes has received such wide acceptance that it shows evidence of dominating psychological thought and has even furnished a groundwork for a new philosophy. As a problem in dissociation and automatism I propose, therefore, to inquire to what degree this hypothesis is justified by actually demonstrated data in our possession today.

The problem may be thus stated: do subconscious states (processes) habitually exist normally, or are they always either artifacts or abnormal phenomena? If they form a part of the normal mind, what is the extent of the subconscious field? There is a very wide tendency at the present day to account for a large variety of phenomena, including both normal and abnormal experiences, by what used to be called "unconscious cerebration" but which is now spoken of as "subconscious thought" or the "secondary consciousness."

Now at the outset, in approaching this problem, we should have a clear idea of what is meant by subconscious ideas and their relation to the personal consciousness. It is difficult to state the theory of a secondary consciousness in a way that will be acceptable to all students, for probably no two observers are agreed as to the interpretation of the facts, or, if the fundamental notion be accepted, whether the theory includes a limited or a large category of facts. All, however, are agreed that, *under certain artificially induced or abnormal conditions,* correlated with our brain processes at any moment of time, there may be a certain number of elementary conscious states of whose existence we are ignorant, but which nevertheless coexist with that habitual waking consciousness which we term "ourself," or our own personality.

Now as to the *conditions* under which this secondary consciousness develops, and as to its *extent* — the number of sensations, emotions and other psychical states composing it, and above all, the degree to which they are organized into a self-acting system (or personality) — there is considerable difference of opinion, so that there may be said to be several theories of the secondary consciousness, according to the point of view of the writer, and the interpretation given to the accepted facts. While all agree that under *special* conditions every mind may be made up of certain states of which we are conscious and certain states of which we are not conscious, some think that in *healthy* minds the secondary consciousness — if existent at all — is limited to only a number of more or less dissociated and isolated states, like sensations and perhaps emotions, without being synthesized into a personal self-unity, or even self-acting system. Others think that these dissociated states are always woven into a systematized unity and are capable of considerable intellectual and independent activity. Some think that these secondary states play but a small subordinate part in our mental lives; others think that they have a very large share in our daily acts, particularly in those acts to which we do not give our conscious volition (habit acts, absent-minded acts, etc.). Still others seek to explain our highest intellectual feats through this secondary consciousness. It will be borne in mind that we are now speaking of normal healthy minds. In diseased minds it is agreed by all that the psychical states making up this secondary consciousness may become highly organized into a self-acting system and become capable of playing a role almost as controlling and independent as the habitual self. But some (Janet) think a doubling of consciousness is always a sign of disease.

Now, subconscious ideas are dissociated ideas — dissociated from the main system of ideas which make up the personal consciousness. They are thrown off, so to speak, as satellites may be supposed to be thrown off from their planet. The term "subconscious" is an unfortunate one, for it is metaphorical, and while descriptive, does not precisely express the true relation of these ideas to the personal consciousness. "Extra-conscious," "coconscious" or dissociated" are more exact terms. Now, being dissociated from our personal consciousness, they are unknown to us. Our knowledge of the existence of such dissociated mental states is largely derived from a study of pathological and artificially induced conditions, where their presence can be positively and accurately determined. The researches of recent years have proved very conclusively not only that the mind may split in two in such a way that certain groups of ideas may be dissociated from the main consciousness, but that a number of these dissociated states may become synthesized among themselves, and that, in this way, is formed a second consciousness, capable of a certain amount of activity. This activity may be manifested contemporaneously with that of our personal consciousness. There is then a doubling of consciousness. The mind becomes dual. Thus in the subject of disintegrated personality just referred to, known as the Misses Beauchamp, a secondary group of dissociated states has existed for many years contemporaneously with the personal consciousness. These secondary states are so extensive and are so well-organized into a personality that I have been able to obtain an autobiography of the subconscious life of this concomitant personality, disclosing a mental life running along side by side with, but unknown to, the personal self from childhood to the present day. The subject is twenty-eight years of age. Similar, though less extensive, manifestations of a double life are common as phenomena of hysteria. In the automatic writing and speech of mediums and of psychological experiment, in the dowsing rod, in so-called post-hypnotic phenomena, and in the automatic acts of artificial and spontaneous abstraction, we have the same manifestations of the splitting of the mind and the formation of an extra-conscious self of which the personal consciousness is ignorant. The dissociated states may or may not take on contemporaneous activity. If they do so, the secondary phenomena thus produced are called *automatisms*, as they occur outside the cognition of the personal self. They form the subconscious fixed ideas of hysteria now so well-known. When the dissociated ideas include the kinesthetic and sensory spheres, we have hysterical paralyses and anesthesias. At times these dissociated ideas break out in insurrections, kick up didos and turn our peaceful mental arrangements topsy-turvy. We then have the hysterical attack.

Allowing for such differences of opinion as have been already stated, there still seems to be a tacit acquiescence on the part of many psychologists in the theory that in normal healthy minds, similar dissociated ideas of greater or less complexity have their place and play a well-regulated part in the mental economy. In other words, according to this theory the normal mind is not a unity any more than the hysterical mind. It requires but a slight extension of this theory to assume, as some do, that these dissociated mental states become normally synthesized into a second consciousness of considerable intellectual capacity, which takes part in our everyday intellectual processes. In every mind, the activity of the primary consciousness is supposed to be accompanied by that of a secondary consciousness. On the basis of actually substantiated data, one would think that this was as far as the hypothesis could be logically carried, but the fact that we are conscious of dissociated ideas gives a certain mysticism to their existence and has offered a temptation to still further extend the hypothesis until, in the hands of certain of its advocates, it has outgrown even all demonstrated pathological facts. The subconscious ideas, instead of being mental states dissociated from the main personality, now become the main reservoir of consciousness, and the personal consciousness becomes a subordinate stream flowing out of this great storage basin of "subliminal" ideas, as they are called. We have within us a great tank of consciousness but we are conscious of only a small portion of its contents. In other words, of the sum-total of conscious states within us, only a small portion forms the personal consciousness. The personal self becomes even an inferior consciousness emerging out of a superior subliminal consciousness present in a transcendental world, and this subliminal conciousness is made the source of flights of genius on the one hand, while it controls the physical processes of the body, on the other. It is hardly necessary to follow this new "tank" hypothesis into its different applications. I merely refer to it as it has unquestionably colored the orthodox conception of subconscious ideas. Thus Professor Stout,[1] while contending against this doctrine, himself apparently influenced by

1 *The Hibbert Journal*, October, 1903.

it, postulates normal dissociated states (he adopts the term "subliminal") and gives them functions of wide scope.

"Consider," he says, "the process of recollecting a name. . . . It may happen that we fail to revive the name while we are trying to do so, and that it suddenly emerges into consciousness after an interval during which we have been occupied with other matters, or have been asleep. This implies that our conscious effort has set going a subliminal process which continues after the conscious effort has ceased."

Professor Stout then goes on to argue that our conscious process has a way of exciting these dissociated states into trains of thought of which we are wholly unconscious and which solve our problems for us while we attend to other things.

It seems to me that these are pure conjectures, although conjectures that may be said to have a high degree of probability. What we need is some sort of proof more reliable than the implications of conscious experience. Certainly there is nothing in conscious experience that demonstrates in a scientific sense that "conscious endeavor" sets in operation a subliminal process. As far as my own conscious experience goes, I am compelled to agree with Mr. Andrew Lang, in that as " 'an ordinary man' I do not find that my conscious activity appeals to 'anything else' but my own conscious processes, or that I am conscious of any such easy way of settling my own problems. As an ordinary man I do not find I can rely upon any other consciousness to write this address but the thoughts which I laboriously elaborate."[1]

"In such cases" [solving problems], he says, "conscious endeavor to find an ideal combination which shall satisfy certain conditions serves only to set in operation subliminal processes which may or may not yield the requisite result. Here also the process may continue after the consciousness which prompted it ceased. The ordin-

1 *The Hibbert Journal*, April, 1904.

ary man, no less than the man of genius, may find that what relatively to *him* are original ideas develop while his thoughts are occupied with disconnected topics, or even while he is asleep. In general, we take an utterly false view of mental construction when we regard it is a mere putting together of data already present in consciousness, analogous to the putting together of the parts of a puzzle spread out on the table before us."

The theory of the normal occurrence of subconscious dissociated thought, as expounded in the "subliminal" doctrine of F. W. H. Myers, seems to have arisen as an interpretation of certain well-known, but exceptional, spontaneous experiences of the kind which Professor Stout accepts as evidence of normal subconscious mental activity, but this theory has a more substantial basis in data which have been obtained through direct objective experimentation. These include (1) various hysterical phenomena, (2) hypnotic experiments, (3) various motor automatisms, particularly automatic writing, and (4) phenomena of absent-mindedness or abstraction. A critical analysis of these data will show that they do not permit of inferences applicable to normal and habitual conditions.

1. That secondary subconscious states, capable of being synthesized into a self, may be developed by disease is a well-attested observation. But, being pathological, they are evidence only of the abnormality of subconscious states.

2. As to hypnotic states, it is sometimes assumed that the hypnotic self represents a persistent consciousness having a continuous existence after the awakening of the personal consciousness. There is no evidence for this. The hypnotic self is a dissociated state of the waking consciousness. On awaking, the synthesis of the original self is again made and the hypnotic dissociation ceases to exist. Nor is there any particular hypnotic state. There may be almost any number of such states in the same individual — as many as there are possible states of dissociation. In the second place, hypnosis is an artifact — an artificial dissociation, not a state of normal life. The phenomena of post-hypnotic suggestion,

which are entirely phenomena of subconscious processes, are likewise artifacts, produced by the methods of the experiment. They prove that the mind may be artificially made to exhibit duality but not that this is true of normal mental life.

3. As to the evidence from automatic writing and similar phenomena, it seems to have been overlooked that these phenomena too are artifacts. Although they are plainly manifestations of dissociation of consciousness and automatism of the dissociated elements, nevertheless this dissociation is the product of the condition of the experiment. Abstraction, which means dissociation of a greater or less degree, is induced and suggestion directly excites the phenomena. But all such experiments have great significance in another respect. The ease with which the mind, in perfectly healthy persons, can be dissociated, and the dissociated states synthesized into an autonomous system, shows that subconscious synthesized states are not always evidence of disease, as maintained by Janet, though they may be artifacts, but that the whole is dependent upon a physiological process. When a physiological stimulus, like the mere sound of a spoken word, a suggested idea, is capable of inciting a dual activity of the mind in healthy university students, the process is unintelligible, unless it is psycho-physiological, that is to say, a normal reaction of the mind to specially devised stimuli. When critically examined, then, the experimental evidence which is relied upon to establish subconscious ideas as normal processes of mentation is found to be fallacious. The resulting phenomena are made subconscious by the very conditions of the experiment. For this reason the problem is impossible to solve by the usual experimental methods. There is, however, some experimental evidence of a different sort which may be utilized, and which I propose presently to point out.

4. The phenomena of absent-mindedness, or abstraction, a normal function, indicate both dissociation and automatism. It is not difficult to demonstrate experimentally that auditory, visual, tactile and other images which are not perceived by the personal consciousness during this state

may be perceived subconsciously. Thus, under proper precautions, I place various objects where they will be within the peripheral field of vision of a suitable subject, C. B. Her attention is strongly attracted listening to a discourse. The objects are not perceived. She is now hypnotized and in hypnosis describes accurately the objects, thus showing that they were subconsciously recognized. It is the same for auditory perceptions of passing carriages, voices, etc. Likewise, on the *motor* side the numerous absent-minded acts of which we are not conscious show intelligent subconscious automatism. C. B., in hypnosis, remembers each step of such an act (putting away a book in the book-case), of which she is completely oblivious when awake.

This duality of the mind in normal absent-mindedness has been pointed out by various observers. Its phenomena simulate those of artificial abstraction as they occur in automatic writing and hysterical states. There is nothing surprising in this, as the term "absent-mindedness" means dissociation of consciousness — a failure to perceive that which before was perceived, and a failure to be conscious of acts intelligently performed. On the other hand, normal absent-mindedness is a distinctly special condition. We don't go about in an absent-minded state, or as if we had lost our heads, when we have work to be done. Absent-minded phenomena are manifestations of the temporary disintegration of the personal self, and doubling of consciousness, but not evidence of the persistence during the ordinary waking life of subconscious states. It does not follow that on waking from revery, complete synthesis does not take place. But here the significant fact, the most significant of all, should not be lost sight of, that in the normal process of abstraction we find evidence of the existence of a normal prearranged mechanism for dissociating consciousness and producing subconscious states. Dissociation is plainly a function of the mind or brain.

Now, the nub of the problem is: Are these subconscious states, in healthy persons, limited to absent-mindedness? And, if not, what part do they play in the mental economy? Indeed, whether so limited or not, what is their extent? *i. e.*

(a) Are they purely isolated phenomena, isolated sensations and perceptions or (b) Are they synthesized, as imagined by Professor Stout, into logical subconscious processes of thought, capable of sustained action, and as imagined by some, sufficiently complex to form a personality — something that we are justified in calling a subconscious self? or (c) Are subconscious states, when synthesized, always either artifacts or pathological?

These questions are at the root of many important problems in abnormal psychology, but are difficult to answer by experimental methods, owing to the danger of artifacts. In illustration of this danger, I may point to the phenomena of subconscious solutions of arithmetical problems, which are sometimes cited in evidence. In favorable subjects, as in an instance under my own observation, it is not difficult by means of suggestion in hypnosis to obtain the solution of arithmetical problems during the waking state by some other consciousness than that of the waking personality. For example, while in hypnosis, two numbers are given to be added or multiplied, say 453+367, or 4362×3, to take actual examples, and the subject awoke instantaneously the moment the last figure is given. The addition or multiplication is correctly solved subconsciously, the subject not having any conscious knowledge that any task whatever has been set.[1] The exact method of mentation by which the problem is extra-consciously solved is learned by catechizing the hypnotic personality. But such experiments are plainly artifacts. The dissociation and automatism are the products of suggestion. The results are of value, however, as cannot be too often insisted upon, in that they show the ease with which duality of the mind may be affected by what is plainly a psycho-physiological stimulus, a suggested idea. But to obtain subconscious phenomena free from artifice, such phenomena must be *spontaneous*. Information regarding the presence and character of subconscious states at any given time can be easily obtained owing to the well-known fact

1 See Chapter V.

that ideas[1] dissociated from the personal consciousness
awake, may become synthesized with this same consciousness in hypnosis and then be remembered. A person in hypnosis may thus be able to analyze and describe the ideas
which were spontaneously present as an extra-conscious-
ness when awake, but which were not then known to the
personal consciousness. This method is far more accurate
than the device of tapping the subconsciousness by automatic writing, though the same in principle. I am obliged
here to refer to a series of observations of this kind which I
have personally made with a view of obtaining light upon
this question, as I know of no others that have been limited
to spontaneous phenomena and are not open to the objection
of artifacts. A systematic examination[2] was made of the personal consciousness in hypnosis regarding the perceptions
and content of the secondary consciousness during definite

1  This word is used as a convenient expression for any state of consciousness.

2  I have adopted this custom of treating the hypnotic self as a sane consciousness instead of a freak fit only to be played with and to be made to perform all sorts of antics. I am certain this method of study will throw more light
on the composition of normal consciousness than that of inducing hallucinations
and other artifacts. The hypnotic self, if treated like a reasonable being, will be
found able to give important information. It knows the waking self, it knows its
own thoughts, and it knows the thoughts of the secondary consciousness. It can
give very valuable information about each. On the other hand, it is easily disintegrated by suggestion; and ideas, hallucinations, and what not, are very easily
created in it. Experiments of this latter kind have their use, but for the purpose
of learning the mode of the working of the normal mind, a still greater advantage is to be obtained by treating it as a rational consciousness, capable of accurately observing and imparting information derived from its own experiences.

I would here insist that it is a mistake to confuse the personal consciousness
in hypnosis with the secondary consciousness when such exists. They are not
identical or coextensive. A hypnotic self, as ordinarily observed, is still the personal consciousness, but in hypnosis the previously dissociated states are synthesized with this self and remembered. The whole becomes then a unity, and
the hypnotic personal consciousness remembers the formerly dissociated ideas
and its own and speaks of them as such. This has given rise to the wrong interpretation that identifies the hypnotic self with the secondary or subconsciousness. But the hypnotic self includes a large part of the waking personal self. On
waking, this part regains the rest of its own syntheses and loses the secondary
states. A failure to recognize these facts has led to much confusion in interpreting abnormal psychological phenomena.

(It should be remembered, however, as stated above (under 2) that there
may be a number of different hypnotic states or integrates, in the same individual. Each may have different memories and so remember different dissociated
states or experiences.)

moments of which the events were *pre-arranged* or otherwise known, the subject not being in a state of absent-mindedness. It is not within the scope of our paper to give the details of these observations, but in this connection I may state briefly a summary of the evidence, reserving the complete observations for future publication. It was found that —

1. A large number of perceptions — visual, auditory, tactile and thermal images, and sometimes emotional states — occurred outside of the personal consciousness, and, therefore, the subject was not conscious of them when awake. The visual images were particularly those of the peripheral vision, such as the extra-conscious perception of a person in the street, who was not recognized by the personal waking consciousness; or the perception of objects intentionally placed in the field of peripheral vision and not perceived by the subject, whose attention was held in conversation. Auditory images of passing carriages, of voices, footsteps, etc., thermal images of heat and cold from the body were similarly found to exist extra-consciously, and to be entirely unknown to the personal waking consciousness.

2. As to the content of the concomitant (dissociated) ideas, it appeared by the testimony of the hypnotic self that, as compared with those of the waking consciousness, the secondary ideas were quite limited. They were, as is always the experience of the subject, made up for the most part of emotions (*e. g.*, annoyances), and sensations (visual, auditory and tactile images of a room, of particular persons, people's voices, etc.). They were not combined into a logical proposition, though in using words to describe them it is necessary to so combine them and, therefore, give them a rather artificial character as 'thoughts.' It is questionable whether the word 'thoughts' may be used to describe mental states of this kind, and the word was used by the hypnotic self subject to this qualification. Commonly, I should infer, a succession of such 'thoughts' may arise, but each is for the most part limited to isolated emotions and sensory images, and lacks the complexity and synthesis of the waking mentation.

3. The memories, emotions and perceptions of which the subject is not conscious when awake are remembered in

hypnosis and described. The thoughts of which the subject is conscious when awake are those which are concentrated on what she is doing. The others, of which she is not conscious, are what may be called side thoughts. These are not logically connected among themselves, are weak, and have little influence on the personal (chief) train of thought. Now, although when awake, the subject is conscious of some thoughts and not of others, both kinds keep running into one another and therefore the conscious and the subconscious are constantly uniting, disuniting and interchanging. *There is no hard and fast line between the conscious and the subconscious, for at times what belongs to one passes into the other, and vice versa.* The waking self is varying the grouping of its thoughts all the time in such a way as to be continually including and excluding the subconscious thoughts. The personal pronoun 'I,' or, when spoken to, 'you,' applied equally to her waking self and to her hypnotic self, *but these terms were not applicable to her unconscious thoughts, which were not self-conscious.* For convenience of terminology, it was agreed to arbitrarily call the thoughts of which the subject is conscious, when awake, the *waking consciousness,* and the thoughts of which, when awake, she is not conscious — the *secondary consciousness.* In making this division the hypnotic self insisted most positively on the distinction, namely, that the secondary consciousness was in no sense a *personality.* The pronoun *I* could not be applied to it. In speaking of the thoughts of this second group of mental states alone, she could not say "I felt this." "I saw that." These thoughts were better described as, for the most part, unconnected, discrete sensations, impressions, and emotions, and were not synthesized into a personality. They were not therefore self-conscious. When the waking self was hypnotized, the resulting hypnotic self acquired the subconscious perceptions of the second consciousness; she then could say "*I*," and the hypnotic "*I*" included what were formerly "subconscious" perceptions. In speaking of the secondary personality by itself, then, it is to be understood that self-consciousness and personality are always excluded. This testimony was verified by test instances of subconscious

perceptions of visual and auditory images of experiences occurring in my presence.

4. *Part played by the secondary consciousness in* (*a*)
*normal mentation.* The hypnotic self testified that the
thoughts of the secondary consciousness do not form a
logical chain. They do not have volition. They are entirely
passive and have no direct control over the subject's voluntary actions.

(*b*) *Part played by the secondary consciousness in absent-mindedness.* (1) Some apparently absent-minded acts
are only examples of amnesia. There is no doubling of consciousness at the time. It is a sort of continuous amnesia
brought about by lack of attention.    (2) In true absent-
mindedness there does occur a division of consciousness along
lines which allow a large field to, and relatively wide synthesis of, the dissociated states. The personal consciousness
is proportionately restricted.    The subconscious thoughts
may involve a certain amount of volition and judgment, as
when the subject subconsciously took a book from the table,
carried it to the bookcase, started to place it on the shelf, and
finding that particular location unsuitable, arranged a place
on another shelf where the book was finally placed. No
evidence, however, was obtained to show that the dissociated
consciousness is capable of wider and more original synthesis
than is involved in adapting habitual acts to the circumstances of the moment.

(*c*) *Solving problems by the secondary consciousness.*
So much is to be found in the literature about subconscious
solutions of problems that the following testimony of the
hypnotic personality is of interest:

> When a problem on which my waking self is en-
> gaged remains unsettled, it is still kept in mind by the
> secondary consciousness, even though put aside by my
> waking self. My secondary consciousness often helps me
> to solve problems which my waking consciousness has
> found difficulty in doing. But it is not my secondary con-
> sciousness that accomplishes the final solution itself. It
> only helps in the following way. Suppose, for instance, I

am trying to translate a difficult passage in Virgil. I work at it for some time and am puzzled. Finally, unable to do it, I put it aside, leaving it unsolved. I decide that it is not worth bothering about and so put it out of my mind. What you do is, you put it *into* your mind: that is to say, you don't put it out of your mind if the problem remains unsolved and unsettled. By putting it *into* your mind I mean that, although the waking consciousness may have put it aside, the problem still remains in the secondary consciousness. In the example I used, the memory of the passage from Virgil would be retained persistently by my secondary consciousness. Then from time to time a whole lot of fragmentary memories and thoughts connected with the passage would arise in this consciousness. Some of these thoughts, perhaps, would be memories of the rules of grammar, or different meanings of words in the passage, in fact, anything I had read, or thought, or experienced in connection with the problem. These would not be logical, connected thoughts, and they would not solve the problem. My secondary consciousness does not actually do this, *i. e.*, in the example taken, translate the passage. The translation is not effected here. But later when my waking consciousness thinks of the problem again, these fragmentary thoughts of my secondary consciousness arise in my mind, and with this information I complete the translation. The actual translation is put together by my waking consciousness.[1] I am not conscious of the fact that these fragments of knowledge existed previously in my secondary consciousness. I do not remember a problem ever to have been solved by the secondary consciousness. It is always solved by the waking self, although the material for solving it may come from the secondary self. When my waking consciousness solves it in this way, the solution seems to come in a miraculous sort of way, sometimes as if it came to me from somewhere else than my own mind. I have sometimes thought, in consequence, that I had solved it in my sleep.

1 Very likely determined by an unconscious process. (M. P.)

The subject of these observations was at the time in good mental and physical condition. Criticism may be made that the subject being one who had exhibited for a long time previously the phenomena of mental dissociation, she now, though for the time being recovered, tended to a greater dissociation and formation of subconscious states than does a normal person, and that the subconscious phenomena were therefore exaggerated. This is true. It is probable that the subconscious *flora* of ideas in this subject are richer than in the ordinary individual. These phenomena probably represent the extreme degree of dissociation compatible with normality. And yet, curiously enough, the evidence tended to show that the more robust the health of the individual and the more stable her mind, the richer the field of these ideas. However this may be, the very exaggerations increase the value of the evidence for the limitation of the extent, independence and activity of the subconscious states. If in such a subject we do not find, as is the case, evidence of subconscious automatism, excepting in absent-mindedness, it is highly improbable that such activity exists in a perfectly healthy subject.

These observations are only suggestive, not conclusive. To solve the whole problem of concomitant, extra, or subconscious states, further and numerous observations are required, but conducted under conditions which shall exclude artifacts and abnormal states. It is interesting, however, here to notice that the direct evidence derived from these observations confirm the theoretical scheme of personal perception offered by Dr. Janet. That scheme is almost a literal representation of the facts as obtained by this method of experimentation.

Summarizing all the evidence which is at our disposal today, derived from actually observed facts, we may say, that *while a greater or less number of isolated dissociated states are constantly occurring under normal conditions, there is no satisfactory evidence that they normally become synthesized among themselves and exhibit automatism excepting in states of abstraction and as artifacts.*

A study of subconscious states is highly important for

the determination of the mechanism of consciousness, and I am convinced that such studies will throw much light upon the problem of how we think.

At this time, considering the fundamental importance of the problem of the subconscious, it has seemed to me wise to stop and review the evidence for the existence of normal dissociated mental states, and this for the further reason of the enormous part which these states play in pathological conditions and because of the credence which has been given to the theory of a normal subconscious self.

If the foregoing review is sound, it would seem that great caution is required in applying the inductions derived from a study of abnormal subconscious phenomena to normal conditions, and that the tendency has been to attribute too extensive a field and too great capabilities to this hidden mental life. The facts at our disposal do not support the hypothesis of a normal subconscious mind excepting within very strict limitations.

## NATURE OF THE DISSOCIATED PROCESS

But the problem of the subconscious brings into stronger relief the still broader problem. What are the factors of the dissociating process by which the duality is brought about? Is the explanation to be found in psychical or in exclusively physiological laws? It was a great advance to show, as has been done, that a large number of abnormal functional phenomena like anesthesia, amnesia, paralysis, aboulia, are all different types of the splitting of consciousness. They must, therefore, be due to some dissociating process. Janet interprets these different mental conditions as *chronic forms of absent-mindedness,* a persistent failure of the personal consciousness to make more than a few syntheses. This failure is the consequence of exhaustion. The dissociation is, therefore, primary and the resulting automatism secondary. Janet is careful to point out that this is not an explanation. It is in fact only a classification. Breuer and Freud, on the other hand, would make the dissociation secondary to the development of what they call the hypnoid state, a group of fixed ideas, which are unable to make the synthesis with the personal consciousness.

None of these theories are satisfactory as explanations. Absent-mindedness is not only insufficient as an explanation of the process, but even as a classification fails to take into account the differences in phenomena, such as the dissociation brought about as artificial abstraction by merely whispering in the subject's ear. I whisper in B IV's ear, and straightway she does not hear but inquires, "Where have you gone to?" I speak aloud and she hears again. (The whispered voice is, of course, heard by a momentarily dissociated group of states which respond.) Why, if this phenomenon is the same as absent-mindedness, and is due to exhaustion, cannot the "personal perception" (Janet) synthesize the whispered voice as well as the conversational voice?[1] Again, multiple personalities with alternating memories are not exhausted, but can make any number of other syntheses, including their own respective memories: Why not also with the lost memories of another personality? There is not a failure of *perception* of the ego, but a splitting of the ego itself. What has produced it?

Any theory, to be sufficient, must take into consideration all the facts not only of abnormal but of normal dissociations, including those artificially induced by experimental devices (suggestion, automatic writing, etc.). When we do this, we find, in the first place, as already pointed out, facts indicating a normal process for dissociating consciousness, through which process normal and abnormal phenomena may be correlated. Normal absent-mindedness, certain types of normal amnesia, sleep, spontaneous somnambulism, hypnosis, etc., can experimentally be shown to be types of dissociation, splitting of the ego (personality) differing from one another in the extent and pattern of the fields of consciousness remaining to the personal ego. The process which brings these states about is probably fundamentally the same as that governing the abnormal splitting of consciousness.

---

1 The whisper is undoubtedly a suggestion that it will not be heard.

In the second place, a study of abnormal and induced dissociation shows that, while normal syntheses and automatisms largely follow psychological laws, the lines of *disaggregation* do not follow the lines mapped out by these laws. For instance they do not follow the boundaries of associated ideas.

The hand that performs automatic writing becomes anesthetic, though the subconscious ideas which control the hand have nothing to do with tactile sensation. A subconscious fixed idea of fear of personal injury robs the personal consciousness of our subject M —— l[1] of perceptions from the peripheral field of vision and from one-half of his body. In another subject all the memories for a certain epoch in her life disappear in consequence of a shock. An emotional shock in A. P., excited by a slight fall during a high kicking act, robs the personal consciousness of the power to move the arm and the leg, which are rigid in contracture. In Madame D., a subject of Charcot and Janet, continuous amnesia for each succeeding moment of the day follows the announcement of a bad piece of news. There are no psychological associations in any of these examples between the ideas and the resulting dissociations, and psychologically we can find no reason why sensory and motor images are dissociated in one case, and memories in another. It would seem from the point of view of our present knowledge that we shall have to look for a complete explanation in some physiological process. All must admit that the final explanation must be in terms of the neuron, in the dissociation of the as yet unknown neuron systems which are correlated with the psychological systems. But without attempting such an explanation, what I wish to point out is that the data of abnormal psychology go to show that the psychological disaggregation does not follow psychical so much as physiological lines. The cleavage is brought about by psychological influences — trauma — (ideas, emotions, etc.) but when the

1 *Boston Medical and Surgical Journal*, June 23, 1904, vol. CL, no. 25, pp. 674-678.

fracture occurs, it tends to follow the physiological map.[1] Just as when a blow shatters a mineral, the lines of fracture follow the natural lines of crystallization, so, while a psychical trauma shatters a psycho-physiological system, the cleavage follows very closely the neuron association systems.

Thus, when Louis Vivé passed into one state in which he had left hemiplegia, into another in which he had right hemiplegia, another with paraplegia, each with its own group of memories, the alterations can only be explained on the ground that these states were determined by some sort of physiological dissociating system. Likewise, when our subject M —— l developed a complete amnesia for the English language, and understood and spoke only German, if we take into account all the phenomena, it would seem this amnesia was determined by physiological dissociation excited by a primarily conscious and later subconscious fear of injury.

Sally Beauchamp's general anesthesia is in no way the result of ideas psychologically in association with it. When B I and B IV exhibit a complete amnesia for each other's lives and display their contradictory traits of character and physiological reactions, it must be because different neurons are brought into activity in each case.

B IV in hypnosis, while slightly groggy from ether, talks intelligently and narrates the history of an adventure of the preceding day. I suggest to her that she shall open her eyes, wake up and be herself, a suggestion I have given a hundred times successfully. She opens her eyes and straightway she does not know me, or her surroundings, or who she herself is. An enormous dissociation of psychologically associated ideas has taken place, whether as the effect of the ether or some other cause I do not know, but according to psychological laws, her syntheses should have been enlarged. I close her eyes again and she regains intelligence, remarking that — "when my eyes are open I do not know who I am."

---

1 It may be thought by some that I have overlooked the role of conflict in the dissociating process, but let us bear in mind that the problem formulated in this section does not touch this issue.

On the other hand, automatism and abnormal *syntheses* seem to be affected largely by psychical laws, particularly that of the law of association of ideas. Abnormal psychology then points strongly to the conclusion that there is a normal physiological dissociating mechanism which is the function of the nervous organization. It is this mechanism which brings about such spontaneous normal states as absent-mindedness, sleep, normal induced states, like hypnosis, and — through its perversions — the dissociations underlying abnormal phenomena.

# CHAPTER XIII

## An Experimental Study of Visions

This study of (visual) hallucinations is of interest from many points of view; historically it would be interesting if we had the data to know the origin of the visions which have influenced the actions of certain characters in history, such as Joan of Arc and Catherine of Sienna. It is said that even Bismarck had a vision which he believed to be supernatural.

It ought to interest the theologian to understand the psychical origin of visions, like those of Saul of Tarsus, Luther, Savonarola, and hosts of saints, which have had such influence upon theological thought. If it had been understood, as we must believe, that such visions were only the pictorial representation in consciousness, according to natural psychical laws, of the fleeting thoughts, prayers, or beliefs, perhaps long forgotten, with which the religious enthusiast had occupied his mind at one time or another, the influence of the Church might have been differently exerted.

For those interested in psychical research, a study of visions may well throw light on many seemingly "occult" phenomena; and for the psychologist, it may be possible to learn, from a study of the laws of the development of visions, their mechanism and the nature of subconscious processes, other facts regarding the organization and functioning of the mind; while finally, by such study, the alienist may be enabled to better understand the hallucinations of the insane. So that from many points of view the subject presents a field for interesting research.

As the nervous system acts by general laws, what is true of the origin and mode of development of vision is probably true of hallucinations of the other senses, of which those of hearing are the most important; so what we have learnt to be true of one, we can predicate as likely to be true of the other. Thus, a study of visions may also enable us to understand those hallucinations of hearing, which, like visions, have figured so conspicuously in the religious history of the past, and which play so large a part in the diseases of the mind.

It is well-known that some people have the faculty of being able to create visions at will by intently gazing at an object. A crystal ball is commonly used for the purpose; the subject gazes into the crystal and, after a few moments of mental concentration, sees something therein — a scene, a person, or anything else, as the case may be. The phenomena have been called crystal visions, from their mode of production. They are not particularly rare, and some, though not very many, experimental observations have been reported. In former times, these visions played a part in occult lore, and, like modern clairvoyance, served to impose on the credulous. So that this part of psychology had its prototype in mysticism, just as chemistry may trace back its origin to alchemy, and astronomy to the romances of astrology. It is not so well-known that it is the fashion for "spiritualistic mediums" to artificially cultivate the art of seeing visions, the method adopted for the purpose being practically that of crystal gazing.[1] The hallucinations of hearing, which these same mediums profess to be communications from spirits of another world (and which some otherwise intelligent people believe), probably have an origin similar to that of visions, and are worthy of study from the point of view of this hypothesis. Visions created artificially by crystal gazing probably do not differ in their mode of genesis from

[1] A patient of mine, having the curiosity to learn something about mediums, undertook (against my advice) to have herself developed by a professional. The "professor" claimed to have developed a very celebrated medium who has since been the object of study by Dr. Hodgson, Professor William James, Professor Lodge, and others. My patient told me that her education consisted in gazing intently, in conjunction with the professor, at a spot in the middle of a table, until she saw a vision at that spot. This was repeated at each lesson. If I remember rightly, a low diet and fatigue were coincident factors. My patient found she was successful beyond her courage, and becoming alarmed, reported to me. These visions, I think, soon got beyond her control and came against her will, but a cessation of the experiments and a little hygienic treatment stopped them.

hose occurring spontaneously in normal people and, there
re good reasons for believing, may be the product of the
ame psychical laws as are some hallucinations, at least, of
he insane. It may, therefore, be inferred without much
danger of error, that a study of artificial visions will throw
ight upon the genesis of the spontaneous variety. The experimental method, in favorable subjects, allows us to study
he phenomena with a fair degree of method, and to so alter
he conditions as to vary the etiological factors.

It is to be hoped that further work will be done in this
ield. I have had an opportunity to make some experiments
of this kind on a particularly favorable subject. In most of
he observations reported hitherto, it has not been possible
o thoroughly investigate the relation of the vision to antecedent events in the subject's life, beyond the evidence of
the waking memory of that person. But in this instance,
the fact that it was possible to hypnotize her and obtain
*two additional and distinct personalities, three in all,* each
with distinct memories, gave an opportunity to search in the
hidden depths of consciousness and obtain information about
facts long forgotten by the normal personality. Further, it
was possible to experimentally study the relation of the subconscious personality to, and the influence of this upon, the
production of visions.

To understand this, it is necessary to state a few facts
regarding the subject. Miss X suffers from what is ordinarily
called neurasthenia, or hystero-neurasthenia, but what I
think is more correctly called hysterical neurasthenia. But
she has no physical stigmata, excepting a possible contraction of the field of vision.[1] She is easily hypnotized; first
passing into a state which resembles that of the ordinary
classical deep stage. After waking, there is complete loss of
memory of this state. During hypnosis she is very susceptible
to suggestion; but, on the whole, there is nothing very remarkable about the mental condition, which does not materially differ from one of the deeper stages of hypnosis as
ordinarily observed. The only points to which I would call

1 At the time these observations were made, this seemed to have disappeared, or, at least, could not be recognized by the finger test.

attention are that Miss X in this stage of hypnosis knows all about Miss X awake, and apparently remembers all that Miss X remembers and some other things besides, which she has forgotten when awake, but Miss X when awake knows nothing of what has occurred in this hypnotic state. For convenience's sake, I have called Miss X, in this stage of hypnosis, X 2, as distinguished from Miss X or X 1.

Now, on commanding X 2 to sleep more deeply, there appears a third personality, whom I have called X 3. This person knows all about both Miss X and X 2, everything they do and think, but is unknown to both. Her memory, also, in some respects, is much fuller than that of either Miss X or X 2, so it comes about that X 3 can tell much in the past life of Miss X that that person has forgotten, and can explain much that the waking personality is at a loss to account for. X 3 even knows all about many of the little absent-minded and half-voluntary doings of Miss X, nor does she hesitate to voluntarily tell of them, although Miss X is morbidly and unnecessarily reserved about her whole life.

I have been able to record a large number of interesting psychical phenomena which were exhibited by this patient, and which I shall report at another time, but the above facts are all that it is necessary to mention in this connection. It may only be added that the characters of the three personalities were very different and distinct. Miss X is reserved, morbidly conscientious, self-contained, serious, deferential, and dignified. X 2 is sad, serious, and gives the impression of weariness and suffering. X 3 is flippant, jovial, free from all physical infirmities, full of fun, reckless, and contemptuous of Miss X, whom she stigmatizes as silly, stupid and dull, and in an apparently heartless way enjoys every trouble that comes to her. X 3 always speaks of Miss X as "She,"[1] and insists that they are different persons — that they don't think the same things or know the same things. She speaks of X 2 as "Miss X asleep." This much will explain the conditions under which the following experiments were made.

---

1　In the following account, She, with a capital S, always refers to Miss X (X 1).

A study of the results obtained shows that the visions could be divided into three groups.

(*a*)     Those which were revivals, of past visual experiences, either conscious or unconscious.

(*b*)     Those which were not revivals, but largely newly created visual representations of a past experience which was not originally visual, *e. g.*, perhaps auditory.

(*c*)     Those which were neither revivals nor representations of any specific past experience (visual or other) so far as known, but fabrications.

Naturally some visions partook more or less of the characteristics of two or more groups, being partly revivals and partly new creations; nevertheless, all could be placed in one or other group according to the chief characteristic.

(*A*) *Experiments in which the visions were revivals of past visual experiences*, either conscious or subconscious.

*Experiment* 1. — In this and all of the experiments, an incandescent electric light globe was used instead of the ordinary glass ball. Of course, the bulb was not connected with the electric wires or circuit, but held free in the hand of the subject as if it were a mirror. This was the first experiment of the kind made with the subject, and in fact the first I had ever made. The idea of making the experiment only occurred to me at the moment, and I picked up the lamp which was lying on my desk, without previously having given any intimation of the nature of the experiment to Miss X, who afterwards told me she had never heard of such phenomena. She was not, therefore, forewarned, and had no idea what was going to happen beyond that suggested by my first remark, which was that she should look into the glass globe, and she would see something in the past or future. Nothing specific as to what she should see was suggested. Miss X, after looking a few seconds, exhibited distinct evidence of fright, so that she kept taking her eyes off the bulb to avoid seeing, and obliged me to insist upon her looking. She afterwards explained this fright as due to a feeling of uncanniness. As she looked, she described to me what she saw. She saw a young woman, in a low-necked dress, a blonde, about twenty-three, sitting in a chair near what was apparently a chimney-piece in a strange room. She was laughing. Standing in front of her was an older man with a dark beard tinged with grey. He was scolding her hard, but the young woman was laughing. Miss X's face during this time was expressive of very lively emotions, and I was obliged to calm her and assure her that it was all right, and there was nothing to be afraid of.

Here I may mention, once for all, the objective characteristics of these visions as they appeared to the subject and were described by Miss X, and also Miss X's mental condition at the time as I observed it. The visions were not seen like small objects reflected in or on the glass bulb, but Miss X stated that the bulb disappeared, and she saw before her the scene she described, which appeared real, the characters being life-size and like living persons. I should infer that she saw them much as one sees the characters on the stage of a theatre, but she saw them, nevertheless, where the bulb was. Perhaps the illustration of looking through an opera-glass at the stage is apposite, for she several times at first broke off from her inspection and examined the bulb to see if there was any explanation of the vision to be found in the glass, much as one who had never seen an opera-glass or a kaleidoscope might examine it for this purpose. To me, as I observed her, she appeared like one who, at a theatre, was completely absorbed by the play, and in that sense was unconscious of surroundings, but not at all in a trance state. Her absorption and the exceeding mobility and expression of her face when describing a vision gave the impression that she was entirely oblivious of myself and surroundings, until spoken to, but not as one hypnotized, but rather as one who is intensely absorbed in the scene of a theatre until she has forgotten where she is. Every feeling: timidity, surprise, interest, seemed to be expressed by the play of her features, and at times, especially at first, she semed rather frightened by the uncanniness of what she saw. Most of her descriptions were given in answer to my questions, which were prodding but never suggestive. They were simply expressions like "What else?" "Go on," "Is there anything more?"

etc. It may be noted, then, as psychologically of interest, that the visions appeared like ordinary hallucinations or vivid dreams, the scenes real, of life-size, but *dissociated* from her surroundings, and not as part of them.

To return, Miss X said she could not see anything more. (It was not noted whether the vision ceased spontaneously.) Upon being interrogated, she could give no explanation of the scene. She could not remember ever having seen the man, or the girl, or the place before. I insisted that the vision must have been a part of her past experience, but she could not recall anything like it. I then hypnotized her, and X 2, the second personality, appeared. X 2 also said she could not remember having seen either of the characters or the room before. She was then placed in deeper hypnosis, and the third personality, X 3 appeared. X 3 immediately, as soon as present, began to smile, then burst out laughing, and at once said she recollected the whole incident. It was at San Antonio, Texas, about seven years ago, when "she" was sixteen years old. They had left the dinner table, she said, and were going upstairs to their room, and on the way passed by an open door of a room. In the room were this young woman and the man, and he was scolding away, and she did not seem to mind it. They were strangers, and "she" only saw them once afterwards, driving in a carriage. X 3 was highly amused at the recollection and the experiment. She was then awakened, and I told Miss X (without giving the source of my information) that she had seen these people in San Antonio, Texas, and gave the particulars as above. She still failed to recollect the incident. The next day, however, she returned and said that after going home she had gone over in her mind her experiences in San Antonio, and by tracing successively in her mind the different events that had occurred there, she had succeeded in bringing back into her memory the whole incident of the crystal vision. In answer to my objection that her recollection was an hallucination and was merely what had been suggested to her by me, she gave a great many more details preceding and following the event of the vision, showing that her memory now is much fuller than that which was shown in the vision. The scene in the room was a mere casual observation, and was not apparently of a nature to make an impression at the time, excepting that it produced some sort of unpleasant feeling, which she always experiences when she hears people scolding. I noticed that she manifested some mental discomfort when she described the man in the vision scolding.

The conclusions to be drawn from this experiment are: first, that in this class of cases, the hallucination represents a past visual experience — a visual picture was reproduced as a whole. Secondly, that the hallucination is in association with certain subconscious groups of mental states (X 3). It is odd that of all the experiences of her past life, such a trivial one should have been selected to emerge from out of the depths of subconscious life into consciousness. The continuous action and succession of events in this and other visions should be noted.

*Experiment* 2. — Miss X looked into the globe and was highly amused. She saw Dr. C. first in a room of the Massachusetts Eye and Ear Infirmary, and then walking down the corridor. She told me that she had seen him there, but never doing what he was doing now. He was fidgeting about in the most nervous way and walking down the corridor in a funny way. She insisted that although she remembered seeing him under the same circumstances as in the vision, she never saw him acting in that way.

Hypnotized. — X 3 is full of fun today and rather rollicking (on this day experiments 3 and 6 were also made); told about the visions and enjoyed the thought of them hugely; spoke with great rapidity, rattling them off as if she were anxious to tell a good story, and enjoyed the telling. She said that one day "She" (X 1) was in the infirmary, in the large operating room, with Dr. C. He was on one side of the table and She on the other. He fidgeted and put one foot on the table and then the other, and moved first one arm and then the other in a nervous way. Miss X copied everything he did, but not intentionally. Dr. C. became so nervous he could not stand it and ran out of the room. X 3 laughed heartily at the recollection. This experiment is interesting only as showing how forgotten and trivial experiences may appear in visions.

*Experiment 3.* — This is an extremely interesting vision, but as it represents a somewhat personal matter, I give only the main facts. Miss X saw two persons walking down the street. One of these, Y, crossed a field to some rocks by the seashore, where Miss X was sitting looking out to sea, with her back to the person approaching. Miss X was about sixteen years of age, dressed as a young girl with her hair down her back. The approaching person went up behind her. She did not see him at first. He had a wild expression in his face, as if insane. "This," she declared to me, "is not true; he never looked like that." It was very disagreeable to see this expression on his face. She repeated "He looks insane." He took some letters or papers out of his pocket and tore them up, and crushed his watch, which he had in his hand. He acted wildly. Miss X kept repeating with some fervor "This is not true, this is not true." In explanation, she remembered that when she was a girl about sixteen the main incident happened; she did see this person walking across the fields to where she was, but she did not see him approach, and none of the rest was true. He simply came up behind her and spoke to her, etc. He did not do any of the things she saw him do in the vision.

*Hypnosis.* — X 3 said it was all true. That She (Miss X) saw him first walking in the street and across the fields, but that Y came up close behind her without her seeing him. Then She saw him and spoke to him, but when She turned her face away, he looked fierce and crunched his teeth. He had his watch in his hand, and crushed it. X 3 insisted that "She" did not see this, did not see the expression of his face, because every time "She" turned round, he smoothed his face out, and when She turned away her head, this fierce expression came again. When I asked X 3 how she could see that, if her head was turned, she kept saying, "I did see it, but 'She' didn't. She doesn't know. I saw it, and that he looked that way. She doesn't know he crunched his watch and tore the papers." (It would appear probable, assuming all this to be literally true, that Miss X must have caught glimpses of this out of the corner of her eye, making use of peripheral as distinct from central vision. These glimpses were not distinct enough to make a conscious impression, but were seen by the hypnotic self, X 3. She may have heard the crunching of the watch and of the papers. It is more than probable that the details in the crystal vision are largely exaggerated, *being created* unconsciously out of the *inferences* which Miss X or X 3 drew from what she saw, a peculiarity of these visions, which is illustrated by some of the other experiments. X 3 probably didn't see as much as she thinks she did, but woman-like, gives her inferences instead of her actual observation.)

*Experiment* 4. — X 3 now (after explaining the last vision) volunteered the following remarkable story, telling it with great gusto and as a joke on Miss X, and speaking with great rapidity, so that it was difficult to follow the sequence of events. The language is substantially that of X 3, but condensed. "She" yesterday received a letter from a photographer. She had it in her hand while walking down Washington Street, and then put it into her pocket (side pocket of jacket) where She kept her watch and money (banknotes). Then as She walked along, She took out the money and tore it to pieces, thinking it was the letter from the photographer. She threw the money into the street. As She tore up the money She said to herself "I wish they would not write on this banknote paper." At my request X 3 repeated the words of the photographer's note, which stated that some photographs were ready. As to the money, there were two ten-dollar notes; this, at my demand, X 3 counted mentally, with some difficulty and concentration of thought. X 3 manifested considerable unwillingness to show me the letter, which she said was in "her" pocket still, and which She still thought to be money. Finally, after some insistence, she did so. It was folded up into a small square, just as one often folds banknotes. The language of the photographer's note was identically the same as quoted by X 3. X 3 said that "She" was absent-minded, and thinking of something else, when She tore up the money. I then gave X 3 the note to put back into her pocket, preparatory to waking her up.

This impish hypnotic personality remarked upon what a joke it would be when She found it there instead of the banknotes. I will say here the heartless cold-blooded delight which this almost Iago-like personality took in the loss of the money, really a very great one to Miss X, was appalling. To X 3 it was a splendid practical joke.

Miss X was now awakened. I asked her whether she did not have some money and had not received a letter from a photographer. She said "Yes," but seemed to think it rather queer my asking these questions. By this time, however, she had become accustomed to being astonished. In reply to a series of questions she said she had not the letter with her, but had torn it up and thrown it into the street (Washington Street). The money she had in her pocket. They were two ten-dollar bills. I asked her to show them to me. She put her hand in her pocket to take them out and brought out the photographer's letter. She evidently received a shock although she tried not to show it. I asked her where the bills were, and after searching her pockets she insisted that she must have left them at home. I remarked that she must have destroyed them by mistake instead of the letter. She refused to admit it. I pointed out the circumstantial evidence. She recognized that it was suspicious but could and would not believe it. The loss meant a great deal to her, and she evidently encouraged herself with a forlorn hope. I then said, taking the glass globe, "We will see whether it is not true. Look in and you will see what you have done." At first she saw indifferent things; then I said, "Think of banknotes and the feeling of tearing them up." Now, to her astonishment, she saw herself walking along Washington Street and in the act of putting the letter in her pocket, then taking out what looked like banknotes, that is, green pieces of paper, and tearing them into pieces and throwing them into the street. The vision, in all its details, corresponded to the account given by the hypnotic personality. Miss X, in answer to my question, said she had once before done a similar thing, namely, in a state of absent-mindedness, she had thrown some banknotes into the fire and had taken the letter which contained them "down town" to pay some bills. The next day, Miss X reported that she was unable to find the money at home, and was satisfied the vision was true. In hypnosis, X 3 now volunteered the information that Miss X ("She") was so much upset by the loss of her money, that in the middle of the night She "had to get up" in her sleep, without knowing it and had taken the remainder of her money and hidden it under "that floppy thing" on the table. "It was now under a red book, a blue book, and that floppy thing" (by this i meant either a tablecloth or a folded up piece of material). "She" knows nothing about it, and thinks She has lost the money and has none left. X 3 does not know how much money there is.

Miss X, on being awakened, is very reticent, does not like my knowing, and will not admit the fact with which I taxed her, *viz.*, that she had lost the rest of her money. (To have this understood, it would be necessary to go into a rather lengthy explanation of the circumstances of Miss X's life, which I hardly feel called upon to do. I will merely say that Miss X had come to Boston to be under my professional care and was in lodgings and had a certain fixed sum for her expenses; the loss of all this money meant financial bankruptcy.) Without further discussion, and *without disclosing my knowledge,* I then presented a glass globe to her; told her to think of the money and she would see what had become of it. She looked into the globe and saw herself in bed in her room. She then saw herself get up, her eyes being closed, and walk up and down the room; she then saw herself going to the bureau drawer, taking out her money, going to the table, taking up the cloth with the books, putting the money on the table, covering it with the cloth and putting the red book and the green book on top of it. The vision thus exactly corresponded[1] to the statement of X 3. Miss X reported at the next visit that she had found the money where she had seen it in the globe.

---

1 Excepting the color of the book, "blue" or "green." This escaped my attention at the time; perhaps it was blue-green, and looked blue to X 3 and green to X, or it may be an error on my part.

## Remarks

It is noteworthy that in this experiment, as well as the preceding one, the vision was a representation of the hypnotic or subliminal consciousness, and not of the waking consciousness. In experiment 3, certain things were portrayed in the vision which the waking consciousness (apparently) never perceived, while in experiment 4 (first part, destruction of bills) an absent-minded act was represented, and in the second part a somnambulic act. It might be held that the first vision of the banknote episode might have been created out of my statement to her, if it were not for the minute fidelity with which the vision corresponded with the account given by X 3, and the corroborating evidence of the second vision when I gave no hint of what would be seen.

(B) *Experiments in which the hallucination was not a revival of a past visual experience, but was largely a newly created visual representation of a past experience other than visual.*

*Experiment 5.* — I will give this in the brief language of my notes: Miss X. looked again into the globe; she saw a room with a bed in it. There was a figure in the bed; the figure threw off the bed clothes and got up. Miss X exclaimed "Why, it is I." (Appeared rather frightened at what she saw, but went on to describe it, largely in answer to my promptings, such as "Go on," "What do you see?" etc.) She saw herself walking to and fro, up and down the room. Then she climbed on to the window sill which is the deep embrasure of a mansard roof. Then she climbed outside the window and from the sill looked down into the street. It was night — the street lamps were lighted, there was also the gas light in the room. As she looked down she felt dizzy. Here Miss X turned away frightened, saying she felt the same dizziness as if she were standing there. She soon continued. She saw herself throw an inkstand into the street below, which she had seen herself take before climbing on to the window. Miss X was again obliged to stop looking be-

cause of dizziness. After a time she returned to the globe
She saw herself go back into the room and walk up and
down; the door opened and she jumped into bed and lay
quiet. Miss L (a friend) entered, went out and returned
several times; brought a poultice which she put on Miss X'
chest; Miss X herself remaining quiet. Then Miss L went
out and Miss X got up an took the poultice, rolled it up into
a little bunch and hid it in a corner, putting a towel over it
Here the experiment ended.

Miss X stated, on being questioned, that she could not
remember any incident like the vision, excepting that she
recognized the room as the first one she occupied when she
came to Boston four or five years ago. It was in the top
story of a house on Columbus Avenue; she was ill there, and
Miss L took care of her. But she did not remember ever having
climbed on to the window, or having thrown an ink
stand out of the window, or any of the incidents of the
vision. She could throw no light on the affair. She was now
lightly hypnotized and X 2 was present. X 2 could add very
little to Miss X's statement. (My notes of X 2's memory are
somewhat confused; it is not plain from them whether or
not she remembered ever having done any of the things
seen in the vision, although it is stated that she had an imperfect memory of the incident. It is possible X 2's statement, as noted, was mixed up with that of X 3, but X 2
remembered being ill in the room described, and that ink
was found in Miss X's shoes. X 2 did not know how it came
there, but Miss L had said that Miss X had poured ink in her
shoes. At any rate, X 2 could not explain the incident as
X 3 did later.)

*Deep hypnosis:* X 3 appeared. With great vivacity and
amusement, X 3 explained the whole scene. (As was customary with her, X 3 spoke of Miss X (X 1) as "She," as if
it were an entirely distinct person and not herself.) "She"
had pneumonia and was delirious, and She imagined She was
on the seashore and was walking up and down the sand. This
was why She walked up and down the room, and She stuck
her toes in the carpet thinking it was the sand. There were
rocks there, and the window sill was one of them, and when

She climbed out upon the window sill, She thought She was climbing upon a rock, and She took up a stone, as She thought, and threw it into the sea. This was the inkstand that She threw into the street. Then when she took the poultice and hid it in the corner She thought She had buried it in the sand. She had not poured ink into her shoes, but her hand shook and She had spilled it into her shoes. Miss L, seeing the ink stains, had inferred that Miss X had poured the ink into the shoes, and had told Miss X so. Hence the statements of X and X 2. X 3 was highly amused at all the mistakes of Miss X's delirium.

## Remarks

It is obvious that this vision was not solely a revival of an optical experience of the past, for Miss X could not have seen *herself* as she did in the vision. The hallucination was rather a new creation corresponding to, and illustrative of, a memory of a past event. But into this new creation a certain number of past optical images entered, as in the scene in the street and the room. Yet even these were originally seen by the delirious consciousness in a different way, that is, as if it were the seashore. The vision rather corresponded to the way in which the third personality, X 3, would have seen delirious X 1 and her surroundings, if she could have seen them. This suggests the relation of the hypnotic personality, X 3, to the delirious consciousness. X 3 observed the delirious Miss X, and was cognizant of her thoughts just as she was of those of the normal Miss X. Just as X 3 knew all about X 1 when in health, so she knew all about X 1 when delirious. But normal X 1 had no recollection of delirious X 1. The hypnotic consciousness is not the delirious consciousness, but bears the same relation to it as it does to the normal consciousness. X 3 was normal while X 1 was delirious. It is a startling idea, that of there being beneath the delirium of a person in fever another healthy personality, a mind unchanged, which is observing everything done, thought and said by the delirious person. It is worth noting in passing that when Miss X saw herself looking into the street, she at that moment actually felt dizzy. That is, as the scene appeared real to her, so looking down into the street of the vision made her dizzy.

*Experiment 6.* — This experiment was interesting, as it showed how a vision could be constructed out of certain past familiar images and certain other experiences of which no optical images could have been received; a new synthesis of images created by the force, if I may use the word, of imagination and known facts. Looking into the globe, Miss X was astonished to see herself sitting on a sofa, the identical sofa on which she was then sitting. *Her eyes were closed,* and she was smoking cigarettes. While Miss X was looking at herself in the globe, she several times turned to look at the sofa on which she was sitting to compare it with that in the globe. They were the same. Her whole expression was one of extreme astonishment and chagrin. She indignantly repudiated the fact, said it was not true, she was not in the habit of smoking cigarettes, and had never smoked one. In giving a further description of herself in the vision, she said her eyes were closed and she looked foolish. The explanation of this vision was that the day before, as a practical joke, I had given a cigarette to X 3, who had taken it in a spirit of fun and smoked it clumsily, showing plainly she had not been accustomed to smoking. X 3 laughed and made merry over the prank, saying it was a great joke on Miss X, who would be "awfully shocked" if She knew it. She pretended it was very wicked — as it was for her. The visionary Miss X's eyes were closed, for I had always obliged X 3 to keep her eyes closed for reasons not necessary to go into here.

## Remarks

It is noteworthy that the vision, so far as it concerned cigarette smoking, represented an experience which belonged only to the hypnotic personality of which Miss X, the superior consciousness, never had any knowledge. From this it might be inferred that visions might present absentminded acts as in the case of experiment No. 4. Secondly, the contents of the vision were partly previous optical images received by the primary consciousness, that of Miss X, *viz.,* images of the sofa and portions of Miss X (X 3 had never had her eyes open·) and partly were syntheses of the third personality's sole *knowledge;* thus the vision was made up of the experiences of two personalities, and only in part of past images. As she had never *seen* herself smoking, the vision was largely an optical representation (not a revival) of impressions from other senses.

(C)   *Experiments in which the vision did not reproduce or represent any past experience, visual or other, so far as known.*

*Experiment 7.* — Miss X looked into the glass globe. She saw an old lady standing in a very steep street leading up over stones; there were steep rocks on one side. The street was like nothing she had ever seen before in this country. (She said *this country,* as if to emphasize the fact that it looked foreign.) She had never seen the old lady before. As she looked, a man on horseback appeared, and the horse knocked the old lady down. The latter seemed to be hurt. Here Miss X turned her head away as if alarmed. On another day, Miss X again saw the same vision. The man's features were also strange to her. The most minute inquiry failed to elicit any fact that would throw light on this vision. Miss X said she had never been abroad, and had never seen any place resembling that of the vision, nor knew of any such accident. When hypnotized, neither of the other two personalities (X 2 and X 3) had any recollection of any such place or event. I am disposed, therefore, to believe that it was probably a visual representation of something she had read, or of some picture she had seen, which would readily pass out of the recollection of even the hypnotic self. As she described the street in detail, it recalled places to me I had seen in Europe, or pictures of foreign scenes.

*Experiment 8.* — Miss X had lost a scarf-pin she valued. I suggested that she should try to find it by looking in the globe. After looking a few minutes, she saw a bed-room with a brass bedstead, and on the dressing-table was a pincushion (described in detail), and in the pincushion were several pins. Amongst them she recognized her own, and exclaimed somewhat excitedly "Why, that is my pin!" Involuntarily she reached out to seize it. During this, her face was very expressive and showed great astonishment. She did not recognize the room, and was certain she had never seen it before, but thought it a city room and not a country one, from its general appearance and furnishing.

In hypnosis, both personalities were also ignorant of this room, but X 3, being asked to tell the last time that Miss X had the scarf-pin, recollected perfectly. "She" (Miss X) came into her room (in the country, not in Boston) one day with a very severe headache, took the pin out of her dress, and stuck it into the head of the couch, then doubled up the pillow and placed it over the place where the pin was, and lay down on the couch with her head on the pillow and rested. "She" forgot all about the pin, and had no recollection of putting the pin where She did, and, in fact, did it rather absent-mindedly. This was several months ago, and X 3 presumed the pin was gone. On Miss X being awakened, I told her what she had done with the pin, but still she had no recollection of the affair.

## Remarks

Probably in this case the vision did not correspond to any known fact in Miss X's experience. The room, I suppose, might be some room she had casually seen but forgotten, but she could not very well have seen her pin in it. Perhaps she might have thought, at some time, that the pin had been found or taken, and was in the possession of someone. Thus the vision might have been constructed in much the same way as the one in which the cigarette figured (experiment No. 6). I was unable to learn whether X 3's story was correct or not, but it probably was, as I had always found her positive recollections accurate. This experiment also illustrates, like No. 4, the effect of suggestion in determining the character of the vision; that is, a vision of a particular thing or subject would occur in preference to any other vision.

I wish that further observations had been made on this subject, especially with a view to determining how far the contents of a vision could be shaped by suggestion, and ascertaining the relation of visions to beliefs, and other thoughts; but various considerations made it desirable to interrupt the experiment at this point. As the laws governing one sense are probably the same as those for another, it is likely that the antecedent relations of hallucinations of hearing are the same as those of hallucinations of vision. This inference is somewhat speculative, but it lends additional value to a knowledge of the origin of visions. If it be true, as is most highly probable, that visions may be an optical representation of pure thoughts and beliefs, this fact gives us something with which to answer Griesinger's question, "Why does the insane patient believe in his hallucinations?" It would seem as Hirst[1] well says, "The patient does not believe himself to be the son of the emperor, because the voice told him so, but he heard the voice making this statement because he believed it."

## CONCLUSIONS

(1) Visions in sane persons may be revivals of past visual experiences, which originally may have been conscious or subconscious. The original subconscious experience may have occurred in a moment of absent-mindedness, or may not have been sufficiently intense to have entered consciousness, or (rarely) may have occurred in somnambulism.

(2) The vision instead of being a revival, may be a newly-created pictorial representation of a past experience other than visual. That is to say, past impressions of one or more senses (touch, hearing) and actions may translate themselves into a representation by another sense as a vision.

(3) It is probable, though not *proved*,[2] that a vision may not reproduce or represent any past experience, visual

1 "The Psychical Mechanism of Delusions." The *Journal of Nervous and Mental Disease*, March, 1898.

2 Other experiments proved this.

or other, but may be newly created out of something the subject has read, heard, or thought. The inference from, and passing thoughts about, known facts may weave themselves into visions. This was probably the origin of the visions of Joan of Arc, and religious enthusiasts in general.

(4) Visions may partake more or less of the characteristics of these classes, being partly revivals, partly representations of actual non-visual experiences, and also of the subject's knowledge, inferences and thoughts.

(5) Generalizing, it is possible that hallucinations of the other senses, especially that of hearing, such, for example, as exhibited by trance mediums, may have a similar origin and composition.

(6) Analogous phenomena may be observed in the attacks of hysterics, where the passing thoughts in the normal state may appear as insistent ideas in the attack.

(7) It is probable that thoughts which have strongly absorbed the mind and expressed the ambition or the ideas and beliefs of the subject may appear as visions. The subjects then are apt to look upon them as inspirations. In this way have arisen the visions of political personages like Joan of Arc, Bismarck, and religious enthusiasts like Luther, Fra Angelico, Catherine of Sienna and others.

(8) Visions, artificially created, may be representations and revivals of the experience of the hypnotic personality, of which experience the waking consciousness has never had knowledge.

(9) Impressions on the sense organs which never entered consciousness (and are therefore neither known nor remembered) may afterwards appear as visions.

# CHAPTER XIV

## Coconscious Images[1]

THE phenomena which I am about to describe are important because, if the evidence upon which they depend is accepted as veridical, they afford *direct* evidence of specific subconscious processes occurring under certain conditions. Even the most ardent of clinical psychologists must admit that the subconscious processes which they postulate to explain their clinical phenomena are based on indirect or circumstantial evidence; that is to say, the postulate of a subconscious process is inferred from the behavior of the phenomena and the logical relation which appears to exist between them and certain antecedent experiences, that give justifiable grounds for the inference of a causal relationship. This causal relation requires the assumption of a subconscious process acting as an intermediary between the conserved antecedent experience and the present observed phenomena. In other words, all takes place *as if* there were this subconscious process.

Now, for the subconscious phenomena about to be described the evidence is direct. I have said that the acceptation of the phenomena depends upon the acceptation of the evidence as trustworthy. If this be not accepted, the phenomena are valueless. The evidence is that of memory derived from introspection. It is the same kind of evidence that must necessarily be used and accepted in all psychological investigations into the content of consciousness. It would seem that if this kind of evidence is accepted, as it is, in one class of psychological investigations, there is no justification in refusing it in another. But, of course, in every

1 Presented at the Eighth Annual Meeting of the American Psychopathological Association, Boston, May 24, 1917.

investigation employing this method, everything depends upon the accuracy of the powers of introspection and trustworthiness of the subject. I have observed these phenomena in three cases only — two of my own and one of Dr. Waterman's. My own cases were studies over a long period of time, and therefore I had an opportunity to weigh carefully the introspective capacity of the subjects, their introspective memories, and their trustworthiness. I have not the slightest doubt regarding any of these points. Dr. Waterman, to whom I am indebted for allowing me to observe the case together with him, has the same confidence. Furthermore, my own cases have been submitted to quite a number of well-known competent observers, and no one has expressed the silghtest doubt regarding their veridical nature.

With respect to the significance and interpretation of the phenomena, I am not prepared to express definite conclusions. They permit, however, of provisional theories which I will offer in the proper place.

## DESCRIPTION OF THE PHENOMENA

The phenomena consist of coconscious "pictures," for the most part visualizations, sometimes auditory "perceptions," which occur outside the field of awareness. I say "coconscious" and "outside the field of awareness" because the subjects in their normal waking state are entirely unaware of them. By no effort of mental concentration or introspection can they possibly bring back memories of such pictures ever having entered the field of consciousness, nor are they aware of them at the moment of occurrence. There is no immediate awareness of them, and it is only by retrospection under the conditions of certain methods of investigation that memories of these coconscious pictures can be recovered.

The method employed was that of retrospection in hypnosis. When the subjects were hypnotized and thereby put into a condition where, as so commonly happens, the capacity for synthesization is enhanced, memories of coconscious phenomena which, it was claimed, had never entered the field of awareness were obtained. These memories were very precise, definite and realistic. There never was any doubt about them as memories, nor any doubt about them as previous realities, that is to say, real psychical occurrences. They were always described as vivid pictures (or auditory sounds, music, etc.) varying in character from a single picture, as of a face or other object, to a succession of pictures, like motion-pictures representing the action of a scene. They were, in other words, similar to the visualizations (belonging to perceptions) which occur normally in the course of conscious thought, as when one thinks of a person or place or scene, only they were more vivid, and, when cinematographic, more complex, and did not appear within the conscious content of awareness. Furthermore, *these visualizations or pictures were not integral elements of the conscious stream of thought (perceptions), but in their content pertained to matter of which the subject was not consciously thinking at the moment.* The matter generally, if not always, was related to antecedent mental experiences (thoughts) with or without secondary elaboration.

The conditions under which these phenomena were observed were various; for instance, they occurred regularly during the course of suggested post-hypnotic acts, often as post-dream phenomena, and as phenomena of repressed thoughts, etc. They will be classified later, after I have given a few examples in order that their nature may be more clearly understood at the outset. For this purpose, I will take a type occurring, perhaps, under the simplest conditions, namely, suggested post-hypnotic phenomena.

## 1. POST-HYPNOTIC PHENOMENA

*Observation* 1: The suggestion was given to the subject in hypnosis that after waking, on the entrance of Dr. Waterman into the room, she was to go to the bookcase, take down a book, take it to the table and place it by the telephone instrument. She then was to take a cigarette from the box and put it in her mouth. The latter suggestion she refused to accept saying that she "would not do it," that "I could not make her do it," etc. Nevertheless I insisted.

This suggestion, after waking, was accurately carried out up to the point of putting the cigarette in her mouth. Instead of doing this, she laughed and, after some hesitation, offered a cigarette to me and to Dr. Waterman.

The subject was then put into three different hypnotic states and the following memories elicited of what occurred subconsciously during the suggested post-hypnotic action. I will give substantially the exact words used in one of these states. (In this state, not in the others, the subject speaks of herself in the third person, as "C.")

You know after you woke her up and went into the other room to summon Dr. Waterman, there began to be pictures in the subconscious portion of her mind. There was a picture of the bookcase, then one of Dr. P. — very bright, much brighter than that of the bookcase — and then there was a picture of a woman walking across the room, taking a book out of the bookcase and then coming back and putting it down by the telephone. (The picture was not of the subject.) She was in black, tall, had gray hair. A picture of you alternated with all the pictures. There was an ornate gold frame,[1] very bright, about your picture. These pictures first came after awaking, before getting up from the sofa (perhaps a minute). C did not see them, but she thought of a bookcase alone and nothing more. Afterwards, she got up and as she proceeded to carry out the act, the pictures still kept coming and going, subconsciously. When she took down the book, a picture of a woman taking down a book came into C2's[2] mind, and each act was accompanied by a picture corresponding to the act, and each picture alternated with a

1 This gold frame frequently appeared under certain conditions and seemed to have a symbolic meaning in that it stood for my authority, suggestions, therapeutic assurances, advice, etc. This symbolism was a perseveration of commands, or assurances that all was well, etc.; i. e., actual therapeutic suggestions and advice given to solve her problems and resolve her mental conflicts.

2 C2 was an arbitrarily agreed upon term to designate, for short, that subconscious portion of the mind in which the pictures, which did not appear in awareness, occurred.

picture of you. After she had laid the book down, she turned to the table where the cigarettes were, when there came a very bright picture of a ballet or chorus girl. The girl had short red skirts of tulle and she was sitting at a table with her feet crossed. A three-cornered hat was on her head, and she was *smoking a cigarette.* She looked very gay. This was when C picked up the box of cigarettes, and as she did so, there came the thought that she would put a cigarette in her mouth and then she felt shocked at the idea. It was with a picture of the ballet girl that the *thought* came to put a cigarette in her mouth, and then she felt shocked at the idea of doing such a thing. No pictures came into her conscious mind, only *two thoughts, one of the bookcase, the other of putting a cigarette in her mouth.* The pictures were subconscious (C2).

The picture of the ballet girl had an interesting history. It transpired that this picture was a replica of a real picture which she had seen elsewhere and which previously had brought to her mind, much to her disapproval, the kind of people who smoke cigarettes. It had made an impression of aversion, for it symbolized her punctilious ideas as to smoking cigarettes. This general aversion, without any specific memory of the picture, was why she had been consciously unwilling to accept the suggestion to smoke them. But smoking cigarettes had been actually associated in her mind with the ballet girl type of person, and apparently this strongly associated idea, symbolized in the form of a previously experienced picture, arose subconsciously at the moment when the suggested act was to be performed. When she felt shocked that she should have the idea of smoking a cigarette, this subconscious picture of a ballet girl appeared.

*Observation* 2: The suggestion was given in hypnosis that the subject was to bring me the next day a *manuscript.* The authorship of this manuscript was symbolized by the letter A for reasons not necessary to go into. This suggestion was carried out, the manuscript being brought in her muff and handed to me without the subject afterwards being aware of what she had done. That is to say, she had no knowledge of the suggestion or of the fact of having carried it out.

The coconscious events were afterwards described in two different hypnotic states as follows, the language of each description of course being somewhat different:

> After the subject was awakened from hypnosis, on her way home, there kept coming and going coconscious visual images of the letter A (rather vague and indistinct) and of the letters MS. These floated in and out, alternating with a *bright* picture of you, much brighter than the others. Then, while she was eating her dinner, there came a picture of her desk where she keeps all her papers — all the copies of all that she has done for you. The picture of the desk was brighter than that of A. The lower drawer was open. There were some hands searching all through the papers and taking out some papers and rolling them and putting an elastic around them. There appeared over and over visual images of hands, desk, manuscript, hands, desk — then there came a picture of her muff and the hands putting the roll of manuscript in the muff, then again a picture of you. These all went through her mind [coconsciously]. First A, then picture of you, then MS, then picture of you, then desk and hands getting papers, then you, then muff, then you, then hands putting papers in muff, then you, then roll of papers in muff, then you, then there was a picture of hands giving the roll to you. These alternated over and over.
>
> Of the pictures, that of you was all that was in C's consciousness. She didn't think about it, but it floated into her mind.

(Note that in this observation one of the pictures, that of me, emerged into consciousness. This, as we shall see later, sometimes happens, and then it may appear as an hallucination.)

The mental condition during the actual carrying out of the post-hypnotic act was described as follows:

After she had gone upstairs, and when she was going to bed, she went to the drawer to take her diary out to write in it and she burrowed down under all those papers and took out that manuscript and rolled it up and put an elastic around it and put it in her muff, but she did not know she had done it. She did it in a perfectly absent-minded way. She was thinking of her conversation with you before she left. She was entirely unconscious of what she was doing. With each act, as above described, a corresponding picture appeared in C2. For example: picture of open drawer — she opened the drawer; hands picking up manuscript — she picked up manuscript, etc.

That all happened last night. This morning she came in with the manuscript in her muff. She had her finger in the roll all the way in, but she did not know it. She had it in her hand when she took her things off, came in here and gave it to you. When she gave it to you, the pictures of you and the hands were very bright in C2, and I think also in C's mind, in an unconscious way. She handed it to you in an absent-minded way. That is, she did not know what she was doing.

Note the fact that these coconscious pictures began to come and go shortly after the suggestion was given in hypnosis and for a long time before the suggestion was to be carried out, showing that some sort of a subconscious process, energized by the suggestion, was in activity, and that this process was apparently the same process as was going on during the carrying out of the suggested act, for the pictures were the same up to the fulfillment. Whether this was a correlated process or a causal process the facts do not absolutely establish, although the natural inference is that it was a causal one.

These same phenomena were frequently observed, when inquired into, following suggestions given for therapeutic purposes. The resulting phenomena of course belong to the same class, namely, suggested post-hypnotic phenomena.

*Observation* 3: On one occasion, *e. g.*, I suggested to the subject in hypnosis that she would be "as hungry as a pig"; I also gave the suggestion of "sleep" to relieve the insomnia of which she had complained. In giving the suggestion "sleep" I had described how sleepy she would be when she went to bed — that her head would droop, droop, etc. It turned out that when I said this, she thought of a child, and it reminded her of a mother putting a child to sleep. Now, later, after waking, there were coconscious pictures of some little pigs scrambling over each other to eat from a trough. This was followed by a picture of me in a frame, but not bright as it had been before. This, again, was followed by a picture of a woman trying to wake a child who was very sleepy. The woman could not wake her. She took the child by the shoulders, and the child's head fell back from one side to the other as when overcome by sleep. These pictures of the sleeping child were faint and shadowy. With pictures of the pigs the subject felt that she must eat something, and with those of the sleeping child, she felt sleepy, and although she did not feel hungry, she drank some milk, and in spite of a certain sadness and depression, she slept fairly well.

This affective state could be correlated with other pictures occurring at this time, alternating or coincident. This correlation will be described later in connection with affective states.

It should be noted that the pictures of the sleeping child were not simply reproductive representations of the thought experienced at the time of the suggestion, but were distinct coconscious elaborations of the same, and therefore fabrications. The same probably is true of the "little pigs."

The above examples make the character of the phenomena clear. Taking the phenomena as a whole, they may be grouped, for convenience of study, into the following types: Those occurring as

1. Phenomena of post-hypnotic suggested acts.
2. After-phenomena of dreams.
3. After-phenomena of repressed thoughts.

4. Phenomena of moods, particularly depressed or exalted states.

5. Symbolisms.

6. Phenomena in the mechanism of hallucinations.

7. Phenomena of perseveration of previous emotional
complexes.

This classification is not exclusive, inasmuch as the characteristics of two or more types may be present in any given
phenomenon. For example, as after-phenomena of dreams,
they may also represent repressed thoughts, giving rise to
and occurring in the dreams; and as phenomena of moods,
they may exhibit the characteristics of any of the other
conditions.

The behavior of the phenomena is comprehensible only
on the theory that they are not the whole subconscious process, but are coconscious elements in a more elaborate underlying process, which cannot be brought to consciousness as
a memory, as can the pictures. For the most part, the pictures and the inferred underlying processes can be logically
interpreted as revivals or perseverations, with or without
secondary elaboration, of antecedent thoughts (experiences).

Sometimes the coconscious phenomenon could be correlated:

(a) with conscious affects: that is to say, the affective state
of exaltation or depression (mood), coloring consciousness, bore no relation to the conscious thoughts of the
subject, but corresponded to these coconscious phenomena of which the subject was unaware;

(b) with somatic phenomena, in an apparently causal relation: as when coconscious images of movements of the
hands or feet were accompanied by such movements;

(c) with conscious thoughts; as when, following or coincident with the images, thoughts pertaining to the objects pictured entered the subject's mind;

(d) with antecedent thoughts of which they were pictorial
representations, sometimes in symbolic and allegorical
form;

(e) with hallucinations, which were simply the emergence
into awareness of the coconscious images.

In giving the records of further observations, the above classification of types will not be strictly followed, in view of the fact that, as already stated, any given phenomenon may exhibit the characteristics of several types.

## 2. AFTER-PHENOMENA OF DREAMS

Coconscious pictures which had been elements of previous dreams frequently occurred. Sometimes, they were accompanied by *somatic phenomena,* which, again, were elements in the dreams. Frequently, *repressed thoughts* which appeared in the dreams also appeared in the pictures. The following are examples:

1. In this dream, she was at the entrance of a great cave. Some one, a figure, came rushing past her with his hand over his (or her) eyes. This figure said "Do not look! You will be blinded!" Suddenly it flashed light in the cave, like a flashlight picture, and she saw a scene there enacted. Then everything became black as if she were blinded, and then it would flash and illuminate the cave and she would again see the enactment of the scene. This happened three or four times in the dream.

Now, after waking, pictures began coming and going coconsciously — of the cave, and of the objects seen there in the dream; and sometimes coincidentally with the occurrence of these pictures, of which of course she was not aware, she would see consciously, *i. e.,* become aware of, a flash of light, just as she did in the dream. Then it was as if again she looked into a brilliantly lighted place and saw there some horrible object (the scene in the dream, although she did not know it to be such). It may be added, although not germane to the point, that at first, after waking, she was unsteady and shaken nervously, but after a time, the picture of me in the frame began to come coconsciously and alternate with the above dream pictures, and with the picture of me, she would become steadier and would think (guided by past experiences), "It is only a dream probably. I won't allow it to upset me. I will be just as calm as I can, and it will probably be all right," etc. When this dream was interpreted, it was not difficult to show that the cave, flashes of light, blindness, etc., symbolized pictorially antecedent thoughts that she had had, and had tried to *repress*.

Such phenomena would seem to compel the conclusion that the *same process which had produced the dream-content continued to function subconsciously during the waking state* and caused the coconscious pictures, on the one hand, and the somatic phenomena, on the other.

It should be noted in passing, for we shall see a more striking example later, that some of the coconscious pictures, namely, the scene in the cave, emerged into consciousness as an hallucination, when the flash of light occurred.

2. The dream was of picking her way over a certain rocky path which was covered with cats. She picked her way to avoid stepping on the cats, and shrank and wriggled as she placed each foot to avoid the cats.

Now, after waking from this dream, during that same day, the subject frequently had a feeling that she was going to step on something disagreeable, and frequently looked to see what she was stepping on, to see if there was something there. Each time, she shrank from this possible something, just as she had done in the dream. Coincident with this feeling of stepping on something disagreeable, there came coconscious pictures of the cats on the rocky path — revivals of the dream cats under her feet.

3. During the afternoon preceding the dream, while tearing up some letters referring to an episode in her life, she was very much disturbed over the false position in which she had been placed: she thought "I cannot move in the matter." The dream symbolized these thoughts: for in it, she was told by a certain person, the writer of the letters, that she could not move, that is, go for help; and thereupon she could not — she became rigid.

Now, the next day, there were coconscious pictures of the person of her dream, and when these pictures came, she could not move a step, even though at the time she was crossing the floor. This happened half a dozen times when she was up, and more often when she was lying down. At such times, she would become rigid for a few seconds, and then the picture of the dream personage would go out of the subconscious, and my picture would come, and she could move.

## 3. REPRESSED THOUGHTS

Many instances of pictures which seemed to be plainly the visualizations of repressed thoughts were observed. An example of these, occurring through the mediation of a dream, has already been given. The following illustrates their occurrence after repression, without such mediation.

On one occasion, the period of ten days or so preceding the anniversary of her husband's death was a time of distressing associated memories, among which was one of the deathbed scene. Now, on a certain day at the beginning of this anniversary period, visualizations of this deathbed scene — of the room and the bed, of her husband sitting on the side of the bed, of Mrs. X supporting him, and of blood coming from his mouth — had been coming and going *coconsciously* and *before* the memory of it came into her consciousness. It was not until the next day that the memory of this scene, along with many associated ideas pertaining to her husband, entered the conscious content of her mind, and then she *consciously* visualized the scene. And whenever she did so, a wave of nausea arose. (During the whole period she suffered from prolonged headache. The deathbed scene itself, she had not actually witnessed, but it had been described to her by a certain Mrs. X, her husband having died away from home. The visualization came from this description.) During this anniversary period, a great many other distressing memories, connected with the last days of her husband, crowded into her mind. She made a great effort, however, to repress them, to put them out of her mind by fixing her thoughts on other things. But, as another subject said, "When you put things out of your mind, you don't put them *out* of your mind, you put them *into* your mind." And so she succeeded in putting them out of her mind, in repressing them, *but only to have them reappear as pictures in* C2, and among these pictures was the visualization of the deathbed scene, which from time to time kept recurring. This particular coconscious visualization was always accompanied by ("caused"?) waves of nausea, just as was the case when she consciously visualized the scene. (The occurrence of nausea, correlated with distressing coconscious visualizations of other scenes, had been noted before.)

### 4 and 5. MOODS AND SYMBOLISMS

Not infrequently these visualizations were manifestly allegorical representations of ideas entertained by the subject, and specifically were expressive of her outlook towards life and the particular problems it presented to her, or of her relations to her environment, etc. These allegories took different shape according to her emotional mood, varying as she was elated or depressed. Evidently there was a close correlation between these coconscious phenomena and the contemporary mood, *i. e.*, the affective coloring of consciousness, the former appearing to determine, or at least reflect the latter, or *vice versa;* or, as may be *more probable,* both being determined by deeper subconscious processes from which the affect emerged. A few examples, out of many that might be given, will make clear what I mean.

1. Often when the subject felt full of courage, but not really happy, according to the introspective statement given by the hypnotic personality, there would be in C2 the picture of a man toiling up a steep mountain-side, with a heavy pack on his back. If she felt hopeful, the mountain looked bright at the top, but if she felt doubt-

ful about accomplishing whatever it was she wanted to do, the mountain top was in the clouds.

Sometimes the road up the mountain seemed very rough, and at others it was smooth, according as she felt. On one occasion, for instance, the subject "was more depressed than she had been for a long time. She felt as if she simply could not bear a disappointment which had come to her. There was not one bright or hopeful thought in her mind. She felt that she had come to the end of her endurance and was ready to give up the fight."

Now the correlated coconscious picture was of a road "so rough as to be almost impassable; the man was bent under the weight of his load, and the top of the mountain was hidden by black clouds." After a psychotherapeutic talk, "the picture was still there but changed. The clouds had lifted from the top of the mountain and the atmosphere had cleared. The man was still toiling up the mountain-side but he stood up straight and the road was not so rough. The man in this picture looked a little like Pilgrim in *Pilgrim's Progress*. He had on a sort of frock, belted at the waist and reaching to his knees and heavy laced boots, quite high. His hair was long and he had no hat. His bundle was slung over his shoulder on a stick." *With the change in this picture, there came a change in the subject's thoughts and feelings:* "She felt some hope and courage, some strength to meet the demand made upon her. She felt that she had exaggerated the importance of the matter which had disturbed her and that she ought to be very thankful that it was no worse, but still felt depressed and sad, though stronger."

It will be agreed, I think, that if the subject had wanted to picture, allegorically, her conception of the road of life which she had to travel and its final goal, according to her mood, she could not have voluntarily done it better. But this allegory cannot be construed as a wholly new original subconscious fabrication of the moment. She had previously often consciously thought of the road of life which she had to travel in similar allegorical terms, and this rough rocky road had appeared in her dreams. Such thoughts therefore, when out of mind, were conserved in the subconscious; and we are permitted to infer, from all that we know of the subconscious, that they took on functional activity and, by some mechanism, manifested themselves through these coconscious pictures. They had, however, in the allegory undergone much secondary elaboration. The coloring of the conscious content of the mind by the affect belonging to a subconscious process is a phenomenon which has been frequently demonstrated.[1] Although in a given instance the subconscious source of the affect may not be clear, in other instances there seems to be no room for doubt.

2. Another set of cinematographic pictures appeared about this time. The scene was my office. I was "blowing bubbles — gorgeous great bubbles — and there were pictures of herself holding out her hands to catch the bubbles. And then the bubbles burst. When the bubble was there she felt elated, and when it burst she felt depressed."

These pictures can be rationally interpreted as an allegorical representation of actual psychotherapeutic experiences. I was in the habit of encouraging her with roseate plans for her future, of what she could do in the way of literary and other work to solve her problem of life. But these plans almost always "burst" and for one reason or another came to naught. This, too, was her point of view and caused considerable unhappiness. With the acceptance of the plans, however, she was always highly elated, but when they finally "burst" she became correspondingly depressed.

3. There were certain lines upon courage which had appealed to her and which appeared at times as visualized words in C2, but without coming into the conscious content of her mind. These lines began:

---

1 *Cf.* Prince: *The Unconscious*, chapters XII, XIII, XXVI.

"Of wounds and sore defeat
I made my battle-stay,
Winged sandals for my feet
I wove of my delay."

When these words appeared, she felt more courageous and had more endurance.

4. Again, it was observed that, at times, in the C2 part of her mind, there was a curious religious connection with her mood.

Thus, when she felt very depressed and rebellious, there was a picture of Christ on the Cross. Correlated with this picture, of which of course there was no awareness, her conscious thoughts at the moment were of undeserved suffering. She realized that suffering is not always a punishment for sin (as Christ's was not), or happiness the reward of virtue. When, on the other hand, she felt peaceful and her mind was more or less at rest, the picture became that of Christ calming the waters. He stood with His hands outstretched. Sometimes there were words there, like, "Let not your heart be troubled," "Yea, though I walk through the valley of the shadow," etc.

5. It was noted that after a therapeutic talk, when she felt "hopeful and sometimes exalted, there would be in C2, coming and going, pictures of meadows with lambs frisking about, children dancing around the May-pole, flowers and music, beautiful landscapes with the sun bright and shining; everything gay and light. When," the testimony ran, "there is music or sound in C2, it is a perception, not a visual picture."

The subject volunteered the suggestion that it seemed to her "that in this C2 part of her mind, could be found the explanation of many seemingly strange things. Certain perceptions may be registered in C2, of which the personality is unconscious, and these perceptions may work themselves out in various ways. This may account, sometimes, for the

moods of depression or gaiety for which we know no reason."
This interpretation is borne out by a number of these phenomena which occurred following conditions of which the
subject was ignorant, even in the state of hypnosis, when
the images were recalled. For instance, when on certain occasions in the course of conversation with the subject in another hypnotic state, of which the one in question had no
knowledge, I had given her information on certain subjects,
coconscious pictures illustrative thereof had later appeared.
Neither the waking nor the informing hypnotic personality,
of course, had memory of these conversations and therefore
was "unconscious" of the source of the images. The subconscious knowledge manifested itself through coconscious visualizations. Thus, on one occasion there was a picture of a
bride; a dead man lying in his coffin, and a woman dressed
in black, like a widow. The bride and the widow were the
same woman. This picture represented what I had told her,
while in a different state of hypnosis, of a certain mutual
acquaintance. The correlated conscious thoughts of the subject at the time concerned the woman of the picture.

6. One of the most elaborate and psychologically interesting of these allegorical and symbolic pictures is the
following:

At one time, she had a habit of putting her hand unconsciously to her left breast, particularly if a stranger
was present or if a number of people were in the room.
I had noticed her doing this several times. On investigation, it was brought out that when she made this gesture,
there developed, coconsciously, pictures of her initials *embroidered* in red, quite large and fanciful, corresponding
to the description of the "scarlet letter" in Hawthorne's
novel of that name. It will be remembered that the letter,
as there described, is an embroidered capital letter.

The history of the development of this phenomenon is
as follows:
I had made use of the subject, incognito, on one occa-

sion, to demonstrate hypnotic phenomena before the medical students at the school. Later, on reading an article of mine on the "Unconscious," she came across a reference to her own case. She did not recognize at the time that this, in connection with the school demonstration, would disclose her identity, but nevertheless, at the moment, there occurred the *coconscious thought* of which she was not aware: "Now she is branded." *And right after that, within a few moments, the coconscious picture of the initials came.* It should be explained that for a long time she had been dominated by the idea that if it should be known that she exhibited subconscious phenomena, a social stigma would be fastened upon her and would affect her standing. This formed a kind of complex which troubled her.

Now, it so happened that a day or two *still later,* she attended a lecture of mine at the hospital, and she noticed that some women students looked at her and whispered among themselves. At the time, she thought that it was because she had been exhibited at the medical school, and was slightly annoyed. When she got home, for some reason or other, it flashed into her mind (emergence of the previous coconscious knowledge?) that I had described in the published article the vision which she reproduced for me at the school. The thought at once came to her, "Now they will know me." She felt "terrible, torn," etc., and wrote me a letter in which she said, "I feel as if I bore three scarlet letters on my breast" (emergence from the coconscious). And when she wrote these words, a coconscious picture of Arthur Dimmesdale developed, and it was after this that she made the gesture of putting her hand to her breast.

For a time the initials and the picture of Arthur Dimmesdale constantly kept coconsciously coming and going, accompanied by the gesture. To take a specific instance: When I first noticed the gesture, I had just asked her about her repressed thoughts, and then the gesture occurred. The question had brought to her mind the thought of her illness, and then, according to the hypnotic personality, the coconscious initials came. It was as if the subconscious "stigma" complex was awakened by thoughts of illness, etc. "After the letters came a picture of Arthur Dimmesdale, and then she put her hand to her breast. The picture of Arthur Dimmesdale resembled that of the description in the book, tall, slender, clerical dress, pale, *with his hands on his breast.*"

When examining this statement, it will be noted that the coconscious initials first followed immediately after a coconscious thought — "Now she is branded" — without conscious awareness thereof. Second, that it was not until a day or two later that the coconscious knowledge flashed into her mind that her identity would be known, and she felt that she bore three scarlet letters on her breast (branded), *coincidentally with the coconscious picture of Arthur Dimmesdale* (and the initials?) Third, the behavior of the whole was *as if* an associated subconscious "stigma" complex was awakened in which the initials and the picture of Arthur Dimmesdale were incorporated as elements. Fourth, it is also worth noting that this subconscious complex, apparently, induced the somatic phenomenon, the gesture, which was performed automatically (involuntarily) and almost, if not wholly, unconsciously.

## 6. HALLUCINATIONS

It has already been stated that occasionally one or more of the visualizations emerged into consciousness. I want now to point out in more detail how such an emergence may result in an hallucination: That is to say, how what is at one moment a coconscious "picture," not integrated with the content of consciousness, may suddenly emerge and the subject become aware of it not as a visual image belonging to the conscious stream of thought, but as an hallucination. In this, we have one mechanism at least by which hallucinations may be produced. More concretely, this mechanism may be stated as follows:

There occurs a subconscious process dissociated from and independent of the stream of consciousness. One element in this process is a visual image. This image emerges and the subject becomes aware of it; but the image is still dissociated from and independent of the content of the stream of consciousness — that is, it is an hallucination. Its behavior is as if it was an image pertaining to a second process, which had not entered awareness and which was (more or less) independent of the conscious train of thought of the moment, but coincident with it. I have observed several examples of this phenomenon. The following is an illustration:

On the anniversary of her wedding, during the day she had been trying to keep out of her mind the thought of what day it was — had tried to make herself think it was just like any other day. But at times the realization of the day would come to her. About 9.30 in the evening, she let herself go — let her thoughts flood through her mind. She was sitting in her room, looking out of the window, thinking of the day and all that it meant, of the members of the family and others who were dead. Then her thoughts began to roam over a future life, wondering if people had any consciousness of this life and knew what was going on — whether they knew each other as here, had memories of this life. In other words, she thought of them as spirits and not as they were in this life.

While she was thinking all this, there developed *co-conscious* pictures of her father and mother and of her relatives who are dead, of herself as a bride, as she was dressed, (although she was not thinking of her herself as a bride at all) and there was a *picture of her dead husband. This was brighter than the others.*

Then suddenly she had a peculiar feeling. She felt a cold draft and turned suddenly and looked towards the hall of the apartment where there was a light (there was none in the room), and there, midway in the room, was a vision of her husband. It was luminous, a brightness, in the centre of which was a figure that merged into the brightness. No sharp outline of form was visible, excepting the face and head, which were *distinct* and *bright*. The whole was radiant.

Now, the point to be noted is that just before the

vision, the coconscious pictures were there. Then, at the moment when the vision appeared, all these pictures vanished *excepting the bright vision of her husband*. This emerged as a conscious image, *i. e.*, she became aware of it, but as an hallucination. This interpretation, based on the subject's retrospection of the events, is fortified by the fact that objectively, as seen in retrospection, the coconscious image and the hallucinatory image were "just the same" in details, were identically appearing pictures. To the subject, from one point of view, it seemed that she had suddenly become aware of something of which she had a moment before been unaware. The image (vision) of her husband had been there before, but it had been coconscious.

## 7. PERSEVERATION

Examples of *perseveration* of antecedent conscious experiences manifested in these coconscious pictures will be found running through many of these observations and need not be further elaborated.

\* \* \*

In my second case, a very large number of observations of the same phenomena were made. They were not, however, so systematically studied with a view to their correlation with other phenomena, but they occurred under the same conditions and exhibited the same characteristics. It would be largely a repetition to record them.

Dr. Waterman has given me the following account of a third case which he permitted me to observe also on one occasion.

### DR. G. A. WATERMAN'S CASE

A woman of thirty applied to me for treatment of her condition which she termed kleptomania. Her trouble consisted in the habit of taking jewelry, whenever she came across it on the counters in stores. She never had taken any of the jewelry home but would find herself with it gathered in her hands; at this juncture she always became frightened at the realization of what she was doing and would put it back on the counter and hurry from the store. A careful analysis of her mental state, at such times, revealed no evidence of any impulse to take the jewelry, nor did she have any desire for it, being the wife of a man in affluent circumstances.

After trying during several visits to discover the mechanism that was giving rise to her troublesome condition, I resorted to hypnosis. A state of complete hypnosis was readily obtained, the patient becoming relaxed and anesthetic. On being asked, in this state, what was the cause of her trouble, she at once replied that it was a dream that she had had a year and a-half previously, of which she had never been conscious in her waking state. The memory of the dream, however, was still as vivid to her in hypnosis as it was the day after she dreamed it.

The patient dreamed that she was standing before a counter on which was displayed a pile of glittering jewels. A burglar stood before her and, in a threatening manner, commanded her to steal the jewels for him. She pleaded to be allowed to go, but he exclaimed, "If you do not steal them, I will have your mother murdered." It seemed at the time that her mother was in an adjacent room, separated from her only by a partition, and she could hear her groaning. Overcome with anxiety for her mother, she seized a handful of jewels, but on looking down at them she realized what she was doing and looked up weeping at the burglar to ask him to let her go. At this point she awoke sobbing. Her husband beside her, who had been awakened by her distress, asked why she was crying and she answered "I don't know, I must have had a bad dream." For she had no conscious memory of her dream. It was shortly after this that she found herself taking jewelry in the stores.

(It happens that two of the elements of this dream were associated with distressing circumstances in the patient's life. — First: the burglar as he appeared in the dream was the same one who had featured in a terrifying experience in the patient's early life; for at the age of twenty, she had been held up by this man at the point of a revolver, and at the time really had a narrow escape. Second: about the time the patient had the dream, her mother had been taken ill and was told that she had hardening of the arteries and could not live very long. This had caused the patient great anxiety. It is therefore natural that both of these factors in her dream were associated with strong emotions.)

While the patient was still hypnotized, she was asked in what way this dream acted on her mind at the time she took jewelry in the stores. She said that whenever she saw jewelry on a counter, this dream recurred to her. It did not come to her consciously, but *the pictures of the dream were coconscious and were going on independently of the train of thought in her conscious mind.*

In order to illustrate the mechanism of her dream and its relation to her trouble, I placed a key in a leather case and put the case on a couch across the room, and, while the patient was still under hypnosis, told her that when she awakened, at the moment I raised the shade next to my desk, she would walk across the room, pick up the case, open it and take out the key. A short time after this, the patient was awakened and while she was arranging her hat at a mirror across the room, I raised the shade. At once, she walked slowly across the room, conversing with me about certain social things, that she had been doing the day before, and, passing behind me, picked up the case on the couch. At this juncture I turned and saw her standing with the key in her hand and looking at it with a puzzled expression. The following conversation ensued:—

Q. — "What are you doing?"

A. — "I do not know."

Q. — "Why have you that key?"

A. — "I don't know."

Q. — "Don't you know that it is a key of my private box?"

A. — "No."

Q. — "Don't you think that some explanation is

needed when you, behind my back, open a case and take the key to my private box?"

Patient flushing and looking embarrassed: "I don't know what to say, I am sure I am very sorry."

Q. — "What was in your mind, what were you thinking of when you did it?"

A. — "I really was only thinking of what I was talking to you about, about going to the theatre, etc."

"Surely," I said, "there must have been some cause. Perhaps it was not in your conscious mind, let us see if we cannot find it."

The patient was hypnotized again and asked what made her open the case and take out the key. She at once replied, *"Why, pictures of myself doing it"*; and, on being further questioned, described the *flow of coconscious pictures of herself performing the act. She said that at the time these pictures were acting in her mind, she herself was correspondingly performing the act.*

After explaining the relationship of the subconscious with the act performed, and making her see the connection between the experiment in the office and her actions in real life, the patient was awakened. She was, of course, amnesic to all that had taken place in hypnosis, but the same explanation was made to her in the waking-state, with the result that she was no longer troubled by her so-called kleptomania.

\*   \*   \*

What is the meaning of these phenomena? With what, if any, normal psychological events can they be identified? What part do they play in the mechanisms by means of which the mind functions? Are they solely abnormal phenomena, or have they normal prototypes, the conditions only (dissociation, repression, etc.) under which they function being abnormal? Have we in them something which throws light on the subconscious workings of the mind?

These are some of the questions which at once come to mind and invite answer.

Looking at them without regard to their relation to the content of consciousness and the conditions under which they occurred — *e. g.*, whether within or without the field of awareness — it is obvious that they must in themselves be psychical events that are found in normal mental processes. For the abnormal is only the normal functioning under altered conditions. It is inconceivable, therefore, that they are new elements of consciousness in the sense of new creations unknown to psychological processes. In fact, they are images, and as such are normal elements of consciousness. Now images occur in the course of normal mentation only in three forms: as

(a) real sensory events, as in perceptions of the environment;

(b) sense elements (imagery) of thought;

(c) hallucinations. In this class dream imagery would be included.

We must see whether the images in question can be identified with, or are akin to, any of these known types, before postulating another species.

The first type (a) — perceptions of the environment — can be excluded at once.

As to their kinship to thought imagery (b): if we accept the theory (fairly well established) that there are normally, as well as abnormally, subconscious processes — processes of a psychical nature which do not enter awareness, and if we assume that these processes are akin to, if not technically identical with, thought, then we should expect that they would include images of the same pattern and behavior as those of conscious thought. They would include visual and auditory images, the so-called secondary sensory elements (perceptions) which are found among the components of the complex called an "idea"; and they would either be more or less persistent and unchanging, or would follow one another in pictorial (cinematographic) sequence correspondingly with the fixity or flux of thought.

Under this hypothesis, the coconscious images recalled in retrospection would be only these particular sensory components of subconscious "ideas." As images, they would not

differ from those of ordinary thought-imagery, except tha
they are coconscious and do not therefore emerge into aware
ness. Why the rest of the subconscious "idea," or process, i
not revived as memory, but only the sensory elements, is an
other question and one which probably cannot be answeree
satisfactorily. The fact would imply that the rest of th
"idea," or thought process, is more intensely dissociated from
awareness than the sense images. But why it should be so
one cannot say. After all, however, what is a thought pro
cess, an "idea," anyway, and what are its other components.
Verbal images (visual, auditory and kinesthetic) may b
components, but not necessarily such, as in deaf mutes. Per
haps images of objects are the most dynamic elements; anc
that is why they alone have sufficient intensity and vividnes
to be recalled in memory. The same problem attaches tc
the imagery of dreams.

Hypothetically, it is conceivable that the rest of th
subconscious process is purely neural and that the activity
of the sense neurons alone has psychical elements (images) a
correlates. Hence memory can only recall the latter.

As to their kinship with hallucinations and particularly
dream imagery (c): their resemblance in behavior and vivid
ness to dream imagery is quite striking and suggests that we
are dealing with the same mechanisms. Indeed, the recur
rence as coconscious images of the dream imagery, fol
lowed by their secondarily resulting somatic and psycho
logical phenomena (e. g., flashes of light and blindness in
one example) in the waking state, would seem to indicate
this identity of the mechanisms. That in dreams the im
agery is only the conscious emergence of a larger subcon
scious mechanism, there is strong evidence to believe. The
same is true of the imagery of "crystal visions," i. e., arti
ficial hallucinations, and hypnagogic hallucinations. In these
phenomena and dreams, the imagery takes on a cinemato
graphic character, as is often the case in the images under
consideration. As indicative of a subconscious process, may
be mentioned the fact that in the production of artificial
hallucinations, the subject, as he "sees" himself in the vision,
knows what the vision-self is thinking about, and feels the

emotion manifested in the expression of the vision-face and exhibits the same expression in his own face. This subconscious process in hallucinations and dreams of this sort, if not technically "thought," must be at least akin to thought. If such be the case, then hallucinatory imagery and dream imagery may be explained as the conscious emergence of the secondary images pertaining to such "thought."

By this process of reasoning, we arrive at the conclusion that the mechanism of the imagery in types b (thought) and c (hallucinations) is (may be) pragmatically the same, and that the coconscious images in question are identical with normal images, but belong to subconscious processes of "thought."

How far the subconscious process pertains only to abnormal conditions and how far to normal conditions is another problem. It is sufficient here to say that a mass of evidence at our disposal indicates that subconscious processes are normal as well as abnormal phenomena.

As to the relations between the coconscious images plus their subconscious processes and other coconscious thoughts — thoughts which may be described, if one prefers, as outside the field of awareness, or focus of attention, or in the background of the mind — and the conscious field, I would offer the following considerations.

In the first place, the images are always (?) expressions of antecedent thoughts, often after secondary elaboration, sometimes in symbolic fashion as in dreams. This shows that such antecedent thoughts, although out of mind, whether because of repression or not, do not necessarily remain passive, but may undergo subconscious incubation, and function actively, but outside the field of awareness.

In the second place, when other coconscious thoughts were recovered in memory by retrospection of the subject, the images in question did not *immediately* pertain to these thoughts, though they might mediately do so. For example, take the coconscious thought "now she is branded" (Obs. 6; symbolism). The images were initial letters and the picture of Arthur Dimmesdale. The "thought" and images did not seem to be a unity, but the images pertained to associated ideas. In other instances there was no apparent association, though it may have been through roots not revealed to the memory of the moment. So always when contemporaneous (or sequential) subconscious thoughts and images were recalled by the subject, they seemed to her separate phenomena, not a unity as in conscious thought and perceptions. They were always described as separate phenomena, as different parts of the mind, for which different terms were used. The interpretation, I would suggest, is this:

Our conscious experiences are integrated into systems of associated thoughts. Any given experience may be linked up with many systems, each one being a different setting and giving a different meaning or significance to the idea. For instance, a shell for a '75 cannon may be integrated with a problem in ballistics, or cannons, or with bloody warfare in the trenches. Again, within each system there are subsystems. Nearly every idea, then, has many ramifications and roots in systematized antecedent experiences. Any thought in the focus of attention or one in the fringe of consciousness of the moment may, through such integration, excite into activity a system outside the field of awareness, and thus awaken coconscious thought. This system, again, through roots, may indirectly excite logically distant systems — *i. e.*, associated subconsciously, say, through a single element, such as a verbal symbol ("shell"). From this system, functioning "subconsciously" (S. M.),[1] images (CCI) may arise outside the field of awareness (coconscious). These images (CCI), when recalled through retrospection, will thus appear to be unsystematized with the contemporaneous coconscious thought (CCT) also recalled in the same way.

---

1 The meanings of these letter-symbols are explained on the next page under figure 21.

This mechanism may be diagrammatically represented
as follows:

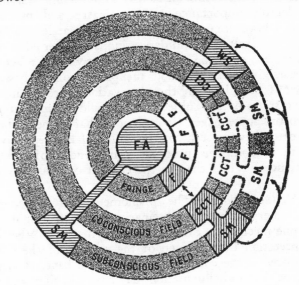

FIG. 21

The field of consciousness and of the subconscious is
represented by circles.

FA — Focus of Attention.

F — Fringe of awareness.

CCT — Coconscious thought outside fringe of awareness (e. g., "Now she is branded") integrated indirectly with
CCI.

CCT', CCT" — Quiescent systems of antecedent experience integrated more or less directly with CCT and
capable of being excited to activity and becoming coconscious thought, or the fringe, or attention.

SM — Subconscious mechanisms pertaining to FA, CCT,
CCT', CCT" and CCI.

CCI — Coconscious images emerging when their SM
is subconsciously stimulated by an associative process.

*Affects:* The emergence into consciousness of the affect, integrated with a subconsciously functioning system, is of considerable importance for psychiatry and psychopathology. I have discussed this phenomenon at length in other writings.[1] Exaltation and depression, and other emotions and feelings, can often be traced to the activity of subconscious processes giving rise to moods inexplicable on the basis of the conscious thoughts. In the observations here recorded, affective states of the subject often could be correlated with the coconscious images. It is obvious that in melancholia we shall often have to seek for the source of the depressive feelings in subconscious processes (the residua of antecedent experiences) rather than in the content of consciousness.

*Hallucinations:* The phenomenon of a coconscious image emerging as an hallucination gives an insight into at least one mechanism of this clinical symptom. Whether the interpretation I have given of the relation of the image to the process is the correct one or not, we have, at any rate, evidence that an hallucination may have its origin and mechanism in a subconscious process, and that this process is the perseveration, with or without secondary elaboration, of antecedent experiences.

In addition to what I have said above, I think we are justified in drawing the following conclusions:

1. Coconscious images are elements of more elaborate subconscious processes.

2. They may be explained as secondary images pertaining to such subconscious processes.

3. They may emerge into consciousness and thereby become hallucinations.

4. The subconscious processes of which they are elements are perseverations and sometimes, after undergoing incubation, elaborations of antecedent experiences.

5. The subconscious processes may construct symbolisms.

---

[1] See: *The Dissociation of a Personality, The Unconscious,* and various articles.

6. They may determine or motivate the conscious streams of thought.

7. They are sometimes derived from repressed thoughts.

8. They often provide the conscious affect.

9. They may induce dreams, on the one hand and, on the other, may be derived from dreams.

10. They may induce somatic phenomena.

# CHAPTER XV

## An Experimental Study of the Mechanism of Hallucinations[1]

I Assume that the members of this Association are familiar with the traditional theories of the mechanism of hallucinations. I shall, therefore, not refer to them beyond remarking that they may be all classed under one or the other of two groups, *viz.*, the anatomico-physiological theories and the psychological theories; and that all are inadequate and unsatisfactory. It remains, therefore, to attack the problem anew and, if possible, by experimental methods. We have open to us several methods of attack:

1. That of inducing artificially hallucinations, particularly visions depicting known antecedent experiences. A study of their content permits of inferences regarding an underlying process related to and derived from the antecedent experiences.

2. Hypnotic methods by which, through introspection, memories of subconscious processes correlated with the hallucination are obtained.

3. Subconscious or so-called automatic script recording subconscious processes during a correlated hallucination.

4. A combination of all three methods.

### 1. Artificial Hallucinations

I have made studies of a large number of artificial hallucinations in the course of many years' experimentation, and

1 Presented at the eleventh annual meeting of the American Psychopathological Association, Atlantic City, June 11, 1921.

some twenty years ago published one such study.[1] They are commonly called "crystal visions," because the usual technique is to direct the attention by the use of a crystal into which the subject gazes (crystal gazing). A crystal of course is not essential. Merely fixing the attention with expectation of the development of the phenomenon is sufficient with susceptible subjects. An examination of the content of visualizations thus produced shows that they are identical in structure and action with many of the hallucinations of the insane as well as with the spontaneous hallucinations of the sane (Joan of Arc, Fra Angelico, Catherine of Sienna, Margaret Mary of the Sacred Heart, Archduke Charles of Austria, *et alii*). They are essentially and psychologically hallucinations artificially induced. (Parenthetically I may remark that it is an extraordinary thing that psychiatrists and psychologists have neglected them as objects of study, as plainly we have here phenomena that can be subjected to experimentation and are capable of giving an insight into the mechanisms of the mind and, as we shall see, into the relation of subconscious processes to conscious processes. One would expect that psychiatrists seeking to determine the mechanism of hallucinations of the insane would begin with artificial hallucinations and that psychologists interested in the problems of imagery would do the same.)

An examination of the content of the hallucinations thus induced reveals that they may be: (*a*) visual memories, *i. e.*, reproductions of past visual experiences; (*b*) visualized memories of past experiences that were not visual (*e. g.*, of knowledge gained in other ways); (*c*) pure fabrications showing constructive imagination which may represent past thoughts (repressed or not), wishes, forebodings, etc., or attempts to solve problems and doubts, answer questions, etc. Further, when the visualizations are of persons, *the thoughts of the vision-personality* (*i. e.*, those underlying the hallucinations) *may emerge into consciousness*; and I may mention in passing that the *affect* pertaining to these thoughts or to elements in the hallucination often wells up

1 See chapter XIII.

into consciousness. (This is a phenomenon of importance bearing on the problem of moods or affectivity.

More important for our present study, the behavior of these hallucinations shows that an active process is going on that is not in awareness (*i e.*, is subconscious) but is inducing the visualization (*e. g.*, when the hallucination has the action of a cinema picture, or represents in visual imagery past thoughts, and is not simply a reproduction or memory of a past visual experience). If we can find out what sort of a process it is, identify it, and discover its relation to the hallucination, we shall advance a step towards solving the problem of hallucinations in the insane.

## 2. Hypnotic Methods (Coconscious Images)

There is another class of phenomena, which I have called *coconscious* images. The finding of these came from hypnotic methods, *i. e.*, introspection in hypnosis. They are as extraordinary as they are interesting, but I do not expect you to believe them until you have confirmed their reality by your own observations. My own findings have, however, been confirmed by Dr. G. A. Waterman in a case of his own.[1] I have found them, according to the evidence of the subjects, in four cases including that of Dr. Waterman, who gave me an opportunity to examine his case.

Coconscious visual images may be defined as psychical images of which the individual is not aware.
They occur as:

1. Phenomena of suggested post-hypnotic acts.

2. After-phenomena of dreams.

3. After-phenomena of repressed thoughts.

4. Phenomena of moods (depressed and exalted states).

5. Phenomena of perseveration of previous emotional complexes (mental systems).

6. Phenomena in the mechanism of hallucinations.

---

1 For a study of these phenomena see chapter on "Coconscious Images."

Because of their behavior, the phenomena in the last class belong to this study. As phenomena of suggested post-hypnotic acts they permit of experimental induction and study. I have found that each step in such an act (in the cases studied) is preceded or accompanied by a subconscious image or picture corresponding to one of the elements of the act performed or to be performed. Such images, occurring with repressed thoughts not in awareness, are interesting from a psychological and psychopathological point of view. Sometimes these subconscious pictures are accompanied by an affect which alone emerges into consciousness, as with artificial hallucinations, and apparently determines the conscious mood.[1]

Now, what strikes me as noteworthy is this: occasionally I have found that *one or more images emerge into consciousness and become an hallucination.*

This observation led me to postulate a theory of visual hallucinations, namely, that in certain instances, at least, *they were the emergence into awareness of imagery belonging to subconscious thought — the same sort of imagery that occurs in conscious thought.*

Auditory hallucinations, similarly, are the emergence of subconscious verbal "images," *i. e.,* sounds of words used in subconscious inarticulate thought or internal speech.

### 3. Subconscious Script

It remained, however, to prove this by a method independent of hypnotic introspection and memory, but one that would reveal the subconscious thought and synchronously the corresponding hallucinatory images after emergence into consciousness, and the correlation of the two. For this purpose the following procedure was devised: (*a*) to induce experimentally subconscious processes; (*b*) to 'tap' the subconscious process while in progress and obtain physical records of it; (*c*) if any hallucinations occurred synchronously to obtain a detailed description of the same; (*d*) to

1 I have discussed this important phenomenon in *The Unconscious*, chaps. XII, XIII, XVII; see also *The Dissociation of a Personality* for numerous observations.

428 STUDIES IN PERSONALITY

correlate by comparison, if possible, the imagery of the hallucination with the ideas expressed in the written record of the subconscious process: and (*e*) to obtain immediate evidence by introspection furnished by the *subconscious* personality with regard to the relation, if any, between the elements of the subconscious process and the imagery of the hallucination and its mechanism.

The technique of 'tapping' the subconscious process suited to the experiments and obtaining physical records of the same is subconscious writing, commonly called 'automatic writing.' (Here I may again venture a parenthetical remark: it is strange that psychologists and those engaged in psychopathological work have so utterly neglected the study of subconscious writing, both as a phenomenon and a mode of investigating the nature and potentialities of processes outside of awareness, and, I may add, of the dynamic structure and mechanism of the mind. The mechanism of this kind of writing still needs to be worked out as well as the relation of the process to the personal consciousness.[1])

To carry out the proposed plan of investigation, it was necessary to have a subject who both experiences hallucinations and can produce automatic (subconscious) script without awareness of what the hand is writing. (The latter is necessary because some automatic writers become aware of the content of the script, as it is being written, although it is subconsciously written in that they are not aware of what will be produced and do not voluntarily produce it.) I fortunately had a subject who answers these two conditions and who had been under my observation for about a year. She came to me as a patient for other reasons. I have therefore an intimate knowledge of her character and personality and can vouch for the *bona fide* nature of the phenomena themselves. She comes of a good and, at one time, wealthy American family, and as a young girl she was, I judge, rather luxuriously brought up; she possesses considerable artistic talent with pencil and brush and has an ambition to develop her

---

1 This important phenomenon has been left to those interested in Psychical Research and Spiritualism, who are concerned solely with the content of the writing and not with its psychology.

voice for dramatic purposes. This is the ambition of her life. These facts are pertinent to an understanding of the content of the script and the hallucinations obtained. She produces automatic script with remarkable facility and has written what would make several volumes in this way, including two or three of fiction and a good deal of verse.

Now, on several occasions she had casually remarked that often while she was automatically writing, she had experienced visualizations and other hallucinatory phenomena which afterwards she discovered corresponded to the content of the script. Being interested in other aspects of the case, I had merely made a note of the fact at the time without further attention. Later, when I took up the question of hallucinations for study, it occurred to me at once that here I had just the subject I wanted at hand. The conditions of the experiments were arranged as follows:

The head of the subject was covered with an opaque cloth to prevent her seeing the script as it was being written automatically by her hand. A pencil was then put into her hand which rested conveniently on a sheet of paper placed on a writing tablet by her side. She was then told to write automatically regarding some subject which I designated in general terms in each experiment; for instance, a memory of some remembered episode in her life, a memory of such an episode but one forgotten by the subject; a fantasy; a fabrication requiring constructive imagination, etc. The object of diversifying the subjects was to obtain products of different kinds of subconscious work (memory, dream-like fantasy, imagination, etc.). If, during the experiment, while the hand was writing, an hallucination developed, the subject was directed to indicate the fact, the moment she saw it, by exclaiming 'picture.' Thereupon, I made a mark on the script at the point where the picture appeared. Likewise, the moment the hallucination disappeared the subject exclaimed, as directed, 'gone,' and the point was similarly marked on the script. Thus, those words of the script which were written during the occurrence of any given hallucination could be identified and could be compared with the latter, and any correlation of the written ideas and the hallucinatory images noted.

In some cases as soon as the hallucination appeared, the subject was required to describe orally the 'picture' in detail. This description was taken down by me *verbatim*. Two things, be it noted, were thus being done by the subject at one and the same time; namely, writing with the hand one thing, of which she was not consciously aware, and describing orally and consciously another thing — two entirely different processes, one subconscious and the other conscious.

In other experiments the subject was not required to describe the details of the hallucination until after it had disappeared, but only to indicate its beginning and ending and its general character, such as of a person, or place, or thing — "a ship on the ocean"; "a street in a city," etc. As soon as it disappeared, the writing was interrupted and the subject was required, while the memory was fresh, to describe the details of the hallucination. This having been done, the writing was resumed and this procedure continued until the script was finished, when, as it happened, *the hallucination always ceased*. This method was found to be the most practical for reasons I will not go into because it would involve a lengthy discussion of the principles underlying the phenomena of subconscious writing.

After the observation was complete, the script and the hallucination, as recorded, were compared and for this purpose arranged in parallel columns. Thus any correlations between the imagery of an hallucination and the synchronously written script could easily be noted.

Finally, after each observation, the method of *subconscious introspection* was used to elicit such evidence as might be obtainable as to what occurred subconsciously during the writing of the script and the hallucination, *i. e.*, what was the character of the subconscious process that produced the script; what (if psychological) was its content; what, if any, psychical elements (such as images) of which the subject was not consciously aware were present; and what, if any, light could be thrown by subconscious introspection upon the relation of the subconscious process to the hallucination?

Very positive introspective testimony as to the source of the imagery of the hallucinations and the relation of those images to the subconscious process was thus elicited. Its credibility must be judged according to the value assigned to the method. A summary of this evidence will be reported in its proper place, after the various scripts and their accompanying hallucinations have been given.

Before giving the results of the experiments, the following facts in the psychological history of the case will enable the reader to understand the rather fantastic content of the text of some of the script and imagery. The subject had at a previous time exhibited the phenomenon of double personality and for this reason had been sent to me for study and readjustment. This phase of the case had been recovered from at the time when the experiments were undertaken. During this previous phase one of the personalities called 'Juliana' had imagined, as a fantasy, that she was the reincarnated soul of a Spanish peasant girl of the thirteenth century and, after the fashion of secondary coconscious personalities of spiritualistic mediums (as in Flournoy's case of 'Hélène Smith'), imagined that she remembered her previous life as such a peasant. A most elaborate and extravagant romance of the thirteenth century had thus been fabricated, beginning with her early girlhood as a rustic peasant and ending in her death in old age after many adventures as a street singer and finally as a great artist with a wonderful voice, having sung and danced before the King's Court and great audiences, one of which was gathered in the Coliseum in Rome. The genesis of this fantasy could be traced, I think, to the day-dreams of the subject as a young girl, and later to dreams under the influence of morphine during a serious illness. But as elements in it there could be recognized, as motivating factors, her life's aspirations. As Juliana, a secondary coconscious personality and also an alternating personality (to whom 'Susie' used to change from time to time) she would play the part seriously and honestly of a Spanish girl, spoke broken English with a foreign accent, and also a suppositious Spanish dialect of the thirteenth century which, of course, was only a mass of neologisms (nicknamed by me the 'lingo'), and, in general, she acted the part well.

After reintegration, the subject consciously and coconsciously remembered in complete detail the so-called 'Spanish fantasy,' and, according to well-known principles, the conserved subconscious systems could be 'tapped' and, as artifacts, brought to light as more or less temporarily dissociated autonomous systems.

In the cure, that is, the reintegration of the two personalities into one normal one, the belief in all this fantasy, previously cherished by Juliana and accepted by the other personality, was, of course, destroyed.

It need only be added that at the time when these observations were undertaken, the subject, owing to reversal in the family fortunes, was obliged to earn her living, and was employed in a large department store in which she rendered excellent service as a saleswoman. She regarded this, however, as only temporary, hoping later to achieve the object of her life-long ambition, to cultivate her voice for a career upon the stage.

I will now give the results of the experiments, not in the order in which they were made, but classified according to the type of content of the script and hallucination.

## A. SUBCONSCIOUS (AUTOMATIC) WRITING ACCOMPANIED BY VISUAL HALLUCINATIONS

*Observation I.* In this observation, both the script and the hallucination record a *memory* of an episode which occurred two or three years ago when the subject, as I have explained, exhibited the secondary personality of 'Juliana.' The subject now consciously remembers the episode here described at the University. (Susie is the name of the normal personality; 'Dr. Jones' is assistant professor of philosophy.) To conceal the identity of the subject, fictitious names, including that of the University, have been substituted throughout.

## 1.  A Memory of a Previous Episode in the Subject's Life

The subject was directed to write automatically an account of some episode in her life, making the selection herself subconsciously.  (Of course neither I nor the subject had any suspicion of what it would be.)

SCRIPT: "I was at Harvard [*University one day with Dr. Jones when I changed into Juliana for Dean Smith and he*] was pleased with me.  I went [*through all sort of gestures as Juliana and*] I spoke 'lingo' for [*the men and they seemed very much interested and the Dean never*] took his eyes off of Juliana."

While the hand was writing this script automatically, without awareness on the part of the subject, the first 'picture' (hallucination) appeared when the word "university" was written and continued until the word "he" was written, when it vanished.  This is indicated in the text by the words in italics enclosed in brackets and designated by the number 1.  Similarly the second picture appeared synchronously with the word "through," and ended after the writing of the words "Juliana and"; the third picture appeared with "the men" and ended after "never."

The hallucination (as described and taken down *verbatim* by me) and the script were now compared to see (*a*) if, and to what extent, the images of the hallucination were synchronized with the "ideas" contained in the script, and (*b*) if the images corresponded to and represented these ideas thus synchronously expressed in the writing after the manner of conscious imagery.

For the sake of clarity, the script and the hallucination are arranged below in parallel columns, each "picture" being set off against those portions of the script that were written during its occurrence.

(I trust this explanation of the phenomena obtained in this experiment and of the form in which they are now presented will be sufficient for a comprehension of all the succeeding observations that follow, as the same plan was adhered to in each.)

| SCRIPT | HALLUCINATION |
|---|---|
| 1. I was at Harvard [*University one day with Dr. Jones when I changed into Juliana for Dean Smith and he*] was pleased with me. | I see Harvard University. The steps going up and the brown stones and the whole front of the building. I see myself as Susie going up the steps and into the building and I go down the hall to Dr. Jones' office. Dr. Jones is there and Dean Smith. They rise and shake hands and then sit down. I sit down as Susie and I see myself sitting in a chair and I turn into Juliana. I rise again as Juliana and shake hands again. They seem pleased. (The whole vision is like a movie.) |
| 2. I went [*through all sorts of gestures as Juliana and*] | I see myself sitting in Dr. Jones' office as Juliana and I am going through all sorts of funny gestures like a foreigner. They laugh. (I cannot hear them.) |
| 3. I spoke 'lingo' for [*the men and they seemed very much interested and the Dean never*] took his eyes off of Juliana. | I see myself as Juliana and I am talking the 'lingo' — ( I can hear the words — but cannot tell what they are). I can hear Dr. Jones' voice as if he is saying this is "an interesting phase" (the exact words). |

If you will take the pains to examine carefully these results and compare the script with the corresponding hallucinations you will note several things:

1. At the moment of the occurrence of the subconscious writing of the words "Harvard University," and the words describing each succeeding step of the original episode, a visualization, or hallucination, or image — call it what you will — corresponding to and representing the ideas or thoughts expressed by the subconsciously written words developed in consciousness. I am particular to express it this way because it must not be forgotten that all we have are certain physical marks (writing) on paper (of which the subject, let it also be not forgotten, was unaware), and a described hallucination. But if we accept the doctrine that automatic script is written by actual coconscious thoughts, not in awareness, rather than by purely physiological pro-

cesses[1] we may with equal accuracy express the facts and avoid pedanticism by the formula: *at the moment of the occurrence of a subconscious memory or thought (not in awareness) of Harvard University and of each succeeding step of the original episode, a visualization corresponding to and representing that thought-memory appears in conscious awareness.*

2. These visualizations resemble and perhaps, we may say, simulate or are identical with the ordinary visualizations of conscious thought, although they may be richer in detail and more vivid.[2]

She subconsciously thinks of being at Harvard University, as had happened on a certain occasion, and almost at once she experiences not only images representing a building at Harvard, but also images of herself in movement, walking up the steps, into the building and down the corridor to 'Dr. Jones' room, as she did in the original episode. And so on with the remainder of the episode in the script.

3. The visualization (hallucination) was much richer in detail than the description of the episode given in the script. I shall come back to this fact and discuss it more fully later. I will merely point out now that this is also true of the imagery of conscious thought and particularly of written thought. When I write "I took such a train for New York," with the thought of having taken the train, I may have an elaborate imagery of the Boston station of the N.Y. and N.H.R.R. crowded with bustling people, of entering the gate with other passengers, of the long train of cars standing by the platform of the station, etc. More or less of all this I may have and do as I write it, according as my mind dwells on the incident and gives time for the thoughts and images to develop. And yet I only precisely

---

1 I am not certain that it makes any difference in our conclusions whether the writing is done by physical or psychical processes. The point is the correlation of imagery with a subconscious process that is equivalent to a thought and corresponds to the image or images.

2 Although this qualification is true by comparison with the imagery of the average run of individuals, it may be doubted if it is true by comparison with the imagery of some persons who are extraordinarily vivid and elaborate visualizers.

think and still more only write, "I took a train." A good visualizer has very rich imagery for very simply expressed thoughts.

4. A moment elapses after the script begins to describe the incident *before* the correlated image develops. For instance, the image of the University building does not develop until after the four words "I was at Harvard," are written. This slight delay in the development of the hallucination is of considerable significance and I will come back to it later after the results of the other experiments are given. We shall find better examples of it and also of the correlation of script and imagery in the more elaborate scripts and hallucinations. In fact, I begin with this simple type of script and imagery that the main principle involved in all the experiments may be first clearly understood.

5. Finally, I would point out that the three 'pictures' in this experiment can be recognized easily as continuations of the same theme. But although this was always the case, we shall find that with most of the other hallucinations there is no obvious continuity to the pictures. The scenes shift as in a dream without apparent relation to one another. The significant fact is that *the continuity will be found in the subconsciously written script* without which the varying hallucinations would not seem to be related to one another and could not be understood or interpreted as manifestations of one and the same theme.

All these points should be borne in mind when studying the phenomena of the other experiments.

*Observation II.* (This was the first and a preliminary experiment to determine the best technique.) The subject was directly to write subconsciously a fabricated story constructed out of her former so-called 'Spanish dreams' — those of the Juliana system, which had as a second personality conceived itself to be the reincarnated soul of a Spanish peasant girl and had created an elaborate fantasy of a previous life in Spain in the thirteenth century. The scenes and personages incorporated in the script had been often previously imagined. The images of the hallucination were therefore reproductions of former imagery. The image of Juliana, for instance, was reproduced exactly as it had always been visualized in the Spanish fantasies. (See Observation IV for a drawing of Juliana and the dancing scene.) The visual images were accompanied by a number of auditory 'images' and also by somatic sensations and feelings. These latter were the same as those which had always been associated with the conception of herself as a Spanish girl. Hence the script begins "I feel I am Spanish through and through."

In this preliminary experiment, the scenes of the hallucination were described in detail from memory after the completion of the script. In thus recalling the scenes, the imagery was revived again and described from the reproduction. The images, both as they occurred in the hallucination and as revived, were said to be very vivid, more vivid than when experienced in the original fantasies, and were likened to the pictures of the 'movies.'

## II. The Spanish Fantasy

SCRIPT: "I feel I am [*Spanish*][1] through and through. [*As I paddled barefooted through brooks*][2] and carried [*jugs of water upon a yoke and danced barefooted before the king of Spain and his Court — Cortes*][3][4]. Also when [*I walked to early mass at the village church or mission at a village called in my time Medesa*][5]. And of [*Father Brazado, the priest who discovered my voice*][6][7]. [*I have a voice. I shall always believe I am a soul.*][8]"

| SCRIPT | HALLUCINATION |
|---|---|
| 1. I feel I am *Spanish* through and through | Indicated by certain strong feelings and somatic sensations which emerged in association with the image of Juliana, a revival of a fantasy of herself in a previous existence as a *Spanish peasant of the thirteenth century.* |
| 2. *As I paddled barefooted through brooks* | *A brook.* Juliana is *walking through it barefooted,* with her skirt doubled up in front but falling behind, showing her petticoat of a very coarse cloth, such as a peasant might wear. (Here the subject remarks, it is "a very pretty picture.") |

[Shift]*

| 3. and carried *jugs of water upon a yoke* | Juliana has *water jugs on a yoke* on her neck carrying them from a fountain in the village. [It is a village, not a city, because she sees earth around the fountain.] ("I feel as if the image that is Juliana is a part of me.") |

[Shift]

| 4. *and danced barefooted before the King of Spain and his Court — Cortes* | Juliana dressed in dancing costume — marble floors — draperies — flickering lights. She is *dancing as Juliana has danced in real life.* The scene is such as if it is a *King's Court* — a lot of people there — men as well as the women are dressed in long robes. That is, the men do not wear knee breeches, etc. (The costumes are such as are represented in pictures of medieval times.) |

[Shift]

| 5. Also when *I walked to early mass at the village church or mission* | A road. At the end of the road a little *church.* A sort of white stucco mission church. Juliana's back is towards her. She is *walking down the road* barefooted *going to the church.* The whole is as plain as a motion picture. I can see the grain waving in the adjoining fields. (I have the feeling as if she is lazy and does not want to go to church.) |

[Shift]

| 6. *at a village called in my time Medesa.* | A sort of square. I can see her uncle Salvator. There is a tent propped up over a lot of vegetables exposed in the market place. A lot of foreign-looking women are walking about. There is a crowd. |

[Shift]

| 7. And of *Father Brazado, the priest who discovered my voice.* | A priest — (a man just as vivid as I can see you) medium height — fat — big fat stomach |

* Note the shifting of the scene after each hallucination, without apparent continuity of action, which is to be found only in the theme of the *script,* that is, in the subconscious process. The exact points in the script where two of the hallucinatory scenes ended are not quite clear in my record, so that the time interval between them and the next ones is not apparent.

dressed in a long black robe. Around his waist is tied a cord, a funny twisted cord like nothing I have seen. (Here she imitates with her fingers the twisting of the cord.) He has a grayish beard and is walking down a roadway. Fields on each side. Juliana, with thick black hair flying behind as if the air is blowing it, short skirts, bare legs, is raking in the fields. I can hear her *singing* in the Spanish 'lingo.'

[Shift]

8. *I have a voice.*

Juliana *vividly singing* in a sort of arena like the Coliseum in Rome. There is a big crowd of heads in the Coliseum. I can hear a voice singing in the 'lingo.'

On examination of the details of the script of the synchronously occurring hallucinatory imagery, we see that the latter is composed of just such images as the thought contained in the script would normally incorporate. The subconscious writes "As I paddled barefooted through brooks," and at that moment the subject consciously sees an hallucinatory Juliana walking barefooted through a brook, her clothes made of coarse cloth tucked up in front, etc. The picture of Juliana was identical with previously imagined pictures of herself as that personality.

The subconscious writes "and carry jugs of water upon a yoke," and thereupon the scene shifts and the subject sees an hallucination of herself as Juliana carrying water jugs on a yoke on her neck from a fountain in a village.

The subconscious writes "and danced barefooted before the King of Spain and his Court" (a scene from a former fantasy) and straightway the picture shifts again and the subject sees an hallucination of just such a scene at an imaginary Spanish Court. (This dancing scene had been previously constructed in subconscious fantasy and several times was reproduced in the course of this and other observations.) (See Observation IV.)

The subconscious writes, "also when I walk to early mass at the village church or mission," and the scene of the hallucination shifts; a little church appears at the end of the road and she sees herself as Juliana walking down the road, etc. The imagery, as in all the other scenes, perfectly corresponds to the thought expressed in the script and is precisely such as a thought of this sort would embody, bearing in mind the Spanish setting and peasant personality. The procedure was the same with the next three scenes. In her previous dissociated personality, she had frequently constructed these same scenes with the same imagery which appeared in corresponding hallucinations. The scene in the Coliseum, for instance, she had previously constructed and had woven it into her fantasy of her previous thirteenth century existence. (Before these experiments were undertaken, I had already heard this scene described in vivid detail.)

The richness of the imagery in each scene should be noted. When, for instance, the script speaks of the priest, "Father Brazado," the corresponding image is not simply of a figure or face, or even a priest, but of a priest portrayed as a personality with particular physical characteristics. It is a piece of character-drawing done after the fashion of a play or novel. This character is also given a setting rich in local color, comprising a roadway and fields in which Juliana appears as a peasant girl at work with her rake. Now all this is derived from a previous fantasy which had been constructed as a dream-like work of fiction. The imagery, in other words, includes and is largely constructed out of images belonging to associated ideas, as happens in normal conscious ideation. One thinks of a certain person, and images of that person in a particular setting of a previous experience arise. Similarly, when the script states, "I have a voice," the image is of a particular experience, when, in fantasy, she sang in the Coliseum to a crowded audience. This experience is a pseudo-memory which arises subconsciously.

This richness in detail and extensiveness of the imagery of an hallucination, transcending the verbal limits of the script, are noticeable in all the observations and will be discussed later with the evidence from subconscious introspection. As already stated, this evidence was elicited after each observation as part of the technique, but it will be more advantageous to consider all this evidence together.

*Observation III.* For the following experiment, the subject was instructed a day or two in advance to be prepared to write automatically, at the next visit, a fabrication in the form of a story or anything else of an imaginative character on any subject she chose *subconsciously* to select, but something distinct from the Spanish dreams of Juliana; that is, something that would be original and not a reproduction of former fabrications. Thus a chance for subconscious incubation was given. The result turned out to be a poetical (?) glorification of the talents which she has always felt consciously, and particularly subconsciously, she possessed, but to which she had been unable to give expression owing to the circumstances of her life. The hallucinations were allegorical in form. It was interesting to watch the hand erasing and altering the phraseology as in conscious composing. There was evident difficulty owing to her not being able to see the writing and, therefore, having to keep the written words in mind.

### III.   A Poetical Glorification of Her Own Talents

SCRIPT: "Open wide thy treasure chest ladened with *gifts*[1] *so rare.*

> *And sing thy song of rapture of beauteous skies so fair.*

> Thy tones will fall as *gems that fell from founts of*[2] *gold*

> *And the echo of thy song shall die away like strains from lutes of gold.*

> Pandora's box is poor compared with all *I hold*[3] *Within, and appears as a box of snuff to the one Who knows, who sees, and who can tell Glorious* [picture grows larger] *splendor of skies of roseate hues, And the heavenly grandeur of azure.*"

## SCRIPT

1. Open wide thy treasure chest ladened with *gifts so rare.*
*And sing thy song of rapture of beauteous skies so fair.*

2. *Thy tones will fall as gems that fell from founts of gold.*
*And the echo of thy song shall die away like strains from lutes of gold.*

3. Pandora's box is poor compared with all *I hold*
*Within, and appears as a box of snuff to the one*
*Who knows, who sees, and who can tell*
*Glorious* [picture grows larger] *splendor of skies of roseate hues,*
*And the heavenly grandeur of azure.*

## HALLUCINATION

A big chest *rises* up in my mind — it is heavily carved — a gorgeous thing. At first it is closed and then it slowly opens. As it opens I see that there are in it beautiful strings of *pearls* and red and white *roses.* I see *vials like cut glass flagons,* and instead of seeing the liquid perfume in the flagons there comes out a sort of vaporous cloud that is perfumed, because I can actually *smell* it. And on the edges of this chest are beautiful birds, like pure white doves. They are alive and it seems as if I hear them *cooing* as in the spring-time. I actually *hear* them coo. Then finally, a foggy vapor seems to cover the whole, to swallow it up, and it disappears. (It all seems to symbolize beautiful things.)

I see a *fountain.* It is beautiful. It is of green malachite. The base of this beautiful fountain is formed of funny little creatures that seem to be half animal and half human. They have the faces of goats, with horns and tails and hoofs. They seem like human beings and yet they are goats. (It seems as if I have seen such things before — such as might be in *Midsummer Night's Dream.)* There are four of these figures holding up a big bowl, that of the fountain, which is about five feet tall. It seems to be located on the edge of a wood. In the background I can see light coming through the foliage. Flowing out of this fountain, the beautiful *crystal water* falls over the edge into a basin at the base. And beautiful *gems* — rubies, emeralds, etc., *fall out over the edge along with the water,* as if they were bubbling out of the bowl, and falling into the basin, they disappear. Around the basin at the base were *lutes,* and harps — *golden instruments.* I can hear beautiful *soft music inwardly.* (I have often heard such inward music before. I have often got out of bed to dance to this inner music.) *The music seems to come from the instruments* although nobody plays upon them. It is very *low, dim, soft music.* (The vision seems to symbolize the natural gifts I have within me.)

First I see a picture of a *woman angel.* She is holding a *jewel box* in her hand and butterflies are flying out of it. It seems to diminish in size until it gets real tiny. While she is holding it and as it becomes small, *rays of light* shoot up over the whole and shut out the angel.

*These rays turn into a beautiful sky.* [This was when the vision grew larger, as indicated in the script.] The sky is *blue* and *pink.* (It is very beautiful.) Then clouds form in the sky and then they break and show the *pink color through.*

The correlation of the several elements of the hallucinations with the *synchronously* written words is strikingly manifest.

The hand writes "Open wide thy treasure chest — ladened with gifts so rare," and in a moment or two she visualizes a treasure chest slowly opening and disclosing gifts of rare value.

The script exhorts her to sing a song of rapture, and at the same time, in the allegorical visual and auditory hallucinations, she both sees and hears beautiful white doves cooing as in the spring-time.

The script compares the tones (or words) of her song to gems falling from a fount of gold, and she straightway visualizes a beautiful fountain from which gems bubble out along with the crystal clear water.

The script compares her song (*i. e.,* musical voice on which is centered her ambition) to the strains of golden lutes, whereupon, synchronously, she visualizes golden lutes and other golden instruments lying at the base of the fountain, and she hears "beautiful soft music inwardly" coming, as it seemed, from the instruments.

The script compares the gifts she holds within herself to those Pandora possessed in her box, to the disparagement of poor Pandora, and, correspondingly, she sees a vision of a "woman angel" (the facsimile of a picture in her possession which she, as it later transpired, imagined was that of Pandora) holding a jewel box in her hand.

The script emphasizes her own marvelous knowledge and gift to describe in song the splendor of roseate skies and the grandeur of the heavenly azure, in comparison with the poor little talents belonging to Pandora and contained in her box, and straightway in the vision only butterflies come out of the box, which diminishes to a tiny size, and Pandora and the box are eclipsed by splendid rays of light which turn into a beautiful sky of pink and blue.

Another point worth noting is the wealth of imagery of the hallucinations. If this imagery may be interpreted to represent symbolically the meaning of the script, it approaches allegory with free use of symbolism and analogies.

For instance: her own personality laden with rare inborn gifts, or talents, is likened to and symbolized by a treasure chest filled with gifts of pearls, roses, cut-glass flagons, etc. As she exhorts herself to display her own gifts, she sees the treasure chest open in display of its contents, and, somewhat astray in her knowledge of mythology and the contents of Pandora's box (as I afterwards discovered) she compares the gifts contained within herself to those of Pandora. Similarly, allegory and symbolism are conspicuous in the rich imagery of the fountain with its gems bubbling out with crystal water. All this reminds us of conscious imagery in composition of poetry, oratory and descriptive writing.

*Observation IV.* In this observation, the script records a subconscious memory of a consciously forgotten episode; *i. e.,* a dream of which the subject has no remembrance, nor of the circumstances, except that during a severe illness years ago and while under the influence of morphine, she had a dream of some sort of Spanish character. This was before the break-up into a double personality and the evolution of 'Juliana.' Indeed, it was out of the fantasies of such night and day-dreams, as I interpret the case, that the Spanish personality later became constructed. The hallucination is particularly interesting as it represents a dream within a dream, with corresponding shifting scenes of which the continuity is to be found in the subconscious script. The hallucination was described orally while the hand was writing the script.

## IV. A Subconscious Memory of a Forgotten Dream

SCRIPT: "Once when I was ill in the *South, I wished I was a strong woman; I wished I was a Spanish girl*, and this is what I dreamed: — that I was a Spanish *maiden of rare beauty and charm*, and then I saw her *sitting on a stump and I seemed to see her dreaming. I¹ see her in a palace where*

---

1 The exact moment of emergence of the last two pictures (3 and 4), by an oversight, was not noted on the script. They are here given approximately.

*there is soft music and there seem to be grapes and flowers
and beautiful pictures and oil urns of colored lights.*

| SCRIPT | HALLUCINATION |
|---|---|
| Once when I was ill in the *South I wished I was a strong woman; I wished I was a Spanish girl* and this is what I dreamed: | (Described orally while the hand was writing.) I see *myself in bed. I'm sick.* I see a room — a bed in it, a brass bed. *I am real weak.* I prop myself up on a pillow. I seem to be like I was *dreaming* — I see myself lying back on the pillow. Now I am *asleep.* |
| [Dream of Susie] that I was a Spanish *maiden of rare beauty and charm* | [Shift] I see *Juliana* going into the woods. She is plump, with poor clothes — her hair is hanging down her back — she is barefooted. [Comment after the cessation of the hallucination; "She was *very pretty.*"] |
| and then I saw her *sitting on a stump of a tree and I seemed to see her* day-dreaming. [Dream of Juliana] | [Shift] *Juliana is sitting on a log.* She seems to be dreaming. As I see her *I seem to see her dream.* |
| *I see her in a palace where there is soft music and there seem to be grapes and flowers and beautiful pictures and oil u r n s of colored lights.* | [Shift] I see *this peasant girl in a beautiful palace* — she has beautiful robes on — there is beautiful statuary in the palace — a lot of gaiety around her — a lot of people as in a court — *soft music* — I hear it — *and a lot of light-colored light from urns and lots of fruit* — beautiful marble mosaic floors — the girl is dancing. |

After this experiment the subject again visualized the 'pictures' of Juliana sitting on the stump of a tree and the scene of the palace, and drew the following illustrations (Figs. 22 and 23) *from the visions which she actually saw as if they were real.* The mechanism of this revisualization was found on examination to be very similar to that of the production of a crystal vision. There was, also, as was claimed, a coconscious wish (" a great desire") to have the coconscious images emerge into consciousness so as to be drawn.

The dancing scene at Court had been frequently visualized and was therefore an already organized construction. She had little more than to think intensely of it, coconsciously, to have it re-appear. It was a repetition of Scene 4, Observation II.

The script begins to tell of an illness which the subject suffered a good many years ago, when living in the South, and after seven words are written, an image of herself ill in bed, in the very same brass bedstead and in the very same

Fig. 22. Juliana drawn by the subject from an hallucination.

room in which she had been ill, appears in consciousness. (It is a visualized memory; for on seeing the vision she recollects the illness, the room and the bedstead.) The whole hallucination is composed of just such images as would accompany the recollection of such an episode as one would experience when one recalls a particularly serious illness that one has suffered in a particular place. She had been prostrated at the time, as she well remembers, and the hallucination portrays her as weak in body, and the script described her thought as wishing to be strong — to be, in fact, the strong peasant Spanish girl whom, in her day-dreaming, she had fabricated as fantasy, and so she goes to sleep and dreams the fulfillment of this wish.

Fig. 23. Juliana dancing before the king (drawn as in Fig. 22).

She dreams (according to the script — whether true or not does not matter, for it is only with the content of the subconscious process at work in writing that we are concerned) she dreams, so the script goes on, that she is a Spanish maiden, and the image of such maiden of "rare beauty and charm" appears as an hallucination, but in a particular setting of the woods. The figure is an image identical with that which she had often fabricated of the Spanish peasant, Juliana, and just such an image as the maiden of the script would in conscious thought evoke. The setting of the woods is not described in the script but, as has been pointed out, the imagery of an hallucination is always richer than the script, and the testimony of the subconscious introspection affirmed that all the details of the hallucinations were elements in the subconscious process, as we shall later see. Then, as the subconsciously written script describes the maiden sitting on a stump of a tree, day-dreaming, straightway a corresponding image of Juliana emerges as an hallucination. (Let us never for one moment forget in studying these phenomena that the subject was entirely unaware of the content of the script — of what the hand had written, and, therefore, whatever images pertained to and emerged from the expressed ideas must have pertained to and emerged from a subconscious process, and — if the script was written by a subconscious process — such as the content of that script would require.)

The script declares that (subconsciously) she sees the imagery of the dream, and this imagery emerges into consciousness as an hallucination of Juliana dancing before the King and his Court — a long previously organized fantasy.

Thus examined, the imagery of the several shifting scenes of this hallucination is precisely such as the content of the script would require and, if we are justified in defining that content as coconscious ideas, we may say such imagery as those *coconscious* ideas would contain.

*Observation V.* The chief interest in the next observation lies in the facts (*a*) that the script was motivated by anxiety and not by a wish, and, therefore, the hallucination was not a wish-fulfillment; and (*b*) that the emotions linked with the subconscious process (a memory) emerged into consciousness along with the images of the memory. The emotions involved were both anxiety and anger, but it would seem that anxiety was the dominant emotion of the subconscious system producing the script, while anger was that which was felt most strongly, at least, by the subject while seeing the hallucination. Apparently during the original episode, of which the hallucination and script were a mem ory, both anger and anxiety were elements. For this observation, it should be said, the subject had been directed to write automatically a memory of some episode in her life of an anxious kind. Of course, neither the subject nor I had any idea of what would be written.

The occasion referred to in the script and reproduced in the hallucination was one when the subject was in the clinic of the commercial establishment (where she was employed) to get her time-card signed for the days she was absent on account of illness. The nurse must pass on such cases.

### V. Memory of an Anxious Episode

| SCRIPT | HALLUCINATION (Described orally and synchronously while the hand was writing) |
|---|---|
| "Yes, I am concerned *if they will sign my time-card, and she is cold in her attitude towards me.*" | I see the nurse sitting down at her desk talking to me in the clinic down at the store, and *I seem to be perplexed about something.* I don't know what. She turns her head and writes something on a card. (She was sort of haughty.) |
| [Note: The script further claimed that she felt (subconsciously), while writing, really *anxious* because it meant much to her if the card were not signed and her pay was 'docked.'] | [Oral comment by the subject:] "A feeling of *doubt* and of being full of *fight* comes to my mind. . . . While seeing the hallucination, I felt worried as if my word was doubted, as if I were put on a level with other girls, who tell a lie whenever they open their mouths. . . . I had that feeling at the time." |

Immediately after the observation was finished, the following questionnaire was put to the subconscious system. The answers were written automatically without the subject's awareness of their content.

Q. "What were you concerned about?"

A. "Whether the nurse will put a D. D. [Don't dock] on my card."

Q. "Were you anxious?"

A. "Yes."

Q. "Was the conscious mind anxious?"

A. "No." [Here, in reply to my question, the subject said, *without knowing what the hand wrote,* that she was not consciously anxious at the time of seeing the hallucination but only resentful.]

Q. "Were you *really* anxious?"

A. "Yes, and it would mean something if I did not get it signed."

### Temporal Relation between Script and Hallucination

It is obvious that there are two possible interpretations of the relation between the script and the hallucinations in these observations. First, the hallucination may be secondary to and a product of the script-producing process; or, second, the hallucination may be primary, and the subconscious process may simply describe in the script such an independent hallucination. The point is crucial: for if the second interpretation be the correct one, the hallucination could well be the product of an independent and unrelated process. In favor of the first interpretation, and against the second, is the fact, to which I have already called attention, that the writing of a given script always began before the correlated images appeared in consciousness. A moment or two always elapsed after the idea began to be written before its hallucinatory image developed. This can easily be recognized by noting the point marked in the script of the emergence of the image. If the script simply described a primary and independent hallucination, we should expect the latter to have appeared first and the description-writing of the imaged idea to follow later. But the reverse was the case.

Then, again, the script is never, technically speaking, a description of the hallucination (such as the subject herself gave when she experienced it), but rather a theme in which the expressed ideas would normally have just such images as appeared in the corresponding hallucination.

Further evidence confirmative of the first interpretation was obtained by subconscious introspection — the next step in the investigation. The evidence of introspection was to the effect, as we shall see, that the subconscious process was primary and the hallucination secondary; and that the latter was due to the emergence into consciousness of images belonging to and first formed in the subconscious process.

*Introspective Evidence from Self-Analysis by the Subconscious Process.* The next step in this study obviously was, as stated in the beginning, to learn what light, if any, the subconscious process itself could throw upon the relation between the images (hallucination) and the writing consciousness; and for this purpose to obtain a self-analysis based on *introspection by the subconscious* process that wrote the script. Such introspection would be similar in every way to the conscious method commonly employed in psychological laboratory investigations. It would make use of retrospective memories of the subconscious content. Its value as evidence would depend, like all introspection, on the accuracy and completeness of subconscious introspection.

The technique in the present investigation consisted in presenting a carefully worded questionnaire to be answered by automatic script and followed often by a rigid cross-examination of the replies, care being taken to suggest no leads or theories.

Accordingly, after each of the first four observations, the subject was submitted to such an examination. The content of the subconscious process, whether or not it contained images and thoughts and, whether or not such images as manifested themselves were in any way related to those of the hallucination, or to the subconscious thoughts (if there were any) producing the script, of course could not be known to the personal consciousness, nor were the answers known until after the interrogation was finished. The self-analysis, introspection and replies were, therefore, necessarily subconscious.

## (Observation I: Harvard University)

The replies of the script following Observation I[1] (the

---

1 As here arranged, the observations are not in the sequence in which they were actually made. This observation was the third following the "Treasure Chest" (No. 3).

scene at "Harvard University") are striking in that, without any suggestion of any theory whatever on my part, or indication of any mechanism by which the hallucination might be formed, the script clearly and explicitly described the origin of the pictures or images in the subconscious process and their later emergence into consciousness as the hallucination. The only possible suggestion was in the question whether or not the pictures were in the subconscious mind also, as well as in the personal consciousness, as surely might well be the case, whatever the mechanism. For subconsciously there is awareness for all that which is in the personal attention. The question only related to a possible memory of a possible *fact,* experienced in the past, not to an opinion or general idea, or other thought. The affirmative answer can scarcely be questioned in view of the fact that subconscious images are not a novel phenomenon, as I have recorded them in at least three other cases; and, secondly, in this case they were repeatedly described to me long before I undertook this investigation, and were then, as well as in these observations, recorded under all sorts of conditions and relations and their behavior correspondingly described. They occurred, so it was testified, spontaneously as well as experimentally. *Furthermore these images had been already described in two preceding observations.* Specifically, the statements of the script in this observation were as follows:

"The thought" arises subconsciously first, "then the pictures [images] are completely formed" and "all is visualized" subconsciously. *"I visualize,"* the script states, *"subconsciously the scene I am writing about just as I do consciously.* [The significance of this sentence is that the subject visualized subconsciously one scene while consciously, during the experiment, the content of her thought was of a different order (the scene of the room, the experimenter, etc.). Hence the eruption of the former was an hallucination.] The images "are in the subconscious mind while writing and then they are shifted into the conscious until they become visions." "When set, so to speak, they are reflected into the conscious mind." *"It takes some time* [a few seconds] *for them to come into the conscious mind."*

(Observation II: The Spanish Fantasy)

A source of confusion and error in drawing conclusions lies in the fact that sometimes the script is written by a subconscious system (*e. g.*, Juliana) differentiated from that from which the images are derived. Speaking *figuratively,* there may be two or more 'layers' or 'strata' of subconscious systems underlying one another. The system that does the writing may then derive its images and thoughts from a deeper and more comprehensive underlying layer or system out of which the writing system has become crystallized as a differentiated system. In such case, the images emerge into this differentiated system from the deeper system and, therefore, the former does not know their origin but simply describes their content or the thoughts which they picture and which accompany them. Where all comes from, it does not know. This is analogous to conscious imagery and thought. I have observed many examples of this kind of phenomenon.

The consequence is that when the special script-producing system is interrogated, the replies are inadequate and indefinite for lack of precise knowledge. Unless this is borne in mind confusion may result. This was the case in Observation II. Practically all the precise information that could be given was that the "vision" originated in "a deeper source of thought" and *first appeared subconsciously* to the writing system. Then, secondarily, the writing of the ideas represented by the images caused the images to emerge into consciousness as hallucinations. But however this may have been, the essential point is that the images *first appeared subconsciously and then burst into consciousness as the hallucination.*

This observation was the first made and only a preliminary one to determine whether any positive results were likely to be obtained, and, if so, what was the best method of experimentation. Hence it was rather superficial. The chief points brought out by the subconscious analysis were:

"The 'pictures' seem to form from what has been written but the personal consciousness is not aware of it."

"The visions originate in the deeper source of thought, and then the writing of them causes the visions to conjure up in the mind of the consciousness that is describing [orally] the visions"; *i. e.*, the "personal consciousness."

"The deeper source of thought, which writes, has, while writing, the ideas contained in the pictures; so much so that that is where the mystery lies."

I am impelled here to insist again, as I have frequently done, that there is no *the* subconscious or *the* unconscious. In the structure of the mind there are greater and lesser systems of potential and dynamic processes which may be motivated by the urge of one or more 'dispositions.' These systems play and interplay with one another; and any one or more, without entering the awareness of the personal attention, may function 'subconsciously.' The concept of an unconscious, of which we read much nowadays, *limited* to primitive instinctive processes, is based on inadequate knowledge of subconscious phenomena and is, therefore, scientifically amateurish. Such concepts belong to philosophy and are bound to go the way of all systems of philosophy after having served their usefulness, even as do scientific theories based on incomplete knowledge.

## (Observation III: The Treasure Chest)

The pictures (images) were first formed in the part of the mind that was answering the questionnaire: "the part that wrote the lines had the pictures and they became visible to the one sitting at your side [the subject]." The process was claimed to be as follows: the thoughts expressed in the versification came subconsciously while on her way to keep an appointment. These thoughts were put into verse only later, during the experiment and while writing, but the images were there before the composition was arranged and the "poetry came from the images."[1]

1 The whole process was quite complex, according to the explanation given. Although the thoughts and images of the verse were in the subconscious system that wrote the script of this observation (III) they did not originate there but in a 'deeper' and more comprehensive subconscious system which was answering the questionnaire. From this 'stratum' they invaded the system that was the author of the script and then the images emerged into consciousness as hallu-

"The thoughts were there first; then when they were grouped together to form the poetry, the visions appeared [to the consciousness of the subject] during the process of the writing"; *i. e.*, while writing the script, the images burst into consciousness as the hallucinations. "It took a few seconds for the images to become realistic to the conscious mind."

The order was:

1. Subconscious thoughts.
2. Subconscious images.
3. Subconscious verse.
4. Emergence of the images as hallucinations.

*As to why the visions had more details than were described in the script,* it was explained that there were subconscious thoughts of all the details of the fountain, but "you cannot write all the details as a vision can be described." In other observations substantially the same explanation was given. Thus, in Observation VI, it was stated that "there is a subconscious process that can create visions quicker than the process of writing." This is emphasized by the fact that some visions are "mostly a memory," as was stated to be the case in one of the hallucinations of that observation. Then again (Observation IV) some hallucinations are recurrences or repetitions of subconsciously visualized scenes which have been already constructed subconsciously in all their details and are later revived and flashed as a whole before the mind.

As to what suggested, *i. e.*, motivated the thoughts of the verse, it was explained, "I am not self-centred but I do know I have a certain amount of talent, and I suppose it was that thought or thoughts that were uppermost in my mind."

### (Observation IV: A Memory of Illness)

In reply to the question, "What work was being done subconsciously during the hallucinations from which the drawings were made?" the script asserted:

cinations. This was the same order of affairs as occurred in the preceding observation (II). This same phenomenon, in kind, I had observed under other circumstances and in different forms.

"The subconscious mind of both Susie and Juliana was at work projecting into the conscious mind the visions of Juliana and the palace, and a great desire to have reproduced the vision in the deepest part of the mind [so that it could be drawn]. Yes, there were images that formed the people — all things were images. The subconscious mind thought it all out, it creates the images; then constant thought pushes them into the conscious mind."

## B.  ARTIFICIALLY INDUCED VISUAL HALLUCINATIONS

A series of observations was now carried out of a character *converse* to the preceding. Instead of producing primarily subconscious script with secondarily resulting correlated images (hallucinations), *artificial hallucinations were experimentally produced and the script employed to describe what, if any, subconscious 'thoughts' occurred during the hallucinations*. The method employed was that of fixing the attention by means of a crystal. No directions were given as to what would be seen in the crystal. That was left to chance.

*Observation VI.* This series of three hallucinations is particularly instructive in that it shows the subconscious connection between hallucinations which apparently, as in dreams, have no obvious continuity by themselves. In the thoughts, subconsciously written, the connection is clearly shown especially in A and B of Hallucination 2, which I have consequently grouped together as one. The vision of her mother in a distant city suddenly, without time interval, shifts to a scene in Boston. The script enables the meaning of the shift to be understood. Subconsciously, as the script explains, she wishes she could go home and see her mother once more sitting in the chair, as she had often seen her, and then, after she had fulfilled this filial wish and obligation, return to Boston and complete her vocal training for the stage. This connected subconscious thought fills in the gap between the hallucinations A and B and explains their meaning.

Likewise, there is a connection between all three hallucinations, although less explicit; notwithstanding, they were separate, interrupted observations, but made within a few minutes of each other. She has an aspiration to go upon the stage in opera and act a certain part, that of a Spanish girl in a scenario which she has thought out (Hallucination 1). To accomplish this it will be necessary to remain East and not only support herself by working but at the same time fit herself by study. But she also longs to see her mother (Hallucination 2). This conflict she has often mentioned. Her solution is, as she also has frequently stated, to return home temporarily and then return to the East. But she has expressed doubts if she would be allowed to return, if she should go home. Her wished-for solution is contained in A and B. In B the images are of herself singing by the side of her teacher, just such images as we should expect would be contained in the thought, though the hallucination is not a memory of a particular experience but a fabrication of an imagined general experience.

But to carry out her aspirations, she needs a better paying position for temporary gain, so she applied for the position of assistant buyer and was called before the judges of the applicants. Hallucination 3 is a memory of that event.

## VI. Three Subconsciously Connected Hallucinations

### HALLUCINATION 1

I see a *theatre stage*. I see a little bit of a body (myself) on this great big stage and I am dressed like a *Spanish girl* and I have my arms up *gesticulating as if singing*. I seem to be gay. I am dressed with a shawl and fringe.

### SCRIPT

I am thinking I would love to make *my appearance on the stage as a singer and impersonate Juliana as a Spanish girl*.

### HALLUCINATION 2

(A) I see my *mother sitting in a chair* and myself leaning over her kissing her.

[Shift]
(B) I am in a *studio by a grand piano*. The teacher is playing, and *I am standing by his side singing*. I never saw the studio before. It is prettily furnished.

### SCRIPT
(A) I wish I could see *my mother sitting in her chair and then* come back East and

(B) *go on with my vocal work*.

| [Shift] HALLUCINATION 3 | SCRIPT |
|---|---|
| I see an *office down at the store* and I can see the *three men I talked* to about the position of assistant buyer; there are three chairs, a desk and myself. (I do not see the rest of the vision — not a complete picture like those I have seen.) | I am thinking of the day I was called to the *office of the judges* to select an assistant buyer to train for the position. |

Following this observation, the writing system was catechized and asked to explain why the hallucination of the studio showed more details than were contained in the automatic writing. The explanation given was that the content of hallucinations was often thought out subconsciously first in detail before they were described, and that "there is a subconscious process that can create visions quicker than the process of writing." The vision of her mother was mostly a memory.

*Observation VII.* The next observation is extremely important in that, on the one hand, it illustrates the principle that script may be produced by more than one subconscious system, and, on the other, it shows a source of error that must be guarded against in such experiments. Otherwise, we may be led astray by a failure to find a correlation between the hallucination and the script. In other words, *an hallucination may emerge from or be determined by another system than that which is writing.* Furthermore, it compels the conclusion that more than one subconscious system may actually function at one and the same time, and in this case three such systems were in operation. That script may be obtained from several distinct systems is well-known, as is attested by the script obtained by mediums in claimed spiritistic communications. Of course, psychological investigations have determined the same principle and the facts (*e. g.,* Flournoy's classical observations in the case of Hélène Smith.[1] I need not mention numerous observations of my own illustrative of this point). It may, therefore, be that the script obtained during an hallucination may show no correlation with the latter. In that case, it may be that that

1 *From India to the Planet Mars.*

script can be obtained from another subconscious system which will contain very intimate correlations. This proved to be the case in this observation, where the unrelated script first obtained was written by the 'Juliana system.' The hallucination consisted of a number of differing and shifting scenes. As the subject saw these scenes she sometimes laughed or commented on them. With this preamble I will now give the record of the observations, giving the hallucination and the corresponding script of the 'Juliana system' first.

## VII. Hallucination of the Fulfillment of an Aspiration

Scenes: 1. Funeral (laughs) — 2. Church — 3. Cemetery (laughs) — 4. New York — 5. Theatre — 6. Big buildings like an apartment house. (Given verbally and synchronously with the script of the 'Juliana system.')

Each scene shifted to the next one, as in a movie, without an apparent time interval. The subject experienced the successive scenes of the hallucination, while the script was being written by the 'Juliana system,' and described each verbally in general terms, such as: "I see a funeral" — "Now I see a church" — "It has changed to a cemetery," etc. The six scenes were accordingly recorded as above. Immediately after the hallucination was completed and nothing further appeared, each scene was taken in its order; and the subject, while the memory was vivid, described the details as given below.

| HALLUCINATION | SCRIPT |
|---|---|
| Details of scenes given from memory immediately after their completion | By the 'Juliana system' written synchronously with the hallucination |
| 1. I saw a *funeral* — a casket on a cart, such as is used for soldiers, with black drapery over it, and a white cross of lilies on the top. I could see the petals. There were black-robed priests carrying huge white candles, and some little boys dressed in white following the casket and shaking incense burners — Streets paved with large rough cobblestones. ["It seems to be in Italy — seems foreign to me."] ["I had a feeling at the time the funeral was Juliana's. That is what made me laugh."] | "I am at last out of this world of toil, and with the angels rest; my soul has wended its way to the heavenly realms.<br><br>"This is a real spirit message now."<br><br>    [Signed] Juliana. |

2. Door of *cathedral*. I could see the tower and on top of it a cross. The funeral procession was entering the door. First the priests, then the casket and finally the little boys.

3. Barren landscape. A *cemetery* — graves far apart — one grave opened and they were putting the casket in it. The priests and the boys were standing around the grave, the boys waving the incense. There was no one else there at the funeral. ["That is the funny thing about it — there were no friends."]

4. I saw myself in *New York*, just as I am now, and I was walking down the street — high buildings on either side — there were busses, automobiles and people — ["I did not recognize the street."]

5. *Theatre* — I was going into it by the main street door. I went down the side aisle to the dressing room and I then saw myself on the stage dressed in Grecian white robe — I was simply standing there ["not acting — I did not know what I was going to do"] — no other actors on the stage — audience in their seats.

6. *Apartment house* — I went in — took elevator — went to an apartment I felt to be mine — let myself in by a latch-key. It was a beautifully furnished apartment, rugs, etc. I saw all the furniture. I threw off a long neckpiece of fur, then I stood at some long windows and looked out. I seemed considerably older than I am now, as if I were more of a woman than I am now — say 36-38 years.

The 'Juliana system' was now interrogated, and it was easily demonstrated that this had no causal relationship with the hallucination, but that the spirit message was written as a jest.

[Here an interesting psychological phenomenon that I have frequently observed and reported developed: namely, the emergence of emotional tones from a subconscious process. While this system was writing the spirit message and during the first part of the interrogation when the system manifested a humorous, almost hilarious, mood, the subject was in high spirits, joyful, and felt the spirit of fun. Later, during the latter part of the interrogation when the 'Juliana system' admitted her tomfoolery and wrote of her past (the period when she was a double personality) the subject remarked without knowing what the hand wrote: "I feel serious, now. All my high spirits and feeling of fun have left me"; and then, as a coconscious confession of previous deception was written, "I have a sad, remorseful feeling."[1] This emergence of the feeling-tones belonging to subconscious processes is of significance in the mechanism of moods and exalted and depressive states. The phenomenon accompanied some of the hallucinations.]

My first thought, in the failure to find in the Juliana script any psychological relationship of imagery with the hallucination, was that the findings would prove to be exceptional and that a different type of mechanism for the hallucination would be disclosed. On further investigation, however, this proved not to be the case, as a correlated script was obtained from another subconscious system — the 'Susie system.' This latter did not attempt to go into the details of the subconscious thoughts. I am sorry now I did not demand this, but my whole attention was concentrated upon the principle and the source of the first obtained script and of the hallucination.[2]

When the subconscious 'Susie system' was tapped, as was now done, this system at once claimed to be the source of the hallucination and wrote the account given below of the 'thoughts' which went on subconsciously in this system while the hallucinations were being formed. I have arranged the 'thoughts,' as given, in a parallel column in opposition to the corresponding hallucination.

1 "I have a final confession to make — that I have told falsehoods, and who can blame me? I was fooled for years by a lying subconscious mind who made me a puppet for its own trickery. Perhaps you will understand. Think of the many years I was fooled into believing I was a soul." This confession refers not to these experiments but to the early period of double personality mentioned above, when the subconscious 'Juliana system' claimed to be the reincarnated soul of a Spanish peasant.

2 This involved considerable work, including rigid cross-examinations of the two systems that wrote. To reproduce here the details of this examination would take us too far out of the way. It is sufficient to say that it transpired that the 'Juliana system' facetiously took control of the pencil and, as a joke, wrote the script pretending to be a spirit message. Although the message was short, the 'Juliana system,' of course, might have gone on writing during the unfolding of the whole hallucination.

| HALLUCINATION<br>Details of scene given from memory immediately after their completion | SCRIPT<br>*By the 'Susie system'* written subsequently to the hallucination and therefore from memory |
|---|---|
| 1. I saw a *funeral* — a casket on a cart such as is used for soldiers, with black drapery over it, and a white cross of lilies on the top. I could see the petals. There were black-robed priests carrying huge white candles and some little boys dressed in white following the casket and shaking incense burners — Streets paved with large rough cobblestones. ["It seems to be in Italy — seems foreign to me."] ["I had a feeling at the time the funeral was Juliana's. That is what made me laugh."] | "I had thoughts of Juliana's passing out of existence and of Susie standing on her **feet alone and gaining fame** from her own conscious efforts and not leaning on any one for support." [Here the 'Susie system' was told to be more explicit.] |
| 2. Door of cathedral. I could see the tower and on top of it a cross. The funeral procession was entering the door. First the priests, then the casket and finally the little boys. | "I had thoughts of a funeral of which I made the Juliana complex the central figure." |
| 3. Barren landscape. A *cemetery* — *graves* far apart — one grave opened and they were putting the casket in it. The priests and the boys were standing around the grave, the boys waving the incense. There was no one else there at the funeral. ["That is the funny thing about it — there were no friends."] | |
| 4. I saw myself in *New York* just as I am now and I was walking down the street — high buildings on either side — there were busses, automobiles and people — ["I did not recognize the street."] | |
| 5. *Theatre* — I was going into it by the main street door. I went down the side aisle to the dressing room and I then saw myself on the stage dressed in Grecian white robe — I was simply standing there ["not acting — I did not know what I was going to do"] — no other actors on the stage — audience in their seats. | "And then I thought, if the Susie complex would struggle she could gain fame as an actress." |
| 6. *Apartment house* — I went in — took elevator — went to an apartment I felt to be mine — let myself in by a latch-key. It was a beautifully furnished apartment, rugs, etc. I saw all the furniture. I threw off a long neck-piece of fur, then I stood at some long windows and looked out. I seemed considerably older than I am now, as if I were more of a woman than I am now — say 36-38 years. | "and maintain her o w n apartment just as s h e pleased, a long standing heart's desire." |

The successive scenes of this hallucination are plainly the pictorial representation of the theme which is briefly set forth in the script of the 'Susie system.' This system, it should be explained, represents the aspirations of the normal self.

The 'Juliana system' is a subconsciously perseverating remnant of the former secondary and alternating personality from which this system has been derived.

*Observation VIII.* In this observation, a series of shifting scenes developed. As each picture appeared, the subject, as in Observation VII, called out the fact and described in general terms the scenes: "I see a street in New York" — "I see a scene in a theatre" — "A ship on the ocean," etc., with a few additional descriptive words. *While these pictures were developing,* the hand automatically wrote the script signed 'Susie.' At the same time, I recorded each picture and marked on the script the moment of its beginning and ending. As in the previous observation, immediately after the completion of the script and the hallucination, the subject described in detail from memory the pictures she had seen, taking them one at a time in the order of succession. This she was easily able to do, as she could vividly revive them rich in detail. Each picture was then compared with those words of the script that were written during the occurrence of that picture. Arranging the pictures with the corresponding script in parallel columns, I would call attention to the striking failure of correlation between the two synchronously occurring phenomena. Careful examination reveals that the hallucinations cannot be regarded as the emerging imagery of the subconscious process producing the script. For example: corresponding to the picture of a ship's dock (4), we have only the word "shall"; and to that of the *hotel* (6), the word "earth." The complete observation may be arranged as follows:

VIII. Hallucination in seven scenes: Visit to Italy

Scenes: 1. Street in New York — 2. Theatre — 3. Ocean — 4. Dock 5. Subway — 6. Hotel — 7. Hotel Room.
(Described in general terms verbally and synchronously with the script of the 'Susie system.')

## SCRIPT OF THE 'SUSIE SYSTEM'

"I am thinkinking [1] of New York and of the [2] fame I shall some day achieve as a great ac[3]tress and of my dreams of long standing shall [4] shall [5] hall mature and I shall travel to various sparts of [6] the earth [7] and I shall become overjoyous of my painstaking efforts and the fruit of my toil.

[Signed] Susie Sub[conscious]."

[NOTE: Observe the halting and stammering at 3, 4, and 5, and imperfect spelling. The script was crabbed and was written slowly and apparently with some difficulty. This corresponds with the theory that the images came from still another train of thought, which inhibited this one.]

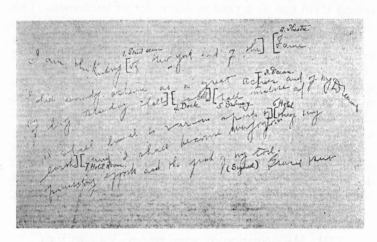

Fig. 24. Facsimile of Script in Observation VIII.

| HALLUCINATION<br>Details given from memory immediately after production | SCRIPT<br>By the 'Susie system,' written synchronously with the hallucination |
| --- | --- |
| 1. Street scene in New York.<br>I saw lots of people — automobile busses — cabs — automobiles — myself — I seemed to be very intent and in a great hurry walking on the sidewalk. | I am thinkinking of New York and of the |

2. Theatre.
I was in a theatre on the stage (not set — only a piano and a man). I was being taught by this man at the piano, singing. (I could not hear my voice.)

fame I shall some day achieve as a great ac

3. Ocean.
I was on a ship in midocean — no land in sight. I was walking on deck with the same man. It was dusk.

tress and of my dreams of long standing shall

4. Dock
I could see baggage being taken off by express and baggage people — lots of people hurrying around holloing for cabs — awful turmoil — I was with the man leaving the ship and on the dock — was geting into a carriage with the man.

shall

5. Subway.
Trains in it. I went down the subway from the carriage and got in the train — doors opened on the side as in London. It was in Italy because I saw funny language like Italian on the billboards. No, it was Spanish language. I don't know where I was. It was Spanish or Italian. The strongest feeling in my mind was Italian.

hall mature and I shall travel the various sparts of

6. Hotel.
Porte-cochere of a big white building. I went in with this man, in a big lobby. I registered myself — I could see this man talking to the clerk as if he knew him. It was as if he was telling the clerk to look after me. He tips his hat and goes away.

the earth

7. Hotel room.
A beautiful room — done in old rose draperies — white furniture — imperial looking, it was so elegant. Different from anything you see in hotels. I was *very tired.* I was walking across the floor — all I could do, and threw myself on the bed. I felt as if I said out loud — "At last I have realized what I long hoped for." ["I don't know what that meant."]
    ["I don't know who the man was — I felt that he was a foreigner — he knew how to sing — as if an impresario."]

and I shall become overjoyous of my painstaking efforts and the fruit of my toil.

Although no detailed correlation between the hallucination and the script can be postulated from the point of view of imagery of specific concrete thoughts, that is, in the sense that the imagery of the hallucination can be recognized as the images of the specific ideas of the script, there was a general correspondence of the themes expressed by both. The script speaks in general terms of her aspirations and their fulfillment: the hallucinations, as a whole, represent a series of imaginary incidents which carry out concretely, as fantasies, these aspirations. But no concrete subconscious thoughts are discovered of which the hallucinations would be the normal images. The first two scenes (New York and Theatre) and the last (Hotel Room) might be interpreted as exceptions, but in a second script, obtained later, we shall see that the imagery precisely corresponds to images that would be expected of this second train of specific thoughts.

Undoubtedly, the general theme of the first script was determined in accordance with a well-known principle: that is to say, by the more specific ideas of a second subconscious process that induced the hallucinations.

In search of another system that might be responsible for the imagery of the hallucinations, the 'Juliana system' was now tapped by automatic writing. This system, after claiming that the pictures belonged to its thoughts, wrote successively, but of course from memory, the 'thoughts' that were subconsciously experienced during each hallucinatory scene. The given data may be tabulated as follows:

| HALLUCINATION | SCRIPT |
|---|---|
| | By 'Juliana system' written, subsequent to the hallucination, from memory. The form correspondingly differs from synchronous script* |
| 1. Street scene in New York. I saw lots of people — automobile busses — cabs — automobiles — myself — I seemed to be very intent and in a great hurry walking on the sidewalk. | I thought I was in New York preparing my voice for an operatic career and I was on my way to the Metropolitan Opera House to see a man who would help me train my voice. That is why I was in a hurry. |
| 2. Theatre. I was in a theatre on the stage — only a piano and man — (not set). | I was thinking that this noted man — I do not know his name but he was there |

* As the script purported to give the content of past thoughts by retrospection, the memories are given in rather general terms, and it was obviously impossible to accurately correlate in time with the 'thoughts' the images within each scene. Therefore, I did not ask for minute details. The danger of artifacts in so doing is obvious.

I was being taught by this man at the piano, singing. (I could not hear my voice.)

[Metropolitan Opera House] and was very much in earnest with my vocal progress; I was thinking I was rehearsing an opera with him that he claimed I would score a success in, and he proposed taking me to Italy to further my studies in that role.

### 3. Ocean.

I was on a ship in mid-ocean — no land in sight. I was walking on deck with the same man. It was dusk.

I was thinking of the trip promised me at the theatre and of being on the liner bound for Italy, where I would resume my studies in the opera of *Traviata;* also that this man would take me there.

### 4. Dock.

I could see baggage being taken off by express and baggage people — lots of people hurrying around holloing for cabs — awful turmoil — I was with the man leaving the ship and on the dock — was getting into a carriage with the man.

I was thinking that we had reached our destination and I was in Italy.

The scene, as near as Susie told it, was a perfect picture of what I was thinking.

### 5. Subway.

Trains in it. I went down the subway from the carriage and got in the train — doors opened on the side as in London. It was in Italy because I saw funny language like Italian on the billboards. No, it was Spanish language. I don't know what it was. It was Spanish or Italian. The strongest feeling in myself was Italian.

I was thinking of passing through a subway. That was my thought — a European one.

### 6. Hotel.

Porte-cochère of a big white building. I went in with this man, in a big lobby. I registered myself — I could see this man talking to the clerk as if he knew him. It was as if he was telling the clerk to look after me. He tips his hat and goes away.

I was thinking I was in Italy and I was very tired after the ocean voyage and very joyous to be in the land of my dreams.

[The script later claimed she was thinking of a hotel also, but forgot to write it. The fatigued condition followed this thought. It is significant of the absence of any intentional fabrication of thoughts to fit the pictures that the script here went on as follows: "I was thinking this noted man was about to return to the hotel for me and take me to an opera-house to try my voice, and I was thinking the place was very dark and cold, and outside it was very bright and sunny." While the pencil was writing this sentence, the subject saw a vision of a theatre corresponding in details to the thought; but there were no such images in the original hallucination. When asked to explain this absence of hallucinatory imagery,

[the script said it could not do so, but that the thought was "not vivid and did not develop into a picture," as obviously is most generally the case; otherwise we all should be having hallucinations.]

7. Hotel room.
A beautiful room — done in old rose draperies — white furniture — imperial looking, it was so elegant. Different from anything you see in hotels. I was *very tired*. I was walking across the floor — all I could do, and threw myself on the bed. I could feel as if I said out loud — "at last I have realized what I long hoped for." ["I don't know what I meant."]
["I don't know who the man was — I felt he was a foreigner — he knew how to sing — as if an impresario."]

I was thinking that my efforts in the future should bring me the reward of such a beautiful chamber, and I thought out each detail of rose and ivory that Susie described,* only she did not tell all the wonderful things.

## C. AUDITORY HALLUCINATIONS

Alongside of the visual hallucinations, it will have been noticed that there occurred auditory hallucinations in a number of instances (Observations I, II, III). Experiments were now undertaken to determine whether or not the mechanism of such auditory phenomena was the same as that of the visual variety. First, such evidence as might be derived from the self-analysis by the subconscious process which induced the hallucination was obtained. In evaluating this evidence, it should be borne in mind that the particular auditory hallucinations to which the subconscious analysis referred were 'messages' from the subconscious to the personal consciousness, or a subconscious *intention* that the words should be heard by the latter. This is not always a condition, as in Observation I and III. The subconscious, however, on numerous occasions has experienced this type of hallucination, as when, for instance, she acted as an amanuensis for the internal voice, and to the dictation of the latter wrote a long story. Such messages were, however, quite common in this

* Referring to the conscious oral description of the hallucination by the subject.

subject just as they are frequently met with in the hallucinations of the insane.

*Observation IX.* The subject heard an internal voice say:
    (*a*)  "Get that smoke out of your lungs";
and again,
    (*b*)  "Tell Dr. Prince the Juliana complex is still holding her ideals."[1]

In response to a searching interrogation as to the mechanism of this and other auditory hallucinations, the subconscious process gave testimony which may be summarized as follows:

In such hallucinations, subconsciously the words are first *intensively thought out and grouped together as auditory sounds or words; that as a result of this intense subconscious thinking, the auditory words emerged into consciousness as the hallucination;* but in addition, in order to produce such an hallucination, there is a subconscious 'striving' or 'aim' to have the thoughts emerge into awareness, a motive to have the thoughts heard; that if there was no such subconscious desire, the subconscious thought would remain 'cut off' or 'away by itself' (*i. e.*, dissociated and not in awareness).

In this way the script explains why sometimes with subconscious thoughts, as in automatic writing, auditory hallucinations occur, and sometimes not. *Intenseness* of thinking and *striving* were required, although the two apparently were considered as identical. The script could not explain the phenomena further. The main point is that when the auditory hallucinations occurred, the words or auditory 'images' were first formed subconsciously and then, as the second step, emerged into awareness as the hallucination. It is obvious, however, that there must be another factor to cause the emergence, as auditory hallucinations do not invariably, or even commonly, accompany automatic writing, and they

---

1 In explanation of this, the script wrote that it referred to a past conversation with me and the "high ideals" she "had theretofore set forth" in regard to smoking cigarettes, which she conceived "harmful." The message apparently resulted from a subconscious memory of this conversation and the reflection: "I felt" (so the pencil wrote) "cigarettes were like morphine and I feel uneasy over them. I must not touch them."

occur when no subconscious volition to this end is in evidence. Perhaps intensity or vividness of the 'images' may be sufficient, and the determining factor. Subconscious desire or volition was insisted upon by the script as the factor in the hallucinations in question, which were plainly of the message type. Accordingly, it was arranged, as a test of this claimed ability, to produce an hallucination by subconscious volition, that the subconscious process was to write (without the knowledge of the personal consciousness, *i. e.*, the subject), a sentence the words of which she would will the subject to hear as an hallucination, and the latter, when she heard an internal voice, was to speak aloud the words internally heard. The two processes — writing and internal speaking — would then occur synchronously and could be recorded. The results were as follows:

*Observation* X. The hand wrote:

(*a*) "I am going to play Princess Theres on the stage."[1]

At the same moment while the hand was writing, without seeing the script and without knowledge (as she averred and I believe) of what was written, the subject exclaimed:

"I am to play Princess Theres on the stage." These words she heard as an internal voice.

(*b*)  (The hand wrote): "I smell cigarettes."

As before, the subject heard a voice and exclaimed:

"I smell cigarettes."

In such observations we have written speech and verbal speech synchronously produced. The words of both were identical. The written words were produced by some process not in awareness and without the knowledge of the subject. The subject pronounced the same words at the same

---

1 This was accompanied by a vision which, as described, was identically the same as that experienced in Observation IV — the same court scene, stage setting, marble floor, herself dancing, etc. When asked to explain how it was that the vision portrayed more than was in the auditory hallucination and the script, the hand wrote: "It had been picturing for years [*i e.*, previously constructed] and all that had to be done was to flash it before the conscious thought like a moving picture." This picture was "intensely thought of subconsciously." (Here intensity rather than volition apparently was the determining factor.)

time, claiming that she heard them internally; and her truthfulness is not open to doubt. That there must be a correlation is manifest, and we must conclude that the same process
which produced the script induced the internal voice. As
this was done by prearranged intention, it must have involved volition of some kind. (Of course I had no knowledge of what the words were to be.)

### D. DREAM IMAGERY

The phenomena elicited in the following record and
analysis of a dream, while not belonging strictly to hallucinations, yet are so closely allied and show such similar mechanisms that I throw it in for good measure.

*Observation XI.* Dream of the Paprika Dance.
"I saw a stage with a huge red pepper in the centre of
the stage, and the lights were dim. Then I heard a loud burst
of music and the scene changed and the large pepper opened
in quarters and a large group of women in bright red tights
were dancing around upon the quartered pepper. Upon their
heads were caps of red, fashioned like the top of a red pepper with the stem serving as a tassel. The stage was now
ablaze with light and just as I awakened it grew dim and
the women scampered away."

After the narration of this dream, which impressed the
dreamer because of its 'completeness,' the beauty of the
music, and the vivid memory of its details, the subject
sketched the two dream scenes. These are here reproduced.

The method of automatic writing was then utilized to
obtain subconscious memories as testimony of (*a*), what, if
any, subconscious mental processes had gone on during the
dream and therefore, of course, during sleep, and (*b*), the
meaning of the dream and the motive for its production. In
response to a rigid cross-examination, the following was testified to by the script.

The idea of the dance had been *subconsciously* thought
out the day before as a novelty for a vaudeville sketch. The
motive was to create something "to put before a producer to

gain an avenue of escape from the miserable shopwork."
Every detail of the scenes was thought out, including the
music. There was also a desire to have the "conscious mind
know of this creation." "In the daytime, the conscious mind

Fig. 25. Drawings of dream imagery

was too busy to take in anything from the subconscious mind." But at night when "the mind was passive" this could be done. So when the mind was asleep "I thought and thought very hard all I had created," the subconscious testified. All the details of the previously thought out scenes now "were grouped together into a finished product." "The intensity of my thoughts created the pictures, first in my complex of thoughts," and then these pictures or images entered "the conscious mind" as the dream. In other words, as with hallucinations, *the normal imagery of thought, but now subconscious thought, emerged into consciousness to become the dream imagery.*[1]

The *meaning* of the scene (that became the dream) was "a passionate dance and atmosphere." "The red pepper bespoke that idea, warmth of the dance and its dancers'" [symbolism]. The motive was not a (subconscious) sexual wish on her part nor was the scene a sexual wish-fulfillment. Nor was there any sexual feeling or desire at the time of constructing this vaudeville novelty, or during the dream. (In reply to a question as to this, the hand wrote emphatically, underscoring twice, "NO!")

The purpose was an artistic one — common we must admit to scenario writers, if we judge by the present-day agitation for censorship of the 'movies' — to create something that would draw and specifically "attract the male attendance." "The idea intended to be conveyed to the public by the red pepper and the movements of the dancers was that of passion." This "the red peppers symbolized because they are hot. The idea struck me," the script explained, "as a novel one, without going into details and dissecting it as you are doing. I thought it a spicy, snappy idea. Now what would you think if you went and viewed it at a theatre?" "The women coming out of the pepper symbolized only beauty of form; nothing more."

The idea of the red pepper was suggested by seeing at

1 Apparently this was not the expectation or intention but only a necessary consequence of the intensity of thought. The intention was to create a condition of bodily nervousness which, as known from previous experience, would result in the subject investigating the cause, etc.

home a paprika can and its highly seasoned contents. *This idea flashed into her mind at the time as a good one.*

This interpretation of the motive of the dream, of course, will be objected to by some critics who will insist that there was a deeper unrevealed and unsuspected 'unconscious' motive in the form of a sexual wish. This criticism cannot be disproved but it is very amateurish in that it shows a lack of familiarity with experimental psychology and an inadequate knowledge of the phenomena of the subconscious. It is equivalent to a denial that other 'unconscious' processes than sexual wishes are capable of constructive imagination.

My chief reason, however, for citing this observation is not the interpretation of the dream but rather to show the analogy between one type of dream-imagery and the imagery of hallucinations, and that, if this observation stands as reliable, the mechanism of the two is identical. This is what should be expected as, after all, dream imagery is one type of hallucinatory phenomenon.

### CONCLUSIONS

1. There is a type of visual hallucination in which the imagery has its source in a dissociated mental process of which the subject is not consciously aware. Such a process is, by definition, a subconscious one.

2. The content of this subconscious process contains images identical with the normal imagery of conscious thought.

3. The hallucination is due to the emergence into consciousness of the previously subconscious images. This emergence necessarily results in an hallucination in that the imagery of the latter is not related to the content of the conscious train of thought but is foreign to the latter. This is a necessary consequence of the imagery being normal elements in a separate dissociated train (mental process).

5. There is a type of auditory hallucination which has essentially the same mechanism.

6. As there is a type of hallucination (visual and au-

ditory) occurring in the insanities, which is identical in form, structure and behavior with that produced experimentally in this study, the conclusion is justified that such hallucinations of the insane are due to the same mechanism.

7. The implication follows that when hallucinations of this type occur in the pathological psychoses, they are indications of the activity of a dissociated subconscious process as a factor in the psychosis.

8. The hallucinatory phenomenon carries the further implication that the genesis and the psychopathology of the psychosis are to be found in the forces which have determined the dissociation and motivated the subconscious process.

9. It is not to be assumed that all hallucinations have the mechanism of the type here studied. It is possible that in those occurring in the intoxication psychoses and in certain forms of organic brain disease, particularly where the hallucination is of a simple unelaborated static structure, the imagery is induced by the direct irritation of the cortical or subcortical neurons. It is difficult, however, to exclude the possibility that the intoxicating agent or organic process simply removes inhibition and permits subconscious dissociated processes to function. Nor can we find any analogy with the known effect of irritation of motor and other areas of the brain. Irritation, as observed, produces simple movements and simple sensory phenomena (noises). Still, the possibility of irritating factors becoming the immediate excitants of organized complexes of neurons underlying the hallucinations cannot be excluded. This theory needs, however, to be proved. Even the irritative theory, as opposed to the psychogenic theory, permits of the interpretation that the irritation excites a dissociated subconscious process from which images emerge into consciousness.

10. The psychological problem of differentiating between normal imagery and hallucination disappears in that they are identical, the hallucination being only the normal imagery of a dissociated subconscious process.

11. If the evidence given by subconscious introspection be not accepted, a possible interpretation of the hallu-

cinatory imagery is that the images do not themselves occur primarily as subconscious elements, but by the same mechanism appear in awareness as the conscious correlates of a coactive dissociated physiological process. In other words, a subconscious process is neural, not psychical. On the other hand, such an interpretation does not take into account a large mass of collateral evidence for the psychical nature of processes occurring outside the field of awareness.

12. Hence, far from an hallucination being a regression to an infantile form of thought (Freud), it is an element in highly developed adult thought processes.

13. The mechanism of the imagery of some dreams is the same as that of the hallucinations of the type here studied.

### EDITORIAL NOTE

The following communication which I received from Dr. Prince in connection with my article "The Freudian Doctrine of Lapses and Its Failings" (*American Journal of Psychology*, 1919) is an interesting sidelight which the author affords in the explanation of slips of the pen, a subject the author has, in contradistinction to Freud, not discussed anywhere in his works.

Thank you for your Freudian article which strikes me as excellent and sound. There is another interpretation of lapses which I have never seen considered. The major premise in all discussions is that we have only one train of thought, *i. e.*, that in the focus of attention. That is not true. We may have two or more trains at the same time (one may be in the fringe) or there may be an oscillation from one to another. Now the "slip" may be caused by a second train during a momentary oscillation or even without such — or images in the fringe may cause it. To explain slips you should examine the whole content of consciousness of the moment. There you will find the explanation. I don't refer to the subconscious of Freud.

MORTON PRINCE.

Prince's referring "slips" to the secondary train of thought and Freud's grounding them to displaced elements in the unconscious, which form a complex touched off by some stimulus of the moment, are both phases of dynamic psychology, in contrast to the physiological theory which ascribes all (or nearly all) lapses to factors in the neural mechanism played upon by the environment or temporary conditions of the individual (blockage, assimilation, perseveration, etc.)

— A. A. R.

# CHAPTER XVI

## THE THEORY OF THE COCONSCIOUS[1]

### 1. DIFFERENT MEANINGS OF THE TERM "SUBCONSCIOUS"

ANY discussion of the subconscious requires an agreement as to the class or classes of facts which shall be comprised under that term. We must discuss specific facts and interpretations of these facts, not mere words — psychological terms; otherwise any discussion will be futile.

It will be agreed that the term *subconscious* is commonly used in the loosest and most reprehensible way to define facts of a different order, interpretations of facts, and philosophical theories. It is often extended in its scope to cover facts of such diverse character that there is no obvious or substantial ground for including them in the same class and referring them to the same basic principles. The same is true of the term "The Unconscious" *(das Unbewusste)* for which "subconscious" is often used as a synonym. To arrive at sound conclusions we must think clearly, and to think clearly we must keep clearly, definitely, in mind the facts and their interpretations for which a given verbal symbol stands and not merely the symbol itself.

I have elsewhere pointed out[2] that of the different meanings which have been given to the term subconscious, there are six which are in frequent use. It will be well to restate these meanings here with slight verbal modifications.

1 Abstract of a paper presented at the Sixth International Psychological Congress, Geneva, August 2-7, 1909. Published in "Rapports et Comptes Rendus," Geneva, Librarie Kundig, 1910.

2 See chapter XVII in this volume.

First: subconsciousness is used to describe that portion of our field of consciousness which, at any given moment, is outside the focus of our attention; a region therefore, as it is conceived, of diminished attention. Subconsciousness here, therefore, means the marginal states or fringe of consciousness of any given moment, and the prefix *sub* designates the diminished or partial awareness that we have for these states out in the corner of our mind's eye.

The second meaning involves a theory which is a *psychological interpretation* of certain physiological facts, abnormal, artificial or normal. It is with this meaning, particularly, that the term is used in abnormal psychology. Subconscious ideas are dissociated or split-off ideas; split-off from the main personal consciousness, from the focus of attention — if that term be preferred — in such fashion that the subject is entirely unaware of them, though they are not inert but active. These split-off ideas may be limited to isolated sensations, like the lost tactile sensations of anesthesia; or may be aggregated into groups or systems. In other words, they form a consciousness coexisting with the primary consciousness; and thereby a doubling of consciousness results. They are therefore better called *coconscious* ideas. The split-off consciousness may display extraordinary activity. The primary personal consciousness, as a general rule, is of course the main and larger consciousness; but under exceptional conditions, as in some types of automatic writing, the personal consciousness may be reduced to rudimentary proportions, while the secondary consciousness may rob the former of the greater part of its faculties and become the dominant consciousness.

The third meaning of the term is another interpretation, but of pure *physiological* principles, of the same phenomena which are attributed by the second meaning to the activity of dissociated ideas. Some psychologists believe that phenomena like automatic writing and speech, the so-called subconscious solution of arithmetical problems, hysterical outbursts, etc., can be best explained as pure neural processes, unaccompanied by any mentation whatsoever. These phenomena become, therefore, purely physiological organic processes of the body. The term subconscious thus becomes equivalent to the old theory of Carpenter's "unconscious cerebration."

The fourth meaning of subconscious, while accepting the psychological interpretation of the second meaning, would have the term include: first, the dissociated coconscious ideas embraced under this second definition above stated; and second, besides these, all those past conscious experiences which are either forgotten and cannot be recalled, or which may be recalled as memories, but for the moment are out of mind because in the march of events our thoughts have passed on and we are thinking about something else. All these potential memories, which are only non-psychical physiological residua or dispositions, are by the definition characterized as subconscious. Thus, plainly, the term is made to define two different classes of facts: namely, coconscious dissociated states, which are psychical and active, and those which are physical, inactive, and dormant, *i. e.*, forgotten or out of mind. These latter are more correctly defined as the *unconscious*.

The fifth meaning is an elaboration and extension of the second (split-off ideas), and thus becomes a *theory* which not only gives an elaborate interpretation of the facts of observation, but becomes a broad generalization in that it propounds a principle of both normal and abnormal life. Under it, the dissociated states become synthesized among themselves into a large self-conscious personality, to which the term "self" is given. Subconscious states thus become personified and are spoken of as the "subconscious self," "subliminal self," "hidden self," "secondary self," etc.; and this subconscious self is conceived of as making up a part of every human mind, whether normal or abnormal, and is supposed to play a very large part in our mental life. Thus, every mind is double; not in the moderate sense of two trains of thought going on at the same time, or being engaged with two distinct and separate series of action at the same time, or even in the sense of there being certain limited discrete perceptions of which the personal consciousness is not aware; but in the sense of having two selves which are often given special domains of their own and spoken of as upper and lower, the waking and submerged selves, etc. This theory (aptly called the layman's theory by Münsterberg), therefore, not only extends the principle of dissociated ideas into normal life, making them constant elements of the human mind, but enlarges the subconscious synthesis into something that is self-conscious and which can speak of itself as an "I."

The sixth use of the term (Myers' doctrine) is an expansion of the fifth meaning and involves a metaphysical doctrine transcending all facts which one can possibly observe in others or, by introspection, find in oneself. It is more specifically described as the "subliminal," which is used as a synonym for subconscious. The subconscious ideas, instead of being mental states dissociated from the main personality, now become the main reservoir of consciousness, and the personal consciousness becomes a subordinate stream flowing out of this great storage basin of "subliminal" ideas, as they are called. We have within us a great tank of consciousness, but we are conscious of only a small portion of its contents. In other words, of the sum-total of conscious states within us only a small portion forms the personal consciousness. The personal self becomes even an inferior consciousness, emerging out of a superior subliminal consciousness, sometimes conceived as part of a transcendental world, and this subliminal consciousness is made the source of flights of genius on the one hand, while, on the other, it controls the physical processes of the body.

The subconscious is always a theoretical interpretation of greater or less probability, of certain phenomena, and postulates certain theoretical facts. Let me define, therefore, the theoretical facts which I shall include in the meanings of the term and to which I shall confine myself in this paper. I use the term "subconscious" in the sense in which it is most commonly used in abnormal psychology.

I. First by the subconscious I would mean those *active processes* which may be interpreted in two ways. Under the one interpretation, (a), they mean that psychical events — call them ideas, sensations, perceptions, emotions or what you will — occur under certain conditions in certain individuals without the individual being aware of them. This interpretation involves the principle of "dissociated," "split-off" ideas — a *doubling of consciousness*. "Subconsciousness" here signifies a *psychical* interpretation of certain observed phenomena which I will presently mention more precisely. The phenomena are ascribed to the dissociated ideas of which they are the physical or psychological manifestations. To define this interpretation, I prefer the term, "COCONSCIOUS," as this term avoids the various meanings of the term "subconscious," and precisely characterizes the interpretation.

Under the other interpretation, (b), the processes which we interpret are not coconscious ideas, but physiological brain processes unaccompanied by consciousness of any kind. Accordingly, these may be properly termed "UNCONSCIOUS CEREBRATION."

II. The second set of so-called subconscious facts, or theoretical facts, that I would include in this discussion should, under a precise terminology, be termed "UNCONSCIOUS." These relate to the dynamic physiological *brain dispositions*, which subserve memory (whether conscious or physiological). They are the physiological brain residua or dispositions which are hypothetically conceived as induced in nervous matter by, or in correlation with, conscious experiences, and which are the mode by which experiences are conserved for purposes of reproduction as memory. It is evident that these facts are not conceived of as psychical in a psychological sense, that they are possessed of nothing of the nature of consciousness. For this reason, from my point of view, they may with accuracy be defined as the "unconscious" in the sense that they do not present themselves as elements of consciousness. Properly speaking, they are nothing but conserved brain conditions, until stimulated into activity, and when this occurs, we have the reproduction of the original experience as psychic memory. It is evident that all psychic experiences, when out of mind or forgotten, are or may be conserved as brain dispositions. It is because these dispositions are capable, when stimulated, of being revived in consciousness that, I take it, such conserved experiences are spoken of by some writers as subconscious.

Whether conserved brain residua, representing previous conscious experiences, can function without reproducing a conscious[1] (*i. e.*, psychic) memory of these experiences is a secondary question, but one which needs to be investigated. Its answer is in part involved in the determination of what interpretation shall be given to the class of facts included in the first category of the subconscious. For if these facts do not require that interpretation which insists that they are the manifestation of psychic events of which the individual is not aware, it is evident that purely physiological processes can imitate psychic processes in the manner, complexity and character of their functioning.

The subconscious, then, may be subdivided for the purposes of this discussion as follows:

Subconscious
- *a)* The *coconscious* (active psychical events or active *unconscious cerebration* according to the interpretation).
- *b)* The *unconscious* (passive physiological brain residua).

Thus, the term "subconscious" is used precisely to define the first set of postulated facts by one class of writers, equally precisely to define the second set by another, and

1 Considerable ambiguity is often introduced into a discussion through the double meaning of the term "conscious." Thus, in one sense, it means awareness of a conscious state, a form of self-consciousness; e. g., "I am conscious of that idea." In the other sense, something that in its nature has the attribute of consciousness as distinguished from that which is not psychical; e. g., "a conscious stream," or "a conscious process," or "a conscious experience," meaning an experience in consciousness. It is thus distinguished from a physiological process, which, having no psychical attribute, is spoken of as unconscious, e. g., unconscious cerebration. It would avoid ambiguity to substitute the term "PSYCHIC" to indicate this latter meaning.

definitely for both by a third group; while others use it loosely without apparently having a clear idea of the differences in the nature of the two sets of facts, or that they are dealing with facts of a different order, and still others disregard the two different interpretations (*a* and *b*) to which the first set is open.

The justification of this last statement is to be found, for example, in the current expression of "repressed (*verdrängte*) ideas." It is assumed or implied by some writers that such ideas persist as psychical events. If so, we only lose our awareness of them, and they necessarily become coconscious. But it is evident that ideas, when repressed, may become merely "unconscious" physiological residua, and it is highly probable that the great mass of repressed ideas are conserved in this form. There is no reason to believe that in this respect repressed ideas differ in general from other ideas that have passed out of mind or are "forgotten." Other writers leave it undetermined as to the form in which repressed ideas are conserved and function, and thus a confused mystical psychology has grown up. The importance of having clear precise knowledge on this point becomes obvious when we remember that repressed ideas are events which occur with great frequency in everyone's daily life and that, therefore, if they still continue in existence, as psychic facts, an enormous *coconscious* life may be created in the mental mechanism of all of us; and when we remember further — a fact of great practical importance — that by one school of abnormal psychologists, an overwhelming rôle is ascribed to the functioning of these assumed coconscious ideas in the production of hysteria, psychasthenia and other pathological phenomena. On the other hand, it is evident that, if repressed ideas become, not coconscious, but merely physiological residua, and if these residua can function without becoming psychical, and produce pathological and other phenomena, this theory involves a theory of "unconscious cerebration" of the first magnitude, one that requires verification for acceptance.

## 2. THE CONCONSCIOUS INTERPRETATION

We have, now, first to consider whether subconscious (coconscious) ideas occur at all; that is to say, whether those phenomena referred to in the first category of the subconscious (mentioned above) justify the interpretation that they are the manifestations of "dissociated," "split-off" ideas of which the subject is not aware, *or* whether they can be adequately interpreted as the manifestations of purely physiological processes which take on all the characteristics of a conscious (psychic) intelligence — so-called unconscious cerebration. This is the important question. It cannot be passed by, as upon it depends the solution of many of the important problems of the hour. It must be met if we would understand the mechanism of thought and of many of those peculiar perversions of mental and physiological processes which present themselves as abnormal life. Some would make of this question one merely of epistemology. To my way of thinking, one might as well say that the determining of the explanation of the phenomena of radioactivity, light and matter, by reference to physical emanations, undulations of the ether, and atoms and molecules, respectively, were pure epistemological questions. In each case we seek simply to determine the forces which express themselves as phenomena. If ideas of which we are not aware occur and function as a part of the mental mechanism, they are definite facts, regardless of the points of view.

The objective and psychological phenomena which we seek to interpret are multiform: the most important being those of automatic writing and speech, the conscious memories of hypnotized subjects, post-hypnotic phenomena resulting from suggestion in hypnosis, pathological phenomena like hysterical attacks, psycholeptic attacks, phobias, motor and sensory automatisms of different kinds, normal and abnormal disturbances of will, memory and thought, etc.

It would require a volume to properly present all this evidence in any adequate way, and therefore I can offer here only a general summary of its most important features and limit myself to a brief discussion of the interpretation of the facts.

\* \* \*

Automatic writing has not received the systematic attention from psychologists which the phenomenon deserves. Whether it be interpreted as the expression of physiological or psychological processes, we have in it the manifestation of dissociated functioning which allows us to study the mechanism of the human mind. It is comparable, in definiteness of functioning, with that of the process of digestion or other complex physiological processes. It gives us an insight of the highest importance into certain modes of activity of the mind or nervous system. One would think that psychologists would avail themselves of the opportunities presented by this phenomenon to study systematically the mechanism of the human mind, and yet systematic studies are rare. The theoretical psychologist seems to prefer to limit himself to armchair discussions of the data of introspection or questions of epistemology, rather than to investigate for himself the concrete phenomena which offer themselves as data for the important doctrine of the subconscious. Investigators in medical psychology, too, promulgate their theories regarding the subconscious or unconscious without giving a thought to this and other precise technical methods of testing their theories.

The same may be said of the evidence furnished by the conscious memories of hypnotized subjects.

Now, for the investigation of the theory of dissociated ideas of which the individual is not aware, automatic writing offers a valuable technical method which cannot be disregarded. Not only is the phenomenon found in pathological individuals, but persons who come within the canons of normality can cultivate the art. As everyone who has had experience with this method knows, script thus produced may have all the intellectual characteristics of that which is produced by a self-conscious intelligence. It may exhibit all the psychological qualities to be found in script which is voluntarily produced by a personality with full possession of its faculties — in the manuscript, for example, of this address from which I am now reading. It may exhibit logical reasoning, mathematical calculation, imagery, original compositions in prose and verse, memory, perceptions, volition; its form may be that characteristic of feeling and emotion. It may show evidence of purpose and foresight. In short, such script may have all the appearance of having been produced by an intelligence of a high order, whatever kind of an intelligence that may be. Yet while the hand is writing all this, the individual, although with his senses alert, entirely aware of his environment and perhaps engaged in thought, is entirely unaware of what his hand is writing or that it is writing at all. There are plainly two intelligences in activity; one, that of the principal personality represented by one stream of thought which he describes, and the other, represented by the script. The first we accept as psychological, for the ordinary common sense reasons which make us believe that other people are conscious as well as ourselves.

For the subject himself the evidence is direct. He knows *he* is a conscious intelligence. He can well say, paraphrasing the famous dictum of Descartes, *cogito, ergo sum:* — "Je pense, donc je suis *conscient*." His second automatic intelligence he and we may doubt. The only thing of which he and we are aware is an objective fact which, so far as that fact shows, may be only the manifestation of pure unconscious cerebration. But I must insist that so far as *we* are concerned, we have just as much a right to doubt the first as the second intelligence. If we doubt the second, we must doubt the first. You reply: "The first knows by direct awareness that it is a conscious intelligence and says so." I answer: "The second does too." It is for the person who denies the second intelligence to disprove his statements.

Suppose we apply the reasoning which makes us believe that other people think as well as ourselves. The second intelligence declares in unequivocal terms that it is a conscious intelligence; that it thinks, feels and acts; that it is a stream of thought distinct from that of the first intelligence; that it has distinct memories, perceptions, feelings and volitions of its own; and that it is consciously aware of all this second mental life. Suppose it, too, says, "*Je pense, donc je suis conscient.*" Shall we say that such statements have not the same force and validity as when made by the primary intelligence? That this awareness is an hallucination? Hardly, as hallucination means consciousness and proves that which we would deny. It must mean that cerebration without consciousness can imitate all the faculties of the conscious intelligence of which it is a facsimile and that it can be as beautiful a liar as the most approved diplomat of any country. It has been said that a diplomat uses language to conceal thought. May we say that the automatic hand uses language not to conceal but to imitate thought? But if all this is lying on the part of unconscious brain processes, may we not ask then why physiological processes should exhibit a lying purpose, and how it comes that we find such a unanimity of lying in so many persons, distributed in all countries and manifested in all times? Quantity of evidence here acquires weight.

But even if the psychological interpretation be accepted, it does not necessarily mean that the second intelligence is synchronous, that is, coconscious with the personal consciousness — a doubling of consciousness. An alternative theory may be taken into account. May there not be a rapid alternation of thought between two systems of ideas, so rapid that the momentary halts in the continuity of each are not appreciable? By this hypothesis, system no. 1 would have amnesia for the momentary periods when no. 2 would be in activity, and this amnesia would give the impression of unawareness for ideas which would apparently be coactive but would really be alternating. With no. 2, on the other hand, the mechanism would be somewhat different. This system, it will be borne in mind, remembers the ideas of both systems. Having no amnesia for no. 1, but complete memory of this system as well as its own, it would be under a false impression that it was aware of its own ideas as a synchronous and co-acting system because of an inability to recognize the rapid oscillations and break in the continuity of each system. Such an hypothesis requires, however, that the systems should not alternate as a whole as in multiple personality, but that single elementary ideas in one system should from instant to instant alternate with the ideas of the other. The systems would not fuse but would form separate synthetic chains. Thus two systems of memory would be formed out of elements which chronologically were broken in continuity and unity. The difficulties raised by such an hypothesis are obvious and yet I do not know how it can be disproved. Certainly in many cases there is a halting in the flow of thought of the principal intelligence, indicating that the activity of the secondary intelligence tends to inhibit the untrammelled flow of the former. The subject himself sometimes testifies that he finds it difficult to think clearly and freely while the secondary intelligence is writing. But on the other hand, in other cases, the subject is unable to recognize any such impairment in his own faculties. Perhaps some method may be invented to determine the fact of discontinuity (if such really exists) of the mental stream and the consequent alternation of the elements of the two streams.

Another piece of evidence must be considered. Sometimes the subject, instead of being completely alert, during the writing by the secondary intelligence, exhibits evidence of impaired consciousness; he becomes drowsy, dull, half-awake; he speaks and acts almost mechanically. This impairment increases until intelligence no. 1 — the principal personality — becomes extinguished, and then we have left intelligence no. 2 alone. We have now an alternating intelligence in place of a subconscious intelligence. This alternating intelligence is plainly, by all the canons of common sense, a conscious intelligence. No one doubts it. It is a personality, but this personality declares that it is the same intelligence that did the writing but a moment before, when the subject was alert and half alert. It manifests memories, narrates its previous thoughts, perceptions, feelings, etc., which occurred while intelligence no. 1 was awake and of which no. 1 was not aware. It remembers all its experiences during what it believes was its previous coconscious existence. It *believes* that the two systems of thought previously coexisted, but of course cannot prove the fact. Here we have continuity of experience and continuity of memory. In the final result, we have a conscious intelligence. Can we stop at any point in the transition from complete alertness of the principal personality through the twilight state to complete extinguishment and the appearance of the alternating state and say: "Here intelligence no. 2 was physiological and here it became psychical?"

Still, granting that intelligence no. 2 was continuously psychical from the beginning, the continuity of memory no. 2 does not prove that the latter was previously synchronously co-active and not a system formed of alternating elements. However strongly these facts may weigh as evidence in favor of the psychical interpretation of the phenomenon of automatic writing, they still stand on the same plane as the contents and testimony of the script so far as concerns the principle of a synchronous doubling of consciousness. The alternating, as opposed to the coconscious hypothesis, still remains untouched.

There remains the testimony of hypnotism and the allied states of secondary personalities. It is well-known that in hypnosis the subject claims to remember, does in fact remember, the tactile impressions given to an anesthetic part of the body, claims that these perceptions were actually perceived by the anesthetic subject who, we know, was actually unaware of them. Can we interpret such memories on the alternating hypothesis, the theory that the perceptions were interjected into the consciousness of the principal personality, which straightway becomes amnesic for them? But any tactile stimulation may be made to be continuous. The amnesia would, in that case, have to be continuous and systematized. Such an interpretation seems far-fetched and extremely improbable.

Again, hypnotic states and secondary personalities quite frequently claim to remember a large stream of coconscious life. Miss Beauchamp[1] and B. C. A.[2] may be taken as examples. These subjects in hypnosis, and in their respective states as secondary personalities, claimed to remember with

1  *The Dissociation of a Personality.*
2  See chapters VIII, IX, X and XI in this volume.

a wealth of detail a stream of rich coconscious life. They claimed that this life was made up of ideas, perceptions, feelings, emotions and volitions which were distinct from those of their respective principal personalities; that the latter were unaware of this life (a fact not to be doubted) and that these coconscious systems willed and performed the acts which were manifested as automatisms. "I am conscious that I think and exist during the life of C" (the principal personality) — says the personality B. "I realize that this is not proof for anyone else, but I *know* it." The secondary personality, in the case of Miss Beauchamp, says the same. These hypnotic and secondary memories are corroborated by the independent observation of other experimenters in other cases, in various countries. They are in accord in principle with the findings in large numbers of experiments in automatic writing carried out by numerous observers in every land.

What weight shall be given to these memories? Shall they be interpreted as hallucinations? Considering the fact of unanimity of the testimony, of the freedom from other hallucinations and delusions, of the logical clearness and precision of ideas of these hypnotic states and secondary personalities, of their intelligence in regard to everything that concerns themselves and their environment, these memories would seem to be valid evidence that in such subjects there does exist a dissociated psychical life of which the principal personality is not aware. Is it a coconscious or is it an alternating one? Whether the dissociated system is a large or small one does not concern us here for the moment. We are only concerned with the principle of dissociation of ideas and synchronous activity. All the evidence goes to show that if dissociated ideas of this kind exist, they vary in complexity and systematization in different individuals according to the conditions of normality and abnormality existing.

Again we are confronted here with the question: are these dissociated psychical systems alternating or synchronous in their activity? In individual instances where the dissociated ideas are of an elementary character, limited, we will say, to visual images or tactile perceptions, it might be that an alternating mechanism would fulfill all the requirements of the case. But this explanation is hardly adequate to satisfy the conditions when the dissociated ideas make up large systems equivalent to personalities, as in the cases of Miss Beauchamp and B. C. A. Here there is a stream of dissociated ideas rivalling in complexity and richness that of the principal personality and apparently, at times at least, exhibiting an equal continuity. In such cases, the conception of a rapid oscillation in consciousness between the elementary ideas of the two systems (like the rapid oscillations of the faradic electric current), with rapid flashes of amnesia, on the part of the one personality for the ideas of the other, and an incapacity of the other personality to be aware of these oscillations or breaks in its own continuity of thought — such a conception is possible but it needs to be proved. Two synchronously functioning systems, — one subconscious, i e., coconscious with the other — seem to be the only adequate interpretation.

I pass over in this discussion the data furnished by the multiform phenomena of other pathological conditions, as they in no way differ in principle from those already cited. The evidence furnished by them is cumulative only. Their value consists rather in the data which they furnish for the determination of the various modes in which coconscious ideas may manifest their activity, the varied parts they play in the mechanism of the mind, and the disturbances that they may directly or indirectly provoke.

There are several points I would here insist upon. One is the unreliability of judgment not based on personal familiarity with the phenomena. To properly weigh and judge evidence of this kind, one must have familiarized himself with the phenomena by actual experimental experience. One is no more qualified to judge the psychological evidence without first having fitted himself by personal acquaintance with the phenomena than in the case of the physical and biological sciences. As in bacteriology, for example, one must have personal knowledge of the facts in order to know what weight should be given to each evidential datum.

The second point I would make is the importance for

psychologists of establishing or disproving the principle of dissociated coconscious ideas and of the evidential value of memory for this purpose. If true ideas, psychological in their nature, can and do occur without being so assimilated with the principal consciousness that the latter is aware of them; if, further, they not only function, but can modify, direct and control the contents and course of self-conscious thought, even to the extent of affecting the will, the mechanism of consciousness cannot be understood without a complete knowledge of the content and influence of these subconscious factors. *Introspection fails as a technical method and gives but a poor, inadequate and partial glimpse into the world of consciousness.* Psychologists must face the problem and meet it. It cannot be shirked. If the mechanism of thought includes ideas of which we are *not* aware, of what use is it to deal only with those ideas of which we *are* aware? Or if ideas are largely determined by processes which are unconscious, how can we solve the whole mechanism of ideation without taking into consideration this physiological part? We cannot even determine the relation and association of ideas, by introspection, if we are not aware of them. In the presence of affects, we cannot determine which ideas have an affective tone, if we do not know the whole existing complex; we may not even be able to determine by introspection the presence of affectivity, although it may be present.

If, again, memory, as met with in hypnotic and other dissociated states, can be relied on to reproduce faithfully the conserved subconscious psychological experiences of which the principal personality was never aware, then we have a method of the first importance for exploring this subconscious field.

By this method, in the cases of Miss Beauchamp and B. C. A., for instance, we are able to obtain evidence of the occurrence, in one and the same mind, of subconscious psychological events of very different orders. We find:

First, a large systematized group or stream of ideas synthesized into a personality.

Secondly, isolated discrete psychical events, in the form of visual pictures, which precede and accompany at times the thoughts and actions of the principal consciousness.

Thirdly, somewhat more complicated ideas — thoughts they may be called — which shift in and out of consciousness, belong to self-consciousness at one moment, are subconscious (coconscious) at the next, and *vice versa*. Many such ideas perhaps never enter the full light of the focus of consciousness, but hang about the fringe where they are only faintly recognized; though forming a part of the complex of the moment, the individual is only partly aware of them. After passing into the coconscious, these are apt to be forgotten and, therefore, are not remembered as ever having played any part in conscious thought. In many subjects it is quite common to find that these marginal ideas play an important part in exciting an obsessional or psycholeptic attack. They are the exciting factor. Following the inrush of the obsession, these associated marginal ideas are forgotten but can be resurrected in abstraction or light hypnosis, when a vivid memory of them is recalled. Hence, introspection completely fails to delineate truthfully the psychological events and to give us a full account of the content of consciousness.

I could give many illustrations of this from my casebook. E. F., for example, while travelling in a street car and conversing on an indifferent subject, suddenly has an attack of her obsession. Introspection fails to reveal any psychological or other exciting cause for the attack. In abstraction (hypnosis?) the whole content of consciousness just preceding and during the attack is revived. It is remembered that while conversing, the thought (of which she was dimly aware at the moment) occurred to her that the car in which she was travelling would pass over a certain bridge of which she has a horror. This dread originated in the fact that she once had a severe attack on this bridge. The thought of the bridge, awakened, only in the fringe of consciousness, by association, called forth the attack, but subsequent amnesia wiped out the ability to recall the thought; and so it is with numerous attacks.

A fourth point needs to be insisted upon: namely, the danger of assuming the presence of coconscious ideas on insufficient evidence. When the accounts of some of the classical cases of hysteria are re-examined, it will be found, I believe, that the evidence does not justify the interpretation at first accepted of the functioning of coconscious ideas, but rather points to a dissociation of personality and a rearrangement of complexes conserved in the "unconscious." The reproduction of these physiological complexes as a new system of ideas or personality will, I believe, answer all the requirements of many cases. Then, again, of recent years a school of medical psychology has grown up that would attribute all sorts of psychological and physiological events in normal and abnormal life to repressed *(verdrängte)* ideas. It is true that it is not always made clear whether the subconscious processes are psychical (coconscious) or whether they are physiological ("unconscious cerebration"). This very ambiguity in the interpretation of what is termed the "unconscious" lends an air of mysticism to the doctrine, which makes it all the more difficult to confirm or refute.

In principle, so far as it postulates subconscious ideas, there is nothing new in this doctrine. It is only a widely extended application in normal and abnormal mental life of a theory which was advanced and fortified by experiment twenty-five years ago by Edmund Gurney in England and Janet in France, and during these many years has been repeatedly confirmed and applied by numerous observers, — Binet, Dessoir, James, Sidis, Coriat, myself and others. This theory of dissociated subconscious ideas, indeed, may be credited to Gurney and Janet as a discovery. At least there is strong evidence in this direction. The new converts to the theory remind one in their enthusiasm of the convert to Christianity who, after hearing the story of the Crucifixion, promptly knocked down the first Jew he met on the street. When remonstrated with, the assailant justified himself on the ground that this was the first time he had heard of the historical facts.

# CHAPTER XVII

## THE SUBCONSCIOUS

### (Contribution to a Symposium)[1]

### I

In the last chapter, six different meanings attaching to the term "subconscious," as used now-a-days, were defined. All but the first and fourth of these meanings involve different interpretations of the same observed facts. For our present purpose, three of these only need to be considered, namely, those which Professor Münsterberg has so clearly distinguished and explained as the points of view of the layman, the physician and the theoretical psychologist. As the first of these three accounts hangs upon the validity of the second, we need only take up for discussion the two last. These two offer interpretations of facts which are not in dispute. Let me state over again the problem:

According to the first of these two interpretations (Professor Münsterberg's and my second type), so-called automatic writing and speech, post-hypnotic phenomena like the solution of arithmetical problems and various abnormal phenomena, the origin of all of which the subject is unaware of, are the manifestations of dissociated ideas unknown to the subject and, on this account, called subconscious. Thus, a "doubling" of consciousness results, consisting of the personal self and the subconscious ideas. I prefer myself the term *coconscious* to "subconscious," partly because it expresses the notion of co-activity of a second con-

---

1 The others who took part in this symposium were the late Prof. Münsterberg, the late Prof. Ribot, Prof. Janet, Prof. Jastrow, and Dr. B. Hart.

sciousness, partly because it avoids the ambiguity of the conventional term, due to its many meanings, and, again, because such ideas are not necessarily *sub*conscious at all; that is, there may be a lack of awareness of them. The coconscious ideas may be very elementary and consist only of sensations and perceptions which have been split off from the personal consciousness, as in hysterical anesthesia, or they may consist of recurring memories of past experiences. Under certain conditions, by a process of synthesizing these ideas, assimilated as they become with a greater or less amount of the personal self, which is thereby attenuated in its powers, quite large dissociated systems of subconscious ideas may be formed and give rise to the complicated phenomena for which an interpretation is desired.

According to the opposing hypothesis, all these phenomena are explainable as the manifestations of purely physiological processes unaccompanied by ideas. The apparently intellectual and purposive acts, as well as volition and memory, are performed by brain processes alone to which no consciousness belongs. Such acts differ only in complexity from such other physiological processes which carry on the digestion and other functions of the body, on the one hand, and the spasmodic jerkings and twitchings, seen in chorea, epilepsy and other abnormal affections, on the other. "Unconscious cerebration," Carpenter called it years ago. Which of these two interpretations is correct? Professor Münsterberg is absolutely right in saying "no fact of abnormal experience can by itself prove that a psychological and not a physiological explanation is needed; it is a philosophical problem which must be settled by principle before the explanation of the special facts begins." The principle is the existence of dissociated subconscious ideas. Are there such things?

With the meaning of this problem well before the mind, it becomes manifest that before the fundamental principle of dissociated ideas is definitely established, it is the sheerest waste of time to discuss larger problems, such as the extent of the subconscious symptoms, whether they belong to the normal as well as the abnormal mind, whether they form a "self," a secondary self (third meaning), etc. These and others are important but secondary problems. Above all, is it a wasteful expenditure of intellectual energy to indulge in metaphysical speculations regarding the existence and functions of a mystical subliminal self (Myers), transcending as it does all experience and everything that even a "subconscious self" can experience. The point, then, which we have to determine at the very beginning of the inquiry is this: Do ideas ever occur outside the synthesis of the personal self-consciousness under any conditions, whether of normal or abnormal life, so that the object becomes unaware of these? Or, putting the question in the form in which it is prescribed to the experimenter: Do phenomena which appear to be the manifestations of a subconscious intelligence necessitate the postulation of dissociated ideas, or are these phenomena compatible with the interpretation that they are due to purely physiological processes without psychical correlates?

## II

The only grounds which I have for believing that my fellow-beings have thoughts like myself are that their actions are like my own, exhibit intelligence like my own, and when I ask them they tell me they have consciousness, which, as described, is like my own. Now, when I observe the so-called automatic actions, I find that they are of a similar character, and when I ask of whatever it is that performs these actions whether it is conscious or not, the written or spoken reply is that it is, and that consciously it feels, thinks and wills the actions, etc. The evidence being the same in the one case as in the other, the presumption is that the automatic intelligence is as conscious as the personal intelligence. The alternative interpretation is not that a physiological process is lying, because lying implies ideas, but that in some way it is able to re-arrange itself and react to another person's ideas, expressed through spoken language, exactly in the same way as a conscious intelligence lies!

The phenomena which occur in the neatest and most precise form and which, from the fact that they can be induced, modified and examined at will, are best adapted for experimental study, are so-called automatic writing and speech. We will, therefore, take these for examination and see if they ever require the interpretation of secondary intelligence of a psychical nature.

When automatic writing is produced in its more highly developed form, the subject with absolutely unclouded mind, with all his senses about him is able to orient, think, and reason as if nothing unusual is occurring. He may watch with unconcerned curiosity the vagaries of the writing pencil. In other words, he is in possession of his normal waking intelligence. Meanwhile his hand automatically produces perhaps long discourses of diverse content. But he is entirely unaware of what his hand is writing and his first knowledge of its content comes after reading the manuscript. We then have intelligence no. 1 together with manifestations which may or may not be interpreted as having been produced by a conscious intelligence no. 2. But writing of this sort is not always produced with intelligence no. 1 as alert as this.

On the contrary, often, and perhaps most frequently, the writer falls into a drowsy condition in which he imperfectly orients his surroundings, and if he is reading aloud, according to the common method of conducting the experiment, he is only dimly conscious of what he is reading. This extinguishing of consciousness in intelligence no. 1 may go further, and he may not hear when spoken to or feel when touched. He reads on mechanically, and without being conscious of what he is reading. In other words, he has become deaf and tactually anesthetic and blind to everything but the printed characters on the page before him, and for even these he is mind-blind. In this state then, there is practically extinguishment of all sense perceptions and intellectual thought, and finally the impairment of consciousness may be carried so far that he actually goes to sleep. Ask intelligence no. 2 what has become of no. 1, and the answer may be, "He has gone to sleep."[1]

---

1 This answer was given by a subject observed while this paper was being prepared.

In other words, intelligence no. 1 has disappeared, but intelligence no. 2 continues.

Now, to interpret the automatic writing produced, when this great impairment of intelligence no. 1 has taken place, as subconscious phenomena and due to subconscious intelligence, whether physiological or psychological, is to overlook the facts as presented. These are not phenomena of a subconscious intelligence but of an alternating intelligence or personality. The complete suppression of intelligence no. 1 has left but one intelligence, that which had been under other conditions intelligence no. 2. Unless the physiological interpretation be maintained, the writing has ceased to be automatic, in the sense in which the term was originally used, and has become what, for the time being, is the primary intelligence, although a different one from that which was originally awake. I say "different" because if we examine the content of the writing, we may find it is made up of memories of past experiences which were entirely forgotten by the original intelligence no. 1, and gives evidence of a personality differing in volitions, sentiments, moods and points of view — in short, of a character differing in a large degree from that of the waking intelligence. The writing may be an original composition involving thought and reason comparable to that exhibited by a normal mind. Such compositions are of great interest because of the light they throw upon the origin and development of secondary personalities, but with that we have nothing to do here. At present, the only interest we have in such compositions is the evidence which they offer for the interpretation of such a personality; that is to say, whether its intelligence is the exhibition of physiological or psychological processes. To arrive at a satisfactory interpretation, we must study the behavior of the personality to its environment. If we speak to it, it answers intelligently in writing, though intelligence no. 1 fails to respond. If we prick the hand, we obtain a similar response from intelligence no. 2 and lack of response from no. 1, and the same holds of the other senses. It exhibits spontaneity of thought and its faculties are curtailed in the motor sphere alone, in which it retains power only to move the muscles of the arm and hand;[1] but even here in the motor sphere, its functions are not necessarily so limited, for it may break out into speech and may exhibit various sporadic movements. It has lost only a general co-ordinating control over the whole body. In the motor sphere, therefore, its loss is not so great as that which has befallen intelligence no. 1. In fact, we have here a condition very similar to that of some persons in deep hypnosis. The main point is that now we have to do with an alternating intelligence, not a co-intelligence. Is it an alternating *consciousness?*

The next thing to note is that in passing from automatic writing, which is performed while intelligence no. 1 is completely alert, to writing which is performed while this intelligence is completely or nearly extinguished, we pass through insensible gradations from one condition to the other and *we must infer that the intelligence must be the same in kind, physiological or psychological, which produced the writing in the one case as in the other.* If the alternating intelligence in the latter case is psychological, the subconscious intelligence in the former must be the same, for there is no place where we can stop and conclude — here the physiological ends and the psychological begins.

In the alternating intelligence producing automatic writing we have an alternating personality. We have here substantially the same condition that is observed, first, in some hypnotic states; second, in trance states; third, "fugues," spontaneous somnambulism and post-epileptic states; fourth, a state not very different from normal sleep with dreams, forgotten on waking; and fifth, certain states of deep abstraction. In none of these has there ever been raised the doubt as to the conscious character of the intelligence. All are "alternating" states and some are alternating personalities. In the first group, suggestions requiring conscious intelligence are comprehended, remembered and acted upon; in the second, writing and speech are manifested which can

---

1 By this is not meant that it has the same degree of knowledge and capacity for intellectual thought possessed by the original personality, no. 1, but only that it has all the different *kinds* of intelligence possessed by a normal person.

only be interpreted as the product of thought; in the third and fourth, the thoughts and dreams can afterwards be regained by certain technical devices; and in the last, the conscious processes are remembered.

\*      \*      \*

Let us go further with our experiment and take a case exhibiting automatic writing where intelligence no. 1 remains unimpaired. We hypnotize such a subject. When asked what sort of intelligence it was that did the writing, he replies that he remembers perfectly the thoughts, sensations and the feelings which made up the consciousness of which intelligence no. 1 was not aware and that this consciousness did the writing. Still, it may be maintained that this in itself is not proof, but that the hypothesis is permissible that these memories are of the nature of hallucinations, and that in hypnosis what were previously physiological processes now have become re-awakened and have given rise in the hypnotic synthesis to psychical memories. We shall then have to go further and seek for additional evidence.

Automatic writers may be divided into two classes; namely, those who, at the moment of writing, are entirely unaware of what the hand is writing; and those in whom, at the moment of writing, ideas, corresponding to written words, surge apparently from nowhere, without logical associative relation into the mind. Mrs. H., for example, is an excellent automatic writer of the second class. At the moment when the pencil writes, ideas, which it is about to express, arise at once in her consciousness so that she is herself in doubt as to whether she writes the sentence volitionally, or whether it is written automatically altogether apart from her will. Sometimes while writing, the ideas come so rapidly that, unable to express them with sufficient celerity with the pencil, she bursts out into voluble speech. To test her doubt, she is given a pencil and told not to write. Then she finds herself without control of her hand; and, in fact, the pencil writes the more fluently the greater the effort she makes to inhibit it. In the midst of a suitable sentence I hold her hand and restrain the writing, and ask her to complete the sentence by word of mouth, which of course she could do if it were her own intelligence, that is no. 1, that was doing the writing; but she cannot complete the ideas, showing that she does not really know what the hand was about to write.

Again, Mrs. B. in hypnosis is told to write automatically when awake, "three times six are eighteen; four times five are twenty." After being awakened she is given something to read aloud; while reading, the hand begins to write as previously directed, but she stops reading with the explanation that she cannot continue because the "absurd sums three times six are eighteen, four times five are twenty," keep coming into her head. She cannot understand why she should think of such things.

Now, are we to conclude that the mechanism of automatic writing in the second class of writers differs from that performed by the first class, and that when the writer is *aware* of the automatic thoughts the writing is done by psychical processes, and that when he is *not aware* of any automatic thoughts it is done by physiological processes? In every other respect, in content of writing and in behavior of the automatic personality to the environment, we find the phenomena are the same. Accordingly it does not seem to me that such an interpretation is justifiable. As I view this question of the subconscious, far too much weight is given to the point of awareness or non-awareness of our conscious processes. As a matter of fact, we find entirely identical phenomena, that is identical in every respect but one — that of awareness — but the one essential and fundamental quality in them is automaticity or independence of the personal consciousness. Doubling and independence of the personal consciousness are, therefore, the test of the subconscious, rather than awareness.

In the content of automatic writing we find evidence which it is difficult to reconcile with a physiological interpretation. This was briefly touched upon before. When studied, the writing, we find, does not consist of words, phrases and paragraphs which might be mere repetitions of memories, whether physiological or psychical, of previous experiences, but occasionally comprises elaborate original compositions. Sometimes, in Mrs. Verrall's writings it consisted of original Latin or Greek compositions;[1] sometimes, as in those who are inclined to a spiritistic interpretation, of fanciful fairy-like fabrications. Sometimes, it exhibits mathematical reasoning, as evidenced by the solution of arithmetical problems. Sometimes, it consists of ingeniously fabricated explanations in answer to questions. Sometimes, it gives indication of a personal character with varying moods and temperaments. Feeling and emotion, whether of anger, hatred or malice, kindness or amiability, are often manifested. If such a document were presented as testamentary evidence in the ordinary course of human affairs, it would seem as if the burden of proof would lie with him who would insist upon interpreting it as without psychological meaning and as only the expression of a physiological activity of the nervous system, without thought.

\* \* \*

Suggestions in hypnosis may result in post-hypnotic phenomena, which are manifestations of an intelligence that cannot possibly be explained by physiological *habits* in many instances, as it exhibits logical re-adjustment of ideas of a high order; for instance, complex arithmetical calculations. The subject is only aware of the final result, being entirely ignorant of the process by which it was arrived at. Later, this process can be recalled in hypnosis as conscious memories. To assume that such a calculation can be performed by a brain process, not accompanied by thought, would seem to require the abandonment of the doctrine of the correlation of mind and brain. In some cases, as with automatic writing, the subject becomes aware of the automatic conscious process though ignorant of its origin. Are we to assume here again that the processes giving rise to the same

1 *Proceedings Soc. Psychical Research*, 1906, vol. XX, part 53.

manifestations, under the same conditions, differ in kind according as whether a subject is aware of them or not — in the former case being psychical, in the latter physiological?

The great variety of phenomena occurring in abnormal conditions are often explained by the patient in hypnosis as the manifestations of ideas (perceptions, hallucinations, memories, emotions, etc.), which are remembered as such, though unknown to the personal consciousness. (This evidence does not differ in kind from that derived from automatic writing.)

After all, as I conceive the matter, the one great difficulty in the mind of those who are unable to accept the psychological interpretation of subconscious phenomena lies in understanding how we can have states of consciousness of which we are unaware. Consciousness is represented as a functioning unity, and it is difficult to accept the notion that all states of consciousness are not so synthesized as to form part of that great system which we dub self-conscious. Thus, consciousness is confused with *self*-consciousness. This has come about because the only immediate experience which anyone has of conscious states is with that which belongs to his self, which is only another way of saying, with that of which he is aware. All conscious states, so far as we experience them, belong to, take part in, or help make up a self, — in fact, the expression, "We experience" implies a self that experiences. It is difficult, therefore, to conceive of a conscious state that is not a *part* of a self-conscious self. It seems queer, then, to think of a state of consciousness, a sensation, a perception, or an idea floating off — so to speak — by its lonesome self and not attached to anything that can be called a self. It is difficult to conceive of anything worthy of being called a sensation or perception, excepting so far as there is a self to experience it; and yet it really is a naïve conception to imagine that we are self-conscious of each and every mental state that is aroused in correlation with our nervous system. Such a conception is very much akin to the naïve notion of scientific materialism which assumes, for the practical purposes of experimentation or other reasons, that phenomenal matter really exists as such. Consciousness, whether in an elementary or complex form, must be correlated with an innumerable number of different physiological brain syntheses. If this is not so, the whole structure of the psychophysiology of the mind and brain falls. We have every reason to assume that some sort of a psychical state occurs when any one of these association-groups is excited to activity. (At any given moment the great mass of them is inhibited.) There is strong reason to believe that though ordinarily there is a harmony in the functioning of these association-groups, yet at times there is considerable disharmony; and there is clinical evidence for believing that there may be some independence of activity, especially under pathological conditions (hallucinations, obsessions, etc.), of different brain syntheses.

Without being obliged to determine what brain synthesis belongs to the personal consciousness at any given moment, we are entitled to ask why we must necessarily be aware of all the conscious states which may belong to each and every brain association-group. Is this not a naive assumption? If it is true that dissociated brain systems can function (as in other parts of the nervous system), and if it is true that they have psychical equivalents, then, our being self-conscious of any given state of consciousness must depend, it would seem, upon whether the brain process, correlated with it, is synthesized in a particular way with the larger system of brain processes correlated at a given moment with the self-conscious personality. And in so far as a brain process can occur detached from the main system of brain processes, so far can consciousness occur without self-consciousness. Unfortunately, we have scarcely a glimmer of knowledge as to the nature of the synthesis, and therefore as to the conditions which determine whether we shall be aware of any conscious state or not. Nor is self-consciousness a necessary element of consciousness. The naïve character of the notion that we must be self-conscious of our consciousness is shown by introspective analysis in intense mental concentration or absent-mindedness. Here is no awareness of self, only a succession of ideas which adjust and re-adjust themselves. It is not until afterwards, on "returning to one's self," that these ideas, through memory, become a part of our self-conscious personality.

It will be noticed that an essential element in the conception of the subconscious, as generally held by students of abnormal phenomena, is the absence of awareness of the personal consciousness for the dissociated ideas. A consideration of the facts in their entirety does not permit of so limited a view from which I am compelled to dissent. Theoretically, a conception so narrow prevents our obtaining a broad view of allied psychological phenomena, obscures our perception of the broad principles underlying them and hinders a correlation of closely related conditions. Dissociation, with activity, independent of the main focus of consciousness, does not necessarily imply or require absence of awareness on the part of the latter, and practically, as we have seen in discussing the phenomena of automatic writing, under the same conditions, a subject is sometimes aware of the dissociated ideas which are actively manifesting themselves, and sometimes not.

The same is true of post-hypnotic and abnormal phenomena. Indeed, even when there is absence of awareness on the part of the personal consciousness, the dissociated coconsciousness may, *per contra,* be aware of the content of the former. For this reason, if for no other, coconsciousness is the preferable term.

The one fundamental principle and criterion of the subconscious is dissociation and co-activity (automatism). When we get rid of this notion of awareness as an essential element, we are able to grasp the relation between the subconsciousness of hysterics and the disaggregation of personality in the psychasthenic. The obsessions, the impulsions, the fears, in short, the imperative ideas are as much disaggregated from the personal consciousness in the psychasthenic as they are in the hysteric, except for the amount of synthesis that gives awareness. Indeed, the hysteric may have a certain amount of awareness, or awareness for some and not for other ideas. The only difference then between an ordinary obsession and a "subconscious" obsession, as commonly viewed, is that the subject is aware of the one and not of the other.

Undoubtedly, the condition of awareness alters considerably the resulting psychical content, as it brings into play various co-operative and modifying and, in some measure, adjusting ideas. This is not the place to enter into a consideration of the difference between psychasthenia and hysteria, or their likeness; but I believe it important to insist that lack of awareness is not an essential factor in the development of the subconscious, and furthermore, that an appreciation of this fact will enable us to better correlate the different varieties of coconscious activities not only in various diseased conditions but with phenomena of normal mental life.

Those who maintain the physiological interpretation seem to me to involve themselves in difficulties far greater than any offered by the psychological interpretation. It is a fundamental interpretation of psycho-physiology that all thought is correlated with physiological activities. Whatever doctrine we adopt, whether that of parallelism or psychophysical identification, every psychical process is correlated with a physiological process and *vice versa*. We cannot conceive of a psychical activity without a corresponding physiological one. How then can we conceive of a physiological process of a complexity and character capable of exhibiting itself as a spontaneous volitional intelligence without corresponding correlated ideas? Surely this needs explanation quite as much as does a lack of awareness of conscious processes. Yet, with a certain modification of our conception of the meaning of the physical, it is possible to reconcile both interpretations.

As a panpsychist I find no difficulty in accepting both a physiological and a psychical interpretation. For those who accept panpsychism, there is no distinction to be made between conscious processes and brain processes of a certain order, except as point of view. They become identified with each other. The psychical is the *reality* of the physical. I cannot conceive of brain processes except as objective phenomena of conscious processes, and I cannot conceive of consciousness except as the reality of "inner life" of brain changes. Hence we may indifferently describe automatic actions as manifestations of physiological activities, if we keep to one set of terms, or of psychical activities if we mix the term. But in doing this let us not straddle and deceive ourselves as to our real position. In thinking in physiological terms we must not confuse ourselves, and, by adopting a terminology, imagine that those physical brain factors are without psychical equivalents. To hold to a purely physiological explanation, without realizing that the psychical is essentially involved here, is to postulate consciousness as a pure epiphenomenon, something that we can shift in and out at our pleasure, when we have brain action, and juggle with as a conjurer juggles with his coins, — "now you see them and now you don't."

It may be that the final explanation of many conscious processes, if we would avoid the entanglement of metaphysics, must be in physiological terms, because it must deal with that which belongs to experience. We can experience physiological "after-effects," and by a simple inference go back to the functioning physiological forerunner, and thus perhaps explain memory, but, as Professor Münsterberg so well points out, it is difficult to see how a comprehensible explanation of memory can be found in "mental dispositions," and on grounds, as I would state them, that such dispositions being out of consciousness, we have no experience of them and can have no conception of what they are like. They become nothing more than metaphysical concepts. For myself, I cannot even think of a "mental disposition," meaning, for instance, a name or mental picture that is not, at the moment, a state of consciousness, whether subconscious or belonging to my self-conscious synthesis. However this may be, I not only say with Professor Münsterberg that "the physiological cerebration is well able to produce the "intellectual result," but would add "it *must* be able to do so." The only question is whether it is accompanied by, belongs to, or *is* another aspect of ideas. This can, to my mind, only be settled by logical inferences from the observed phenomena, and I have endeavored in what has gone before to marshal the evidence, so far as it exists today, in substantiation of this interpretation.

# CHAPTER XVIII

## The Mechanism and Interpretation of Dreams[1]

1. Methods of Investigation.
2. The Material of Dreams.
3. The Motive and Meaning of the Dream.
4. The Subconscious Process and Mechanism.
5. The Persistence of Dream Symbolism as Hysterical Stigmata.

### 1. METHODS OF INVESTIGATION

The problem of the mechanism and interpretation of dreams involves the question whether dreams are to be regarded as mere fantastic imagery without law and order, or whether all the phenomena of the mind can be reduced to an orderly and intelligible sequence of events, as is the case in the physical universe. If the latter be true, then every mental event ought to be related to and determined by an antecedent event. The difficulty of the problem lies principally in the complexity of psychical phenomena; the difficulty of ascertaining all the antecedent events or data; the necessity of depending upon memory to reproduce past mental experiences which contain the data, and the possible fallacies of the final logical interpretation.

Notwithstanding these difficulties, recent investigations under the leadership of Freud have shown that often dreams

---

1 Presented in abstract at the Annual Meeting of the American Psychological Association in Boston, Dec. 29, 30, 31, 1909, and at the first Annual Meeting of the American Psychopathological Association in Washington, May 2, 1910. The whole paper was read at the meeting of the New York Psychological Association, Jan. 4, 1910.

can be so related to antecedent psychical events that they can be recognized as no haphazard vagaries, but as orderly determined phenomena capable of logical interpretation. If a dream is causally related to antecedent mental experiences, the solution of the problem of dreams requires the determination of: (1) those experiences which were the motivating cause of the dream, and those which were the source of the psychological material out of which the content of the dream was fabricated; (2) the nature and mechanism of the motivating process which determined the dream, both as to its occurrence and form; (3) the logical meaning, if any, of the dream itself. All this will become clearer as we go on.

It goes without saying that the data upon which we must depend for the determination of the mechanism and interpretation of dreams are, as I have said, the memories of subjects upon whom the observations are made. These memories are: first, those of the dream itself; and second, those of psychologically related past experiences of the subject. This second class of experiences includes: (a) a large number of past acts of the individual, of his perceptions of, and his relations to, the environment; of his waking thoughts of which he was at one time aware, and of the feelings (affects) which accompanied any given mental process; (b) mental experiences of which the individual was not conscious or was only dimly aware (subconscious thoughts); (c) sensory stimuli which may have been physiologically active during the sleeping state. The problem is to determine the relation, if any, between the dream and such antecedent mental and physiological experiences and co-active sensory stimuli.

It is evident that to determine such relations, it is necessary to obtain all the data, i. e., memories of all the events that enter into the relation. At the outset we are met with certain difficulties in obtaining the data.

In the first place, as to the dream factor, it is well-known that some people do not remember their dreams at all; others remember them very imperfectly. A very serious doubt arises whether any one remembers his dreams completely from end to end in all their details. (I am of course speaking of memories in the normal waking state.) Even when apparently remembered, the dream often very quickly vanishes, in its details at least, before we can tell it. That the dream was fuller than the memory of it reveals, can often be shown by restoring the memory by artificial devices (abstraction, hypnotism, automatic writing, crystal vision, etc.). We then obtain records of a dream much fuller than we supposed had occurred. This is in agreement with what we know of allied phenomena. A dream may be defined clinically as an hallucinatory delirium occurring in a state of dissociation. A dreamer is awake or, if you prefer, partially awake, in the sense that although not aware of his surroundings he has a stream of consciousness, but his consciousness is a delirium. We find the same inability to remember other kinds of deliria and the mental content of other dissociated states after return to the normal condition — such states, I mean, as abstraction, pre-sleeping states, hysterical crises, trances, psycholeptic attacks, hypnosis, suggested post-hypnotic phenomena, etc.[1] The amnesia for a dream conforms, therefore, to these other types of amnesia. In other words, in the normal waking state there is a difficulty in synthesizing the dissociated mental processes with those of the waking personality. Besides, we never can recall the sensory stimulations that are active during sleep.

In the second place, we all know that at any given moment (*e. g.*, that of the observation) it is not always, and probably never, possible to synthesize, *i. e.*, recall all our past experiences, and, therefore, we may not be able to recall those related to the dream. Our waking memories, therefore, are inadequate to solve the problem of dreams.

To overcome the difficulty of remembering our past mental and physiological experiences, an ingenious method has been devised by Freud of putting the individual under investigation in a state of concentration of attention or abstraction. Then, under certain precautions, which include

---

1 The forgetting of a dream is only a particular example of amnesia for dissociated states. Any sufficient explanation of this amnesia must not disregard other types, but must be in harmony with them. The failure of Freud's explanation of this amnesia to satisfy other types is, to my mind, a fatal objection to his theory.

the surrender of all critical reflection, there flood into the mind memories of past experiences which cannot be recalled under ordinary conditions. When the attention is concentrated on a particular element of the dream, the memories are those which have associative relations to this element; then the problem is to interpret the causal relation. For example, the dream may be interpreted as the imaginary fulfillment of a wish contained in the revived memories (Freud).

This method I made use of in these observations, but it was extended to conditions which gave far richer results than were obtained in the normal waking state. That is to say, in addition to the latter method it was combined with certain hypnotic procedures to be presently described. Furthermore, it was supplemented by another method of voluntary recollection in combination with these same procedures. The reason for the employment of these methods was to obtain all possible data which had associative relations to the dreams. Every one knows, or ought to know, that if, instead of stimulating memory in the normal state, we make use of various artificial states, we can recover memories in each state which are not recovered in the others. In other words, all possible memories cannot be recovered in any given state whether waking or artificial. Of our large storehouse of conserved experiences, some can be stimulated into memory in one state and others in another. Suppose a person remembers, apparently, a dream and relates it. If we put that person into a given state of hypnosis, we may find that his memory of the dream is fuller, and he recalls a larger number of details; we put him into another state and he recalls a still larger number; in the third state, a larger number still, perhaps so many that there are no lacunae that can be detected. Or, we may use automatic writing and crystal visions with the same results. Likewise, and more important for the results, in each of these different states memories of past experiences may be recovered which cannot possibly be recovered in the others or in the waking state, even though in the last the technique of abstraction and concentration of the attention is employed.

Furthermore, besides these memories of simply forgotten mental experiences, experiments have shown that in some one or other of these artificial states memories can be obtained of (a) ideas which were once merely coconscious in the mind, *i. e.*, of which the subject was never aware; (b) of ideas which streamed through the mind, like a phantasmagoria, just before going to sleep, twixt sleeping and waking; (c) of ideas occurring during intense absent-mindedness, and (d) of ideas, including repressed ideas, which have been so completely forgotten as to be beyond voluntary recall. Many of these memories cannot be recovered in the waking state, whatever technique be employed. A study of these memories, thus recovered, will show a close and inferentially causal relation between many of them and the subsequent dream.

We must conclude from such observations that memories induced in the waking state alone cannot be relied upon to give us all the required data to determine the mechanism, material, and interpretation of dreams, and therefore that the method in many cases at least is inadequate.

For the purpose of the observations which were the basis of this study, a subject was made use of who could be dissociated into several hypnotic states, *a*, *b*, *c.*, etc. In each state, the memories differed from those of the others as well as from those of the waking personality C. The combination of all the memories, therefore, gives us a much larger mass of data than could be obtained from the subject in her normal waking condition. When awake, the subject could not remember her dreams at all, or only very imperfectly. They could be recovered only in hypnosis in the state *b*. Then the subject remembered them in remarkable detail and with great vividness.

For the purpose of the analysis of the dreams, several or all of the following states were made use of, according to the requirements of the analysis:

1. The normal personality C.
2. Hypnotic state *c*.
3. Hypnotic state *b*.

4. Dissociated group Alpha (by automatic writing).

The methods employed were the following two:

First, such memories as could be recalled by ordinary volitional effort of the subject in each of the first four states were obtained. By this method, in the secondary states, particularly state 3 and 4, *memories were recovered which failed to develop by the second method (Freud's) in the normal waking condition C.*

Secondly, the subject in each of the first three states was put into the condition of abstraction,[1] and thus free associated memories were obtained by the Freudian method. (This was not applicable to the fourth state in which automatic writing was required.) By this method, associative memories would arise that failed to develop by the "voluntary" method whether in the hypnotic or waking state.

By each method, the memories obtained in the first, second, third, and (so far as applicable) fourth states, noticeably differed according to the state in which they were invoked. For instance, the memories in abstraction, associated with *climbing a hill,* in one dream were, in:

normal state C: of a childhood experience of climbing a hill; of climbing a hill in the White Mountains during married life, etc.

hypnosis *c;* of scene in an observatory; of scene in the country; on top of a hill, etc.

hypnosis *b;* of the dream itself and associated thoughts; of the thoughts of the pre-sleeping state, etc.

---

1 I use this term for lack of a better one. It is a passive state in which the attention is concentrated on the content of the inflowing ideas with surrender of critical reflection upon these ideas. I believe that this state of mind is identical, as it was intended to be, with that used by Freud, although I do not think he defines it as "abstraction." I see no reason to differentiate it from abstraction. I have been in the habit for many years of using this form of abstraction (but without surrender of critical reflection) for the purpose of resurrecting dissociated memories. When a person is in hypnosis, the abstraction reaches a higher degree than when he is waking, easily passes into a "hypnoid" condition, and memories are resurrected which are not obtained in the waking state. It was particularly when this method was applied to *b* that the rich flow of memories of events directly preceding the dream occurred. Without abstraction, *b* could recall, for example, but few of the pre-sleeping thoughts.

It should be kept in mind that the waking personality C and the hypnotic state *c* do not remember the dreams, or only imperfectly, and therefore the accounts of the dream were always obtained from the hypnotic state *b*, who remembers them with extraordinary precision and vividness, and in great detail.

After the dream was recovered in state *b*, it was read to the subject when awake and alert (C). This sufficed, of course, to give the information to the hypnotic state *c*. (Alpha had its own source of knowledge.) Then the associative memories were recovered in each state by the two methods described. As will be seen, the absence of true memory in the waking state for the dream did not prevent the inflow of associations in any state.

I will not take the time to consider the possible objections to these methods. Obviously the chief are that few persons can be hypnotized to the extent of this subject, that the observations were confined to a single person, and the possible fabrication by hypnotized subjects. The last objection ought to be confined to those who have a theoretical or only specialized rather than wide knowledge of hypnotism. The first would equally apply to the study of a rare disease. It only limits the material for investigation. The second has its advantages as well as its disadvantages, for it enables us by the examination of a large number of dreams in the same person to search the whole field of the unconscious, and, by comparison of all the dreams, to discover certain persistent conserved ideas which run through and influence the psychical life of the individual.

Owing to the extremely private nature of dreams, I am obviously limited in my selection for publication, and therefore am unable to make use of some which psychologically are the most instructive and thoroughgoing illustrations of the conclusions arrived at. The six instances I shall make use of, however, will, I believe, prove to be sufficient. The fifth dream is selected from some in which the abstraction method was not used. It is instructive in showing the value of the hypnotic voluntary memories alone, without the use of the Freudian method, in revealing the underlying motivating idea and meaning of the dream. In other dreams also I have found these memories sufficient.

## 2. THE MATERIAL OF DREAMS

A study of the analyses of quite a large number of dreams shows that a very large part of the psychological material out of which the dreams were fashioned was furnished by the previous waking thoughts of the dreamer, particularly those disconnected ideas which coursed in a passive, fleeting way through the mind *just before going to sleep.* This pre-sleeping state has certain marked characteristics which distinguish it from the alert state of waking life. We cannot go into this here, although it is worthy of study in itself. It resembles, if it is not identical with, what Sidis calls the hypnoidal state. Suffice it to say that ideas course through the mind in what appears to be a disconnected fashion, although probably determined by associations. Memories of the preceding day and of past thoughts which express the interests, desires, fears, anxieties of the psychological life and mental attitudes of the individual float in a stream through the mind like a phantasmagoria. The state passes gradually and insidiously into sleep. One marked peculiarity of this state is that amnesia for its thoughts rapidly develops. Not only after waking is there little or no memory for the content of the pre-sleeping consciousness, but if the subject arouses himself, or is aroused while in this state, he cannot recall his previous thoughts or does so imperfectly and with difficulty. At least I find that this is the case with myself. After waking, few persons can recall their pre-sleeping thoughts. Yet it was found that in certain hypnotic and dissociated states of the person whose dreams form the subject of this study, these thoughts were recalled with precision and vividness, although she could not recall them in the normal waking state C.

Now, I have found in studying these dreams that whenever pains were taken to recover the pre-sleeping thoughts *certain elements of these pre-sleeping ideas invariably appeared in the content of the dream.* These ideas furnished the material out of which, to a large extent, the dream was formed. Just as a patchwork quilt is put together out of pieces of cloth cut from various garments, so the dream was fashioned from the elements of other thoughts, and particularly the pre-sleeping thoughts. The dream[1] was a mosaic of which the pieces were culled from various preceding mental experiences. Let us take, for example, the following actual dream:

## Dream 1

"C was somewhere and saw an old woman who appeared to be a *Jewess*. She was holding a *bottle* and a *glass*, and seemed to be drinking *whiskey*; then this woman changed into her own *mother* who had the bottle and glass, and appeared likewise to be drinking whiskey; then the door opened and her *father* appeared. He had on her *husband's dressing gown*, and he was holding *two sticks of wood* in his hand."

Recovering by the above-described technical methods the associated memories of the preceding day, particularly those of the pre-sleeping period, we find that on the morning of that day she had visited, as a social worker, a *Jewess*. Later, after retiring to bed, feeling somewhat faint, she took a teaspoonful of *whiskey*. This reminded her of her *mother*, who had been an invalid, and who used to have beside her bed a *glass* of *whiskey* and water, which she sometimes took at night. This made her think how one day her (the subject's) husband had sent her mother a *bottle of whiskey*, and how on that day she had telephoned to her mother, but the mother did not come to the 'phone. Instead, her sister came, and she, C, asked why the mother did not come, and said, "Is mamma tipsy?" The sister did not at once understand, and she had to repeat this question several times, and they laughed heartily over it. It became a family joke. Then it also came to her mind that she had rung the bell for some *wood* in the course of the day, but that it had not been sent up to her apartment; she felt annoyed in consequence. Then again her

1 Freud's manifest dream-content.

thoughts were occupied with going abroad (as she was planning to do) and she thought of her *father*, how she used to read with him a good deal about going abroad, and how he used to tell her about Europe, and she also thought that her son would need a new *dressing gown* before they started abroad because his was too thick and heavy; and that reminded her of her *husband's dressing gown* which had been a nuisance in travelling because it was so hard to pack on account of being too heavy.

All these thoughts floated through her mind just before going to sleep. Analyzing the memories of them and of the day, it is clear that we have practically all of the elements out of which the dream-scene was constructed: *Jewess, mother, father, bottle of whiskey, glass, husband's dressing gown, two sticks of wood*. A Jewess had occupied several hours of her time and a great deal of thought during the day.

In other dreams, again before falling asleep, the subject thinks of the riding school and a beautiful horse there, and a beautiful horse appears in the dream; that she "is like a child crying for the moon," and in the dream she rides to the moon on the horse; that it is so much trouble to get clothes made by the dressmaker that she would rather go without clothes, and in a dream she is naked; she thinks of the beautifully decorated ballroom in the Pension Building at Washington, at the time of the President's inauguration, and in her dream she is in a beautiful ballroom; of going to the theatre, for which she has a longing, and in her dream she is there; and so on *ad infinitum*. Of course, the various elements of a given dream originally appeared respectively in the content of separate and different thoughts, out of which they are selected for the dream. None, or few, of these presleeping thoughts can be recalled when awake, but only in hypnosis.

Another source of these dream elements, although I found it a less rich one, was, as Freud has pointed out as a result of his studies, the thoughts of the preceding day, and even earlier mental experiences. The same may be said of *ideas and feelings which have dominated the psychological life of the subject through a long period of time*. These latter exhibited certain special peculiarities in the dream. They were apt to be *symbolized;* and for the purpose, made use of the material from the two sources just mentioned. Thus, her previous and dominating idea of life was, and is, that it is a hard and difficult path to follow, and this idea appears in the dreams as a particular "steep, rocky path" she is climbing; the subject feels herself singularly alone in life (which is the case) and in her dreams she is always alone, either really by herself, or, if in a crowd or accompanied by others, she feels she is not of them, but off by herself and socially isolated; she has been in the habit of looking upon life as wild, and she is threatened by wild men in her dream, and so on. She has certain apprehensions and anxieties, and these symbolize themselves in one way or another. She has a horror of cats, a regular phobia, and cats constantly appear in her dreams, when the horror of the future looms before her.

An analysis of a large number of dreams reveals the fact that these persisting and dominating ideas, those that may be said to be the symbolized personal expression of her own individuality or of her relations to her environment, or of her view of life run through a large number of dreams, often in a stereotyped form.

This stereotyping of dream imagery is well worth noting in studying both the material and its symbolization in the dream content. It would escape notice if a large number of dreams were not recorded in the same individual. Thus, the rocky path, always the same identical path, occurs over and over again. Likewise, climbing a mountain, near the top of which she meets an old man, and the sudden appearance or changing of dream objects into cats. Stones, gloomy forests, dark places, etc., also recur frequently.

It would seem that certain dream experiences (images), having been strongly conserved as a complex in the unconscious as brain residua or neurograms, were stimulated from time to time, after the manner of an obsession, by the recurring dominating ideas which they symbolize to the subject in the waking state as well as in the dream state.

Still another class of mental experiences which I was able to recognize as the source of the material for dreams was certain subconscious ideas of which the subject *had not been aware;* at least this was the case if we are to trust the memories of the hypnotic state. These ideas had their origin in the personal consciousness, but having been repressed, had gone into the subconscious (or unconscious) and there flowered.

The influence of somatic stimuli (sensory impressions) in determining the content, though it could be recognized, was of minor importance.

Thus far I have spoken only of the material out of which the dreams were constructed.

### 3. THE MOTIVE AND MEANING OF THE DREAM

Equally important for the understanding of dreams is the motive of the dream and its meaning as a whole. Though the dream may be a patchwork made out of the material furnished by the thoughts of the immediate or remote past, the question may still be put whether the dream has a meaning, or is it a senseless thing, as until recently has been supposed?

Did, for example, the picture of the Jewess holding a bottle and glass, and appearing to be drinking, and did the father, in an old dressing gown, carrying two sticks of wood, have any logical meaning, or were they simply hallucinatory fantasies?

It was a brilliant stroke of genius that led Freud to the discovery that dreams are not the meaningless vagaries that they were previously supposed to be, but when interpreted through the method of psychoanalysis may be found to have a logical and intelligible meaning. This meaning, however, is generally hidden in a mass of symbolism which can only be unravelled by a searching investigation into the previous mental experiences of the dreamer. Such an investigation requires, as I have already pointed out, the resurrection of all the associated memories pertaining to the elements of the dream.

When this is done, the conclusion is forced upon us, I believe, that even the most fantastic dream may express some intelligent idea, though that idea may be hidden in symbolism. My own observations confirm those of Freud, so far as to show that running through each dream there is an intelligent *motive;* so that the dream can be interpreted as expressing some idea or ideas which the dreamer previously has entertained. At least, all the dreams I have subjected to analysis justify this interpretation. I would say here, however, that I do not wish to be understood as extending this conclusion beyond the dreams actually studied (some dozen or more in number), although I have no doubt that this conclusion will be found to be a fairly general truth. I am all the more cautious in generalizations because I am unable to confirm that of Freud, that every dream can be interpreted as "the imaginary fulfillment of a wish," which is the motive of the dream.

That sometimes a dream can be recognized as the fulfillment of a wish there can be no question, but that every dream, or that the majority of dreams are such, I have been unable to verify, even after subjecting the individual to the most exhaustive analysis. On the contrary, I find, if my interpretations are correct, that some dreams are rather the expression of the nonfulfillment of a wish; some seem to be that of the fulfillment of a fear or anxiety; some, that of an emotional attitude of mind, etc. Nor, when the dream has been the expression of a wish, has it been, excepting occasionally, of a "repressed wish" (Freud), but rather an avowed and justified wish. It also seems to me that the methods Freud employs are inadequate to justify the wide generalizations that he draws. Nor do his data in my opinion justify his interpretation of the mechanism of the process underlying the dream, and, in many cases, of its meaning. Such interpretations, when all is said and done, are after all questions of inductive logic.

Let me speak more specifically about the dream-motive and meaning. I can illustrate the principle better, perhaps, by an analogy.

In the Corcoran Gallery, at Washington, there is a picture by Watts, known as Love and Life, a photograph of which I have before me. In this picture, Life is represented by a female figure treading a narrow rocky path along the edge of a precipice. This figure, limp and weary, is guided by another figure personifying Love, who holds her by the hand and helps her over the obstacles of the path, and prevents her from falling over the precipice. In this picture the artist symbolizes, in a pictorial representation with paint and canvas, a conception of life which we may suppose has been constructed out of the ideas and feelings which had been previously deposited by the general mental experiences of his life. The picture is, therefore, a condensed visual representation of ideas which had been previously elaborated and experienced in his consciousness.

Now, let us suppose that instead of representing these ideas on canvas, the artist had dreamed such a visual representation of these ideas. On waking from the dream, he might or he might not have remembered his antecedent ideas of which the dream was a visual representation. Suppose he had not remembered them. He would have been at a loss to understand the meaning of his dream. If the dream had consisted of only the narrow rocky path on the edge of a precipice, without the figure of Love, or without both figures, in all probability he would not have recognized any relation between the image and his previous ideas of life.

Now, if by any technical method we could recall to his mind his previous ideas, and if he should find among them the idea of a narrow rocky path associated with an idea of the path of life which we must all tread, if he recalled that he had once conceived of life as that sort of a path, it is clear that he would recognize the dream as the symbolized expression of his previous conception of life. He would justly conclude that this conception in some way underlay and directly determined the dream, just as in fact such ideas had expressed themselves symbolically through the intention of the artist in the painted picture.

In an analogous way, if we take any given dream from actual life and subject it to analysis by resurrecting all the memories associated with the elements of the dream, we find as a fact amongst the memories certain ones which can be so closely related to the dream that the latter can be interpreted logically as a condensed symbolical expression of them.

In principle, there would seem to be very little difference whether the ideas of the individual are expressed symbolically in the visual images of paint and canvas, or in the visual images of a dream.

Now let us take the actual dream of the *Jewess, who appeared to be drinking, and the father entering the room with two sticks of wood,* and see if any similar meaning can be found in the dream dressed up in the symbols of the dream contents. When I first examined this dream, I thought it was only a simple fantasy, and was surprised, when all the associative memories connected with each component element of the dream were obtained, to find that it might well be the symbolic representation of very specific previous thoughts of the dreamer. Instead of being a simple affair, it was found to be very complicated.

I can only give an abstract of the analysis, as a full report of all the data would cover about seventeen pages of typewritten manuscript. The reproduction of these memories in the different states by the methods I have already described occupied several hours.

In the first place, the dream may be divided into two parts or scenes: first, that of the drinking scene; and secondly, that beginning with the door opening, and the father bringing two sticks of wood.

We have seen how the elements of the content of this dream were found almost entirely in the material of the pre-sleeping thoughts.

As to the first scene, a rich collection of memories was obtained. It appeared that on the previous morning, the subject had walked with a *poor Jewess* through the slums, and had passed by some men who had been *drinking*. This led her at the time to think of the lives of these poor people, of the *temptations* to which they were exposed; of how little we know of this side of life and of its *temptations*. She wondered what the effect of such surroundings, particularly of seeing people *drinking*, would have upon the child of the Jewess. She wondered if such people ought to be condemned if they yielded to drink and other temptations. She thought that she herself would not blame such people if they yielded, and that we ought not to *condemn* them. Then, in the psychological analysis, came memories of her mother, whose character she admired, and *who never condemned* anyone. She remembered how her mother, who was an invalid, always had a glass of *whiskey* and water on her table at night, and how the family used to joke her about it. Then came memories again of her husband sending *bottles of whiskey* to her mother; of the latter *drinking* it at night; of the men whom she had seen *drinking*.

These, very briefly, were the experiences, accompanied by strong feeling-tones, which were called up as associative memories of this scene of the dream. With these in mind, it is not difficult to construct a logical though symbolic meaning of it. In the dream, *a* Jewess (not *the* Jewess, but a type) is in the act of drinking whiskey — in other words, the poor, whom the Jewess represents, yield to the temptation which the dreamer had thought of with considerable intensity of feeling during the day. The dreamer's own judgment, after considerable cogitation, had been that such people were not to be condemned. Was she right? The dream answers the question, for the Jewess changes in the dream to her mother, for whose judgment she had the utmost respect. Her mother now drinks the whiskey as she had actually done in life, a logical justification (in view of her mother's fine character and liberal opinion) of her own belief, which was somewhat intensely expressed in her thoughts of that morning, a belief in not condemning poor people who yield to such temptations. *The dream-scene is, therefore, the symbolical representation and justification of her own belief[1] and answers the doubts and scruples that beset her mind.*

The second scene is capable of a simpler interpretation. It is the fulfillment of a wish. It will be remembered that the subject wished for and had ordered some *firewood* to be sent to her room on that day. In the pre-sleeping state, the recollection of the fact and the feeling of annoyance had recurred. In the dream, the *wish had been fulfilled*; the wood

---

1 The symbolic expression of beliefs and symbolic answers to doubts and scruples is quite common in another type of symbolism, *viz.*, visions. Religious and political history is replete with examples.

was brought, but it was her *father* who brought it — two sticks, this number, probably, because she was in the habit of putting two sticks on the fire, and the number, therefore, that she wished at the moment. Very possibly her father, in her husband's dressing gown, can be interpreted as an example of what Freud calls "condensation," the fusion in this case of two persons in one with a common trait. Both her father and her husband would naturally have been inclined to gratify her wishes. On the principle of "condensation," the former, dressed in the latter's dressing gown, would symbolize this trait. Her father and this dressing gown had their origin, as we have seen, in the pre-sleeping states, and were made use of by the dream process to do what the hotel management had neglected, and thus to perform the imaginary fulfillment of a wish.

I might have done better perhaps to have taken for my first example in interpretation a dream of which the meaning was more obvious and perhaps more convincing, but I selected the foregoing dream chiefly because it aptly illustrates the source of its material in the pre-sleeping thoughts.

Before going further, I would like to make clear that I am only concerned at this point with the interpretation or the meaning of the dreams. The mechanism is another matter. By mechanism I mean the nature and working of the process by which the motivating process or thoughts, whether a wish or a fear, or a belief previously entertained, fashions the dream out of the material furnished by other previous thoughts, and expresses itself. This mechanism, as we shall see, is a complicated process and deals with the continuance of these motivating thoughts as a subconscious process of some kind, whether coconscious or unconscious. We shall also see that this mechanism introduces us to the mechanism of some of the phenomena of hysteria and of other psychoneuroses.

How far the conclusions arrived at in this study, both as to interpretation of the motive and the mechanism, are in agreement and disagreement with those of Freud and his school will appear as we proceed.

## Dream 2

"A hill — she was toiling up the hill; could hardly get up; had the sensation of someone or something following her. She said, '*I must not show that I am frightened, or this thing will catch me.*' Then she came where it was lighter, and she could see two clouds or *shadows*, one black and one red, and she said, 'My God, it is *A and B!* If I don't have help I am lost.' (She meant that she would change again.[1]) She began to call 'Dr. Prince! Dr. Prince!' and you were there and you laughed, and said, 'Well, you will have to fight the damned thing yourself.' Then she woke up *paralyzed* with fright."

### PSYCHOLOGICAL ANALYSIS

*Pre-sleeping thoughts obtained through memories of state b in abstraction.*

She thought during the days before the dream that life was a *struggle*; that she must not be *afraid of changing*; she was so depressed she was afraid she would change to A. She thought she *must not be afraid*; then she thought it was hard work not to be afraid. She thought perhaps it would be a good thing if she could be B, and be happy. She felt so discouraged she did not care much; she thought it was such a *struggle*, that if Dr. P. *did not help her*, she would surely change; she thought he was tired of her; she did not blame him; she thought the future looked as black as night; these were not thoughts; I mean these disconnected ideas just floated through her mind — she was almost asleep.

*Associative memories of the dream.* For purposes of consideration, I will give merely a *résumé* of the results in the different states of the analysis of this and the other dreams obtained, noting only those memories which seem to have a relation to the dream.

*Climbing or toiling up a hill* has been a frequently recurring episode in distressing dreams. The recurrence of this

---

1 *i. e.*, relapse into dissociated personalities.

particular action suggests that it expresses a strongly organized idea. The act of toiling up a hill, in her mind, symbolizes a mental attitude towards life, which is so deeply rooted that it has almost the characteristic of an insistent idea. Symbolically, it is her conception of life. She looks upon life, on its moral side, as a constant *struggle and toil* against difficulties; she seems to be always battling with the practical problems of life. The idea that "life was a struggle," was indeed one of the pre-sleeping thoughts. The same idea is symbolized in other dreams by the rocky path she is treading. In everyday life it comes out in many directions. This idea is temperamental rather than justified by the actual conditions of life (aside from illness), but nevertheless exists. She belongs to the type that "takes life hard."

The *material* out of which this symbolism was fabricated may have been furnished by any one of a number of actual experiences in climbing hills, the memories of which recurred in association with the dream in one or other of the states examined. The most probable material was an experience, of which the memory is conserved, of climbing a hill in the White Mountains several years previously. The climbing of this hill had very strong emotional accompaniments, and therefore was likely to present mental recurrences. These accompaniments, moreover, had a very intimate relation to those experiences of her past life, which are the basis of her present attitude of mind towards life, and constituted a veritable trauma.

The *sensation that somebody or something was following* her may be traced to two ideas which had been frequently in her mind in the past and during the days immediately preceding the dream. It may be, therefore, interpreted as having a double meaning. To appreciate this, it will be necessary to explain the situation. During the previous few weeks she had been going through a period of stress and strain resulting in much mental perturbation. She had thought that if she did not get hold of herself, she might disintegrate again into the personalities A and B. She had been free from disintegration, that is, completely synthesized into the normal personality for a year and a-half. The idea of disintegrating, therefore, became a terror to her, and loomed up as a dreadful possibility. This possibility even expressed itself as a feeling at times that A and B were near or about. In the earlier days, when disintegration actually occurred, she often had the thought that *she must not be afraid of relapsing,* because fear might bring about a relapse, the dreaded result; and during the days preceding the dream, this thought, *viz.,* that she must not be afraid of changing, often occupied her thoughts. We have seen that this idea was prominent in the pre-sleeping thoughts. She had a dread that fear would tend to disintegrate her; hence in the dream she said to herself, "I must not show that I am frightened or this thing will catch me": "This thing," interpreted through these associated memories would mean the disintegration into A and B.

The second set of associative memories, which may be symbolized by this part of the dream, is the fear of suicide, which is linked with illness. That is to say, in her mind the consequences of relapsing again into a condition of double personality are so terrifying that suicide has seemed to her preferable. It had loomed up as a possible solution of her psychological difficulties, and, at times, as a choice of evils, seemed preferable. At times she had felt "rather haunted" by the idea of suicide, and had "a subconscious feeling that suicide is dogging my steps." It may be fairly said then that disintegration and suicide are so closely linked that both were symbolized by the dream-feeling "of someone or something following her."

Next in the dream she sees two clouds or *shadows,* one was black and one red. Now, as a fact in everyday life, whenever she thinks of herself as A or B, she actually visualizes a cloud which she seems to see over her left shoulder. When she thinks of A the cloud is *black,* and when of B it is *red.* This is an example of colored thinking. Here then the waking fear, persisting in the dream, becomes fulfilled in the form of a symbol which has been furnished by the material of everyday life.

Recognizing the clouds she exclaims, "My God, it is A and B." This expression is a recurrent memory and almost the identical words she has used to herself in times past, when she came to herself and found that she had been through a change to one or the other of the two personalities, "My God!" she would exclaim, "I have lost time again," meaning, "I have changed to A or B."

In the dream she continues, "If I don't have help I am lost" (the dream-thought being "change" again), and she began to call for her physician. Shortly before the dream, she had actually "thought that if she didn't have help she would be lost," and in the pre-sleeping state "that if Dr. P. did not help her, she would surely change." During the period of alternations of personality she had often appealed to me as her physician for help, so that this dream expression was a simple recurrence of many previous experiences.

In the dream I appear and laugh, and answer her appeal by saying, "Well, you will have to fight the damned thing yourself." This again is in substance a recurring experience. I had often, as her associated memories showed, laughingly brushed aside her fears and treated them lightly. I had often lectured her upon the undesirability of her depending upon me to pull her out of her difficulties, and exhorted her to *depend* more upon herself and to use her willpower, etc. I must confess that I am responsible for the profanity, which is also a recurrent experience, and is a memory based on fact.

Interpreting the dream as a whole, with the record of the associated memories before me, by no effort of the imagination can I see in this dream any fulfillment of a wish. I cannot find that the principles of distortion or of substitution, or any other form of interpretation, help us in that respect. It would plainly seem to be in part the symbolical representation of a fear which had been oppressing her during the preceding days of stress and storm, and in part the imaginary *fulfillment of another fear* — that of being refused help.

## Dream 3

"She was in the rocky path of Watts's,[1] barefooted; stones hurt her feet, few clothes, cold, could hardly climb that path; she saw you there, and she called you to help her, and you said, 'I cannot help you, you must help yourself.' She said, 'I can't, I can't.' 'Well, you have got to. Let me see if I cannot hammer it into your head.' You picked up a stone and hammered her head, and with every blow you said 'I can't be bothered, I can't be bothered.' And every blow sent a weight down into her heart so she felt heavy-hearted. She woke and saw you pounding with a stone; you looked cross."

The subject went on to recall that she had telephoned me in the morning asking for medical assistance. "You said, over the telephone, 'I cannot possibly come to see you to-day. I have engagements all the day and into the evening. I will send Dr. W., you must not depend on me. I didn't say anything about it, but it played ducks and drakes with me the other night,'" etc. [that is when I neglected other engagements to make her a professional visit because of an attack of migraine from which she was suffering].

### PSYCHOLOGICAL ANALYSIS

The rocky path of Watts's picture (Love and Life) like "toiling up a hill" symbolizes, as we shall see more fully in another dream, her dominating idea of life, and, as in the picture, she was treading the stones barefooted; that she had few clothes and was cold may be well referred to the somatic peripheral impressions actually experienced at the time, for "she was cold while she was asleep."

The call for "help" has a special significance. It referred to "help" through certain psychological work which she had undertaken, and for which she depended upon my assistance. As work it meant more than the word would

1 See "Dream 5."

seem to signify because to her mind it meant the solution of one of the problems of her present life, and, as she thought, from a medical point of view, her salvation. She had been told that she must have an interest in life, and for this purpose had taken up this psychological work; she had been fitting herself for it for some time by study; now it seemed to her this new object of life had been taken from her. For it so happened that after patiently waiting for about a month for certain promised material which was necessary, I had been unable to see her, even when she required medical assistance, and had advised her, both in response to the telephone message and on several other occasions, that it would be desirable, on account of the great demand on my time, that she should put herself in the hands of another physician. This, womanlike, she interpreted as being equivalent to losing the opportunity to carry on her work. The work meant her salvation, and yet she must get along alone without it; she had tried hard to forget herself, to lose herself in this work; to solve the problem of life in this way, and now the work was to be taken from her; she felt that it was unjust. These thoughts, the analysis showed, went through her mind over and over again. They were accompanied by an intense emotional tone of despair, because the loss had a double significance — that of inability to pursue her chosen calling, and that of the one thing which she thought would save her from relapsing into her former state of disintegration. All this emotion was accentuated by the fact that she was ill at the time from an attack of migraine, and also in a state of nervous instability.

So she makes the same appeal in her dreams, as she toils up the hill of life, and I tell her that she must help herself, just as over the telephone I had said, "You must not depend upon me." Although I had referred to medical assistance — in *her* mind, through the interpretation which she actually put upon it, my refusal was identified with the loss of work. She felt that going to another physician would be of no use, as it was this particular work alone that would help. Hence, in the dream she said, "I can't help myself." "Well, you have got to," I replied; "let me see if I can't *hammer* it into your head. I can't be bothered." Here we have a recurrence of a pre-sleeping thought which was, "I must not *bother* him; I should think I would get that *into my head* after a while"; and then, "If my heart was not like a *stone* I should weep"; and so in her dream I hammer it into her head with a stone.

Furthermore, after telephoning, she thought, "I must not *bother* him, he can't be *bothered*"; and this thought, with the others, recurred again and again in her mind. It was one of the pre-sleeping thoughts, and so it recurs again in the dream, for I said, "I can't be bothered, I can't be bothered." With every blow of the stone she became heavy-hearted, *as she did when the same thoughts dominated her mind while awake.*

All this that I have described comes out clearly in the memories which were reproduced in the psychological analysis, particularly those of the pre-sleeping state.

The interpretation of the dream as a whole, thus, would seem to be clear. It is simply a dramatic symbolic reproduction of a dominating idea of life, of her wish and of her disappointment. It is an imaginary fulfillment, not of a wish, but of a loss or disappointment; indeed it might be regarded as the non-fulfillment of a wish.

### Dream 4

Shortly before the last dream, the subject "dreamt that she was in a great *ballroom* where everything was very *beautiful*. She was walking about and a man came up to her and asked, 'Where is your escort?' She replied, '*I am alone.*' He then said, 'You cannot stay here, we do not want any *lone women.*'

"In the next scene she was in a *theatre* and was going to sit down, when someone came and said the same thing to her: 'You can't stay here, we do not want any *lone women here.*' Then she was in ever so many places, but wherever she went, she had to leave because she was *alone;* they would not let her stay. Then she was in the street; there was a great crowd, and she saw her husband quite a little way ahead, and struggled to get to him through the crowd. When she got quite near, she saw . . . [what we may interpret as a symbolical representation of happiness]. Then sickness and nausea came over her, and she thought there was no place for her there either."

## PSYCHOLOGICAL ANALYSIS

It appears that the subject had been confined to her apartment during the whole of the preceding week, completely *alone*. The day preceding the dream, she had missed her son (W.) very much, and had thought of him all day, and had wished that some one would come in to see her. She had thought of going to Washington to visit some friends, and had also thought of her visit there last year, and of the *ballroom* in the Pension Building where the presidential inaugural ball was held; of how *beautifully* it was decorated; she thought also of having gone to the *Opéra Comique* with her son, and that if he were only with her now they could go out together. She had felt *very lonely*.

This feeling of *loneliness* has often been a more or less persisting and dominating idea. While circumstances have forced upon her a life of seclusion, she nevertheless feels that she cannot be *alone* any more; that she must have some society; must have her friends and not continue in her lonely way of living. At times, in the intensity of this feeling, she walks the rooms feeling the situation keenly. She says to herself that she "*cannot be alone.*" This feeling results in depression and sadness. The subject has often remarked when remonstrated with that people did not want *a lone woman,*" meaning an odd woman, at social entertainments, and in consequence she has often refused invitations.

On the day following the dream, she kept thinking that there was no place for her in the world, though she did not remember the dream. This symbolized idea of loneliness has been found to run through a number of dreams. At one time she is walking alone along a steep rocky road, parallel to another smooth pleasant road filled with her friends, but where she is not allowed. At another time, she is at an open-air concert in a garden where are many people, but she sits alone.

In the light of these facts, the action of this dream was nothing but the symbolical expression of a recurrent thought to which strong feeling was attached. As to the scene of the beautiful ballroom of the first part of the dream, the *material* is plainly to be found in the thoughts of the preceding day. Invited to visit Washington, she recalled the room in the Pension Building, as she saw it last March, decorated for the inaugural ball; she had thought it very beautiful.

The scene in the theatre owes its origin to the fact that her mind had dwelt upon having gone to the theatre with her son in Paris about six weeks previously. She now thought that if her son were with her they could go out together in the evening; that being alone she could not enjoy such pleasure.[1]

In the street scene *"she struggled to get through the crowd."* From the associated memories, this would seem to symbolize a thought which has run a great deal through her mental life; namely, that of her "great struggle to overcome herself, and get somewhere," that is, achieve the end in view. In the dream she struggles, but only to be disappointed in the end. The analysis of this scene would carry us too far into the intimacy of her life to justify our entering upon it.

## INTERPRETATION

The analysis of this dream substantially carries with it its interpretation. The material out of which it is constituted, the ballroom, theatre, feeling of loneliness, the undesirability of "lone women," all this may be found in the thoughts of the preceding day, and in a certain insistent idea which has run through her mental life. The dream is plainly a symbolical representation of this insistent idea or belief, and, in its action, the dream became a fulfillment of the truth of this belief in that she found no place for herself in the social world.

1 I had frequently advised her going to the theatre in the evening, and she always replied that she could not go alone.

## Dream 5

"She dreamed that she was in a dark gloomy rocky place, and she was walking with difficulty, as she always does in her dream, over this rocky path, and all at once the place was filled with cats. They were everywhere, under her feet and hanging on the trees, which were full of them. She turned in terror to go back, and there in her path was a frightful creature like a wild man of the woods. His hair was hanging down his face and neck; he had a sort of skin over him for covering; his legs and arms were bare and he had a club. A wild figure. Behind him were hundreds of men like him — the whole place was filled with them, so that in front were cats and behind were wild men. This man said to her that she would have to go forward through those cats, and that if she made a sound they would all come down on her and smother her, but if she went through them without making a sound she would never again feel any regret about the past . . . (mentioning certain specific matters. which included two particular systems of ideas known as the Y and Z complexes, all of which had troubled her. These will be referred to later). She realized that she must choose between death from the wild men and the journey over the cats, so she started forward.

Now, in her dream of course she had to step on the cats (the subject here shivers and shudders) and the horror of knowing that they would come on her if she screamed caused her to make such an effort to keep still that the muscles of her throat contracted in her dream (they actually did contract, I could feel them). She waded through the cats without making a sound, and then she saw her mother and tried to speak to her. She reached out her hands and tried to say, 'O mamma!' but she could not speak, and then she woke up feeling nauseated, frightened, and fatigued, and wet with perspiration. Later, after waking, when she tried to speak, she could only whisper."[1]

1 The subject woke with complete aphonia, which persisted until relieved by appropriate suggestion. This persistence of the physical effect of dream ideas is of considerable interest and was observed following other dreams.

An analysis by the abstraction method was not made of this dream, nor was there any attempt to recover the pre-sleeping thoughts. Therefore the source of the material out of which the pattern of the dream was formed was not wholly determined. The solution is accordingly not complete, so far as concerns the appearance of certain elements (*e. g.,* the mother) out of which the dream was constructed. The data for the interpretation were obtained from ordinary memories of the subject in the various states (C, *c* and *b*). In these, it is easy to find the motivating thoughts of which the dream is a symbolical representation. The analysis, therefore, as I have explained at the beginning, is additionally instructive in showing, as was the case in other dreams, the value of the ordinary hypnotic memories.

## PSYCHOLOGICAL ANALYSIS

When narrating the dream, in hypnosis, the subject said that the "rocky path of the dream was a literal *visual reproduction of the path*[1] *in Watts's picture called Love and Life.*" This picture she had recently seen during a visit to Washington where it hangs in the Corcoran Gallery. "Neither of the figures appears in the dream, but the figure of Life symbolizes a part of her feelings and attitude of mind towards life in general." The picture, as a whole, "minus the figure of Love, symbolizes what she has dreamed many times."

After waking from hypnosis, when catechized about the picture, the subject said that "the painting by Watts had interested her greatly, more than any picture she had ever seen, because the figure of Life in its look of helplessness typified her attitude of mind in some respects; if the figure of Love was removed, the picture would represent the way life seems to her — cold, bare, bleak, and lonely."

*In the dream, while under the emotional influence of this "dark, gloomy, rocky place," a swarm of cats suddenly loom before her.* It appears that this subject has a horror of cats, a regular phobia, which can be traced to a fright which

---

1 In addition to the path there were trees in the dream picture.

she received from a cat when she was five or six years of age. All her life she has dreamed of cats, and they constantly appear in her nightmares. It would seem to be a firmly organized and conserved complex which recurs over and over again in such dissociated states. As cats are associated with the affects of terror and apprehension, so anything that awakens this emotion in dreams is liable to excite the pictures of cats as symbols of fear. A study of a number of dreams in which cats appear seems to justify the interpretation that *apprehension,* aroused by the difficulties which beset the path of life and block the future, is symbolized, in a stereotyped way, by the awakening of this terror-producing cat complex. For example, she dreams she is in a rowboat, under distressing circumstances; she endeavors to row the boat which contains her husband, who is ill; a storm comes up, the boat is tossed about, the waves dash over it, and its passage is blocked, so to speak, by the storm. Then she is overwhelmed with terror as the waves turn to cats, which almost smother her and swamp the boat. Again, in another dream she is in a dark, gloomy, narrow canyon through which she makes her way, under the guidance of a friendly hand, out towards the light and open. Then the stones on the steep hillsides roll down upon her, and change to cats which block her way, and she awakes in terror. All these dreams are logically and consistently interpreted as the symbolic expression of certain struggles, anxieties, and apprehensions for the present and future.

Returning to our dream, *she turns to go back, and is confronted by the "wild men."*

For several years, because of trouble and illness, the subject has been in the habit of thinking of life as being "wild." She has often used the word "wild" to express this feeling. This idea would seem to be symbolized in the dream by the wild men, much as an artist might so express it in a picture.

As these men threaten her with death if she goes *back,* she has felt strongly that she must not think of the *past;* that it is madness, it tears her to pieces; that no matter how distressing the present may be, no matter how impossible the future may seem, she must look forward, not back; she thinks of life with a feeling of terror as in her dream she thinks of the cats in front.

In the dream she is promised that if she goes forward without making a *sound* (*i. e.*, speaking or complaining) she will never again have any regrets about the past, *i. e.*, suffer because of what she has lost and other troubles. This is almost a literal reiteration of what she has said to herself.

She often thinks that she must keep things to herself; that she must be *uncomplaining* and self-reliant; she tells herself this every day, and she sometimes thinks that if she can only bear her troubles bravely, surely, by-and-by, she will be happier.

## INTERPRETATION

In the analysis of these memories we have substantially the solution of the dream. In it are to be found nearly all the elements which go to make up the motive, and most of the material. The rocky path and the wild men, preventing her from going back under penalty of death, would seem to be a symbolic representation of her idea of life; that the past is full of trouble, that she must not think of it, that it is madness to do so. But as she thinks of the future with equal terror, and of cats with terror, so her imperative journey forward over the cats would symbolize her feeling towards the future, which seems impossible. The reward promised in her dream, if she will go forward without making a sound, is typified by her real feeling, that if she will be brave without complaining she will sometime in the future be rewarded by happiness, symbolized by her mother.

Although this dream can be interpreted in part as the fulfillment of a wish, for she passed over the terrifying obstacles which blocked her path and attained happiness, leaving the past with its regrets behind, yet the wish, as in the other dreams, was not a repressed wish, but an avowed wish. Moreover, this is not the whole meaning. The dream would rather seem to be principally a symbolic representation of her idea of life in general, and of the moral precepts with which she has endeavored to inspire herself, and which she has endeavored to live up to in order to obtain happiness.

There are three points to which I would direct attention: first, the character of the promised reward in this dream is of considerable significance, and gives a possible clue to the genetic factor in the production of the dream. The psychological equilibrium of the subject had been for a long time disturbed by a system of ideas which was known as the Z complex, and more recently by an episode known as the Y complex. The latter was the motive of one of the dreams that was analyzed. Both were characterized by regrets. The Z complex represents what, she believes, she has been "cheated" out of in life, and might well be expressed by the lines,

> *Of all sad words of tongue or pen,*
> *The saddest are these — it might have been.*

Both complexes had recurred with considerable force during the week, as well as the day preceding the dream. On grounds of *expediency only,* she had recently repressed them — put them out of her mind again and again, and thought she had done so successfully, but, according to the hypnotic consciousness, they had gone into the coconscious; she was not then aware of them, but they were still coconsciously present and, according to this testimony, caused at times depression. The thoughts of these complexes particularly colored her conception of life. The wild man referred specifically to these ideas when he told her she would "have no regrets for the past." These repressed and subconscious thoughts may be, therefore, the fundamental and genetic factor in the production of the dream. On the one hand they are largely responsible for her present conception of and attitude toward life, and, on the other, they have stimulated the counter resolution to repress such thoughts, to go forward, not backward, without complaining, hoping thus to attain happiness. These thoughts, however, *were not unacceptable*. On the contrary, she had constantly justified them. Nevertheless, of these thoughts the dream was almost a literal dramatic, if symbolic, representation.

The second point is the persistence of the physical effect of the dream — the aphonia. In the dream, and after waking, she had lost the use of her voice and could speak only in a whisper until relieved by therapeutic suggestion. To this phenomenon I shall return later.

The third point is the fact of only partial remembrance of the dream in the normal waking state, with slightly fuller memory in one hypnotic state, and complete memory in another hypnotic state. In the waking state, C, the subject could only remember being in a lonely place, and seeing there a lot of cats, a giant or witch, as well as her mother. In the c state, she further recalled the rocky path of Watts's picture. In other words, there may be incomplete or no synthesis of memory for a dissociated process in one state and complete synthesis in another. That we may only incompletely or not at all remember our dreams is a trite fact, but the experimental evidence that the dream experience and the conservation of the same may far exceed our memory is worth bearing in mind. Amnesia for dreams is thus in harmony with a long series of analogous amnesias for dissociated states (hypnosis, trance, dissociated personality, deliria, etc.).

## Dream 6

"This dream occurred twice on succeeding nights. She dreamed she was in the same *rocky dark path* she is always in, — Watt's path — but with trees besides (there are always trees, or a hillside, or a canyon). The *wind* was blowing very hard, and she could hardly walk on account of something, as is always the case. Someone, a *figure*, came rushing past her with his hands over his (or her) eyes. This figure said, '*Don't look, you will be blinded.*' She was at the entrance of a great *cave;* suddenly it *flashed light* in the cave, like a flashlight picture, and there, down on the ground *you* were lying, and you were *bound round and round* with bonds of some kind, and your clothes were torn and dirty, and your face was covered with blood, and you looked terribly anguished; and all over you there were just hundreds of little gnomes or pygmies or brownies, and they were *torturing you.* Some of them had axes, and were chopping on your legs and arms, and some were sawing you. Hundreds of them had little things like joss-sticks, but shorter, which were red hot at the ends, and they were jabbing them into you. It was something like Gulliver and the little creatures running over him. You saw C, and you said, 'O Mrs. C., for heaven's sake get me out of this damned hole.' (You always swear in C's dreams.) She was horrified, and said, 'O Dr. Prince, I am coming,' but she *could not move,* she was rooted to the spot; and then it all went away, everything became black, as if she was *blinded,* and then it would flash again and illuminate the cave, and she would see you again. This happened three or four times in the dream. She kept saying, 'I am coming,' and *struggled to move,* and she woke up saying it. In the same way *she could not move when she woke up, and she could not see.*"

## INTERPRETATION

In order not to weary the reader with the details of the analysis of this dream, I shall merely sum up the results. The dream proved to be a symbolic representation of the subject's conception of life (the rocky path); of her dread of the future, which for years she has said she dared not face; of her feeling that the future was *"blind"* in that she could not "see anything ahead"; of the thought that she would be overwhelmed, "lost," "swept away," if she looked into and realized this future, and she *must not look.* And yet there are moments in life when she realizes vividly the future; and so in the dream one of these moments occurs when she looks into the cave (the future), and in the flash of light the realization comes, — she sees her son (metamorphosed through substitution of another person) tortured, as she has thought of him "tortured" and handicapped (bound) by the moral "pin-pricks" of life. Then follows the symbolic representation (paralysis) of her utter "helplessness" to aid either him or anyone else or alter the conditions of her own life. Finally follows the prophesied consequences of this realization. She is overcome by blindness, and to this extent the dream is a fulfillment of a fear.

Nearly every element of the motive and material of this dream could be found in the thoughts, either of the pre-sleeping state or of previous periods of her life. The elements of the dream and the determining factors can be placed in parallel columns.

| *Dream Elements* | *Source and Symbolic Meaning* |
|---|---|
| Rocky path | Watts's pathway; symbolic conception of life |
| Wind | Old phobia for wind storms, of frequent occurrence in dreams in association with fear. |
| A figure (vague) | Her own thoughts personified. |
| "Don't look, you will be blinded." | Memories: "Did not dare look." "Did not dare face her troubles." Would be "lost," "swept away," "overwhelmed." "Life is all blind, I do not see anything ahead."[1] |
| Cave into which she looked. | Future into which she dared not look. |
| Flashes of light. | Flashes of realization of the future, which she frequently had. |
| M. P. bound and tortured. | Son (by substitution) "tortured," as with "pin-pricks," by being "bound" and hampered by the conditions of his life.[2] |

---

[1] "She has often felt that she was following a blind path in life, that the future is blind. . . . Years ago she told someone that she felt as if she was walking on a narrow precipice and she did not dare to look down or she would be lost, swept away by her troubles, and in the dream she kept her head turned away so as to keep her footing on the path."

[2] The source of this substitution and this helplessness is to be found in the pre-sleeping thoughts. Before going to sleep, she wished she could do some-

Paralysis.

"Feeling of helplessness against every-thing." "Felt powerless to help," not only the actors in the dream, but the troubles which beset her in life.

Blinded.

Overwhelmed by glimpses of the fu-ture which she had to face (word association and substitution); ful-fillment of fear or prophecy.

In this dream, as in the others, we find no "unaccept-able" and "repressed wish," no "conflict" with "censoring thoughts," no "compromise," no "resistance" and no "dis-guise" in the dream content to deceive the dreamer, — elements and processes fundamental in the Freudian school of psychology. We do find a symbolism which is a perfectly clear and simple representation of previous openly avowed ideas (wishes, fears, etc.), which not only were entertained without restraint, but which dominated the mental life of the dreamer. The source of the dream material and of the motivating thoughts was found in the thoughts of the pre-sleeping state, and in those of the subject's everyday life. The relation of the motivating thoughts to the content of the dream, as a factor in its mechanism, will be discussed later.

The persistence of the paralysis and the partial blind-ness after waking should be noted in passing. Four or five times during the day, she had a recurrence of the flashes of light when she seemed to look into a brilliantly lighted place and to see some terrible object. This was followed by mo-mentary absolute blindness. Such phenomena are of great interest, as they throw light upon the psycho-physiological

thing to show her gratitude to M. P. for the medical care she received, but felt her utter helplessness; and then, planning for her son's education at Harvard, she imagined him, for reasons not necessary to go into here, tortured, etc., by certain necessary restrictions which would be imposed upon him, and herself helpless against this treatment; so both persons were associated with the idea of her own helplessness and, through the process of "condensation" (Freud), thus appear in the dream as one person.

processes at work and give an insight into the pathology of certain hysterical phenomena. They will be considered later.

These six dreams which I have given are fairly illustrative and typical of all the dreams of this subject that were studied. I have been limited in my selection, as I have said, by the fact that some relate too intimately to private affairs to be published. Some of the best and most exhaustively analyzed, too, were of this nature. Of a large number collected, some were naturally, considering the time required for an analysis, more completely studied than others. I have not found, however, any psychological principle involved in the other dreams that is not to be found in those already given, so that we may regard them as typical.

## 4. THE SUBCONSCIOUS PROCESS AND MECHANISM

More interesting than the interpretation of the dreams are: first, the mechanism by which the motive expresses itself and makes use of the material; secondly, the evidence which this mechanism offers towards the elucidation of many allied phenomena in pathological conditions; and, thirdly, the light which dreams throw upon the hidden habits and processes of thought which tend to disturb the mental equilibrium of the subject and often lead to the development of the psychoneuroses.

1. Taking the last item first, it must be evident from a consideration of the dreams which have been analyzed above, that the fears, anxieties, and other disturbing thoughts, like regrets and remorse and longings, may express themselves in dreams. It is these thoughts which have a strong feeling-tone and, therefore, are more likely to be conserved, and to manifest themselves in dissociated states, and also, as we know, to disrupt the psychopathic individual of unstable equilibrium. Among these thoughts may be some which the individual will not entertain, and therefore, seeks to repress. I have not found, however, in the dreams studied that repressed thoughts appeared more frequently than those of equal feeling-tone which were not repressed. In-

deed, on the contrary, they were of insignificant frequency.[1] We know, as a fact of clinical experience, that the persistent recurrence of ideas of a distressing character tends to disrupt the mental life of persons of a certain temperament, and to lead to psychoneurotic conditions. It is not always easy to extract from the patient a precise description of such ideas, whether because of reticence regarding his inner life or because of a real lack of appreciation or memory of their content. Through the analysis of our subject's dreams, her mental life was laid bare and a clue to the true psychogenetic factor of certain disturbances was obtained, and thereby an intelligent comprehension gained of the psychoneurotic condition present.

2. As to the mechanism of the dream process and its identification with that which underlies various other psychoneurotic phenomena, we are here entering upon difficult ground, full of pitfalls, and, for this reason, requiring searching observations and great caution in interpretation.

We may begin with one fundamental principle, namely, that of the conservation of mental experiences. We have seen that the dream *material* is to be found in the thoughts of the previous recent life of the dreamer, particularly those that occurred in the pre-sleeping state immediately before the dream, and during the preceding day. The *motive* of the dream was traced in every instance to strongly organized systems of ideas which were deeply rooted in the mind of the subject, and represented her mental attitude towards her environment or the problems of her daily life. According to the principle of conservation, both sets of ideas were conserved, as shown by the fact that they could be recovered by the methods of psychological analysis.

It is not necessary to go into the problem of conservation beyond recalling here that we have reason to believe that mental experiences are stored up as some sort of brain dispositions. We must assume that every experience retained as a potential memory leaves a counterpart record in the

---

1 In only one of the six dreams here given, *viz.*, the fifth, were repressed thoughts in evidence, and these were not unacceptable to the subject but were justified in her mind, nor was the dream a fulfillment of them.

neurons. This record is commonly spoken of as "brain residua," "brain dispositions," "vestigia," and "the unconscious." There are various theoretical objections to these terms, particularly to that of "the unconscious" because of its ambiguity resulting from differences in its connotation. I have suggested the word *neurogram* to define these hypothetical brain changes which are deposited by the experiences of life.

Now, the material of the dream and the motive of the dream could be traced, in every instance, to neurograms so deposited. The dream always expressed, in symbolic form, previous thoughts, while its content was made up of the elements of previous thoughts and present sensory experiences. A neurogram is something which, *ex hypothesi,* when stimulated can function and reproduce the original experience, *i. e.,* memory, and so far as the elements of a dream are recurrences of the elements of previous mental experiences, they are merely memories, and the dream itself a patchwork of memories. In some dreams, recorded in the literature, the recognition of a large part, at least, of a dream as pure memory is easy enough.

But dreams are something more than patchwork of memories. Taking as a whole the dreams recorded here and others of my collection, we shall find in their construction certain characteristics which give the dream a logical and intelligent design.

These are first: a motive running through the content of many of the dreams, as in a story constructed by a dramatist. They sometimes have a sort of plot, as if an intelligence other than that of the consciousness of the dreamer had planned the development and had foreseen the outcome. The dreamer has a feeling of being followed by something, — she does not know what. It turns out to be two symbolical creatures, A and B. In another dream she sees something lying under a tree; she asks what it is, and not receiving the information, proceeds to investigate, and it turns out to be a certain person with a broken leg. Again, she is told, like Bluebeard's wife, not to look into a certain place under warning of punishment. In her case, the place is a cave in which the secrets of the future are to be seen. She looks and sees a sight which, symbolic of the future, fills her with terror, and she is punished for her curiosity. Such dreams have the appearance of having been planned by an intelligence which is distinct from the dream consciousness, and which, from the beginning, foresees the ending.

Secondly, while the motive and the component parts of the dream are reproductions of various thoughts which were previously experienced by the subject, in every instance the reproductions are not of their original form, but sensory hallucinations (visual and auditory) are substituted to a large extent for the original thoughts, which are thus only symbolically reproduced or expressed. For instance, the thought that life is "wild" is expressed by the vision of a wild man who speaks (auditory hallucination) the ideas she has thought. The idea that she is alone in the world and that there is no place for a "lone woman" is reproduced by a visual scene of herself wandering alone in various places and of being turned out of them because alone, without an escort. The idea that life is a toil and struggle is represented by an hallucinatory image of a hill or a rocky path up which she is toiling, etc.

Now how did it come about that the neurograms which were deposited by these ideas did not reproduce, as memory, the original thoughts in their original form, but became distorted into symbolic hallucinatory representations of them, fabricated often into a story? That is not what commonly occurs in waking life under the ordinary conditions of everyday life. I say "commonly" and "under the ordinary conditions" advisedly, for under certain conditions, as I will point out later, this symbolic reproduction does occur occasionally.

If this question of the *why* cannot be completely answered with our present knowledge — and I doubt if it can — what sort of psychological process or processes is involved in dreams? And do dreams stand alone, or are they only a particular type of psychological symbolism? If the last is true, any complete theory of the process and mechanism of dreams must satisfy the conditions of other types.

According to the well-known theory of Freud, the

mechanism is a very complicated process and involves the previous repression of a wish, which thereby becomes dissociated and "unconscious." There results a conflict at the time of the dream between this dissociated idea (which is the true dream-thought) and a repressing "censor" (censoring thoughts), and finally a compromise by which the true dream-thought (the latent content) manifests itself in the distorted form of the dream (the manifest content) by which the underlying true dream is disguised so as not to be recognizable. The dream, according to this theory, is always, as maintained by Freud, the "imaginary fulfillment of a wish." The amnesia following the dream is interpreted as the work of the "censor."

It is not my intention here to enter into a criticism and discussion of this theory. Suffice it to say that I have not been able to verify it in the dreams which were the object of this study, although Freud's method of analysis was conscientiously made use of. As I have already said, and as I believe any one can assure himself by a study of the six dreams embodied in this paper, I have been unable to find any evidence of repression, of previously dissociated ideas, of a "censor," or of a compromise. Nor have the dreams, as I have interpreted them, represented the "imaginary fulfillment of a wish" more than that of a fear or anxiety or other attitude of mind towards life. Nor can I accept the view that the amnesia following the dream differs in principle from that so commonly observed for dissociated states in general, or that it is the handiwork of a "censor."

On the other hand, the results of this study justify the view that the conscious dream, as remembered, is not a fantasy, but a logical, though symbolic, representation of ideas which to a certain extent are distorted, *i. e.*, so far as this is required by the conditions of symbolism. These ideas, in every instance, had been previously entertained by the dreamer and could be recovered as memories. Further, the interpretation seems to be substantiated that they were the motive of the dream and therefore were continued during the dream as some kind of a *logical intelligent process* (coconscious or unconscious, psychological or physiological).

This motivating process may be regarded correctly as the *true* dream (Freud's "latent content") which manifested itself in the symbolism of the remembered dream (Freud's "manifest content"). In these respects, and so far, then, this study is confirmatory of Freud's interpretation.

What sort of a process the "true dream" is, and by what mechanism it manifests itself in the distorted symbolism is another problem.

As to the *process*, if the interpretation is correct that the dream-content is a symbolism of some other thought — this thought, or the process which stands for it, must be subconscious.[1] In other words, it is inconceivable that the dream consciousness can be the whole of the process; it must be only a part of it, and the other part can be only subconscious, as it does not appear in the consciousness of the dreamer. The hypothesis which would answer all the requirements of the case is this: the dream process consists of two parts, one is the dream consciousness and the other is subconscious. The subconscious process is that which may be called the true dream and represents those previous thoughts which, by analysis, were found to furnish the motive of the dream — the motivating thoughts. This subconscious process manifests itself in consciousness not directly by its own previously correlated thoughts, but indirectly through symbolic pictures, verbal expressions, etc., which are apt to be incomprehensible in meaning until the "true dream-thoughts" of the subconscious dream process are discovered and thereby interpreted. Expressing this in other words, it may be said that the motivating "thoughts" of the subconscious process emerge into the consciousness of the dreamer in a symbolic form. This is substantially the conclusion which Freud reached, so far as concerns the process, as a result of his studies. In principle, the process is similar to that involved in the well-proven subconscious solving of problems. If, for example, it is a mathematical problem, a

---

1 Coconscious or unconscious. For the purpose of the hypothesis it does not matter which. Those who accept the psychological interpretation of such dream processes would hold that they were true subconscious "thoughts" (coconscious); those who hold to the physiological interpretation — that they were brain processes, *i. e.*, "unconscious." I am inclined to the former view.

number pops into the consciousness of the individual, or he sees an hallucinatory number as a visual symbol. He may have no idea what it may mean until it is discovered that it is the answer to a particular problem, perhaps given to him in hypnosis. The calculation has been done by a subconscious process, and the answer alone emerges into consciousness.

That part of the *mechanism* by which the subconscious calculation process on the one hand, and the subconscious dream process on the other, become converted into their corresponding results in consciousness is another problem still, and one to which I do not think we are at present able to offer a solution. The elaborate mechanism proposed by Freud (which is the cornerstone of his psychology) to account for the peculiar "distortion" of the "true dream-thoughts" in the symbolism, I have not found, as I have already said, to be confirmed by the results of this study. I will pass over for the present this part of the mechanism and return to it later.

Assuming, for the moment, the subconscious dream process, it will help us to understand this process and its relation to the dream if we examine more closely the facts as revealed by psychological analysis. In all the dreams, the symbolic representation of the motivating thoughts was a selection of those particular elements from the material furnished by past experiences which had an *associative relation* to the motivating thoughts. It will be remembered, for instance, that in the fifth dream, that of the wild men, the motive of the dream was the conception of life and certain precepts of conduct which the subject had laid down for herself for the attainment of future happiness. Both sets of ideas had recurred over and over again and were conserved as neurograms. They recurred again in the dream, not in their original form as thoughts, but in a symbolic representation, which was a fabricated scene in which a rocky path, wild men, cats, etc., appeared and took part in the action, which was really the acting out of her own previous thoughts. It was much as if these had constructed a charade, the action and scene of which were taken from associated thoughts of the dreamer.

Now, according to the hypothesis, these neurograms which pertained to the subject's conception of life and conduct (the motive of the dream) proceeded to function during a dissociated state ("sleep") but they functioned subconsciously; hence they did not appear in the dreamer's consciousness as conscious memory. What they did do was to stimulate certain elements of associative thoughts (neurograms). These were Watts's rocky path, wild men, cats. All this material belonged to thoughts which had strong associations with the fundamental dream motive. The subconscious process appropriated, by some kind of mechanism, this material and wove it, with some of the ideas which were correlated with its own neurograms, into a dream consciousness the content of which was a dramatic scene. This scene, as I have said, was a symbolic representation of the ideas pertaining to the subconsciously functioning neurograms, and consisted partly of sensory hallucinations and partly of thoughts. Thus, according to this hypothesis, one portion of the dream process is subconscious and one portion is the dream consciousness, and the elements of the latter stand in associative relation to the former.

The first question that proposes itself when weighing the probability of the truth of such an hypothesis is whether there are any analogous phenomena which can provide us with data such as to support it. As we are dealing with dissociated mental life we would naturally expect to find such data, if they exist, amongst the phenomena of the dissociations, although we should also expect to find them particularly in special conditions in normal life.

More than this, dreams plainly are only a particular type of the phenomena of hallucinatory symbolism; they do not stand alone, and, therefore, it is amongst these other types that we must look for the data which will afford a basis for an hypothesis. Further, any explanation of dream symbolism must also be consistent with the facts of all other types of hallucinatory symbolism.

The question which we have put may at once be answered in the affirmative for, when we marshal the facts furnished by these other types, we do find many analogous phenomena supporting the hypothesis of a subconscious process which manifests itself in consciousness through symbolic representation.

Symbolism as an hallucinatory phenomenon occurs in numerous and multiform conditions.

(*a*) Perhaps the simplest form of symbolism is the well-known hallucinatory phenomenon which can be experimentally produced by stimulation of the anesthetic skin of an hysteric. In a suitable subject, if the anesthetic hand be *pricked* five times the subject sees as a *visual* hallucination the number *five* written perhaps on the back of an hallucinatory hand.[1]

Here the stimuli are not only perceived but they are apperceived. By some process or other, of which the subject is not aware, the stimuli are counted, the specific ideas relating to their number and the part pricked are translated into another sense-process which symbolically represents the idea. This idea is not that of the implement used to stimulate the anesthetic skin, or any other relation of the subject to the environment, but only of the number of times the hand was pricked, as if in answer to a question. The symbolic answer alone arises in consciousness — a visualized number written on a visualized hand. There plainly must be some process of which the subject is unaware (*i e.*, subconscious), which performs the apperception and then thrusts into consciousness its symbolic representation. The phenomenon, therefore, instead of being simple, as it might appear to be at first sight, is a highly complicated one and involves both subconscious and conscious elements.

(*b*) In artificial hallucinations representing past experiences, we have a similar but more elaborate symbolism. A given individual looks into a crystal and sees a scene enacted, which may be a personally lived experience of his own life, or the representation of something which was read in a book, or overheard in conversation, or previously entertained ideas and mental concepts. Here the visual hallucination not only reproduces as a visual memory the original

1 See Sidis, Prince, and Linenthal: "The Pathology of Hysteria." *Boston Medical and Surgical Journal*, June 23, 1904.

sense-impressions but symbolically represents the thought and actions pertaining to the original experience. For instance, a subject sees enacted a murder scene which faithfully portrays in visual symbols a murder scene that had been read in a novel. Synchronously with the visual symbolism, the thoughts with their emotional tone, which were a part of the original experience, may not only be symbolically expressed by the hallucinatory scene but may arise again in the mind of the visualizer, just as often occurs in dreams. I have made a large number of such observations.

The same but more elaborate symbolism may be recognized in spontaneous hallucinations. I have reported two very striking incidents of this kind.[1] One was of Miss B., who saw in my presence as a vision a certain person who, in hallucinatory words, reproached her for a certain action. Although the action was performed in a dissociated state and, therefore, not remembered, the hallucinatory symbolism represented the pricking of her conscience. Here it was not the original scene that was reproduced, but a censure of the scene. These censuring *thoughts* translated themselves into an appropriate symbolism similar to what we observe in dreams. For her, lacking the memory of the scene which I alone knew, the symbolism had no meaning.

The other incident was a spontaneous hallucinatory experience by the subject B. C. A. While in a slightly dissociated state, she heard certain consoling words addressed to her. These words came from her husband, who was dead, and whom she saw as an hallucination. The motive and material of this hallucination could be traced to previous mental experiences of the subject, as in the dreams already described.

Mrs. Verrall, in her account of automatic writing, records a spontaneous hallucination which symbolically represented what had once been described in spoken words to the percipient.

An excellent illustration of this type of hallucinatory symbolism is the historical vision of Archduke Francis Charles (the father of the present Emperor of Austria) who

---

1 *The Dissociation of a Personality*, 2d edition, pp. 508, 509; and *Journal of Abnormal Psychology*, vol. III, p. 337.

"was also greatly troubled in his mind as to his right to waive his claim to the crown in favor of his son. According to his own statement, he only finally made up his mind when, while earnestly praying for guidance in his perplexity, he had a *vision of the spirit of his father, the late Emperor Francis, laying his hand on the head of his youthful grandson and thus putting all his own doubts to rest.*"[1] The remarkable likeness of this vision, in its construction, to that of the first scene of the first dream described above is worth noting. Not only were both visual hallucinations (the one while asleep and the other while awake) but both symbolized an abstract idea in the conventional dream-form.

These phenomena introduce us to a still more complicated form of symbolism — the condensation, dramatization and elaboration of abstract ideas in visual and auditory symbols. This is well exemplified in the hallucinations which so frequently accompany sudden religious conversion. These hallucinatory symbolisms represent the ideas which from time to time in the past have consciously occupied the mind of the individual. The words heard by St. Paul, for instance, in the light of modern data, can well be interpreted as the expression of doubts and scruples which once entered his mind. All such hallucinatory symbolisms — whether artificial or spontaneous — can only be explained on the theory that, besides the hallucination, there is a subconscious motivating process which expresses itself symbolically in consciousness. The hallucination is not a pure memory, but something that is fabricated, and there must be some unconscious process that does the fabrication. We must assume that there are two parts to the process, one subconscious, due to the functioning of neurograms belonging to previous experiences, or, as James has so well expressed it, "to the subconscious incubation and maturing of motives deposited by the experiences of life"; and one in consciousness, the hallucination through which the subconscious process manifests itself symbolically. As in dreams, the motive of the hallucination is found in the previous motives of life, and the material through which the motive is symbolically expressed

1 Sir Horace Rumbold: *Francis Joseph and His Times;* p. 151. (Italics mine.)

is found in the previous thoughts of the converted person, particularly those of recent date.

(c)   Analogous phenomena we find in those most valuable of psychological phenomena for the investigation of the processes of the human mind — the so-called "post-hypnotic suggestions." In calculation experiments of this kind, I have found that coconscious pictures of numbers arise, and although the subject is not aware of these coconscious pictures, a memory of them can be recovered (in some subjects) in hypnosis. These visualized numbers pop up coconsciously from time to time and arrange themselves in certain positions, until finally the completed number, which is the answer to the calculation appears. But plainly these numbers do not give the process by which they are presented; they give only the results. The very fact of their coming and going shows that there must be a deeper underlying "unconscious"[1] process. The appearance of the numbers reminds one of the appearance of the electrically-flashed transparent numbers in the Boston Subway. These numbers in the subway flash into our consciousness the information of the order in which certain cars will arrive, but the mechanism which flashes the numbers — an employee stationed some distance away working an electrical apparatus — is hidden from our awareness.

In the performance of some post-hypnotic phenomena following suggestions, the coconscious pictures and the "unconscious" process are quite complicated. The motive in such phenomena is to be found "in the deposited experiences of life," i. e., the previous suggestion. The selection of numbers to express the motive is a necessary consequence of the experiment. In some experiments, on the other hand, the coconscious pictures were elaborate symbolisms of the motive, e. g., a ballet girl, dressed in red, with her feet on the table, was a symbol of the kind of person who, the subject thought, smoked cigarettes. The hypnotic suggestion — one

1 I use the word "unconscious" here (as distinct from coconscious) in the sense of some process which has no psychical equivalent in the consciousness or coconsciousness of the subject, who is, of course, unaware of it. I pass over for the present the nature of this "unconscious" process.

objected to — was that the subject should smoke a cigarette after waking; the material for the coconscious symbolism was easily found in a previous mental experience of the subject, namely, a picture of a ballet girl dressed in red, which hung in the apartment of the subject and was the original of the coconscious picture.[1]

When we survey, then, the field of other types of hallucinatory symbolic phenomena, we find, underlying them all, a subconscious process of which the content of the symbolism is a manifestation. The process is in principle the same in all types; there is nothing unique in the process of the dreams which were the object of this study. It is one which is met with in various analogous phenomena. Whether this principle is universally true of dreams can be determined only by extensive studies.

I have emphasized the analogy between dreams and other types of hallucinatory symbolism. I would also emphasize the fact that in these other types, evidence of repressed unacceptable ideas, of a "censor," of conflict with the repressing censoring thoughts, of a compromise and final disguisement of the underlying subconscious "thoughts" is lacking. I do not mean by this that no part of this mechanism is ever present in any examples of such types. Such an assertion, of course from the nature of the case, would be incapable of substantiation; but in large numbers of examples it is inconceivable that this mechanism could be in play. With St. Paul, for example, it may have been true that he had refused to entertain and admit to himself the evidence of Christianity and had repressed such ideas; but it is preposterous logic to assume that the hallucinatory words, "Saul, Saul, why persecutest thou me?" were a disguisement of the true thought and intended not to be understood by Saul.

1 I have collected a large number of observations of these extraordinarily interesting phenomena, which I believe have not been noted thus far by other students. In the subconscious manifestation of certain subjects they play a very important part. I am happy to say that Dr. G. A. Waterman has confirmed my observations in one of my cases (the subject of this study). For brief accounts which I have previously given to these phenomena see, *The Dissociation of a Personality*, p. 350; *The Psychological Review*, March-May, 1905; and the *Journal of Abnormal Psychology*, vol. I, v. 49.

See especially chapter XIII of this volume.

The same may be said of the hallucinatory words in the two examples I have given on page 553. Yet such an interpretation would be required by this hypothetical mechanism of Freud.

On the whole, the dreams I have collected and studied in their various characteristics comport exceedingly closely, in principle, with the other types. If the mechanism of Freud is true of dreams, it ought to be true of other types of hallucinatory symbolism. One very suggestive type of hallucination is that of an artificial (crystal) vision which is an exact portrayal of a previous dream. The whole dream, from beginning to end, and in all its details, unfolds itself in the crystal like a reel in one of the "moving pictures." The similarity between the two phenomena becomes more apparent in the case where the crystal gazer loses his apperception of his environment, which disappears, and he seems to himself to be within the scene of the crystal. It is a natural inference that the same mechanism which is at work in the one case must be at work in the other. This may be so, in which case we should not be justified in assuming a different mechanism for dreams than for visions.

Yet another interpretation is possible. A vision of a dream scene, being a repetition of an experience, is open, in large part, to explanation on the principle of memory, or the reproduction of a conserved experience (the dream), but this is not wholly the case, for the gazer often sees the figure of *himself and his relation to the dream environment.* These elements of the vision are plainly not a reproduction of an experience, for the dreamer does not see himself. In this detail, the vision is plainly a translation of his own subconscious knowledge into the visual symbol. Similarly, I have secured artificial visions of sleep-walking acts. In the vision, unconscious acts (*i e.,* the unconscious dropping of a letter from the hand) were portrayed, while the outer facial expression of the figure in the crystal, indicative of mirth or sadness, revealed the inner thoughts of the somnambulist.

As to the *characteristics* of the symbolism of the dreams, they were not fundamentally different from those which can be observed in certain other types, particularly in the visions of religious mystics. Of the four characteristics which Freud has insisted upon as fundamental to dreams and as constituting the mechanism (wrongly termed, I think) by which the true dream-thought becomes "distorted," three — "condensation," "dramatization," and "secondary elaboration" — can be easily recognized in many such visions,[1] and they were prominent in the dreams of my subject. By "condensation," a symbol represents more than a single idea; as the national flag stands for a host of ideas, so climbing the hill of life (dream 2), or the rocky path of life (dreams 5 and 6), the red and black shadows (dream 2), "cats," etc., are symbolic condensations of complex ideas. So likewise, dramatization and secondary elaboration of the true dream-thoughts may be easily recognized in the dreams and in the necessarily condensed analyses I have given. But these characteristics are essential in a greater or less degree to all symbolism, particularly the pictorial variety, and there is nothing peculiar in this respect in dreams. In Margaret Mary's historical vision of the Sacred Heart[2] they are strikingly manifest. On the other hand, Freud's fourth characteristic, the "displacement" of the emotion, pertaining to the underlying true dream, to an inconsequential element in the ("manifest") dream content, I have not noticed in the dreams I have collected, nor do I think it observable in other types of symbolism, though I have not made an extended search for this characteristic. In my collection, the emotion appeared to be always associated with those elements of the "manifest" content which represented the emotional thoughts of the true dream. There was therefore no "disguise" of the latter.

As to that part of the *mechanism* by which the motivating thoughts (*i. e.,* the subconscious process) fabricate the symbolism (out of the material furnished by the pre-sleeping thoughts and those of the preceding day), we have already seen that those elements of this material are selected

---

[1] For example, compare Saint Margaret Mary's vision of the Sacred Heart and the hallucinatory experiences of one of Starbuck's cases, both quoted in James's *Varieties of Religious Experience*, p. 343 and p. 352.

[2] *Loc. cit.*

which have an associative relation with the motive. The law of association may thus explain — so far as it explains anything — the selection of the different pieces of the dream content. But *why* does the subconscious content manifest itself through the particular action adopted, in preference to any other course? As the motivating thoughts were not unacceptable and repressed in any of the dreams I have collected, it was not for the purpose of disguisement.

In drawing conclusions I feel it wiser to confine myself entirely to the results of my own observations. The question does not permit of a satisfying answer. Until we can delve down beneath the threshold of consciousness, and until we know more of what goes on in the subconscious process, it will be impossible to answer the question of the "why" in any satisfactory manner. If the subconscious process is a thinking consciousness, and if we knew what it was thinking about during a dream, we could say probably why it manifested itself as it did; if it is only a brain process, and we knew the laws of its functioning, we could also answer the question. Considering the limitations of our knowledge in this respect, any solution at present can only be conjectural. Take, *e. g.*, the first dream. The history shows, with almost certainty, that the pre-sleeping thoughts and those of the preceding day "suggested" or awakened the subconscious "thoughts" (process) of this dream, and, therefore, were responsible for the dream. The analysis justifies this inference. This being the case, we should expect that the material of the dream would be taken by association from these causative forethoughts. Now, let us suppose that the subconscious "thought" was, "Poor people, like the Jewess, are not to be condemned for drinking whiskey; for my mother, who was beyond criticism, would not have condemned them." And let us further suppose that it is a function of a subconscious process (in fact commonly manifested) to give rise to visual images in consciousness. In this case, it is not difficult to understand that the subconscious thought might well induce (through associated memories brought out in the analysis) conscious pictures of the Jewess and her mother as in the scene, and thus manifest itself symbolically in the dream scene.

That this is not a mere fanciful hypothesis, but has experimental support, I could show by citing from a large number of experiments and other observations I have made, in which suggested or spontaneous subconscious processes were accompanied by coconscious pictures. Each step in the process was accompanied by its corresponding and illustrative picture. But this is a problem for another and independent study, and I prefer to leave it for the present where it is. Finally, I would say that I would not be understood as affirming that the conclusions arrived at in this study can be extended *in toto* to the dreams of all individuals. It may be that in particular subjects, dissociated subconscious processes more readily are formed and take on functional activity than in normally stable individuals. In the latter class it may be that dreams are determined by other processes, including those of normal thought. Further studies are required. On the other hand, we do not know as yet to what extent even everyday thought, which seems so free from other determining influences than those of the "personal consciousness" is in reality determined by subconscious processes. This is probably far more the case than we imagine. Though there may be grave doubts regarding the mechanism and other theories of Freud, we are under obligation to him for emphasizing the importance of the subconscious in normal everyday life.

### 5. THE PERSISTENCE OF DREAM SYMBOLISM AS HYSTERICAL STIGMATA

Another instructive class of facts, in this connection, is the persistence of certain of the dream phenomena after waking. For instance, in the fifth dream, the subject tries to speak to her mother, but finds she has lost her voice. This followed the dream-thought that she must not speak (make a sound) and an intense muscular effort not to cry out as she passed over the cats. (The dream analysis pointed to an actual spasm of the muscles of the throat during this effort.)

Now, on waking, the *aphonia* persisted. She could not speak any more than in the dream.

Likewise, in the sixth dream, the subject was blinded or partially blinded; on waking, this partial blindness persisted. In the dream, the blindness followed a tremendously brilliant flash of light (as of a flashlight) which lighted up a cave and revealed a distressing picture. This flash was followed momentarily by absolute darkness (as if blinded). This phenomenon was repeated several times. Now, after waking, not only was there *persistent partial blindness*, but *flashes of light* followed by absolute darkness were repeated several times during the course of the day, and in each flash she saw, vaguely and obscurely, what she had seen in her dream — it was as if she "looked into a brilliantly lighted place (the cave) and saw there some terrible object but she [I] did not know what it was." In other words, the symbolism of the dream was partially repeated as an hallucination when the subject was in her normal waking state.

Another phenomenon of the same type was the persisting *paralysis* after waking. In the sixth dream, her helplessness was symbolized by inability to move, *i. e.*, paralysis. "She could not move hand or foot for about five minutes." Amongst the other dreams I have collected is one in which she was told by a certain person in the dream that she could not move, and in the dream she could not; she became rigid. The next day, from time to time coconscious "pictures" developed. When these "pictures" came, she could not move a step even though she was at the time crossing the floor. This happened half a dozen times, when she was up and about, and more often when she was lying down. At such times she would become rigid for a few seconds; then the picture of X would go out and the picture of Y would come and she could move.

Following other dreams, after waking, the subject had a *visual hallucination* of a person whom she vividly saw in her room. This phenomenon occurred on several occasions. The hallucinations were not always of the same person. On recovering the memory of the dream, it was found that the visions were always of a person who had been a conspicuous object in the dream. The dream process, in other words, persisted after waking.

On other occasions, the subject had peculiar sensori-motor *phenomena* — sort of tics. During the course of the day, she frequently had the feeling that she was going to step on something disagreeable and each time looked to see what she was stepping on — to see if there was something there. Each time she shrank from this possible something. It was found that, correspondingly, in the dream, she imagined that she was picking her way over Watts's rocky path, which was covered with cats. She picked her way to avoid stepping on the cats, as she placed each foot.

On numerous occasions in the dream, a violent *headache, with nausea,* suddenly developed at the emotional crisis of the nightmare. After waking, severe headache and nausea, simulating and previously diagnosed as migraine, persisted until relieved by simple suggestion (Dream 4). These head-aches had resisted all therapeutic measures, in the hands of numerous physicians, until I discovered this pathology through the dreams.

Finally, I may say, although not completing the number of somatic phenomena, which were observed to follow the dreams, *depression and fatigue* have been common phe-nomena. These could be traced to the persistence of the same phenomena as elements of dreams.

Now, the first thing to be noted in these physiological phenomena — the aphonia, the blindness, the paralysis, the headache, the hallucinations, the tics, the depression and fa-tigue, — is that in the dream they were primarily due to *psychical* causes, certain ideas, and were elements in a process of which the dream consciousness was also a part. Of this there can be no question, considering that they were only elements of a dream; and all were instantaneously relieved by suggestion. (I put aside for the moment the question of the relation of the dream phenomena to the second or larger "unconscious" process.)

The second thing to be noted is that the persistence of

the phenomena during the waking state shows that in that state a secondary process was still in activity; and it is hardly to be doubted that this process was the same as that which induced the phenomena in the dream. There is no avoidance of the conclusion *that the phenomena were the persistence of the dream process — or part of it — in the waking state.* This dream process in the waking state was certainly subconscious (whether coconscious or unconscious); for the subject was unaware of it. It must have been through the continued activity of such a subconscious process that the vocal function, in one case, and the visual function and the general muscular innervation, in another, were inhibited. Through such continued activity, the flashes of light, the visual hallucinations, the sensori-motor phenomena (tics), etc., all must have been produced.

But there was still other evidence of some subconscious process at work in the production of this symbolism. The method of psychological analysis brought out that, after waking, *coconscious* pictures of the dream cave and its contents, in one case, and of cats in the rocky path, in the other, began to come and go (of this, of course, the subject was not aware) and sometimes, when these coconscious pictures came, she would be aware of the flashes of light and of the feeling of stepping on cats. In other words, the functioning of the unconscious dream process would produce part of the dream symbolism in the waking consciousness and part in the coconscious. The conscious elements of each complemented the other and substantially reproduced this part of the dream.

Here we have, it seems to me, evidence which forces the conclusion of an unconscious process revealing itself through conscious and somatic phenomena. I have collected a large amount of similar evidence from the phenomena of post-hypnotic suggestions.

As the somatic phenomena (aphonia, blindness, paralysis, hallucinations, etc.) were identical with those phenomena which clinically are known as hysterical, these observations clearly open the door to the interpretation of hysteria. Into this great subject, of course, I cannot go here.

There is one principle, however, which I would dwell upon for a moment. I have pointed out that the hysterical stigmata following the dreams were originally in the dream either symbolic representations or immediate representations of certain previously conceived ideas; aphonia, that she must not speak; the blindness, that if she looked into the future she would be metaphorically blinded or overwhelmed; the paralysis, that she was helpless, etc. We have seen that these subconscious activities were carried over into the waking state and underlay the persisting hysterical stigmata. It necessarily follows, therefore, that these hysterical stigmata must still be regarded as symbolic manifestations of the ideas which originally gave rise to them and which continued to function as a subconscious process. I would further point out that in the absence of any knowledge of the dream, it would have been impossible to have traced the true relationship between these stigmata and the ideas of which they were symbols, or, indeed, of the genesis of the stigmata at all.

These considerations suggest the question whether we may not logically consider all the conventional stigmata of hysteria from this point of view, and investigate them as possible symbolisms of hidden processes of thought. In such an investigation, the direct connection between a stigma and the mental content would rarely be obvious and could only be ascertained by the same method of searching psychological analysis as is employed in the examination of dreams.

I will here simply illustrate the principle of symbolism suggested above (meaning thereby not so-called "conversion") by the following examples of an hysterical symptom: We all know that contractures and paralysis are very common in hysteria. We also know that in hysteria these contractures can often be modified, removed and reinduced by suggestion. I have here the photograph of hysterical contractures, which could be removed and induced again at will by the suggesting influence of a tuning fork, as will be seen in the photograph. It is, again, well-known that contractures can be induced in highly suggestible normal people by the same influence.

Now, what is the process by which such contractures are brought about? They plainly are not voluntary motor innervations. The subject himself cannot voluntarily create or remove them. They must be due to some unconscious process, but one which can be directly influenced by an idea, whether suggested or autochthonous. Is it not possible that if the patient, shown in the photograph, had been subjected to psychological analysis, we should have resurrected memories of ideas previously entertained by the patient in some period of her life and since acting subconsciously, which were symbolized by the contracture and the paralysis? The content of these ideas might be, and probably would be, very far removed from the specific conception of a contracture. In her dreams we might have found them symbolically expressed, as were the other stigmata in the subject upon whom the above observations were made. In the hysteric, the contractures followed a slight accident. We might have been able to resurrect memories of fear of injuries and their possible consequences; memories of specific accidents occurring to people who had been maimed and paralyzed, fallacious ideas of disease, etc. Out of such ideas, subconsciously functioning, it is possible that the actual contractures developed as a symbolic representation, as was the case in the hysterical phenomena I have described above.

However that may be, and whatever the exact mechanism, it has become convincingly clear that an understanding of the psychoneuroses and of dreams can only be obtained through a study of the phenomena of the subconscious (coconscious and unconscious) in all their protean forms. As has been shown so often, a knowledge of the subconscious opens the door to an understanding not only of the great psychoneuroses, of which hysteria is the most striking example, but as well of the mental processes of normal everyday life, waking and sleeping. Our present knowledge of subconscious processes which do not enter our awareness, but probably take part in and determine every process of thought, is but surface deep, and we know little of the mode of working of their complex mechanism. Though we can recognize the manifestation of these mechanisms, we are able as yet to determine only very imperfectly the "how" and the "why" of their production. It remains for future researches to solve these problems, but they can be solved only by the same methods of observation and experiment which in other departments of science have given reliable results and placed our knowledge on a sound basis.

PART IV

# CHAPTER XIX

## WHY THE BODY HAS A MIND AND THE SURVIVAL OF CONSCIOUSNESS AFTER DEATH[1]

### I

HOWEVER interesting such historical *résumés* of thought and knowledge may be, I am going to put aside the temptation to set out with the customary historical exposition of the various theories of mind and body that have been held by philosophers and scientists of all times, and approach the question entirely from the standpoint of present-day science. What we are all interested in, what you are interested in, is the question: Does modern science, do the amazing discoveries of science that have been revealed in recent years, of physics and chemistry, and psychology and neurology, and indeed of palaeontology and anthropology, throw any further light, more than we have always had, on this baffling, intriguing problem, all-important for human satisfaction?

Many of us, fortunately not all, doubting souls that we be, yet earnestly longing for spiritual acquiescence in our brief mundane life, insistently ask for an answer to this question. You all remember the often quoted remark of Carlyle when told that Margaret Fuller "accepted the universe." "Gad, she had better!" exclaimed Carlyle. Yet seething, restless human nature, unsatisfied with blind faith and impelled by a constant urge to know, asks again and again of science what assurance it can give that personal existence may not be merely an ephemeral phase of a small portion of the universe. This desire for assurance, often involving the

---

1 A lay sermon delivered under the auspices of the Phillips Brooks House Association (Harvard University), November 22nd, 1925.

assuaging of poignant sorrow, finds expression in modern spiritualism and gives an explanation of the blind faith of many noble minds, often keen intellects, in the tawdry phenomena of the spiritualistic *séance*, or, at best, in unscientific and logically inadequate evidence of surviving spirits, evidence that would be given scant hearing in any other domain of intelligent inquiry. So if modern science can contribute anything of a positive character that will enable us to have anything like a real understanding of the nature of the mind and its relation to the body, it may be able, or at least it ought to be able, to have something to say in respect to the possibility of the mind surviving the body after death.

It is not superfluous, I think, to point out, in passing, that whatever theories have been held in respect to these problems, whatever speculations have been indulged in by philosophers and scientists from Aristotle to Descartes, and in recent times, Spencer and George H. Lewes, and Huxley, and Clifford, and others, they have all been based upon the actual scientific knowledge of their day. They may very properly be regarded as the logical interpretation of the facts laboriously and slowly achieved by contemporary science, but considered from differing points of view. But it was contemporary science; let us not forget that. As new facts are accumulated, old facts take on new meanings, and new interpretations are called for. The older theories held only for their day; or rather the evaluation of those theories, for they were derived from the relatively simple contemporary scientific knowledge, which only justified their being assigned to a place in the category of speculation.

This knowledge, for all its positiveness and self-satisfaction, was relatively meagre; and, riddled with gaps of the unknown, it terminated in blank walls beyond which there were only hypotheses and speculations. And such, we must admit, it is today, however relatively advanced.

Moreover, after passing in review the various theories that have been offered, it becomes obvious that what changes have taken place in thought have been rather in the reappraisal of old theories than in the conception of new ones. For science has no new data from which to advance a theory of mind that has not already been suggested. So any modern theory of mind derives its sanction from a revaluation of an ancient concept, that new value being justified only by facts newly acquired. The same is true of many other theories of science, particularly in biology. The concept of evolution, with which Darwin's name is so classically linked, was in his time no new doctrine, but as old as Greek philosophy. It was only from the accumulation of new facts by Darwin that it received a new and higher evaluation and was removed from the category of philosophical speculation. So, in discussing the nature of mind, any theory is entitled to a higher appraisal than it has already received only by reason of the accumulation of a new knowledge that can give us a deeper insight into the nature of the universe, of things material and immaterial.

So, let the dead bury the dead, and let us dip at once into the present-day problems of consciousness and treat the question in the light, if there be light, of present-day knowledge. Let us make a *tabula rasa* of our minds, if we can, and wipe out, as with a sponge, all inherited "traditional" concepts which, ingrained as accepted formulae and beliefs, necessarily, in accordance with psychological laws, conflict with, repress and make us blind to new points of view and new interpretations of old facts in the light of new ones. A poor figure of speech, I fear, that of the sponge, for modern psychology has taught us that when concepts are deeply scratched and grooved into the mind, it takes more than a sponge, rather a grindstone, to polish it off into a *tabula rasa*. And this is particularly true when the accepted concepts are tinged with feeling-tones and, it may be, vibrate with deep and often overpowering emotion, when stirred, though unwittingly, by a problem that is quick to awaken suspicion of questioning religious faith and belief in immortality.

Let it be enough, then, to say of past speculations dealing with the nature of consciousness that it is an old, old problem. And let us frankly recognize that we are dealing with animal consciousness as well as that of proud *homo sapiens*. We cannot, if we would honestly study this difficult problem, leave out of consideration any of the data at our disposal. We cannot, if we would be candid, make a selection from the facts which we are called to investigate and explain, and thereby limit ourselves to human experience. That would be an eclectic science with a vengeance. If we admit that animals have "intelligence," which is to say consciousness, similar in kind to that of man, however inferior in degree, we must include such consciousness amongst the data involved in the problem.

It thus becomes a biological problem and may be formulated, as we shall see: "Why the body has a mind."[1]

If we are prepared to refuse to believe that animals have consciousness — that our pet dog that leaps into our lap, expresses unbounded joy, distinguishes his master from a stranger and carries out his commands; that howls with every expression of pain when punished; that our favorite horse, highly trained to obey the most delicate signals, who comes at call to eat sugar out of our hands; that the wild bird that takes flight at the slightest sound of danger and the ape that behaves sometimes better than a human being — if we are prepared to assert that these animals have no emotions, or conscious perceptions of their environment, no cognition; that their eyes and brains, like as they are unto our own, do not see with visual images, that their ears do not hear with sound, that their skins do not feel with pain; if we are prepared to insist that they are merely mechanical puppets, automata, that all this behavior is but the expression of mechanical reflex action of the nervous system, unaccompanied by any of the forms of consciousness which we experience in ourselves, then we have, of course, simplified the problem by eliminating the greater part of the data of which we have to give an account. On the other hand, we have at the same time made it more difficult of solution, because we have eliminated so many of the data, in many respects the most instructive, and reduced the problem to that of human consciousness. It can no longer be treated as a biological problem that pertains to life in general.

I venture to think that common-sense people will ac-

---

1 This formula was suggested by C. A. Strong's book, *Why the Mind Has a Body*, the argument of which was based on my earlier book, *The Nature of Mind and Human Automatism* (1885).

cept without reserve the possession of consciousness by, at least, their *own* animal pets. We are, then, with this admission, justified in treating the problem of consciousness as a biological one, and so I shall do. But when so regarded, at once its range becomes enormously extended. For at one end of the scale of animal life it reaches down to the behavior of the lower orders of animals, such as the bees and ants, the fish and the reptiles. It may even perhaps extend to the amoeba, in which, low form of life though it is, so eminent a biologist as Jennings has felt compelled to postulate some kind of consciousness. At the other end of the scale it reaches up through the mammals, the ape, the gorilla, the Neanderthal man and other semi-human types amongst which science has been searching for the lineal ancestor from which present *homo sapiens* has descended. It is the nature of consciousness as occurring in all these different forms of animal life of which we must take and give an account. Otherwise no account would be complete or final.

Very well then; if it is agreed, as I think it must be, that animals have consciousness, let us begin with animals. I am sure you will agree with me that this will be a far better way, for then the question will cease to be one of you and me, and all personal interest and bias will be eliminated. As soon as and so long as we talk about our own consciousness — about your consciousness and my consciousness — we meet with what the psychologists call resistances, unwitting though they be. These resistances, of which we may not be consciously aware, emanate from deeply ingrained "inherited" concepts and beliefs which, according to the teachings of modern psychology, inhibit and prevent any unbiased examination of new interpretations in the light of newly discovered data. There is no gainsaying the fact that the belief in dualism, which is a synonym for animism, a belief in mind as an entity apart and distinct from the body, is so generally accepted, has been so deeply ingrained in the mind of the vast majority of human beings from the time of early childhood, that any attempt to utilize the newly acquired data and concepts of science in giving an explanation of consciousness and matter in any other terms becomes a question which touches our personality. Moreover, when any habit of thought, which means opinion and prejudice and point of view, has become firmly fixed, intellectual freedom, when it is in question, becomes the rarest of intellectual traits, a *rara avis* indeed. Indeed, we are all "Fundamentalists" in some field of thought and experience. There are political fundamentalists — the "die hards"; scientific fundamentalists — the skeptics; social fundamentalists — the aristocrats; as well as religious fundamentalists. And it is well that it is so, for it is the basis of conservatism; and, if it were otherwise, the world would be turned topsy-turvy in a frenzy for the new. Lucky that every new movement or thought meets with psychological resistance.

Lord Grey in the opening passage of his illuminating memoirs expresses this psychological principle far more pleasantly and, I fear, more convincingly than I can hope to do. He is speaking about contemporary opinions regarding the events which led up to the Great War, but what he says is equally applicable to strongly intrenched opinion in other fields: "Many of the war generation," he writes, "have formed opinions that nothing will modify, and are dominated by predilections or prejudices that have become an inseparable part of their lives. With such people mental digestion ceases to be able to assimilate anything except what nourishes convictions already formed; all else is rejected or resented; and new material or reflections about the war are searched, not for the truth, but for fuel to feed the flame of preconceived opinion."

And, likewise, it is in accordance with psychological law, *viz.*, that when the conventional conception of the nature of our own consciousness is brought into question, suspicions, though unconscious and unavowed, spring into being. There is fear that the consequences of any new interpretation may eventuate in the weakening of the moral values of our ideals, or in the negation of some valued religious concept such as immortality, touching, as they do, the happiness and the aspirations and spiritual welfare of all of us.

Let us, therefore, talk about apes and dogs and crawfish and such things — that is not personal. Let us approach the problem we have taken in hand as a broad biological one and therefore as one of animal consciousness; of that of your pet dog. Perhaps we shall be able to arrive at some satisfactory solution, or rather theory — for that is all we can hope for in the light of present knowledge — and perhaps not. But if we are fortunate enough to do so, we can then see how far our personal resistance will allow us to apply our solution to our own consciousness.

## II

The problem of the nature of mind is inextricably involved in that of the mind-body problem, the relation of conscious processes to their correlated brain processes, and one cannot be considered apart from the other. Indeed they are one and the same. But in dealing with these questions, we are met with the two very old rival hypotheses of dualism and monism. I shall have something more to say about these hypotheses later. Meanwhile the first question to be answered, if it can be answered, is: What is the relation of the consciousness of animals to their bodily processes; or, more specifically, to their brain processes?

Do their conscious processes determine their bodily behavior, and, if so, what is the relation between the two by which one acts upon the other? By what relation are desire, feeling and sensation so associated with brain processes that the former determine the behavior of the animal? For whatever view be held of the mind-body problem, there is no escaping the indubitable fact that, when viewed *physiologically,* the activity of the muscular system, the gland system and that of the organs of the body generally, make, with the activity of the nervous system — of which we need now only consider brain processes — one continuous closed system in which there is no place for the intercalation of consciousness. From the ingoing stimulus through the brain and out to the muscular system and organs of the body, eventuating in behavior, there is only one chain of events; and this chain is purely physical — nerves, spinal cord, brain, muscles. It is a purely physical circuit. And plainly, behavior of the animal, though it experiences desire, feeling and sensation, is and necessarily must be determined by the brain process as the central impulse-sending factor in this chain of physical events. Where, then, does consciousness come in? What part does it play? How can it play any part? If the brain process determines the behavior of the animal, how can desire and feeling and sensation do it too? Can it be that the brain process induces feeling, and then, in turn, feeling induces the outgoing brain process? That would mean that a certain quantity of energy of the physical process disappears to be replaced by an equivalent quantity of feeling; and correspondingly this quantity of feeling disappears to be replaced by an equivalent quantity of energy. For that is what the law of "correlation of forces," one of the fundamentals of physics, would require, as John Fiske pointed out, many years ago, as a weighty objection to "materialism." The impossibility of bringing feeling, or consciousness, into the physical equation is manifest. Indeed, *as so stated*, the law would be senseless. Furthermore, aside from this incompatibility, this conception includes the postulate that feeling can act upon atoms and molecules, conceived as material realities. But as Lange, the German philosopher, declared, "Were it possible for a single cerebral atom to be removed by 'thought' so much as the millionth of a millimeter out of the path due to it by the laws of mechanics, the whole 'formula of the universe' would become inapplicable and senseless."

## III

In the latter part of the last century, wide public interest in this question was aroused by the discussions of eminent physicists, biologists and psychologists, such as Tyndall, Huxley, Herbert Spencer, Bain, and the brilliant mathematician, Clifford. They spoke from the point of view and in the light of the knowledge given them by the science of their time. Tyndall, whose addresses gave rise to considerable hostile feeling, formulated the question in the following terms: —

"The discussion . . . turns on the question: Do states

of consciousness enter as links in the chain of antecedence and sequence which give rise to bodily actions and to other states of consciousness; or are they merely *by-products,* which are not essential to the physical processes going on in the brain? Speaking for myself, it is certain that I have no power of imagining states of consciousness interposed *between* the molecules of the brain, and influencing the transference of motion among the molecules. The thought 'eludes all mental presentation,' and hence the logic seems of iron strength, which claims for the brain an automatic action uninfluenced by states of consciousness. But it is, I believe, admitted by those who hold the automatic theory that states of consciousness are produced by the marshalling of the molecules of the brain; and this production of consciousness by molecular motion is to me quite as unthinkable as the production of molecular motion by consciousness. If, therefore, unthinkability be the proper test, I must equally reject both classes of phenomena. I, however, reject neither, and thus stand in the presence of two incomprehensibles instead of one incomprehensible."

Huxley, in a famous address, accepted the logic of "iron strength" and committed himself frankly to the opinion that the "consciousness of brutes and men would appear to be related to the mechanism of the body simply as a collateral product of its working, and to be as completely without the power of modifying that working as the steam whistle, which accompanies the work of a locomotive engine, is without influence upon its machinery."

Again: "It seems to me that in men as in brutes there is no proof that any state of consciousness is the cause of change in the motion of matter of the organism. If these positions are well based, it follows that our mental conditions are simply the symbols in consciousness of the changes which take place automatically in the organism; and that, to take an extreme illustration, the feeling we call volition is not the cause of a voluntary act, but the symbols of that state of the brain which is the immediate cause of the act."

The lecture in which he gave expression to this view exposed him, in consequence, to a storm of vituperation and abuse, which might have overwhelmed a less fearless and able man than Professor Huxley.[1]

I cite the views of these two famous scientists because they expressed the attempts of science of that day to answer the question before us in the light of the existing knowledge, and they well present the insoluble difficulty of the doctrine of two entities and parallelism. My attempt will be to avoid this difficulty and to answer the question in the light of the present-day knowledge and concepts of science. Very possibly the answer of today will have to be revised at some future day in the light of still newer knowledge.

The logic of Huxley and Tyndall was met, as I have said, by a storm of protest as, I think, it should have been met, not because the logic was faulty, but because the premise which they accepted of the nature of the atom and the molecule, that is to say, of the nature of matter, we now know to be untrue. The concept of matter has become completely revolutionized. This is the key to the whole problem as I hope to be able to make evident. And yet it is curious that there are some psychologists of standing today, belonging to the new behavioristic school, who are "steam whistlers," as we may call them, still holding that consciousness has nothing to do with the behavior of man or animal and that, therefore, we are all automata.

There are, then, three theories that have been advanced to explain the nature of the mind and its relation to bodily processes. Two are comprehended as *Dualism* and one as *Monism*. Of the dualistic theories — often regarded as doctrines, so accepted have they become as beliefs — one may be termed *epiphenomenalism* or *parallelism*. It postulates consciousness as a unique entity which has nothing in common with physical events. Accepting the concept, as laid down by the older science, of the nature of atoms and molecules, and accepting the "unthinkability" of this entity acting upon *such* atoms and molecules and entering into the chain of those physical brain events which physiologically are proven to determine bodily actions, it is perforce com-

1 See my *Nature of Mind and Human Automatism*, 1885, pp. 23, 24 and 107.

pelled, by the logic of "iron strength," to suppose that conscious processes proceed contemporaneously side by side with and parallel to the physical processes of the brain. Feeling, desire, volition, can have nothing to do with determining the activities of the animal. No matter how intelligent and purposeful this behavior may seem, it is only the mechanical resultant of purely reflex processes. Consciousness is only an epiphenomenon and animals are automata. Such is the doctrine of parallelism.

Of course, this theory is extended to man, otherwise it would have no interest for us here. But in thus extending it, it disregards the common-sense view derived from human experience that our desires and volitions do determine and are responsible for our behavior. It takes no account of the fact that, as a matter of common sense, society, in all its relations, in its codes of law and morals, is based upon the principle that our consciousness *is* the cause of our actions and that the responsibility for these rests upon our conscious will, not upon the gray matter of our brains.

I have thought it wise to dwell for a moment on this, as it seems to me, outgrown theory, because there are not wanting, as already intimated, true scientific explanations of human and animal behavior.

The second form which dualism takes is *interactionism.* It accepts the older concepts of the atom and molecule of science but disregards the logic of "iron strength." It also accepts parallelism and the proven facts of physiology; but resting, by analogy with the common experiences of man, on common sense, it maintains that consciousness of brutes does act upon atoms and molecules, and that consciousness is the cause of bodily behavior, though we may not know the *how.* That is the mystery, one that is accepted as inexplicable. It may be worth while pointing out here that the spiritualistic interpretation of the phenomena of which we now-a-days hear so much, propagated by spiritualists and alleged to be due to disembodied minds acting on mediums, is based on the theory of interactionism.

The third hypothesis, *monism,* rejected in the past, but on philosophical grounds, the notion of the nature of matter

— of the atom and the molecule — as conceived by science in the latter part of the last century, and in this rejection it has been vindicated by the new knowledge of modern science. It also accepted the logic of "iron strength" which gripped the "steam whistlers" and parallelists; but in rejecting their notion of matter, it rejected their major premise. Their conclusion, therefore, fell to the ground. And this was maintained for another reason: that the conclusion was not in accordance with common sense and common human experience, when the theory was extended to man.

Now, on the basis of the new concept of matter which the new knowledge offers, science itself is, as I believe, for the first time in a position to give its support to monism and offer an hypothesis which gives us an insight into the nature of mind and its relation to bodily processes. Viewed from the standpoint of this concept, the notion that "states of consciousness" may "enter as links in the chain of antecedence and sequence which give rise to bodily actions" is not only *not* unthinkable, but is quite intelligible; and it renders comprehensible both *that* and *how* feeling and thought are the cause of behavior. This new knowledge of matter even allows us to go further and say that a cerebral atom *can* be moved by "thought," without the whole "formula of the universe" becoming "inapplicable and senseless," though Lange's statement was wholly sound under the old criterion of the atom. Indeed, I think it is well within bounds to say that the new concepts of science are destined to give us an entirely new conception of the universe. As one writer on the atom has said, "for the first time in centuries there exists the material which a genius could synthesize into a universal science, in which physics and chemistry, biology and geology will lose their identities in a common set of principles."[1]

I trust it must be apparent from what has been said that the problems of the nature of mind and its relation to the body cannot be separated and that they are in reality one problem. But the key to the problem is the nature of "matter." Indeed, so it seems to me, *that*, rather than the nature

1  John Mills, *Within the Atom*, p. 9.

of mind, is the real problem. So long as the old notion of matter prevailed, it was impossible from the standpoint of science to find a solution. And it must be kept in mind that it is only from this standpoint that we are viewing the question, not from that of philosophy and epistemology. So long as physics and chemistry had offered an incomplete and erroneous notion of the nature of atoms and molecules, how was it possible for physical science to find an adequate theory of the correlation of mind and body? Was it not futile for science to attempt to correlate mind with something that does not exist? I say "does not exist," for matter, as it used to be conceived, it is now agreed as a result of modern researches in physics and chemistry, has no real existence. Is it any wonder that Huxley, in 1874, in a lay sermon, much as this modest address may be regarded, found it impossible to reconcile the facts of consciousness with those of the material world?

## IV

Let me premise that any theory which would offer an adequate explanation of the problem we have in hand must satisfy certain conditions.

1. It must recognize and take into consideration the immateriality — the spirituality, if you like so to term it — of mind.

2. It must recognize and accept the physical and physiological conception of the continuing chain of events of the nervous system by which behavior is determined.

3. It must provide for consciousness entering into that chain of events, which Huxley and Tyndall thought was unthinkable.

4. It must recognize and accept the psychological conception that volition and feeling and other conscious processes are the cause of our actions.

5. It must recognize and be compatible with the law of correlation of forces and conservation of energy.

6. It must recognize and accept the modern conception of physics and chemistry with regard to the nature of

"matter" and "force" and reconcile these with the immateriality of physical processes.

7. It must recognize and explain the apparent duality of mind and matter.

8. It must not be incompatible with any known established fact.

"Some job," you will say. If I am rash enough to undertake it, it is because for the first time we have the material to take the problem out of the field of philosophy and approach it from the standpoint of science.

The modern conception of matter clarifies and simplifies the physical data of the problem, though the nature of the problem itself remains the same. In the days of Huxley and Tyndall, the atom was supposed to be the unanalyzable unit of matter. It is only in recent years that it has been shown that the atom of every element is, on the contrary, a sort of microcosmic solar system; for every atom is a complex of units of negative and positive electricity, the units of the former revolving in orbits around a nucleus of the latter. The significance of this conception for our problem I cannot express in language better than I have elsewhere used. In sum and substance "matter," as we know it through our senses, has disappeared, having been resolved into negative and positive electricity, or, more specifically, units of the same in motion, acting and reacting upon one another and associated with, or more probably being in themselves, units of energy. Consequently all the physical and chemical properties of so-called "matter" are nothing but the activities of electricity.

This is a marvelous conception and a marvelous reconstruction of our knowledge. The properties of matter, such as mass, hardness, crystallization, atomic weight, chemical affinity and reactions, are resolved into the activity and manifestations of units of electricity; while that which we apprehend directly as heat and light and indirectly as ultraviolet rays, X-rays, radio rays, and other rays, are modes of electro-magnetic motions, shot out by the energy of such units.

When we look out upon the world of objects about us, we must recast our mode of viewing them and thinking. We must learn to think in terms of those mysterious concepts, electricity and energy, if we would try to resolve the deeper ultimate problems of life and mind, as well as those of the physical world. When we look out upon the rocks and houses and trees and plants and animals, we must try to view them in terms of billions upon billions of negative and positive electrons — electrical units in tremendous activity and motion, sometimes sending out units of energy into the world of space and always acting upon our senses in such fashion that we apprehend them all, not as they are, but as material objects. The only known constituent of the ponderable matter of the universe is electricity.

But what about the brain processes of the physiologist? These we apprehend *as such* in the same way as we apprehend the rest of our material world. And, though we conceive them in the form of atomic or molecular activity, physical or chemical, they too disappear under the analysis of the physicist. Let us not forget that we must, likewise, learn to think of these activities as those of enormously complex groups (called atoms and molecules) of units of electricity, and groups of groups, motivated by and associated with units of energy and, perhaps, radiating energy.

But what is a unit of electricity, the electron, from the standpoint of the physicist? Here we are apt to be misled by the limitation and connotations of language. As Bertrand Russell warns us, "Our imagination is so incurably concrete and pictorial that we have to express scientific laws, as soon as we depart from the language of mathematics, in language which asserts much more than we mean to assert. We speak of the electron as if it were a little hard lump of matter, but no physicist really means to assert that it is. We speak of it as if it had a certain size, but that also is more than we really mean."

In the name of exact science, then, what do physicists mean? I fear, in spite of Bertrand Russell's charitable words, that some have just such an "incurably concrete and pictorial imagination," that they mean just what their language implies, and that it is only the rather rare physicist of profounder and more philosophic thought that is not misled by word symbols.

If the electron could speak what would it say? "Ho, ho!" it would say: "So you think I am a little hard lump of something that you can weigh and measure? Not a bit of it! That is the way your 'incurably concrete and pictorial imagination' sees me, because that is the way I affect your visual apparatus, your visual sense. You only apprehend me objectively through your poor, little, limited, inadequate senses as a negative or positive electron. I am the *reality* of the universe. I am the *energy* of the universe. I am the *immateriality* of the universe. You cannot see me as I really am. Don't you know you can never know what I really am by your methods? I am the Unknown and Unknowable of physics. You only see and know me from *without*. I know myself from *within*. You know and see only what I do. You discover only the laws of my behavior and you call me electricity and energy. But these are only word-pictures or concepts of your own mind. Sometimes you are pleased to call me 'force,' but that is a concept derived from your own conscious experience. You are conscious when you meet with resistance, or when you move your body and material objects, of a feeling of exerting force or energy. But that is a subjective feeling. Nevertheless, when you see motion of other things, when you see me moving, you think in terms of feeling and say I have 'force'; that the activities of all electrons are determined by force. But that is only a subjective concept of yours; you are thinking anthropomorphically. All you see and know is that things *happen*, and the conditions of their happening are your laws. Why, you do not know. *I*, a mysterious electron, know but I will not tell, because you would not understand. I am the great mystery.

"But we electrons are just units of that which you are pleased to postulate and call energy and force and electricity. But we are not what you mean by these names. You know very well that your postulates are only convenient concepts of physics to work with; that they are symbols of something else; and, when taken literally, lead to misunderstandings.

And so I say we are units of the *reality of those concepts* — of the real universe, the universe from within. We are immaterial. It is our behavior that you apprehend and measure and you call our behavior electrons.

"When we immaterial units are marshalled in certain groups, numbers and configurations and move in certain orbits, you apprehend a whole group *through your senses* as atoms of the elements — hydrogen and oxygen and carbon and nitrogen and gold and silver, and all the rest. And when we behave in a certain way, you recognize our behavior as the chemical and physical properties of these atoms. And when those groups of us that you recognize as atoms of hydrogen are collocated with those groups that you recognize as an atom of oxygen, we become what you perceive as a molecule of water, or some other compound. And the physical and chemical properties of this compound are only our more complex behavior. We do lots of things that I cannot stop now to tell you about; and if I did, you could not understand, because you only know us from without as physical. We know ourselves from within as immaterial.

"But you know very well that as we become marshalled in greater and greater numbers in more complex combinations, in what you call and apprehend as atoms, and compounds of atoms, until we verily swarm like bees as molecules of organic substances, then the properties of the compounds *correspondingly* vary until they even exhibit the phenomena of life, and in the brain processes we emerge as the activities of mind."

And what would the philosophically-minded physicist say to all this? He would say that the electron is right: and he would agree that when we think of brain processes of an animal — don't forget we are talking of your pet dog — we must learn to think of processes, physical or chemical, in terms of their final analysis; that is, processes of which the component factors are mysterious concepts termed units of negative and positive electricity, or mysterious units of energy, which are probably one and the same thing.

Beyond this the objective methods of science cannot

give us the faintest idea of what concretely a brain process of a dog, or any animal, or a human being, is. We must not overlook that fact.

And we must not forget, what the physicist sometimes does forget, that electrons are not ultimates. In a sense they are only word-pictures. *They are only phenomenal manifestations of an unknown something.* And the unknown something is that which is postulated as the energy of the universe. But the nature of this something, the physicist cannot even guess at. He can only postulate concepts — *the immaterial* entities, electricity and energy, to account for certain phenomena which he apprehends as and calls matter. But these entities are not only unknown but unknowable by the objective methods of science. The postulated something may be "spiritual," if we wish to so term it, or of the order of the physical, or something else that is *not matter.* Whatever it is, it is not material in the sense of the material phenomenal world, as known to physics, which it is supposed to explain. It is *immateriality.*[1]

This is no new conception. It has long been held by philosophy and is not strange to science. Nevertheless I would ask you to dwell for a moment upon the significance of the conception, hackneyed though it be, *viz.*, the immateriality of that which we apprehend by the laws of our senses as matter. So long as the old notions of matter prevailed — that atoms were the ultimates of science — it was only philosophy that could fully grasp that, while we are living in a real universe, this real universe is totally and absolutely unlike the universe of our senses. But in these latter days when "matter" has been resolved into the phenomena of energy, called electricity, which is itself immaterial and the ultimate nature of which is unknowable, it is easier for our minds to think of the universe as immaterial. I cannot see that language has any positive term which is applicable to the real universe without connoting something that we

---

1 In this and some other passages below I have drawn freely from the text of a previous address of my own. "Three Fundamental Errors of the Behaviorist and the Reconciliation of the Purposive and Mechanistic Concepts" (Powell Lecture, Clark Univerity. Dec. 15. 1927; published in *Psychologies of 1925*, Clark University, 1926), in which I made use of this same theory of mind.

do not mean. The most we can do is to define the real universe in negative terms, telling what it is not, and so say it is "immateriality." We might call it "spiritual," though that term has been pre-empted in its common usage and implies more than we would mean. At any rate, the real universe is immaterial, though that immateriality manifests itself to us objectively through that which we apprehend as energy and electricity.

## V

The physicist now has finished his job and has gone as far as he can go. So he hands over his concepts to representatives of two other branches of science, to the psychologist and the physiologist, and he says to them: "Here is my new material: what can you do with it to solve your problem? Can you, O Psychologist, explain by means of it how volition and feeling can determine behavior? And you, O Physiologist, can you now understand how consciousness can enter into the chain of physical events in the brain?"

And these two scientists both say, "Thank you; you have now given us for the first time in centuries the material which enables us to form a comprehensible theory of the nature of mind and its relation to the body. At last you have taken the problem out of philosophy, and we can answer the question, why the body has a mind and the mind has a body.

"Your ultimate unknown something," these scientists say, "your immaterial energy of the universe is the same *in kind*, is of the same nature, as mind. The same in kind," they say, "because mind does not come into being, does not emerge, until the units of the immaterial universe are assembled in those extremely complex combinations, configurations, and arrangements that are to be found in the nervous system."

If this be true, then you must see that that portion of the immaterial energy which reveals itself to our senses( in, for example, the dog or the ape) as (hypothetical) brain process, is the immaterial reality of that process, is the consciousness of the animal. They are one and the same thing, immaterial mind being the reality, and brain process the mode in which it is objectively apprehended as matter. We may say that *mind is made out of the same immateriality as is the phenomenal universe.* This immateriality bursts into flower, emerges as consciousness, when its units are collocated in enormous numbers, in certain highly complex combinations, and become activated in a correspondingly complex manner. This immateriality, and consequently the elements of which mind is composed, are the reality of the universe. There would, indeed, seem to be no reason why we should not say, as not contradicting anything we know, that physical energy-in-itself and psychical energy are identical in kind. And out of the immaterial energy of the phenomenal physical universe, consciousness or mind has emerged in the process of "emergent evolution." Expressed again in another way we may say, if I may repeat what I have said elsewhere, consciousness is the *reality* of a particular combination of units of energy, of the energy of the universe in itself, the unknowable of physics, the brain processes (of the physiologist) "from within." Thus, the psychical becomes identified with that which is postulated by the physicist as the unknowable energy of the universe, by the physiologist as the brain process. Hence the theory is essentially monism. For mind and so-called "matter" have in their essence become identified. Indeed the real problem is, as we shall further see, one of *identification.*[1] It is not an easy notion for the imagination to grasp, for it cannot be pictured in concrete images. It can be formulated only in abstract terms as a concept, or after the fashion of a mathematical formula.

Obviously then, says the psychologist, it makes no difference whether you explain behavior in terms of nervous processes or of volition and feeling, for they are one and the same thing. And the physiologist says: "Of course, consciousness enters into the chain of physical events of the nervous system; for the immaterial reality of the physical brain process is consciousness."

[1] See my paper "The Identification of Mind and Matter," *Philosophical Review,* 1904, vol. XIII, no. 4.

Finally, testing the theory by the eight conditions laid down at the beginning, it is easy to see that it satisfies each and all. It accepts the immateriality or spirituality of mind; it is compatible with the physiological principle that brain processes (as well as mind) determine behavior; it renders intelligible how consciousness can and does enter into the chain of physical events; it satisfies common sense, which demands that feeling and volition are the cause of bodily activities and are not simply "symbols in consciousness"; it satisfies the law of correlation of forces and conservation of energy; it accepts the modern conception of matter and "force" and recognizes and explains the apparent duality of mind and matter; it does not contradict any known fact of consciousness or physical science.

Now, see how by this theory the real problem interestingly shifts. It is no longer the old parlous problem of parallelism, which has been the thorn in the flesh of psychological science. The theory relegates the epiphenomenalism of the steam-whistle to that limbo where such absurdities belong. Interactionism, too, disappears as a problem; for, there being *only* one process, there ceases to be the question of how one kind of process, the mental, can act upon another of a different kind. Instead of these the real problem becomes; if consciousness and so called "matter" are identical in kind, how is it to be explained that animal consciousness — feeling, image, color, pain — can appear under such different forms as units of electricity and electro-magnetic motion? Surely, in ourselves, our experiences of the two are totally unlike. Here is a seeming paradox — but seeming only.

The answer is simple and obvious. Electricity and energy are the mode in which the immaterial *reality* of the brain process — *i. e.*, the animal consciousness — is apprehended, actually (or ideally), through the senses by another organism, the reaction of this organism to the reality; in fact it is the only mode by which, if apprehended by a second organism, it could be apprehended. For a moment's reflection must make it clear that, if apprehended through the senses, it must be in terms of those senses; if through the visual sense, it must be apprehended as visual perception — form and motion, if through the auditory sense, as sound; if through the tactile sense, as tactile perception; and so with the other senses.

## VI

We have been considering solely animal consciousness. But you and I know that that was only a sort of camouflage. All along we have had the thought of human consciousness in the background of our minds, and the realization that what was true of animals must be true of man. We knew perfectly well that that was where we were coming out. Indeed, the assumption that animals have consciousness was based on our own consciousness and the fact that the two were alike in kind, though not in complexity and degree. Well, then, the principle of continuity forces the acceptance of the application of this monistic theory to man. For in the continuous line of ascent, from the lowest order of mammals up through the dog, the ape, the Neanderthal and other types of prehistoric man to man as he exists today, there is no stopping-place where we are entitled to say that consciousness becomes different in kind, undergoes a change in its intrinsic nature and in its relation to the ultimates of the brain processes. Still further, descending to the very lowest levels of animal life, meeting at each stage, as we go down, evidences of more and more primitive and even primordial types of consciousness until we reach what we can only postulate as mere sensibility in the amoeba, we realize that we have in this monistic theory a principle that is capable of explaining the problems of life and mind in terms of a universal concept. For this concept allows us to interpret the manifestations of both in terms of varying complexity and arrangement of units of the energy of the universe.[1]

We can now answer the question, "why the body has

1 For the development of this biological conception of consciousness, I would refer to my paper "Awareness, Consciousness, Coconsciousness and Animal Intelligence, from the Point of View of the Data of Abnormal Psychology — a Biological Theory of Consciousness"; (*Intern. Cong. of Psychol.*, Oxford 1923) published in *Psychologies of 1925*, Clark University, 1926.

a mind." When the marshalling of the units of the immaterial, the spiritual energy of the universe, which is the body,
reaches a certain complexity — this immaterial body *is* the
mind.

If this theory of the relation of consciousness to the
physiological processes of the body be the legitimate interpretation of the modern theory of matter and energy, bearing as it does on the question of the survival of consciousness
after dissolution of the body, what has science to say to this
question?    The average man is not interested in scientific
theories, and to him this is the only question of practical interest. Well, the history of science and of human thought
ought to teach us humility and it is wise not to dogmatize
or feel sure that we have attained the ultimate truth. But I
can see no escape from what seems to me the logic of "iron
strength" that compels the conclusion that if consciousness is
the resultant of an enormously complex organization of units
of that immaterial entity which is the real universe and
which manifests itself, but only objectively, to science in an
unreal form as "matter," that when that particular organization has become disintegrated by death, the mind itself
must cease to exist. This would seem to be the inexorable
logic of the hypothesis; and there would seem to be no other
hypothesis that does not leave the problem of the relation of
consciousness to the body as an inscrutable mystery, or lead
to consequences that are, as Tyndall said, unthinkable.

But mind you, I have said not "survival," but survival
of *consciousness* as we empirically know it. Whether there
is any other kind of survival, a survival of some entity of
which we have no experience, a soul — as distinct from the
mind, that is something beyond the province of science,
something about which science can have no opinion whatever.

The principle of continuity, again, rejects the notion of
the survival of consciousness unless we grant that same survival to every species of animal to which we ascribe mind,
including the prehistoric Neanderthal man and his like.

There are also a vast number of facts in the realm of
pathological consciousness, such, for example, as the mind
of the idiotic cretin, not restored but generated to normal-

ity by a few doses of an extract of the thyroid gland — a fact which seems almost impossible to reconcile with any theory of survival of consciousness. For what would have survived if the glandular extract had not been given? But to consider such facts of pathology here would carry us too far afield.

Thus, we can say that for the first time physics and chemistry, physiology, psychology and biology have furnished us the material which some genius some day can "synthesize into a universal science in which these and other sciences will lose their identity in a common set of principles."

### EDITORIAL NOTE

The juxtaposition of epiphenomenalism and parallelism, on page 578, as synonyms, may lead to misunderstanding. Parallelism is, as the term suggests, a neutral view which would assign equal importance to body and mind as fundamental unresolvable entities or categories, or as two phases of the selfsame "stuff" (the *identity* theory), while epiphenomenalism clearly makes matter the primal substratum with the mental as a momentary flash, issuing from it. Dr. Prince's psychical monism would tend to regard the physical as of a piece with the mental. In other words, what is looked upon as matter is to him and others who share the theory such stuff as dreams are made of, *viz.*, psychical material.

— A. A. R.

# CHAPTER XX

## HUGHLINGS-JACKSON ON THE CONNECTION BETWEEN THE MIND AND THE BRAIN

RUNNING through the later writings of Hughlings-Jackson, or at least through such of them as deal with the more abstract problems of nervous pathology, will be found a very decided opinion regarding the relation between the mind and the nervous system. This distinguished neurologist has consistently and repeatedly maintained a view regarding this relationship which has occupied a more or less prominent place in his writings. It is true that this theme has not, so far as the writer knows, ever been presented as the main topic under discussion, yet it has been emphasized so often, and in such decided language that, considering Hughlings-Jackson's standing as a neurologist, it is desirable that it should not be allowed to pass without careful examination.

A passage wherein this view has been as distinctly expressed as anywhere else, is the following: "Now, I speak of the relation of consciousness to nervous states. The doctrine I hold is, first, that states of consciousness (or synonymously, states of mind) are utterly different from nervous states; second, that the two things occur together — that for every mental state there is a correlative nervous state; third, that although the two things occur in parallelism, there is no interference of one with the other. This may be called the doctrine of concomitance. Thus in the case of visual perception, there is an unbroken physical circuit, complete reflex action, from sensory periphery through highest centres back to muscular periphery. The visual image, a purely mental state, occurs in parallelism with — *arises during* (not *from*) — the activities of the two highest links of this purely physical chain — so to speak, it 'stands outside' these links.

"It seems to me that the doctrine of concomitance is at any rate convenient in the study of nervous diseases. It, or an essentially similar doctrine, is held by Hamilton, J. S. Mill, Clifford, Spencer, Max Müller, Bain, Huxley, Du Bois Reymond, Laycock, Tyndall, Hermann, and David Ferrier.

"Those who accept the doctrine of concomitance do not believe that volitions, ideas, and emotions produce movements or any other physical states. They would not say that an hysterical woman did not do this or that because she lacked will; that an aphasic did not speak because he had lost the memory of words, and that a comatose patient did not move because he had lost consciousness. On the contrary, they would give, or try to find, materialistic explanations of physical inabilities. I do not try to show what is the nature of the relation between mental and nervous states."[1]

Again: "We must be very careful both in ophthalmological and neurological studies not to confound sensations — colors for an example, which are states of mind — with activities of sensory elements, which are states of body. We must not speak of any mental states as occurring *from,* but as arising *during* discharges; only physical effects, such as movements, arise *from* nervous discharges."[2]

From these quotations it will be seen that Hughlings-Jackson sharply differentiates the psychical from the physical, and widens the chasm between them to proportions as great as it ever attained in the past. He lends the authority of his name to what may be called the popular opinion. If this opinion be correct, all well and good; but if it be erroneous — as many competent to judge believe — it is time that this statement be challenged.

I hope to be able to show in the course of these pages that this doctrine of "concomitance," as just expressed, is one that leads to consequences more fallacious than even the crassest materialism.

I cannot help suspecting that Hughlings-Jackson has not completely grasped the full meaning of this problem.

1 "Evolution and Dissolution of the Nervous System."

2 "Ophthalmology and Diseases of the Nervous System."

To group together Hamilton, Clifford, Spencer, Bain, Huxley, and Tyndall, to say nothing of the others, as holding essentially the same doctrine, is to my mind much the same thing as putting Salisbury, Gladstone, Chamberlain, and Labouchère into one political boat, and saying they hold essentially the same opinions. If one does not see the fundamental difference between the opinions of Clifford and Huxley, one can scarcely have a clear idea of the matter.

Not the least of Hughlings-Jackson's sins is the seduction of his pupil, Mercier,[1] who has even more vehemently expressed himself to the same effect, though both claim the authority of Spencer for their opinions. But anyone familiar with Spencer will hardly hold him responsible for such errors. Mercier writes, "Try to think of a feeling passing along a nerve. . . . The axis cylinders are grey threads of protein substance, which is made up, like all other matter, of molecules swinging in space. Now, where is pain? Is it in the molecules or in the intervening space? And how does it pass along the nerve? Does it jump from molecule to molecule, or does it flow in the interstices? If the former, pain must be solid; if the latter, it must be a fluid, both of which hypotheses are manifestly nonsense. . . . But it may be said: 'pain, we know, is not really in the nerves; it is in the brain.' Again the same problem awaits us: the brain is made up of cells and fibres. Is pain in the cells? Is it in the fibres?" etc. "Let us try to imagine," he continues, "an idea of food producing a movement — say, of carrying food to the mouth. . . . Try to imagine the idea of a beefsteak binding two molecules together. It is impossible. Equally impossible is it to imagine a similar idea loosening the attractive force between two molecules."

I agree with Mercier that such hypotheses are "manifestly nonsense"; but they are nonsense because of the nonsense connoted by the terms "matter" and "mind" as employed by Mercier. But notwithstanding that, we (who hold the views which will be presently explained) are in full accord with him on this point, nevertheless we maintain that

1 *The Nervous System and the Mind.*

Hughlings-Jackson and Mercier are at fault in allowing themselves to be "driven to the conclusion that pain and matter are things with no community in nature, are facts of totally different orders, and cannot be reduced to any common term." Still more, our contention is that no one could seriously propose the question, "Can the idea of a beef-steak bind two molecules together?" as one at all involved in the problem, without having a total misconception of the nature of the subject under discussion; no one could ask such a question and possess a correct idea of the nature of matter. These extraordinary hypotheses are relevant only on the supposition that matter, that molecules and motion, have objective reality, as we know them, and that they are not merely states of consciousness. I can imagine the horror with which Spencer would contemplate such notions being imputed to him after all he has written to discredit them.

But there is one very serious objection to Hughlings-Jackson's views, which may as well be stated here. "Those who accept the doctrine of concomitance," he naïvely remarks, as if it were no objection to this hypothesis, "do not believe that volitions, ideas and emotions produce movements, or any other physical states." This is the position taken by Huxley, who once said "The consciousness of brutes [and men] would appear to be related to the mechanism of their body simply as a collateral product of its working, and to be as completely without the power of modifying that working as the steam whistle, which accompanies the work of a locomotive engine, is without influence upon its machinery. . . . And to take an extreme illustration, the feeling we call volition is not the cause of a voluntary act, but the symbol of that state of the brain which is the immediate cause of that act."

Mercier with much emphasis adopts, if I interpret him correctly, the same "steam-whistle" opinion, though expressing himself in different language.

And they are right so far as this conclusion is a logical consequence of their premises. It is the inevitable conclusion to which they must be driven. If mind is something that stands entirely apart from molecules and motion, if it has only a parallel existence with cerebral processes, it cannot enter as a link in the chain of events, and consciousness can have nothing to do with governing our actions. We are nothing, as Huxley has said, but automata.

Now, I do not wish to speak except with the highest deference for those who hold opposing views. I know how easy it is for the mind to deceive itself in matters of this kind; how difficult it is to free one's self from the ideas which by long habit are connoted by language, and which consequently prevent our viewing a thing from a new aspect. But I do wish to emphasize the fact that any doctrine which ultimately leads to denial of volition as a cause of action is, as Mercier would say, "nonsense," and doomed to failure. If a man is moved to sympathy at the misery of a beggar and, following his sympathy, he gives a dollar to that beggar, the giver is satisfied that his feelings of sympathy — his states of consciousness — directly control his muscular acts and move his fingers to take a dollar bill out of his pocket and give it away. This is a fact of direct experience, and is worth a whole volume of scientific erudition.

If, under the influence of anger, I strike a man, there is little use in my trying to shift the responsibility from my temper to the shoulders of my gray matter, and in my telling the world that my outburst of temper was only a sort of "steam whistle"; that it told me what my right hand was going to do, but had no more to do with the hitting than had that of the judge on the bench who is going to try my case.

Popular language correctly expresses the facts in such cases, and any scientific doctrine which attempts to explain the relation of mind to body and does not recognize this truth will never be accepted by common-sense people. The contention of those who hold the doctrine which will be developed later is that the "steam-whistle" advocates have been logically driven to their conclusion; but the reason for this is that though their logic is faultless, their premises are wrong, the conditions of the problem not being thoroughly understood. Well-known truths regarding the nature of so-called "matter" have, in practice, been neglected, or their full bearing on the question has been overlooked. That there is a solution of this question, which, on the one hand, does not disregard these truths, and, on the other hand, recognizes volition as a cause of muscular action, seems likely. This solution thus far has been, for the most part, neglected; but the reason for this is plainly because it has not been understood, and not because any serious objection has been urged against its final conclusions.

This matter is not one which purely concerns the psychologist, with whom it has hitherto been customary to leave it as a question of metaphysics. It concerns as much the alienist and the neurologist, and even the general practising physician, with all of whom it is a matter of real practical importance. How can one understand, for example, how a psychical shock, such as would be incurred in a railway disaster, can produce not only mental perturbation but disturbances of the various physiological functions of the body, known as somatic? How can one really understand how such a shock could cause disturbances of the heart, the viscera, neuralgic pain in various parts of the body, tumor, vaso-motor disturbances, spasms, and what-not, unless one has a clear conception of the relation between mental action and cerebral action? How understand the true genesis of neuro-mimesis and hysteria, with all their protean manifestations, or conversely, how can one possess any distinct picture of the mode by which a purely physical concussion, or disturbance of the circulation, causes an impairment of speech, reasoning powers and other mental faculties, unless he has a definite idea of the relation between these two classes of facts? It we look back to the time when mind was regarded as something apart from the body, and consider the views which obtained in those days regarding the nature of insanity and the barbarous treatment of the insane, which was their natural consequence, we realize what the practical results have been, in these later years, from obtaining a knowledge of the dependence of a diseased mind on a diseased brain; and if we can penetrate deeper still into the inner recesses of the nervous system, and can extract the secret of the more intimate relation between the mind and the brain matter, we can scarcely doubt that much that is now obscure in the pathology of many neuroses and psychoses would become intelligible. How then can it be denied that this question is a practical one, and one which the neurologist should seek to understand?

The negative view to which Dr. Hughlings-Jackson has repeatedly given expression — that we have no knowledge whatsoever regarding the subject, and that we stand face to face with a great mystery — is that which is popularly held; although amongst those who have thought much on the subject there is a weighty minority who believe that a satisfactory solution has been found. This solution has not been generally accepted, and, indeed, I think I keep well inside the limits of moderation in saying that it has not been really understood by one out of every ten even of those who have undertaken to write upon the question. For this reason, various false conceptions are usually to be found underlying every discussion of this most perplexing problem. And yet it is this minority view towards which opinion is gradually converging.

That every mental act is accompanied by a physical change in the brain has become an accepted axiom, and yet, having due regard to the accuracy of language, it may be said that *such a statement is absolutely false, and is the basis of most of the fallacious views on the subject.* This may seem paradoxical, and probably will be challenged by every reader who has followed me thus far, and yet it is a fact which I hope to be able to make clear before I have finished.

"Does the mental action follow the physical action, or does the physical action follow the mental?" "How do neural vibrations in the brain become transformed into thought and feeling?" These are questions which are frequently asked, and the questioner shakes his head and tells us there is no use trying to answer them. The essayist, if he be an essayist, says that these questions are insoluble, and that we are as far as ever from obtaining a solution of the mystery. This is perfectly true. We are as far as ever from doing this, and it is safe to say that we never shall answer these questions, for the simple reason that the questions themselves are mere nonsense. They involve assumptions which are not true, and therefore the questions are absurdities and cannot be answered. We cannot say how brain action is transformed into thought, because it is not "transformed" at all. Nor shall we be able to discover whether mental action follows the physical, or *vice versa*, because neither follows the other. The erroneous assumption here is that there are two different facts (the mental and the physical), each having a separate and independent existence *in the same individual*, whereas there is in reality only *one fact*, and one thing cannot very well be transformed into or follow itself.

That we have two different and separate conceptions — one, the so-called mental facts, the other, the so-called physical facts — is perfectly true; they form a part of common experience. But whether there are two different and separate existences corresponding to these conceptions is another matter and something which cannot be left to common experience to determine. For aught that appears on the surface, there may be but one real existence, or fact, which is the basis of both conceptions, and, without anticipating further the argument, it may be said that this is the explanation to which the best thought at the present day is tending. I am not referring to the notion that mental and physical facts are but "different aspects of one and the same underlying thing" — a most hazy and confused notion — but to a very different idea. I prefer that this idea shall be developed later as we go on, rather than incur the risk of being misunderstood at the outset before the ground has been prepared. I shall have, then, to ask the reader to temporarily suspend his judgment and to follow me with open-mindedness to the end, and to try to get at my real meaning, which, I fear, my words will but poorly express.

I take it that the reason why this question has escaped a satisfactory explanation is because we have not examined sufficiently deeply into the nature of the facts under investigation, and have not reduced them to their lowest terms. In matters of this kind it is essential that we should first resolve the facts into their component elements and find out what manner of things they are — whether they are what they seem to be on the surface, or something else, before attempting to deal with them. I say in matters of this kind, because in other fields of inquiry — in the physical sciences, for example — it is not essential that we should make this preliminary inquiry into the exact nature of the things whose phenomena we are investigating.

If you, who are interested in chemistry, wish to learn the exact amount of sulphuric acid and zinc necessary to produce a given amount of sulphate of zinc, or desire to ascertain the chemical action which takes place in the process; or if I wish to know the laws of electro-magnetism, it is not necessary that either of us should know the exact nature of material bodies, nor that we should have more than a common expert knowledge of chemical substances and of the nature of electricity. Whatever error may exist in our conceptions of these material facts will be the same on both sides of the equation, and may be neglected. It is not even necessary to know the nature of electricity, for whatever it be — whether a fluid, as was formerly held, or whether a mode of motion — it is only its laws that we are investigating; while, underlying these, electricity itself persists as a constant unvarying factor, and any result that may be arrived at will not be affected by any error in our notion of electrical force. We are dealing from beginning to end with facts of the same order or class, which have equivalent values so far as their intrinsic nature is concerned.

Likewise, in dealing with problems in neurology, if, for example, we wish to determine the relations between a peripheral stimulation and a resultant motor action, it is not necessary to know the essential nature of nerve force or the exact chemical composition of the protoplasm of nerve cells or the true nature of the brain-matter, because these are constant factors in the reaction, and bear the same relation to the ingoing stimulation as to the outgoing one.

So, too, in dealing with matters of psychology. If we wish to study the laws of memory, or of volition, or of the association of ideas, it is not necessary to go deeply into the nature of mind for similar reasons. Thought, sensations, feelings are all facts of the same order, just as zinc, sulphuric acid, electricity, and heat are all material facts, and therefore of the same class. The one class is psychical — the other class material; and so long as we are only dealing with facts of one class, it is not necessary to reduce them to their lowest terms; but when we wish to ascertain the relation between facts of two different orders — between psychical facts, on the one hand, and physical facts, on the other — to learn if they have anything in common, discover their likeness or unlikeness, it becomes necessary to resolve them into their component elements before attempting to compare them. In other words, if $x$ is on both sides of the equation, its value may be neglected, but if $x$ is on the one side and $y$ on the other, the equation cannot be established until the value of $x$ and $y$ are known.

Pursuing, then, our inquiry along these lines, let us see what is the composition of a psychical state and what that of a cerebral state. It will be, perhaps, more convenient to consider the latter first. When we speak of cerebral activity, it has been agreed that we mean a form of molecular motion — *neural vibration,* it is often called. The exact nature of this motion has not been made out, but there can be no doubt that nerve-force can be reduced to some form of motion, just as electricity, heat, light and other physical forms of energy may all be shown to be modes of motion. In other words, the so-called "nervous current" which transmits a peripheral impression from the skin or the ear to the central nervous system is no other than an oscillation of the molecules of the axis-cylinders of the nerves. The motion of one molecule is communicated to its neighbor, and so on, until the wave of motion has reached the central organ, just as heat and light waves are transmitted through the air and ether respectively, or electricity through solid bodies. When this motion reaches the cerebral centres, what happens? The same thing is repeated. The motion is taken up by the cells and fibres of the brain. If the peripheral impression has come from the ear or from the eye, the protoplasmic molecules in the temporal lobe, in the one case, and in the parieto-occipital lobe, in the other, join in the oscillation, and if muscular action ensues, the molecular agitation is transmitted again along the motor nerves to the muscles, where it is converted into muscular energy. Thus far it will be noticed that we have had to deal with modes of motion, purely physical processes, and we have come across nothing like mental activity, nothing like the sounds and visual pictures which are supposed to arise at the instant when the molecular wave reaches the temporal and occipital lobes; and assuredly we never shall see anything of such psychical states as long as we only look at the process from one point of view. Unless we go behind the scenes, as it were, and see what all these molecular processes really are, we shall be as blind to the mental process as Nelson was to the signal for retreat at Copenhagen when he put his blind eye to the telescope and said he didn't see it.

This failure to find even the first rudiment of mind, in tracing the chain of neural motion from the periphery to the centre and back again, is what has led Hughlings-Jackson to fall into the same pit into which Huxley stumbled, when the latter said that consciousness was as completely without the power of modifying the working of the body as the "steam whistle which accompanies the work of a locomotive engine is without influence upon its machinery."

So Jackson, with his mind only on the physical process, says that "the visual image, a purely mental state, occurs in parallelism with — *arises during* (not *from*) — the activities of the two highest links of this purely physical chain; so to speak, it 'stands outside' of these links." He does not "believe that volitions, ideas, and emotions produce movements or any other physical states. He would not say that an hysterical woman did not do this or that because she lacked will; that an aphasic did not speak because he had lost the memory of words; that a comatose patient did not move because he had lost consciousness. On the contrary, [he] would give or try to find materialistic explanations of physical inabilities."

The logical process by which these conclusions were reached is plain enough, but it reduces the whole matter to an absurdity. All our conscious experience tells us that our feelings are the causes of our actions. This is a fact which each man can prove for himself as often as he wishes to try. The facts of consciousness are as trustworthy as those of the physical world, but all this experience Hughlings-Jackson is willing to pitch overboard simply because, when examining physiological processes by purely physiological methods, he fails to come across anything like a mental state. It is perfectly true that bodily actions are the resultant of physical processes in the brain, but it also may be true that they are the resultant of mental states; and our failure to see this may be due to faulty methods employed in investigating them. At any rate, we are not justified in casting aside either the evidence of our own consciousness or the evidence of physical research without attempting to reconcile the two, however contradictory in appearance. This reconciliation can only be accomplished by inquiring more deeply into the *real* nature of cerebral motion.

Cerebral motion is equivalent to molecular oscillation. But what is motion, and what manner of things are these molecules? A molecule of nervous protoplasm, for example, is something of definite shape and size and color and density, just like any lump of protoplasm of which, with myriads of other molecules, it is an insignificant part. And all these peculiarities distinguish a protoplasmic molecule from another kind of molecule of muscular substance, for example, which is of different size, shape, color, etc. But what *are* these properties? Anyone who has given any special attention to this question now-a-days is well aware that all these properties as we know them are neither more nor less than our own states of consciousness; and that, in fact, our whole knowledge of the material world is nothing more than a series of such states. Further, any inferences that we may draw from a study of the material universe are nothing more than inferences that we may draw regarding a series of states of consciousness that we have under certain conditions.

This is a truth that no follower of Herbert Spencer will be prepared to deny, and although it seems to me that few, if any, of those who have thought on the subject would dispute the truth of the statement, I am free to admit that

daily experience convinces me that the number of even cultivated persons who have thought at all deeply on the matter
is exceedingly small.

Our knowledge of a molecule, then, is nothing more
nor less than a series of sensations of our own, and when we
talk about a material world as being something without
kinship with anything else, we are talking nonsense; or
speaking more politely, we are making assertions unsupported
by the evidence of the most rudimentary experience. For
the only objective (material) world we know is a series of
conscious states, and therefore something entirely akin to
each one's consciousness; while the thing-in-itself we know
nothing whatsoever about, and therefore, we are not justified in making any assertions about it at all. Beyond our
own sensations of grayness, of hardness, of smell, etc., we
know no more what a molecule of protoplasm, or any other
molecule, *really* is — we know no more what the molecule-
in-itself is — than we know whether angels' wings are tied
on with pink ribbons or blue ribbons.

It will be well to stop and ponder for a while upon this,
to take in its full meaning. Very few of even those who have
fully recognized the truth of each individual fact involved
have completely realized the full force of all the facts as a
whole. Even John Fiske, who never loses an occasion to insist upon this peculiarity of our knowledge of the objective
world, and is most intolerant of everyone else who has not
grasped it, seems to forget all about it himself when he
comes to consider the deductions to which these individual
truths lead. Otherwise I cannot understand how he can so
entirely misconstrue Clifford as he has done. For John Fiske
to eulogize Clifford is to me very much like Robert Inger-
soll appealing to the Archbishop of Canterbury to confirm
his own heretical opinions.

But can we derive any help regarding the true nature
of a molecule from the ultimate analysis to which the physicist seeks to reduce such material bodies? A molecule of any
substance, whether gaseous, liquid, or solid, is never at rest,
and is always in motion. The direction and extent of this
motion differs according as it is a gaseous, liquid, or solid

molecule. In a gaseous condition molecules fly about, for the most part, in straight lines; in a liquid, being always in contact, they slide around each other, moving about in all directions through the whole extent of the liquid; while in a solid, although every molecule is in motion, each is confined to a fixed path of limited extent in which it oscillates to and fro, much as a ball suspended from the ceiling by an elastic cord would oscillate up and down. These are the conceptions, at least, which, physicists teach us, represent the most probable composition of matter. By means of this constant motion of the molecules, many of the properties of a substance may be explained.

It is possible that we may even go further than this. Sir William Thompson has advanced the hypothesis, supporting it by a series of mathematical calculations, that all molecules are but vortex rings (motion) in an incompressible, frictionless fluid — the ether.[1] All matter is then but a form of the ether, and matter differs from the ether only in the size and arrangement of the vortex rings. One of the beauties of this hypothesis is that the properties of material bodies, such as hardness, elasticity, etc., are reduced to one common basis, motion, and accounted for by differences in the size and rapidity of rotation of the vortex rings. Without stopping to consider some of the modifications of this theory, which have been suggested to meet the objections that have been raised to it, it is probable that some such conception as this will be the ultimate analysis of matter on the part of physics, and it will be shown that all material molecules are only points of motion in a universal fluid, and that one kind of matter differs from another kind only in the kind of its motion.

Assuming, now, that the results of these investigations are correct, and that atoms and molecules are simply points of motion, are we any nearer a knowledge of the true nature of such bodies? A few moments' reflection will convince

1 In the light of the modern development of physical theory, the preceding paragraphs and part of what follows are, to be sure, antiquated, but they are included for obvious historical reasons.

anyone that we are as far as ever from such knowledge. The problem has been simplified, that is all. Instead of knowing matter as a group of conscious states, called color and hardness, and size and shape, etc., we have reduced our knowledge to terms of one sense — of vision. All the other modes by which we know the object have been reduced to this one. But our knowledge now is none the less subjective, a mode of our own consciousness. What is there behind these vortex rings, — the thing-in-itself? Of this we have no direct knowledge. It is the great unknown universe. What shall we call it? Shall we call it *force*? If we do, we shall use a term which derives all its significance from our own conscious experience, from our states of muscular sense and tactile sense, and apply it to something of which we have no experience. The idea of force means nothing except so far as it represents certain sensations — feelings of effort and feelings of resistance. And if we use this term to express an unknown element in the universe, we shall endow that element, of which we have no experience, and can have no experience, with qualities which have no meaning except as states of mind.

Stop for a moment, and try to conceive what manner of thing this unknown universe in which we live is. What is this material world, which we know only as states of mind — as color, hardness, motion, force, etc? By what name shall we call it? We cannot call it power, force, activity, motion, for these names all derive their meaning from states of our consciousness; therefore we cannot use them to describe that which is not consciousness, and, so far as we know, does not resemble any conscious experience. We have no language to define it because we have no experience of it to give us language; no mental conception corresponds to it. It is the unknown *x*.

But in spite of this limitation of our powers, there is another way by which we may obtain a hint, if only a hint, of the nature of this object world. But first, let us turn from the contemplation of this material world of molecules to the world of mind. Will a similar analysis resolve states of consciousness into a known and unknown element? If so, we can never understand the relationship between cerebral activity and mental activity. I hold not. We may, as Spencer has endeavored to do, resolve complex states of mind into simpler states. We may perhaps resolve any state of consciousness into a number of psychical shocks which have blended into a single feeling, just as a musical note may be resolved into a number of individual sounds, which in consciousness blend into one. In this way, a sort of psychical unit may be obtained, of which all mental states are compounds. In a similar way the material world may be resolved into "simple pulsations, or rhythmical movements of ether-atoms."

But after all has been resolved into psychical shocks, that shock is still a state of mind, and it cannot be reduced by analysis any farther. It cannot be shown to be still further compounded, and more important still, it is not something that, like the physical world, is known in terms of something else. It is known directly and immediately in terms of itself. Therefore it is absolutely known. Mind is an ultimate, a reality — something that we know just as it exists, not a picture of something else. It is known by direct experience. The real nature of the material world we know nothing about. The real nature of mind we know all about. Our sensations of pleasure and pain are really just as we know them.

This being so, my contention and the contention of those who hold the same view is that the relation between a mental fact and a cerebral fact is satisfactorily explained in the following way: — a mental state of pain is a real fact belonging either to ourselves or to another person. For the purpose of clearness of presentation, let us consider another person's pain. This is a real fact. Cerebral molecular motion is a group of conscious states not in that person but in ourselves, and therefore it is a symbol of a something else in that other person. This something else is his pain. *The pain is the thing-in-itself; the neural vibration is the visual picture which one person would have if his optic apparatus could be affected by the mental state of pain in another person.*

Mental states are the reality of [what appears to another person as] molecular vibrations in the brain.

To thoroughly realize the meaning of this conception, we must keep vividly before us the fact that no such thing as a "molecular vibration" occurs, as such, in any one's brain. Something occurs there, of course. But what we call a molecular vibration is only a group of conscious states which is our mental picture of an apparently unknown activity, and caused in one person by this apparently unknown activity in another. I say "apparently" unknown, for in this case it happens to be known, *i. e.*, it is consciousness.

An important corollary follows from this. It was seen that we know nothing of the real nature of the material "forces" of the world. There is one exception to this, namely, cerebral "force." This we do know. The real nature of cerebral "force" is consciousness.

But if mind is the reality of cerebral processes, it is obvious that the statement with which we started out is true, *viz.*, that there are not two separate processes occurring synchronously side by side, and correlated with one another *in the same individual*. There is only one process — the psychical. The physical is only an objective presentation of it in another person, just as a man pictured in a mirror is only a representation of the real man in the street. There are not two men. The real man is the real agent in the chain of circumstances making up his life. Therefore cerebral processes (which, as we know them, are a picture) are not transformed into, nor do they precede nor follow the psychical process, which is the real thing.

In a paper like this, it is, of course, out of the question to adduce any extensive proofs of these postulates, even if it were possible to *prove,* in the sense in which this word is ordinarily used in the physical sciences, hypotheses of this kind. I have already set forth, as I believe, in my work on *The Nature of Mind* elaborate and cogent reasons on which this explanation of the relation of the mind to the brain rests. At best, all that can be asked is that such an hypothesis shall satisfactorily explain all the conditions of the problem, and that it shall not be incompatible with any known fact. If it shall be found that there is no known fact with which it is not in harmony, and that it does not conflict with any known law, the theory must be accepted as satisfactory. This we, who hold it, contend to be the case.

It makes comprehensible how a stimulation of the body "gives rise to a psychical process"; and conversely, how a psychical process occasions a physical process. It is in harmony with and explains the fact of everyone's conscious experience that his feelings and volitions are the cause of his actions, and are not only a sort of "steam whistle" without power of modifying the workings of his body. It bridges over the chasm between mind and matter, and recognizes, while it makes intelligible, their known differences. It gives an interpretation of the universe as a whole.

In order to avoid any misunderstanding, and to anticipate a possible criticism, it is proper to make one qualification of the statement that bodily processes give rise to mental processes, and *vice versa*. This qualification must be considered as largely verbal if the real nature of the processes is kept in mind, but still an adherence to the strict meaning of language requires that it be made.

It has always been a difficulty to conceive how motion in a sensory nerve on reaching the brain could give rise to feeling, and again, how feeling could give rise to motion in outgoing nerves. Strictly speaking, this does not occur. "Motion" in a sensory nerve, as has been already explained, is only somebody's group of conscious states, and, therefore, a mental picture of unknown activities in a nerve. Indeed, a nerve is only a similar mental picture of the unknown. Now, it is the unknown activity which occasions feeling and other states of mind, and it is the unknown activity again, pictured as motion in motor nerves, which is occasioned in turn by feeling. As what we call motion is only somebody's picture or symbol, naturally it cannot cause your mental state. To insist on this refinement of language is, however, pedantic, except for the purpose of calling attention to the facts.

There is one point which it is desirable should receive perhaps some further explanation — at least, those who have not yet quite grasped the full meaning of this theory may think it necessary.

If cerebral motion is only a picture of the real thing, say a musical sound, why is it that the picture appears as *motion*, a so-called objective fact, while the real thing is a musical sound? The answer is not difficult, and those who have followed me thus far must have anticipated it.

Let us suppose that one of us should show a kaleidoscope to some one, who not only had never seen such a thing before, but was totally ignorant of the effect of prisms, mirrors, etc., on light — in fact, was totally ignorant of the most rudimentary knowledge of optics and of the physical sciences. Such a person might be an inhabitant of some uncivilized island in the Pacific. Suppose such a person, looking through the kaleidoscope, sees a wonderful variegated mosaic of colors. We can easily imagine how his curiosity would be excited by what he saw. He would, probably, at once examine the other end of the tube, but only to find there, in a glass box, a lot of little pieces of colored glass thrown higgledy-piggledy together, and nothing at all like the beautiful mosaic that he has seen. He will, probably, still ask where is the picture he has seen and if you point again to the little box of broken glass he will not believe you. You tell him to look once more through the tube, and as he looks you turn the kaleidoscope, and he sees a succession of changing pictures, each a symmetrical pattern of brilliant colors. Again he takes his eye from the tube to examine the farther end, but, as before, he finds only a handful of pieces of broken glass, comparatively dull in color, tumbling over each other without order or method. You tell him that is what he sees, but, incredulous, he shakes his head and will not believe you. He insists there is something inside the tube which he sees. You continue to expostulate and tell him there is nothing there, but he retorts that there must be two things, not one. He sees an ever-changing panorama of symmetrical and orderly designs, brilliant with transmitted light, and you are only showing a lot of dull glass tumbling about, and without brilliancy. He says there are two processes totally unlike each other. He can find no similarity between the two, and therefore is confident there must be something inside the tube. So you take the apparatus to pieces, and show him there is nothing inside but some mirrors arranged in a peculiar way. If you have amused yourself sufficiently with his curiosity, and if you think him sufficiently intelligent, you will probably explain to him why it is that these pieces of glass appear so different when viewed through the tube. It is an optical illusion. They can appear as if arranged symmetrically only because they are seen through an apparatus which, arranged according to the laws of optics, compel anything seen through it to appear in a form different from that when seen with the naked eye.

So it is with mind and a cerebral molecule. If we could *optically* experience a feeling as a pain or as a musical sound, in ourselves or another person, as we can ideally — that feeling could only appear to us as it would be modified by our optical apparatus — just as the pieces of glass were modified in the kaleidoscope. If our visual apparatus were affected by a state of consciousness in another person, it would be an absolute necessity that we should see that state of consciousness (pain, sound), not as it really is but as a visual image, *viz.*, a molecular motion. The *reality* of that motion would be the other person's state of consciousness. This would be the thing-in-itself. Hence it follows that cerebral molecules and motion, which are commonly said to be correlated in each person's brain with his psychical processes, are only the modes by which *one* person apprehends *another's* conscious states. Consciousness is not correlated with molecular motion in the same individual, but only with states of consciousness (*i. e.*, the mental picture of molecular motion) in another person.

APPENDIX

# APPENDIX

## HISTORY OF THE DISCOVERY OF COCONSCIOUS IDEAS.[1]

THE subconscious is no modern theory. Elsewhere,[2] I have had occasion to remind the reader that, as a concept in a scheme of metaphysics, "unconscious ideas" — *i. e.,* ideas of which we are not conscious, have long been recognized. Leibniz was the first to maintain, on theoretical grounds and by *a priori* reasoning, the existence of ideas of which we are not aware, as did likewise Kant, influenced by Leibniz, and later Schelling, and Herbart; while Hartmann evolved the unconscious into a biological and metaphysical system.

"To have ideas," says Kant, "and yet not be conscious of them — there seems to be a contradiction in that — for how can we know that we have them if we are not conscious of them? Nevertheless, we may become aware indirectly that we have an idea, although we be not directly cognizant of the same." (*Anthropology, sec. 5.*) And again, "innumerable are the sensations and perceptions whereof we are not conscious, although we must undoubtedly conclude that we have them, obscure ideas as they may be called (to be found in animals as well as in man). The clear ideas are but an infinitely small fraction of these same, exposed to consciousness. That only a few spots on the great chart of our minds are illuminated may well fill us with amazement in contemplating this nature of ours."

1 This hitherto unpublished paper was written some twenty years ago for a volume on the *Coconscious,* which was never finished, having been laid aside, because of the pressure of other work. More recently (1926), in slightly expanded form, it was given as a lecture in the Department of Abnormal and Dynamic Psychology, Harvard University.

2 *The Unconscious,* p. 250.

"Unconscious ideas" says Herbart, are such "as are in consciousness without our being aware of them."

Hartmann included all physiological processes of the nervous system in the Unconscious, and attributed to them special attributes (will, purpose, etc.).

It was not until the end of the last century that the subconscious was made the field of scientific research and concrete processes demonstrated by what may be properly regarded as experimental methods. This was the work of Edmund Gurney in England and Pierre Janet in France.

The theory of the subconscious, as developed in philosophy, did not recognize that many phenomena, now classed as abnormal, are manifestations of subconscious processes. These phenomena, in one form or another, are as old as the hills. They have occurred at all times and in all parts of the world ever since the human mind has been what it is today. In the form of manifestations of trances, witchcraft, demoniac possessions, crystal gazing, visions, religious experiences, hallucinatory voices, supernormal phenomena of various kinds, hysterical crises, etc., they have been observed from all time. But the discovery that such and less dramatic phenomena, and many that can be artificially induced, are due to a splitting of the mind into conscious and subconscious fragments or systems, and to the independent activity of the latter, is a modern discovery. The discovery has been far-reaching in its effects, opening up, as it did, a rich field of research, from which there have been gathered numerous findings that have given a vivid insight into human personality and human consciousness.

From this fundamental principle, the modern philosophical and psychological theories of the subconscious have been evolved and finally elaborated into those of the psychoanalytic schools, on the one hand, and those which seem to me, at least, to be the sounder theories of experimental psychology, on the other.

The credit for priority in demonstrating that the mind can be so dissociated as to exhibit two or more independent foci of activity, in the sense that synchronous manifestations of different intelligent activities, of one of which the personal consciousness is unaware, can be obtained under experimental and pathological conditions belongs, as I have said, to the late Edmund Gurney of England and Pierre Janet of France. If the title to discovery necessarily depends upon demonstration, these two workers in the field of experimental psychology may be justly regarded as the discoverers of this important principle.

The publication of Janet's work in France[1] antedated that of Gurney in England[2] by a few months, but each worked independently without knowledge of what the other was doing and along different lines and by different methods.

Gurney's work, brilliant as it was original and sound, was cut short by his untimely death. Had he lived, he undoubtedly would have done much to elucidate the problems which his researches opened up. His method was that of suggesting in hypnosis a mathematical problem under such conditions that the solution could be carried out only after the subject was restored to the waking state, when he had no memory of what had been suggested. The answer was given by automatic writing while the subject was consciously engaged in another task requiring concentration of attention. The suggested problem, being mathematical, necessitated intelligent mental action. Such test problems, of course, could be varied indefinitely; and he made them of various degrees of complexity.[3]

1 Les actes inconscients et le dédoublement de la personnalité": *Revue Philosophique*, 1886, vol. XI, p. 577.

2 Peculiarities of Certain Post-Hypnotic States": *Proc. Soc. Psychical Res'ch.* April, 1887, vol. IV, p. 268.

3 The principle is illustrated by the two following experiments selected from Gurney's second series:—

The subject, Wells, was told, in hypnosis, to multiply 12s/ 3¾d by 8, and then suddenly awakened the instant after the suggestion was given. Of course there was no memory of what had happened in the hypnotic state. The subject was then made to repeat aloud "God save the Queen" with every other word left out. While his mind was thus occupied, his hand, in accordance with the customary method of "automatic writing," wrote correctly the answer to the sum, but without the subject's conscious knowledge of what the hand was writing.

Again, "Wells was told to work out the sum, '13 loaves at 5d each, and was instantly awakened as usual. He wrote, '13 loaf at 5d is 5s/-5d.' When hypnotized again, and asked to say what he had written, he replied, '13 loaf—oh, I've put *loaf* instead of *loaves* — at 5d is 5s/-5d. I've written the 13 twice — see — but I crossed it out.' He then proceeded, by a long roundabout process, to work the problem out, arriving at the correct answer again."

One should note certain points in these simple but important observations which, it may be remarked, raise other questions which, even at this day, need further systematic research. The points I now refer to are:

*First,* the content of the automatic writing is of the kind that, according to common experience, would be ascribed to an intelligence, as it involved not only writing but the intelligent answer to a mathematical calculation.

*Second,* the calculation was done by some process not in awareness.

*Third,* the subject's main personal consciousness was occupied at the time with another problem, *viz.,* repeating a verse with every other word left out, a task requiring some concentration of thought.

*Fourth,* the absence of awareness, if deception is excluded, of the problem to be solved and of the content of the writing.

The interpretation put upon these results by Gurney was that the arithmetical problem was solved, not by a physiological reflex, but by some sort of consciousness of which the personal self was not aware. "Intelligent automatism" and a "secondary intelligence" were explanatory terms used by him. The final proof of the correctness of this interpretation, he believed, was found in the fact that when the subject was re-hypnotized in such experiments, "he recalled the whole process" of doing the sum, including such errors as were made. Gurney was not, however, as explicit as could be desired as to what was remembered: *i. e.,* whether only the *writing* of the figures on the paper, or the content of the *thoughts* of that "intelligence" which did the writing, a matter of some importance, if not for the proof of *an* "intelligence" at least for the nature of this intelligence.[1]

(I may say here, parenthetically, that I have recovered, in hypnosis, a complete memory of the thoughts of the co-conscious intelligence that did the writing, even to a detailed account of each step in the mental computation.) Gurney,

1 Of course, automatic writing was known long before Gurney's experiments. It was the interpretation of this phenomenon and the demonstration of its correctness which gave them their importance.

also, failed to realize, as we would at this late date expect, considering it was pioneer work, the possibility that the automatically written computation might have been written by a rapidly oscillating *alternating* intelligence. This alternative interpretation is suggested by the fact that in automatic writing there is often considerable inhibition of the personal consciousness, so that the subject falters, stumbles and finds difficulty in speaking while the script is being produced. This stumbling gives an opportunity for an alternating intelligence to write between the hesitations of speech. To eliminate this possibility is a very difficult problem in research. It has been held that because of this inhibition of conscious speech, the writing is not done by a true cointelligence but by an alternating one. This reasoning is fallacious in that it does not take into account all conscious processes. That there should be considerable inhibition of speech, even to a total degree, is what should be expected. For language processes which involve neurological pathways, and especially the same language processes, cannot, obviously, be utilized at one and the same time by two different intelligences. But language is not the whole of consciousness. A person may lose completely the processes of language, both of speech and understanding, without being deprived of conscious intelligence, as is shown in aphasia. There are other conscious processes. So during automatic writing, the subject, although unable to speak, may be perfectly aware of the environment, perceive the situation, see and hear and have emotions and desires. Contemporaneously with such a consciousness, a co-intelligence may manifest itself by writing, without the personal intelligence being aware of the content of the script.

While Gurney was pursuing his researches on coconscious intelligence, Janet was occupied in similar studies along different lines and in a different field. Janet worked with a certain hysterical subject and was able, by means of hypnotic writing, to tap the coconscious system of pathologically dissociated ideas and carry on more or less lengthy conversations of which the personal consciousness of the hysteric was unaware. With this subject, he began also that long series of brilliant experiments on hysterics which resulted in the demonstration that the lost memories in hysterical amnesia and the lost tactile and other sensations underlying the anesthesia of the hysteric were lost to the personal consciousness, not because they were obliterated, but because they were dissociated and, in some instances, made up an independent system of ideas which thereby became subconscious. He also demonstrated, among other things, that many of the "crises" of hysteria were due to the automatic activity of these dissociated ideas (memories, etc.). Gurney's and Janet's work gave the first stimulus to experimental investigations in subconscious phenomena.

But, it must be admitted, these studies attracted interest in only narrow circles, principally amongst those engaged in psychical research in England and America and a few psychologists in France and Germany who had been stimulated by the teachings of the great Charcot. The medical profession and psychologists in general remained indifferent and seemed to regard such investigations as belonging to the occult. Indeed, they seemed to be unable to understand them and grasp their significance. In the narrow circles I have mentioned, the new discoveries excited a keen interest. F. W. H. Myers and Henry Sidgwick in England, William James and Boris Sidis in this country, A. Binet in France, Max Dessoir and Breuer and Freud in Germany and Austria, were of the outstanding few who had the vision to see the extent of the new field the gates of which had been opened.

Without attempting to give, in historical sequence, a complete record of the early work which was done in this field since the appearance of Gurney's and Janet's original contributions, it is sufficient to note that numerous investigations have been carried on and a large number of data have been collected. These have not only confirmed the basic findings, but have considerably enlarged our knowledge of the subconscious. It is not necessary here to mention more than a few of the earlier contributions. It is significant that the confirmatory observations were contributed from no one locality or country.

In France, about two years later (1889), Binet, later

eminent as the originator of intelligence tests, was able in his studies of the automatic unconscious movements of anesthetic limbs,[1] to obtain co-ordinated, purposeful movements of which the subject was unaware and of a character which seemed to justify the interpretation that they were governed by an intelligence of some kind other than that of the personal self. This keen student of psychological phenomena later contributed additional observations of great value for the solution of problems belonging to the subconscious.

In America, William James, whose imagination was keenly stirred by the possibilities opened up by this new field of research, and with that remarkable vision which could picture the meaning which a new discovery might have for a new conception of human intelligence, took up with enthusiasm these pioneer researches and gave an account of them entitled "The Hidden Self" in a popular magazine. He also made a contribution of his own in January, 1889.[2]

Noting that in Janet's *anesthetic* subjects, "the hand which wrote expressed an intelligence perfectly perceptive of those skin-sensations of which the usual intelligence, expressing itself by word of mouth, was ignorant," the happy thought occurred to him that, conversely, the usual intelligence of ordinary non-hysterical automatic writers might be also transiently ignorant of the sensations of the writing hand and arm. Accordingly, experimenting on a healthy subject, he found that this was the case "in certain instances, at least," and that the automatic consciousness was in possession of the sensations lost to the consciousness which expressed itself by word of mouth.

About the same time, in the winter of 1889, I took up the problems of the subconscious as a field of research. Experimenting on two hysterical subjects, one with anesthesia

1 "Recherches sur les altérations de la conscience chez les hystériques": *Rev. de Philos.*, February, 1889. Review by F. W. H. Myers, *Proc. Soc. Psychical Res'ch*, vol. XV, p. 200.

2 "Notes on Automatic Writing," *Proc. Amer. Soc. Psychical Res'ch*, March, 1889, vol. I, p. 548.

of the hand and one without anesthesia, I was able, among other things, to confirm[1] the fact that sensations lost by the hand, owing to the hysterical anesthesia, were somehow and somewhere recorded, — for they were remembered in hypnosis — and to obtain automatic writing that was not only indicative of intelligence, but which recorded the suggestions given in hypnosis to be carried out after waking and for which there was no waking memory. Afterwards, in hypnosis, the subject remembered even the mistakes committed in the automatic writing, such as the failure to dot an *i* and cross a *t*. Further, the writing recorded remarks made to the subject in hypnosis, but not intended to be reproduced in the automatic writing. The hand of the patient, not previously anesthetic, became so, as in Janet's experiment, while writing automatically; and the lost sensations became synthesized with the intelligence that expressed itself through the writing hand. I was also able to record various other subconscious phenomena showing purposive intelligent actions and, among them, paralysis subconsciously induced as a "defense reaction."

In 1889, Sidis published his studies in the psychology of suggestion,[2] dealing largely with subconscious problems, to which he contributed many valuable data and important generalizations.

Passing to Germany, we may note that the Berlin psychologist, Max Dessoir, contributed (1889) an important monograph on the doubling of personality,[3] based on personal observations; and two years later (1891), Breuer and Freud of Vienna, five years after Janet's first publication, published their classical studies in hysteria in which, like Janet, they offered evidence to show that in this disease there was a splitting of personality, with automatism of the split-off groups of conscious states. Their researches, therefore,

---

[1] "Some of the Revelations of Hypnotism, Post-Hypnotic Suggestions, Automatic Writing and Double Personality." *Boston Med. and Surg. Journ.*, May 15, 1890.

[2] *The Psychology of Suggestion.*

[3] *Das Doppel-Ich.* Schriften der Gesellschaft für Experimental-Psychologie zu Berlin.

were also confirmatory of those of Janet and previous investigators. They offered, however, a different and sounder
interpretation of the mechanism in hysteria, in that they
held that the dissociation was due to repressions from conflict, while Janet thought it was due to inability to synthesize the split-off consciousness because of feebleness or exhaustion (*épuisement*) of the "personal" consciousness.

Thus it was that by these early researches the actuality
of concrete subconscious processes was established on a basis
of experimentation and scientific observation, and the concept taken out of the field of philosophy.

For my purpose, it is unnecessary to follow the history
of subsequent investigations, which, for the most part, were
directed towards the development of the theory. The principle had been demonstrated.

All this was simple enough. But it was only the beginning; just as the discovery of the germ by Pasteur as the
cause of fermentation was the beginning of the science of
bacteriology and infectious diseases. There remained the
application of the principle to a large number of complex
conditions and the working out of the *why*, the *how*, and
the *what* — *why* the mind is disrupted, and its mental
processes disturbed; *how*, by what mechanism this is done
and the psycho-physiological phenomena produced; *what*
particular subconscious processes are the causal factors in
specific conditions? Here, in answer to these questions,
divergent interpretations have arisen and created the different schools to which I have referred.

It is in the great field of abnormal psychology that
subconscious ideas come out into strong relief in practical
life, and play an extravagant part in throwing the whole
organism into disharmony with its environment. On the
other hand, artificially induced manifestations, like automatic writing, hypnotism, hallucinatory and post-hypnotic
phenomena, multiple and dissociated personalities, etc., are
artifacts and, as such, being under the control of the experimenter, are of especial value in demonstrating the principle of psychical dissociation and subconscious activity.
More than this, they can be utilized to explore the subcon-

scious and to artificially create psychophysiological phenomena identical in every way with those occurring in
normal everyday life and abnormal life. Thus, the mechanisms of conflicts, inhibitions, amnesia, hallucinations,
anxieties, obsessions, etc., can be studied. But, in abnormal
conditions, subconscious activity reaches enormous proportions, becoming enucleated, so to speak, by repression, incubation, and their motivating urges from the complexity of
processes in which the mechanisms of normal mental life are
obscured. In hysterical "crises" and motor automatisms,
obsessions, fears, hallucinations, delusions, inhibitions and
conflicts, of which the subject is unaware, we find examples
of such activity.

In this field, then, the subconscious is well studied; and
if the abnormal, as Virchow defined it, is only the normal
functioning under altered conditions, and as an ultimate
analysis of all disease processes, shows us an exaggeration, a
caricature of normal functioning, then the study of abnormal mental life must throw the clearest light on the mechanism of the normal mind. There is one thing of which we can
be certain, nothing can occur as an abnormal phenomenon
that is not effected by a normal mechanism, by a mechanism
which already exists, preformed in the mind and body, and
by which normal functioning is performed. Thus, the prototype of every abnormal phenomenon is found in normal
conditions. Hallucinations, delusions, conflicts, obsessing
fears, for example, are phenomena of everyday life. Disease
must make use of the same mechanism to produce its manifestations, though conditions of life may throw those mechanisms out of gear and so prevent the adaptation of the
personality to its environment, and in doing this, produce
the exaggerated and distressing phenomena we call *abnormal*.
And so it is that by the study of the abnormal we gain an
insight into the normal.

The part taken by subconscious processes in the activities of the mind in normal everyday life — I have now in
mind such activities as thinking, the determination of meaning, beliefs, prejudices, affections, solutions of problems, etc.
— presents a more difficult problem than those met with in

abnormal conditions. The snag that we are up against in making use of experimental methods — the only adequate methods — is that in the so-called "tapping" of the subconscious, we necessarily create artifacts which are not the conditions of everyday life. And yet, there are numerous data derived from other methods which compel the interpretation that our normal complexes of the kind I have just mentioned have roots in subconscious dispositions deposited by the experiences of life, dating back even to childhood. These dispositions are, we must believe, an integral part of our mental functionings and, when activated, whether coconscious or unconscious, play an important, and even predominant, part in determining our conscious processes; and in such processes I would include our emotional attitudes, feelings and the meanings which ideas have for us. We have only one mind, and that mind includes subconscious as well as conscious processes, all being normally functionally integrated.

But no clinical observations of abnormal conditions depending solely on the method of associative memories, as employed exclusively by one school of psychopathologists, can give us an adequate concept of the subconscious, any more than the physicist can arrive at an adequate theory of the "ether" (if there be an ether), or of cosmic energy by the study of the phenomenon of light alone. Associative memories may, in concrete cases, give an adequate insight into the particular subconscious processes responsible for the specific mental behavior under investigation. But that is not the same thing as the determination of a general concept of the subconscious as an integral factor of the human mind. To reach a comprehensive understanding of the subconscious activity of the mind, experimental methods must be employed in both normal and abnormal conditions. Furthermore, to obtain a comprehensive conception of the subconscious, every kind of subconscious phenomenon must be taken into consideration — motor phenomena of various kinds, such as so-called automatic writing and drawing; subconscious perceptions, images and hallucinations; volitions and affective phenomena. To these must be added various forms of intellectual activities, such as the solution of problems of all kinds; the incubation and maturation of the experiences of life, and their numerous motivations; deep-seated desires and aspirations; reasoning, memories and constructive imagination, the last often manifested in poetical and prose compositions. All these are open to experimental research.

How futile, then, to limit a concept of the subconscious to only one or more primitive instincts, or to attribute all subconscious activity to a single instinct as the motivating principle. None of these conditions or phenomena I have mentioned can be neglected and all experimental methods should be used according to their adaptability to the case. I feel justified in the opinion because in such experimental researches, of an intensive character, I have been engaged for nearly forty years[1] and have reached conclusions regarding the nature, functioning and relative evaluation of subconscious activities, which seem to me to be compelling from this laborious experience.

The final analysis of the subconscious must involve its nature — psychological or physiological — the extent and complexity of its field, what it can do and cannot do, and how it does it, its motivations, its dynamic relations and integrations with conscious processes and the various mechanisms involved, its correlations with the various functions of the body and the part it plays in general in normal life. For such an undertaking the first requisite is a thorough understanding of the part it plays in the artificial and abnormal phenomena which are attributable to its activity. As already said, it is from the data supplied by the study of abnormal psychology and experimental artifacts that the present-day theory of the subconscious originated and has derived its demonstration.

It will be further noticed that the work which has been done in demonstrating the manifestations of secondary intelligence and in carrying on those observations which have led to the interpretation of coconscious ideas has come from

1 In this year, 1928, I am enabled to add a goodly number of years as a sort of valedictory to the span in the original paper.

clinicians and students of the new school of experimental psychology. This interpretation has not been wholly accepted by the academic psychologists, who deal with normal psychology. Nor has it been universally adopted by those clinicians who have, from their own researches, accepted the principle of subconscious processes in normal and abnormal life. One school — the psychoanalytic — prefers to remain non-committal on the nature of the subconscious, leaving it open whether subconscious processes are psychological or physiological, or both. There is still an attitude of strong skepticism in some quarters[1] where it is held that the phenomena are entirely interpretable on the theory of physiological processes, or what was called many years ago by Carpenter "unconscious cerebration."

These psychologists maintain the physiological as opposed to the psychological interpretation. They hold that automatic writing and speech, all the apparently subconscious intellectual acts, including those showing foresight, design, volition, reason and memory, and the various groups of abnormal phenomena, are the expression of only brain processes to which no consciousness belongs. They are, therefore, physiological automatisms — "unconscious cerebration." According to this view, such acts differ only in complexity from those other physiological processes which carry on the digestive and other functions of the body, on the one hand, and the spasmodic jerkings and twitchings seen in chorea, epilepsy and other affections, on the other.

With this great and fundamental difference in view between the theoretical psychologists and the experimental investigators, it is incumbent, before entering upon a study of the subconscious, to present the grounds on which the psychological interpretation is based.[2]

---

1 Compare: A. H. Pierce, "An Appeal from the Prevailing Doctrine of a Detached Subconsciousness" in *Studies in Philosophy and Psychology;* Münsterberg and Ribot in "A Symposium on the Subconscious," *Jour. of Abnormal Psychol.*, April, 1907. Also Pierce's review of the "Symposium," *Jour. of Philos., Psychol. & Scient. Methods*, Sept. 12, 1907; and Morton Prince: "Prof. Pierce's version of the late 'Symposium' on the Subconscious." *Jour. Philos., Psychol. & Scient. Methods*, Jan. 30, 1908.

2 For a general statement of the argument see chapters XVI and XVII of this volume.

EXTRACTS

# EXTRACTS

# I

*from*

## "THE DESIRABILITY OF INSTRUCTION IN PSYCHOPATHOLOGY IN OUR MEDICAL SCHOOLS AND ITS INTRODUCTION AT TUFTS"

*Boston Medical and Surgical Journal,*
Vol. CLIX, No. 16, pp. 497-499, Oct. 15, 1908

NOT so many years ago the Harvard bacteriological laboratory consisted of a little oven up in a corner of the gallery of the physiological laboratory in the old medical school. There Dr. Ernst was allowed to cook his germs and experiment. Dr. Ernst, as I remember it, had urged the introduction of bacteriology in the school and the establishment of a laboratory, but such was the skepticism regarding the value of bacteriology that the best that the faculty could be prevailed upon to provide was this little out-of-the-way corner as a tentative measure. Just previous to this Koch had announced his discovery of the bacillus as the cause of tuberculosis, or, as we had been taught in the school (following the views of Niemeyer) of chronic catarrhal pneumonia.

Still many expert practitioners did not hesitate to express themselves as skeptical of the soundness of Koch's alleged discovery, and bacteriology was taught in none of our medical schools. Though considerable work had been done in Europe in bacteriology, as yet America had not joined the procession.

The position of psychopathology today is not so very different from what was at that time the position of bacteriology. During the past twenty years a large amount of experimental work in this field has been done in Europe and America, but as yet the great body of the medical profession has not informed itself, either through mastering the literature or by repetition of the experimental observations, of the results of this work. And yet discoveries of the first importance have been made.

. . . . . . . . .

The present-day enthusiasm for psychotherapeutics is, I fear, to a large extent misdirected and unintelligently aplied. Every younger practitioner desires to employ the method and every older one is struggling under the self-satisfying impression that he has always employed it — *intelligently.* In simple cases this last is undoubtedly the case, especially when all that is required is common sense, a knowledge of human nature and the experience of a man of the world. But in complex cases it is far from being the case. The trouble is that many want to practise psychotherapeutics but few wish to acquire a knowledge of psychopathology. To do so is a laborious, time-consuming task. What would we think of a physician, or layman, who wished to treat heart disease, who felt himself an expert in the procedure, but who cared nothing about the physiology of the heart, about the work of the valves and of the musculature, about the disease processes that affect the organ and the secondary effects of heart disease on the other organs of the body? As intelligent therapeutics of the heart is based upon a knowledge of the physiology and pathology of the organ, so intelligent psychotherapeutics must be based on a knowledge of the physiology of the mind and pathology of its diseases.

Common observation has shown that when the mental mechanism becomes dissociated, its processes perverted or when associations which are disadvantageous for the individual become formed, not only are abnormal mental syndromes — like fixed ideas, persistent fatigue, weakness of the will, etc. — established, but the physiological functions of the body are deranged in all sorts of ways, with the result that physical symptoms become a prominent part of the morbid picture. In mild cases mental and physical hygiene, such as has been practised from time immemorial, is all sufficient to insure a cure. But in the severer cases experience shows that it is necessary to go deeper and, by methods specially adapted to the particular case, to determine the exact pathological process present and then to reintegrate the disorganized mental mechanism or substitute healthy mental complexes for perverted complexes, or re-educate the mind, etc., as the case may be. Here the technique of what may fairly be called a scientific psychotherapy comes into play; measures based on the exact psychopathic conditions present, instead of the empirical measures which experience, without knowing the Why, has shown, will work successfully in milder types. Because of the latter fact, and because certain distinguished teachers have laid stress in a general way on the moral factor in treatment, it is frequently claimed, even by those holding an honorable place in medicine, that modern psychotherapy is nothing more than what has been the practice of all physicians in all times. Such a claim could not be made by any one who has trained himself by actual experience with investigations in psychopathology. To assert otherwise is to exhibit an entire ignorance of the subject; it is worse than ignorance, it is childish. It is the same as saying that modern aseptic surgery does not differ from the surgery of the pre-Listerian period, because cleanliness has always been a surgical tenet and successful operations have been performed without aseptic precautions. The difference is one of technique; the aseptic technique is based on the principles of bacterial pathology, while previous methods of cleanliness were entirely empirical. So, rational psychotherapy, based on the principles of psychopathology, becomes similarly a matter of rational technique. This does not deny that empirical psychotherapy may often be effective, like empirical surgery. On the contrary, the methods of psychotherapy, as taught by Dubois and others, the so-called rest-cure of Weir Mitchell, the isolation treatment of Charcot, as well as the practice of all wise practitioners, testify to the efficacy of moral influences in restoring, in the ordinary run of cases, healthy bodily processes. This is particularly the case when the unhealthy state results from disordered mental habits, auto-suggestion, morbid introspection, worry, stress and strain, etc. But these methods are all empirical. Even the widely read work of Dubois shows that his methods are based on little more than the results of clinical experience, while his theories exhibit a woeful lack of training in the physiology of the mind and psychopathology. To mention only two points: No one who is well trained in these subjects would venture to maintain, as does the author, that "persuasion" is in principle different from "suggestion" and, therefore, to deny to the latter that efficacy which is claimed for the former. Nor would such a one deny the efficacy of suggestion (persuasion) in hypnosis if he had had the scientific erudition and experience of clinicians like Forel and was master of his subject.

While empirical methods are sufficient in certain cases, many can only be touched by methods based on the special pathology of the disease. But whether or not empirical methods are efficient, it is the aim and object of scientific medicine to investigate the laws of disease and the principles underlying empirical procedures, to the end that the art of treatment may have a rational foundation.

In advocating the introduction of psychopathology into the curriculum of medical schools I ought to state somewhat specifically the field which is intended to be covered. Without attempting to give a definite program, I would suggest the following as a tentative plan. (The classification is not strictly accurate but will serve the purpose.)

*Mental physiology.* — Mechanism of memory, including physiological (unconscious) memories (spinal cord and ganglia). Meaning of the unconscious. Formation and conservation of unconscious complexes. Meaning of the subconscious and coconscious. Integrative action of the nervous system. Habit formation. Emotion. Influence of psychical processes on the functions of the viscera (digestive, vasomotor, secretory, respiratory systems, etc.). Coenesthesia. Hypnosis (theory and phenomena). Suggestion. Idea complexes.

*Dissociations of the mind.* — Anesthesia. Paralysis. Amnesia. Abstraction. Hypnoidal states. Sleep. Trance states. Fatigue. Subconscious ideas and their activity. Unconscious processes. Aboulia.

*Syntheses.* — Sensory automatisms (visual and auditory hallucinations). Paraesthesias. Pain. Motor automatisms (spasms, contractures). Recurrent mental states. Obsessions. Impulsions. Fixed ideas. Delusions. Unconscious mental complexes and their influences. Dreams.

*Special pathology.* — Neurasthenia. Hysteria. Psychasthenia. Hypochondriasis. Phobias. Habit psychoses and neuroses. Mimicry. Psycholeptic attacks. Recurrent sensorimotor attacks. Amnesic states. Dissociated personality. Fugues. Tics.

*Methods of examination besides the ordinary clinical methods.* — Psychoanalysis. Abstraction. Hypnoidization. Hypnosis. Automatic writing. Artificial hallucinations. Psychogalvanic tests. Word reaction tests.

*Principles of psychotherapeutics based on psychopathology.*

It has been decided to introduce such a course in Tufts College Medical School this year. This, I believe, will be the first attempt to give systematic instruction in this subject in a medical school. I regret that it will not be possible to carry out in full even such an incomplete program as I have outlined. This is owing to the lack of psychopathic wards to supply the clinical material. To adequately teach psychopathology, we should have the resources of a hospital at our disposal. Unlike other large cities, there is not a hospital in Boston which provides beds for even a neurological service (if we except the *two* (!) beds at the Massachusetts General Hospital and the Long Island Hospital). The difficulty of teaching psychopathology without the material which only a hospital affords will be appreciated if one imagines what would be the result to medical education if our teachers of internal medicine and surgery were deprived of their hospital services. However, we propose to take the initiative, relying upon such opportunities for clinical material as may offer, and hoping that either the powers which determine the policies of our hospitals or some good philanthropist will soon provide wards or hospitals in the interest of patients and of medical science.

## II

*from*

### "THE EDUCATIONAL TREATMENT OF NEURASTHENIA AND CERTAIN HYSTERICAL STATES"

(Read at the Annual Meeting of the Massachusetts
Medical Society, June 8, 1898)

*Education and Mental Therapeutics.* The next part of the treatment, and at the same time the one that is most difficult and interesting, is what I call the education of the patient. It is upon this that we must rely for the suppression of the individual symptoms, the acquisition of strength and the development of habits of body and mind that will enable the patient to return to the wear and tear of life without breaking down. The preliminary step in the treatment is the study of the origin, history, and groupings of individual symptoms. It is surprising to find, after a searching inquiry which involves every detail concerning the origin and character of the symptoms, and the conditions under which they arise, how often what seems to be a mere chaos of unrelated mental and physical phenomena will resolve itself into a series of logical events, and law and order be found to underlie the symptomatic tangle. By such a study we can determine what symptoms are pure habit symptoms of the kind which Dr. Taylor today has already described and of which he has given us examples; what symptoms are pure manifestations of hysteria; what are due to faulty ideation or auto-suggestion; what fatigue is due to real physical exhaustion and is true fatigue and what is false fatigue; what pains are due to the diffusion of effort and association and what are due to some real underlying physical cause; what symptoms are due to real disease of organs like the heart or stomach and what to mimicry. After unravelling the symptoms in this way it will be surprising to find how much facilitated will be the removal of them.

. . . . . . . .

Having gained the patient's confidence and co-operation, the rules I would lay down are these: First, remove all interfering mental states that prevent the subsidence of symptoms; these are: (*a*), a fixed idea or belief in the seriousness of the condition and the existence of real organic disease. (*b*), a belief in the danger or incurability of the state. (*c*), a fear or *apprehension* that any harm can come to the patient from incautious actions, like exercise and doing various things. (*d*), subconscious fixed ideas or memories producing hysteric symptoms.

One of the commonest hampering mental states is a belief on the part of the patient that doing things which bring on symptoms are likely to produce serious harm. Most patients do not mind disagreeable feelings so much as they fear that anything that produces them might do them serious and lasting harm. A patient, for example, refuses to go about not because he minds fatigue, but because he thinks that fatigue means serious damage. Another fears to move because of cardiac symptoms, which he imagines or has been told indicate heart disease, but does not mind them if he can be assured and really believe there is no cardiac trouble. It is surprising sometimes to see the almost immediate beneficial effects produced by the mere acceptance of the idea that symptoms do not mean disease or lasting injury. With the acceptance of this idea, symptoms sometimes subside at once.

The next point is the instruction of the patient in the meaning of symptoms. The patient should be allowed to understand the cause and meaning of each discomfort; for example, when symptoms are pure habits, due to association of ideas and actions, when fatigue is a false or habit fatigue this should be explained. It is my habit to give a great deal of time to this instruction. It is important to take the patient into your confidence and explain the nature of such symptoms as if one were explaining to a colleague; and above all, when the case is of hysteria to say so frankly, and not conceal the fact but explain its nature. Next, when tendencies to emotional states exist, states of anger at trivial things, anxiety, fear, worry, nervous shocks, accompanied as these usually are by somatic symptoms, to educate the patient to control and suppress all such emotional states. Here tact, character and individuality on the part of the physician come in.

*Suppression of individual symptoms by appropriate therapeutic agents.* — Now comes in one of the most important parts of the treatment, namely, the daily suppression of individual symptoms by proper therapeutic agents. Symptoms should, if possible, be suppressed as fast as they arise without being allowed to gather headway and grow, in order that faulty habits and reactions of the nervous system may be broken up at once. It is preferable that the patient should make visits to the physician's office rather than the reverse. When a patient makes a pilgrimage, as it were, for the distinct purpose of being alleviated, the effect of the treatment is generally heightened. For the suppression of symptoms, one of the most valuable therapeutic agents, and one which I find myself making use of more and more in practice, is *direct and educational* suggestion. This occupies a very prominent place in every case. It may be used in various forms and for different purposes. As to the form which is used, I have rarely of late been obliged to resort to the hypnotic state, but have obtained all the influence that I have needed in a waking state, using for the purpose static electricity where it can be had; the faradic or galvanic battery will sometimes answer. At the same time that the electricity is applied the direct suggestion is given, and the patient may be further *instructed* in the nature and cause of her symptoms and disease, and what is to be expected. In a waking state, a suggestion is more efficacious if given symbolically so to speak, through some material agent. I myself rely almost entirely upon some form of electricity. I would not overlook the purely physical effect of electricity in neurasthenia. I believe it has a physical influence especially in suppressing painful feelings, and removing fatigue sensations. I would therefore make use, at one and the same time, of both influences, the mental and the physical. In some cases the physical and in some cases the mental influence predominates. To illustrate, a patient is directed to come daily at first to the physician's office. The patient's symptoms, we will say, are headache, insomnia, backache and fatigue. The static douche and sparks are used, the present and future effect expected insisted upon; if possible the patient is not allowed to leave until some, or complete, relief has been obtained. The beneficial effect of drugs should not be neglected. Often sedatives like bromide are valuable. Gouty and rheumatic tendencies should be corrected, and the diet carefully regulated of course when dyspeptic symptoms exist.

My plan is to take each symptom individually in turn, no matter in what part of the body it may be, and by appropriate therapeutic agents to endeavor to dispel it as fast as it appears.

In some but rare cases of hysteria it may be necessary to go down to the lowest strata of consciousness, and for this purpose the hypnotic state may be necessary. One advantage of hypnosis in such cases as this, is that in this state we can often learn from the patient the causes and origin of symptoms which in the waking state are forgotten. For example, Miss F. suffers from attacks of pain in the left side, with various other symptoms, coming on under peculiar circumstances. It is related in hypnosis that they all date from a certain episode involving an emotional shock. The physical character of such pains is at once demonstrated, and their removal facilitated by suggestion. Many such instances might be cited.

A further value of hypnotic suggestion is that you are sometimes able to make in the hypnotic state criticisms of the patient's habits which will be resented in a waking state. Ordinarily hypnosis is not necessary. Besides suggestions directed to the individual symptoms, others should be given directed to the state itself. For example, that there is no real disease at all, only a lack of harmony in the working of the system, according to the view taken by the physician, always being particular to state the truth and exactly what the physician believes. Suggestions should also be given to counteract fixed ideas, fears, apprehensions, and expectations of the patient, and by such suggestions to anticipate future accidents that may arise.

*Avoidance of artificial cultivation of symptoms.* — Just as education is a most potent factor for good, it may have an equal influence for evil. Caution is therefore most desirable against unintentionally suggesting all sorts of possible evil consequences that may result either from the actions of the patient or from the disease. The physician should be cautious against suggesting himself, or allowing others to suggest, either directly or by innuendo, that fatigue, pain, insomnia, or any discomfort, will be likely to supervene under certain circumstances, and above all that any real lasting injury can be done the patient by any effort of any kind. This does not mean that rigid rules of conduct should not be prescribed; on the contrary they should be, but it should be done with intelligence and judgment. I have seen more than one neurasthenic whose symptoms have been the pure result of unintentional cultivation.

### III

*from*
"THE CRIMINAL RESPONSIBILITY OF INSANE PERSONS"

(Chairman's Address Before the Section on Nervous and Mental Diseases of the American Medical Association, at Atlantic City, June, 1907)

*The Journal of the American Medical Association*
November 16, 1907, Vol. XLIX

THE law says that "it must be clearly proved that at the time of committing the act the accused" did not know it was wrong. If these words are to be taken literally it is probable that very few insane persons know at this particular time their act to be wrong, though they have such a knowledge before and after. At that moment, particularly if the act is connected with a delusion, the insane mind is in such a condition of dissociation that no knowledge, *i. e.,* no ideas beyond the very limited ones concerned in the specific action performed occupy the contracted field of his consciousness. The individual knows nothing or very little beyond what he is at the moment doing. For all else his mind is a blank, owing to a contraction of the field of consciousness. There is amnesia for all related knowledge and there is an absolute impossibility of synthesizing his dissociated memories and related ideas with the ideas which effect the specific act. So great is the dissociation that it is not uncommon for a person, after the committal of a crime, to have only a hazy, indistinct memory or none at all for his previous act. Cases of even sane persons are not uncommon where a crime performed in a moment of great excitement is followed by greater or less amnesia for the act. The emotion dissociates all but a fragment of a person's knowledge. In this respect, then, the law, if literally construed, is so broad as to exculpate many mentally deranged persons who might well be held to be responsible. It is hard to see how Thaw, for instance, if insane, could be convicted under this provision of the law. Is the law to be construed literally in one of its parts and freely in another, according to the case which it is desired to cover?

This brings us to what, in my judgment, is the true psychological conception of knowledge. We may know a person's name, and yet at a given moment we may have amnesia for it and not be able to synthesize it with our personal consciousness. The same is true of all knowledge. So long as we can not synthesize our knowledge with our personal consciousness, that knowledge ceases to be a part of our personality and can not take an effective part in our reasoning processes. Our reason, strictly speaking, is deranged. A person with a delusion of persecution, for instance, that his food is being poisoned, can not synthesize logically conflicting ideas (which should normally be corrective) with that system which constitutes his delusion. You may point out that others eat and drink the same food, but, though he knows in one sense the fact, owing to the dementia always present, or other defect, the knowledge remains isolated and does not become a part of his mental synthesis which, therefore, persists as a delusion. In other words, his reason does not normally function. This, I take it, is the psychological principle underlying the empirical, though, in my judgment, substantially correct construction placed on the term "knowing" by Justice Stephen; namely, the ability to "judge calmly and reasonably of the moral or legal character of a proposed act." Of what use is it to know unless you can make use of your knowledge by the reasoning process? It is not only stored away knowledge, but the integrity of the reasoning process, the process of synthesizing knowledge with the personality which constitutes responsibility. One might almost say it is the integrity of personality. Indeed, one sees in epileptic automatism, fugues and similar dream states the principle of disintegrated personality with irresponsibility illustrated in its extreme form.

．．．．．．．．

The controversy which has so long existed between the medical and legal profession over the responsibility of the insane will, I believe, if carefully analyzed be found to be largely due to the entirely different conceptions of insanity entertained by the two professions. The legal conception of insanity must be based entirely on book knowledge and has very little relation with the facts. The medical man's conception is that of the mental and physical behavior of the insane as actually observed and which can not be described so as to be appreciated by a person without practical experience. With these differences there naturally arises a difference in view.

But in the hundredth case where the accused would be found to be insane, under the procedure suggested, and where responsibility is questioned, what should be the test?

I doubt very much whether any single formula can be devised which will meet all the requirements, or at least I doubt whether any such formula can be devised which will be sufficiently simple to be presented to a jury of laymen and be understood. The formula proposed by Mercier may be as good as any; it is, "The actor must will the act; intend the harm; desire primarily his own gratification. Furthermore, the act must be unprovoked, and the actor must know and appreciate the circumstances in which the act is done," in order to incur responsibility by a harmful act. This seems to me somewhat complicated for the jury to thoroughly take in and is, furthermore, open to the same objection as the formula of the judges, in that a great deal depends on the interpretation of the term "know and appreciate the circumstances." I confess that I should not know myself exactly how this phrase should be interpreted, and it is probable that it would only follow the fate of the present formula and be interpreted in different ways by different judges.

I would submit for consideration whether, in the rare case in which the question of responsibility would be raised as to a person who had been judged insane after committal to an asylum for observation, the wisest procedure would not be to have the full observations of those who have carefully followed the case in the asylum presented to the jury. From these statements, which should include the presence or absence of hallucinations and delusions and obsessions, the condition of the will, the intellect, the emotions, the reasoning process and, in fact, a complete analysis of the mental condition, the jury could judge of the responsibility of the insane person without being limited by any legal formula. This, practically I believe, is what juries do to a large extent today, disregarding all formulas laid down by the court and deciding from what seems to them to be the merits of the case. Where the question of insanity, however, is determined not in an asylum by unbiased observers, but in court under the present thoroughly rotten system of expert testimony, the alleged facts as found are contradictory and trials are apt to result in disagreements or unsatisfactory verdicts. . . . If the condition of insanity were determined, not in open court as a result of a battle between experts lined up on either side, but under observation in an asylum by experts appointed by the court, I believe it would be found that in a vast majority of cases those persons who were found to be clinically insane would be found to be also irresponsible by any formula which is soundly based on psychological and psychiatric principles.

## IV

*from*

### "A CRITIQUE OF PSYCHOANALYSIS"[1]
*Archives of Neurology and Psychiatry*
December, 1921, Vol. VI, pp. 610-621

Let me say at the outset that there are two principles which, in my judgment, must be accepted as contributions of the highest importance to our knowledge, and for these we are indebted to the genius of Freud. One of these is the doctrine or the theory of repression and the other is that of conflict. They are intimately related, for it is through conflict that repression is induced. Before speaking of these I feel called on to say a few words about the subconscious, for this underlies and is the basis not only of the doctrines of psychoanalysis but of the theories of psychopathology of every modern school of research. The theory of the subconscious is not novel, nor was it originated by Freud, though that seems to be the impression of many writers on psychoanalysis. As a philosophical concept of the unconscious, of which I will later speak, it dates back as far as Leibniz and Kant, and, later, Schelling, Herbart and Hartmann, the last having evolved it into a biological and metaphysical system. Freud converted it into a debatable doctrine peculiar to psychoanalysis. It remained for Pierre Janet, in France, and Edmund Gurney, in England, to take it out of the field of philosophical speculation and demonstrate by the inductive method its concrete reality as mental processes underlying certain psychological phenomena. This real pioneer work, in 1886-1887, laid the basis by the use of experimental methods, for every theory of modern psychopathology that makes use of subconscious processes. It was comparable in the field of psychology to the demonstration of radioactivity by physicists as intra-atomic processes essential for the explanation of certain physical phenomena. In using the word "demonstration" it must not be lost sight of,

---

1 Throughout the article, the unusual form "psychanalysis" occurs.

however, that both radioactivity and subconscious processes are logically only theories, though as theories they have attained the highest probability of truth.

Dissociation with the formation of subconscious processes that, motivated by their own emotional impulsive force, take on autonomous activity and induce psychological and physiological phenomena, had been demonstrated previously, as I have said, by Pierre Janet and Edmund Gurney, working independently, and their conclusions were confirmed (1889 to 1890) by Alfred Binet, William James, Max Dessoir and myself. But later Freud with Breuer (1891) discovered and applied the principle and mechanism of repression to explain the dissociation in the psychoneuroses. This although only a particular application of the dynamic principle was a marked advance. It is Freud's great contribution to our knowledge of the psychoneuroses. Its importance can scarcely be exaggerated. Nevertheless, it must not be forgotten that dissociation may be effected by simple failure of normal inhibition without repression from conflict, though this is not recognized by psychoanalysts.

The motivation, however, of the succeeding subconscious processes became another problem, and the debatable doctrine of the repressed sexual wish, and particularly of an infantile sexual wish, was insisted on by Freud as furnishing an almost universal motive, or urge, impelling these processes to fulfill a sexual aim.

Without further discussion of this wearisome question, I want to point out only that the valuable theory of repression does not require the acceptance of the doctrine of the sexual nature of the conflict and of the repressed subconscious processes. That is an entirely different problem. It is to Freud's credit, too, that the basis of his investigation was the search for the "Why." No complete solution of the problem of repression, dissociation and subconscious activity and no complete understanding of the resulting phenomena can be attained without answering the question of the "Why." "How" and "That" are inadequate explanations. But while the Freudian psychology has been most stimulating in directing a search for the "Why," its own answer was and is, in my judgment, radically wrong and has had a most baneful influence.

Repression, as I have said, necessarily implies and requires conflict.

The recognition of mental conflicts and their disturbing effects on the individual is as old as literature itself, but we are indebted to Freud for the recognition of them as factors in the mechanism of repression and the important part they play in the maladjustment of the individual to the environment and the induction of the psychoneuroses. This does not mean, however, that we must necessarily accept the universally sexual nature of the conflict, or the very special mechanisms postulated through which it is conceived that the subconscious process fulfills its aim, or the symptoms are compromise-formations. After recognizing and giving due credit for the theories of repression and conflict, I must think that the greater part of the remainder of the doctrines of psychoanalysis are not only unsubstantiated, but cannot be reconciled with a large body of facts which have been gained by other methods of research and which must be taken into consideration. Furthermore, nearly all the facts which have been advanced as the result of psychoanalytic methods are open to other interpretations than those which the fundamental doctrines of psychoanalysis postulate.

. . . . . . . . . .

I have no intention, least of all desire, to enter into any disputatious discussion of this theory. I want only to indicate the point of view from which I approach this problem and to record my dissent from any such limited theory of the subconscious. Without denying that some subconscious processes may have these characteristics (reserving an exception, as the lawyers say, to the extreme infantile origin postulated), to hold that all, or that subconscious processes generally, are of the character stated is to take a far too narrow view of the phenomena. One may say, if one likes, that he will call unconscious only those which have the characteristics mentioned and so arbitrarily define the subconscious. But that does not alter the fact that there are vast numbers of processes that are subconscious and that have not any of the six characteristics contained in the definition and particularly of repressed sexual wishes, or even of having been repressed at all, and that these take part in conflicts and repression with resulting phenomena. The statement contained in the theory is simply not true. One might as well define men (*qua men*) as criminals, or even as sexual criminals, repressed in jail, and disregard all other men who are not criminals and not in prison.

. . . . . . . .

The instincts and instinctive processes and the behavior to which they give rise have been the object of study to earnest students of human and animal behavior, and their investigations have presented important results. There is by no means, it is true, an agreement of interpretation, but the theories advanced are impressive and must be taken into consideration.

All this work is entirely ignored by the Freudian school of psychoanalysts and until recently by all psychoanalysts; and yet some of the interpretations of instinctive processes derived from such studies offer explanations of human behavior which are entitled at least to consideration. None of these theories may be true but one or more of them offer explanations which are as probable and adequate as that represented by the libido.

. . . . . . . .

Again, take the doctrine of symbolisms. That symbolisms occur as mental phenomena no one questions, but the universality of specific symbolisms occurring in all minds, in all places, and in all ages, is, to my way of thinking, an extravagance which passes the bounds of inductive science. The postulation of a symbolism may be necessary to explain the connection between a mental phenomenon and some selected antecedent experience in order to interpret the latter as the causal factor, in accordance with one or other Freudian doctrine; but it does not follow that the causal factor may not be some other equally well-demonstrated one, utilizing some much simpler mechanism. As a matter of fact, I believe that when such phenomena can be submitted to other technical methods of investigation, it will be found that in the great majority of cases we can find evidences of subconscious processes which are subject to an entirely different interpretation than that requiring a symbolism.

So I might run through the various doctrines, concepts, or hypotheses, call them what you will, of psychoanalysis, and I believe that evidence could be presented that would equally well support other interpretations than those which make up the body of doctrine maintained by psychoanalysis.

. . . . . . . . . .

The failure of the psychoanalytic method is due to the fact that the findings require and depend on too elaborate, intricate, and, however ingenious, debatable interpretations, which themselves depend on debatable theoretical mechanisms and forces, and the method itself is not only inexact and inadequate but open to artifacts of the most subtle kind, particularly in the selection of the data. The conception of the subconscious and the theoretical structure built upon it approaches more nearly a philosophy than a science, and with philosophy we are not concerned.

### Psychoanalysis as a Method of Therapeutics

Time will not permit me to more than touch on psychoanalysis as a method of therapeutics. That cures may be effected by this method may be admitted as by any method of mental therapeutics whether of Christian science, faith, suggestion, amulets, charms, re-education or what not. Successful therapeutics is no proof of the truth of the concepts accepted as articles of belief.

### The Influence of the Freudian Psychology on Psychological and Psychiatric Thought

After having thus criticized the psychoanalytic method and the validity of the doctrines, it would be ungenerous not to bear a well-deserved tribute to the influence of the psychoanalytic school on contemporaneous thought. I regret that the time at my disposal will not permit me to do full justice to this aspect of the subject. There can be no question that

Freud, supported by a large group of enthusiastic followers, has compelled the attention of psychologists and physicians and forced them to take heed. Previously scant attention or courtesy was paid to any researches in dynamic or subconscious processes.

. . . . . . . .

This, to my mind, is the great gain for which we must be thankful to Freud — the acceptance of the dynamic approach and the dynamic conception of aberrations of the normal personality however manifested. It is the search for the "Why" which is the final step in dynamic pathology. Undoubtedly there is at present a tendency to go too far in the search for functional causes and mechanisms and to overlook the conditions of organic disease. Sometimes one would think that there is no such thing as organic disease to consider. We must keep at least one foot on the ground and not soar all the time, or too high.

While the war forced the dynamic point of view on a reluctant profession, it has also given the *coup de grâce* to many of the Freudian concepts and in particular to the sexual wish as the universal determinant of the psychoneuroses. In other words, the Freudian doctrine of the "Why" — of the libido and the unconscious sexual wish — broke down as a result of general experience with the war neuroses. Nevertheless, the main and important point is that neurologists and psychiatrists, while far from being in agreement as to the particular causal factors, mechanisms and processes that produce the symptomatic phenomena of the psychoneuroses, generally recognize that the explanation of the latter is to be found in the conflicting instinctive attitudes, strivings, impulses and reactions of human personality.

But what shall be said, on the one hand, of the mental processes of those who, motivated by the Will to Disbelieve, have steadfastly refused even to listen to any such explanations or weigh the evidence on which they are based; and, on the other hand, of those who, motivated by the Will to Believe, regardless of the canons of logic, of conflicting facts and inadequate methods of research, untrained in scientific methods of precision and without a comprehensive background of knowledge of the great store of psychological phenomena accumulated by experimental psychology, have accepted as proved the *ex-cathedra* dicta of a psychoanalytic master and become devout, faithful believers in doctrines which have never at best been more than working hypotheses, if not mere philosophical speculations based on selected data? In these two types of mind we have a psychological phenomenon equaling in interest those involved in the problems of the psychoneuroses.

When I was a boy I read in an essay by the French critic Sainte-Beuve a sentence which has always stuck in my memory and which I like to think has influenced for good my mental tendencies. The subject of the essay was a modern miracle called the "Holy Thorn." The sentence ran something like this: "Some people see in this miracle a special intervention of Providence; but I can see in it only the humiliation of the human mind."

## V

*from*

### "THOUGHT-TRANSFERENCE"
Boston Medical and Surgical Journal, February 3, 1887.

If called upon to summarize the evidence as it stands, I should say that; *First,* all the evidence *that we possess, such as it is,* goes to prove that certain persons, under certain favorable conditions, can become cognizant of the thoughts of another without any communication by the senses. *Second,* that the best *working* hypothesis that we possess is in favor of direct thought-transference as an explanation. *Third, a priori,* there is nothing inherently impossible or improbable in the hypothesis. *Fourth,* the subject must be considered as still *sub judice,* and needs further investigation to settle the question beyond possibility of doubt.

Before dismissing the subject, I wish to say a few words in regard to the nature of the evidence before us: There are two objections or arguments which are commonly employed against thought-transference: One is that similar claims have been made almost from time immemorial by spiritualists, clairvoyants, and the like; that all sorts of equally extraordinary performances have been done by this sort of people; but as each has been investigated, it has broken down and failed to stand the tests of rigid examination; or, if not, that no thorough examination has been allowed. Furthermore the performances of professional jugglers, like Herman and Keller, are cited as evidence showing how easy it is to impose upon even the cleverest observer.

To my mind, objections of this sort are most illogical and unscientific. There is not the slightest parallel between the two cases. In the first place, no one can find the slightest similarity between professional mediums and the earnest, conscientious, responsible people who have conducted the investigations, many of them skilled by profession in experimental methods of research; nor even between the former and the "mind readers", like the Liverpool young ladies, Miss R. and Miss E., and the Creery children.

In the second place, no physical experiments in the laboratory have been more under the control of the chemist and physiologist than have these. The subjects have given themselves up to the experimenters, not occasionally and fitfully, but day after day. Any and every sort of condition has been cheerfully acquiesced in when imposed. They have seemed, judging by the reports, to take the same interest in studying the question as any one else. Nor are the conditions complex. It seems as if the only essential conditions of the experiment apparently requisite are to see that the subject or percipient does not get any clues to the agent's thought through any one of the five senses — touch, taste, smell, sight, and hearing.

The first three are easily excluded. It would seem as if the latter two could easily be. No paraphernalia are used; no dark closets; no strange rooms; no attempt to regulate the experiment. The subjects, too, in no case have been trained professionals, and, in one case, only children. It seems strange, at first sight, that so many adult intelligences could be deceived under such conditions by such youthful minds. The experiments, too, have not been carried out by one set of people only; on the contrary, the same subjects and different subjects have been examined by independent observers, and each has confirmed the results previously obtained.

The second objection, referred to as usually raised, is that the existence of thought-transference is so inherently improbable that the chances are far greater that there has been some error in the observations than that the hypothesis is true. This objection, in the first place, overlooks the distinction between the facts and the interpretation of the facts which I have already insisted upon. Further, in my judgment, it seems to me far from the truth. Whether I admit thought-transference or not, I see no valid ground on which to base such an assumption nor, so far as I know, has any been given. If thought-transference directly contradicts some well-established law, as perpetual motion would that of gravitation, then it might be said that it is inherently improbable. But no established law is controverted by it. If, again, the theory of thought-transference maintained that there was a constant influence of one mind upon another or others, that all minds act and interact upon one another in the course of the ordinary affairs of life, or that complicated processes of thought were transferred from one individual to another, then it might with reason be said that there was an inherent improbability against the theory. For if this were the case, the probability of the fact having so long escaped detection would be small, while the disastrous consequences to society would be so great that it might be doubted whether progress in civilization could go on.

But the theory is far less extensive that this. The conditions under which thought-transference can take place, if at all, are very limited, while the ideas themselves are very simple. The number of people, too, who possess the alleged faculty is comparatively very small. It is necessary that the agent, who is as essential for success as the percipient, shall concentrate his attention, to the exclusion of all other thoughts, on a particular idea. If he cannot do this, the experiment will probably fail. The percipient must likewise put himself into a state which may be called expectant attention, excluding as far as possible all consciousness of surroundings. The idea to be transferred must be simple, such as a mental picture of an object, not too complicated in structure, a number, a taste, or a pain. The more complicated the idea the greater the liability of failure, complete or partial. It seems to me that one of the strongest points in favor of the theory is the failures themselves. They are just what would be expected under the theory. A careful analysis of the failures will show, I think, that their character comports exactly with what would be predicted from the theory itself. Space and time will not allow me to go into this here. But, in conclusion, we may say the experiments furnish two classes of facts; namely, successes and failures, both of which furnish strong presumptive evidence for the theory. But still, in spite of this strong presumptive evidence, it is given by too few experiments, and the subjects have been too sparse to justify us in accepting the hypothesis without further confirmation.

It may not be out of place, before concluding, to caution you not to confuse these phenomena with those of muscle-reading as performed by so-called professional mind-readers. The latter class of experiments have of late been so exhaustively discussed that it is not worth while to more extensively refer to them here. Those who are interested will find in the *Nineteenth Century* for December 1886, a very entertaining article by Mr. Stuart Cumberland, a very successful professional, who has retired from the business. He now furnishes the public with a very complete explanation of how the tricks are done.

### EDITORIAL NOTE

Although Dr. Prince was interested in psychical research, in the sense, that he would not ignore any phenomena which had some pretense to authenticity, thus showing that he had an open mind, he had never expressed himself as accepting any of the claims made by experimenters, even of repute.

In spite of the favorable attitude he seems to take on the subject of transference, his stand may best be summarized in the conclusion "In spite of this strong presumptive evidence, it is given by too few experimenters, and the subjects have been too sparse to justify us in accepting the hypothesis without further confirmation."

In the introduction to the translation of Morton Prince's The Case of Miss

# VI

*from*

"A WORLD CONSCIOUSNESS AND FUTURE PEACE"

(Address before the Concordia Association of Japan at
Tokyo, at a garden party given by Baron
Shibusaya, June 13th, 1916)

*The Journal of Abnormal Psychology,* October-November, 1916

## A World Consciousness

What hope does psychology hold out to civilization?
The common ideals of a collective consciousness respect and
protect the rights of individuals and regulate their relations
to one another *within* the nation. May it not be that, with
time, fostered by systematic worldwide teaching, there may
be developed an international consciousness, or world consciousness so far as concerns international relations? And
may it not be that the principles of such a consciousness will
regulate the nations in their relations to one another to the
same extent that the social and national consciousness within
a single nation regulates the relations of the people to one
another, and, in the United States today, the relations of
the sovereign states of the American Union to one another?

Beauchamp, the foremost authority on psychic research in Germany, Professor
T. K. Oesterreich intimates that the Beauchamp case offered numerous observations of a parapsychic nature but that Prince had suppressed them, and had
declined to make them accessible to the then American champion of occult
phenomena, James H. Hyslop.

"Morton Prince," Oesterreich asserts, "had a deep aversion for the admissi-
bility of parapsychic processes *und so zog er es vor, das ihm nicht restlos
schulmassig deutbare Beobachtungsmaterial zuverschweigen.*

"It is deplorable," he continues, "that the great merit which Morton Prince
had won through the publication of the Miss Beauchamp case had a setback
through his very behavior in this regard. Still more regrettable is it that we
consequently are not cognizant of the Beauchamp case in its full scope, but
know only that Prince's report suppresses everything known which scientifically
could be most important because fundamentally new.

"Can there be a more depressing proof of the tragic meaning of mere faith
(sic) and the weakness of the truth impulse even in the realm of science?"

The above has been cited as an antidote for those who may consider the
extract from the article on telepathy as showing a weakness the other way.

— A. A. R.

In such a world consciousness there would grow up common habits of mind that would become second nature — common points of view, common ideals of right and wrong in the dealings of one nation with another.

Likewise, conceptions of humanity, of liberty, and of the obligations of one people to another would have a common meaning, which is not the case today. In a consciousness of this kind, among the international habits of thought would be that of respecting the rights and interests of other nations whether large countries like China or small ones like Serbia, and the habit of repressing desires which have for an object the selfish aggrandizement of a nation at the expense of weaker ones. Such a world consciousness would mean desire, grown into habit and customs, to respect the rights of foreign peoples under international law, which, in turn, would be truly the expression of world ideals and desires, not of selfish interests as today, and the habit of looking to arbitration and conciliation to compose the conflicting interests of nation. The imponderable force of such a consciousness would offer the strongest support to international law — the power behind the law — and out of such ideals and such desires, when established, there would necessarily develop a general will to peace and a will to fulfill the obligations imposed by the ideals.

Theoretically the attainment of a world consciousness of this kind is psychologically possible, and if ever attained it would necessarily have the same binding force in regulating international conduct as has the social consciousness within a nation today. To reach such an end the old world-habit of mind — the habit of thinking in war terms, of turning at first thought to war as a necessary means of settling international disputes, must be broken. A world conscience will be the censor which, like the social censor, will threaten with the *taboo* a breach of treaties of international customs, codes, and habits of conduct. The ideals of the German autocracy and of the German military caste as taught, by their philosophers and publicists like Treitschke and Nietzsche and military writers like Bernhardi and their Kaiser, such ideals as "Might makes Right," "World Empire or Downfall," "It is the duty of great nations to make war on weak nations," "Little nations have no rights which powerful nations are bound to respect," and "Nothing shall happen in this world without Germany being consulted," in short "Kultur" and the worship of force, all such military ideals must give place to the ideals of that collective consciousness of the German people that govern them in their relations to each other within the Empire and to a newly created collective consciousness of the world. The war attitude of mind of the German autocracy and military caste, which, like a mental disease has permeated and taken possession of the soul of the German people in its attitude towards other nations, must give place to a world consciousness.

If such a world consciousness should be developed, one nation will understand another because the ideals of the common consciousness will have the same meaning. We shall think in the same language though we do not speak it. It is not through militarism, nor by piling up armaments, nor by a "league to enforce peace" that a world peace can be perpetually maintained. Such methods can be only temporary. Nor in the future when all nations shall be equally armed to the teeth and all the peoples of all the nations mobilized into armies, as will be the case after this war, can even just aspirations be attained and international disputes and conflicts of interest be settled by arms, because there must result a deadlock of forces. Some other mode must be found. May not these legitimate aims be reached without war when the great nations arrive at an international consciousness, with common ideals, a common understanding, and a common will.[1]

A world consciousness in international relations — that is the vision I see, the dream that psychology permits us to have. May that dream come true!

1 The thesis of such a world consciousness which Lord Haldane ably presented from a legal standpoint and which I have endeavored to develop along psychological lines necessarily, of course, assumes the co-operation of an international police of some kind, just as the social consciousness is supplemented by a civic and national police. There are "Apache" or bandit nations as there are bandits within the social organization of every nation, and in the case of revolutions the rights of foreign nationals must be protected from mob violence.

INDEXES

# INDEX OF NAMES[1]

1  Characters from fiction are italicized. ,

# INDEX OF SUBJECTS